Religious Liberty and the American Supreme Court

Religious Liberty and the American Supreme Court

The Essential Cases and Documents

Vincent Phillip Muñoz

ROWMAN & LITTLEFIELD PUBLISHERS, INC.
Lanham • Boulder • New York • Toronto • Plymouth, UK

Published by Rowman & Littlefield Publishers, Inc.
A wholly owned subsidary of The Rowman & Littlefield Publishing Group, Inc.
4501 Forbes Boulevard, Suite 200, Lanham, Maryland 20706
www.rowman.com

10 Thornbury Road, Plymouth PL6 7PP, United Kingdom

British Library Cataloguing in Publication Information Available

Library of Congress Cataloging-in-Publication Data

Religious liberty and the American Supreme Court : the essential cases and documents / [edited
by] Vincent Phillip Muñoz.
    pages cm
  Includes bibliographical references and index.
  ISBN 978-1-4422-0827-8 (cloth : alk. paper) — ISBN 978-1-4422-0829-2 (electronic) 1. Freedom
of religion—United States—Cases. 2. Church and state—United States—Cases. 3. Freedom
of religion—United States—Sources. 4. Church and state—United States—Sources. I. Muñoz,
Vincent Phillip, editor of compilation.
  KF4783.A52.R45 2013
  342.7.08'52—dc23   2013007912

∞™ The paper used in this publication meets the minimum requirements
of American National Standard for Information Sciences—Permanence of
Paper for Printed Library Materials, ANSI/NISO Z39.48-1992.

Printed in the United States of America

For my students

The establishment of Civil and Religious Liberty was the Motive which induced me to the Field; the object is attained, and it now remains to be my earnest wish and prayer, that the Citizens of the United Sates would make a wise and virtuous use of the blessings, placed before them.

George Washington
Letter to the Reformed German Congregation of New York
November 27, 1783

Every government degenerates when trusted to the rulers of the people alone. The people themselves, therefore, are its only safe depositories. And to render them safe, their minds must be improved to a certain degree.

Thomas Jefferson
Notes on the State of Virginia, 1782

A popular Government, without popular information, or the means of acquiring it, is but a Prologue to a Farce or a Tragedy; or, perhaps both. Knowledge will forever govern ignorance: And a people who mean to be their own Governors, must arm themselves with the power which knowledge gives.

James Madison
Letter to W. T. Barry
August, 4, 1822

Contents

II. HISTORICAL DOCUMENTS

Cases by Subject Matter

This supplemental table of contents is offered to direct readers to cases by subject matter. It must be noted that the line between Free Exercise Clause cases and Establishment Clause cases is not always clear. (It was not until the mid-twentieth century that the Court began distinguishing the First Amendment's "free exercise" and "establishment" text as separate clauses demarcating separate meanings.) The groupings below are nonexclusive; some cases appear in more than one category. Bold numbers indicate chapter numbers.

Within the Free Exercise Clause case categorization, "direct" or "indirect" burden refers to the type of restriction placed on religion by the state. Direct burden cases involve laws and regulations that specify disabilities on religion as such. Indirect burden cases involve state action that incidentally affects religious individuals or institutions in the application of a more generally applicable statute or regulation that does not specify or target religion as such. A law that specifically made "the performance of a Catholic mass" illegal would be a direct burden; a generally applicable building code that limited the construction size of a new Catholic church building would be an indirect burden.

Free Exercise Clause Cases: Direct Burdens

Free Exercise Clause Cases: Indirect Burdens

Free Exercise/Free Speech Clause Cases

Establishment Clause Cases: Religion in the Public Square

Establishment Clause Cases: Government and Religious Schools

Establishment Clause Cases: Religion and Public Schools

Notes on the Text

This volume is intended for citizens and students who seek to understand the U.S. Supreme Court's church-state jurisprudence. The cases and documents presented comprise the most important legal materials pertaining to the First Amendment's protection of religious liberty. The included Supreme Court cases are presented chronologically, which, it is hoped, will help the reader grasp how various First Amendment church-state doctrines were developed and have changed over time.

In presenting cases chronologically, this volume breaks from usual casebook practice of grouping cases by subject matter. This arrangement, while perhaps more useful to the practicing lawyer, hides the fact that many cases do not neatly fit into to one subject area alone. Equally importantly, trends and doctrines in Establishment Clause cases alter and influence free exercise decision making (and vice versa). How decisions under one clause constrain and influence decisions under the other (or ought to) can easily be overlooked if cases are presented thematically instead of chronologically. Moreover, thematic arrangement obscures the larger narrative arc of the Court's development of doctrine. This volume is intended to help readers discover not only what the law is but how it came to be what it is. That aim, we believe, is best served by the chronological arrangement of cases. To aid students and teachers interested in specific church-state subject matters, however, a supplemental table of contents by subject matter has also been provided.

The cases in this volume are excerpted. Every effort has been made to include the most important doctrinal, analytical, philosophical, and historical passages in each excerpted opinion. Nonetheless, the dedicated student who wishes a more complete understanding of a case or opinion ought to read its full text. Lost in the excerpting process, in particular, is how justices rely on and interpret precedents. For purposes of space, case citations have been removed unless a citation is needed to identify the location of a quotation or was deemed of particular importance.

Case citations refer to the *United States Reports*, the official record of the proceedings of the U.S. Supreme Court. Under the commonly accepted citation protocol, "*Wallace v. Jaffree*, 472 U.S. 38 (1985)" indicates that the case *Wallace v. Jaffree* can be found in volume 472 of the *United States Reports* starting on page 38 and that the case was decided in the year 1985. Citations within an opinion to precedents often have the following format: "*Lemon v. Kurtzman*, 403 U.S. 602, 612–613 (1971)." This citation indicates a reference to pages 612–613 of *Lemon v. Kurtzman*. In the footnote in the following quote, "330 U.S., at 16" indicates a reference to page 16 of volume 330 of the

United States Reports. For the three most recent cases in this volume, page numbers to the *United States Reports* were unavailable at the time of publication. As noted on the first pages of those case excerpts, the citation and page numbers used refer to the *Supreme Court Reporter*.

For all but the three most recent cases, page references within the opinion's text refer to the original pagination in the *United States Reports*. In the following example from Justice Rehnquist's dissent in *Wallace v. Jaffree*, page 92 of the *United States Reports* begins with the words "between church and State."

> This language from *Reynolds*, a case involving the Free Exercise Clause of the First Amendment rather than the Establishment Clause, quoted from Thomas Jefferson's letter to the Danbury Baptist Association the phrase "I contemplate with sovereign reverence that act of the whole American people which declared that their legislature should 'make no law respecting an establishment of religion, or prohibiting the free exercise thereof,' thus building a wall of separation [92] between church and State."[1]
>
> It is impossible to build sound constitutional doctrine upon a mistaken understanding of constitutional history, but unfortunately the Establishment Clause has been expressly freighted with Jefferson's misleading metaphor for nearly 40 years.
>
> [1]*Reynolds* is the only authority cited as direct precedent for the "wall of separation theory." 330 U.S., at 16. *Reynolds* is truly inapt; it dealt with a Mormon's Free Exercise Clause challenge to a federal polygamy law.

For the most part, footnotes in the justices' opinions have been eliminated. In cases where original footnotes are present, the note number is the original number used in the opinion. In the example above, note 1 was the first note in Justice Rehnquist's opinion. Depending on the excerpt, the first note of an opinion may not start with the number 1 and numbers may not proceed sequentially. Clarifying material added to text and footnotes by the editor appears in brackets. Editorial footnotes added to the cases are marked by asterisks.

Acknowledgments

Several friends and colleagues helped me complete this book. Don Drakeman and Matthew Frank provided especially thoughtful comments on an early draft of the introduction and made helpful suggestions about which cases and documents to include. Rick Garnett, Michael Uhlmann, and Allen Hertzke also provided helpful suggestions for the table of contents. Professors Uhlmann and Hertzke additionally tested drafts of the manuscript in their church-state seminars, helping me to improve the excerpts for classroom use. Thank you to them and their students. Two of my best students, Matthew Shapanka and Colin Littlefield, made valuable contributions throughout the research, excerpting, and editing processes, as did Jennifer Smith, my assistant at Notre Dame's Tocqueville Program for Inquiry into Religion and Public Life. Jon Sisk at Roman & Littlefield provided the insight, encouragement, and patience needed to see this project through to the end. Margaret Cabaniss produced the exceptionally thorough index in a remarkably short amount of time. Thank you to her and to her three little assistants, John, Thomas, and Stephen. Miguel Buckenmeyer helped with the book's cover design.

This project was conceived when I was the William E. Simon Fellow in Religion & Public Life at Princeton University's James Madison Program. Thank you to its benefactors and stewards, especially Robby George and Brad Wilson. Patrick Deneen, in his capacity as director of Georgetown University's Tocqueville Forum, provided office space while I worked on the manuscript in Washington, DC. Access to the treasures of our nation's capital afforded one unexpected benefit, for which I am deeply grateful—my amazingly beautiful, patient, and loving wife, Jennifer, who makes all that I do possible.

Religious Liberty and the American Supreme Court was made possible, in part, by support from the Institute for Scholarship in the Liberal Arts, College of Arts and Letters, University of Notre Dame. My thanks to ISLA's director, Thomas Merluzzi, and to John McGreevy, dean of the College of Arts and Letters.

Introduction

"Congress shall make no law respecting an establishment of religion, or prohibiting the free exercise thereof."

—First Amendment, Constitution of the United States of America

In June 2002, a divided three-judge panel of the Ninth Circuit Federal Court of Appeals ruled public school teacher-led recitations of the Pledge of Allegiance unconstitutional. Public reaction was swift and severe. Senator Robert Byrd (D-WV) called the judge who authored the opinion "stupid." House Speaker Dennis Hastert (R-IL) concluded, "Obviously, the liberal court in San Francisco has gotten this one wrong." Senator Majority Leader Tom Daschle (D-SD) summed up the general sentiment of Congress in a more nonpartisan tone: "This decision is nuts." The president agreed. According to his White House spokesman, George W. Bush's reaction was, "This is ridiculous."

The Ninth Circuit's ruling might have been surprising, even shocking, but it is not quite right to call it "stupid" or "ridiculous"—at least not if you are knowledgeable about the history of the Supreme Court's church-state jurisprudence. The opinion by the allegedly liberal San Francisco judge (who was appointed by Ronald Reagan) was solidly within existing Supreme Court precedents. In fact, Justice Antonin Scalia (another Reagan appointee) had suggested ten years earlier that if pushed to its logical outcome, the Court's Establishment Clause jurisprudence rendered the Pledge of Allegiance unconstitutional.[1] The real story behind the pledge case was not how an unmoored and irresponsible judge abused his power; rather, it was how a federal circuit court, respectful of its duty to follow established Supreme Court precedents, found itself obliged to rule the phrase "under God" in the Pledge of Allegiance unconstitutional if recited in the nation's public schools.

The Ninth Circuit's decision eventually was set aside on a technicality, but the Supreme Court precedents that guided the circuit court's original three-judge panel remain in effect. Understanding those precedents requires that we return to the Supreme Court's first significant Establishment Clause decision, *Everson v. Board of Education* (1947). And understanding *Everson* requires a return to the Court's first significant free exercise decision, *Reynolds v. United States* (1879). To comprehend where the Court is now and how it arrived there, we have to return to the commencement of its church-state doctrinal

---

1. *Lee v. Weisman*, 505 U.S. 577, 639 (1992).

journey. This introduction, accordingly, proceeds historically. By focusing on landmark decisions, key opinions, and leading dissents, it aims to explain how the Supreme Court has created America's current church-state constitutional law. Understanding the paths taken and doctrines adopted by the Supreme Court, which have not always been consistent and perhaps not even coherent, is the first step for students, citizens, and judges to evaluate whether America's highest court has accurately, intelligently, and prudently interpreted the First Amendment's protections of religious freedom.

The Turn to the Founders and the Establishment of a "Wall of Separation"

The First Amendment's protection of religious freedom is usually divided into two parts: the Establishment Clause ("Congress shall make no law respecting an establishment of religion") and the Free Exercise Clause ("or prohibiting the free exercise thereof"). The Court handed down its most influential Establishment Clause decision in *Everson v. Board of Education* (1947), the landmark case in which the Court invoked Thomas Jefferson and James Madison to rule that the First Amendment erected a "wall of separation" between church and state. In turning to the Founders for guidance, *Everson* followed the precedent established in *Reynolds v. United States* (1879), the Court's first significant free exercise decision. With *Reynolds*, accordingly, we begin.

Reynolds arrived at the Supreme Court through a challenge to a federal statute that criminalized bigamy and polygamy. George Reynolds, a practicing member of the Church of Jesus Christ of Latter-Day Saints (commonly known as the Mormon Church), was convicted of having married two women, sentenced to two years at hard labor, and fined $500. At the time, the Mormon Church encouraged polygamy (it has since disavowed the practice), and Reynolds, Brigham Young's secretary, was a church member in good standing. Reynolds's appeal contended that the First Amendment's Free Exercise Clause shielded him from the antipolygamy law. The Supreme Court, not persuaded, unanimously upheld Reynolds's conviction, in the process interpreting the First Amendment's Free Exercise Clause for the first time.

In a move that still influences church-state jurisprudence, the Court cited Thomas Jefferson to reach its decision. Recognizing that the word "religion" is not defined in the Constitution, Chief Justice Morrison Waite stated that it would be most appropriate to turn to "the history of the times in the midst of which the provision was adopted" to ascertain the First Amendment's meaning.[2] The Founders' efforts to protect religious freedom, Waite contended, culminated in Virginia with the adoption of Jefferson's Bill for Establishing Religious Freedom. "In the preamble of this act religious freedom is defined," the chief justice wrote.

> After a recital "that to suffer the civil magistrate to intrude his powers into the field of opinion, and to restrain the profession or propagation of principles on supposition of their ill tendency, is a dangerous fallacy which at once destroys all religious liberty," it is declared "that it is time enough for the rightful purposes of civil government for its officers to interfere when principles break out into overt acts against peace and good order." In these two sentences is found the true distinction between what properly belongs to the church and what to the State.[3]

2. *Reynolds v. United States*, 98 U.S. 145, 162 (1879).
3. *Reynolds v. United States*, 98 U.S. 145, 163 (1879).

According to the Court, the Free Exercise Clause was intended to protect beliefs and not actions. Thus, the First Amendment did not protect George Reynolds's bigamy.

Reynolds was a Free Exercise Clause case, but its most dramatic impact on church-state law would be felt nearly seventy years later in *Everson v. Board of Education* (1947), the Court's first significant Establishment Clause case. *Everson* involved a challenge to a New Jersey school district's policy that reimbursed parents for costs associated with transporting their children to and from public and Catholic schools. The Court used the case to apply the Establishment Clause against the states and to implement what has come to be known as the separationist approach to the First Amendment.[4]

The issue of incorporating the Establishment Clause could (and probably should) have been thoroughly considered, debated, and evaluated. The text's awkward phrase "respecting an establishment" could have been interpreted in a jurisdictional manner. So viewed, "respecting" would have indicated that the national government lacked jurisdiction over religious establishments and therefore could not make its own establishment or interfere with state authority over religious establishments. This interpretation would have recognized federalism as a central tenet of the Establishment Clause. Just like the Tenth Amendment, the Establishment Clause would have been understood to resist application against state governments.

Justice Hugo Black, author of *Everson*'s majority opinion, bypassed the entire incorporation issue with the wave of his pen. In one sentence, he simply said that the Fourteenth Amendment had already made the First Amendment applicable to the states. For authority he cited *Murdock v. Pennsylvania* (1943).[5] *Murdock*, however, was a Free Exercise Clause case. In this way, Black quietly and efficiently managed to eliminate the possible federalism component of the Establishment Clause without making a substantive legal argument. Although the case was decided 5–4, no justices disagreed with him on this point.

The Court's nine justices also all agreed that the Establishment Clause erected a wall of separation between church and state. As set forth by Black's majority opinion, that meant at least the following:

> Neither a state nor the Federal Government can set up a church. Neither can pass laws which aid one religion, aid all religions, or prefer one religion over another. Neither can force nor influence a person to go to or to remain away from church against his will or force him to profess a belief or disbelief in any religion. No person can be punished for entertaining or professing religious beliefs or disbeliefs, for church attendance or non-attendance. No tax in any amount, large or small, can be levied to support any religious activities or institutions, whatever they may be called, or whatever form they may adopt to teach or practice religion. Neither a state nor the Federal Government can, openly or secretly, participate in the affairs of any religious organizations or groups and vice versa.[6]

While pathbreaking, Justice Black's opinion obscured the originality of his doctrinal creation. Just before the above-cited passage, he stated matter-of-factly that the Court had previously recognized that the First Amendment's terms "had the same objective and were intended to provide the same protection against governmental intrusion on

---

4. The Bill of Rights originally only imposed restrictions against the national government. In the twentieth century, the Supreme Court applied aspects of the Bill of Rights against the states through a process of "incorporation." The textual vehicle for incorporation has been the Fourteenth Amendment.

5. *Everson v. Board of Education*, 330 U.S. 1, 8 (1947).

6. *Everson v. Board of Education*, 330 U.S. 1, 15–16 (1947).

religious liberty as the Virginia statute."[7] To substantiate the point, he cited three previous cases. But none of those cases actually said what Justice Black implied they did.[8] Without calling attention to his enterprise, Justice Black effectively created out of whole cloth the modern-day Establishment Clause. Ever since, most Establishment Clause Supreme Court decisions have turned on the question of how high the "wall" stands, not whether the Founders built it. While his specific doctrine has not decided each and every case, Black's *Everson* opinion established the parameters within which subsequent Courts have approached the text.

Justice Black and the Court added more bricks to the wall in *McCollum v. Board of Education* (1948), a case decided one year after *Everson*. Like many Establishment Clause disputes, *McCollum* concerned religion in public schools—specifically, whether Protestant, Catholic, and Jewish teachers could, under the approval and supervision of school authorities, conduct voluntary religion classes during the school day on public school grounds. At the time, such instruction was widespread, involving more the two million school children throughout the nation. Without detailed argumentation or a precise account of how it reached its decision, the Court terminated such programs on the grounds that they violated the wall of separation between church and state.

The Court's next significant case, *Zorach v. Clauson* (1952), brought into question the wall's strength. In response to *McCollum*, New York City permitted its public schools to release students during the school day, on written request from their parents, so that they could leave school grounds to attend religious instruction or devotional exercises at local religious centers. Justices Black, Felix Frankfurter, and Robert Jackson viewed the case as another straightforward violation of the requirements of separationism. But a six-member majority upheld the released-time program, in part because it involved neither religious instruction in public school classrooms nor the expenditure of public funds. In an often-quoted passage, the Court's majority declared, "We are a religious people whose institutions presuppose a Supreme Being."[9]

Clauson, however, would turn out to be a relatively small setback in the separationist construction project. In two bold and controversial school prayer decisions in the early 1960s, the Court rededicated itself to building the wall and thoroughly separating state institutions from religion. In *Engel v. Vitale* (1962), the Court found public school teacher-led recitation of the "Regents' prayer" unconstitutional. The New York State Board of Regents, the government agency in charge of the New York public school system, had composed the following prayer and prescribed its use at the beginning of the public school day: "Almighty God, we acknowledge our dependence upon Thee, and we beg Thy blessings upon us, our parents, our teachers and our Country." The Court held 6–1 that the prayer violated the Establishment Clause, even if the state did not force students to recite it.

---

7. *Everson v. Board of Education*, 330 U.S. 1, 13 (1947).

8. On page 13 of his *Everson* opinion, Black offered the following citation: "*Reynolds v. United States*, 98 U.S. at page 164; *Watson v. Jones*, 13 Wall. 679; *Davis v. Beason*, 133 U.S. 333." *Watson v. Jones* lacks a single reference to the Virginia statute. *Beason*, similarly, references neither the Virginia statute nor its relationship to the First Amendment. Justice Field's majority opinion in the case quotes Justice Waite's opinion in *Reynolds* at length, but it does not refer to Jefferson's Virginia statute. *Davis*, 133 U.S. 333, 343–44 (1890) (quoting *Reynolds*, 98 U.S. 145, 165–66 [1879]). In *Reynolds*, the Court did say that "the controversy upon this general subject [of religious establishment] . . . seemed at last to culminate in Virginia" and the passing of Jefferson's Virginia statute (*Reynolds v. United States*, 98 U.S. 145, 163 [1879]). *Reynolds* then said that Jefferson's letter to the Danbury Baptist Association—not the Virginia statute—"may be accepted almost as an authoritative declaration of the scope and effect of the [First] [A]mendment." But, more importantly, that "scope and effect," according to the *Reynolds* Court, was that the state could regulate beliefs but not actions. Under the cover of *Reynolds*, Justice Black took a different phrase from Jefferson's Danbury letter and made it the cornerstone of Establishment Clause jurisprudence.

9. *Zorach v. Clausen*, 343 U.S. 306, 313 (1952).

The following year, in *Abington School District v. Schempp* (1963), the Court struck down school-administered daily Bible readings and recitations of the Lord's Prayer in public schools. Pennsylvania law required that "at least ten verses from the Holy Bible shall be read, without comment, at the opening of each public school on each school day." The law allowed children to be excused from reading the Bible or from being present when it was read upon the written request of a parent or guardian. Maryland's public schools were governed by a similar law, which was also examined in the case. According to Justice Potter Stewart, *Schempp*'s lone dissenter, to disallow such religious activities in the public school would amount to "the establishment of a religion of secularism."[10] An eight-member majority disagreed. Citing *Everson*, the majority found state-sponsored Bible reading and prayer in public school to violate the "wholesome [state] neutrality" toward religion mandated by the Establishment Clause.[11]

Whether the Court's separationist wall is neutral toward religion and whether the First Amendment even requires state neutrality toward religion remain topics of significant dispute. To further complicate matters, the same year the Court decided *Schempp* it also embarked on an approach to the Free Exercise Clause that appears to favor religious over nonreligious individuals. To this line of cases we now turn.

The Free Exercise Clause and Religious Exemptions

While implementing its separationist Establishment Clause jurisprudence, the Court developed a seemingly more accommodationist approach to the Free Exercise Clause. As noted above, in *Reynolds* the Court interpreted the Free Exercise Clause to protect beliefs but not actions. After incorporating the clause to apply against the states in *Cantwell v. State of Connecticut* (1940), the Court applied *Reynolds*'s belief-action dichotomy against Jehovah's Witnesses in *Minersville School District v. Gobitis* (1940). The World War II–era case involved Jehovah's Witness children expelled from their public school for refusing to participate in daily salutations to the American flag and recitations of the Pledge of Allegiance.[12] An eight-member majority ruled in favor of the school district, unsympathetic to the children's religious objections to worshipping, in their view, a graven image.

Just two years later, however, a new court majority seemed to take a different tack. Following the *Gobitis* decision, a West Virginia school district implemented a new state law by requiring daily recitations of the Pledge of Allegiance and the corresponding flag salute. Soon thereafter, several Jehovah's Witness children were expelled from West Virginia public schools. When their case reached the Supreme Court in *West Virginia State Board of Education v. Barnette* (1943), the Court struck down the school district policy. Writing for a six-member majority, Justice Jackson concluded that "compelling the flag salute and pledge transcends constitutional limitations . . . and invades the sphere of intellect and spirit which it is the purpose of the First Amendment to our Constitution to reserve from all official control."[13]

Some think *Barnette* reversed *Gobitis* by granting Jehovah's Witness children religious exemptions from the school district's policy. A more precise reading of the Court's

---

10. *Abington School District v. Schempp*, 374 U.S. 203, 313 (1963).
11. *Abington School District v. Schempp*, 374 U.S. 203, 222 (1963).
12. At the time, the recited text of the Pledge of Allegiance was as follows: "I pledge allegiance to my flag, and to the Republic for which it stands; one nation indivisible, with liberty and justice for all." While the words were spoken, teachers and pupils extended their right hands in salute to the flag.
13. *West Virginia State Board of Education v. Barnette*, 319 U.S. 624, 642 (1943).

opinion, however, reveals that the majority struck down mandatory flag salutes and pledge recitations for all school children, not just those who held religious objections to the exercises. The majority made clear that while religious beliefs did provide the Jehovah's Witnesses' motivation in the case, its decision did not "turn on one's possession of particular religious views or the sincerity with which they are held."[14] And as the quotation above shows, the Court majority invoked the First Amendment as a whole, not just the Free Exercise Clause, to render its decision. After *Barnette*, no government entity could compel any child to say the Pledge of Allegiance or salute the flag.[15]

Twenty years later, in *Sherbert v. Verner* (1963), the Court did adopt the exemption approach to free exercise. The case presented perhaps one of the most sympathetic litigants in church-state legal history. Adell Sherbert was fired from her textile job of thirty-five years when she refused to accept a six-day-a-week schedule that included Saturdays. A Seventh-Day Adventist, Sherbert considered Saturday her sabbath. For years she had had an agreement to work five days a week and not on Saturdays. Unable to find a new job because of her unwillingness to work on her sabbath, Sherbert applied for state unemployment benefits. South Carolina officials denied her application, however, on the grounds that alternative work (which required Saturday labor) was in fact available.

In a precedent-setting decision, the Supreme Court found that South Carolina violated the Free Exercise Clause when it denied Sherbert unemployment benefits. Writing for the Court, Justice William Brennan explained the judgment:

> The ruling [by the South Carolina Employment Security Commission] forces her [Sherbert] to choose between following the precepts of her religion and forfeiting benefits, on the one hand, and abandoning one of the precepts of her religion in order to accept work, on the other hand. Governmental imposition of such a choice puts the same kind of burden upon the free exercise of religion as would a fine imposed against appellant for her Saturday worship.[16]

Under what would become known as the *Sherbert* test, the Court ruled that the Free Exercise Clause requires the state to have "a compelling state interest" and to use the "least restrictive means" possible when enacting or enforcing legislation that burdens an individual's religion. As implemented by the Court, it did not matter if government action burdened religion directly or indirectly or if the state intended to burden religion. Under *Sherbert*, religious individuals possessed a presumptive constitutional right to exemptions from burdensome laws, save only the "compelling state interest" and "least restrictive means" conditions.

Sherbert's exemption approach to free exercise went unchallenged for nearly thirty years until the Court, shockingly, overthrew the doctrine for most cases in *Employment Division v. Smith* (1990). All the more surprisingly to some, Justice Scalia authored the change. *Smith* involved claims for unemployment compensation by two drug-rehabilitation counselors. The state employment division found that the counselors had been fired with cause (they had tested positive for using a hallucinogenic) and accordingly denied their applications for state unemployment benefits. The counselors did not contest the results of their positive drug tests, but in their legal appeal, they explained that they had used peyote while participating in a Native American Church ritual. That practice, they contended, was protected by the Free Exercise Clause.

---

14. *West Virginia State Board of Education v. Barnette*, 319 U.S. 624, 634 (1943).
15. It should be noted that in their concurring opinion in *Barnette*, Justices Black and Douglas focused on the religious element of the case and suggested that the school district policy trespassed the Constitution in its application against "conscientious objectors."
16. *Sherbert v. Verner*, 374 U.S. 398, 405 (1963).

Rather than requiring Oregon to show a "compelling state interest" to justify its burden on the counselors' religious practices, the Supreme Court dramatically narrowed the *Sherbert* test. In a complicated (and, to many, unpersuasive) majority opinion that cited *Reynolds* and *Gobitis*, Justice Scalia wrote that the Court had only applied *Sherbert's* exemption standard in "hybrid" situations that involved more than one constitutional right. For most cases, the Court held, the state had no constitutional obligation to grant religious exemptions from laws that indirectly burdened religious beliefs or exercises. The *Smith* approach to the Free Exercise Clause permitted neutral laws of general applicability to impose indirect burdens on religion.

The *Lemon* Test, the Endorsement Test, and Critiques of Separationism

Scalia's narrowing of the *Sherbert* test helped to alleviate a striking tension in the Court's church-state jurisprudence. More than one critic had noted that the Court's exemption-granting free exercise rule adopted in *Sherbert* did not easily square with its separationist approach to the Establishment Clause. The *Sherbert* test required the government to extend to religious individuals special consideration for exemptions when they felt burdened by state action. At the same time, the Establishment Clause prohibited the government from preferring or advancing religion over nonreligion. The Court's Establishment Clause seemed to prohibit the preferential action demanded by the Court's Free Exercise Clause. As Justice Stewart noted in his concurring opinion in *Sherbert*, "There are many situations where legitimate claims under the Free Exercise Clause will run into head-on collision with the Court's . . . construction of the Establishment Clause."[17]

Stewart was referring to *Vitale* and *Schempp*, the public school prayer cases discussed above. About a decade after these decisions were handed down, the Court attempted to articulate a systematic approach to the Establishment Clause in *Lemon v. Kurtzman* (1971). The case involved various types of government aid to private religious schools, a large majority of which were Catholic. The Court set forth what came to be known as the *Lemon* test, a three-part analytical tool to evaluate state action. In order to pass constitutional muster, governmental practices must do the following:

1. have a secular legislative purpose,
2. not have the primary effect of either advancing or inhibiting religion, and
3. not result in an "excessive government entanglement" with religion.

A violation of any of the test's prongs would render state action unconstitutional.

The Court's decision to strike down the state aid challenged in *Lemon* rested on the "excessive entanglement" prong, the *Lemon* test's most novel feature. Also new in *Lemon* was the Court's justification for why "excessive entanglement" between church and state violated the Constitution. According to Chief Justice Warren Burger's majority opinion, "One of the principal evils against which the First Amendment was intended to protect" was "political division along religious lines."[18] Government funding of religious schools, Burger said, threatened to divide the community. On one side, he said, would stand "partisans of parochial schools, understandably concerned with rising costs and sincerely dedicated to both the religious and secular educational missions of their schools"; on the other side would be "those who oppose state aid, whether for

---

17. *Sherbert v. Verner*, 374 U.S. 398, 414 (1963).
18. *Lemon v. Kurtzman*, 403 U.S. 602, 622 (1971).

constitutional, religious, or fiscal reasons." One side would "promote political action to achieve their goals," and in response their opponents would "employ all of the usual political campaign techniques to prevail." Candidates for political office would then "be forced to declare and voters to choose." This might sound like the ordinary functioning of a representative democracy, but according to Burger such political activity posed an existential danger: "Many people confronted with issues of this kind will find their votes aligned with their faith," and "the potential divisiveness of such conflict is a threat to the normal political process."[19] Policies and politics likely to align religious faith with voting patterns, Burger reasoned, could cause political division along religious lines and would therefore unconstitutionally entangle church and state.

The *Lemon* test remains a standing precedent often identified as the benchmark for Establishment Clause analysis. A majority opinion by Justice David Souter in *McCreary County v. American Civil Liberties Union of Kentucky* (2005) employed it to strike down a pair of Ten Commandments displays in county courthouses. Yet *Lemon* has never lacked critics. Perhaps Burger himself, the test's formulator, implicitly levied the most telling censure. In *Marsh v. Chambers* (1983), the chief justice authored a majority opinion upholding the state of Nebraska's legislative chaplaincy. His opinion turned to history, noting that government-funded legislative chaplains date back to the American founding and that the same Congress that drafted the First Amendment also approved of a chaplain. What Burger did not say, however, spoke loudest: nowhere in his opinion did he invoke or cite the *Lemon* test. He likely avoided it because, in the words of Justice Brennan's dissent, that legislative prayer has a "pre-eminently religious" purpose would seem to be "self-evident."[20] Brennan did not level the charge directly, but Burger apparently abandoned the *Lemon* test because it failed to reach the outcome he thought proper. Given the history that Burger did present, his opinion implicitly (and maybe unwittingly) suggested that the *Lemon* test was inconsistent with the Founders' practices and original intentions.

Perhaps because of *Lemon*'s perceived shortcoming, Justice Sandra Day O'Connor moved to modify the approach during the following term. In her first church-state opinion, the newly appointed associate justice advanced her "endorsement test" in a concurrence in *Lynch v. Donnelly* (1984). Under O'Connor's approach, judicial inquiry would ask whether a state action "intends to convey a message of endorsement or disapproval of religion."[21] By focusing on and striking down state endorsements of religion, O'Connor suggested that the Court would no longer have to attempt to measure the effects of any state action on religion, thereby clarifying Establishment Clause adjudication.

O'Connor's long tenure as the fifth and decisive vote in Establishment Clause disputes ensured that the "endorsement test" remained at the center of church-state jurisprudence for over two decades. This does not mean the approach was necessarily well regarded or enthusiastically embraced. Critics were quick to point out that evaluating a legislator's intentions is hardly a matter of hard science. It is not always possible to know what a single legislator (not to mention a legislative body as a whole) intended in drafting or passing a particular law. Moreover, if legislators know that their intentions might be evaluated later by a court, they have an incentive to deliberately plant constitutionally acceptable intentions in the legislative record. These problems and others would lead to a host of criticisms of the endorsement test and proposals for alternative approaches.

Perhaps the boldest critique came from then–Associate Justice William Rehnquist in *Wallace v. Jaffree* (1985). Rehnquist aimed to uproot the wall of separation with a histori-

---

19. *Lemon v. Kurtzman*, 403 U.S. 602, 622 (1971).
20. *Lemon v. Kurtzman*, 403 U.S. 602, 797 (1971).
21. *Lynch v. Donnelly*, 465 U.S. 668, 691 (1984).

cal pickax. The case evaluated a law that mandated a moment of silence "for prayer or voluntary meditation" in Alabama's public elementary schools. Citing *Lemon* and the endorsement test, a six-member majority struck down the practice. Rehnquist dissented, rejecting the entire foundation upon which the majority had constructed its opinion. "It is impossible to build sound constitutional doctrine," he declared, "upon a mistaken understanding of constitutional history." *Everson*'s first mistake, he said, was to turn to Jefferson. The author of the letter to the Danbury Baptist Association, from which Justice Black took the phrase "a wall of separation," was in Paris at the time of the adoption of the First Amendment; accordingly, Rehnquist suggested, Jefferson had nothing to do with its drafting and should not be consulted on its interpretation. Moreover, the records of the Establishment Clause in the First Congress, Rehnquist continued, reveal not separationism but rather the idea that government should not prefer one religion over others. Numerous official political acts by various Founding Fathers, he said, confirmed nonpreferentialism, including official presidential proclamations of days of prayer and thanksgiving; the reenactment in 1789 of the Northwest Ordinance of 1787, which declared, "[Religion], morality, and knowledge, being necessary to good government and the happiness of mankind, schools and the means of education shall forever be encouraged"; land grants to support religion; and early commentaries on the Constitution by leading jurists, including Joseph Story.

Since Rehnquist's dissent in *Jaffree*, nonpreferentialism has often been considered the main alternative to separationism. Other justices, however, have not firmly embraced the approach, including those often sympathetic to Rehnquist's judgments. Instead, *Everson*'s other critics have tended to offer their own alternative doctrines and Establishment Clause tests.

In *County of Allegheny v. American Civil Liberties Union* (1989), Justice Anthony Kennedy blasted O'Connor's endorsement test and offered his own approach to the Establishment Clause. The case involved holiday displays in two downtown Pittsburgh government buildings. The first display, located at the top of the Grand Staircase of the Allegheny County Courthouse, consisted of a crèche depicting the Christian nativity scene. The second display, which was down the street outside the city-county building, included an eighteen-foot Chanukah menorah, or candelabra, and a forty-five-foot, decorated Christmas tree. In a split 5–4 decision, the Court found the nativity scene unconstitutional but held the joint menorah/Christmas tree display constitutional. According to Justice O'Connor, who cast the decisive fifth vote, the nativity display endorsed religion, whereas the menorah/Christmas tree display did not.

Kennedy issued a three-part critique of the endorsement test. He said it failed to accord with history, especially with the founding, which was full of governmental actions endorsing religion. Next, he claimed that the endorsement test embraced a "jurisprudence of minutiae" because it required judges to determine whether a disclaimer sign or inclusion of a secular figurine offset the religious elements in a display, thereby neutralizing possible governmental endorsement of religion.[22] Perhaps his most vigorous critique, however, regarded the endorsement test's callous indifference to religion:

> If government is to participate in its citizens' celebration of a holiday that contains both a secular and a religious component, enforced recognition of only the secular aspect would signify the callous indifference toward religious faith that our cases and traditions do not require; for by commemorating the holiday only as it is celebrated by nonadherents, the government would be refusing to acknowledge the plain fact, and the historical reality,

---

22. *County of Allegheny v. American Civil Liberties Union*, 492 U.S. 573, 674 (1989).

that many of its citizens celebrate its religious aspects as well. Judicial invalidation of government's attempts to recognize the religious underpinnings of the holiday would signal not neutrality but a pervasive intent to insulate government from all things religious.[23]

To replace the endorsement test, Kennedy advocated his own two-part approach. The Establishment Clause, he said, should prevent the government from the following:

1. coercing anyone to support or participate in any religion or its exercise, and
2. granting direct benefits in such a way that establishes a religion or tends to do so.

It should not prevent, Kennedy emphasized, government recognition or acknowledgment of religion.

Justice Scalia signed on to Justice Kennedy's *Allegheny County* opinion, but three years later Scalia wrote his own fiery critique of the Court's Establishment Clause jurisprudence, with Kennedy as one of his targets. The occasion for Scalia's colorful opinion was *Lee v. Weisman* (1992), a public school prayer case from Rhode Island in which a public junior high school invited a Jewish rabbi to offer prayers at its eighth-grade graduation. The Supreme Court ruled, 5–4, that the school's invitation, coupled with its instruction to the rabbi to compose nondenominational prayers, violated the Establishment Clause.

Justice Kennedy wrote the majority opinion (joined by Justice O'Connor), explaining, "The undeniable fact is that the school district's supervision and control of a high school graduation ceremony places public pressure, as well as peer pressure, on attending students to stand as a group or, at least, maintain respectful silence during the invocation and benediction. This pressure, though subtle and indirect, can be as real as any overt compulsion."[24]

Justice Scalia's irate dissenting opinion mocked Kennedy's "psychological coercion" test. "The Court's notion," Scalia wrote,

> that a student who simply *sits* in "respectful silence" during the invocation and benediction (when all others are standing) has somehow joined—or would somehow be perceived as having joined—in the prayers is nothing short of ludicrous. We indeed live in a vulgar age. But surely "our social conventions" have not coarsened to the point that anyone who does not stand on his chair and shout obscenities can reasonably be deemed to have assented to everything said in his presence. Since the Court does not dispute that students exposed to prayer at graduation ceremonies retain (despite "subtle coercive pressures") the free will to sit, there is absolutely no basis for the Court's decision.[25]

Scalia then noted that right before the students were asked to stand for the rabbi's prayer, they were asked to stand for the Pledge of Allegiance. Given that the First Amendment prohibits students from being coerced to say the pledge (*West Virginia State Board of Education v. Barnette*), he pointed out that public school–directed Pledge of Allegiance recitations would also be unconstitutional under Kennedy's coercion standard.[26]

As an alternative, Scalia advanced his own approach to the Establishment Clause, which might be deemed "legal coercion": "The coercion that was a hallmark of historical establishments of religion was coercion of religious orthodoxy and of financial support by

---

23. *County of Allegheny v. American Civil Liberties Union*, 492 U.S. 573, 663–664 (1989).
24. *Lee v. Weisman*, 505 U.S. 577, 593 (1992).
25. *Lee v. Weisman*, 505 U.S. 577, 637–638 (1992). Emphasis in the original.
26. *Lee v. Weisman*, 505 U.S. 577, 638–639 (1992).

force of law and threat of penalty."[27] Under Scalia's Establishment Clause, only government actions such as forced attendance of state religious services, direct regulation of religious practices as such, and civil disabilities imposed on religious dissenters amount to constitutional violations. Other than Justice Clarence Thomas, he persuaded no justices to sign on to his "legal coercion" standard. And in time, Thomas issued his own caveat.

The criticisms of *Everson* and its progeny by Rehnquist, Kennedy, and Scalia accepted *Everson's* underlying assumption that the Establishment Clause could unproblematically by applied against the states. In a series of short but provocative passages across multiple opinions, Justice Thomas expressed doubts about this modern-day Establishment Clause orthodoxy. He initially raised eyebrows in *Zelman v. Simmons-Harris* (2002), a school voucher case. Thomas's concurring opinion noted that the Establishment Clause originally applied only to the federal government and "on its face . . . places no limit on the States with regard to religion." He equivocated about incorporation. After recognizing that the Fourteenth Amendment "fundamentally restructured the relationship between individuals and the States," Thomas said that "it may well be that state action [in the context of the Establishment Clause] should be evaluated on different terms than similar action by the Federal Government." Quoting *Walz v. Tax Commission* (1970), he seemed to suggest that those terms were "strict neutrality," but then he concluded, "Thus, while the Federal Government may 'make no law respecting an establishment of religion,' the States may pass laws that include or touch on religious matters so long as these laws do not impede free exercise rights or any other individual religious liberty interest."[28] This last sentence seemed to suggest that in his view the Establishment Clause ought not apply against the states.

Thomas made that exact argument more explicitly two years later in *Elk Grove Unified School District v. Newdow* (2004), the Pledge of Allegiance case with which this chapter began. In his *Newdow* concurrence, Thomas wrote, "The text and history of the Establishment Clause strongly suggest that it is a federalism provision intended to prevent Congress from interfering with state establishments." The Framers, he continued, "made clear that Congress could not interfere with state establishments, notwithstanding any argument that could be made based on Congress' power under the Necessary and Proper Clause." Unlike the Free Exercise Clause, "the Establishment Clause does not purport to protect individual rights"; thus, Thomas concluded, "it makes little sense to incorporate [it]."[29]

One year later, he reasserted his federalism interpretation in *Van Orden v. Perry* (2005), one of the two Ten Commandments cases decided by the Court on the last day of its 2004 term.[30] Thomas insisted that "this case would be easy if the Court were willing to abandon the inconsistent guideposts it has adopted for addressing Establishment Clause challenges, and return to the original meaning of the Clause." The case would have been "easy" because "if the Establishment Clause does not restrain the states, then it has no application here, where only state action is at issue." Thomas did not, however, conclude his analysis by recognizing every state's right to establish a religion and, therefore, to post the Ten Commandments. Instead, he suggested that "even if the [Establishment] Clause is incorporated, or if the Free Exercise Clause limits the power of State to establish religion," the Court should return to the original meaning of the word

27. *Lee v. Weisman*, 505 U.S. 577, 640 (1992).
28. *Zelman v. Simmons-Harris*, 536 U.S. 639, 678–679 (2002).
29. *Elk Grove Unified School District v. Newdow*, 542 U.S. 1, 49–50 (2004).
30. On the same day that the Court handed down its decision in *Van Orden*, it also handed down its decision in *McCreary County v. American Civil Liberties Union of Kentucky*, 545 U.S. 844 (2005). Both cases involved Ten Commandments displays on government property.

"establishment." "The Framers understood an establishment," he claimed, "necessarily to involve actual legal coercion."[31] Citing Justice Scalia's opinion in *Lee v. Weisman* (1992), he then defined legal coercion as "coercion of religious orthodoxy *by force of law and threat of penalty.*"[32] It should be noted that Justice Thomas did not contend that a return to the original meaning of the word "establishment" amounted to a return to the original meaning of the Establishment Clause. He left it ambiguous regarding whether the prohibition against legal coercion, precisely speaking, was a product of the incorporated Establishment Clause or the Free Exercise Clause.

Non-Establishment and Free Exercise Today

This introduction has attempted to make clear that the Establishment Clause remains a matter of significant dispute. On the current Supreme Court, four justices appear to embrace some version of separationism (Ruth Bader Ginsburg, Stephen Breyer, Elena Kagan, and Sonia Sotomayor). Two justices (Scalia and Thomas) have embraced a "legal coercion" standard, although they do not reach that point in the same manner. Justice Kennedy has advanced a "psychological coercion" approach. Chief Justice John Roberts and Justice Samuel Alito have not articulated their understanding of the Establishment Clause, although, given their judicial philosophies, they likely fall somewhere in the coercion zone between Scalia and Kennedy.

Free exercise jurisprudence is a bit less murky but by no means clear. As discussed above, *Employment Division v. Smith* (1990) severely truncated the exemption approach adopted in *Sherbert v. Verner* (1963). Despite congressional efforts effectively to overturn *Smith* legislatively with the Religious Freedom Restoration Act (1993) (struck down as applied to state governments in *City of Boerne v. Flores* [1997]), *Smith* remains the guiding precedent for most free exercise cases. How many justices agree with *Smith* and would vote to uphold it, however, is unclear.

The current unsettled status of First Amendment church-state law suggests the necessity and advisability of a thorough and critical study of the Supreme Court's religious liberty jurisprudence. Only by grasping how different justices conceive the underlying purposes of the First Amendment's religion clauses and by evaluating the adequacy of their corresponding doctrinal interpretations can students and citizens understand how their constitutional rights are judicially protected and judge whether those protections adequately safeguard their fundamental freedom of religious liberty.

---

31. *Van Orden v. Perry*, 545 U.S. 677, 692–693 (2005).
32. *Van Orden v. Perry*, 545 U.S. 677, 693 (2005). Emphasis in the original. Quoting *Lee v. Weisman*, 505 U.S. 577, 640 (1992) (Scalia, J., dissenting).

❶

Reynolds v. United States

98 U.S. 145 (1879)

Vote: 9—Waite, Clifford, Swayne, Miller, Field, Strong, Bradley, Hunt, Harlan
   0

Opinion announcing the opinion of the Court: Waite
Concurring opinion: Field

George Reynolds, secretary to Mormon Church leader Brigham Young, was indicted for violating a federal statute prohibiting bigamy. Reynolds resided in Utah, at the time a federal territory. Subject to imprisonment for a term of up to five years, he was convicted by a jury and sentenced to two years at hard labor and a $500 fine. Reynolds appealed his conviction, citing, among other things, the Free Exercise Clause of the First Amendment.

MR. CHIEF JUSTICE WAITE delivered the opinion of the court.

. . . [161] On the trial, the plaintiff in error, the accused, proved that at the time of his alleged second marriage he was, and for many years before had been, a member of the Church of Jesus Christ of Latter-Day Saints, commonly called the Mormon Church, and a believer in its doctrines; that it was an accepted doctrine of that church "that it was the duty of male members of said church, circumstances permitting, to practise polygamy; . . . that this duty was enjoined by different books which the members of said church believed to be of divine origin, and among others the Holy Bible, and also that the members of the church believed that the practice of polygamy was directly enjoined upon the male members thereof by the Almighty God, in a revelation to Joseph Smith, the founder and prophet of said church; that the failing or refusing to practise polygamy by such male members of said church, when circumstances would admit, would be punished, and that the penalty for such failure and refusal would be damnation in the life to come." He also proved "that he had received permission from the recognized authorities in said church to enter into polygamous marriage; . . . that Daniel H. Wells, one having authority in said church to perform the marriage ceremony, married the said defendant on or about the time the crime is alleged to have been committed, to some woman by the name of Schofield, and that such marriage ceremony was performed under and pursuant to the doctrines of said church."

Upon this proof he asked the court to instruct the jury that if they found from the evidence that he "was married as [162] charged—if he was married—in pursuance of and in conformity with what he believed at the time to be a religious duty, that the verdict must be 'not guilty.'" This request was refused, and the court did charge "that there must have been a criminal intent, but that if the defendant, under the influence of a religious belief that it was right—under an inspiration, if you please, that it was right—deliberately married a second time, having a first wife living, the want of consciousness of evil intent—the want of understanding on his part that he was committing a crime—did not excuse him; but the law inexorably in such case implies the criminal intent."

Upon this charge and refusal to charge the question is raised, whether religious belief can be accepted as a justification of an overt act made criminal by the law of the land. The inquiry is not as to the power of Congress to prescribe criminal laws for the Territories, but as to the guilt of one who knowingly violates a law which has been properly enacted, if he entertains a religious belief that the law is wrong.

Congress cannot pass a law for the government of the Territories which shall prohibit the free exercise of religion. The first amendment to the Constitution expressly forbids such legislation. Religious freedom is guaranteed everywhere throughout the United States, so far as congressional interference is concerned. The question to be determined is, whether the law now under consideration comes within this prohibition.

The word "religion" is not defined in the Constitution. We must go elsewhere, therefore, to ascertain its meaning, and nowhere more appropriately, we think, than to the history of the times in the midst of which the provision was adopted. The precise point of the inquiry is, what is the religious freedom which has been guaranteed.

Before the adoption of the Constitution, attempts were made in some of the colonies and States to legislate not only in respect to the establishment of religion, but in respect to its doctrines and precepts as well. The people were taxed, against their will, for the support of religion, and sometimes for the support of particular sects to whose tenets they could not and did not subscribe. Punishments were prescribed for a failure to attend upon public worship, and sometimes for entertaining [163] heretical opinions. The controversy upon this general subject was animated in many of the States, but seemed at last to culminate in Virginia. In 1784, the House of Delegates of that State having under consideration "a bill establishing provision for teachers of the Christian religion," postponed it until the next session, and directed that the bill should be published and distributed, and that the people be requested "to signify their opinion respecting the adoption of such a bill at the next session of assembly."

This brought out a determined opposition. Amongst others, Mr. Madison prepared a "Memorial and Remonstrance," which was widely circulated and signed, and in which he demonstrated "that religion, or the duty we owe the Creator," was not within the cognizance of civil government. At the next session the proposed bill was not only defeated, but another, "for establishing religious freedom," drafted by Mr. Jefferson, was passed. In the preamble of this act religious freedom is defined; and after a recital "that to suffer the civil magistrate to intrude his powers into the field of opinion, and to restrain the profession or propagation of principles on supposition of their ill tendency, is a dangerous fallacy which at once destroys all religious liberty," it is declared "that it is time enough for the rightful purposes of civil government for its officers to interfere when principles break out into overt acts against peace and good order." In these two sentences is found the true distinction between what properly belongs to the church and what to the State.

In a little more than a year after the passage of this statute the convention met which prepared the Constitution of the United States. Of this convention Mr. Jefferson was not a member, he being then absent as minister to France. As soon as he saw the draft of the Constitution proposed for adoption, he, in a letter to a friend, expressed his disappointment at the absence of an express declaration insuring the freedom of religion, but was willing to accept it as it was, trusting that the good sense and honest intentions of the people would bring about the necessary alterations. [164] Five of the States, while adopting the Constitution, proposed amendments. Three—New Hampshire, New York, and Virginia—included in one form or another a declaration of religious freedom in the changes they desired to have made, as did also North Carolina, where the convention at first declined to ratify the Constitution until the proposed amendments were acted upon. Accordingly, at the first session of the first Congress the amendment now under consideration was proposed with others by Mr. Madison. It met the views of the advocates of religious freedom, and was adopted. Mr. Jefferson afterwards, in reply to an address to him by a committee of the Danbury Baptist Association, took occasion to say: "Believing with you that religion is a matter which lies solely between man and his God; that he owes account to none other for his faith or his worship; that the legislative powers of the government reach actions only, and not opinions—I contemplate with sovereign reverence that act of the whole American people which declared that their legislature should 'make no law respecting an establishment of religion or prohibiting the free exercise thereof,' thus building a wall of separation between church and State. Adhering to this expression of the supreme will of the nation in behalf of the rights of conscience, I shall see with sincere satisfaction the progress of those sentiments which tend to restore man to all his natural rights, convinced he has no natural right in opposition to his social duties." Coming as this does from an acknowledged leader of the advocates of the measure, it may be accepted almost as an authoritative declaration of the scope and effect of the amendment thus secured. Congress was deprived of all legislative power over mere opinion, but was left free to reach actions which were in violation of social duties or subversive of good order.

Polygamy has always been odious among the northern and western nations of Europe, and, until the establishment of the Mormon Church, was almost exclusively a feature of the life of Asiatic and of African people. At common law, the second marriage was always void, and from the earliest history of England polygamy has been treated as an offence against society. After the establishment of the ecclesiastical [165] courts, and until the time of James I., it was punished through the instrumentality of those tribunals, not merely because ecclesiastical rights had been violated, but because upon the separation of the ecclesiastical courts from the civil the ecclesiastical were supposed to be the most appropriate for the trial of matrimonial causes and offences against the rights of marriage, just as they were for testamentary causes and the settlement of the estates of deceased persons.

By the statute of 1 James I., the offence, if committed in England or Wales, was made punishable in the civil courts, and the penalty was death. As this statute was limited in its operation to England and Wales, it was at a very early period re-enacted, generally with some modifications, in all the colonies. In connection with the case we are now considering, it is a significant fact that on the 8th of December, 1788, after the passage of the act establishing religious freedom, and after the convention of Virginia had recommended as an amendment to the Constitution of the United States the declaration in a bill of rights that "all men have an equal, natural, and unalienable right to the free exercise of religion, according to the dictates of conscience," the legislature of that State substantially enacted the statute of James I., death penalty included, because, as recited in the preamble, "it hath been doubted whether bigamy or polygamy be punishable by the laws of this Commonwealth." From that day to this we think it may safely be said there never has been a time in any State of the Union when polygamy has not been an offence against society, cognizable by the civil courts and punishable with more or less severity. In the face of all this evidence, it is impossible to believe that the constitutional guaranty of religious freedom was intended to prohibit legislation in respect to this most important feature of social life. Marriage, while from its very nature a sacred obligation, is nevertheless, in most civilized nations, a civil contract, and usually regulated by law. Upon it society may be said to be built, and out of its fruits spring social relations and social obligations and duties, with which government is necessarily required to deal. In fact, according as monogamous or polygamous marriages are allowed, do we find the principles on which the government of [166] the people, to a greater or less extent, rests. Professor Lieber says, polygamy leads to the patriarchal principle, and which, when applied to large communities, fetters the people in stationary despotism, while that principle cannot long exist in connection with monogamy. Chancellor Kent observes that this remark is equally striking and profound. An exceptional colony of polygamists under an exceptional leadership may sometimes exist for a time without appearing to disturb the social condition of the people who surround it; but there cannot be a doubt that, unless restricted by some form of constitution, it is within the legitimate scope of the power of every civil government to determine whether polygamy or monogamy shall be the law of social life under its dominion.

In our opinion, the statute immediately under consideration is within the legislative power of Congress. It is constitutional and valid as prescribing a rule of action for all those residing in the Territories, and in places over which the United States have exclusive control. This being so, the only question which remains is, whether those who make polygamy a part of their religion are excepted from the operation of the statute. If they are, then those who do not make polygamy a part of their religious belief may be found guilty and punished, while those who do, must be acquitted and go free. This would be introducing a new element into criminal law. Laws are made for the government of actions, and while they cannot interfere with mere religious belief and opinions, they may with practices. Suppose one believed that human sacrifices were a necessary part of religious worship, would it be seriously contended that the civil government under which he lived could not interfere to prevent a sacrifice? Or if a wife religiously believed it was her duty to burn herself upon the funeral pile of her dead husband, would it be beyond the power of the civil government to prevent her carrying her belief into practice?

So here, as a law of the organization of society under the exclusive dominion of the United States, it is provided that plural marriages shall not be allowed. Can a man excuse his practices to the contrary because of his religious belief? [167] To permit this would be to make the professed doctrines of religious belief superior to the law of the land, and in effect to permit every citizen to become a law unto himself. Government could exist only in name under such circumstances.

A criminal intent is generally an element of crime, but every man is presumed to intend the necessary and legitimate consequences of what he knowingly does. Here the accused knew he had been once married, and that his first wife was living. He also knew that his second marriage was forbidden by law. When, therefore, he married the second time, he is presumed to have intended to break the law. And the breaking of the law is the crime. Every act necessary to constitute the crime was knowingly done, and the crime was therefore knowingly committed. Ignorance of a fact may sometimes be taken as evidence of a want of criminal intent, but not ignorance of the law. The only defence of the accused in this case is his belief that the law ought not to have been enacted. It matters not that his belief was a part of his professed religion: it was still belief, and belief only.

In *Regina v. Wagstaff*, the parents of a sick child, who omitted to call in medical attendance because of their religious belief that what they did for its cure would be effective, were held not to be guilty of manslaughter, while it was said the contrary would have been the result if the child had actually been starved to death by the parents, under the notion that it was their religious duty to abstain from giving it food. But when the offence consists of a positive act which is knowingly done, it would be dangerous to hold that the offender might escape punishment because he religiously believed the law which he had broken ought never to have been made. No case, we believe, can be found that has gone so far. . . .

2

Church of the Holy Trinity v. United States

143 U.S. 457 (1892)

Vote: 9—Field, Harlan, Gray, Blatchford, Lamar, Fuller, Brewer, Brown, Shiras
  0

Opinion announcing the opinion of the Court: Brewer

In 1887, the Church of the Holy Trinity, an Episcopal church in New York, contracted with E. Walpole Warren, an English clergyman residing in London, to become the church's rector and pastor. The church subsequently was convicted of violating the Alien Contract Labor Act of 1885, a federal law that prohibited "the importation and migration of foreigners and aliens under contract or agreement to perform labor in the United States, its Territories, and the District of Columbia."

  The Alien Contract Labor Act made it illegal for employers to pay the migration costs of aliens under contract to perform "labor or service of any kind" in the United States. The intent of the legislation, as expressed in a House committee report, was "to restrain and prohibit the immigration or importation of laborers who would have never seen our shores but for the inducements and allurements of men whose only object is to obtain labor at the lowest possible rate, regardless of the social and material well-being of our own citizens and regardless of the evil consequences which result to American laborers from such immigration." Referring to such laborers, the report continued,

> This class of immigrants care nothing about our institutions, and in many instances never even heard of them; they are men whose passage is paid by the importers; they come here under contract to labor for a certain number of years; they are ignorant of our social condition, and that they may remain so they are isolated and prevented from coming into contact with Americans. They are generally from the lowest social stratum, and live upon the coarsest food and in hovels of a character before unknown to American workmen. They, as a rule, do not become citizens, and are certainly not a desirable acquisition to the body politic. The inevitable tendency of their presence among us is to degrade American labor, and to reduce it to the level of the imported pauper labor.*

---

*Congressional Record, 48th Cong., 5359.

MR. JUSTICE BREWER delivered the opinion of the court.

. . . [458] It must be conceded that the act of the corporation is within the letter of this section, for the relation of rector to his church is one of service, and implies labor on the one side with compensation on the other. Not only are the general words labor and service both used, but also, as it were to guard against any narrow interpretation and emphasize a breadth of meaning, to them is added "of any kind;" and, further, as noticed by the Circuit Judge in his opinion, the fifth section, which makes specific exceptions, among them professional actors, artists, lecturers, singers and domestic [459] servants, strengthens the idea that every other kind of labor and service was intended to be reached by the first section. While there is great force to this reasoning, we cannot think Congress intended to denounce with penalties a transaction like that in the present case. It is a familiar rule, that a thing may be within the letter of the statute and yet not within the statute, because not within its spirit, nor within the intention of its makers. This has been often asserted, and the reports are full of cases illustrating its application. This is not the substitution of the will of the judge for that of the legislator, for frequently words of general meaning are used in a statute, words broad enough to include an act in question, and yet a consideration of the whole legislation, or of the circumstances surrounding its enactment, or of the absurd results which follow from giving such broad meaning to the words, makes it unreasonable to believe that the legislator intended to include the particular act. As said in Plowden, 205: "From which cases, it appears that the sages of the law heretofore have construed statutes quite contrary to the letter in some appearance, and those statutes which comprehend all things in the letter they have expounded to extend to but some things, and those which generally prohibit all people from doing such an act they have interpreted to permit some people to do it, and those which include every person in the letter, they have adjudged to reach to some persons only, which expositions have always been founded upon the intent of the legislature; which they have collected sometimes by considering the cause and necessity of making the act, sometimes by comparing one part of the act with another, and sometimes by foreign circumstances." . . .

[463] It will be seen that words as general as those used in the first section of this act were by that decision limited, and the intent of Congress with respect to the act was gathered partially, at least, from its title. Now, the title of this act is, "An act to prohibit the importation and migration of foreigners and aliens under contract or agreement to perform labor in the United States, its Territories and the District of Columbia." Obviously the thought expressed in this reaches only to the work of the manual laborer, as distinguished from that of the professional man. No one reading such a title would suppose that Congress had in its mind any purpose of staying the coming into this country of ministers of the gospel, or, indeed, of any class whose toil is that of the brain. The common understanding of the terms labor and laborers does not include preaching and preachers; and it is to be assumed that words and phrases are used in their ordinary meaning. So whatever of light is thrown upon the statute by the language of the title indicates an exclusion from its penal provisions of all contracts for the employment of ministers, rectors and pastors.

Again, another guide to the meaning of a statute is found in the evil which it is designed to remedy; and for this the court properly looks at contemporaneous events, the situation as it existed, and as it was pressed upon the attention of the legislative body. The situation which called for this statute was briefly but fully stated by Mr. Justice Brown when, as District Judge, he decided the case of *United States v. Craig*, 28 Fed.

Rep. 795, 798: "The motives and history of the act are matters of common knowledge. It had become the practice for large capitalists in this country to contract with their agents abroad for the shipment of great numbers of an ignorant and servile class of foreign laborers, under contracts, by which the employer agreed, upon the one hand, to prepay their passage, while, upon the other hand, the laborers agreed to work after their arrival for a certain time at a low rate of wages. The effect of this was to break down the labor market, and to reduce other laborers engaged in like occupations to the level [464] of the assisted immigrant. The evil finally became so flagrant that an appeal was made to Congress for relief by the passage of the act in question, the design of which was to raise the standard of foreign immigrants, and to discountenance the migration of those who had not sufficient means in their own hands, or those of their friends, to pay their passage."

It appears, also, from the petitions, and in the testimony presented before the committees of Congress, that it was this cheap unskilled labor which was making the trouble, and the influx of which Congress sought to prevent. It was never suggested that we had in this country a surplus of brain toilers, and, least of all, that the market for the services of Christian ministers was depressed by foreign competition. Those were matters to which the attention of Congress, or of the people, was not directed. So far, then, as the evil which was sought to be remedied interprets the statute, it also guides to an exclusion of this contract from the penalties of the act. . . .

[465] We find, therefore, that the title of the act, the evil which was intended to be remedied, the circumstances surrounding the appeal to Congress, the reports of the committee of each house, all concur in affirming that the intent of Congress was simply to stay the influx of this cheap unskilled labor.

But beyond all these matters no purpose of action against religion can be imputed to any legislation, state or national, because this is a religious people. This is historically true. From the discovery of this continent to the present hour, there is a single voice making this affirmation. . . .

[467] Coming nearer to the present time, the Declaration of Independence recognizes the presence of the Divine in human affairs in these words: "We hold these truths to be self-evident, that all men are created equal, that they are endowed by their Creator with certain unalienable Rights, that among these are Life, Liberty, and the pursuit of Happiness." "We, therefore, the Representatives of the United States of America, in General Congress, Assembled, appealing to the Supreme Judge of the world for the rectitude of our intentions, do, in the Name and by Authority of the good People of these Colonies, solemnly publish and declare," etc.; "And for the support [468] of this Declaration, with a firm reliance on the Protection of Divine Providence, we mutually pledge to each other our Lives, our Fortunes, and our sacred Honor."

If we examine the constitutions of the various States we find in them a constant recognition of religious obligations. Every constitution of every one of the forty-four States contains language which either directly or by clear implication recognizes a profound reverence for religion and an assumption that its influence in all human affairs is essential to the well being of the community. This recognition may be in the preamble, such as is found in the constitution of Illinois, 1870: "We, the people of the State of Illinois, grateful to Almighty God for the civil, political and religious liberty which He hath so long permitted us to enjoy, and looking to Him for a blessing upon our endeavors to secure and transmit the same unimpaired to succeeding generations," etc.

It may be only in the familiar requisition that all officers shall take an oath closing with the declaration "so help me God." It may be in clauses like that of the constitution of Indiana, 1816, Article XI, section 4: "The manner of administering an oath or affirmation shall be such as is most consistent with the conscience of the deponent, and shall be esteemed the most solemn appeal to God." Or in provisions such as are found in Articles 36 and 37 of the Declaration of Rights of the Constitution of Maryland, 1867: "That as it is the duty of every man to worship God in such manner as he thinks most acceptable to Him, all persons are equally entitled to protection in their religious liberty; wherefore, no person ought, by any law, to be molested in his person or estate on account of his religious persuasion or profession, or for his religious practice, unless, under the color of religion, he shall disturb the good order, peace or safety of the State, or shall infringe the laws of morality, or injure others in their natural, civil or religious rights; nor ought any person to be compelled to frequent or maintain or contribute, unless on contract, to maintain any place of worship, or any ministry; nor shall any person, otherwise competent, be deemed incompetent as a witness, or juror, on account of his religious belief: Provided, He [469] believes in the existence of God, and that, under His dispensation, such person will be held morally accountable for his acts, and be rewarded or punished therefor, either in this world or the world to come. That no religious test ought ever to be required as a qualification for any office of profit or trust in this State other than a declaration of belief in the existence of God; nor shall the legislature prescribe any other oath of office than the oath prescribed by this constitution." Or like that in Articles 2 and 3, of Part 1st, of the Constitution of Massachusetts, 1780: "It is the right as well as the duty of all men in society publicly and at stated seasons, to worship the Supreme Being, the great Creator and Preserver of the universe. . . . As the happiness of a people and the good order and preservation of civil government essentially depend upon piety, religion and morality, and as these cannot be generally diffused through a community but by the institution of the public worship of God and of public instructions in piety, religion and morality: Therefore, to promote their happiness and to secure the good order and preservation of their government, the people of this commonwealth have a right to invest their legislature with power to authorize and require, and the legislature shall, from time to time, authorize and require, the several towns, parishes, precincts and other bodies-politic or religious societies to make suitable provision, at their own expense, for the institution of the public worship of God and for the support and maintenance of public Protestant teachers of piety, religion and morality in all cases where such provision shall not be made voluntarily." Or as in sections 5 and 14 of Article 7, of the constitution of Mississippi, 1832: "No person who denies the being of a God, or a future state of rewards and punishments, shall hold any office in the civil department of this State. . . . Religion, morality and knowledge being necessary to good government, the preservation of liberty, and the happiness of mankind, schools and the means of education, shall forever be encouraged in this State." Or by Article 22 of the constitution of Delaware, 1776, which required all officers, besides an oath of allegiance, to make and subscribe the following declaration: "I, A.B., do profess [470] faith in God the Father, and in Jesus Christ His only Son, and in the Holy Ghost, one God, blessed for evermore; and I do acknowledge the Holy Scriptures of the Old and New Testament to be given by divine inspiration."

Even the Constitution of the United States, which is supposed to have little touch upon the private life of the individual, contains in the First Amendment a declaration common to the constitutions of all the States, as follows: "Congress shall make no law respecting an establishment of religion, or prohibiting the free exercise thereof," etc. And also provides in Article 1, section 7, a provision common to many constitutions, that the Executive shall have ten days (Sundays excepted) within which to determine whether he will approve or veto a bill.

There is no dissonance in these declarations. There is a universal language pervading them all, having one meaning; they affirm and reaffirm that this is a religious nation. These are not individual sayings, declarations of private persons: they are organic utterances; they speak the voice of the entire people. . . .

[471] If we pass beyond these matters to a view of American life as expressed by its laws, its business, its customs and its society, we find everywhere a clear recognition of the same truth. Among other matters note the following: The form of oath universally prevailing, concluding with an appeal to the Almighty; the custom of opening sessions of all deliberative bodies and most conventions with prayer; the prefatory words of all wills, "In the name of God, amen"; the laws respecting the observance of the Sabbath, with the general cessation of all secular business, and the closing of courts, legislatures, and other similar public assemblies on that day; the churches and church organizations which abound in every city, town and hamlet; the multitude of charitable organizations existing every where under Christian auspices; the gigantic missionary associations, with general support, and aiming to establish Christian missions in every quarter of the globe. These, and many other matters which might be noticed, add a volume of unofficial declarations to the mass of organic utterances that this is a Christian nation. In the face of all these, shall it be believed that a Congress of the United States intended to make it a misdemeanor for a church of this country to contract for the services of a Christian minister residing in another nation?

[472] Suppose in the Congress that passed this act some member had offered a bill which in terms declared that, if any Roman Catholic church in this country should contract with Cardinal Manning to come to this country and enter into its service as pastor and priest; or any Episcopal church should enter into a like contract with Canon Farrar; or any Baptist church should make similar arrangements with Rev. Mr. Spurgeon; or any Jewish synagogue with some eminent Rabbi, such contract should be adjudged unlawful and void, and the church making it be subject to prosecution and punishment, can it be believed that it would have received a minute of approving thought or a single vote? Yet it is contended that such was in effect the meaning of this statute. The construction invoked cannot be accepted as correct. It is a case where there was presented a definite evil, in view of which the legislature used general terms with the purpose of reaching all phases of that evil, and thereafter, unexpectedly, it is developed that the general language thus employed is broad enough to reach cases and acts which the whole history and life of the country affirm could not have been intentionally legislated against. It is the duty of the courts, under those circumstances, to say that, however broad the language of the statute may be, the act, although within the letter, is not within the intention of the legislature, and therefore cannot be within the statute.

3

Bradfield v. Roberts

175 U.S. 291 (1899)

Vote: 9—Harlan, Gray, Fuller, Brewer, Brown, Shiras, White, Peckham, McKenna
  0

Opinion announcing the opinion of the Court: Peckham

In March 1897, Congress appropriated $30,000 to be used toward construction of hospital buildings in Washington, DC. In August 1897, the district commissioners contracted with Providence Hospital to build a new facility. The hospital, incorporated in 1864, was owned and operated by the Sisters of Charity, a group of Catholic nuns.

As part of the building appropriation, the district commissioners and the hospital directors agreed that two-thirds of the capacity of the federally funded building would be reserved for the city's indigent patients and that the hospital would be paid $250 per annum (68 cents per day) for the care of each of those patients. The agreement also stipulated that persons able to pay for their treatments would "have the privilege of selecting their own physicians and nurses . . . at the expense of the patient making the request."

This case resulted from a taxpayer challenge to the Catholic hospital receiving federal funds.

MR. JUSTICE PECKHAM, after stating the facts, delivered the opinion of the court.

. . . [296] The act shows that the individuals named therein and their successors in office were incorporated under the name of "The Directors of Providence Hospital," with power to [297] receive, hold and convey personal and real property, as provided in its first section. By the second section the corporation was granted "full power and all the rights of opening and keeping a hospital in the city of Washington for the care of such sick and invalid persons as may place themselves under the treatment and care of the said corporation." The third section gave it full power to make such by-laws, rules and regulations that might be necessary for the general accomplishment of the objects of the hospital, not inconsistent with the laws in force in the District of Columbia. Nothing is said about religion or about the religious faith of the incorporators of this institution in the act of incorporation. It is simply the ordinary case of the incorporation of a hospital for the purposes for which such an institution is generally conducted. It is claimed that the allegation in the complainant's bill, that the said "Providence Hospital is a private eleemosynary corporation, and that to the best of complainant's knowledge and belief it is composed of members of a monastic order or sisterhood of the Roman Catholic Church, and is conducted under the auspices of said church; that the title to its property is vested in the Sisters of Charity of Emmitsburg, Maryland," renders the agreement void for the reason therein stated, which is that Congress has no power to make "a law respecting a religious establishment," a phrase which is not synonymous with that used in the Constitution, which prohibits the passage of a law "respecting an establishment of religion."

If we were to assume, for the purpose of this question only, that under this appropriation an agreement with a religious corporation of the tenor of this agreement would be invalid, as resulting indirectly in the passage of an act respecting an establishment of religion, we are unable to see that the complainant in his bill shows that the corporation is of the kind described, but on the contrary he has clearly shown that it is not.

The above-mentioned allegations in the complainant's bill do not change the legal character of the corporation or render it on that account a religious or sectarian body. Assuming [298] that the hospital is a private eleemosynary corporation, the fact that its members, according to the belief of the complainant, are members of a monastic order or sisterhood of the Roman Catholic Church, and the further fact that the hospital is conducted under the auspices of said church, are wholly immaterial, as is also the allegation regarding the title to its property. The statute provides as to its property and makes no provision for its being held by any one other than itself. The facts above stated do not in the least change the legal character of the hospital, or make a religious corporation out of a purely secular one as constituted by the law of its being. Whether the individuals who compose the corporation under its charter happen to be all Roman Catholics, or all Methodists, or Presbyterians, or Unitarians, or members of any other religious organization, or of no organization at all, is of not the slightest consequence with reference to the law of its incorporation, nor can the individual beliefs upon religious matters of the various incorporators be inquired into. Nor is it material that the hospital may be conducted under the auspices of the Roman Catholic Church. To be conducted under the auspices is to be conducted under the influence or patronage of that church. The meaning of the allegation is that the church exercises great and perhaps controlling influence over the management of the hospital. It must, however, be managed pursuant to the law of its being. That the influence of any particular church may be powerful over the members of a non-sectarian and secular corporation, incorporated for a certain defined purpose and with clearly stated powers, is surely not sufficient to convert such a corporation into a religious or sectarian body. That fact does not alter the legal character of the corporation, which is incorporated under an act of Congress, and its powers, duties and character are to be solely measured by the charter under which it alone has any legal existence. There is no allegation that its hospital work is confined to members of that church or that in its management the hospital has been conducted so as to violate its charter in the smallest degree. It is simply the case of a secular corporation being managed by people [299] who hold to the doctrines of the Roman Catholic Church, but who nevertheless are managing the corporation according to the law under which it exists. The charter itself does not limit the exercise of its corporate powers to the members of any particular religious denomination, but on the contrary those powers are to be exercised in favor of any one seeking the ministrations of that kind of an institution. All that can be said of the corporation itself is that it has been incorporated by an act of Congress, and for its legal powers and duties that act must be exclusively referred to. As stated in the opinion of the Court of Appeals, this corporation "is not declared the trustee of any church or religious society. Its property is to be acquired in its own name and for its own purposes; that property and its business are to be managed in its own way, subject to no visitation, supervision or control by any ecclesiastical authority whatever, but only to that of the Government which created it. In respect then of its creation, organization, management and ownership of property it is an ordinary private corporation whose rights are determinable by the law of the land, and the religious opinions of whose members are not subjects of inquiry."

It is not contended that Congress has no power in the District to appropriate money for the purpose expressed in the appropriation, and it is not doubted that it has power to authorize the Commissioners of the District of Columbia to enter into a contract with the trustees of an incorporated hospital for the purposes mentioned in the agreement in this case, and the only objection set up is the alleged "sectarian character of the hospital and the specific and limited object of its creation."

The other allegations in complainant's bill are simply statements of his opinion in regard to the results necessarily flowing from the appropriation in question when connected with the agreement mentioned.

The act of Congress, however, shows there is nothing sectarian in the corporation, and "the specific and limited object of its creation" is the opening and keeping a hospital in the city of Washington for the care of such sick and invalid persons as [300] may place themselves under the treatment and care of the corporation. To make the agreement was within the discretion of the Commissioners, and was a fair exercise thereof.

The right reserved in the third section of the charter to amend, alter or repeal the act leaves full power in Congress to remedy any abuse of the charter privileges.

Without adverting to any other objections to the maintenance of this suit, it is plain that complainant wholly fails to set forth a cause of action, and the bill was properly dismissed by the Court of Appeals, and its decree will, therefore, be

Affirmed.

Cantwell v. State of Connecticut

310 U.S. 296 (1940)

Vote: 9—Hughes, McReynolds, Stone, Roberts, Black, Reed, Frankfurter, Douglas, Murphy

  0

Opinion announcing the opinion of the Court: Roberts

Newton Cantwell and his two sons, Jesse and Russell, members of the Jehovah's Witnesses, were arrested in New Haven, Connecticut. On the day of their arrests, the Cantwells had gone door-to-door on Cassius Street in New Haven to proselytize. Each carried books and pamphlets on religious subjects, a portable phonograph, and a set of phonograph records that introduced and described the books. The Cantwells asked those who responded to their door calls for permission to play one of the records. If permission was granted, they asked the person to buy the book described. Upon a refusal to purchase the book, the Cantwells solicited a contribution toward the publication of the pamphlets. If a contribution was received, a pamphlet was delivered upon the condition that it would be read. At the time, Cassius Street passed through a Roman Catholic neighborhood.

One of the Cantwells' phonograph records, describing a book titled Enemies, *included an attack on Catholicism. Jesse Cantwell stopped two men in the street, asked for and received permission to play a phonograph record, and played the* Enemies *record. Both men happened to be Catholic and were incensed by the record's contents. One of the men testified that he felt like hitting Cantwell. When asked, "Did you do anything else or have any other reaction?" he answered, "No, sir, because he said he would take the Victrola and he went." The other man testified that he was tempted to throw Cantwell off the street and that he told Cantwell he had better get off the street before something happened to him. He also said that was the end of the matter, as Cantwell picked up his books and walked up the street. There was no evidence that Jesse Cantwell was personally offensive or entered into any argument with those he interviewed.*

Each Cantwell was charged with violating a Connecticut licensing solicitation statute and the common-law offense of inciting a breach of the peace. * *In relevant part, the*

---

*The Connecticut Supreme Court held that the charge was not assault, breach of the peace, or making threats but invoking or inciting others to a breach of the peace and that the facts supported conviction for that offense. The U.S. Supreme Court vacated Cantwell's breach-of-the-peace conviction.

licensing solicitation statute under which the appellants were charged and convicted provided the following:

> *No person shall solicit money, services, subscriptions or any valuable thing for any alleged religious, charitable or philanthropic cause, from other than a member of the organization for whose benefit such person is soliciting or within the county in which such person or organization is located unless such cause shall have been approved by the secretary of the public welfare council. Upon application of any person in behalf of such cause, the secretary shall determine whether such cause is a religious one or is a bona fide object of charity or philanthropy and conforms to reasonable standards of efficiency and integrity, and, if he shall so find, shall approve the same and issue to the authority in charge a certificate to that effect.*

On appeal to the Connecticut Supreme Court, the convictions of all three on the statutory offense were affirmed. The Cantwells appealed to the Supreme Court, contending that their convictions violated the Free Exercise Clause.

Mr. Justice ROBERTS, delivered the opinion of the Court.

. . . [303] First. We hold that the [licensing solicitation] statute, as construed and applied to the appellants, deprives them of their liberty without due process of law in contravention of the Fourteenth Amendment. The fundamental concept of liberty embodied in that Amendment embraces the liberties guaranteed by the First Amendment. The First Amendment declares that Congress shall make no law respecting an establishment of religion or prohibiting the free exercise thereof. The Fourteenth Amendment has rendered the legislatures of the states as incompetent as Congress to enact such laws. The constitutional inhibition of legislation on the subject of religion has a double aspect. On the one hand, it forestalls compulsion by law of the acceptance of any creed or the practice of any form of worship. Freedom of conscience and freedom to adhere to such religious organization or form of worship as the individual may choose cannot be restricted by law. On the other hand, it safeguards the free exercise of the chosen form of religion. Thus the Amendment embraces two concepts—freedom to believe and freedom to act. The first is absolute but, in the nature of things, the [304] second cannot be. Conduct remains subject to regulation for the protection of society. The freedom to act must have appropriate definition to preserve the enforcement of that protection. In every case the power to regulate must be so exercised as not, in attaining a permissible end, unduly to infringe the protected freedom. No one would contest the proposition that a state may not, by statute, wholly deny the right to preach or to disseminate religious views. Plainly such a previous and absolute restraint would violate the terms of the guarantee. It is equally clear that a state may by general and non-discriminatory legislation regulate the times, the places, and the manner of soliciting upon its streets, and of holding meetings thereon; and may in other respects safeguard the peace, good order and comfort of the community, without unconstitutionally invading the liberties protected by the Fourteenth Amendment. The appellants are right in their insistence that the Act in question is not such a regulation. If a certificate is procured, solicitation is permitted without restraint but, in the absence of a certificate, solicitation is altogether prohibited.

The appellants urge that to require them to obtain a certificate as a condition of soliciting support for their views amounts to a prior restraint on the exercise of their religion within the meaning of the Constitution. The State insists that the Act, as construed by the Supreme Court of Connecticut, imposes no previous restraint upon the dissemination of religious views or teaching but merely safeguards against the perpetration of frauds under the cloak of religion. Conceding that this is so, the question remains whether the method adopted by Connecticut to [305] that end transgresses the liberty safeguarded by the Constitution.

The general regulation, in the public interest, of solicitation, which does not involve any religious test and does not unreasonably obstruct or delay the collection of funds, is not open to any constitutional objection, even though the collection be for a religious purpose. Such regulation would not constitute a prohibited previous restraint on the free exercise of religion or interpose an inadmissible obstacle to its exercise.

It will be noted, however, that the Act requires an application to the secretary of the public welfare council of the State; that he is empowered to determine whether the cause is a religious one, and that the issue of a certificate depends upon his affirmative action. If he finds that the cause is not that of religion, to solicit for it becomes a crime. He is not to issue a certificate as a matter of course. His decision to issue or refuse it involves appraisal of facts, the exercise of judgment, and the formation of an opinion. He is authorized to withhold his approval if he determines that the cause is not a religious one. Such a censorship of religion as the means of determining its right to survive is a denial of liberty protected by the First Amendment and included in the liberty which is within the protection of the Fourteenth.

The State asserts that if the licensing officer acts arbitrarily, capriciously, or corruptly, his action is subject to judicial correction. Counsel refer to the rule prevailing in Connecticut that the decision of a commission or an administrative official will be reviewed upon a claim that "it works material damage to individual or corporate rights, or invades or threatens such rights, or is so unreasonable as to justify judicial intervention, or is not consonant with justice, or that a legal duty has not [306] been performed." It is suggested that the statute is to be read as requiring the officer to issue a certificate unless the cause in question is clearly not a religious one; and that if he violates his duty his action will be corrected by a court.

To this suggestion there are several sufficient answers. The line between a discretionary and a ministerial act is not always easy to mark and the statute has not been construed by the State court to impose a mere ministerial duty on the secretary of the welfare council. Upon his decision as to the nature of the cause, the right to solicit depends. Moreover, the availability of a judicial remedy for abuses in the system of licensing still leaves that system one of previous restraint which, in the field of free speech and press, we have held inadmissible. A statute authorizing previous restraint upon the exercise of the guaranteed freedom by judicial decision after trial is as obnoxious to the Constitution as one providing for like restraint by administrative action.

Nothing we have said is intended even remotely to imply that, under the cloak of religion, persons may, with impunity, commit frauds upon the public. Certainly penal laws are available to punish such conduct. Even the exercise of religion may be at some slight inconvenience in order that the state may protect its citizens from injury. Without doubt a state may protect its citizens from fraudulent solicitation by requiring a stranger in the community, before permitting him publicly to solicit funds for any purpose, to establish his identity and his authority to act for the cause which he purports to represent. The state is likewise free to regulate the time [307] and manner of solicitation generally, in the interest of public safety, peace, comfort or convenience. But to condition the solicitation of aid for the perpetuation of religious views or systems upon a license, the grant of which rests in the exercise of a determination by state authority as to what is a religious cause, is to lay a forbidden burden upon the exercise of liberty protected by the Constitution. . . .

Minersville School District v. Gobitis

310 U.S. 586 (1940)

Vote: 8—Hughes, McReynolds, Roberts, Black, Reed, Frankfurter, Douglas, Murphy
*   1—Stone*

Opinion announcing the opinion of the Court: Frankfurter
Concurring in the result: McReynolds
Dissenting opinion: Stone

Lillian Gobitis, aged twelve, and her brother William, aged ten, were expelled from the public schools of Minersville, Pennsylvania, for refusing to salute the national flag as part of a daily school exercise. The local school board required both teachers and pupils to participate in the ceremony. At the time, the recited text of the Pledge of Allegiance was as follows: "I pledge allegiance to my flag, and to the Republic for which it stands; one nation indivisible, with liberty and justice for all." While the words were spoken, teachers and pupils extended their right hands in salute.

The Gobitis family, who were Jehovah's Witnesses, believed that the Bible forbade exercises such as the flag salute with the Pledge of Allegiance. To comply with Pennsylvania's compulsory school-attendance law, the family enrolled the children in private schools. To be relieved of the financial burden thereby entailed, they brought suit, seeking to enjoin Minersville authorities from exacting participation in the flag-salute ceremony as a condition of the children's attendance at the public schools.

Mr. Justice FRANKFURTER delivered the opinion of the Court.

. . . [593] Centuries of strife over the erection of particular dogmas as exclusive or all-comprehending faiths led to the inclusion of a guarantee for religious freedom in the Bill of Rights. The First Amendment, and the Fourteenth through its absorption of the First, sought to guard against repetition of those bitter religious struggles by prohibiting the establishment of a state religion and by securing to every sect the free exercise of its faith. So pervasive is the acceptance of this precious right that its scope is brought into question, as here, only when the conscience of individuals collides with the felt necessities of society.

Certainly the affirmative pursuit of one's convictions about the ultimate mystery of the universe and man's relation to it is placed beyond the reach of law. Government may not interfere with organized or individual expression of belief or disbelief. Propagation of belief—or even of disbelief in the supernatural—is protected, whether in church or chapel, mosque or synagogue, tabernacle or meetinghouse. Likewise the Constitution assures generous immunity to the individual from imposition of penalties for offending, in the course of his own religious activities, the religious views of others, be they a minority or those who are dominant in government.

But the manifold character of man's relations may bring his conception of religious duty into conflict with the secular interests of his fellow-men. When does the constitutional guarantee compel exemption from doing what society thinks necessary for the promotion of some great common end, or from a penalty for conduct which appears dangerous to the general good? To state the [594] problem is to recall the truth that no single principle can answer all of life's complexities. The right to freedom of religious belief, however dissident and however obnoxious to the cherished beliefs of others—even of a majority—is itself the denial of an absolute. But to affirm that the freedom to follow conscience has itself no limits in the life of a society would deny that very plurality of principles which, as a matter of history, underlies protection of religious toleration. Our present task then, as so often the case with courts, is to reconcile two rights in order to prevent either from destroying the other. But, because in safeguarding conscience we are dealing with interests so subtle and so dear, every possible leeway should be given to the claims of religious faith.

In the judicial enforcement of religious freedom we are concerned with a historic concept. The religious liberty which the Constitution protects has never excluded legislation of general scope not directed against doctrinal loyalties of particular sects. Judicial nullification of legislation cannot be justified by attributing to the framers of the Bill of Rights views for which there is no historic warrant. Conscientious scruples have not, in the course of the long struggle for religious toleration, relieved the individual from obedience to a general law not aimed at the promotion or restriction of religious beliefs. The mere possession of religious convictions [595] which contradict the relevant concerns of a political society does not relieve the citizen from the discharge of political responsibilities. The necessity for this adjustment has again and again been recognized. In a number of situations the exertion of political authority has been sustained, while basic considerations of religious freedom have been left inviolate. *Reynolds v. United States; Davis v. Beason; Selective Draft Law Cases; Hamilton v. Regents.* In all these cases the general laws in question, upheld in their application to those who refused obedience from religious conviction, were manifestations of specific powers of government deemed by the legislature essential to secure and maintain that orderly, tranquil, and free society without which religious toleration itself is unattainable. Nor does the freedom of speech assured by Due Process move in a more absolute circle of immunity than that enjoyed by religious freedom. Even if it were assumed that freedom of speech goes beyond the historic concept of full opportunity to utter and to disseminate views, however heretical or offensive to dominant opinion, and includes freedom from conveying what may be deemed an implied but rejected affirmation, the question remains whether school children, like the Gobitis children, must be excused from conduct required of all the other children in the promotion of national cohesion. We are dealing with an interest inferior to none in the hierarchy of legal values. National unity is the basis of national security. To deny the legislature the right to select appropriate means for its attainment presents a totally different order of problem from that of the propriety of subordinating the possible ugliness of littered streets to the free expression of opinion through distribution of handbills. [596] Situations like the present are phases of the profoundest problem confronting a democracy—the problem which Lincoln cast in memorable dilemma: "Must a government of necessity be too strong for the liberties of its people, or too weak to maintain its own existence?" No mere textual reading or logical talisman can solve the dilemma. And when the issue demands judicial determination, it is not the personal notion of judges of what wise adjustment requires which must prevail.

Unlike the instances we have cited, the case before us is not concerned with an exertion of legislative power for the promotion of some specific need or interest of secular society—the protection of the family, the promotion of health, the common defense, the raising of public revenues to defray the cost of government. But all these specific activities of government presuppose the existence of an organized political society. The ultimate foundation of a free society is the binding tie of cohesive sentiment. Such a sentiment is fostered by all those agencies of the mind and spirit which may serve to gather up the traditions of a people, transmit them from generation to generation, and thereby create that continuity of a treasured common life which constitutes a civilization. "We live by symbols." The flag is the symbol of our national unity, transcending all internal differences, however large, within the framework of the Constitution. This Court has had occasion to say that ". . . the flag is the symbol of the nation's power, the emblem of freedom in its truest, best sense. . . . [I]t signifies government resting on the consent of the governed; liberty regulated by law; the protection of the weak against the strong; security against the exercise of arbitrary power; and absolute safety for free institutions against foreign aggression." *Halter v. Nebraska*, 205 U.S. 34, 43.

[597] The case before us must be viewed as though the legislature of Pennsylvania had itself formally directed the flag-salute for the children of Minersville; had made no exemption for children whose parents were possessed of conscientious scruples like those of the Gobitis family; and had indicated its belief in the desirable ends to be secured by having its public school children share a common experience at those periods of development when their minds are supposedly receptive to its assimilation, by an exercise appropriate in time and place and setting, and one designed to evoke in them appreciation of the nation's hopes and dreams, its sufferings and sacrifices. The precise issue, then, for us to decide is whether the legislatures of the various states and the authorities in a thousand counties and school districts of this country are barred from determining the appropriateness of various means to evoke that unifying sentiment without which there can ultimately be no liberties, civil or religious. To stigmatize legislative judgment in providing for this universal gesture of respect for the symbol of our national life in the setting of the common school as a lawless inroad on that freedom of conscience which the Constitution protects, would amount to no less than the pronouncement of pedagogical and psychological dogma in a field where courts possess no marked and certainly no [598] controlling competence. The influences which help toward a common feeling for the common country are manifold. Some may seem harsh and others no doubt are foolish. Surely, however, the end is legitimate. And the effective means for its attainment are still so uncertain and so unauthenticated by science as to preclude us from putting the widely prevalent belief in flag-saluting beyond the pale of legislative power. It mocks reason and denies our whole history to find in the allowance of a requirement to salute our flag on fitting occasions the seeds of sanction for obeisance to a leader.

The wisdom of training children in patriotic impulses by those compulsions which necessarily pervade so much of the educational process is not for our independent judgment. Even were we convinced of the folly of such a measure, such belief would be no proof of its unconstitutionality. For ourselves, we might be tempted to say that the deepest patriotism is best engendered by giving unfettered scope to the most crochety [*sic*] beliefs. Perhaps it is best, even from the standpoint of those interests which ordinances like the one under review seek to promote, to give to the least popular sect leave from conformities like those here in issue. But the courtroom is not the arena for debating issues of educational policy. It is not our province to choose among competing considerations in the subtle process of securing effective loyalty to the traditional ideals of democracy, while respecting at the same time individual idiosyncrasies among a people so diversified in racial origins and religious allegiances. So to hold would in effect make us the school board for the country. That authority has not been given to this Court, nor should we assume it.

We are dealing here with the formative period in the development of citizenship. Great diversity of psychological and ethical opinion exists among us concerning the best way to train children for their place in society. Be- [599] cause of these differences and because of reluctance to permit a single, iron-cast system of education to be imposed upon a nation compounded of so many strains, we have held that, even though public education is one of our most cherished democratic institutions, the Bill of Rights bars a state from compelling all children to attend the public schools. *Pierce v. Society of the Sisters of the Holy Names of Jesus and Mary.* But it is a very different thing for this Court to exercise censorship over the conviction of legislatures that a particular program or exercise will best promote in the minds of children who attend the common schools an attachment to the institutions of their country. . . .

That the flag-salute is an allowable portion of a school program for those who do not invoke conscientious scruples is surely not debatable. But for us to insist that, though the ceremony may be required, exceptional immunity must be [600] given to dissidents, is to maintain that there is no basis for a legislative judgment that such an exemption might introduce elements of difficulty into the school discipline, might cast doubts in the minds of the other children which would themselves weaken the effect of the exercise.

The preciousness of the family relation, the authority and independence which give dignity to parenthood, indeed the enjoyment of all freedom, presuppose the kind of ordered society which is summarized by our flag. A society which is dedicated to the preservation of these ultimate values of civilization may in self-protection utilize the educational process for inculcating those almost unconscious feelings which bind men together in a comprehending loyalty, whatever may be their lesser differences and difficulties. That is to say, the process may be utilized so long as men's right to believe as they please, to win others to their way of belief, and their right to assemble in their chosen places of worship for the devotional ceremonies of their faith, are all fully respected.

Judicial review, itself a limitation on popular government, is a fundamental part of our constitutional scheme. But to the legislature no less than to courts is committed the guardianship of deeply-cherished liberties. Where all the effective means of inducing political changes are left free from interference, education in the abandonment of foolish legislation is itself a training in liberty. To fight out the wise use of legislative authority in the forum of public opinion and before legislative assemblies rather than to transfer such a contest to the judicial arena, serves to vindicate the self-confidence of a free people.

Mr. Justice STONE dissenting.

. . . [601] The law which is thus sustained is unique in the history of Anglo-American legislation. It does more than suppress freedom of speech and more than prohibit the free exercise of religion, which concededly are forbidden by the First Amendment and are violations of the liberty guaranteed by the Fourteenth. For by this law the state seeks to coerce these children to express a sentiment which, as they interpret it, they do not entertain, and which violates their deepest religious convictions. It is not denied that such compulsion is a prohibited infringement of personal liberty, freedom of speech and religion, guaranteed by the Bill of Rights, except in so far as it may be justified and supported as a proper exercise of the state's power over public education. Since the state, [602] in competition with parents, may through teaching in the public schools indoctrinate the minds of the young, it is said that in aid of its undertaking to inspire loyalty and devotion to constituted authority and the flag which symbolizes it, it may coerce the pupil to make affirmation contrary to his belief and in violation of his religious faith. And, finally, it is said that since the Minersville School Board and others are of the opinion that the country will be better served by conformity than by the observance of religious liberty which the Constitution prescribes, the courts are not free to pass judgment on the Board's choice.

Concededly the constitutional guaranties of personal liberty are not always absolutes. Government has a right to survive and powers conferred upon it are not necessarily set at naught by the express prohibitions of the Bill of Rights. It may make war and raise armies. To that end it may compel citizens to give military service, *Selective Draft Law Cases*, and subject them to military training despite their religious objections. *Hamilton v. Regents*. It may suppress religious practices dangerous to morals, and presumably those also which are inimical to public safety, health and good order. *Davis v. Beason*. But it is a long step, and one which I am unable to take, to the position that government may, as a supposed educational measure and as a means of disciplining the young, compel public affirmations which violate their religious conscience. . . .

[W]here there are competing demands of the interests of government and of liberty under the Constitution, and where the performance of governmental functions is brought into conflict with specific constitutional restrictions, there must, when that is possible, be reasonable accommodation between them so as to preserve the essentials of both and . . . it is the function of courts to determine whether such accommodation is reasonably possible. . . . So here, even if we believe that such compulsions will contribute to national unity, there are other ways to teach loyalty and patriotism which are the sources of national unity, than by compelling the pupil to affirm that which he does not believe and by [604] commanding a form of affirmance which violates his religious convictions. Without recourse to such compulsion the state is free to compel attendance at school and require teaching by instruction and study of all in our history and in the structure and organization of our government, including the guaranties of civil liberty which tend to inspire patriotism and love of country. I cannot say that government here is deprived of any interest or function which it is entitled to maintain at the expense of the protection of civil liberties by requiring it to resort to the alternatives which do not coerce an affirmation of belief.

The guaranties of civil liberty are but guaranties of freedom of the human mind and spirit and of reasonable freedom and opportunity to express them. They presuppose the right of the individual to hold such opinions as he will and to give them reasonably free expression, and his freedom, and that of the state as well, to teach and persuade others by the communication of ideas. The very essence of the liberty which they guaranty is the freedom of the individual from compulsion as to what he shall think and what he shall say, at least where the compulsion is to bear false witness to his religion. If these guaranties are to have any meaning they must, I think, be deemed to withhold from the state any authority to compel belief or the expression of it where that expression violates religious convictions, whatever may be the legislative view of the desirability of such compulsion. . . .

[606] The Constitution expresses more than the conviction of the people that democratic processes must be preserved at all costs. It is also an expression of faith and a command that freedom of mind and spirit must be preserved, which government must obey, if it is to adhere to that justice and moderation without which no free govern- [607] ment can exist. For this reason it would seem that legislation which operates to repress the religious freedom of small minorities, which is admittedly within the scope of the protection of the Bill of Rights, must at least be subject to the same judicial scrutiny as legislation which we have recently held to infringe the constitutional liberty of religious and racial minorities.

With such scrutiny I cannot say that the inconveniences which may attend some sensible adjustment of school discipline in order that the religious convictions of these children may be spared, presents a problem so momentous or pressing as to outweigh the freedom from compulsory violation of religious faith which has been thought worthy of constitutional protection.

Jones v. Opelika; Bowden v. Fort Smith; Jobin v. Arizona

316 U.S. 584 (1942)

Vote: 5—Roberts, Reed, Frankfurter, Byrnes, Jackson
    4—Stone, Black, Douglas, Murphy

Opinion announcing the opinion of the Court: Reed
Dissenting opinions: Stone, Black, Murphy

The Court's decision below extended to cases from Alabama, Arkansas, and Arizona in which Jehovah's Witnesses had been convicted for selling books without the appropriate local licenses. The practice of many Jehovah's Witnesses at the time was to go door-to-door or approach individuals on the street and offer religious books and pamphlets in exchange for contributions. Sometimes books and pamphlets were given away without charge.

The City of Opelika, Alabama, charged and convicted petitioner Jones of selling books without a license, operating as a book agent without a license, and operating as a transient agent, dealer, or distributor of books without a license. The license fee for book agents (Bibles excepted) was $10 per annum. The license fee for transient agents, dealers, or distributors of books was $5. The licenses were subject to revocation—potentially without notice—at the discretion of the City Commission.

Petitioner Bowden was convicted of violating a Fort Smith, Arkansas, licensing ordinance that applied to all peddlers of "dry goods, notions, wearing apparel, household goods or other articles not herein or otherwise specifically mentioned." The licensing fees were $25 per month, $10 per week, or $2.50 per day.

Petitioner Jobin was convicted of violating a Casa Grande, Arizona, ordinance that required transient merchants, peddlers, and street vendors to obtain a $25-per-quarter business license.

MR. JUSTICE REED delivered the opinion of the Court.

. . . [593] We turn to the constitutional problem squarely presented by these ordinances. There are ethical principles of greater value to mankind than the guarantees of the Constitution, personal liberties which are beyond the power of government to impair. These principles and liberties belong to the mental and spiritual realm, where the judgments and decrees of mundane courts are ineffective to direct the course of man. The rights of which our Constitution speaks have a more earthy quality. They are not absolutes to be exercised independently of other cherished privileges, protected by the same organic instrument. Conflicts in the exercise of rights arise, and the conflicting forces seek adjustments in the courts, as do these parties, claiming on the one side the freedom of religion, speech and the press, guaranteed by the Fourteenth Amendment, and on the other the right to employ the sovereign power explicitly reserved to the State by the Tenth Amendment to ensure orderly living, without which constitutional guarantees of civil liberties would be a mockery. Courts, no more than Constitutions, can intrude into the consciences of men or compel them to believe contrary to their faith or think contrary [594] to their convictions; but courts are competent to adjudge the acts men do under color of a constitutional right, such as that of freedom of speech or of the press or the free exercise of religion, and to determine whether the claimed right is limited by other recognized powers, equally precious to mankind. So the mind and spirit of man remain forever free, while his actions rest subject to necessary accommodation to the competing needs of his fellows. . . .

[597] When proponents of religious or social theories use the ordinary commercial methods of sales of articles to raise propaganda funds, it is a natural and proper exercise of the power of the State to charge reasonable fees for the privilege of canvassing. Careful as we may and should be to protect the freedoms safeguarded by the Bill of Rights, it is difficult to see in such enactments a shadow of prohibition of the exercise of religion or of abridgement of the freedom of speech or the press. It is prohibition and unjustifiable abridgement which are interdicted, not taxation. Nor do we believe it can be fairly said that because such proper charges may be expanded into unjustifiable abridgements they are therefore invalid on their face. The freedoms claimed by those seeking relief here are guaranteed against abridgement by the Fourteenth Amendment. Its commands protect their rights. The legislative power of municipalities must yield when [598] abridgement is shown. If we were to assume, as is here argued, that the licensed activities involve religious rites, a different question would be presented. These are not taxes on free will offerings. But it is because we view these sales as partaking more of commercial than religious or educational transactions that we find the ordinances, as here presented, valid. A tax on religion or a tax on interstate commerce may alike be forbidden by the Constitution. It does not follow that licenses for selling Bibles or for manufacture of articles of general use, measured by extrastate sales, must fall. It may well be that the wisdom of American communities will persuade them to permit the poor and weak to draw support from the petty sales of religious books without contributing anything for the privilege of using the streets and conveniences of the municipality. Such an exemption, however, would be a voluntary, not a constitutionally enforced, contribution.

In the ordinances of Casa Grande and Fort Smith, we have no discretionary power in the public authorities to refuse a license to any one desirous of selling religious literature. No censorship of the material which enters into the books or papers is authorized. No religious symbolism is involved, such as was urged against the flag salute in *Minersville School District v. Gobitis*. For us there is no occasion to apply here the principles taught by that opinion. Nothing more is asked from one group than from another which uses similar methods of propagation. We see nothing in the collection of a nondiscriminatory license fee, uncontested in amount, from those selling books or papers, which abridges the freedoms of worship, speech or press. As to the claim that even small license charges, if valid, will impose upon the itinerant colporteur a crushing aggregate, [599] it is plain that if each single fee is, as we assume, commensurate with the activities licensed, then though the accumulation of fees from city to city may in time bulk large, he will have enjoyed a correlatively enlarged field of distribution. The First Amendment does not require a subsidy in the form of fiscal exemption. Accordingly, the challenge to the Fort Smith and Casa Grande ordinances fails.

There is an additional contention by petitioner as to the Opelika ordinance. It is urged that, since the licenses were revocable, arbitrarily, by the local authorities, there can be no true freedom for petitioners in the dissemination of information, because of the censorship upon their actions after the issuance of the license. But there has been neither application for, nor revocation of, a license. The complaint was bottomed on sales without a license. It was that charge against which petitioner claimed the protection of the Constitution. This issue he had standing to raise. From what has been said previously, it follows that the objection to the unconstitutionality of requiring a license fails. There is no occasion, at this time, to pass on the validity of the revocation section, as it does not affect his present defense.

In *Lovell v. Griffin*, we held invalid a statute which placed the grant of a license within the discretion of the licensing authority. By this discretion, the right to obtain a license was made an empty right. Therefore the formality of going through an application was naturally not deemed a prerequisite to insistence on a constitutional right. Here we have a very different situation. A license is required that may properly be required. The fact that such a license, if it were granted, may subsequently [600] be revoked does not necessarily destroy the licensing ordinance. The hazard of such revocation is much too contingent for us now to declare the licensing provisions to be invalid. *Lovell v. Griffin* has, in effect, held that discretionary control in the general area of free speech is unconstitutional. Therefore, the hazard that the license properly granted would be improperly revoked is far too slight to justify declaring the valid part of the ordinance, which is alone now at issue, also unconstitutional.

MR. CHIEF JUSTICE STONE [dissenting]:

. . . [608] The First Amendment is not confined to safeguarding freedom of speech and freedom of religion against discriminatory attempts to wipe them out. On the contrary, the Constitution, by virtue of the First and the Fourteenth Amendments, has put those freedoms in a preferred position. Their commands are not restricted to cases where the protected privilege is sought out for attack. They extend at least to every form of taxation which, because it is a condition of the exercise of the privilege, is capable of being used to control or suppress it.

[609] Even were we to assume—what I do not concede—that there could be a lawful non-discriminatory license tax of a percentage of the gross receipts collected by churches and other religious orders in support of their religious work, we have no such tax here. The tax imposed by the ordinances in these cases is more burdensome and destructive of the activity taxed than any gross receipts tax. The tax is for a fixed amount, unrelated to the extent of the defendants' activities or the receipts derived from them. It is thus the type of flat tax which, when applied to interstate commerce, has repeatedly been deemed by this Court to be prohibited by the commerce clause. When applied, as it is here, to activities involving the exercise of religious freedom, its vice is emphasized in that it is levied and paid in advance of the activities taxed, and applied at rates well calculated to suppress those activities, save only as others may volunteer to pay the tax. It requires a sizable out-of-pocket expense by someone who may never succeed in raising a penny in his exercise of the privilege which is taxed.

The defendants' activities, if taxable at all, are taxable only because of the funds which they solicit. But that solicitation is for funds for religious purposes, and the present taxes are in no way gauged to the receipts. The taxes are insupportable either as a tax on the dissemination of ideas or as a tax on the collection of funds for religious purposes. For on its face a flat license tax restrains in advance the freedom taxed and tends inevitably to suppress its exercise. The First Amendment prohibits all laws abridging freedom of press and religion, not merely some laws or all except tax laws. It is true that the constitutional guaranties of freedom of press and religion, like the commerce clause, make no distinction between fixed-sum [610] taxes and other kinds. But that fact affords no excuse for courts, whose duty it is to enforce those guaranties, to close their eyes to the characteristics of a tax which render it destructive of freedom of press and religion.

We may lay to one side the Court's suggestion that a tax otherwise unconstitutional is to be deemed valid unless it is shown that there are none who, for religion's sake, will come forward to pay the unlawful exaction. The defendants to whom the ordinances have been applied have not paid it and there is nothing in the Constitution to compel them to seek the charity of others to pay it before protesting the tax. It seems fairly obvious that if the present taxes, laid in small communities upon peripatetic religious propagandists, are to be sustained, a way has been found for the effective suppression of speech and press and religion despite constitutional guaranties. The very taxes now before us are better adapted to that end than were the stamp taxes which so successfully curtailed the dissemination of ideas by eighteenth century newspapers and pamphleteers, and which were a moving cause of the American Revolution. Vivid recollections of the effect of those taxes on the freedom of press survived to inspire the adoption of the First Amendment.

Freedom of press and religion, explicitly guaranteed by the Constitution, must at least be entitled to the same freedom from burdensome taxation which it has been thought that the more general phraseology of the commerce clause has extended to interstate commerce. Whatever doubts may be entertained as to this Court's function to relieve, unaided by Congressional legislation, from burdensome taxation under the commerce clause, [611] it cannot be thought that that function is wanting under the explicit guaranties of freedom of speech, press and religion. In any case, the flat license tax can hardly become any the less burdensome or more permissible, when levied on activities within the protection extended by the First and Fourteenth Amendments both to the orderly communication of ideas, educational and religious, to persons willing to receive them and to the practice of religion and the solicitation of funds in its support.

In its potency as a prior restraint on publication, the flat license tax falls short only of outright censorship or suppression. The more humble and needy the cause, the more effective is the suppression.

MR. JUSTICE BLACK, MR. JUSTICE DOUGLAS and MR. JUSTICE MURPHY join in this opinion.

MR. JUSTICE MURPHY, with whom the CHIEF JUSTICE, MR. JUSTICE BLACK, and MR. JUSTICE DOUGLAS concur, dissenting.

When a statute is challenged as impinging on freedom of speech, freedom of the press, or freedom of worship, those historic privileges which are so essential to our political welfare and spiritual progress, it is the duty of this Court to subject such legislation to examination, in the light of the evidence adduced, to determine whether it is so drawn as not to impair the substance of those cherished freedoms in reaching its objective. Ordinances that may operate to restrict the circulation or dissemination of ideas on religious or other subjects should be framed with fastidious care and precise language to avoid undue encroachment on these fundamental liberties. And the protection of the Constitution must be extended to all, not [612] only to those whose views accord with prevailing thought but also to dissident minorities who energetically spread their beliefs. Being satisfied by the evidence that the ordinances in the cases now before us, as construed and applied in the state courts, impose a burden on the circulation and discussion of opinion and information in matters of religion, and therefore violate the petitioners' rights to freedom of speech, freedom of the press, and freedom of worship in contravention of the Fourteenth Amendment, I am obliged to dissent from the opinion of the Court.

It is not disputed that petitioners, Jehovah's Witnesses, were ordained ministers preaching the gospel, as they understood it, through the streets and from house to house, orally and by playing religious records with the consent of the householder, and by distributing books and pamphlets setting forth the tenets of their faith. It does not appear that their motives were commercial, but only that they were evangelizing their faith as they saw it. . . .

[613] There is no suggestion in any of these three cases that petitioners were perpetrating a fraud, that they were demeaning themselves in an obnoxious manner, that their activities created any public disturbance or inconvenience, that private rights were contravened, or that the literature distributed was offensive to morals or created any "clear and present danger" to organized society.

The ordinance in each case is sought to be sustained as a system of non-discriminatory taxation of various businesses, [614] professions, and vocations, including the distribution of books for which contributions are asked, for the sole purpose of raising revenue. Any inclination to take the position that petitioners, who were proselytizing by distributing informative literature setting forth their religious tenets, and whose activities were wholly unrelated to any commercial purposes, were not within the purview of these occupational tax ordinances, is foreclosed by the decisions of the state courts below to the contrary. As so construed, the ordinances, in effect, impose direct taxes on the dissemination of ideas and the distribution of literature, relating to and dealing with religious matters, for which a contribution is asked in an attempt to gain converts, because those were petitioners' activities. Such taxes have been held to violate the Fourteenth Amendment, and that should be the holding here.

Freedom of Speech and Freedom of the Press.

. . . [620] The exercise, without commercial motives, of freedom of speech, freedom of the press, or freedom of worship are not proper sources of taxation for general revenue purposes. In dealing with a permissible regulation of these freedoms and the fee charged in connection therewith, we emphasized the fact that the fee "was not a revenue tax, but one to meet the expense incident to the administration of the Act and to the maintenance of public order," and stated only that, "There is nothing contrary to the Constitution in the charge of a fee limited to the purpose stated." *Cox v. New Hampshire*, 312 U.S. 569, 577. The taxes here involved are ostensibly for revenue purposes; they are not regulatory fees. Respondents do not show that the instant activities of Jehovah's Witnesses create special problems causing a drain on the municipal coffers, or that these taxes are commensurate with any expenses entailed by the presence of the Witnesses. In the absence of such a showing, I think no tax whatever can be levied on petitioners' activities in distributing their literature or disseminating their ideas. If the guaranties of freedom of speech and freedom of the press are to be preserved, municipalities should not be free to raise general revenue by taxes on the circulation of information and opinion in noncommercial causes; other sources can be found, the taxation of which will not choke off ideas. Taxes such as the instant ones violate petitioners' right to freedom of speech and freedom of the press, protected against state invasion by the Fourteenth Amendment.

Freedom of Religion.

Under the foregoing discussion of freedom of speech and freedom of the press, any person would be exempt from taxation upon the act of distributing information or [621] opinion of any kind, whether political, scientific, or religious in character, when done solely in an effort to spread knowledge and ideas, with no thought of commercial gain. But there is another, and perhaps more precious, reason why these ordinances cannot constitutionally apply to petitioners. Important as free speech and a free press are to a free government and a free citizenry, there is a right even more dear to many individuals—the right to worship their Maker according to their needs and the dictates of their souls and to carry their message or their gospel to every living creature. These ordinances infringe that right, which is also protected by the Fourteenth Amendment.

Petitioners were itinerant ministers going through the streets and from house to house in different communities, preaching the gospel by distributing booklets and pamphlets setting forth their views of the Bible and the tenets of their faith. While perhaps not so orthodox as the oral sermon, the use of religious books is an old, recognized and effective mode of worship and means of proselytizing. For this, petitioners were taxed. The mind rebels at the thought that a minister of any of the old established churches could be made to pay fees to the community before entering the pulpit. These taxes on petitioners' efforts to preach the "news of the Kingdom" should be struck down because they burden petitioners' right to worship the Deity in their own fashion and to spread the gospel as they understand it. There is here no contention that their manner of worship gives rise to conduct which calls for regulation, and these ordinances are not aimed at any such practices.

One need only read the decisions of this and other courts in the past few years to see the unpopularity of Jehovah's [622] Witnesses and the difficulties put in their path because of their religious beliefs. An arresting parallel exists between the troubles of Jehovah's Witnesses and the struggles of various dissentient groups in the American colonies for religious liberty which culminated in the Virginia Statute for Religious Freedom, the Northwest Ordinance of 1787, and the First Amendment. In most of the colonies there was an established church, and the way of the dissenter was hard. All sects, including Quaker, Methodist, Baptist, Episcopalian, Separatist, Rogerine, and Catholic, suffered. Many of the non-conforming ministers were itinerants, and measures were adopted to curb their unwanted activities. The books of certain denominations were banned. Virginia and Connecticut had burdensome licensing requirements. Other states required oaths before one could preach which many ministers could not conscientiously take. [623] Research reveals no attempt to control or persecute by the more subtle means of taxing the function of preaching, or even any attempt to tap it as a source of revenue.[20]

---

20. The Stamp Act of 1765 exempted "any books containing only matters of devotion or piety." MacDonald, *Documentary Source Book of American History* (3d ed., 1934), p. 128.

By applying these occupational taxes to petitioners' non-commercial activities, respondents now tax sincere efforts to spread religious beliefs, and a heavy burden falls upon a new set of itinerant zealots, the Witnesses. That burden should not be allowed to stand, especially if, as the excluded testimony in No. 280 [*Jones*] indicates, the accepted clergymen of the town can take to their pulpits and distribute their literature without the impact of taxation. Liberty of conscience is too full of meaning for the individuals in this Nation to permit taxation to prohibit or substantially impair the spread of religious ideas, even though they are controversial and run counter to the established notions of a community. If this Court is to err in evaluating claims that freedom of speech, freedom of the press, and freedom of religion have been invaded, far better that it err in being overprotective of these precious rights.

MR. JUSTICE BLACK, MR. JUSTICE DOUGLAS, MR. JUSTICE MURPHY:

The opinion of the Court sanctions a device which in our opinion suppresses or tends to suppress the free exercise of a religion practiced by a minority group. This is but another step in the direction which *Minersville School District v. Gobitis* took against the same religious minority, and is a logical extension of the principles upon which that decision rested. Since we joined in the opinion in the *Gobitis* case, we think this is an appropriate [624] occasion to state that we now believe that it also was wrongly decided. Certainly our democratic form of government, functioning under the historic Bill of Rights, has a high responsibility to accommodate itself to the religious views of minorities, however unpopular and unorthodox those views may be. The First Amendment does not put the right freely to exercise religion in a subordinate position. We fear, however, that the opinions in these and in the *Gobitis* case do exactly that.

7

Murdock v. Pennsylvania
(City of Jeannette)*

319 U.S. 105 (1943)

Vote: 5—Stone, Black, Douglas, Murphy, Byrnes
4—Roberts, Reed, Frankfurter, Jackson

Opinion announcing the opinion of the Court: Douglas
Dissenting opinions: Reed, Frankfurter

A year after its initial decision in Opelika, *the Supreme Court ordered a reargument of* Jones v. Opelika *along with the present case. The facts in* Murdock *were similar to those in* Opelika. *Jehovah's Witnesses went door-to-door in the City of Jeannette, Pennsylvania, distributing literature and asking for contributions in return for religious books and pamphlets. Books cost twenty-five cents; pamphlets, five cents. Sometimes, lesser sums were accepted or materials were given away if an interested person was without funds.*

Several Jehovah's Witnesses were convicted of violating a City of Jeannette ordinance that required "all persons canvassing for or soliciting within said Borough, orders for goods, paintings, pictures, wares, or merchandise of any kind, or persons delivering such articles under orders so obtained or solicited" to procure a business license. The licensing fees were $1.50 for one day, $7 for one week, $12 for two weeks, and $20 for three weeks.

MR. JUSTICE DOUGLAS delivered the opinion of the Court.

. . . [108] The First Amendment, which the Fourteenth makes applicable to the states, declares that "Congress shall make no law respecting an establishment of religion, or prohibiting the free exercise thereof; or abridging the freedom of speech, or of the press . . ." It could hardly be denied that a tax laid specifically on the exercise of those freedoms would be unconstitutional. Yet the license tax imposed by this ordinance is, in substance, just that.

---

*Together with No. 481, *Perisich v. Pennsylvania (City of Jeannette)*, No. 482, *Mowder v. Pennsylvania (City of Jeannette)*, No. 483, *Seders v. Pennsylvania (City of Jeannette)*, No. 484, *Lamborn v. Pennsylvania (City of Jeannette)*, No. 485, *Maltezos v. Pennsylvania (City of Jeannette)*, No. 486, *Anastasia Tzanes v. Pennsylvania (City of Jeannette)*, and No. 487, *Ellaine Tzanes v. Pennsylvania (City of Jeannette)*, also on writs of certiorari, 318 U.S. 748, to the Superior Court of Pennsylvania.

Petitioners spread their interpretations of the Bible and their religious beliefs largely through the hand distribution of literature by full or part time workers. They claim to follow the example of Paul, teaching "publickly, and from house to house." Acts 20:20. They take literally the mandate of the Scriptures, "Go ye into all the world, and preach the gospel to every creature." Mark 16:15. In doing so they believe that they are obeying a commandment of God.

The hand distribution of religious tracts is an age-old form of missionary evangelism—as old as the history of printing presses. It has been a potent force in various religious movements down through the years. This form of evangelism is utilized today on a large scale by various religious sects whose colporteurs carry the Gospel to thousands [109] upon thousands of homes and seek through personal visitations to win adherents to their faith. It is more than preaching; it is more than distribution of religious literature. It is a combination of both. Its purpose is as evangelical as the revival meeting. This form of religious activity occupies the same high estate under the First Amendment as do worship in the churches and preaching from the pulpits. It has the same claim to protection as the more orthodox and conventional exercises of religion. It also has the same claim as the others to the guarantees of freedom of speech and freedom of the press.

The integrity of this conduct or behavior as a religious practice has not been challenged. Nor do we have presented any question as to the sincerity of petitioners in their religious beliefs and practices, however misguided they may be thought to be. Moreover, we do not intimate or suggest in respecting their sincerity that any conduct can be made a religious rite and by the zeal of the practitioners swept into the First Amendment. *Reynolds v.* [110] *United States* and *Davis v. Beason* denied any such claim to the practice of polygamy and bigamy. Other claims may well arise which deserve the same fate. We only hold that spreading one's religious beliefs or preaching the Gospel through distribution of religious literature and through personal visitations is an age-old type of evangelism with as high a claim to constitutional protection as the more orthodox types. The manner in which it is practiced at times gives rise to special problems with which the police power of the states is competent to deal. But that merely illustrates that the rights with which we are dealing are not absolutes. We are concerned, however, in these cases merely with one narrow issue. There is presented for decision no question whatsoever concerning punishment for any alleged unlawful acts during the solicitation. Nor is there involved here any question as to the validity of a registration system for colporteurs and other solicitors. The cases present a single issue—the constitutionality of an ordinance which as construed and applied requires religious colporteurs to pay a license tax as a condition to the pursuit of their activities.

The alleged justification for the exaction of this license tax is the fact that the religious literature is distributed with a solicitation of funds. Thus it was stated, in *Jones v. Opelika*, p. 597, that when a religious sect uses "ordinary commercial methods of sales of articles to raise propaganda funds," it is proper for the state to charge "reasonable fees for the privilege of canvassing." Situations will arise where it will be difficult to determine whether a particular activity is religious or purely commercial. The distinction at times is vital. As we stated only the other day, in *Jamison v. Texas*, 318 U.S. 413, 417, "The states can prohibit the use of the streets for [111] the distribution of purely commercial leaflets, even though such leaflets may have 'a civic appeal, or a moral platitude' appended. *Valentine v. Chrestensen*, 316 U.S. 52, 55. They may not prohibit the distribution of handbills in the pursuit of a clearly religious activity merely because the handbills invite the purchase of books for the improved understanding of the religion or because the handbills seek in a lawful fashion to promote the raising of funds for religious purposes." But the mere fact that the religious literature is "sold" by itinerant preachers rather than "donated" does not transform evangelism into a commercial enterprise. If it did, then the passing of the collection plate in church would make the church service a commercial project. The constitutional rights of those spreading their religious beliefs through the spoken and printed word are not to be gauged by standards governing retailers or wholesalers of books. The right to use the press for expressing one's views is not to be measured by the protection afforded commercial handbills. It should be remembered that the pamphlets of Thomas Paine were not distributed free of charge. It is plain that a religious organization needs funds to remain a going concern. But an itinerant evangelist, however misguided or intolerant he may be, does not become a mere book agent by selling the Bible or religious tracts to help defray his expenses or to sustain him. Freedom of speech, freedom of the press, freedom of religion are available to all, not merely to those who can pay their own way. As we have said, the problem of drawing the line between a purely commercial activity and a religious one will at times be difficult. On this record it plainly cannot be said that petitioners were engaged in a commercial rather than a religious venture. It is a distortion of the facts of record to describe their activities as the occupation of selling books and pamphlets. And the Pennsylvania court did not rest the judgments of conviction on that basis, though it did find [112] that petitioners "sold" the literature. The Supreme Court of Iowa in *State v. Mead*, 230 Iowa 1217, described the selling activities of members of this same sect as "merely incidental and collateral" to their "main object which was to preach and publicize the doctrines of their order." That accurately summarizes the present record.

We do not mean to say that religious groups and the press are free from all financial burdens of government. We have here something quite different, for example, from a tax on the income of one who engages in religious activities or a tax on property used or employed in connection with those activities. It is one thing to impose a tax on the income or property of a preacher. It is quite another thing to exact a tax from him for the privilege of delivering a sermon. The tax imposed by the City of Jeannette is a flat license tax, the payment of which is a condition of the exercise of these constitutional privileges. The power to tax the exercise of a privilege is the power to control or suppress its enjoyment. Those who can tax the exercise of this religious practice can make its exercise so costly as to deprive it of the resources necessary for its maintenance. Those who can tax the privilege of engaging in this form of missionary evangelism can close its doors to all those who do not have a full purse. Spreading religious beliefs in this ancient and honorable manner would thus be denied the needy. Those who can deprive religious groups of their colporteurs can take from them a part of the vital power of the press which has survived from the Reformation.

It is contended, however, that the fact that the license tax can suppress or control this activity is unimportant [113] if it does not do so. But that is to disregard the nature of this tax. It is a license tax—a flat tax imposed on the exercise of a privilege granted by the Bill of Rights. A state may not impose a charge for the enjoyment of a right granted by the Federal Constitution. Thus, it may not exact a license tax for the privilege of carrying on interstate commerce (*McGoldrick v. Berwind-White Co.*, 309 U.S. 33, 56–58), although it may tax the property used in, or the income derived from, that commerce, so long as those taxes are not discriminatory. A license tax applied to activities guaranteed by the First Amendment would have the same destructive effect. It is true that the First Amendment, like the commerce clause, draws no distinction between license taxes, fixed sum taxes, and other kinds of taxes. But that is no reason why we should shut our eyes to the nature of the tax and its destructive influence. The power to impose a license tax on the exercise of these freedoms is indeed as potent as the power of censorship which this Court has repeatedly struck down. . . .

[114] The taxes imposed by this ordinance can hardly help but be as severe and telling in their impact on the freedom [115] of the press and religion as the "taxes on knowledge" at which the First Amendment was partly aimed. They may indeed operate even more subtly. Itinerant evangelists moving throughout a state or from state to state would feel immediately the cumulative effect of such ordinances as they become fashionable. The way of the religious dissenter has long been hard. But if the formula of this type of ordinance is approved, a new device for the suppression of religious minorities will have been found. This method of disseminating religious beliefs can be crushed and closed out by the sheer weight of the toll or tribute which is exacted town by town, village by village. The spread of religious ideas through personal visitations by the literature ministry of numerous religious groups would be stopped.

The fact that the ordinance is "nondiscriminatory" is immaterial. The protection afforded by the First Amendment is not so restricted. A license tax certainly does not acquire constitutional validity because it classifies the privileges protected by the First Amendment along with the wares and merchandise of hucksters and peddlers and treats them all alike. Such equality in treatment does not save the ordinance. Freedom of press, freedom of speech, freedom of religion are in a preferred position.

It is claimed, however, that the ultimate question in determining the constitutionality of this license tax is whether the state has given something for which it can ask a return. That principle has wide applicability. But it is quite irrelevant here. This tax is not a charge for the enjoyment of a privilege or benefit bestowed by the state. The privilege in question exists apart from state authority. It is guaranteed the people by the Federal Constitution.

Considerable emphasis is placed on the kind of literature which petitioners were distributing—its provocative, [116] abusive, and ill-mannered character and the assault which it makes on our established churches and the cherished faiths of many of us. But those considerations are no justification for the license tax which the ordinance imposes. Plainly a community may not suppress, or the state tax, the dissemination of views because they are unpopular, annoying or distasteful. If that device were ever sanctioned, there would have been forged a ready instrument for the suppression of the faith which any minority cherishes but which does not happen to be in favor. That would be a complete repudiation of the philosophy of the Bill of Rights.

Jehovah's Witnesses are not "above the law." But the present ordinance is not directed to the problems with which the police power of the state is free to deal. It does not cover, and petitioners are not charged with, breaches of the peace. They are pursuing their solicitations peacefully and quietly. Petitioners, moreover, are not charged with or prosecuted for the use of language which is obscene, abusive, or which incites retaliation. Nor do we have here, as we did in *Cox v. New Hampshire* and *Chaplinsky v. New Hampshire*, state regulation of the streets to protect and insure the safety, comfort, or convenience of the public. Furthermore, the present ordinance is not narrowly drawn to safeguard the people of the community in their homes against the evils of solicitations. As we have said, it is not merely a registration ordinance calling for an identification of the solicitors so as to give the authorities some basis for investigating strangers coming into the community. And the fee is not a nominal one, imposed as a regulatory measure and calculated to defray the expense of protecting those on the streets and at home against the abuses of solicitors. [117] Nor can the present ordinance survive if we assume that it has been construed to apply only to solicitation from house to house. The ordinance is not narrowly drawn to prevent or control abuses or evils arising from that activity. Rather, it sets aside the residential areas as a prohibited zone, entry of which is denied petitioners unless the tax is paid. That restraint and one which is city-wide in scope (*Jones v. Opelika*) are different only in degree. Each is an abridgment of freedom of press and a restraint on the free exercise of religion. They stand or fall together.

The judgment in *Jones v. Opelika* has this day been vacated. Freed from that controlling precedent, we can restore to their high, constitutional position the liberties of itinerant evangelists who disseminate their religious beliefs and the tenets of their faith through distribution of literature. The judgments are reversed and the causes are remanded to the Pennsylvania Superior Court for proceedings not inconsistent with this opinion.

The following dissenting opinions are applicable to *Jones v. Opelika* and to *Murdock v. Pennsylvania*. . . .

MR. JUSTICE REED, dissenting:

. . . [120] In the opinion in *Jones v. Opelika* on the former hearing, attention was called to the differentiation between these cases of taxation and those of forbidden censorship, prohibition or discrimination. There is no occasion to repeat what has been written so recently as to the constitutional right to tax the money-raising activities of religious or didactic groups. There are, however, other reasons, not fully developed in that opinion, that add to our conviction that the Constitution does not prohibit these general occupational taxes.

The real contention of the Witnesses is that there can be no taxation of the occupation of selling books and pamphlets because to do so would be contrary to the due process clause of the Fourteenth Amendment, which now is held to have drawn the contents of the First Amendment into the category of individual rights protected [121] from state deprivation. Since the publications teach a religion which conforms to our standards of legality, it is urged that these ordinances prohibit the free exercise of religion and abridge the freedom of speech and of the press. . . .

None of the provisions of our Constitution is more venerated by the people or respected by legislatures and the courts than those which proclaim for our country the freedom of religion and expression. While the interpreters of the Constitution find the purpose was to allow the widest practical scope for the exercise of religion and the dissemination of information, no jurist has ever conceived that the prohibition of interference is absolute. Is subjection to nondiscriminatory, nonexcessive taxation in the distribution of religious literature, a prohibition of the exercise of religion or an abridgment of the freedom of the press? . . .

[123] The available evidence of Congressional action shows clearly that the draftsmen of the amendments had in mind the practice of religion and the right to be heard, rather than any abridgment or interference with either by taxation [124] in any form. The amendments were proposed by [125] Mr. Madison. He was careful to explain to the Congress the meaning of the amendment on religion. The draft was commented upon by Mr. Madison when it read:

"no religion shall be established by law, nor shall the equal rights of conscience be infringed." 1 Annals of Congress 729.

He said that he apprehended the meaning of the words on religion to be that Congress should not establish a religion and enforce the legal observation of it by law, nor compel men to worship God in any manner contrary to their conscience. *Id.*, 730. No such specific interpretation of the amendment on freedom of expression has been found in the debates. The clearest is probably from Mr. Benson, who said that

> "The committee who framed this report proceeded on the principle that these rights belonged to the people; they conceived them to be inherent; and all that they meant to provide against was their being infringed by the Government." *Id.*, 731–32. . . .

[127] Is there anything in the decisions of this Court which indicates that church or press is free from the financial [128] burdens of government? We find nothing. Religious societies depend for their exemptions from taxation upon state constitutions or general statutes, not upon the Federal Constitution. This Court has held that the chief purpose of the free press guarantee was to prevent previous restraints upon publication. . . .

It may be said, however, that ours is a too narrow, technical and legalistic approach to the problem of state taxation of the activities of church and press; that we should look not to the expressed or historical meaning of the First Amendment but to the broad principles of free speech and free exercise of religion which pervade our national way of life. It may be that the Fourteenth Amendment guarantees these principles rather than the more definite concept expressed in the First Amendment. This would mean that as a Court, we should determine what sort of liberty it is that the due process clause of [129] the Fourteenth Amendment guarantees against state restrictions on speech and church.

But whether we give content to the literal words of the First Amendment or to principles of the liberty of the press and the church, we conclude that cities or states may levy reasonable, non-discriminatory taxes on such activities as occurred in these cases. Whatever exemptions exist from taxation arise from the prevailing law of the various states. The constitutions of Alabama and Pennsylvania, with substantial similarity to the exemption provisions of other constitutions, forbid the taxation of lots and buildings used exclusively for religious worship. These are the only exemptions of the press or church from taxation. We find nothing more applicable to our problem in the other constitutions. Surely this unanimity of specific state action on exemptions of religious bodies from taxes would not have occurred throughout our history, if it had been conceived that the genius of our institutions, as expressed in the First Amendment, was incompatible with the taxation of church or press.

Nor do we understand that the Court now maintains that the Federal Constitution frees press or religion of any tax except such occupational taxes as those here levied. Income taxes, ad valorem taxes, even occupational taxes are presumably valid, save only a license tax on sales of religious books. Can it be that the Constitution permits a tax on the printing presses and the gross income of a metropolitan newspaper but denies the right to lay an occupational tax on the distributors of the same papers? Does the exemption apply to booksellers or distributors of magazines or only to religious publications? And, if the latter, to what distributors? Or to what books? Or is this Court saying that a religious [130] practice of book distribution is free from taxation because a state cannot prohibit the "free exercise thereof" and a newspaper is subject to the same tax even though the same Constitutional Amendment says the state cannot abridge the freedom of the press? It has never been thought before that freedom from taxation was a perquisite attaching to the privileges of the First Amendment. The National Government grants exemptions to ministers and churches because it wishes to do so, not because the Constitution compels. Where camp meetings or revivals charge admissions, a federal tax would apply, if Congress had not granted freedom from the exaction.

It is urged that such a tax as this may be used readily to restrict the dissemination of ideas. This must be conceded but the possibility of misuse does not make a tax unconstitutional. No abuse is claimed here. The ordinances in some of these cases are the general occupation license type covering many businesses. In the *Jeannette* prosecutions, the ordinance involved lays the usual tax on canvassing or soliciting sales of goods, wares and merchandise. It was passed in 1898. Every power of taxation or regulation is capable of abuse. Each one, to some extent, prohibits the free exercise of religion and abridges the freedom of the press, but that is hardly a reason for denying the power. If the tax is used oppressively, the law will protect the victims of such action.

This decision forces a tax subsidy notwithstanding our accepted belief in the separation of church and state. Instead of all bearing equally the burdens of government, this Court now fastens upon the communities the entire cost of policing the sales of religious literature. . . . [131] The distributors of religious literature, possibly of all informatory publications, become today privileged to carry on their occupations without contributing their share to the support of the government which provides the opportunity for the exercise of their liberties.

Nor do we think it can be said, properly, that these sales of religious books are religious exercises. . . . The record shows that books entitled "Creation" and "Salvation," as well as Bibles, were offered for sale. We shall assume the first two publications, also, are religious books. Certainly there can be no dissent from the statement that [132] selling religious books is an age-old practice, or that it is evangelism in the sense that the distributors hope the readers will be spiritually benefited. That does not carry us to the conviction, however, that when distribution of religious books is made at a price, the itinerant colporteur is performing a religious rite, is worshipping his Creator in his way. Many sects practice healing the sick as an evidence of their religious faith or maintain orphanages or homes for the aged or teach the young. These are, of course, in a sense, religious practices but hardly such examples of religious rites as are encompassed by the prohibition against the free exercise of religion.

And even if the distribution of religious books was a religious practice protected from regulation by the First Amendment, certainly the affixation of a price for the articles would destroy the sacred character of the transaction. The evangelist becomes also a book agent.

The rites which are protected by the First Amendment are in essence spiritual—prayer, mass, sermons, sacrament—not sales of religious goods. The card furnished each Witness to identify him as an ordained minister does not go so far as to say the sale is a rite. It states only that the Witnesses worship by exhibiting to people "the message of said gospel in printed form, such as the Bible, books, booklets and magazines, and thus afford the people the opportunity of learning of God's gracious provision for them." On the back of the card appears: "You may contribute twenty-five cents to the Lord's work and receive a copy of this beautiful book." The sale of these religious books has, we think, relation to their religious exercises, similar to the "information march," said by the Witnesses to be one of their "ways of worship" and by this Court to be subject to regulation by license in *Cox v. New Hampshire*, 312 U.S. 569, 572, 573, 576. . . .

[133] The limitations of the Constitution are not maxims of social wisdom but definite controls on the legislative process. We are dealing with power, not its abuse. This late withdrawal of the power of taxation over the distribution activities of those covered

by the First Amendment fixes what seems to us an unfortunate principle of tax exemption, capable of indefinite extension. We had thought that such an exemption required a clear and certain grant. This we do not find in the language of the First and Fourteenth Amendments. We are therefore of the opinion the judgments below should be affirmed.

[134] MR. JUSTICE ROBERTS, MR. JUSTICE FRANKFURTER, and MR. JUSTICE JACKSON join in this dissent. MR. JUSTICE JACKSON has stated additional reasons for dissent in his concurrence in *Douglas v. Jeannette*.

MR. JUSTICE FRANKFURTER, dissenting:

. . . [135] It cannot be said that the petitioners are constitutionally exempt from taxation merely because they may be engaged in religious activities or because such activities may constitute an exercise of a constitutional right. It will hardly be contended, for example, that a tax upon the income of a clergyman would violate the Bill of Rights, even though the tax is ultimately borne by the members of his church. A clergyman, no less than a judge, is a citizen. And not only in time of war would neither willingly enjoy immunity from the obligations of citizenship. It is only fair that he also who preaches the word of God should share in the costs of the benefits provided by government to him as well as to the other members of the community. And so, no one would suggest that a clergyman who uses an automobile or the telephone in connection with his work thereby gains a constitutional exemption from taxes levied upon the use of automobiles or upon telephone calls. Equally alien is it to our constitutional system to suggest that the Constitution of the United States exempts church-held lands from state taxation. Plainly, a tax measure is not invalid under the federal Constitution merely because it falls upon persons engaged in activities of a religious nature.

[136] Nor can a tax be invalidated merely because it falls upon activities which constitute an exercise of a constitutional right. The First Amendment of course protects the right to publish a newspaper or a magazine or a book. But the crucial question is—how much protection does the Amendment give, and against what is the right protected? It is certainly true that the protection afforded the freedom of the press by the First Amendment does not include exemption from all taxation. A tax upon newspaper publishing is not invalid simply because it falls upon the exercise of a constitutional right. Such a tax might be invalid if it invidiously singled out newspaper publishing for bearing the burdens of taxation or imposed upon them in such ways as to encroach on the essential scope of a free press. If the Court could justifiably hold that the tax measures in these cases were vulnerable on that ground, I would unreservedly agree. But the Court has not done so, and indeed could not.

The vice of the ordinances before us, the Court holds, is that they impose a special kind of tax, a "flat license tax, the payment of which is a condition of the exercise of these constitutional privileges [to engage in religious activities]." But the fact that an occupation tax is a "flat" tax certainly is not enough to condemn it. A legislature undoubtedly can tax all those who engage in an activity upon an equal basis. The Constitution certainly does not require that differentiations must be made among taxpayers upon the basis of the size of their incomes or the scope of their activities. Occupation taxes normally are flat taxes, and the Court surely does not mean to hold that a tax is bad merely because all taxpayers pursuing the very same activities and thereby demanding the same governmental services are treated alike. Nor, as I have indicated, can a tax be invalidated because the exercise of a constitutional privilege is conditioned upon its payment. It depends upon the nature of the condition that [137] is imposed, its justification, and the extent to which it hinders or restricts the exercise of the privilege.

As I read the Court's opinion, it does not hold that the taxes in the cases before us in fact do hinder or restrict the petitioners in exercising their constitutional rights. It holds that "The power to tax the exercise of a privilege is the power to control or suppress its enjoyment." . . .

The power to tax, like all powers of government, legislative, executive and judicial alike, can be abused or perverted. The power to tax is the power to destroy only in the sense that those who have power can misuse it. Mr. Justice Holmes disposed of this smooth phrase as a constitutional basis for invalidating taxes when he wrote "The power to tax is not the power to destroy while this Court sits." *Panhandle Oil Co. v. Knox*, 277 U.S. 218, 223. The fact that a power can be perverted does not mean that every exercise of the power is a perversion of the power. Thus, if a tax indirectly suppresses or controls the enjoyment of a constitutional privilege which a legislature cannot directly suppress or control, of course it is bad. But it is irrelevant that a tax can suppress or control if it does not. The Court holds that "Those who can tax the exercise of this religious practice can make its exercise so costly as to deprive it of resources necessary for its maintenance." But this is not the same as saying that "Those who do tax the exercise of this religious practice have made its exercise so costly as to deprive it of the resources necessary for its maintenance."

[138] The Court could not plausibly make such an assertion because the petitioners themselves disavow any claim that the taxes imposed in these cases impair their ability to exercise their constitutional rights. We cannot invalidate the tax measures before us simply because there may be others, not now before us, which are oppressive in their effect. The Court's opinion does not deny that the ordinances involved in these cases have in no way disabled the petitioners to engage in their religious activities. It holds only that "Those who can tax the privilege of engaging in this form of missionary evangelism can close its doors to all those who do not have a full purse." I quite agree with this statement as an abstract proposition. Those who possess the power to tax might wield it in tyrannical fashion. It does not follow, however, that every exercise of the power is an act of tyranny, or that government should be impotent because it might become tyrannical. The question before us now is whether these ordinances have deprived the petitioners of their constitutional rights, not whether some other ordinances not now before us might be enacted which might deprive them of such rights. To deny constitutional power to secular authority merely because of the possibility of its abuse is as valid as to deny the basis of spiritual authority because those in whom it is temporarily vested may misuse it. . . .

[139] It is strenuously urged that the Constitution denies a city the right to control the expression of men's minds and the right of men to win others to their views. But the Court is not divided on this proposition. No one disputes it. All members of the Court are equally familiar with the history that led to the adoption of the Bill of Rights and are equally zealous to enforce the constitutional protection of the free play of the human spirit. Escape from the real issue before us cannot be found in such generalities. The real issue here is not whether a city may charge for the dissemination of ideas but whether the states have power to require those who need additional facilities to help bear the cost of furnishing such facilities. Street hawkers make demands upon municipalities that involve the expenditure of dollars and cents, whether they hawk printed matter or other things. As the facts in these cases show, the cost of maintaining the peace, the additional demands upon governmental facilities for assuring security, involve outlays

which have to be met. To say that the Constitution forbids the states to obtain the necessary revenue from the whole of a class that enjoys these benefits [140] and facilities, when in fact no discrimination is suggested as between purveyors of printed matter and purveyors of other things, and the exaction is not claimed to be actually burdensome, is to say that the Constitution requires not that the dissemination of ideas in the interest of religion shall be free but that it shall be subsidized by the state. Such a claim offends the most important of all aspects of religious freedom in this country, namely, that of the separation of church and state.

The ultimate question in determining the constitutionality of a tax measure is—has the state given something for which it can ask a return? There can be no doubt that these petitioners, like all who use the streets, have received the benefits of government. Peace is maintained, traffic is regulated, health is safeguarded—these are only some of the many incidents of municipal administration. To secure them costs money, and a state's source of money is its taxing power. There is nothing in the Constitution which exempts persons engaged in religious activities from sharing equally in the costs of benefits to all, including themselves, provided by government.

I cannot say, therefore, that in these cases the community has demanded a return for that which it did not give. Nor am I called upon to say that the state has demanded unjustifiably more than the value of what it gave, nor that its demand in fact cramps activities pursued to promote religious beliefs. No such claim was made at the bar, and there is no evidence in the records to substantiate any such claim if it had been made. Under these circumstances, therefore, I am of opinion that the ordinances in these cases must stand.

MR. JUSTICE JACKSON joins in this dissent.

West Virginia State Board of Education v. Barnette

319 U.S. 624 (1943)

Vote: 6—Stone, Black, Douglas, Murphy, Byrnes, Jackson
   3—Roberts, Reed, Frankfurter

Opinion announcing the opinion of the Court: Jackson
Concurring opinions: Black and Douglas, Murphy
Dissenting opinion: Frankfurter

Following the Supreme Court decision in Minersville School District v. Gobitis *(1940), the West Virginia legislature amended its statutes to require all West Virginia schools to conduct courses of instruction in history, civics, and the constitutions of the United States and of the state "for the purpose of teaching, fostering and perpetuating the ideals, principles and spirit of Americanism, and increasing the knowledge of the organization and machinery of the government." To implement the law, the state's board of education adopted a resolution that ordered the flag salute to become "a regular part of the program of activities in the public schools" and declared that all teachers and pupils "shall be required to participate in the salute honoring the Nation represented by the Flag; provided, however, that refusal to salute the Flag be regarded as an Act of insubordination, and shall be dealt with accordingly."*

The resolution originally required the "commonly accepted salute to the Flag," which it defined. Some civic groups—including the Parent and Teachers Association, the Boy and Girl Scouts, and the Red Cross—objected on account of the salute "being too much like Hitler's." Some modification appears to have been made in deference to these objections, but no concessions were made to religious objections articulated by Jehovah's Witnesses. In the end, a "stiff-arm" salute was required—the saluter was to keep the right hand raised with palm turned up while the following was repeated: "I pledge allegiance to the flag of the United States of America and to the Republic for which it stands; one nation, indivisible, with liberty and justice for all." Failure to participate in the exercise was considered "insubordination" and dealt with by expulsion. Readmission to school was conditioned on compliance. Expelled children were to be considered "unlawfully absent," which meant their parents or guardians were liable to prosecution for violating the state's compulsory school-attendance laws. If convicted, parents were subject to a $50 fine and a thirty-day jail term.

The Jehovah's Witnesses involved in this case subscribed to a literal interpretation of Exodus 20:4–5, which reads, "Thou shalt not make unto thee any graven image, or any likeness of anything that is in heaven above, or that is in the earth beneath, or that is in the water under the earth; thou shalt not bow down thyself to them nor serve them." They considered the flag to be an "image" included within this command and, accordingly, refused to salute it.

Several Jehovah's Witness children were expelled from West Virginia public schools. Officials threatened to send some of them to reformatories maintained for criminally inclined juveniles. Parents of expelled children were prosecuted or threatened with prosecution for causing delinquency.

Mr. Justice JACKSON delivered the opinion of the Court.

. . . [631] As the present Chief Justice [Stone] said in dissent in the *Gobitis* case, the State may "require teaching by instruction and study of all in our history and in the structure and organization of our government, including the guaranties of civil liberty which tend to inspire patriotism and love of country." 310 U.S. at page 604. Here, however, we are dealing with a compulsion of students to declare a belief. They are not merely made acquainted with the flag salute so that they may be informed as to what it is or even what it means. The issue here is whether this slow and easily neglected route to aroused loyalties constitutionally may be short-cut by substituting a compulsory salute and slogan. . . .

[633] Here it is the State that employs a flag as a symbol of adherence to government as presently organized. It requires the individual to communicate by word and sign his acceptance of the political ideas it thus bespeaks. Objection to this form of communication when coerced is an old one, well known to the framers of the Bill of Rights.

It is also to be noted that the compulsory flag salute and pledge requires affirmation of a belief and an attitude of mind. It is not clear whether the regulation contemplates that pupils forego any contrary convictions of their own and become unwilling converts to the prescribed ceremony or whether it will be acceptable if they simulate assent by words without belief and by a gesture barren of meaning. It is now a commonplace that censorship or suppression of expression of opinion is tolerated by our Constitution only when the expression presents a clear and present danger of action of a kind the State is empowered to prevent and punish. It would seem that involuntary affirmation could be commanded only on even more immediate and urgent grounds than silence. But here the power of com- [634] pulsion is invoked without any allegation that remaining passive during a flag salute ritual creates a clear and present danger that would justify an effort even to muffle expression. To sustain the compulsory flag salute we are required to say that a Bill of Rights which guards the individual's right to speak his own mind, left it open to public authorities to compel him to utter what is not in his mind.

Whether the First Amendment to the Constitution will permit officials to order observance of ritual of this nature does not depend upon whether as a voluntary exercise we would think it to be good, bad or merely innocuous. Any credo of nationalism is likely to include what some disapprove or to omit what others think essential, and to give off different overtones as it takes on different accents or interpretations. If official power exists to coerce acceptance of any patriotic creed, what it shall contain cannot be decided by courts, but must be largely discretionary with the ordaining authority, whose power to prescribe would no doubt include power to amend. Hence validity of the asserted power to force an American citizen publicly to profess any statement of belief or to engage in any ceremony of assent to one presents questions of power that must be considered independently of any idea we may have as to the utility of the ceremony in question.

Nor does the issue as we see it turn on one's possession of particular religious views or the sincerity with which they are held. While religion supplies appellees' motive for enduring the discomforts of making the issue in this case, many citizens who do not share these religious views [635] hold such a compulsory rite to infringe constitutional liberty of the individual. It is not necessary to inquire whether nonconformist beliefs will exempt from the duty to salute unless we first find power to make the salute a legal duty.

The *Gobitis* decision, however, assumed, as did the argument in that case and in this, that power exists in the State to impose the flag salute discipline upon school children in general. The Court only examined and rejected a claim based on religious beliefs of immunity from an unquestioned general rule. The question which underlies the [636] flag salute controversy is whether such a ceremony so touching matters of opinion and political attitude may be imposed upon the individual by official authority under powers committed to any political organization under our Constitution. . . .

[640] Lastly, and this is the very heart of the *Gobitis* opinion, it reasons that "National unity is the basis of national security," that the authorities have "the right to select appropriate means for its attainment," and hence reaches the conclusion that such compulsory measures toward "national unity" are constitutional. *Id.*, 310 U.S. at page 595. Upon the verity of this assumption depends our answer in this case.

National unity as an end which officials may foster by persuasion and example is not in question. The problem is whether under our Constitution compulsion as here employed is a permissible means for its achievement.

Struggles to coerce uniformity of sentiment in support of some end thought essential to their time and country have been waged by many good as well as by evil men. Nationalism is a relatively recent phenomenon but at other times and places the ends have been racial or territorial security, support of a dynasty or regime, and particular plans for saving souls. As first and moderate methods to attain unity have failed, those bent on its accomplishment must resort to an ever-increasing severity. [641] As governmental pressure toward unity becomes greater, so strife becomes more bitter as to whose unity it shall be. Probably no deeper division of our people could proceed from any provocation than from finding it necessary to choose what doctrine and whose program public educational officials shall compel youth to unite in embracing. Ultimate futility of such attempts to compel coherence is the lesson of every such effort from the Roman drive to stamp out Christianity as a disturber of its pagan unity, the Inquisition, as a means to religious and dynastic unity, the Siberian exiles as a means to Russian unity, down to the fast failing efforts of our present totalitarian enemies. Those who begin coercive elimination of dissent soon find themselves exterminating dissenters. Compulsory unification of opinion achieves only the unanimity of the graveyard.

It seems trite but necessary to say that the First Amendment to our Constitution was designed to avoid these ends by avoiding these beginnings. There is no mysticism in the American concept of the State or of the nature or origin of its authority. We set up government by consent of the governed, and the Bill of Rights denies those in power any legal opportunity to coerce that consent. Authority here is to be controlled by public opinion, not public opinion by authority.

The case is made difficult not because the principles of its decision are obscure but because the flag involved is our own. Nevertheless, we apply the limitations of the Constitution with no fear that freedom to be intellectually and spiritually diverse or even contrary will disintegrate the social organization. To believe that patriotism will not flourish if patriotic ceremonies are voluntary and spontaneous instead of a compulsory routine is to make an unflattering estimate of the appeal of our institutions to free minds. We can have intellectual individualism [642] and the rich cultural diversities that we owe to exceptional minds only at the price of occasional eccentricity and abnormal attitudes. When they are so harmless to others or to the State as those we deal with here, the price is not too great. But freedom to differ is not limited to things that do not matter much. That would be a mere shadow of freedom. The test of its substance is the right to differ as to things that touch the heart of the existing order.

If there is any fixed star in our constitutional constellation, it is that no official, high or petty, can prescribe what shall be orthodox in politics, nationalism, religion, or other matters of opinion or force citizens to confess by word or act their faith therein. If there are any circumstances which permit an exception, they do not now occur to us.

We think the action of the local authorities in compelling the flag salute and pledge transcends constitutional limitations on their power and invades the sphere of intellect and spirit which it is the purpose of the First Amendment to our Constitution to reserve from all official control.

[643] Mr. Justice BLACK and Mr. Justice DOUGLAS, concurring.

We are substantially in agreement with the opinion just read, but since we originally joined with the Court in the *Gobitis* case, it is appropriate that we make a brief statement of reasons for our change of view.

Reluctance to make the Federal Constitution a rigid bar against state regulation of conduct thought inimical to the public welfare was the controlling influence which moved us to consent to the *Gobitis* decision. Long reflection convinced us that although the principle is sound, its application in the particular case was wrong. We believe that the statute before us fails to accord full scope to the freedom of religion secured to the appellees by the First and Fourteenth Amendments.

The statute requires the appellees to participate in a ceremony aimed at inculcating respect for the flag and for this country. The Jehovah's Witnesses, without any desire to show disrespect for either the flag or the country, interpret the Bible as commanding, at the risk of God's displeasure, that they not go through the form of a pledge of allegiance to any flag. The devoutness of their belief is evidenced by their willingness to suffer persecution and punishment, rather than make the pledge.

No well-ordered society can leave to the individuals an absolute right to make final decisions, unassailable by the State, as to everything they will or will not do. The First Amendment does not go so far. Religious faiths, honestly held, do not free individuals from responsibility to conduct themselves obediently to laws which are either imperatively necessary to protect society as a whole from grave [644] and pressingly imminent dangers or which, without any general prohibition, merely regulate time, place or manner of religious activity. Decision as to the constitutionality of particular laws which strike at the substance of religious tenets and practices must be made by this Court. The duty is a solemn one, and in meeting it we cannot say that a failure, because of religious scruples, to assume a particular physical position and to repeat the words of a patriotic formula creates a grave danger to the nation. Such a statutory exaction is a form of test oath, and the test oath has always been abhorrent in the United States.

Words uttered under coercion are proof of loyalty to nothing but self-interest. Love of country must spring from willing hearts and free minds, inspired by a fair administration of wise laws enacted by the people's elected representatives within the bounds of express constitutional prohibitions. These laws must, to be consistent with the First Amendment, permit the widest toleration of conflicting viewpoints consistent with a society of free men.

Neither our domestic tranquillity [sic] in peace nor our martial effort in war depend on compelling little children to participate in a ceremony which ends in nothing for them but a fear of spiritual condemnation. If, as we think, their fears are groundless, time and reason are the proper antidotes for their errors. The ceremonial, when enforced against conscientious objectors, more likely to defeat than to serve its high purpose, is a handy implement for disguised religious persecution. As such, it is inconsistent with our Constitution's plan and purpose.

Mr. Justice MURPHY, concurring.

 . . . [645] The right of freedom of thought and of religion as guaranteed by the Constitution against State action includes both the right to speak freely and the right to refrain from speaking at all, except in so far as essential operations of government may require it for the preservation of an orderly society—as in the case of compulsion to give evidence in court. Without wishing to disparage the purposes and intentions of those who hope to inculcate sentiments of loyalty and patriotism by requiring a declaration of allegiance as a feature of public education, or unduly belittle the benefits that may accrue therefrom, I am impelled to conclude that such a requirement is not essential to the maintenance of effective government and orderly society. To many it is deeply distasteful to join in a public chorus of affirmation of private belief. By some, in- [646] cluding the members of this sect, it is apparently regarded as incompatible with a primary religious obligation and therefore a restriction on religious freedom. Official compulsion to affirm what is contrary to one's religious beliefs is the antithesis of freedom of worship which, it is well to recall, was achieved in this country only after what Jefferson characterized as the "severest contests in which I have ever been engaged." . . .

Mr. Justice FRANKFURTER, dissenting.

One who belongs to the most vilified and persecuted minority in history is not likely to be insensible to the freedoms guaranteed by our Constitution. Were my purely personal attitude relevant I should wholeheartedly associate myself with the general libertarian views in the Court's opinion, representing as they do the thought and [647] action of a lifetime. But as judges we are neither Jew nor Gentile, neither Catholic nor agnostic. We owe equal attachment to the Constitution and are equally bound by our judicial obligations whether we derive our citizenship from the earliest or the latest immigrants to these shores. As a member of this Court I am not justified in writing my private notions of policy into the Constitution, no matter how deeply I may cherish them or how mischievous I may deem their disregard. The duty of a judge who must decide which of two claims before the Court shall prevail, that of a State to enact and enforce laws within its general competence or that of an individual to refuse obedience because of the demands of his conscience, is not that of the ordinary person. It can never be emphasized too much that one's own opinion about the wisdom or evil of a law should be excluded altogether when one is doing one's duty on the bench. The only opinion of our own even looking in that direction that is material is our opinion whether legislators could in reason have enacted such a law. In the light of all the circumstances, including the history of this question in this Court, it would require more daring than I possess to deny that reasonable legislators could have taken the action which is before us for review. Most unwillingly, therefore, I must differ from my brethren with regard to legislation like this. I cannot bring my mind to believe that the "liberty" secured by the Due Process Clause gives this Court authority to deny to the State of West Virginia the attainment of that which we all recognize as a legitimate legislative end, namely, the promotion of good citizenship, by employment of the means here chosen. . . .

[649] When Mr. Justice Holmes, speaking for this Court, wrote that "it must be remembered that legislatures are ultimate guardians of the liberties and welfare of the people in quite as great a degree as the courts," *Missouri, Kansas & Texas R. Co. v. May*, 194 U.S. 267, 270, he went to the very essence of our constitutional system and the democratic conception of our society. He did not mean that for only some phases of civil government this Court was not to supplant legislatures and sit in judgment upon the right or wrong of a challenged measure. He was stating the comprehensive judicial duty and role of this Court in our constitutional scheme whenever legislation is sought to be nullified on any ground, namely, that responsibility for legislation lies with legislatures, answerable as they are directly to the people, and this Court's only and very narrow function is to determine whether within the broad grant of authority vested in legislatures they have exercised a judgment for which reasonable justification can be offered.

The framers of the federal Constitution might have chosen to assign an active share in the process of legislation to this Court. They had before them the well-known example of New York's Council of Revision, which had been functioning since 1777. After stating that "laws inconsistent with the spirit of this constitution, or with the public good, may be hastily and unadvisedly passed," the state constitution made the judges of New York part of the legislative process by providing that "all bills which have passed the senate and assembly shall, before they become laws," be presented to a Council of which the judges constituted a majority, "for their revisal and consideration." Art. III, New York Constitution of 1777. Judges exercised this legislative function in New York [650] for nearly fifty years. But the framers of the Constitution denied such legislative powers to the federal judiciary. They chose instead to insulate the judiciary from the legislative function. They did not grant to this Court supervision over legislation.

The reason why from the beginning even the narrow judicial authority to nullify legislation has been viewed with a jealous eye is that it serves to prevent the full play of the democratic process. The fact that it may be an undemocratic aspect of our scheme of government does not call for its rejection or its disuse. But it is the best of reasons, as this Court has frequently recognized, for the greatest caution in its use.

[651] Under our constitutional system the legislature is charged solely with civil concerns of society. If the avowed or intrinsic legislative purpose is either to promote or to discourage some religious community or creed, it is clearly within the constitutional restrictions imposed on legislatures and cannot stand. But it by no means follows that legislative power is wanting whenever a general non-discriminatory civil regulation in fact touches conscientious scruples or religious beliefs of an individual or a group. Regard for such scruples or beliefs undoubtedly presents one of the most reasonable claims for

the exertion of legislative accommodation. It is, of course, beyond our power to rewrite the state's requirement, by providing exemptions for those who do not wish to participate in the flag salute or by making some other accommodations to meet their scruples. That wisdom might suggest the making of such accommodations and that school administration would not find it too difficult to make them and yet maintain the ceremony for those not refusing to conform, is outside our province to suggest. Tact, respect, and generosity toward variant views will always commend themselves to those charged with the duties of legislation so as to achieve a maximum of good will and to require a minimum of unwilling submission to a general law. But the real question is, who is to make such accommodations, the courts or the legislature?

This is no dry, technical matter. It cuts deep into one's conception of the democratic process—it concerns no less the practical differences between the means for making these accommodations that are open to courts and to legislatures. A court can only strike down. It can only say, "This or that law is void." It cannot modify or qualify, it cannot make exceptions to a general require- [652] ment. And it strikes down not merely for a day. At least the finding of unconstitutionality ought not to have ephemeral significance unless the Constitution is to be reduced to the fugitive importance of mere legislation. When we are dealing with the Constitution of the United States, and more particularly with the great safeguards of the Bill of Rights, we are dealing with principles of liberty and justice "so rooted in the traditions and conscience of our people as to be ranked as fundamental"—something without which "a fair and enlightened system of justice would be impossible." *Palko v. Connecticut*, 302 U.S. 319, 325. If the function of this Court is to be essentially no different from that of a legislature, if the considerations governing constitutional construction are to be substantially those that underlie legislation, then indeed judges should not have life tenure and they should be made directly responsible to the electorate. There have been many but unsuccessful proposals in the last sixty years to amend the Constitution to that end.

Conscientious scruples, all would admit, cannot stand against every legislative compulsion to do positive acts in conflict with such scruples. We have been told that such compulsions override religious scruples only as to major concerns of the state. But the determination of what is major and what is minor itself raises questions of policy. For the way in which men equally guided by reason appraise importance goes to the very heart of policy. Judges should be very diffident in setting their judgment against that of a state in determining what is and what is not a major concern, what means are appropriate to proper ends, and what is the total social cost in striking the balance of imponderables.

What one can say with assurance is that the history out of which grew constitutional provisions for religious equal- [653] ity and the writings of the great exponents of religious freedom—Jefferson, Madison, John Adams, Benjamin Franklin—are totally wanting in justification for a claim by dissidents of exceptional immunity from civic measures of general applicability, measures not in fact disguised assaults upon such dissident views. The great leaders of the American Revolution were determined to remove political support from every religious establishment. They put on an equality the different religious sects—Episcopalians, Presbyterians, Catholics, Baptists, Methodists, Quakers, Huguenots—which, as dissenters, had been under the heel of the various orthodoxies that prevailed in different colonies. So far as the state was concerned, there was to be neither orthodoxy nor heterodoxy. And so Jefferson and those who followed him wrote guaranties of religious freedom into our constitutions. Religious minorities as well as religious majorities were to be equal in the eyes of the political state. But Jefferson and the others also knew that minorities may disrupt society. It never would have occurred to them to write into the Constitution the subordination of the general civil authority of the state to sectarian scruples.

The constitutional protection of religious freedom terminated disabilities, it did not create new privileges. It gave religious equality, not civil immunity. Its essence is freedom from conformity to religious dogma, not freedom from conformity to law because of religious dogma. Religious loyalties may be exercised without hindrance from the state, not the state may not exercise that which except by leave of religious loyalties is within the domain of temporal power. Otherwise each individual could set up his own censor against obedience to laws conscientiously deemed for the public good by those whose business it is to make laws.

The prohibition against any religious establishment by the government placed denominations on an equal foot- [654] ing—it assured freedom from support by the government to any mode of worship and the freedom of individuals to support any mode of worship. Any person may therefore believe or disbelieve what he pleases. He may practice what he will in his own house of worship or publicly within the limits of public order. But the lawmaking authority is not circumscribed by the variety of religious beliefs, otherwise the constitutional guaranty would be not a protection of the free exercise of religion but a denial of the exercise of legislation.

The essence of the religious freedom guaranteed by our Constitution is therefore this: no religion shall either receive the state's support or incur its hostility. Religion is outside the sphere of political government. This does not mean that all matters on which religious organizations or beliefs may pronounce are outside the sphere of government. Were this so, instead of the separation of church and state, there would be the subordination of the state on any matter deemed within the sovereignty of the religious conscience. Much that is the concern of temporal authority affects the spiritual interests of men. But it is not enough to strike down a non-discriminatory law that it may hurt or offend some dissident view. It would be too easy to cite numerous prohibitions and injunctions to which laws run counter if the variant interpretations of the Bible were made the tests of obedience to law. The validity of secular laws cannot be measured by their conformity to religious doctrines. It is only in a theocratic state that ecclesiastical doctrines measure legal right or wrong.

An act compelling profession of allegiance to a religion, no matter how subtly or tenuously promoted, is bad. But an act promoting good citizenship and national allegiance is within the domain of governmental authority and is therefore to be judged by the same considerations of power and of constitutionality as those involved in the many [655] claims of immunity from civil obedience because of religious scruples.

That claims are pressed on behalf of sincere religious convictions does not of itself establish their constitutional validity. Nor does waving the banner of religious freedom relieve us from examining into the power we are asked to deny the states. Otherwise the doctrine of separation of church and state, so cardinal in the history of this nation and for the liberty of our people, would mean not the disestablishment of a state church but the establishment of all churches and of all religious groups.

The subjection of dissidents to the general requirement of saluting the flag, as a measure conducive to the training of children in good citizenship, is very far from being the first instance of exacting obedience to general laws that have offended deep religious scruples. Compulsory vaccination, see *Jacobson v. Massachusetts*, 197 U.S. 11, food inspection regulations, see *Shapiro v. Lyle*, D.C., 30 F.2d 971, the obligation to bear arms, see *Hamilton v. Regents*, 293 U.S. 245, 267, testimonial duties, see *Stansbury v. Marks*, 2 Dall. 213, compulsory medical treatment, see *People v. Vogelgesang*, 221 N.Y. 290—

these are but illustrations of conduct that has often been compelled in the enforcement of legislation of general applicability even though the religious consciences of particular individuals rebelled at the exaction.

Law is concerned with external behavior and not with the inner life of man. It rests in large measure upon compulsion. Socrates lives in history partly because he gave his life for the conviction that duty of obedience to secular law does not presuppose consent to its enactment or belief in its virtue. The consent upon which free government rests is the consent that comes from sharing in the process of making and unmaking laws. The state is not shut out from a domain because the individual conscience may deny the state's claim. The individual con- [656] science may profess what faith it chooses. It may affirm and promote that faith—in the language of the Constitution, it may "exercise" it freely—but it cannot thereby restrict community action through political organs in matters of community concern, so long as the action is not asserted in a discriminatory way either openly or by stealth. One may have the right to practice one's religion and at the same time owe the duty of formal obedience to laws that run counter to one's beliefs. Compelling belief implies denial of opportunity to combat it and to assert dissident views. Such compulsion is one thing. Quite another matter is submission to conformity of action while denying its wisdom or virtue and with ample opportunity for seeking its change or abrogation. . . .

[658] When dealing with religious scruples we are dealing with an almost numberless variety of doctrines and beliefs entertained with equal sincerity by the particular groups for which they satisfy man's needs in his relation to the mysteries of the universe. There are in the United States more than 250 distinctive established religious denominations. In the state of Pennsylvania there are 120 of these, and in West Virginia as many as 65. But if religious scruples afford immunity from civic obedience to laws, they may be invoked by the religious beliefs of any individual even though he holds no membership in any sect or organized denomination. Certainly this Court cannot be called upon to determine what claims of conscience should be recognized and what should be rejected as satisfying the "religion" which the Constitution protects. That would indeed resurrect the very discriminatory treatment of religion which the Constitution sought forever to forbid. And so, when confronted with the task of considering the claims of immunity from obedience to a law dealing with civil affairs because of religious scruples, we cannot conceive religion more narrowly than in the terms in which Judge Augustus N. Hand recently characterized it:

> "It is unnecessary to attempt a definition of religion; the content of the term is found in the history of the human race and is incapable of compression into a few words. Religious belief arises from a sense of the inadequacy of rea- [659] son as a means of relating the individual to his fellow-men and to his universe. . . . [It] may justly be regarded as a response of the individual to an inward mentor, call it conscience or God, that is for many persons at the present time the equivalent of what has always been thought a religious impulse."
> *United States v. Kauten*, 2 Cir., 133 F.2d 703, 708. . . .

[664] Saluting the flag suppresses no belief nor curbs it. Children and their parents may believe what they please, avow their belief and practice it. It is not even remotely suggested that the requirement for saluting the flag involves the slightest restriction against the fullest opportunity on the part both of the children and of their parents to disavow as publicly as they choose to do so the meaning that others attach to the gesture of salute. All channels of affirmative free expression are open to both children and parents. Had we before us any act of the state putting the slightest curbs upon such free expression, I should

not lag behind any member of this Court in striking down such an invasion of the right to freedom of thought and freedom of speech protected by the Constitution. . . .

[670] Of course patriotism cannot be enforced by the flag salute. But neither can the liberal spirit be enforced by judicial invalidation of illiberal legislation. Our constant preoccupation with the constitutionality of legislation rather than with its wisdom tends to preoccupation of the American mind with a false value. The tendency of focusing attention on constitutionality is to make constitutionality synonymous with wisdom, to regard a law as all right if it is constitutional. Such an attitude is a great enemy of liberalism. Particularly in legislation affecting freedom of thought and freedom of speech much which should offend a free-spirited society is constitutional. Re- [671] liance for the most precious interests of civilization, therefore, must be found outside of their vindication in courts of law. Only a persistent positive translation of the faith of a free society into the convictions and habits and actions of a community is the ultimate reliance against unabated temptations to fetter the human spirit.

9

Follett v. Town of McCormick

321 U.S. 573 (1944)

Vote: 6—Stone, Black, Reed, Douglas, Murphy, Byrnes
     3—Roberts, Frankfurter, Jackson

Opinion announcing the opinion of the Court: Douglas
Concurring opinions: Reed, Murphy
Dissenting opinion: Roberts, Frankfurter, and Jackson

Follett, a Jehovah's Witness, made his living from the "contributions" he received when he went door-to-door distributing books in his hometown of McCormick, South Carolina. He was convicted of violating a McCormick ordinance that required book-selling agents to obtain a business license. The cost of the license was $1 per day or $15 per year. Follett had no other source of income.

MR. JUSTICE DOUGLAS delivered the opinion of the Court.

. . . [574] The ordinance in this case is in all material respects the same as the ones involved in *Jones v. Opelika* [575] and *Murdock v. Pennsylvania*. In those cases, the tax imposed was also a license tax—"a flat tax imposed on the exercise of a privilege granted by the Bill of Rights" and therefore an unconstitutional exaction. *Murdock v. Pennsylvania*, p. 113. In those cases members of Jehovah's Witnesses had also been found guilty of "peddling" or "selling" literature within the meaning of the local ordinances. But since they were engaged in a "religious" rather than a "commercial" venture, we held that the constitutionality of the ordinances might not be measured by the standards governing the sales of wares and merchandise by hucksters and other merchants. "Freedom of press, freedom of speech, freedom of religion are in a preferred position." *Murdock v. Pennsylvania*, p. 115. We emphasized that the "inherent vice and evil" of the flat license tax is that "it restrains in advance those constitutional liberties" and "inevitably tends to suppress their exercise." p. 114.

The Supreme Court of South Carolina recognized those principles but distinguished the present case from the *Murdock* and *Opelika* decisions. It pointed out that the appellant was not an itinerant but was a resident of the town where the canvassing took place, and that the principle of the *Murdock* decision was applicable only to itinerant preachers. It stated, moreover, that appellant earned his living "by the sale of books," that his "occupation was that of selling books and not that of colporteur," that "the sales proven were more commercial than religious." It concluded that the "license was required for the selling of books, not for the spreading of religion."

[576] We pointed out in the *Murdock* case that the distinction between "religious" activity and "purely commercial" activity would at times be "vital" in determining the constitutionality of flat license taxes such as these. 319 U.S. p. 110. But we need not determine here by what tests the existence of a "religion" or the "free exercise" thereof in the constitutional sense may be ascertained or measured. For the Supreme Court of South Carolina conceded that "the book in question is a religious book"; and it concluded "without difficulty" that "its publication and distribution come within the words, 'exercise of religion,' as they are used in the Constitution." We must accordingly accept as *bona fide* appellant's assertion that he was "preaching the gospel" by going "from house to house presenting the gospel of the kingdom in printed form." Thus we have quite a different case from that of a merchant who sells books at a stand or on the road.

The question is therefore a narrow one. It is whether a flat license tax as applied to one who earns his livelihood as an evangelist or preacher in his home town is constitutional. It was not clear from the records in the *Opelika* and *Murdock* cases to what extent, if any, the Jehovah's Witnesses there involved were dependent on "sales" or "contributions" for a livelihood. But we did state that an "itinerant evangelist" did not become "a mere book agent by selling the Bible or religious tracts to help defray his expenses or to sustain him." 319 U.S. p. 111. Freedom of religion is not merely reserved for those with a long purse. Preachers of the more orthodox faiths are not engaged in commercial undertakings because they are dependent on their calling for a living. [577] Whether needy or affluent, they avail themselves of the constitutional privilege of a "free exercise" of their religion when they enter the pulpit to proclaim their faith. The priest or preacher is as fully protected in his function as the parishioners are in their worship. A flat license tax on that constitutional privilege would be as odious as the early "taxes on knowledge" which the framers of the First Amendment sought to outlaw. *Grosjean v. American Press Co.*, 297 U.S. 233, 245–248. A preacher has no less a claim to that privilege when he is not an itinerant. We referred to the itinerant nature of the activity in the *Murdock* case merely in emphasis of the prohibitive character of the license tax as so applied. Its unconstitutionality was not dependent on that circumstance. The exaction of a tax as a condition to the exercise of the great liberties guaranteed by the First Amendment is as obnoxious as the imposition of a censorship or a previous restraint. For, to repeat, "the power to tax the exercise of a privilege is the power to control or suppress its enjoyment." *Murdock v. Pennsylvania*, p. 112.

But if this license tax would be invalid as applied to one who preaches the Gospel from the pulpit, the judgment below must be reversed. For we fail to see how such a tax loses its constitutional infirmity when exacted from those who confine themselves to their own village or town and spread their religious beliefs from door to door or on the street. The protection of the First Amendment is not restricted to orthodox religious practices any more than it is to the expression of orthodox economic views. He who makes a profession of evangelism is not in a less preferred position than the casual worker.

This does not mean that religious undertakings must be subsidized. The exemption from a license tax of a preacher who preaches or a parishioner who listens does [578] not mean that either is free from all financial burdens of government, including taxes on income or property. We said as much in the *Murdock* case. But to say that they, like other citizens, may be subject to general taxation does not mean that they can be required to pay a tax for the exercise of that which the First Amendment has made a high constitutional privilege.

MR. JUSTICE REED, concurring:

My views on the constitutionality of ordinances of this type are set out at length in *Jones v. Opelika*, 316 U.S. 584, and in a dissent on the rehearing of the same case, 319 U.S. 117. These views remain unchanged but they are not in accord with those announced by the Court.

My understanding of this Court's opinions in *Murdock v. Pennsylvania* and *Jones v. Opelika*, 319 U.S. 103, is that distribution of religious literature in return for money when done as a method of spreading the distributor's religious beliefs is an exercise of religion within the First Amendment and therefore immune from interference by the requirement of a license. These opinions are now the law of the land.

As I see no difference in respect to the exercise of religion between an itinerant distributor and one who remains in one general neighborhood or between one who is active part time and another who is active all of his time, there is no occasion for me to state again views already rejected by a majority of the Court. Consequently, I concur in the conclusion reached in the present case.

It is wise to remember that the taxing and licensing power is a dangerous and potent weapon which, in the hands of unscrupulous or bigoted men, could be used to suppress freedoms and destroy religion unless it is kept within appropriate bounds.

[579] Separate [dissenting] opinion of MR. JUSTICE ROBERTS, MR. JUSTICE FRANKFURTER, and MR. JUSTICE JACKSON.

The present decision extends the rule announced in *Jones v. Opelika*, 319 U.S. 103, and *Murdock v. Pennsylvania*.

The ordinance in question is not, in the words of the First Amendment, a law "prohibiting the free exercise" of religion. At the outset it should be observed that the ordinance is not discriminatory. It lays a tax on the pursuit of occupations by which persons earn their living in [580] the Town of McCormick. It does not single out persons pursuing any given occupation and exempt others. If it were attacked as a denial of the equal protection of the laws the contention would be frivolous. There is no suggestion that the purpose is other than to raise revenue necessary for the support of government from all who enjoy the service and protection of government, and to adjust the tax laid on the appellant in the light of the aid he derives from such service and protection.

Secondly, the ordinance lays no onerous burden on the occupation of the appellant or any other citizen. The tax in question is wholly unlike that considered in *Grosjean v. American Press Co.*, 297 U.S. 233, which had the unmistakable purpose of hitting at one out of many occupations and hitting so hard as to discourage or suppress the pursuit of that calling. The Court there said (p. 250):

> "It is not intended by anything we have said to suggest that the owners of newspapers are immune from any of the ordinary forms of taxation for support of the government. But this is not an ordinary form of tax, but one single in kind, with a long history of hostile misuse against the freedom of the press."

What then is the law under attack? It is a revenue measure applying generally to those earning their living in the community. It is a monetary exaction reasonably related to the cost of maintaining society by governmental protection, which alone renders civil liberty attainable.

Follett is not made to pay a tax for the exercise of that which the First Amendment has relieved from taxation. He is made to pay for that for which all others similarly situated must pay—an excise for the occupation of street vending. Follett asks exemption because street vending [581] is, for him, also part of his religion. As a result, Follett will enjoy a subsidy for his religion. He will save the contribution for the cost of government which everyone else will have to pay.

The present decision extends and reaches beyond what was decided in *Murdock v. Pennsylvania.* There the community asserted the right to subject transient preachers of religion to taxation; there the court emphasized the "itinerant" aspect of the activities sought to be subjected to the exaction. The emphasis there was upon the casual missionary appearances of Jehovah's Witnesses in the town and the injustice of subjecting them to a general license tax. Here, a citizen of the community, earning his living in the community by a religious activity, claims immunity from contributing to the cost of the government under which he lives. The record shows appellant "testified that he obtained his living from the money received from those with whom he placed books, that he had no other source of income."

Unless the phrase "free exercise," embodied in the First Amendment, means that government must render service free to those who earn their living in a religious calling, no reason is apparent why the appellant, like every other earner in the community, should not contribute his share of the community's common burden of expense. In effect the decision grants not free exercise of religion, in the sense that such exercise shall not be hindered or limited, but, on the other hand, requires that the exercise of religion be subsidized. Trinity Church, owning great property in New York City, devotes the income to religious ends. Must it, therefore, be exempt from paying its fair share of the cost of government's protection of its property?

We cannot ignore what this decision involves. If the First Amendment grants immunity from taxation to the exercise of religion, it must equally grant a similar exemption [582] to those who speak and to the press. It will not do to say that the Amendment, in the clause relating to religion, is couched in the imperative and, in the clause relating to freedom of speech and of press, is couched in the comparative. The Amendment's prohibitions are equally sweeping. If exactions on the business or occupation of selling cannot be enforced against Jehovah's Witnesses they can no more be enforced against publishers or vendors of books, whether dealing with religion or other matters of information. The decision now rendered must mean that the guarantee of freedom of the press creates an immunity equal to that here upheld as to teaching or preaching religious doctrine. Thus the decision precludes nonoppressive, nondiscriminatory licensing or occupation taxes on publishers, and on news vendors as well, since, without the latter, the dissemination of views would be impossible. This court disavowed any such doctrine with respect to freedom of the press in *Grosjean v. American Press Co.*, and it is unthinkable that those who publish and distribute for profit newspapers and periodicals should suggest that they are in a class apart, untouchable by taxation upon their enterprises for the support of the government which makes their activities possible.

Not only must the court, if it is to be consistent, accord to dissemination of all opinion, religious or other, the same immunity, but, even in the field of religion alone, the implications of the present decision are startling. Multiple activities by which citizens earn their bread may, with equal propriety, be denominated an exercise of religion as may preaching or selling religious tracts. Certainly this court cannot say that one activity is the exercise of religion and the other is not. The materials for judicial [583] distinction do not exist. It would be difficult to deny the claims of those who devote their lives to the healing of the sick, to the nursing of the disabled, to the betterment of social and economic conditions, and to a myriad other worthy objects, that their respective callings, albeit they earn their living by pursuing them, are, for them, the exercise of religion. Such a belief, however earnestly and honestly held, does not entitle the believers to be free of contribution to the cost of government, which itself guarantees them the privilege of pursuing their callings without governmental prohibition or interference.

We should affirm the judgment.

10

Everson v. Board of Education of Ewing Township

330 U.S. 1 (1947)

Vote: 5—Vinson, Black, Reed, Douglas, Murphy
  4—Frankfurter, Jackson, Rutledge, Burton

Opinion announcing the opinion of the Court: Black
Dissenting opinions: Jackson, Rutledge

Pursuant to a New Jersey statute authorizing local school boards to make rules and contracts for transporting schoolchildren to and from school, the Board of Education of Ewing Township authorized reimbursement of expenditures for public bus transportation of pupils to and from public and Catholic schools. The fares amounted to about $40 per year per pupil. A township taxpayer challenged the constitutionality of reimbursements to parents of children attending parochial school.

Mr. Justice BLACK delivered the opinion of the Court.

. . . [4] Since there has been no attack on the statute on the ground that a part of its language excludes children attending private schools operated for profit from enjoying state payment for their transportation, we need not consider this exclusionary language; it has no relevancy to any constitutional question here presented.[1] . . .

[8] The New Jersey statute is challenged as a "law respecting an establishment of religion." The First Amendment, as made applicable to the states by the Fourteenth, *Murdock v. Commonwealth of Pennsylvania*, 319 U.S. 105, commands that a state "shall make no law respecting an establishment of religion, or prohibiting the free exercise

---

1. Appellant does not challenge the New Jersey statute or the resolution on the ground that either violates the equal protection clause of the Fourteenth Amendment by excluding payment for the transportation of any pupil who attends a "private school run for profit." Although the township resolution authorized reimbursement only for parents of public and Catholic school pupils, appellant does not allege, nor is there anything in the record which would offer the slightest support to an allegation, that there were any children in the township who attended or would have attended, but for want of transportation, any but public and Catholic schools. It will be appropriate to consider the exclusion of students of private schools operated for profit when and if it is proved to have occurred, is made the basis of a suit by one in a position to challenge it, and New Jersey's highest court has ruled adversely to the challenger. Striking down a state law is not a matter of such light moment that it should be done by a federal court *ex mero motu* on a postulate neither charged nor proved, but which rests on nothing but a possibility.

thereof." These words of the First Amendment reflected in the minds of early Americans a vivid mental picture of conditions and practices which they fervently wished to stamp out in order to preserve liberty for themselves and for their posterity. Doubtless their goal has not been entirely reached; but so far has the Nation moved toward it that the expression "law respecting an establishment of religion," probably does not so vividly remind present-day Americans of the evils, fears, and political problems that caused that expression to be written into our Bill of Rights. Whether this New Jersey law is one respecting the "establishment of religion" requires an understanding of the meaning of that language, particularly with respect to the imposition of taxes. Once again, therefore, it is not inappropriate briefly to review the background and environment of the period in which that constitutional language was fashioned and adopted.

A large proportion of the early settlers of this country came here from Europe to escape the bondage of laws which compelled them to support and attend government favored churches. The centuries immediately before and contemporaneous with the colonization of America had been filled with turmoil, civil strife, and persecutions, generated in large part by established sects determined to [9] maintain their absolute political and religious supremacy. With the power of government supporting them, at various times and places, Catholics had persecuted Protestants, Protestants had perse-cuted Catholics, Protestant sects had persecuted other Protestant sects, Catholics of one shade of belief had persecuted Catholics of another shade of belief, and all of these had from time to time persecuted Jews. In efforts to force loyalty to whatever religious group happened to be on top and in league with the government of a particular time and place, men and women had been fined, cast in jail, cruelly tortured, and killed. Among the offenses for which these punishments had been inflicted were such things as speak-ing disrespectfully of the views of ministers of government-established churches, non-attendance at those churches, expressions of non-belief in their doctrines, and failure to pay taxes and tithes to support them.

These practices of the old world were transplanted to and began to thrive in the soil of the new America. The very charters granted by the English Crown to the individuals and companies designated to make the laws which would control the destinies of the colonials authorized these individuals and companies to erect religious establishments which all, whether believers or non-believers, would be required to support and attend. An exercise of [10] this authority was accompanied by a repetition of many of the old world practices and persecutions. Catholics found themselves hounded and proscribed because of their faith; Quakers who followed their conscience went to jail; Baptists were peculiarly obnoxious to certain dominant Protestant sects; men and women of varied faiths who happened to be in a minority in a particular locality were persecuted because they steadfastly persisted in worshipping God only as their own consciences dictated. And all of these dissenters were compelled to pay tithes and taxes to support government-sponsored churches whose ministers preached inflammatory sermons designed to strengthen and consolidate the established faith by generating a burning hatred against dissenters. [11] These practices became so commonplace as to shock the freedom-loving colonials into a feeling of abhorrence. The imposition of taxes to pay ministers' salaries and to build and maintain churches and church property aroused their indignation. It was these feelings which found expression in the First Amend-ment. No one locality and no one group throughout the Colonies can rightly be given entire credit for having aroused the sentiment that culminated in adoption of the Bill of Rights' provisions embracing religious liberty. But Virginia, where the established church had achieved a dominant influence in political affairs and where many excesses attracted wide public attention, provided a great stimulus and able leadership for the movement. The people there, as elsewhere, reached the conviction that individual religious liberty could be achieved best under a government which was stripped of all power to tax, to support, or otherwise to assist any or all religions, or to interfere with the beliefs of any religious individual or group.

The movement toward this end reached its dramatic climax in Virginia in 1785–86 when the Virginia legislative body was about to renew Virginia's tax levy for the support of the established church. Thomas Jeffer- [12] son and James Madison led the fight against this tax. Madison wrote his great "Memorial and Remonstrance" against the law. In it, he eloquently argued that a true religion did not need the support of law; that no person, either believer or non-believer, should be taxed to support a religious institution of any kind; that the best interest of a society required that the minds of men always be wholly free; and that cruel persecutions were the inevitable result of government-established religions. Madison's "Remonstrance" received strong support throughout Virginia, and the Assembly postponed consideration of the proposed tax measure until its next session. When the proposal came up for consideration at that session, it not only died in committee, but the Assembly enacted the famous "Virginia Bill for Religious Liberty" originally written by Thomas Jefferson. The preamble to that Bill stated among other things that

> "Almighty God hath created the mind free; that all attempts to influence it by temporal punishments, or burthens, or by civil incapacitations, tend only to beget habits of hypocrisy and meanness, and are [13] a departure from the plan of the Holy author of our religion who being Lord both of body and mind, yet chose not to propagate it by coercions on either . . . ; that to compel a man to furnish contributions of money for the propagation of opinions which he disbelieves, is sinful and tyrannical; that even the forcing him to support this or that teacher of his own religious persuasion, is depriving him of the comfortable liberty of giving his contributions to the particular pastor, whose morals he would make his pattern. . . ."

And the statute itself enacted

> "That no man shall be compelled to frequent or support any religious worship, place, or ministry whatsoever, nor shall be enforced, restrained, molested, or burthened, in his body or goods, nor shall otherwise suffer on account of his religious opinions or belief. . . ."

This Court has previously recognized that the provisions of the First Amendment, in the drafting and adoption of which Madison and Jefferson played such leading roles, had the same objective and were intended to provide the same protection against governmental intrusion on religious liberty as the Virginia statute. *Reynolds v. United States*, 98 U.S. at page 164; *Watson v. Jones*, 13 Wall. 679; *Davis v. Beason*, 133 U.S. 333. Prior to the adoption of the Fourteenth Amendment, the First Amendment did not apply as a restraint against the states. Most of them did soon provide similar constitutional protections [14] for religious liberty. But some states persisted for about half a century in imposing restraints upon the free exercise of religion and in discriminating against particular religious groups. . . .

The meaning and scope of the First Amendment, preventing establishment of religion or prohibiting the free exercise thereof, in the light of its history and the evils it [15] was designed forever to suppress, have been several times elaborated by the decisions of this Court prior to the application of the First Amendment to the states by the

Fourteenth. The broad meaning given the Amendment by these earlier cases has been accepted by this Court in its decisions concerning an individual's religious freedom rendered since the Fourteenth Amendment was interpreted to make the prohibitions of the First applicable to state action abridging religious freedom. There is every reason to give the same application and broad interpretation to the "establishment of religion" clause. The interrelation of these complementary clauses was well summarized in a statement of the Court of Appeals of South Carolina, quoted with approval by this Court, in *Watson v. Jones*, 13 Wall. 679, 730: "The structure of our government has, for the preservation of civil liberty, rescued the temporal institutions from religious interference. On the other hand, it has secured religious liberty from the invasions of the civil authority."

The "establishment of religion" clause of the First Amendment means at least this: Neither a state nor the Federal Government can set up a church. Neither can pass laws which aid one religion, aid all religions, or prefer one religion over another. Neither can force nor influence a person to go to or to remain away from church against his will or force him to profess a belief or disbelief in any religion. No person can be punished for entertain- [16] ing or professing religious beliefs or disbeliefs, for church attendance or non-attendance. No tax in any amount, large or small, can be levied to support any religious activities or institutions, whatever they may be called, or whatever form they may adopt to teach or practice religion. Neither a state nor the Federal Government can, openly or secretly, participate in the affairs of any religious organizations or groups and vice versa. In the words of Jefferson, the clause against establishment of religion by law was intended to erect "a wall of separation between Church and State." *Reynolds v. United States*, 98 U.S. at page 164.

We must consider the New Jersey statute in accordance with the foregoing limitations imposed by the First Amendment. But we must not strike that state statute down if it is within the state's constitutional power even though it approaches the verge of that power. New Jersey cannot consistently with the "establishment of religion" clause of the First Amendment contribute tax-raised funds to the support of an institution which teaches the tenets and faith of any church. On the other hand, other language of the amendment commands that New Jersey cannot hamper its citizens in the free exercise of their own religion. Consequently, it cannot exclude individual Catholics, Lutherans, Mohammedans, Baptists, Jews, Methodists, Non-believers, Presbyterians, or the members of any other faith, because of their faith, or lack of it, from receiving the benefits of public welfare legislation. While we do not mean to intimate that a state could not provide transportation only to children attending public schools, we must be careful, in protecting the citizens of New Jersey against state-established churches, to be sure that we do not inadvertently prohibit New Jersey from extending its general State law benefits to all its citizens without regard to their religious belief. [17] Measured by these standards, we cannot say that the First Amendment prohibits New Jersey from spending tax-raised funds to pay the bus fares of parochial school pupils as a part of a general program under which it pays the fares of pupils attending public and other schools. It is undoubtedly true that children are helped to get to church schools. There is even a possibility that some of the children might not be sent to the church schools if the parents were compelled to pay their children's bus fares out of their own pockets when transportation to a public school would have been paid for by the State. The same possibility exists where the state requires a local transit company to provide reduced fares to school children including those attending parochial schools, or where a municipally owned transportation system undertakes to carry all school children free of charge. Moreover, state-paid policemen, detailed to protect children going to and from church schools from the very real hazards of traffic, would serve much the same purpose and accomplish much the same result as state provisions intended to guarantee free transportation of a kind which the state deems to be best for the school children's welfare. And parents might refuse to risk their children to the serious danger of traffic accidents going to and from parochial schools, the approaches to which were not protected by policemen. Similarly, parents might be reluctant to permit their children to attend schools which the state had cut off from such general government services as ordinary police and fire protection, connections for sewage disposal, public [18] highways and sidewalks. Of course, cutting off church schools from these services, so separate and so indisputably marked off from the religious function, would make it far more difficult for the schools to operate. But such is obviously not the purpose of the First Amendment. That Amendment requires the state to be a neutral in its relations with groups of religious believers and non-believers; it does not require the state to be their adversary. State power is no more to be used so as to handicap religions, than it is to favor them.

This Court has said that parents may, in the discharge of their duty under state compulsory education laws, send their children to a religious rather than a public school if the school meets the secular educational requirements which the state has power to impose. See *Pierce v. Society of Sisters*. It appears that these parochial schools meet New Jersey's requirements. The State contributes no money to the schools. It does not support them. Its legislation, as applied, does no more than provide a general program to help parents get their children, regardless of their religion, safely and expeditiously to and from accredited schools.

The First Amendment has erected a wall between church and state. That wall must be kept high and impregnable. We could not approve the slightest breach. New Jersey has not breached it here.

Mr. Justice JACKSON, dissenting.

I find myself, contrary to first impressions, unable to join in this decision. I have a sympathy, though it is not ideological, with Catholic citizens who are compelled by law to pay taxes for public schools, and also feel constrained by conscience and discipline to support other schools for their own children. Such relief to them as [19] this case involves is not in itself a serious burden to taxpayers and I had assumed it to be as little serious in principle. Study of this case convinces me otherwise. The Court's opinion marshals every argument in favor of state aid and puts the case in its most favorable light, but much of its reasoning confirms my conclusions that there are no good grounds upon which to support the present legislation. In fact, the undertones of the opinion, advocating complete and uncompromising separation of Church from State, seem utterly discordant with its conclusion yielding support to their commingling in educational matters. The case which irresistibly comes to mind as the most fitting precedent is that of Julia who, according to Byron's reports, "whispering 'I will ne'er consent,'—consented." . . .

[21] II

Whether the taxpayer constitutionally can be made to contribute aid to parents of students because of their attendance at parochial schools depends upon the nature of those schools and their relation to the Church. The Constitution says nothing of education. It lays no obligation on the states to provide schools and does not undertake to regulate state systems of education if they see fit to maintain them. But they cannot, through school policy any more than through other means, invade rights secured [22] to citizens by the Constitution of the United States. One of our basic rights is to be free of taxation to support a transgression of the constitutional command that the authorities "shall make no law respecting an establishment of religion, or prohibiting the free exercise thereof." . . .

[23] It is no exaggeration to say that the whole historic conflict in temporal policy between the Catholic Church and non-Catholics comes to a focus in their respective school policies. The Roman Catholic Church, counseled by experience in many ages and many lands and with all sorts and conditions of men, takes what, from the viewpoint of its own progress and the success of its mission, is a wise estimate of the importance of education to religion. It does not leave the individual to pick up religion by chance. It relies on early and indelible indoctrination in the faith and order of the Church by the word and example of persons consecrated to the task.

Our public school, if not a product of Protestantism, at least is more consistent with it than with the Catholic culture and scheme of values. It is a relatively recent development dating from about 1840. It is organized on [24] the premise that secular education can be isolated from all religious teaching so that the school can inculcate all needed temporal knowledge and also maintain a strict and lofty neutrality as to religion. The assumption is that after the individual has been instructed in worldly wisdom he will be better fitted to choose his religion. Whether such a disjunction is possible, and if possible whether it is wise, are questions I need not try to answer.

I should be surprised if any Catholic would deny that the parochial school is a vital, if not the most vital, part of the Roman Catholic Church. If put to the choice, that venerable institution, I should expect, would forego its whole service for mature persons before it would give up education of the young, and it would be a wise choice. Its growth and cohesion, discipline and loyalty, spring from its schools. Catholic education is the rock on which the whole structure rests, and to render tax aid to its Church school is indistinguishable to me from rendering the same aid to the Church itself.

III

It is of no importance in this situation whether the beneficiary of this expenditure of tax-raised funds is primarily the parochial school and incidentally the pupil, or whether the aid is directly bestowed on the pupil with indirect benefits to the school. The state cannot maintain a Church and it can no more tax its citizens to furnish free carriage to those who attend a Church. The prohibition against establishment of religion cannot be circumvented by a subsidy, bonus or reimbursement of expense to individuals for receiving religious instruction and indoctrination.

The Court, however, compares this to other subsidies and loans to individuals and says, "Nor does it follow that a law has a private rather than a public purpose because [25] it provides that tax-raised funds will be paid to reimburse individuals on account of money spent by them in a way which furthers a public program." Of course, the state may pay out tax-raised funds to relieve pauperism, but it may not under our Constitution do so to induce or reward piety. It may spend funds to secure old age against want, but it may not spend funds to secure religion against skepticism. It may compensate individuals for loss of employment, but it cannot compensate them for adherence to a creed.

It seems to me that the basic fallacy in the Court's reasoning, which accounts for its failure to apply the principles it avows, is in ignoring the essentially religious test by which beneficiaries of this expenditure are selected. A policeman protects a Catholic, of course—but not because he is a Catholic; it is because he is a man and a member of our society. The fireman protects the Church school—but not because it is a Church school; it is because it is property, part of the assets of our society. Neither the fireman nor the policeman has to ask before he renders aid "Is this man or building identified with the Catholic Church." But before these school authorities draw a check to reimburse for a student's fare they must ask just that question, and if the school is a Catholic one they may render aid because it is such, while if it is of any other faith or is run for profit, the help must be withheld. To consider the converse of the Court's reasoning will best disclose its fallacy. That there is no parallel between police and fire protection and this plan of reimbursement is apparent from the incongruity of the limitation of this Act if applied to police and fire service. Could we sustain an Act that said police shall protect pupils on the way to or from public schools and Catholic schools but not [26] while going to and coming from other schools, and firemen shall extinguish a blaze in public or Catholic school buildings but shall not put out a blaze in Protestant Church schools or private schools operated for profit? That is the true analogy to the case we have before us and I should think it pretty plain that such a scheme would not be valid.

The Court's holding is that this taxpayer has no grievance because the state has decided to make the reimbursement a public purpose and therefore we are bound to regard it as such. I agree that this Court has left, and always should leave to each state, great latitude in deciding for itself, in the light of its own conditions, what shall be public purposes in its scheme of things. It may socialize utilities and economic enterprises and make taxpayers' business out of what conventionally had been private business. It may make public business of individual welfare, health, education, entertainment or security. But it cannot make public business of religious worship or instruction, or of attendance at religious institutions of any character. There is no answer to the proposition more fully expounded by Mr. Justice RUTLEDGE that the effect of the religious freedom Amendment to our Constitution was to take every form of propagation of religion out of the realm of things which could directly or indirectly be made public business and thereby be supported in whole or in part at taxpayers' expense. That is a difference which the Constitution sets up between religion and almost every other subject matter of legislation, a difference which goes to the very root of religious freedom and which the Court is overlooking today. This freedom was first in the Bill of Rights because it was first in the forefathers' minds; it was set forth in absolute terms, and its strength is its rigidity. It was intended not only to keep the states' hands out of religion, but to [27] keep religion's hands off the state, and above all, to keep bitter religious controversy out of public life by denying to every denomination any advantage from getting control of public policy or the public purse. Those great ends I cannot but think are immeasurably compromised by today's decision. . . .

[28] Mr. Justice FRANKFURTER joins in this opinion.

Mr. Justice RUTLEDGE, with whom Mr. Justice FRANKFURTER, Mr. Justice JACKSON and Mr. Justice BURTON agree, dissenting.

"Congress shall make no law respecting an establishment of religion, or prohibiting the free exercise thereof. . . ." U.S. Const. Am. Art. I.

"Well aware that Almighty God hath created the mind free; . . . that to compel a man to furnish contributions of money for the propagation of opinions which he disbelieves, is sinful and tyrannical; . . .

We, the General Assembly, do enact, That no man shall be compelled to frequent or support any religious worship, place, or ministry whatsoever, nor shall be enforced, restrained, molested, or burthened in his body or goods, nor shall otherwise suffer on account of his religious opinions or belief. . . ."[1]

[29] I cannot believe that the great author of those words, or the men who made them law, could have joined in this decision. Neither so high nor so impregnable today as yesterday is the wall raised between church and state by Virginia's great statute of religious freedom and the First Amendment, now made applicable to all the states by the Fourteenth. New Jersey's statute sustained is the first, if indeed it is not the second breach to be made by this Court's action. That a third, and a fourth, and still others will be attempted, we may be sure. For just as *Cochran v. Louisiana State Board of Education*, 281 U.S. 370, has opened the way by oblique ruling for this decision, so will the two make wider the breach for a third. Thus with time the most solid freedom steadily gives way before continuing corrosive decision.

This case forces us to determine squarely for the first time what was "an establishment of religion" in the First Amendment's conception; and by that measure to decide whether New Jersey's action violates its command. . . .

[31] I

Not simply an established church, but any law respecting an establishment of religion is forbidden. The Amendment was broadly but not loosely phrased. It is the compact and exact summation of its author's views formed during his long struggle for religious freedom. In Madison's own words characterizing Jefferson's Bill for Establishing Religious Freedom, the guaranty he put in our national charter, like the bill he piloted through the Virginia Assembly, was "a Model of technical precision, and perspicuous brevity." Madison could not have confused "church" and "religion," or "an established church" and "an establishment of religion."

The Amendment's purpose was not to strike merely at the official establishment of a single sect, creed or religion, outlawing only a formal relation such as had prevailed in England and some of the colonies. Necessarily it was to uproot all such relationships. But the object was broader than separating church and state in this narrow sense. It was to create a complete and permanent separation of the [32] spheres of religious activity and civil authority by comprehensively forbidding every form of public aid or support for religion. In proof the Amendment's wording and history unite with this Court's consistent utterances whenever attention has been fixed directly upon the question.

"Religion" appears only once in the Amendment. But the word governs two prohibitions and governs them alike. It does not have two meanings, one narrow to forbid "an establishment" and another, much broader, for securing "the free exercise thereof." "Thereof" brings down "religion" with its entire and exact content, no more and no less, from the first into the second guaranty, so that Congress and now the states are as broadly restricted concerning the one as they are regarding the other.

No one would claim today that the Amendment is constricted, in "prohibiting the free exercise" of religion, to securing the free exercise of some formal or creedal observance, of one sect or of many. It secures all forms of religious expression, creedal, sectarian or nonsectarian wherever and however taking place, except conduct which trenches

---

1. "A Bill for Establishing Religious Freedom," enacted by the General Assembly of Virginia, January 19, 1786.

upon the like freedoms of others or clearly and presently endangers the community's good order and security. For the protective purposes of this phase of the basic freedom street preaching, oral or by distribution of [33] literature, has been given "the same high estate under the First Amendment as . . . worship in the churches and preaching from the pulpits." And on this basis parents have been held entitled to send their children to private, religious schools. *Pierce v. Society of Sisters.* Accordingly, daily religious education commingled with secular is "religion" within the guaranty's comprehensive scope. So are religious training and teaching in whatever form. The word connotes the broadest content, determined not by the form or formality of the teaching or where it occurs, but by its essential nature regardless of those details.

"Religion" has the same broad significance in the twin prohibition concerning "an establishment." The Amendment was not duplicitous. "Religion" and "establishment" were not used in any formal or technical sense. The prohibition broadly forbids state support, financial or other, of religion in any guise, form or degree. It outlaws all use of public funds for religious purposes.

II

No provision of the Constitution is more closely tied to or given content by its generating history than the religious clause of the First Amendment. It is at once the refined product and the terse summation of that history. The history includes not only Madison's authorship and the proceedings before the First Congress, but also the long and intensive struggle for religious freedom in America, more especially in Virginia, of which the Amend- [34] ment was the direct culmination. In the documents of the times, particularly of Madison, who was leader in the Virginia struggle before he became the Amendment's sponsor, but also in the writings of Jefferson and others and in the issues which engendered them is to be found irrefutable confirmation of the Amendment's sweeping content.

For Madison, as also for Jefferson, religious freedom was the crux of the struggle for freedom in general. *Remonstrance*, Par. 15.* Madison was coauthor with George Mason of the religious clause in Virginia's great Declaration of Rights of 1776. He is credited with changing it from a mere statement of the principle of tolerance to the first official legislative pronouncement that freedom of conscience and religion are inherent rights of the individual. He sought also to have the Declara- [35] tion expressly condemn the existing Virginia establishment. But the forces supporting it were then too strong.

Accordingly Madison yielded on this phase but not for long. At once he resumed the fight, continuing it before succeeding legislative sessions. As a member of the General Assembly in 1779 he threw his full weight behind Jefferson's historic Bill for Establishing Religious Freedom. That bill was a prime phase of Jefferson's broad program of democratic reform undertaken on his return from the Continental Congress in 1776 and submitted for the General Assembly's consideration in 1779 as his proposed revised Virginia code. With Jefferson's departure for Europe in 1784, Madison became the Bill's prime [36] sponsor. Enactment failed in successive legislatures from its introduction in June 1779, until its adoption in January, 1786. But during all this time the fight for religious freedom moved forward in Virginia on various fronts with growing intensity. Madison led throughout, against Patrick Henry's powerful opposing leadership until Henry was elected governor in November, 1784.

---

*Justice Rutledge attached Madison's "Memorial and Remonstrance" as an appendix to his opinion. Madison's document can be found in this volume on pages 582–86.

The climax came in the legislative struggle of 1784–1785 over the Assessment Bill. See Supplemental Appendix hereto. This was nothing more nor less than a taxing measure for the support of religion, designed to revive the payment of tithes suspended since 1777. So long as it singled out a particular sect for preference it incurred the active and general hostility of dissentient groups. It was broadened to include them, with the result that some subsided temporarily in their opposition. As altered, the bill gave to each taxpayer the privilege of designating which church should receive his share of the tax. In default of designation the legislature applied it to pious uses. But what is of the utmost significance here, "in [37] its final form the bill left the taxpayer the option of giving his tax to education."

Madison was unyielding at all times, opposing with all his vigor the general and non-discriminatory as he had the earlier particular and discriminatory assessments proposed. The modified Assessment Bill passed second reading in December, 1784, and was all but enacted. Madison and his followers, however, maneuvered deferment of final consideration until November, 1785. And before the Assembly reconvened in the fall he issued his historic "Memorial and Remonstrance."

This is Madison's complete, though not his only, interpretation of religious liberty. It is a broadside attack upon all forms of "establishment" of religion, both general and particular, nondiscriminatory or selective. Reflecting not only the many legislative conflicts over the Assessment Bill and the Bill for Establishing Religious Freedom but also, for example, the struggles for religious incorporations and the continued maintenance of the glebes, the "Remonstrance" is at once the most concise and the most accurate statement of the views of the First Amendment's author concerning what is "an establishment of religion." Because it behooves us in the dimming distance of time not [38] to lose sight of what he and his coworkers had in mind when, by a single sweeping stroke of the pen, they forbade an establishment of religion and secured its free exercise, the text of the "Remonstrance" is appended at the end of this opinion for its wider current reference, together with a copy of the bill against which it was directed.

The "Remonstrance," stirring up a storm of popular protest, killed the Assessment Bill. It collapsed in committee shortly before Christmas, 1785. With this, the way was cleared at last for enactment of Jefferson's Bill for Establishing Religious Freedom. Madison promptly drove it through in January of 1786, seven years from the time it was first introduced. This dual victory substantially ended the fight over establishments, settling the issue against them.

The next year Madison became a member of the Constitutional Convention. Its work done, he fought valiantly to secure the ratification of its great product in Virginia as elsewhere, and nowhere else more effectively. Madison was certain in his own mind that under the Constitution "there is not a shadow of right in the general government to intermeddle with religion" and that "this subject is, for the honor of America, perfectly free and [39] unshackled. The Government has no jurisdiction over it. . . ." Nevertheless he pledged that he would work for a Bill of Rights, including a specific guaranty of religious freedom, and Virginia, with other states, ratified the Constitution on this assurance.

Ratification thus accomplished, Madison was sent to the first Congress. There he went at once about performing his pledge to establish freedom for the nation as he had done in Virginia. Within a little more than three years from his legislative victory at home he had proposed and secured the submission and ratification of the First Amendment as the first article of our Bill of Rights.

All the great instruments of the Virginia struggle for religious liberty thus became warp and woof of our constitutional tradition, not simply by the course of history, but by the common unifying force of Madison's life, thought and sponsorship. He epitomized the whole of that tradition in the Amendment's compact, but nonetheless comprehensive, phrasing.

As the "Remonstrance" discloses throughout, Madison opposed every form and degree of official relation between religion and civil authority. For him religion was a wholly private matter beyond the scope of civil power [40] either to restrain or to support. Denial or abridgment of religious freedom was a violation of rights both of conscience and of natural equality. State aid was no less obnoxious or destructive to freedom and to religion itself than other forms of state interference. "Establishment" and "free exercise" were correlative and coextensive ideas, representing only different facets of the single great and fundamental freedom. The "Remonstrance," following the Virginia statute's example, referred to the history of religious conflicts and the effects of all sorts of establishments, current and historical, to suppress religion's free exercise. With Jefferson, Madison believed that to tolerate any fragment of establishment would be by so much to perpetuate restraint upon that freedom. Hence he sought to tear out the institution not partially but root and branch, and to bar its return forever.

In no phase was he more unrelentingly absolute than in opposing state support or aid by taxation. Not even "three pence" contribution was thus to be exacted from any citizen for such a purpose. *Remonstrance*, Par. 3. [41] Tithes had been the life blood of establishment before and after other compulsions disappeared. Madison and his coworkers made no exceptions or abridgments to the complete separation they created. Their objection was not to small tithes. It was to any tithes whatsoever. "If it were lawful to impose a small tax for religion the admission would pave the way for oppressive levies." Not the amount but "the principle of assessment was wrong." And the principle was as much to prevent "the interference of law in religion" as to restrain religious intervention in political matters. In this field the authors of our freedom would not tolerate "the first experiment on our liberties" or "wait till usurped power had strengthened itself by exercise, and entangled the question in precedents." *Remonstrance*, Par. 3. Nor should we.

In view of this history no further proof is needed that the Amendment forbids any appropriation, large or small, from public funds to aid or support any and all religious exercises. But if more were called for, the debates in the First Congress and this Court's consistent expressions, whenever it has touched on the matter directly, supply it. [42] By contrast with the Virginia history, the congressional debates on consideration of the Amendment reveal only sparse discussion, reflecting the fact that the essential issues had been settled. Indeed the matter had become so well understood as to have been taken for granted in all but formal phrasing. Hence, the only enlightening reference shows concern, not to preserve any power to use public funds in aid of religion, but to prevent the Amendment from outlawing private gifts inadvertently by virtue of the breadth of its wording. In the [43] margin are noted also the principal decisions in which expressions of this Court confirm the Amendment's broad prohibition.

[44] III

Compulsory attendance upon religious exercises went out early in the process of separating church and state, together with forced observance of religious forms and ceremonies. Test oaths and religious qualification for office followed later. These things none devoted to our great tradition of religious liberty would think of bringing back. Hence today, apart from efforts to inject religious training or exercises and sectarian issues into the public schools, the only serious surviving threat to maintaining that complete and permanent separation of religion and civil power which the First Amendment commands is through use of the taxing power to support religion, religious establishments, or establishments having a religious foundation whatever their form or special religious function.

Does New Jersey's action furnish support for religion by use of the taxing power? Certainly it does, if the test remains undiluted as Jefferson and Madison made it, that money taken by taxation from one is not to be used or given to support another's religious training or belief, or indeed one's own. Today as then the furnishing of "con- [45] tributions of money for the propagation of opinions which he disbelieves" is the forbidden exaction; and the prohibition is absolute for whatever measure brings that consequence and whatever amount may be sought or given to that end.

The funds used here were raised by taxation. The Court does not dispute nor could it that their use does in fact give aid and encouragement to religious instruction. It only concludes that this aid is not "support" in law. But Madison and Jefferson were concerned with aid and support in fact not as a legal conclusion "entangled in precedents." *Remonstrance*, Par. 3. Here parents pay money to send their children to parochial schools and funds raised by taxation are used to reimburse them. This not only helps the children to get to school and the parents to send them. It aids them in a substantial way to get the very thing which they are sent to the particular school to secure, namely, religious training and teaching.

Believers of all faiths, and others who do not express their feeling toward ultimate issues of existence in any creedal form, pay the New Jersey tax. When the money so raised is used to pay for transportation to religious schools, the Catholic taxpayer to the extent of his proportionate share pays for the transportation of Lutheran, Jewish and otherwise religiously affiliated children to receive their non-Catholic religious instruction. Their parents likewise pay proportionately for the transportation of Catholic children to receive Catholic instruction. Each thus contributes to "the propagation of opinions which he disbelieves" in so far as their religions differ, as do others who accept no creed without regard to those differences. Each [46] thus pays taxes also to support the teaching of his own religion, an exaction equally forbidden since it denies "the comfortable liberty" of giving one's contribution to the particular agency of instruction he approves.

New Jersey's action therefore exactly fits the type of exaction and the kind of evil at which Madison and Jefferson struck. Under the test they framed it cannot be said that the cost of transportation is no part of the cost of education or of the religious instruction given. That it is a substantial and a necessary element is shown most plainly by the continuing and increasing demand for the state to assume it. Nor is there pretense that it relates only to the secular instruction given in religious schools or that any attempt is or could be made toward allocating proportional shares as between the secular and the religious instruction. It is precisely because the instruction is religious and relates to a particular faith, whether one or another, that parents send their children to religious schools under the *Pierce* doctrine. And the very purpose of the state's contribution is to defray the cost of conveying the pupil to the place where he will receive not simply secular, but also and primarily religious, teaching and guidance.

Indeed the view is sincerely avowed by many of various faiths, that the basic purpose of all education is or should be religious, that the secular cannot be and should not be separated from the religious phase and emphasis. Hence, [47] the inadequacy of public or secular education and the necessity for sending the child to a school where religion is taught. But whatever may be the philosophy or its justification, there is undeniably an admixture of religious with secular teaching in all such institutions. That is the very reason for their being. Certainly for purposes of constitutionality we cannot contradict the whole basis of the ethical and educational convictions of people who believe in religious schooling.

Yet this very admixture is what was disestablished when the First Amendment forbade "an establishment of religion." Commingling the religious with the secular teaching does not divest the whole of its religious permeation and emphasis or make them of minor part, if proportion were material. Indeed, on any other view, the constitutional prohibition always could be brought to naught by adding a modicum of the secular.

An appropriation from the public treasury to pay the cost of transportation to Sunday school, to weekday special classes at the church or parish house, or to the meetings of various young people's religious societies, such as the Y.M.C.A., the Y.W.C.A., the Y.M.H.A., the Epworth League, could not withstand the constitutional attack. This would be true, whether or not secular activities were mixed with the religious. If such an appropriation could not stand, then it is hard to see how one becomes valid for the same thing upon the more extended scale of daily instruction. Surely constitutionality does not turn on where or how often the mixed teaching occurs.

Finally, transportation, where it is needed, is as essential to education as any other element. Its cost is as much a part of the total expense, except at times in amount, as the cost of textbooks, of school lunches, of athletic equipment, of writing and other materials; indeed of all other [48] items composing the total burden. Now as always the core of the educational process is the teacher-pupil relationship. Without this the richest equipment and facilities would go for naught. But the proverbial Mark Hopkins conception no longer suffices for the country's requirements. Without buildings, without equipment, without library, textbooks and other materials, and without transportation to bring teacher and pupil together in such an effective teaching environment, there can be not even the skeleton of what our times require. Hardly can it be maintained that transportation is the least essential of these items, or that it does not in fact aid, encourage, sustain and support, just as they do, the very process which is its purpose to accomplish. No less essential is it, or the payment of its cost, than the very teaching in the classroom or payment of the teacher's sustenance. Many types of equipment, now considered essential, better could be done without.

For me, therefore, the feat is impossible to select so indispensable an item from the composite of total costs, and characterize it as not aiding, contributing to, promoting or sustaining the propagation of beliefs which it is the very end of all to bring about. Unless this can be maintained, and the Court does not maintain it, the aid thus given is outlawed. Payment of transportation is no more, nor is it any the less essential to education, whether religious or secular, than payment for tuitions, for teachers' salaries, for buildings, equipment and necessary materials. Nor is it any the less directly related, in a school giving religious instruction, to the primary religious objective all those essential items of cost are intended to achieve. No rational line can be drawn between payment for such larger, but not more necessary, items and payment for transportation. The only line that can be so drawn is one between more dollars and less. Certainly in this [49] realm such a line can be no valid constitutional measure.

Now, as in Madison's time, not the amount but the principle of assessment is wrong. *Remonstrance*, Par. 3.

IV

. . . [52] It is not because religious teaching does not promote the public or the individual's welfare, but because neither is furthered when the state promotes religious education, that the Constitution forbids it to do so. Both legislatures and courts are bound by that distinction. . . .

[53] The reasons underlying the Amendment's policy have not vanished with time or diminished in force. Now as when it was adopted the price of religious freedom is double. It is that the church and religion shall live both within and upon that freedom. There cannot be freedom of religion, safeguarded by the state, and intervention by the church or its agencies in the state's domain or dependency on its largesse. Madison's *Remonstrance*, Par. 6, 8. The great condition of religious liberty is that it be maintained free from sustenance, as also from other interferences, by the state. For when it comes to rest upon that secular foundation it vanishes with the resting. *Id.*, Par. 7, 8. Public money devoted to payment of religious costs, educational or other, brings the quest for more. It brings too the struggle of sect against sect for the larger share or for any. Here one by numbers alone will benefit most, there another. That is precisely the history of societies which have had an established religion and dissident [54] groups. *Id.*, Par. 8, 11. It is the very thing Jefferson and Madison experienced and sought to guard against, whether in its blunt or in its more screened forms. *Ibid*. The end of such strife cannot be other than to destroy the cherished liberty. The dominating group will achieve the dominant benefit; or all will embroil the state in their dissensions. *Id.*, Par. 11.

Exactly such conflicts have centered of late around providing transportation to religious schools from public funds. The issue and the dissension work typically, in Madison's phrase, to "destroy that moderation and harmony which the forbearance of our laws to intermeddle with Religion, has produced amongst its several sects." *Id.*, Par. 11. This occurs, as he well knew over measures [55] at the very threshold of departure from the principle. *Id.*, Par. 3, 9, 11. . . .

[57] This is not therefore just a little case over bus fares. In paraphrase of Madison, distant as it may be in its present form from a complete establishment of religion, it differs from it only in degree; and is the first step in that direction. *Id.*, Par. 9. Today as in his time "the same authority which can force a citizen to contribute three pence only . . . for the support of any one religious establishment, may force him" to pay more; or "to conform to any other establishment in all cases whatsoever." And now, as then, "either . . . we must say, that the will of the Legislature is the only measure of their authority; and that in the plenitude of this authority, they may sweep away all our fundamental rights; or, that they are bound to leave this particular right untouched and sacred." *Remonstrance*, Par. 15. The realm of religious training and belief remains, as the Amendment made it, the kingdom of the individual [58] man and his God. It should be kept inviolately private, not "entangled . . . in precedents" or confounded with what legislatures legitimately may take over into the public domain.

V

[59] The problem then cannot be cast in terms of legal discrimination or its absence. This would be true, even though the state in giving aid should treat all religious instruction alike. Thus, if the present statute and its application were shown to apply equally to all religious schools [60] of whatever faith, yet in the light of our tradition it could not stand. For then the adherent of one creed still would pay for the support of another, the

childless taxpayer with others more fortunate. Then too there would seem to be no bar to making appropriations for transportation and other expenses of children attending public or other secular schools, after hours in separate places and classes for their exclusively religious instruction. The person who embraces no creed also would be forced to pay for teaching what he does not believe. Again, it was the furnishing of "contributions of money for the propagation of opinions which he disbelieves" that the fathers outlawed. That consequence and effect are not removed by multiplying to all-inclusiveness the sects for which support is exacted. The Constitution requires, not comprehensive identification of state with religion, but complete separation. . . .

Illinois ex rel. McCollum v. Board of Education

333 U.S. 203 (1948)

Vote: 8—Vinson, Black, Frankfurter, Douglas, Murphy, Jackson, Rutledge, Burton
    1—Reed

Opinion announcing the opinion of the Court: Black
Concurring opinions: Frankfurter, Jackson
Dissenting opinion: Reed

This case resulted from the efforts of Jewish, Catholic, and Protestant citizens in Illinois to provide religious education in public schools during the school day. Justice Black sets forth the relevant facts at the beginning of his majority opinion. At the time of the case, Illinois had a compulsory education law (punishable by fines) that, with exceptions, required parents to send their children, aged seven to sixteen, to tax-supported public schools or to private or parochial schools that met state educational standards. By law, pupils were to remain in attendance during regular school hours. Similar "released time" arrangements had existed in the United States for decades. In his concurring opinion, Justice Frankfurter reported that in 1947 alone two million schoolchildren in some twenty-two hundred communities participated in similar programs.

Mr. Justice BLACK delivered the opinion of the Court.

[207] Although there are disputes between the parties as to various inferences that may or may not properly be drawn from the evidence concerning the religious program, the following facts are shown by the record without dispute. In 1940 interested members of the Jewish, Roman Catholic, and a few of the Protestant faiths formed a voluntary association called the Champaign Council on Religious Education. They obtained permission from the Board of Education to offer classes in religious instruction to public school pupils in grades four to nine inclusive. Classes were made up of pupils whose parents signed printed cards requesting that their children be permitted to attend; they were held weekly, thirty minutes for [208] the lower grades, forty-five minutes for the higher. The council employed the religious teachers at no expense to the school authorities, but the instructors were subject to the approval and supervision of the superintendent of schools. The classes were taught in three [209] separate religious groups by Protestant teachers,

Catholic priests, and a Jewish rabbi, although for the past several years there have apparently been no classes instructed in the Jewish religion. Classes were conducted in the regular classrooms of the school building. Students who did not choose to take the religious instruction were not released from public school duties; they were required to leave their classrooms and go to some other place in the school building for pursuit of their secular studies. On the other hand, students who were released from secular study for the religious instructions were required to be present at the religious classes. Reports of their presence or absence were to be made to their secular teachers.

The foregoing facts, without reference to others that appear in the record, show the use of tax-supported property for religious instruction and the close cooperation between the school authorities and the religious council in promoting religious education. The operation of the state's compulsory education system thus assists and is integrated with the program of religious instruction carried on by separate religious sects. Pupils compelled by law to go to school for secular education are released [210] in part from their legal duty upon the condition that they attend the religious classes. This is beyond all question a utilization of the tax-established and tax-supported public school system to aid religious groups to spread their faith. And it falls squarely under the ban of the First Amendment (made applicable to the States by the Fourteenth) as we interpreted it in *Everson v. Board of Education*. There we said: "Neither a state nor the Federal Government can set up a church. Neither can pass laws which aid one religion, aid all religions, or prefer one religion over another. Neither can force or influence a person to go to or to remain away from church against his will or force him to profess a belief or disbelief in any religion. No person can be punished for entertaining or professing religious beliefs or disbeliefs, for church attendance or nonattendance. No tax in any amount, large or small, can be levied to support any religious activities or institutions, whatever they may be called, or whatever form they may adopt to teach or practice religion. Neither a state nor [211] the Federal Government can, openly or secretly, participate in the affairs of any religious organizations or groups, and vice versa. In the words of Jefferson, the clause against establishment of religion by law was intended to erect 'a wall of separation between Church and State.'" *Id.*, at pages 15, 16 of 330 U.S. The majority in the *Everson* case, and the minority as shown by quotations from the dissenting views in our notes 6 and 7, agreed that the First Amendment's language, properly interpreted, had erected a wall of separation between Church and State. They disagreed as to the facts shown by the record and as to the proper application of the First Amendment's language to those facts.

Recognizing that the Illinois program is barred by the First and Fourteenth Amendments if we adhere to the views expressed both by the majority and the minority in the *Everson* case, counsel for the respondents challenge those views as dicta and urge that we reconsider and repudiate them. They argue that historically the First Amendment was intended to forbid only government preference of one religion over another, not an impartial governmental assistance of all religions. In addition they ask that we distinguish or overrule our holding in the *Everson* case that the Fourteenth Amendment made the "establishment of religion" clause of the First Amendment applicable as a prohibition against the States. After giving full consideration to the arguments presented we are unable to accept either of these contentions.

To hold that a state cannot consistently with the First and Fourteenth Amendments utilize its public school system to aid any or all religious faiths or sects in the dissemination of their doctrines and ideals does not, as counsel urge, manifest a governmental hostility to religion or religious teachings. A manifestation of such hostility would be at war with our national tradition as embodied in the First Amendment's guaranty of the free [212] exercise of religion. For the First Amendment rests upon the premise that both religion and government can best work to achieve their lofty aims if each is left free from the other within its respective sphere. Or, as we said in the *Everson* case, the First Amendment had erected a wall between Church and State which must be kept high and impregnable.

Here not only are the state's tax-supported public school buildings used for the dissemination of religious doctrines. The State also affords sectarian groups an invaluable aid in that it helps to provide pupils for their religious classes through use of the state's compulsory public school machinery. This is not separation of Church and State.

Mr. Justice FRANKFURTER delivered the following opinion, in which Mr. Justice JACKSON, Mr. Justice RUTLEDGE and Mr. Justice BURTON join.

We dissented in *Everson v. Board of Education* because in our view the Constitutional principle requiring separation of Church and State compelled invalidation of the ordinance sustained by the majority. Illinois has here authorized the commingling of sectarian with secular instruction in the public schools. The Constitution of the United States forbids this. . . .

[214] The evolution of colonial education, largely in the service of religion, into the public school system of today is the story of changing conceptions regarding the American democratic society, of the functions of State-maintained education in such a society, and of the role therein of the free exercise of religion by the people. The modern public school derived from a philosophy of freedom reflected in the First Amendment. It is appropriate to recall that the "Remonstrance" of James Madison, an event basic in the history of religious liberty, was called forth by a proposal which involved support to religious education. See Mr. Justice Rutledge's opinion in the *Everson* case, 330 U.S. at pages 36, 37. As the momentum for popular education increased and in turn evoked strong claims for State support of religious education, contests not unlike that which in Virginia had produced Madison's "Remonstrance" appeared in various form in other States. New York and Massachusetts provide famous chapters in the history that established dissociation of religious teaching from State-maintained schools. In New York, the rise of the common schools led, despite fierce sectarian opposition, to the barring of tax funds to church schools, and later to any school in which sectarian doctrine was [215] taught. In Massachusetts, largely through the efforts of Horace Mann, all sectarian teachings were barred from the common school to save it from being rent by denominational conflict. The upshot of these controversies, often long and fierce, is fairly summarized by saying that long before the Fourteenth Amendment subjected the States to new limitations, the prohibition of furtherance by the State of religious instruction became the guiding principle, in law and feeling, of the American people. . . .

Separation in the field of education, then, was not imposed upon unwilling States by force of superior law. In this respect the Fourteenth Amendment merely reflected a principle then dominant in our national life. To the extent that the Constitution thus made it binding upon the States, the basis of the restriction is the whole experience of our people. Zealous watchfulness against fusion of secular and religious activities by Government itself, through any of its instruments but especially through its educational agencies, was the democratic response of the American community to the particular needs of a young and growing nation, unique in the composition of its [216] people. A totally different situation elsewhere, as illustrated for instance by the English provisions for religious education in State-maintained schools, only serves to illustrate that free societies are not cast in one mold. Different institutions evolve from different historic circumstances.

It is pertinent to remind that the establishment of this principle of separation in the field of education was not due to any decline in the religious beliefs of the people. Horace Mann was a devout Christian, and the deep religious feeling of James Madison is stamped upon the "Remonstrance." The secular public school did not imply indifference to the basic role of religion in the life of the people, nor rejection of religious education as a means of fostering it. The claims of religion were not minimized by refusing to make the public schools agencies for their assertion. The non-sectarian or secular public school was the means of reconciling freedom in general with religious freedom. The sharp confinement of the public schools to secular education was a recognition of the need of a democratic society to educate its children, insofar as the State undertook to do so, in an atmosphere free from pressures in a realm in which pressures are most resisted and where conflicts are most easily and most bitterly engendered. Designed to serve as perhaps the most powerful agency for promoting cohesion among a heterogeneous democratic people, the public school must keep scrupu- [217] lously free from entanglement in the strife of sects. The preservation of the community from divisive conflicts, of Government from irreconcilable pressures by religious groups, of religion from censorship and coercion however subtly exercised, requires strict confinement of the State to instruction other than religious, leaving to the individual's church and home, indoctrination in the faith of his choice.

This development of the public school as a symbol of our secular unity was not a sudden achievement nor attained without violent conflict. While in small communities of comparatively homogeneous religious beliefs, the need for absolute separation presented no urgencies, elsewhere the growth of the secular school encountered the resistance of feeling strongly engaged against it. But the inevitability of such attempts is the very reason for Constitutional provisions primarily concerned with the protection of minority groups. And such sects are shifting groups, varying from time to time, and place to place, thus representing in their totality the common interest of the nation.

Enough has been said to indicate that we are dealing not with a full-blown principle, nor one having the definiteness of a surveyor's metes and bounds. But by 1875 the separation of public education from Church entanglements, of the State from the teaching of religion, was firmly established in the consciousness of the nation. In [218] that year President Grant made his famous remarks to the Convention of the Army of the Tennessee:

> "Encourage free schools and resolve that not one dollar appropriated for their support shall be appropriated for the support of any sectarian schools. Resolve that neither the state nor the nation, nor both combined, shall support institutions of learning other than those sufficient to afford every child growing up in the land the opportunity of a good common school education, unmixed with sectarian, pagan, or atheistical dogmas. Leave the matter of religion to the family altar, the church, and the private school, supported entirely by private contributions. Keep the church and state forever separated."

So strong was this conviction, that rather than rest on the comprehensive prohibitions of the First and Fourteenth Amendments, President Grant urged that there be written into the United States Constitution particular elaborations including a specific prohibition against the use of public funds for sectarian education,[6] such as had [219] been written into many State constitutions. By 1894, in urging the adoption of such a provision in the New York Constitution, Elihu Root was able to summarize a century of the nation's history: "It is not a question of religion, or of creed, or of party; it is a question of declaring and maintaining the great American principle of eternal separation between Church and State." The extent to which [220] this principle was deemed a presupposition of our Constitutional system is strikingly illustrated by the fact that every State admitted into the Union since 1876 was compelled by Congress to write into its constitution a requirement that it maintain a school system "free from sectarian control." . . .

[226] How does "released time" operate in Champaign? Public school teachers distribute to their pupils cards supplied by church groups, so that the parents may indicate whether they desire religious instruction for their children. For those desiring it, religious classes are conducted in the regular classrooms of the public schools by teachers of religion paid by the churches and appointed by them, but, as the State court found, "subject to the approval and supervision of the Superintendent." The courses do not profess to give secular instruction in subjects concerning religion. Their candid purpose is sectarian teaching. While a child can go to any of the religious classes offered, a particular sect wishing a teacher for its devotees requires the permission of the school superintendent "who in turn will determine whether or not it is practical for said group to teach in said school [227] system." If no provision is made for religious instruction in the particular faith of a child, or if for other reasons the child is not enrolled in any of the offered classes, he is required to attend a regular school class, or a study period during which he is often left to his own devices. Reports of attendance in the religious classes are submitted by the religious instructor to the school authorities, and the child who fails to attend is presumably deemed a truant.

Religious education so conducted on school time and property is patently woven into the working scheme of the school. The Champaign arrangement thus presents powerful elements of inherent pressure by the school system in the interest of religious sects. The fact that this power has not been used to discriminate is beside the point. Separation is a requirement to abstain from fusing functions of Government and of religious sects, not merely to treat them all equally. That a child is offered an alternative may reduce the constraint; it does not eliminate the operation of influence by the school in matters sacred to conscience and outside the school's domain. The law of imitation operates, and nonconformity is not an outstanding characteristic of children. The result is an obvious

6. President Grant's Annual Message to Congress, December 7, 1875, 4 Cong. Rec. 15 et seq.; Ames, *The Proposed Amendments to the Constitution of the United States during the First Century of Its History*, H. Doc. No. 353, Pt. 2, 54th Cong., 2d Sess., pp. 277, 278. In addition to the first proposal, "The Blaine Amendment," five others to similar effect are cited by Ames. The reason for the failure of these attempts seems to have been in part "That the provisions of the State constitutions are in almost all instances adequate on this subject, and no amendment is likely to be secured." *Id.*

In the form in which it passed the House of Representatives, the Blaine Amendment read as follows: "No State shall make any law respecting an establishment of religion, or prohibiting the free exercise thereof; and no religious test shall ever be required as a qualification to any office or public trust under any State. No public property, and no public revenue of, nor any loan of credit by or under the authority of, the United States, or any State, Territory, District, or municipal corporation, shall be appropriated to, or made or used for, the support of any school, educational or other institution, under the control of any religious or anti-religious sect, organization, or denomination, or wherein the particular creed or tenets of any religious or anti-religious sect, organization, or denomination shall be taught. And no such particular creed or tenets shall be read or taught in any school or institution supported in whole or in part by such revenue or loan of credit; and no such appropriation or loan of credit shall be made to any religious or anti-religious sect, organization, or denomination, or to promote its interests or tenets. This article shall not be construed to prohibit the reading of the Bible in any school or institution; and it shall not have the effect to impair rights of property already vested. . . ." H. Res. 1, 44th Cong., 1st Sess. (1876).

pressure upon children to attend. Again, while the Champaign school population represents only a fraction of the more than two hundred and fifty sects of the nation, not even all the practicing sects in Champaign are willing or able to provide religious instruction. The children belonging to these non-participating sects will thus have inculcated in them a feeling of separatism when the school should be the training ground for habits of community, or they will have religious instruction in a faith which is not that of [228] their parents. As a result, the public school system of Champaign actively furthers inculcation in the religious tenets of some faiths, and in the process sharpens the consciousness of religious differences at least among some of the children committed to its care. These are consequences not amenable to statistics. But they are precisely the consequences against which the Constitution was directed when it prohibited the Government common to all from becoming embroiled, however innocently, in the destructive religious conflicts of which the history of even this country records some dark pages. . . .

[231] Separation means separation, not something less. Jefferson's metaphor in describing the relation between Church and State speaks of a "wall of separation," not of a fine line easily overstepped. The public school is at once the symbol of our democracy and the most pervasive means for promoting our common destiny. In no activity of the State is it more vital to keep out divisive forces than in its schools, to avoid confusing, not to say fusing, what the Constitution sought to keep strictly apart. "The great American principle of eternal separation"—Elihu Root's phrase bears repetition—is one of the vital reliances of our Constitutional system for assuring unities among our people stronger than our diversities. It is the Court's duty to enforce this principle in its full integrity. [232] We renew our conviction that "we have staked the very existence of our country on the faith that complete separation between the state and religion is best for the state and best for religion." *Everson v. Board of Education*, 330 U.S. at page 59. If nowhere else, in the relation between Church and State, "good fences make good neighbors."

Mr. Justice REED, dissenting.

. . . [240] I find it difficult to extract from the [majority and concurring] opinions any conclusion as to what it is in the Champaign plan that is unconstitutional. Is it the use of school buildings for religious instruction; the release of pupils by the schools for religious instruction during school hours; the so-called assistance by teachers in handing out the request cards to pupils, in keeping lists of them for release and records of their attendance; or the action of the principals in arranging an opportunity for the classes and the appearance of the Council's instructors? None of the reversing opinions say whether the purpose of the Champaign plan for religious instruction during school hours is unconstitutional or whether it is some ingredient used in or omitted from the formula that makes the plan unconstitutional. . . .

[244] The phrase "an establishment of religion" may have been intended by Congress to be aimed only at a state church. When the First Amendment was pending in Congress in substantially its present form, "Mr. Madison said, he apprehended the meaning of the words to be, that Congress should not establish a religion, and enforce the legal observation of it by law, nor compel men to worship God in any manner contrary to their conscience." Passing years, however, have brought about acceptance of a broader meaning, although never until today, I believe, has this Court widened its interpretation to any such degree as holding that recognition of the interest of our nation in religion, through the granting, to qualified representatives of the principal faiths, of opportunity

to present religion as an optional, extracurricular subject during released school time in public school buildings, was equivalent to an establishment of religion. A reading of the general statements of eminent statesmen of former days, referred to in the opinions in this and *Everson v. Board of Education*, will show that circumstances such as those in this case were far from the minds of the authors. The words and spirit of those statements may be wholeheartedly accepted without in the least impugning the judgment of the State of Illinois.

[245] Mr. Jefferson, as one of the founders of the University of Virginia, a school which from its establishment in 1819 has been wholly governed, managed and controlled by the State of Virginia, was faced with the same problem that is before this Court today: The question of the constitutional limitation upon religious education in public schools. In his annual report as Rector, to the President and Directors of the Literary Fund, dated October 7, 1822, approved by the Visitors of the University of whom Mr. Madison was one, Mr. Jefferson set forth his views at some length. These suggestions of Mr. Jefferson were [246] adopted and ch. II, 1, of the Regulations of the University of October 4, 1824, provided that:

"Should the religious sects of this State, or any of them, according to the invitation held out to them, establish within, or adjacent to, the precincts of the University, schools for instruction in the religion of their sect, the students of the University will be free, and expected to attend religious worship at the establishment of their respective sects, in the morning, and in time to meet their school in the University at its stated hour."

[247] Thus, the "wall of separation between church and State" that Mr. Jefferson built at the University which he founded did not exclude religious education from that school. The difference between the generality of his statements on the separation of church and state and the specificity of his conclusions on education are considerable. A rule of law should not be drawn from a figure of speech.

Mr. Madison's "Memorial and Remonstrance against Religious Assessments" relied upon by the dissenting Justices in *Everson* is not applicable here. Mr. Madison was one of the principal opponents in the Virginia General Assembly of A Bill Establishing a Provision for Teachers of the Christian Religion. The monies raised by the taxing section of that bill were to be appropriated "by the Vestries, Elders, or Directors of each religious society, . . . to a provision for a Minister or Teacher [248] of the Gospel of their denomination, or the providing places of divine worship, and to none other use whatsoever. . . ." The conclusive legislative struggle over this act took place in the fall of 1785 before the adoption of the Bill of Rights. The "Remonstrance" had been issued before the General Assembly convened and was instrumental in the final defeat of the act which died in committee. Throughout the "Remonstrance," Mr. Madison speaks of the "establishment" sought to be effected by the act. It is clear from its historical setting and its language that the "Remonstrance" was a protest against an effort by Virginia to support Christian sects by taxation. Issues similar to those raised by the instant case were not discussed. Thus, Mr. Madison's approval of Mr. Jefferson's report as Rector gives, in my opinion, a clearer indication of his views on the constitutionality of religious education in public schools than his general statements on a different subject.

This Court summarized the amendment's accepted reach into the religious field, as I understand its scope, in *Everson v. Board of Education*. The Court's opinion quotes the gist of the Court's reasoning in *Everson*. I agree as there stated that none of our governmental entities can "set up a church." I agree that they cannot "aid" all or any religions or prefer one "over another." But "aid" must be understood as a purposeful assistance directly to the church itself or to some religious group or organization doing religious work of such a character that it may fairly be said to be performing ecclesiastical functions. "Prefer" must give an advantage to one "over another." I agree that pupils cannot "be released in part from their legal duty" of school attendance upon condition that they attend religious classes. But as Illinois has held that it is within the discretion of the School Board to permit absence from school for religious instruc- [249] tion no legal duty of school attendance is violated. If the sentence in the first opinion, concerning the pupils' release from legal duty, is intended to mean that the Constitution forbids a school to excuse a pupil from secular control during school hours to attend voluntarily a class in religious education, whether in or out of school buildings, I disagree. Of course, no tax can be levied to support organizations intended "to teach or practice religion." I agree too that the state cannot influence one toward religion against his will or punish him for his beliefs. Champaign's religious education course does none of these things.

It seems clear to me that the "aid" referred to by the Court in the *Everson* case could not have been those incidental advantages that religious bodies, with other groups similarly situated, obtain as a by-product of organized society. This explains the well-known fact that all churches receive "aid" from government in the form of freedom from taxation. The *Everson* decision itself justified the transportation of children to church schools by New Jersey for safety reasons. . . .

[253] The practices of the federal government offer many examples of this [voluntary and educational] kind of "aid" by the state to religion. The Congress of the United States has a chaplain for each House who daily invokes divine blessings and guidance for [254] the proceedings. The armed forces have commissioned chaplains from early days. They conduct the public services in accordance with the liturgical requirements of their respective faiths, ashore and afloat, employing for the purpose property belonging to the United States and dedicated to the services of religion. Under the Servicemen's Readjustment Act of 1944, eligible veterans may receive training at government expense for the ministry in denominational schools. The schools of the District of Columbia have opening exercises which "include a reading from the Bible without note or comment, and the Lord's prayer."

In the United States Naval Academy and the United States Military Academy, schools wholly supported and completely controlled by the federal government, there are a number of religious activities. Chaplains are attached to both schools. Attendance at church services on Sunday is compulsory at both Military and Naval Academies. At West Point the Protestant services are [255] held in the Cadet Chapel, the Catholic in the Catholic Chapel, and the Jewish in the Old Cadet Chapel; at Annapolis only Protestant services are held on the reservation, midshipmen of other religious persuasions attend the churches of the city of Annapolis. These facts indicate that both schools since their earliest beginnings have maintained and enforced a pattern of participation in formal worship.

With the general statements in the opinions concerning the constitutional requirement that the nation and the states, by virtue of the First and Fourteenth Amendments, may "make no law respecting an establishment of religion," I am in agreement. But, in the light of the meaning given to those words by the precedents, customs, and practices which I have detailed above, I cannot agree with the Court's conclusion that when pupils compelled by law to go to school for secular education are released from school so as to attend the religious classes, churches are unconstitutionally aided. Whatever may be the wisdom of the arrangement as to the use of the school buildings made with The Champaign Council of Religious Education, it is clear to me that past practice shows such cooperation between the schools and a non-ecclesiastical body is not forbidden by the First Amendment. When actual church services have always been permitted on government property, the mere use of the school buildings by a non-sectarian group for religious education ought not to be condemned as an establishment of religion. For a non-sectarian organization to give the type of instruction here offered cannot be said to violate our rule as to the establishment of religion by the state. The prohibition of enactments respecting the establishment of religion do [256] not bar every friendly gesture between church and state. It is not an absolute prohibition against every conceivable situation where the two may work together any more than the other provisions of the First Amendment— free speech, free press—are absolutes. If abuses occur such as the use of the instruction hour for sectarian purposes, I have no doubt, in view of the *Ring* case, that Illinois will promptly correct them. If they are of a kind that tend to the establishment of a church or interfere with the free exercise of religion, this Court is open for a review of any erroneous decision. This Court cannot be too cautious in upsetting practices embedded in our society by many years of experience. A state is entitled to have great leeway in its legislation when dealing with the important social problems of its population. A definite violation of legislative limits must be established. The Constitution should not be stretched to forbid national customs in the way courts act to reach arrangements to avoid federal taxation. Devotion to the great principle of religious liberty should not lead us into a rigid interpretation of the constitutional guarantee that conflicts with accepted habits of our people. This is an instance where, for me, the history of past practices is determinative of the meaning of a constitutional clause not a decorous introduction to the study of its text.

12

Zorach v. Clauson

343 U.S. 306 (1952)

Vote: 6—Vinson, Reed, Douglas, Burton, Clark, Minton
3—Black, Frankfurter, Jackson

Opinion announcing the opinion of the Court: Douglas
Dissenting opinions: Black, Frankfurter, Jackson

New York City permitted its public schools to release students during school hours,
on written request by their parents, so that they could leave the school buildings and
grounds to attend religious instruction or devotional exercises at local religious centers.
Students not released were required to stay in their classrooms. The program involved
neither religious instruction in public schools nor the expenditure of public funds.

The program's regulations required the religious organizations and parents to as-
sume full responsibility for attendance at the religious schools. The participating reli-
gious organizations were required to report to the public schools the names of children
released who failed to attend religious instruction. Only one hour per week of released
time was permitted, and the hour of release was to be the same for all religious schools.
No announcement of any kind was to be made in the public schools relative to the pro-
gram. Students who were released were to be dismissed from school in the usual way.
There was to be no comment by any principal or teacher on the attendance or nonat-
tendance of any pupil at the religious instruction.

MR. JUSTICE DOUGLAS delivered the opinion of the Court.

. . . [308] This "released time" program involves neither religious instruction in public
school classrooms nor the expenditure [309] of public funds. All costs, including the application blanks, are paid by the religious organizations. The case is therefore unlike *McCol-*
lum v. Board of Education, which involved a "released time" program from Illinois. In that
case the classrooms were turned over to religious instructors. We accordingly held that the
program violated the First Amendment which (by reason of the Fourteenth Amendment)
prohibits the states from establishing religion or prohibiting its free exercise.

Appellants, who are taxpayers and residents of New York City and whose children
attend its public schools, challenge the present law, contending it is in essence not different from the one involved in the *McCollum* case. Their argument, stated elaborately

in various ways, reduces itself to this: the weight and influence of the school is put behind a program for religious instruction; public school teachers police it, keeping tab on students who are released; the classroom activities come to a halt while the students who are released for religious instruction are on leave; the school is a crutch on which the churches are leaning for support in their religious training; without the cooperation of the schools this "released time" program, [310] like the one in the *McCollum* case, would be futile and ineffective. . . .

The briefs and arguments are replete with data bearing on the merits of this type of "released time" program. Views pro and con are expressed, based on practical experience with these programs and with their implications. We do not stop to summarize these materials nor to burden the opinion with an analysis of them. For they involve considerations not germane to the narrow constitutional issue presented. They largely concern the wisdom of the system, its efficiency from an educational point of view, and the political considerations which have motivated its adoption or rejection in some communities. Those matters are of no concern here, since our problem reduces itself to whether New York by this system has either prohibited the "free exercise" of religion or has made a law "respecting an establishment of religion" within the meaning of the First Amendment.

[311] It takes obtuse reasoning to inject any issue of the "free exercise" of religion into the present case. No one is forced to go to the religious classroom and no religious exercise or instruction is brought to the classrooms of the public schools. A student need not take religious instruction. He is left to his own desires as to the manner or time of his religious devotions, if any.

There is a suggestion that the system involves the use of coercion to get public school students into religious classrooms. There is no evidence in the record before us that supports that conclusion. The present record indeed tells us that the school authorities are neutral in this regard and do no more than release students whose parents so request. If in fact coercion were used, if it were established that any one or more teachers were using their office to persuade or force students to take the religious instruction, a wholly different case would be presented. Hence we put aside that claim of coercion [312] both as respects the "free exercise" of religion and "an establishment of religion" within the meaning of the First Amendment.

Moreover, apart from that claim of coercion, we do not see how New York by this type of "released time" program has made a law respecting an establishment of religion within the meaning of the First Amendment. There is much talk of the separation of Church and State in the history of the Bill of Rights and in the decisions clustering around the First Amendment. There cannot be the slightest doubt that the First Amendment reflects the philosophy that Church and State should be separated. And so far as interference with the "free exercise" of religion and an "establishment" of religion are concerned, the separation must be complete and unequivocal. The First Amendment within the scope of its coverage permits no exception; the prohibition is absolute. The First Amendment, however, does not say that in every and all respects there shall be a separation of Church and State. Rather, it studiously defines the manner, the specific ways, in which there shall be no concert or union or dependency one on the other. That is the common sense of the matter. Otherwise the state and religion would be aliens to each other—hostile, suspicious, and even unfriendly. Churches could not be required to pay even property taxes. Municipalities would not be permitted to render police or fire protection to religious groups. Policemen who helped parishioners into their places of worship would violate the Constitution. Prayers in our legislative halls; the appeals [313] to the Almighty in the messages of the Chief Executive; the proclamations making Thanksgiving Day a holiday; "so help me God" in our courtroom oaths—these and all other references to the Almighty that run through our laws, our public rituals, our ceremonies would be flouting the First Amendment. A fastidious atheist or agnostic could even object to the supplication with which the Court opens each session: "God save the United States and this Honorable Court."

We would have to press the concept of separation of Church and State to these extremes to condemn the present law on constitutional grounds. The nullification of this law would have wide and profound effects. A Catholic student applies to his teacher for permission to leave the school during hours on a Holy Day of Obligation to attend a mass. A Jewish student asks his teacher for permission to be excused for Yom Kippur. A Protestant wants the afternoon off for a family baptismal ceremony. In each case the teacher requires parental consent in writing. In each case the teacher, in order to make sure the student is not a truant, goes further and requires a report from the priest, the rabbi, or the minister. The teacher in other words cooperates in a religious program to the extent of making it possible for her students to participate in it. Whether she does it occasionally for a few students, regularly for one, or pursuant to a systematized program designed to further the religious needs of all the students does not alter the character of the act.

We are a religious people whose institutions presuppose a Supreme Being. We guarantee the freedom to worship as one chooses. We make room for as wide a variety of beliefs and creeds as the spiritual needs of man deem necessary. We sponsor an attitude on the part of government that shows no partiality to any one group and that lets each flourish according to the zeal of its adherents and the appeal of its dogma. When the state [314] encourages religious instruction or cooperates with religious authorities by adjusting the schedule of public events to sectarian needs, it follows the best of our traditions. For it then respects the religious nature of our people and accommodates the public service to their spiritual needs. To hold that it may not would be to find in the Constitution a requirement that the government show a callous indifference to religious groups. That would be preferring those who believe in no religion over those who do believe. Government may not finance religious groups nor undertake religious instruction nor blend secular and sectarian education nor use secular institutions to force one or some religion on any person. But we find no constitutional requirement which makes it necessary for government to be hostile to religion and to throw its weight against efforts to widen the effective scope of religious influence. The government must be neutral when it comes to competition between sects. It may not thrust any sect on any person. It may not make a religious observance compulsory. It may not coerce anyone to attend church, to observe a religious holiday, or to take religious instruction. But it can close its doors or suspend its operations as to those who want to repair to their religious sanctuary for worship or instruction. No more than that is undertaken here. . . .

[315] In the *McCollum* case the classrooms were used for religious instruction and the force of the public school was used to promote that instruction. Here, as we have said, the public schools do no more than accommodate their schedules to a program of outside religious instruction. We follow the *McCollum* case. But we cannot expand it to cover the present released time program unless separation of Church and State means that public institutions can make no adjustments of their schedules to accommodate the religious needs of the people. We cannot read into the Bill of Rights such a philosophy of hostility to religion.

MR. JUSTICE BLACK, dissenting.

Illinois ex rel. McCollum v. Board of Education held invalid as an "establishment of religion" an Illinois system under which school children, compelled by law to go to public schools, were freed from some hours of required school work on condition that they attend special religious classes held in the school buildings. Although the classes were taught by sectarian [316] teachers neither employed nor paid by the state, the state did use its power to further the program by releasing some of the children from regular class work, insisting that those released attend the religious classes, and requiring that those who remained behind do some kind of academic work while the others received their religious training. We said this about the Illinois system:

> "Pupils compelled by law to go to school for secular education are released in part from their legal duty upon the condition that they attend the religious classes. This is beyond all question a utilization of the tax-established and tax-supported public school system to aid religious groups to spread their faith. And it falls squarely under the ban of the First Amendment. . . ." *McCollum v. Board of Education*, at pp. 209–210.

I see no significant difference between the invalid Illinois system and that of New York here sustained. Except for the use of the school buildings in Illinois, there is no difference between the systems which I consider even worthy of mention. In the New York program, as in that of Illinois, the school authorities release some of the children on the condition that they attend the religious classes, get reports on whether they attend, and hold the other children in the school building until the religious hour is over. As we attempted to make categorically clear, the *McCollum* decision would have been the same if the religious classes had not been held in the school buildings. We said:

> "Here not only are the State's tax-supported public school buildings used for the dissemination of religious doctrines. The State also affords sectarian groups an invaluable aid in that it helps to provide pupils for their religious classes through use of the State's compulsory public school machinery. *This* is [317] not separation of Church and State." (Emphasis supplied.) *McCollum v. Board of Education*, at p. 212.

McCollum thus held that Illinois could not constitutionally manipulate the compelled classroom hours of its compulsory school machinery so as to channel children into sectarian classes. Yet that is exactly what the Court holds New York can do. . . .

[318] Here the sole question is whether New York can use its compulsory education laws to help religious sects get attendants presumably too unenthusiastic to go unless moved to do so by the pressure of this state machinery. That this is the plan, purpose, design and consequence of the New York program cannot be denied. The state thus makes religious sects beneficiaries of its power to compel children to attend secular schools. Any use of such coercive power by the state to help or hinder some religious sects or to prefer all religious sects over nonbelievers or vice versa is just what I think the First Amendment forbids. In considering whether a state has entered this forbidden field the question is not whether it has entered too far but whether it has entered at all. New York is manipulating its compulsory education laws to help religious sects get pupils. This is not separation but combination of Church and State.

The Court's validation of the New York system rests in part on its statement that Americans are "a religious people whose institutions presuppose a Supreme Being." This was at least as true when the First Amendment was adopted; and it was just as true when eight Justices of this Court invalidated the released time system in *McCollum* on the premise that a state can no more "aid all religions" than it can aid one. It was precisely because Eighteenth [319] Century Americans were a religious people divided into many fighting sects that we were given the constitutional mandate to keep Church and State completely separate. Colonial history had already shown that, here as elsewhere zealous sectarians entrusted with governmental power to further their causes would sometimes torture, maim and kill those they branded "heretics," "atheists" or "agnostics." The First Amendment was therefore to insure that no one powerful sect or combination of sects could use political or governmental power to punish dissenters whom they could not convert to their faith. Now as then, it is only by wholly isolating the state from the religious sphere and compelling it to be completely neutral, that the freedom of each and every denomination and of all nonbelievers can be maintained. It is this neutrality the Court abandons today when it treats New York's coercive system as a program which merely "encourages religious instruction or cooperates with religious authorities." The abandonment is all the more dangerous to liberty because of the Court's legal exaltation of the orthodox and its derogation of unbelievers. . . .

[320] State help to religion injects political and party prejudices into a holy field. It too often substitutes force for prayer, hate for love, and persecution for persuasion. Government should not be allowed, under cover of the soft euphemism of "co-operation," to steal into the sacred area of religious choice.

MR. JUSTICE FRANKFURTER, dissenting.

. . . [323] The deeply divisive controversy aroused by the attempts to secure public school pupils for sectarian instruction would promptly end if the advocates of such instruction would consent to have the school "close its doors or suspend its operations"— that is, dismiss classes in their entirety, without discrimination—instead of seeking to use the public schools as the instrument for securing attendance at denominational classes. The unwillingness of the promoters of this movement to dispense with such use of the public schools betrays a surprising want of confidence in the inherent power of the various faiths to draw children to outside sectarian classes—an attitude that hardly reflects the faith of the greatest religious spirits.

MR. JUSTICE JACKSON, dissenting.

This released time program is founded upon a use of the State's power of coercion, which, for me, determines its unconstitutionality. Stripped to its essentials, the plan has two stages: first, that the State compel each student to yield a large part of his time for public secular [324] education; and, second, that some of it be "released" to him on condition that he devote it to sectarian religious purposes.

No one suggests that the Constitution would permit the State directly to require this "released" time to be spent "under the control of a duly constituted religious body." This program accomplishes that forbidden result by indirection. If public education were taking so much of the pupils' time as to injure the public or the students' welfare by encroaching upon their religious opportunity, simply shortening everyone's school day would facilitate voluntary and optional attendance at Church classes. But that suggestion is rejected upon the ground that if they are made free many students will not go to the Church. Hence, they must be deprived of freedom for this period, with Church attendance put to them as one of the two permissible ways of using it.

The greater effectiveness of this system over voluntary attendance after school hours is due to the truant officer who, if the youngster fails to go to the Church school, dogs him back to the public schoolroom. Here schooling is more or less suspended during the "released time" so the nonreligious attendants will not forge ahead of the churchgoing absentees. But it serves as a temporary jail for a pupil who will not go to Church. It takes more subtlety of mind than I possess to deny that this is governmental constraint in support of religion. It is as unconstitutional, in my view, when exerted by indirection as when exercised forthrightly.

As one whose children, as a matter of free choice, have been sent to privately supported Church schools, I may challenge the Court's suggestion that opposition to this plan can only be antireligious, atheistic, or agnostic. My evangelistic brethren confuse an objection to compulsion with an objection to religion. It is possible to hold a faith with enough confidence to believe that what should be [325] rendered to God does not need to be decided and collected by Caesar.

The day that this country ceases to be free for irreligion it will cease to be free for religion—except for the sect that can win political power. The same epithetical jurisprudence used by the Court today to beat down those who oppose pressuring children into some religion can devise as good epithets tomorrow against those who object to pressuring them into a favored religion. And, after all, if we concede to the State power and wisdom to single out "duly constituted religious" bodies as exclusive alternatives for compulsory secular instruction, it would be logical to also uphold the power and wisdom to choose the true faith among those "duly constituted." We start down a rough road when we begin to mix compulsory public education with compulsory godliness. . . .

⓭

Torcaso v. Watkins

367 U.S. 488 (1961)

Vote: 9—Warren, Black, Frankfurter, Douglas, Clark, Harlan, Brennan, Whittaker, Stewart

    0

Opinion announcing the opinion of the Court: Black

Article 37 of the Declaration of Rights of the Maryland Constitution declared, "No religious test ought ever to be required as a qualification for any office of profit or trust in this State, other than a declaration of belief in the existence of God." The appellant, Torcaso, was appointed to the office of notary public by the governor of Maryland but was refused a commission to serve because he would not declare his belief in God.

MR. JUSTICE BLACK delivered the opinion of the Court.

. . . [489] There is, and can be, no dispute about the purpose or effect of the Maryland Declaration of Rights requirement before us—it sets up a religious test which was designed to [490] and, if valid, does bar every person who refuses to declare a belief in God from holding a public "office of profit or trust" in Maryland. The power and authority of the State of Maryland thus is put on the side of one particular sort of believers—those who are willing to say they believe in "the existence of God." It is true that there is much historical precedent for such laws. Indeed, it was largely to escape religious test oaths and declarations that a great many of the early colonists left Europe and came here hoping to worship in their own way. It soon developed, however, that many of those who had fled to escape religious test oaths turned out to be perfectly willing, when they had the power to do so, to force dissenters from their faith to take test oaths in conformity with that faith. This brought on a host of laws in the new Colonies imposing burdens and disabilities of various kinds upon varied beliefs depending largely upon what group happened to be politically strong enough to legislate in favor of its own beliefs. The effect of all this was the formal or practical "establishment" of particular religious faiths in most of the Colonies, with consequent burdens imposed on the free exercise of the faiths of nonfavored believers.

There were, however, wise and far-seeing men in the Colonies—too many to mention—who spoke out against test oaths and all the philosophy of intolerance behind them. One of these, it so happens, was George Calvert (the first Lord Baltimore), who took a most important part in the original establishment of the Colony of Maryland. He was a Catholic and had, for this reason, felt compelled by his conscience to refuse to take the Oath of Supremacy in England at the cost of resigning from high governmental office. He again refused to take that oath when it was demanded by the Council of the Colony of [491] Virginia, and as a result he was denied settlement in that Colony. A recent historian of the early period of Maryland's life has said that it was Calvert's hope and purpose to establish in Maryland a colonial government free from the religious persecutions he had known—one "securely beyond the reach of oaths. . . ."

When our Constitution was adopted, the desire to put the people "securely beyond the reach" of religious test oaths brought about the inclusion in Article VI of that document of a provision that "no religious Test shall ever be required as a Qualification to any Office or public Trust under the United States." Article VI supports the accuracy of our observation in *Girouard v. United States*, 328 U.S. 61, 69, that "[t]he test oath is abhorrent to our tradition." Not satisfied, however, with Article VI and other guarantees in the original Constitution, the First Congress proposed and the States very shortly thereafter [492] adopted our Bill of Rights, including the First Amendment. That Amendment broke new constitutional ground in the protection it sought to afford to freedom of religion, speech, press, petition and assembly. . . .

[495] We repeat and again reaffirm that neither a State nor the Federal Government can constitutionally force a person "to profess a belief or disbelief in any religion." Neither can constitutionally pass laws or impose requirements which aid all religions as against non-believers, and neither can aid those religions based on a belief in the existence of God as against those religions founded on different beliefs.

In upholding the State's religious test for public office the highest court of Maryland said:

> "The petitioner is not compelled to believe or disbelieve, under threat of punishment or other compulsion. True, unless he makes the declaration of belief he cannot hold public office in Maryland, but he is not compelled to hold office."

The fact, however, that a person is not compelled to hold public office cannot possibly be an excuse for barring him [496] from office by state-imposed criteria forbidden by the Constitution. This was settled by our holding in *Wieman v. Updegraff*. We there pointed out that whether or not "an abstract right to public employment exists," Congress could not pass a law providing ". . . that no federal employee shall attend Mass or take any active part in missionary work."

This Maryland religious test for public office unconstitutionally invades the appellant's freedom of belief and religion and therefore cannot be enforced against him.

14

Braunfeld v. Brown

366 U.S. 599 (1961)

Vote: 6—Warren, Black, Frankfurter, Clark, Harlan, Whittaker
    3—Douglas, Brennan, Stewart

Opinion announcing the judgment of the Court: Warren
Separate opinion: Frankfurter
Opinion concurring and dissenting: Brennan
Dissenting opinions: Douglas, Stewart

A 1959 Pennsylvania blue law restricted commerce within the state on Sundays. Specifically, the law held,

> *Whoever engages on Sunday in the business of selling, or sells or offers for sale, on such day, at retail, clothing and wearing apparel, clothing accessories, furniture, housewares, home, business or office furnishings, household, business or office appliances, hardware, tools, paints, building and lumber supply materials, jewelry, silverware, watches, clocks, luggage, musical instruments and recordings, or toys, excluding novelties and souvenirs, shall, upon conviction thereof in a summary proceeding for the first offense, be sentenced to pay a fine of not exceeding one hundred dollars ($100), and for the second or any subsequent offense committed within one year after conviction for the first offense, be sentenced to pay a fine of not exceeding two hundred dollars ($200) or undergo imprisonment not exceeding thirty days in default thereof.*

Each separate sale or offer to sell constituted a separate offense.

Appellants were merchants engaged in the retail sale of clothing and home furnishings in Philadelphia. They were also members of the Orthodox Jewish faith, which required the closing of their places of business and total abstention from all manner of work from nightfall each Friday until nightfall each Saturday.

MR. CHIEF JUSTICE WARREN announced the judgment of the Court and an opinion in which MR. JUSTICE BLACK, MR. JUSTICE CLARK, and MR. JUSTICE WHITTAKER concur.

[600] This case concerns the constitutional validity of the application to appellants of the Pennsylvania criminal statute, enacted in 1959, which proscribes the Sunday retail

sale of certain enumerated commodities. Among the questions presented are whether the statute is a law [601] respecting an establishment of religion and whether the statute violates equal protection. Since both of these questions, in reference to this very statute, have already been answered in the negative, *Two Guys from Harrison-Allentown, Inc., v. McGinley*, and since appellants present nothing new regarding them, they need not be considered here. Thus, the only question for consideration is whether the statute interferes with the free exercise of appellants' religion. . . .

Appellants contend that the enforcement against them of the Pennsylvania statute will prohibit the free exercise [602] of their religion because, due to the statute's compulsion to close on Sunday, appellants will suffer substantial economic loss, to the benefit of their non-Sabbatarian competitors, if appellants also continue their Sabbath observance by closing their businesses on Saturday; that this result will either compel appellants to give up their Sabbath observance, a basic tenet of the Orthodox Jewish faith, or will put appellants at a serious economic disadvantage if they continue to adhere to their Sabbath. Appellants also assert that the statute will operate so as to hinder the Orthodox Jewish faith in gaining new adherents. And the corollary to these arguments is that if the free exercise of appellants' religion is impeded, that religion is being subjected to discriminatory treatment by the State.

In *McGowan v. Maryland*, at pp. 437–440, we noted the significance that this Court has attributed to the development of religious freedom in Virginia in determining the scope of the First Amendment's protection. We observed that when Virginia passed its Declaration of Rights in 1776, providing that "all men are equally entitled to the free exercise of religion," Virginia repealed its laws which in any way penalized "maintaining any opinions in matters of religion, forbearing to repair to church, or the exercising any mode of worship whatsoever." But Virginia retained its laws prohibiting Sunday labor.

We also took cognizance, in *McGowan*, of the evolution of Sunday Closing Laws from wholly religious sanctions to legislation concerned with the establishment of a day of community tranquillity [*sic*], respite and recreation, a day when the atmosphere is one of calm and relaxation rather than one of commercialism, as it is during the other six days of the week. We reviewed the still growing state [603] preoccupation with improving the health, safety, morals and general well-being of our citizens.

Concededly, appellants and all other persons who wish to work on Sunday will be burdened economically by the State's day of rest mandate; and appellants point out that their religion requires them to refrain from work on Saturday as well. Our inquiry then is whether, in these circumstances, the First and Fourteenth Amendments forbid application of the Sunday Closing Law to appellants.

Certain aspects of religious exercise cannot, in any way, be restricted or burdened by either federal or state legislation. Compulsion by law of the acceptance of any creed or the practice of any form of worship is strictly forbidden. The freedom to hold religious beliefs and opinions is absolute. Thus, in *West Virginia State Board of Education v. Barnette* this Court held that state action compelling school children to salute the flag, on pain of expulsion from public school, was contrary to the First and Fourteenth Amendments when applied to those students whose religious beliefs forbade saluting a flag. But this is not the case at bar; the statute before us does not make criminal the holding of any religious belief or opinion, nor does it force anyone to embrace any religious belief or to say or believe anything in conflict with his religious tenets.

However, the freedom to act, even when the action is in accord with one's religious convictions, is not totally free from legislative restrictions. As pointed out in *Reynolds v. United States*, at p. 164, legislative power over mere opinion is forbidden but it may reach people's actions when they are found to be in violation of important social duties or subversive of good order, even when [604] the actions are demanded by one's religion. This was articulated by Thomas Jefferson when he said:

"Believing with you that religion is a matter which lies solely between man and his God, that he owes account to none other for his faith or his worship, that *the legislative powers of government reach actions only, and not opinions*, I contemplate with sovereign reverence that act of the whole American people which declared that their legislature should 'make no law respecting an establishment of religion, or prohibiting the free exercise thereof,' thus building a wall of separation between church and State. Adhering to this expression of the supreme will of the nation in behalf of the rights of conscience, I shall see with sincere satisfaction the progress of those sentiments which tend to restore to man all his natural rights, convinced he has no natural right in opposition to his social duties." (Emphasis added.)

And, in the *Barnette* case, the Court was careful to point out that "The freedom asserted by these appellees does not bring them into collision with rights asserted by any other individual. It is such conflicts which most frequently require intervention of the State to determine where the rights of one end and those of another begin. . . . It is . . . to be noted that the compulsory flag salute and [605] pledge requires *affirmation of a belief* and an *attitude of mind*." 319 U.S., at 630, 633. (Emphasis added.)

Thus, in *Reynolds v. United States*, this Court upheld the polygamy conviction of a member of the Mormon faith despite the fact that an accepted doctrine of his church then imposed upon its male members the duty to practice polygamy. And, in *Prince v. Massachusetts* this Court upheld a statute making it a crime for a girl under eighteen years of age to sell any newspapers, periodicals or merchandise in public places despite the fact that a child of the Jehovah's Witnesses faith believed that it was her religious duty to perform this work.

It is to be noted that, in the two cases just mentioned, the religious practices themselves conflicted with the public interest. In such cases, to make accommodation between the religious action and an exercise of state authority is a particularly delicate task, *id.*, at 165, because resolution in favor of the State results in the choice to the individual of either abandoning his religious principle or facing criminal prosecution.

But, again, this is not the case before us because the statute at bar does not make unlawful any religious practices of appellants; the Sunday law simply regulates a secular activity and, as applied to appellants, operates so as to make the practice of their religious beliefs more expensive. Furthermore, the law's effect does not inconvenience all members of the Orthodox Jewish faith but only those who believe it necessary to work on Sunday. And even these are not faced with as serious a choice as forsaking their religious practices or subjecting themselves to criminal prosecution. Fully recognizing that the alternatives [606] open to appellants and others similarly situated—retaining their present occupations and incurring economic disadvantage or engaging in some other commercial activity which does not call for either Saturday or Sunday labor—may well result in some financial sacrifice in order to observe their religious beliefs, still the option is wholly different than when the legislation attempts to make a religious practice itself unlawful.

To strike down, without the most critical scrutiny, legislation which imposes only an indirect burden on the exercise of religion, i.e., legislation which does not make unlawful the religious practice itself, would radically restrict the operating latitude of the legislature. Statutes which tax income and limit the amount which may be deducted for religious contributions impose an indirect economic burden on the observance of the religion of the citizen whose religion requires him to donate a greater amount to his church; statutes which require the courts to be closed on Saturday and Sunday impose a similar indirect burden on the observance of the religion of the trial lawyer whose religion requires him to rest on a weekday. The list of legislation of this nature is nearly limitless.

Needless to say, when entering the area of religious freedom, we must be fully cognizant of the particular protection that the Constitution has accorded it. Abhorrence of religious persecution and intolerance is a basic part of our heritage. But we are a cosmopolitan nation made up of people of almost every conceivable religious preference. These denominations number almost three hundred. Consequently, it cannot be expected, much less required, that legislators enact no law regulating conduct that may in some way result in an economic disadvantage to some religious sects and not to others because of the special practices of the various religions. We do not believe that such an effect is an absolute test [607] for determining whether the legislation violates the freedom of religion protected by the First Amendment.

Of course, to hold unassailable all legislation regulating conduct which imposes solely an indirect burden on the observance of religion would be a gross oversimplification. If the purpose or effect of a law is to impede the observance of one or all religions or is to discriminate invidiously between religions, that law is constitutionally invalid even though the burden may be characterized as being only indirect. But if the State regulates conduct by enacting a general law within its power, the purpose and effect of which is to advance the State's secular goals, the statute is valid despite its indirect burden on religious observance unless the State may accomplish its purpose by means which do not impose such a burden.

As we pointed out in *McGowan v. Maryland*, at pp. 444–445, we cannot find a State without power to provide a weekly respite from all labor and, at the same time, to set one day of the week apart from the others as a day of rest, repose, recreation and tranquillity [*sic*]—a day when the hectic tempo of everyday existence ceases and a more pleasant atmosphere is created, a day which all members of the family and community have the opportunity to spend and enjoy together, a day on which people may visit friends and relatives who are not available during working days, a day when the weekly laborer may best regenerate himself. This is particularly true in this day and age of increasing state concern with public welfare legislation.

[608] Also, in *McGowan*, we examined several suggested alternative means by which it was argued that the State might accomplish its secular goals without even remotely or incidentally affecting religious freedom. *Ante*, at pp. 450–452. We found there that a State might well find that those alternatives would not accomplish bringing about a general day of rest. We need not examine them again here. However, appellants advance yet another means at the State's disposal which they would find unobjectionable. They contend that the State should cut an exception from the Sunday labor proscription for those people who, because of religious conviction, observe a day of rest other than Sunday. By such regulation, appellants contend, the economic disadvantages imposed by the present system would be removed and the State's interest in having all people rest one day would be satisfied.

A number of States provide such an exemption, and this may well be the wiser solution to the problem. But our concern is not with the wisdom of legislation but with its constitutional limitation. Thus, reason and experience teach that to permit the exemption might well undermine the State's goal of providing a day that, as best possible, eliminates the atmosphere of commercial noise and activity. Although not dispositive of the issue, enforcement problems would be more difficult since there would be two or more days to police rather than one and it would be more difficult to observe whether violations were occurring.

Additional problems might also be presented by a regulation of this sort. To allow only people who rest on a day other than Sunday to keep their businesses open on that day might well provide these people with an economic advantage over their competitors who must [609] remain closed on that day; this might cause the Sunday-observers to complain that their religions are being discriminated against. With this competitive advantage existing, there could well be the temptation for some, in order to keep their businesses open on Sunday, to assert that they have religious convictions which compel them to close their businesses on what had formerly been their least profitable day. This might make necessary a state-conducted inquiry into the sincerity of the individual's religious beliefs, a practice which a State might believe would itself run afoul of the spirit of constitutionally protected religious guarantees. Finally, in order to keep the disruption of the day at a minimum, exempted employers would probably have to hire employees who themselves qualified for the exemption because of their own religious beliefs, a practice which a State might feel to be opposed to its general policy prohibiting religious discrimination in hiring. For all of these reasons, we cannot say that the Pennsylvania statute before us is invalid, either on its face or as applied.

[610] MR. JUSTICE BRENNAN, concurring and dissenting.

I agree with THE CHIEF JUSTICE that there is no merit in appellants' establishment and equal-protection claims. I dissent, however, as to the claim that Pennsylvania has prohibited the free exercise of appellants' religion. . . .

The Court has demonstrated the public need for a weekly surcease from worldly labor, and set forth the considerations of convenience which have led the Commonwealth of Pennsylvania to fix Sunday as the time for that respite. I would approach this case differently, from the point of view of the individuals whose liberty is—concededly—curtailed by these enactments. For the values of the First Amendment, as embodied in the Fourteenth, look primarily towards the preservation of personal liberty, rather than towards the fulfillment of collective goals.

The appellants are small retail merchants, faithful practitioners of the Orthodox Jewish faith. They allege—and the allegation must be taken as true, since the case comes to us on a motion to dismiss the complaint—that ". . . one who does not observe the Sabbath [by refraining from labor] . . . cannot be an Orthodox Jew." [611] In appellants' business area Friday night and Saturday are busy times; yet appellants, true to their faith, close during the Jewish Sabbath, and make up some, but not all, of the business thus lost by opening on Sunday. "Each of the plaintiffs," the complaint continues, "does a substantial amount of business on Sundays, and the ability of the plaintiffs to earn a livelihood will be greatly impaired by closing their business establishment on Sundays." Consequences even more drastic are alleged: "Plaintiff, Abraham Braunfeld, will be unable to continue in his business if he may not stay open on Sunday and he will thereby lose his capital investment." In other words, the issue in this case—and we do not understand either appellees or the Court to contend otherwise—is whether a State may put an individual to a choice between his business and his religion. The Court today holds that it may. But I dissent, believing that such a law prohibits the free exercise of religion. . . .

[613] Admittedly, these laws do not compel overt affirmation of a repugnant belief, as in *Barnette*, nor do they prohibit outright any of appellants' religious practices, as did the federal law upheld in *Reynolds v. United States* (1878), cited by the Court. That is, the laws do not say that appellants must work on Saturday. But their effect is that appellants

may not simultaneously practice their religion and their trade, without being hampered by a substantial competitive disadvantage. Their effect is that no one may at one and the same time be an Orthodox Jew and compete effectively with his Sunday-observing fellow tradesmen. This clog upon the exercise of religion, this state-imposed burden on Orthodox Judaism, has exactly the same economic effect as a tax levied upon the sale of religious literature. And yet, such a tax, when applied in the form of an excise or license fee, was held invalid in *Follett v. Town of McCormick*. All this the Court, as I read its opinion, concedes.

What, then, is the compelling state interest which impels the Commonwealth of Pennsylvania to impede [614] appellants' freedom of worship? What overbalancing need is so weighty in the constitutional scale that it justifies this substantial, though indirect, limitation of appellants' freedom? It is not the desire to stamp out a practice deeply abhorred by society, such as polygamy, as in *Reynolds*, for the custom of resting one day a week is universally honored, as the Court has amply shown. Nor is it the State's traditional protection of children, as in *Prince v. Massachusetts* (1944), for appellants are reasoning and fully autonomous adults. It is not even the interest in seeing that everyone rests one day a week, for appellants' religion requires that they take such a rest. It is the mere convenience of having everyone rest on the same day. It is to defend this interest that the Court holds that a State need not follow the alternative route of granting an exemption for those who in good faith observe a day of rest other than Sunday.

It is true, I suppose, that the granting of such an exemption would make Sundays a little noisier, and the task of police and prosecutor a little more difficult. It is also true that a majority—21—of the 34 States which have general Sunday regulations have exemptions of this kind. We are not told that those States are significantly noisier, or that their police are significantly more burdened, than [615] Pennsylvania's. Even England, not under the compulsion of a written constitution, but simply influenced by considerations of fairness, has such an exemption for some activities. The Court conjures up several difficulties with such a system which seem to me more fanciful than real. Non-Sunday observers might get an unfair advantage, it is said. A similar contention against the draft exemption for conscientious objectors (another example of the exemption technique) was rejected with the observation that "its unsoundness is too apparent to require" discussion. *Selective Draft Law Cases*, 245 U.S. 366, 390 (1918). However widespread the complaint, it is legally baseless, and the State's reliance upon it cannot withstand a First Amendment claim. We are told that an official inquiry into the good faith with which religious beliefs are held might be itself unconstitutional. But this Court indicated otherwise in *United States v. Ballard* (1944). Such an inquiry is no more an infringement of religious freedom than the requirement imposed by the Court itself in *McGowan v. Maryland*, p. 420, decided this day, that a plaintiff show that his good-faith religious beliefs are hampered before he acquires standing to attack a statute under the Free-Exercise Clause of the First Amendment. Finally, I find the Court's mention of a problem under state antidiscrimination statutes almost chimerical. Most such statutes provide that hiring may be made on a religious basis if religion is a bona fide occupational qualification. It happens, moreover, that Pennsylvania's statute has such a provision.

In fine, the Court, in my view, has exalted administrative convenience to a constitutional level high enough to [616] justify making one religion economically disadvantageous. The Court would justify this result on the ground that the effect on religion, though substantial, is indirect. The Court forgets, I think, a warning uttered during the congressional discussion of the First Amendment itself: ". . . the rights of conscience are, in their nature, of peculiar delicacy, and will little bear the gentlest touch of governmental hand. . . ."

⑮

Engel v. Vitale

370 U.S. 421 (1962)

Vote: 6—Warren, Black, Douglas, Clark, Harlan, Brennan
    1—Stewart

Opinion announcing the opinion of the Court: Black
Concuring opinion: Douglas
Dissenting opinion: Stewart
Not participating in the decision: Frankfurter
Not participating in the consideration or decision: White

The New York State Board of Regents—a governmental agency to which the New York legislature granted broad supervisory, executive, and legislative powers over the state's public school system—composed the following prayer and recommended its recitation in New York's public schools: "Almighty God, we acknowledge our dependence upon Thee, and we beg Thy blessings upon us, our parents, our teachers and our Country."

The prayer was published as a part of the regents' "Statement on Moral and Spiritual Training in the Schools," which declared, "We believe that this Statement will be subscribed to by all men and women of good will, and we call upon all of them to aid in giving life to our program."

The Board of Education of Union Free School District No. 9, New Hyde Park, New York, acting in its official capacity under state law, directed the school district's principal to cause the "Regents' prayer" to be said aloud by each class in the presence of a teacher at the beginning of each school day. Teachers either led the recitation or selected a student to do so. Along with the prayer, the board of education adopted a regulation that stated, "Neither teachers nor any school authority shall comment on participation or non-participation . . . nor suggest or request that any posture or language be used or dress be worn or be not used or not worn." Provision was also made for excusing children, upon written request of a parent or guardian, from the saying of the prayer or from the room in which the prayer was said. A letter implementing and explaining this regulation was sent to each taxpayer and parent in the school district.

MR. JUSTICE BLACK delivered the opinion of the Court.

. . . [424] We think that by using its public school system to encourage recitation of the Regents' prayer, the State of New York has adopted a practice wholly inconsistent with the Establishment Clause. There can, of course, be no doubt that New York's program of daily classroom invocation of God's blessings as prescribed in the Regents' prayer is a religious activity. It is a solemn avowal of divine faith and supplication for the blessings of the Almighty. . . .

[425] The petitioners contend among other things that the state laws requiring or permitting use of the Regents' prayer must be struck down as a violation of the Establishment Clause because that prayer was composed by governmental officials as a part of a governmental program to further religious beliefs. For this reason, petitioners argue, the State's use of the Regents' prayer in its public school system breaches the constitutional wall of separation between Church and State. We agree with that contention since we think that the constitutional prohibition against laws respecting an establishment of religion must at least mean that in this country it is no part of the business of government to compose official prayers for any group of the American people to recite as a part of a religious program carried on by government. . . .

[429] By the time of the adoption of the Constitution, our history shows that there was a widespread awareness among many Americans of the dangers of a union of Church and State. These people knew, some of them from bitter personal experience, that one of the greatest dangers to the freedom of the individual to worship in his own way lay in the Government's placing its official stamp of approval upon one particular kind of prayer or one particular form of religious services. They knew the anguish, hardship and bitter strife that could come when zealous religious groups struggled with one another to obtain the Government's stamp of approval from each King, Queen, or Protector that came to temporary power. The Constitution was intended to avert a part of this danger by leaving the government of this country in the hands of the people rather than in the hands of any monarch. But this safeguard was not enough. Our Founders were no more willing to let the content of their prayers and their privilege of praying whenever they pleased be influenced by the ballot box than they were to let these vital matters of personal conscience depend upon the succession of monarchs. The First Amendment was added to the Constitution to stand as a guarantee that neither the power nor the prestige of the Federal Government would be used to control, support or influence the kinds of prayer the American people can say—[430] that the people's religions must not be subjected to the pressures of government for change each time a new political administration is elected to office. Under that Amendment's prohibition against governmental establishment of religion, as reinforced by the provisions of the Fourteenth Amendment, government in this country, be it state or federal, is without power to prescribe by law any particular form of prayer which is to be used as an official prayer in carrying on any program of governmentally sponsored religious activity.

There can be no doubt that New York's state prayer program officially establishes the religious beliefs embodied in the Regents' prayer. The respondents' argument to the contrary, which is largely based upon the contention that the Regents' prayer is "non-denominational" and the fact that the program, as modified and approved by state courts, does not require all pupils to recite the prayer but permits those who wish to do so to remain silent or be excused from the room, ignores the essential nature of the program's constitutional defects. Neither the fact that the prayer may be denominationally neutral nor the fact that its observance on the part of the students is voluntary can serve to free it from the limitations of the Establishment Clause, as it might from the Free Exercise Clause, of the First Amendment, both of which are operative against the States by virtue of the Fourteenth Amendment. Although these two clauses may in certain instances overlap, they forbid two quite different kinds of governmental encroachment upon religious freedom. The Establishment Clause, unlike the Free Exercise Clause, does not depend upon any showing of direct governmental compulsion and is violated by the enactment of laws which establish an official religion whether those laws operate directly to coerce nonobserving individuals or not. This is not to say, of course, that [431] laws officially prescribing a particular form of religious worship do not involve coercion of such individuals. When the power, prestige and financial support of government is [*sic*] placed behind a particular religious belief, the indirect coercive pressure upon religious minorities to conform to the prevailing officially approved religion is plain. But the purposes underlying the Establishment Clause go much further than that. Its first and most immediate purpose rested on the belief that a union of government and religion tends to destroy government and to degrade religion. The history of governmentally established religion, both in England and in this country, showed that whenever government had allied itself with one particular form of religion, the inevitable result had been that it had incurred the hatred, disrespect and even contempt of those who held contrary beliefs. That same history showed that many people had lost their respect for any religion that had relied upon the support of government to spread its faith. The Establishment Clause [432] thus stands as an expression of principle on the part of the Founders of our Constitution that religion is too personal, too sacred, too holy, to permit its "unhallowed perversion" by a civil magistrate.[15] Another purpose of the Establishment Clause rested upon an awareness of the historical fact that governmentally established religions and religious persecutions go hand in hand. The Founders knew that only a few years after the Book of Common Prayer became the only accepted form of religious services in the established Church of England, an Act of Uniformity was passed to compel all Englishmen to attend those services and to make it a criminal offense to conduct or attend religious gatherings of any other kind—a law [433] which was consistently flouted by dissenting religious groups in England and which contributed to widespread persecutions of people like John Bunyan who persisted in holding "unlawful [religious] meetings . . . to the great disturbance and distraction of the good subjects of this kingdom. . . ."[18] And they knew that similar persecutions had received the sanction of law in several of the colonies in this country soon after the establishment of official religions in those colonies. It was in large part to get completely away from this sort of systematic religious persecution that the Founders brought into being our Nation, our Constitution, and our Bill of Rights with its prohibition against any governmental establishment of religion. The New York laws officially prescribing the Regents' prayer are inconsistent both with the purposes of the Establishment Clause and with the Establishment Clause itself.

It has been argued that to apply the Constitution in such a way as to prohibit state laws respecting an [434] establishment of religious services in public schools is to indicate a hostility toward religion or toward prayer. Nothing, of course, could be more wrong. The history of man is inseparable from the history of religion. And perhaps it is not too much to say that since the beginning of that history many people have devoutly believed that "More things are wrought by prayer than this world dreams of." It was doubtless largely due to men who believed this that there grew up a sentiment that caused men to leave the cross-currents of officially established state religions and religious persecution in Europe and come to this country filled with the hope that they could find a place in which they could pray when they pleased to the God of their faith in the language they chose. And there were men of this same faith in the [435] power of

---

15. [James Madison,] *Memorial and Remonstrance against Religious Assessments.*

18. Bunyan's own account of his trial is set forth in *A Relation of the Imprisonment of Mr. John Bunyan,* reprinted in *Grace Abounding and The Pilgrim's Progress* (Brown ed. 1907), at 103–132.

prayer who led the fight for adoption of our Constitution and also for our Bill of Rights with the very guarantees of religious freedom that forbid the sort of governmental activity which New York has attempted here. These men knew that the First Amendment, which tried to put an end to governmental control of religion and of prayer, was not written to destroy either. They knew rather that it was written to quiet well-justified fears which nearly all of them felt arising out of an awareness that governments of the past had shackled men's tongues to make them speak only the religious thoughts that government wanted them to speak and to pray only to the God that government wanted them to pray to. It is neither sacrilegious nor antireligious to say that each separate government in this country should stay out of the business of writing or sanctioning official prayers and leave that purely religious function to the people themselves and to those the people choose to look to for religious guidance.

[436] It is true that New York's establishment of its Regents' prayer as an officially approved religious doctrine of that State does not amount to a total establishment of one particular religious sect to the exclusion of all others—that, indeed, the governmental endorsement of that prayer seems relatively insignificant when compared to the governmental encroachments upon religion which were commonplace 200 years ago. To those who may subscribe to the view that because the Regents' official prayer is so brief and general there can be no danger to religious freedom in its governmental establishment, however, it may be appropriate to say in the words of James Madison, the author of the First Amendment:

> "[I]t is proper to take alarm at the first experiment on our liberties. . . . Who does not see that the same authority which can establish Christianity, in exclusion of all other Religions, may establish with the same ease any particular sect of Christians, in exclusion of all other Sects? That the same authority which can force a citizen to contribute three pence only of his property for the support of any one establishment, may force him to conform to any other establishment in all cases whatsoever?"[22] . . .

[437] MR. JUSTICE DOUGLAS, concurring.

It is customary in deciding a constitutional question to treat it in its narrowest form. Yet at times the setting of the question gives it a form and content which no abstract treatment could give. The point for decision is whether the Government can constitutionally finance a religious exercise. Our system at the federal and state levels is presently honeycombed with such financing. Nevertheless, I think it is an unconstitutional undertaking whatever form it takes.

First, a word as to what this case does not involve.

[438] Plainly, our Bill of Rights would not permit a State or the Federal Government to adopt an official prayer and penalize anyone who would not utter it. This, however, is not that case, for there is no element of compulsion or coercion in New York's regulation requiring that public schools be opened each day with the following prayer:

> "Almighty God, we acknowledge our dependence upon Thee, and we beg Thy blessings upon us, our parents, our teachers and our Country." . . .

---

22. [James Madison,] *Memorial and Remonstrance against Religious Assessments.*

In short, the only one who need utter the prayer is the teacher; and no teacher is complaining of it. Students can stand mute or even leave the classroom, if they desire. . . .

[439] The question presented by this case is therefore an extremely narrow one. It is whether New York oversteps the bounds when it finances a religious exercise.

What New York does on the opening of its public schools is what we do when we open court. Our Crier has from the beginning announced the convening of the Court and then added "God save the United States and this Honorable Court." That utterance is a supplication, a prayer in which we, the judges, are free to join, but which we need not recite any more than the students need recite the New York prayer.

What New York does on the opening of its public schools is what each House of Congress does at the opening [440] of each day's business. Reverend Frederick B. Harris is Chaplain of the Senate; Reverend Bernard Braskamp is Chaplain of the House. Guest chaplains of various denominations also officiate.

[441] In New York the teacher who leads in prayer is on the public payroll; and the time she takes seems minuscule as compared with the salaries appropriated by state legislatures and Congress for chaplains to conduct prayers in the legislative halls. Only a bare fraction of the teacher's time is given to reciting this short 22-word prayer, about the same amount of time that our Crier spends announcing the opening of our sessions and offering a prayer for this Court. Yet for me the principle is the same, no matter how briefly the prayer is said, for in each of the instances given the person praying is a public official on the public payroll, performing a religious exercise in a governmental institution. It is said that the [442] element of coercion is inherent in the giving of this prayer. If that is true here, it is also true of the prayer with which this Court is convened, and of those that open the Congress. Few adults, let alone children, would leave our courtroom or the Senate or the House while those prayers are being given. Every such audience is in a sense a "captive" audience.

At the same time I cannot say that to authorize this prayer is to establish a religion in the strictly historic meaning of those words. A religion is not established in the usual sense merely by letting those who choose to do so say the prayer that the public school teacher leads. Yet once government finances a religious exercise it inserts a divisive influence into our communities. The New York Court said that the prayer given does not conform to all of the tenets of the Jewish, Unitarian, and Ethical Culture groups. One of the petitioners is an agnostic.

"We are a religious people whose institutions presuppose a Supreme Being." *Zorach v. Clauson*, 343 U.S. 306, 313. Under our Bill of Rights free play is given for [443] making religion an active force in our lives. But "if a religious leaven is to be worked into the affairs of our people, it is to be done by individuals and groups, not by the Government." *McGowan v. Maryland*, 366 U.S. 420, 563 (dissenting opinion). By reason of the First Amendment government is commanded "to have no interest in theology or ritual" (*id.*, at 564), for on those matters "government must be neutral." *Ibid.* The First Amendment leaves the Government in a position not of hostility to religion but of neutrality. The philosophy is that the atheist or agnostic—the nonbeliever—is entitled to go his own way. The philosophy is that if government interferes in matters spiritual, it will be a divisive force. The First Amendment teaches that a government neutral in the field of religion better serves all religious interests.

My problem today would be uncomplicated but for *Everson v. Board of Education*, 330 U.S. 1, 17, which allowed taxpayers' money to be used to pay "the bus fares of parochial school pupils as a part of a general program under which" the fares of pupils attending public and other schools were also paid. The *Everson* case seems in retrospect to be out of line with the First Amendment. . . .

[444] MR. JUSTICE STEWART, dissenting.

. . . [445] With all respect, I think the Court has misapplied a great constitutional principle. I cannot see how an "official religion" is established by letting those who want to say a prayer say it. On the contrary, I think that to deny the wish of these school children to join in reciting this prayer is to deny them the opportunity of sharing in the spiritual heritage of our Nation.

The Court's historical review of the quarrels over the Book of Common Prayer in England throws no light for me on the issue before us in this case. England had then and has now an established church. Equally unenlightening, I think, is the history of the early establishment and later rejection of an official church in our own States. For we deal here not with the establishment of a state church, which would, of course, be constitutionally impermissible, but with whether school children who want to begin their day by joining in prayer must be prohibited from doing so. Moreover, I think that the Court's task, in this as in all areas of constitutional adjudication, is not responsibly aided by the uncritical invocation of metaphors like the "wall of separation," a phrase nowhere to [446] be found in the Constitution. What is relevant to the issue here is not the history of an established church in sixteenth century England or in eighteenth century America, but the history of the religious traditions of our people, reflected in countless practices of the institutions and officials of our government.

At the opening of each day's Session of this Court we stand, while one of our officials invokes the protection of God. Since the days of John Marshall our Crier has said, "God save the United States and this Honorable Court." Both the Senate and the House of Representatives open their daily Sessions with prayer. Each of our Presidents, from George Washington to John F. Kennedy, has upon assuming his Office asked the protection and help of God.

[449] The Court today says that the state and federal governments are without constitutional power to prescribe any particular form of words to be recited by any group of the American people on any subject touching religion. One of the stanzas of "The Star-Spangled Banner," made our National Anthem by Act of Congress in 1931, contains these verses:

> "Blest with victory and peace, may the heav'n rescued land
> Praise the Pow'r that hath made and preserved us a nation!
> Then conquer we must, when our cause it is just,
> And this be our motto 'In God is our Trust.'"

In 1954 Congress added a phrase to the Pledge of Allegiance to the Flag so that it now contains the words "one Nation under God, indivisible, with liberty and justice for all." In 1952 Congress enacted legislation calling upon the President each year to proclaim a National Day of Prayer. Since 1865 the words "IN GOD WE TRUST" have been impressed on our coins.

[450] Countless similar examples could be listed, but there is no need to belabor the obvious. It was all summed up by this Court just ten years ago in a single sentence:

"We are a religious people whose institutions presuppose a Supreme Being." *Zorach v. Clauson*, 343 U.S. 306, 313.

I do not believe that this Court, or the Congress, or the President has by the actions and practices I have mentioned established an "official religion" in violation of the Constitution. And I do not believe the State of New York has done so in this case. What each has done has been to recognize and to follow the deeply entrenched and highly cherished spiritual traditions of our Nation—traditions which come down to us from those who almost two hundred years ago avowed their "firm Reliance on the Protection of divine Providence" when they proclaimed the freedom and independence of this brave new world.

I dissent.

16

Abington School District v. Schempp*
374 U.S. 203 (1963)

Vote: 8—*Warren, Black, Douglas, Clark, Harlan, Brennan, White, Goldberg*
    1—*Stewart*

Opinion announcing the opinion of the Court: Clark
Concurring opinions: Douglas, Brennan, Goldberg
Dissenting opinion: Stewart

The Court's decision in Abington School District v. Schempp *encompassed two cases—one from Pennsylvania, the other from Maryland—pertaining to Bible reading and prayer at the beginning of the public school day. Pennsylvania law required that*

> *at least ten verses from the Holy Bible shall be read, without comment, at the opening of each public school on each school day. Any child shall be excused from such Bible reading, or attending such Bible reading, upon the written request of his parent or guardian.*

The appellees, Edward Lewis Schempp, his wife Sidney, and their children, Roger and Donna, were members of the Unitarian Church in Germantown, Philadelphia, Pennsylvania. The Schempp children attended the Abington Senior High School, a public school operated by appellant district. Each morning at Abington Senior High School between 8:15 and 8:30 a.m., opening exercises were conducted pursuant to aforementioned statute. Under the supervision of a teacher, selected students enrolled in the school's radio and television course gathered in the school's workshop studio, read ten verses of the Holy Bible, and recited the Lord's Prayer. The students' voices were broadcast throughout the school over an intercom. Students in each classroom were asked to stand and recite the prayer in unison. The exercises concluded with the flag salute and announcements.
    Participation in the opening exercises was voluntary as directed by the statute. The student reading the verses from the Bible selected the passages and read from any version of the Bible he or she chose, although the school only furnished copies of the King James Bible. No prefatory statements were issued, no questions asked or solicited, no comments or explanations made, and no interpretations given at or during the exercises. Students and parents were advised that a student could absent him- or herself from the classroom or, should he or she elect to remain, not participate in the exercises. In schools without

---

*Decided together with *Murray v. Curlett.*

an intercom, the Bible reading and the recitation of the Lord's Prayer were conducted by the homeroom teacher, who chose the text of the verses and read them him- or herself or had them read by students in rotation or by volunteers. This was followed by a standing recitation of the Lord's Prayer, together with the Pledge of Allegiance.

The Maryland case was prompted by a challenge to similar exercises in Baltimore's public schools. In 1905, the Board of School Commissioners of Baltimore City adopted a rule, pursuant to the Annotated Code of Maryland, that provided for the holding of opening exercises in the schools of the city, consisting primarily of the "reading, without comment, of a chapter in the Holy Bible and/or the use of the Lord's Prayer." The petitioners, Madalyn Murray and her son, William J. Murray III, were both professed atheists.

MR. JUSTICE CLARK delivered the opinion of the Court.

. . . [214] III

Almost a hundred years ago in *Minor v. Board of Education of Cincinnati,* Judge Alphonso Taft, father [215] of the revered Chief Justice, in an unpublished opinion stated the ideal of our people as to religious freedom as one of

"absolute equality before the law, of all religious opinions and sects. . . .
    The government is neutral, and, while protecting all, it prefers none, and it disparages none."

Before examining this "neutral" position in which the Establishment and Free Exercise Clauses of the First Amendment place our Government it is well that we discuss the reach of the Amendment under the cases of this Court.

First, this Court has decisively settled that the First Amendment's mandate that "Congress shall make no law respecting an establishment of religion, or prohibiting the free exercise thereof" has been made wholly applicable to the States by the Fourteenth Amendment. . . .

[216] Second, this Court has rejected unequivocally the contention that the Establishment Clause forbids only governmental preference of one religion over another. Almost 20 years ago in *Everson,* at 15, the Court said that "[n]either a state nor the Federal Government can set up a church. Neither can pass laws which aid one religion, aid all religions, or prefer one religion over another." . . .

[222] V

The wholesome "neutrality" of which this Court's cases speak thus stems from a recognition of the teachings of history that powerful sects or groups might bring about a fusion of governmental and religious functions or a concert or dependency of one upon the other to the end that official support of the State or Federal Government would be placed behind the tenets of one or of all orthodoxies. This the Establishment Clause prohibits. And a further reason for neutrality is found in the Free Exercise Clause, which recognizes the value of religious training, teaching and observance and, more particularly, the right of every person to freely choose his own course with reference thereto, free of any compulsion from the state. This the Free Exercise Clause guarantees. Thus, as we have seen, the two clauses may overlap. As we have indicated, the Establishment Clause has been directly considered by this Court eight times in the past score of years and, with only one Justice dissenting on the point, it has consistently held that the clause withdrew all legislative power respecting religious belief or the expression thereof. The test may be stated as follows: what are the purpose and the primary effect of the enactment? If either is the advancement or inhibition of religion then the enactment exceeds the scope of legislative power as circumscribed by the Constitution. That is to say that to withstand the strictures of the Establishment Clause there must be a secular legislative purpose and a primary effect that neither advances nor inhibits religion. *Everson v. Board of Education; McGowan v. Maryland*, at 442. The Free Exercise Clause, likewise considered many times here, withdraws from legislative power, state and federal, the exertion of any restraint on the free exercise [223] of religion. Its purpose is to secure religious liberty in the individual by prohibiting any invasions thereof by civil authority. Hence it is necessary in a free exercise case for one to show the coercive effect of the enactment as it operates against him in the practice of his religion. The distinction between the two clauses is apparent—a violation of the Free Exercise Clause is predicated on coercion while the Establishment Clause violation need not be so attended. . . .

[225] It is insisted that unless these religious exercises are permitted a "religion of secularism" is established in the schools. We agree of course that the State may not establish a "religion of secularism" in the sense of affirmatively opposing or showing hostility to religion, thus "preferring those who believe in no religion over those who do believe." *Zorach v. Clauson*, at 314. We do not agree, however, that this decision in any sense has that effect. In addition, it might well be said that one's education is not complete without a study of comparative religion or the history of religion and its relationship to the advancement of civilization. It certainly may be said that the Bible is worthy of study for its literary and historic qualities. Nothing we have said here indicates that such study of the Bible or of religion, when presented objectively as part of a secular program of education, may not be effected consistently with the First Amendment. But the exercises here do not fall into those categories. They are religious exercises, required by the States in violation of the command of the First Amendment that the Government maintain strict neutrality, neither aiding nor opposing religion.

Finally, we cannot accept that the concept of neutrality, which does not permit a State to require a religious exercise even with the consent of the majority of those [226] affected, collides with the majority's right to free exercise of religion. While the Free Exercise Clause clearly prohibits the use of state action to deny the rights of free exercise to anyone, it has never meant that a majority could use the machinery of the State to practice its beliefs. . . .

The place of religion in our society is an exalted one, achieved through a long tradition of reliance on the home, the church and the inviolable citadel of the individual heart and mind. We have come to recognize through bitter experience that it is not within the power of government to invade that citadel, whether its purpose or effect be to aid or oppose, to advance or retard. In the relationship between man and religion, the State is firmly committed to a position of neutrality. Though the application of that rule requires interpretation of a delicate sort, the rule itself is clearly and concisely stated in the words of the First Amendment. . . .

[227] MR. JUSTICE DOUGLAS, concurring.

I join the opinion of the Court and add a few words in explanation.

While the Free Exercise Clause of the First Amendment is written in terms of what the State may not require of the individual, the Establishment Clause, serving the same goal of individual religious freedom, is written in different terms.

Establishment of a religion can be achieved in several ways. The church and state can be one; the church may control the state or the state may control the church; or the relationship may take one of several possible forms of a working arrangement between the two bodies. Under all of these arrangements the church typically has a place in the state's budget, and church law usually governs such matters as baptism, marriage, divorce and separation, at least for its members and sometimes for the entire body politic. Education, too, is usually high on the priority [228] list of church interests. In the past schools were often made the exclusive responsibility of the church. Today in some state-church countries the state runs the public schools, but compulsory religious exercises are often required of some or all students. Thus, under the agreement Franco made with the Holy See when he came to power in Spain, "The Church regained its place in the national budget. It insists on baptizing all children and has made the catechism obligatory in state schools."

The vice of all such arrangements under the Establishment Clause is that the state is lending its assistance to a church's efforts to gain and keep adherents. Under the First Amendment it is strictly a matter for the individual and his church as to what church he will belong to and how much support, in the way of belief, time, activity or money, he will give to it. "This pure Religious Liberty"

> "declared . . . [all forms of church-state relationships] and their fundamental idea to be oppressions of conscience and abridgments of that liberty which God and nature had conferred on every living soul."[5]

In these cases we have no coercive religious exercise aimed at making the students conform. The prayers announced are not compulsory, though some may think they have that indirect effect because the nonconformist student may be induced to participate for fear of being called an "oddball." But that coercion, if it be present, [229] has not been shown; so the vices of the present regimes are different.

These regimes violate the Establishment Clause in two different ways. In each case the State is conducting a religious exercise; and, as the Court holds, that cannot be done without violating the "neutrality" required of the State by the balance of power between individual, church and state that has been struck by the First Amendment. But the Establishment Clause is not limited to precluding the State itself from conducting religious exercises. It also forbids the State to employ its facilities or funds in a way that gives any church, or all churches, greater strength in our society than it would have by relying on its members alone. Thus, the present regimes must fall under that clause for the additional reason that public funds, though small in amount, are being used to promote a religious exercise. Through the mechanism of the State, all of the people are being required to finance a religious exercise that only some of the people want and that violates the sensibilities of others.

The most effective way to establish any institution is to finance it; and this truth is reflected in the appeals by church groups for public funds to finance their religious schools. Financing a church either in its strictly religious activities or in its other activities is equally unconstitutional, as I understand the Establishment Clause. Budgets for one activity may be technically separable from budgets for others. But the institution is an inseparable whole, a living organism, which is strengthened in proselytizing when it is strengthened in any department by contributions from other than its own members.

[230] Such contributions may not be made by the State even in a minor degree without violating the Establishment Clause. It is not the amount of public funds expended; as

---

5. Cobb, [Religious Liberty in America (1902),] at 2.

this case illustrates, it is the use to which public funds are put that is controlling. For the First Amendment does not say that some forms of establishment are allowed; it says that "no law respecting an establishment of religion" shall be made. What may not be done directly may not be done indirectly lest the Establishment Clause become a mockery.

MR. JUSTICE BRENNAN, concurring.

[231] When John Locke ventured in 1689, "I esteem it above all things necessary to distinguish exactly the business of civil government from that of religion and to settle the just bounds that lie between the one and the other," he anticipated the necessity which would be thought by the Framers to require adoption of a First Amendment, but not the difficulty that would be experienced in defining those "just bounds." The fact is that the line which separates the secular from the sectarian in American life is elusive. The difficulty of defining the boundary with precision inheres in a paradox central to our scheme of liberty. While our institutions reflect a firm conviction that we are a religious people, those institutions by solemn constitutional injunction may not officially involve religion in such a way as to prefer, discriminate against, or oppress, a particular sect or religion. Equally the Constitution enjoins those involvements of religious with secular institutions which (a) serve the essentially religious activities of religious institutions; (b) employ the organs of government for essentially religious purposes; or (c) use essentially religious means to serve governmental ends where secular means would suffice. The constitutional mandate expresses a deliberate and considered judgment that such matters are to be left to the conscience of the citizen, and declares as a basic postulate of the relation between the citizen and his government that "the rights of conscience are, in their nature, of peculiar delicacy, and will little bear the gentlest touch of governmental hand. . . ."[2]

I join fully in the opinion and the judgment of the Court. I see no escape from the conclusion that the exercises [232] called in question in these two cases violate the constitutional mandate. The reasons we gave only last Term in *Engel v. Vitale* for finding in the New York Regents' prayer an impermissible establishment of religion, compel the same judgment of the practices at bar. The involvement of the secular with the religious is no less intimate here; and it is constitutionally irrelevant that the State has not composed the material for the inspirational exercises presently involved. It should be unnecessary to observe that our holding does not declare that the First Amendment manifests hostility to the practice or teaching of religion, but only applies prohibitions incorporated in the Bill of Rights in recognition of historic needs shared by Church and State alike. While it is my view that not every involvement of religion in public life is unconstitutional, I consider the exercises at bar a form of involvement which clearly violates the Establishment Clause.

The importance of the issue and the deep conviction with which views on both sides are held seem to me to justify detailing at some length my reasons for joining the Court's judgment and opinion.

I

. . . [234] Plainly, the Establishment Clause, in the contemplation of the Framers, "did not limit the constitutional proscription to any particular, dated form of state-supported

---

2. Representative Daniel Carroll of Maryland during debate upon the proposed Bill of Rights in the First Congress, August 15, 1789, I Annals of Cong. 730.

theological venture." "What Virginia had long practiced, and what Madison, Jefferson and others fought to end, was the extension of civil government's support to religion in a manner which made the two in some degree interdependent, and thus threatened the freedom of each. The purpose of the Establishment Clause was to assure that the national legislature would not exert its power in the service of any purely religious end; that it would not, as Virginia and virtually all of the Colonies had done, make of religion, as religion, an object of legislation. . . . The Establishment Clause withdrew from the sphere of legitimate legislative concern and competence a specific, but comprehensive, area of human conduct: man's belief or disbelief in the verity of some transcendental idea and man's expression in action of that belief or disbelief." *McGowan v. Maryland*, at 465–466 (opinion of Frankfurter, J.).

In sum, the history which our prior decisions have summoned to aid interpretation of the Establishment Clause permits little doubt that its prohibition was designed comprehensively to prevent those official involvements of religion which would tend to foster or discourage religious worship or belief.

But an awareness of history and an appreciation of the aims of the Founding Fathers do not always resolve concrete problems. The specific question before us has, for example, aroused vigorous dispute whether the architects of the First Amendment—James Madison and Thomas Jefferson particularly—understood the prohibition against any "law respecting an establishment of [235] religion" to reach devotional exercises in the public schools. It may be that Jefferson and Madison would have held such exercises to be permissible—although even in Jefferson's case serious doubt is suggested by his admonition against "putting the Bible and Testament into the hands of the children at an age when their judgments are not sufficiently matured for religious inquiries. . . ." But [236] I doubt that their view, even if perfectly clear one way or the other, would supply a dispositive answer to the question presented by these cases. A more fruitful inquiry, it seems to me, is whether the practices here challenged threaten those consequences which the Framers deeply feared; whether, in short, they tend to promote that type of interdependence between religion and state which the First Amendment was designed to prevent. Our task is to translate "the majestic generalities of the Bill of Rights, conceived as part of the pattern of liberal government in the eighteenth century, into concrete restraints on officials [237] dealing with the problems of the twentieth century. . . ." *West Virginia State Board of Education v. Barnette*, 319 U.S. 624, 639.

A too literal quest for the advice of the Founding Fathers upon the issues of these cases seems to me futile and misdirected for several reasons: First, on our precise problem the historical record is at best ambiguous, and statements can readily be found to support either side of the proposition. The ambiguity of history is understandable if we recall the nature of the problems uppermost in the thinking of the statesmen who fashioned the religious guarantees; they were concerned with far more flagrant intrusions of government into the realm of religion than any that our century has witnessed. While it is clear to me that the Framers meant the Establishment Clause to prohibit more than the creation of an established federal church such as existed in England, I have no doubt that, in their preoccupation with the imminent question of established churches, they gave no distinct [238] consideration to the particular question whether the clause also forbade devotional exercises in public institutions.

Second, the structure of American education has greatly changed since the First Amendment was adopted. In the context of our modern emphasis upon public education available to all citizens, any views of the eighteenth century as to whether the exercises at bar are an "establishment" offer little aid to decision. Education, as the

Framers knew it, was in the main confined to private schools more often than not under strictly sectarian supervision. Only gradually did control of education pass largely
to public officials. It would, therefore, [239] hardly be significant if the fact was that the
nearly universal devotional exercises in the schools of the young Republic did not provoke criticism; even today religious ceremonies in church-supported private schools
are constitutionally unobjectionable.

[240] Third, our religious composition makes us a vastly more diverse people than
were our forefathers. They knew differences chiefly among Protestant sects. Today the
Nation is far more heterogeneous religiously, including as it does substantial minorities not only of Catholics and Jews but as well of those who worship according to no
version of the Bible and those who worship no God at all. [241] In the face of such
profound changes, practices which may have been objectionable to no one in the time
of Jefferson and Madison may today be highly offensive to many persons, the deeply
devout and the nonbelievers alike.

Whatever Jefferson or Madison would have thought of Bible reading or the recital of
the Lord's Prayer in what few public schools existed in their day, our use of the history of
their time must limit itself to broad purposes, not specific practices. By such a standard,
I am persuaded, as is the Court, that the devotional exercises carried on in the Baltimore
and Abington schools offend the First Amendment because they sufficiently threaten in
our day those substantive evils the fear of which called forth the Establishment Clause of
the First Amendment. It is "a constitution we are expounding," and our interpretation of
the First Amendment must necessarily be responsive to the much more highly charged
nature of religious questions in contemporary society.

Fourth, the American experiment in free public education available to all children
has been guided in large measure by the dramatic evolution of the religious diversity
among the population which our public schools serve. The interaction of these two important forces in our national life has placed in bold relief certain positive values in the
consistent application to public institutions generally, and public schools particularly, of
the constitutional decree against official involvements of religion which might produce
the evils the Framers meant the Establishment Clause to forestall. The public schools are
supported entirely, in most communities, by public funds—funds exacted not only from
parents, nor alone from those who hold particular religious views, nor indeed from those
who subscribe to any creed at all. It is implicit in the history and character of American
public education that the public schools serve a uniquely [242] public function: the training of American citizens in an atmosphere free of parochial, divisive, or separatist influences of any sort—an atmosphere in which children may assimilate a heritage common
to all American groups and religions. This is a heritage neither theistic nor atheistic, but
simply civic and patriotic. . . .

[253] III

No one questions that the Framers of the First Amendment intended to restrict exclusively the powers of the Federal Government. Whatever limitations that Amendment
now imposes upon the States derive from the Fourteenth Amendment. The process of
absorption of the religious guarantees of the First Amendment as protections against the
States under the Fourteenth Amendment began with the Free Exercise Clause. . . .

[254] The absorption of the Establishment Clause has, however, come later and by
a route less easily charted. It has been suggested, with some support in history, that
absorption of the First Amendment's ban against congressional legislation "respecting

an establishment of religion" is conceptually impossible because the Framers meant the Establishment Clause also to foreclose any attempt by Congress to disestablish the existing official state churches. Whether or not such was the understanding of the Framers and whether such a purpose would have inhibited the absorption of the Establishment Clause at the threshold of the Nineteenth Century are questions not dispositive of our present inquiry. For it is [255] clear on the record of history that the last of the formal state establishments was dissolved more than three decades before the Fourteenth Amendment was ratified, and thus the problem of protecting official state churches from federal encroachments could hardly have been any concern of those who framed the post–Civil War Amendments. Any such objective of the First Amendment, having become historical anachronism by 1868, cannot be thought to have deterred the absorption of the Establishment Clause to any greater degree than it would, for example, have deterred the absorption of the Free Exercise Clause. That no organ of the Federal Government possessed in 1791 any power to restrain the interference of the States in religious matters is indisputable. It is equally plain, on the other hand, that the Fourteenth Amendment created a panoply of new federal rights for the protection of citizens of the various States. And among those rights was freedom from such state governmental involvement in the affairs of religion as the Establishment Clause had originally foreclosed on the part of Congress.

[256] It has also been suggested that the "liberty" guaranteed by the Fourteenth Amendment logically cannot absorb the Establishment Clause because that clause is not one of the provisions of the Bill of Rights which in terms protects a "freedom" of the individual. See Corwin, *A Constitution of Powers in a Secular State* (1951), 113–116. The fallacy in this contention, I think, is that it underestimates the role of the Establishment Clause as co-guarantor, with the Free Exercise Clause, of religious liberty. The Framers did not entrust the liberty of religious beliefs to either clause alone. The Free Exercise Clause "was not to be the full extent of the Amendment's guarantee of freedom from governmental intrusion in matters of faith." *McGowan v. Maryland*, at 464 (opinion of Frankfurter, J.).

Finally, it has been contended that absorption of the Establishment Clause is precluded by the absence of any intention on the part of the Framers of the Fourteenth Amendment to circumscribe the residual powers of the States to aid religious activities and institutions in ways which fell short of formal establishments. That argument relies in part upon the express terms of the [257] abortive Blaine Amendment—proposed several years after the adoption of the Fourteenth Amendment—which would have added to the First Amendment a provision that "[n]o State shall make any law respecting an establishment of religion. . . ."* Such a restriction would have been superfluous, it is said, if the Fourteenth Amendment had already made the Establishment Clause binding upon the States.

The argument proves too much, for the Fourteenth Amendment's protection of the free exercise of religion can hardly be questioned; yet the Blaine Amendment would also have added an explicit protection against state laws abridging that liberty. Even if we assume that the draftsmen of the Fourteenth Amendment saw no immediate connection between its protections against state action infringing personal liberty and the

---

*The Blaine Amendment, in full, stated, "No State shall make any law respecting an establishment of religion, or prohibiting the free exercise thereof; and no money raised by taxation in any State for the support of public schools, or derived from any public fund therefor [*sic*], nor any public lands devoted thereto, shall ever be under the control of any religious sect; nor shall any money so raised or lands so devoted be divided between religious sects or denominations."

guarantees of the First Amendment, it is certainly too late in the day to suggest that their assumed inattention to the question dilutes the force of these constitutional guarantees in their application to the States. It is enough to conclude [258] that the religious liberty embodied in the Fourteenth Amendment would not be viable if the Constitution were interpreted to forbid only establishments ordained by Congress. . . .

[266] IV

I turn now to the cases before us. The religious nature of the exercises here challenged seems plain. Unless *Engel v. Vitale* is to be overruled, or we are to engage in wholly disingenuous distinction, we cannot sustain [267] these practices. Daily recital of the Lord's Prayer and the reading of passages of Scripture are quite as clearly breaches of the command of the Establishment Clause as was the daily use of the rather bland Regents' Prayer in the New York public schools. Indeed, I would suppose that, if anything, the Lord's Prayer and the Holy Bible are more clearly sectarian, and the present violations of the First Amendment consequently more serious. . . .

[278] But three further contentions have been pressed in the argument of these cases. These contentions deserve careful consideration, for if the position of the school authorities were correct in respect to any of them, we would be misapplying the principles of *Engel v. Vitale*.

A

First, it is argued that however clearly religious may have been the origins and early nature of daily prayer and Bible reading, these practices today serve so clearly secular educational purposes that their religious attributes may be overlooked. I do not doubt, for example, that morning devotional exercises may foster better discipline in the classroom, and elevate the spiritual level on which the school day opens. The Pennsylvania Superintendent of Public Instruction, testifying by deposition in the *Schempp* case, offered his view that daily Bible reading "places upon the children or those hearing the reading of this, and the atmosphere which goes on in the reading . . . one of the last vestiges of moral value [279] that we have left in our school system." The exercise thus affords, the Superintendent concluded, "a strong contradiction to the materialistic trends of our time." Baltimore's Superintendent of Schools expressed a similar view of the practices challenged in the *Murray* case, to the effect that "[t]he acknowledgement of the existence of God as symbolized in the opening exercises establishes a discipline tone which tends to cause each individual pupil to constrain his overt acts and to consequently conform to accepted standards of behavior during his attendance at school." These views are by no means novel.

It is not the business of this Court to gainsay the judgments of experts on matters of pedagogy. Such decisions must be left to the discretion of those administrators charged with the supervision of the Nation's public schools. The limited province of the courts is to determine whether the means which the educators have chosen to achieve legitimate pedagogical ends infringe the constitutional freedoms of the First Amendment. The secular purposes which devotional exercises are said to serve fall into two categories—those which depend upon an immediately religious experience shared by the participating children; and those which appear sufficiently divorced from the religious content of the devotional material that they can be served equally by nonreligious [280] materials. With respect to the first objective, much has been written about the moral and spiritual values of infusing some religious influence or instruction into the public school classroom. To the extent that only religious materials will serve this purpose, it seems to me that the purpose as well as the means is so plainly religious that the exercise is necessarily forbidden by the Establishment Clause. The fact that purely secular benefits may eventually result does not seem to me to justify the exercises, for similar indirect nonreligious benefits could no doubt have been claimed for the released time program invalidated in *McCollum*.

The second justification assumes that religious exercises at the start of the school day may directly serve solely secular ends—for example, by fostering harmony and tolerance among the pupils, enhancing the authority of the teacher, and inspiring better discipline. To the extent that such benefits result not from the content of the readings and recitation, but simply from the holding of such a solemn exercise at the opening assembly or the first class of the day, it would seem that less sensitive materials might equally well serve the same purpose. I have previously suggested that *Torcaso* and the *Sunday Law Cases* forbid the use of religious means to achieve secular [281] ends where nonreligious means will suffice. That principle is readily applied to these cases. It has not been shown that readings from the speeches and messages of great Americans, for example, or from the documents of our heritage of liberty, daily recitation of the Pledge of Allegiance, or even the observance of a moment of reverent silence at the opening of class, may not adequately serve the solely secular purposes of the devotional activities without jeopardizing either the religious liberties of any members of the community or the proper degree of separation between the spheres of religion and government. Such substitutes would, I think, be unsatisfactory or inadequate only to the extent that the present activities do in fact serve religious goals. While I do not question the judgment of experienced educators that the challenged practices may well achieve valuable secular ends, it seems to me that the State acts unconstitutionally if it either sets about to attain even indirectly religious ends by religious means, or if it uses religious means to serve secular ends where secular means would suffice.

B

Second, it is argued that the particular practices involved in the two cases before us are unobjectionable [282] because they prefer no particular sect or sects at the expense of others. Both the Baltimore and Abington procedures permit, for example, the reading of any of several versions of the Bible, and this flexibility is said to ensure neutrality sufficiently to avoid the constitutional prohibition. One answer, which might be dispositive, is that any version of the Bible is inherently sectarian, else there would be no need to offer a system of rotation or alternation of versions in the first place, that is, to allow different sectarian versions to be used on different days. The sectarian character of the Holy Bible has been at the core of the whole controversy over religious practices in the public schools throughout its long and often bitter history. To [283] vary the version as the Abington and Baltimore schools have done may well be less offensive than to read from the King James version every day, as once was the practice. But the result even of this relatively benign procedure is that majority sects are preferred in approximate proportion to their representation in the community and in the student body, while the smaller sects suffer commensurate discrimination. So long as the subject matter of the exercise is sectarian in character, these consequences cannot be avoided.

The argument contains, however, a more basic flaw. There are persons in every community—often deeply devout—to whom any version of the Judeo-Christian Bible is offensive. There are others whose reverence for the Holy Scriptures demands private study or reflection and to whom public reading or recitation is sacrilegious, as one of the expert witnesses at the trial of the *Schempp* case explained. To such persons it is not the fact of using the Bible in the public schools, nor the content of any particular version, that is offensive, but only the manner in [284] which it is used. For such persons, the anathema of public communion is even more pronounced when prayer is involved. Many deeply devout persons have always regarded prayer as a necessarily private experience. One Protestant group recently commented, for example: "When one thinks of prayer as sincere outreach of a [285] human soul to the Creator, 'required prayer' becomes an absurdity." There is a similar problem with respect to comment upon the passages of Scripture which are to be read. Most present statutes forbid comment, and this practice accords with the views of many religious groups as to the manner in which the Bible should be read. However, as a recent survey discloses, scriptural passages read without comment frequently convey no message to the younger children in the school. Thus there has developed a practice in some schools of bridging the gap between faith and understanding by means of "definitions," even where "comment" is forbidden by statute. The present practice therefore poses a difficult dilemma: While Bible reading is almost universally required to be without comment, since only by such a prohibition can sectarian interpretation be excluded from the classroom, [286] the rule breaks down at the point at which rudimentary definitions of Biblical terms are necessary for comprehension if the exercise is to be meaningful at all.

It has been suggested that a tentative solution to these problems may lie in the fashioning of a "common core" of theology tolerable to all creeds but preferential to none. But as one commentator has recently observed, "[h]istory is not encouraging to" those who hope to fashion a "common denominator of religion detached from its manifestation in any organized church." Sutherland, *Establishment According to Engel*, 76 Harv. L. Rev. 25, 51 (1962). Thus, the notion of a "common core" litany or supplication offends many deeply devout worshippers who do not find clearly sectarian practices objectionable. Father Gustave Weigel has recently expressed [287] a widely shared view: "The moral code held by each separate religious community can reductively be unified, but the consistent particular believer wants no such reduction."[66] And, as the American Council on Education warned several years ago, "The notion of a common core suggests a watering down of the several faiths to the point where common essentials appear. This might easily lead to a new sect—a public school sect—which would take its place alongside the existing faiths and compete with them."[67] Engel is surely authority that nonsectarian religious practices, equally with sectarian exercises, violate the Establishment Clause. Moreover, even if the Establishment Clause were oblivious to nonsectarian religious practices, I think it quite likely that the "common core" approach would be sufficiently objectionable to many groups to be foreclosed by the prohibitions of the Free Exercise Clause.

C

A third element which is said to absolve the practices involved in these cases from the ban of the religious guarantees of the Constitution is the provision to excuse or

---

66. Quoted in Kurland, *The Regents' Prayer Case: "Full of Sound and Fury, Signifying . . . ,"* 1962 Supreme Court Review (1962), 1, 31.

67. Quoted in Harrison, *The Bible, the Constitution and Public Education*, 29 Tenn. L. Rev. 363, 417 (1962). See also Dawson, *America's Way in Church, State, and Society* (1953), 54.

exempt students who wish not to participate. Insofar as these practices are claimed to violate the Establishment [288] Clause, I find the answer which the District Court gave after our remand of *Schempp* to be altogether dispositive:

> "The fact that some pupils, or theoretically all pupils, might be excused from attendance at the exercises does not mitigate the obligatory nature of the ceremony. . . . The exercises are held in the school buildings and perforce are conducted by and under the authority of the local school authorities and during school sessions. Since the statute requires the reading of the 'Holy Bible,' a Christian document, the practice, as we said in our first opinion, prefers the Christian religion. The record demonstrates that it was the intention of the General Assembly of the Commonwealth of Pennsylvania to introduce a religious ceremony into the public schools of the Commonwealth." 201 F. Supp., at 819.

Thus the short, and to me sufficient, answer is that the availability of excusal or exemption simply has no relevance to the establishment question, if it is once found that these practices are essentially religious exercises designed at least in part to achieve religious aims through the use of public school facilities during the school day. . . .

[293] To summarize my views concerning the merits of these two cases: The history, the purpose and the operation of the daily prayer recital and Bible reading leave no doubt that these practices standing by themselves constitute an impermissible breach of the Establishment Clause. Such devotional exercises may well serve legitimate nonreligious purposes. To the extent, however, that such purposes [294] are really without religious significance, it has never been demonstrated that secular means would not suffice. Indeed, I would suggest that patriotic or other nonreligious materials might provide adequate substitutes—inadequate only to the extent that the purposes now served are indeed directly or indirectly religious. Under such circumstances, the States may not employ religious means to reach a secular goal unless secular means are wholly unavailing. I therefore agree with the Court that the judgment in *Schempp* must be affirmed, and that in *Murray* must be reversed.

V

These considerations bring me to a final contention of the school officials in these cases: that the invalidation of the exercises at bar permits this Court no alternative but to declare unconstitutional every vestige, however slight, of cooperation or accommodation between religion and government. I cannot accept that contention. While it is not, of course, appropriate for this Court to decide questions not presently before it, I venture to suggest that religious exercises in the public schools present a unique problem. For not every involvement of religion in public life violates the Establishment Clause. Our decision in these cases does not clearly forecast anything about the constitutionality of other types of interdependence between religious and other public institutions.

Specifically, I believe that the line we must draw between the permissible and the impermissible is one which accords with history and faithfully reflects the understanding of the Founding Fathers. It is a line which the Court has consistently sought to mark in its decisions expounding the religious guarantees of the First Amendment. What the Framers meant to foreclose, and what our decisions under the Establishment Clause have forbidden, [295] are those involvements of religious with secular institutions which (a) serve the essentially religious activities of religious institutions; (b) employ the organs of government for essentially religious purposes; or (c) use essentially religious means to serve governmental ends, where secular means would suffice. When the secular and religious institutions become involved in such a manner, there inhere in the relationship precisely those dangers—as much to church as to state—which the Framers feared would subvert religious liberty and the strength of a system of secular government. On the other hand, there may be myriad forms of involvements of government with religion which do not import such dangers and therefore should not, in my judgment, be deemed to violate the Establishment Clause. Nothing in the Constitution compels the organs of government to be blind to what everyone else perceives—that religious differences among Americans have important and pervasive implications for our society. Likewise nothing in the Establishment Clause forbids the application of legislation having purely secular ends in such a way as to alleviate burdens upon the free exercise of an individual's religious beliefs. Surely the Framers would never have understood that such a construction sanctions that involvement which violates the Establishment Clause. Such a conclusion can be reached, I would suggest, only by using the words of the First Amendment to defeat its very purpose. . . .

[296] *A. The Conflict between Establishment and Free Exercise.*—There are certain practices, conceivably violative of the Establishment Clause, the striking down of which might seriously interfere with certain religious liberties also protected by the First Amendment. Provisions for churches and chaplains at military establishments for those in the armed services may afford one such example. [297] The like provision by state and federal governments for chaplains in penal institutions may afford another example. It is argued that such provisions may be assumed to contravene the Establishment Clause, yet be sustained on constitutional grounds as necessary to secure to the members of the Armed Forces and prisoners those rights of worship guaranteed under the Free Exercise Clause. Since government has deprived such persons of the opportunity [298] to practice their faith at places of their choice, the argument runs, government may, in order to avoid infringing the free exercise guarantees, provide substitutes where it requires such persons to be. Such a principle might support, for example, the constitutionality of draft exemptions for ministers and divinity students, cf. *Selective Draft Law Cases*, 245 U.S. 366, 389–390; of the excusal of children from school on their respective religious holidays; and of the allowance by government of temporary use of public buildings by religious organizations when their own churches have become unavailable because of a disaster or emergency.

Such activities and practices seem distinguishable from the sponsorship of daily Bible reading and prayer recital. For one thing, there is no element of coercion present in the appointment of military or prison chaplains; the soldier or convict who declines the opportunities for worship would not ordinarily subject himself to the suspicion or obloquy of his peers. Of special significance to this distinction is the fact that we are here usually dealing [299] with adults, not with impressionable children as in the public schools. Moreover, the school exercises are not designed to provide the pupils with general opportunities for worship denied them by the legal obligation to attend school. The student's compelled presence in school for five days a week in no way renders the regular religious facilities of the community less accessible to him than they are to others. The situation of the school child is therefore plainly unlike that of the isolated soldier or the prisoner.

The State must be steadfastly neutral in all matters of faith, and neither favor nor inhibit religion. In my view, government cannot sponsor religious exercises in the public schools without jeopardizing that neutrality. On the other hand, hostility, not neutrality, would characterize the refusal to provide chaplains and places of worship for prisoners and soldiers cut off by the State from all civilian opportunities for public communion, the withholding of draft exemptions for ministers and conscientious objectors, or the denial of the temporary use of an empty public building to a congregation whose place of worship has been destroyed by fire or flood. I do not say that government must provide chaplains or draft exemptions, or that the courts should intercede if it fails to do so.

B. Establishment and Exercises in Legislative Bodies.—The saying of invocational prayers in legislative chambers, state or federal, and the appointment of legislative chaplains, might well represent no involvements of the kind prohibited by the Establishment Clause. Legislators, federal and state, are mature adults who may presumably absent themselves from such public and cere- [300] monial exercises without incurring any penalty, direct or indirect. It may also be significant that, at least in the case of the Congress, Art. I, 5, of the Constitution makes each House the monitor of the "Rules of Its Proceedings" so that it is at least arguable whether such matters present "political questions" the resolution of which is exclusively confided to Congress. Finally, there is the difficult question of who may be heard to challenge such practices.

C. Non-Devotional Use of the Bible in the Public Schools.—The holding of the Court today plainly does not foreclose teaching about the Holy Scriptures or about the differences between religious sects in classes in literature or history. Indeed, whether or not the Bible is involved, it would be impossible to teach meaningfully many subjects in the social sciences or the humanities without some mention of religion. To what extent, and at what points in the curriculum, religious materials should be cited are matters which the courts ought to entrust very largely to the experienced officials who superintend our Nation's public schools. They are experts in such matters, and we are not. We should heed Mr. Justice Jackson's caveat that any attempt by this Court to announce curricular standards would be "to decree a uniform, rigid and, if we are consistent, an unchanging standard for countless school boards represent- [301] ing and serving highly localized groups which not only differ from each other but which themselves from time to time change attitudes." *Illinois ex rel. McCollum v. Board of Education, supra,* at 237. . . .

We do not, however, in my view usurp the jurisdiction of school administrators by holding as we do today that morning devotional exercises in any form are constitutionally invalid. But there is no occasion now to go further and anticipate problems we cannot judge with the material now before us. Any attempt to impose rigid limits upon the mention of God or references to the Bible in the classroom would be fraught with dangers. If it should sometime hereafter be shown that in fact religion can play no part in the teaching of a given subject without resurrecting the ghost of the practices we strike down today, it will then be time enough to consider questions we must now defer.

D. Uniform Tax Exemptions Incidentally Available to Religious Institutions.— Nothing we hold today questions the propriety of certain tax deductions or exemptions which incidentally benefit churches and religious institutions, along with many secular charities and nonprofit organizations. If religious institutions benefit, it is in spite of rather than because of their religious character. For religious institutions simply share benefits which government makes generally available to educational, charitable, and eleemosynary groups. There is no indication that taxing authorities have used such benefits in any way to subsidize worship or foster belief in God. And as [302] among religious beneficiaries, the tax exemption or deduction can be truly nondiscriminatory, available on equal terms to small as well as large religious bodies, to popular and unpopular sects, and to those organizations which reject as well as those which accept a belief in God.

E. Religious Considerations in Public Welfare Programs.—Since government may not support or directly aid religious activities without violating the Establishment

Clause, there might be some doubt whether nondiscriminatory programs of governmental aid may constitutionally include individuals who become eligible wholly or partially for religious reasons. For example, it might be suggested that where a State provides unemployment compensation generally to those who are unable to find suitable work, it may not extend such benefits to persons who are unemployed by reason of religious beliefs or practices without thereby establishing the religion to which those persons belong. Therefore, the argument runs, the State may avoid an establishment only by singling out and excluding such persons on the ground that religious beliefs or practices have made them potential beneficiaries. Such a construction would, it seems to me, require government to impose religious discriminations and disabilities, thereby jeopardizing the free exercise of religion, in order to avoid what is thought to constitute an establishment.

The inescapable flaw in the argument, I suggest, is its quite unrealistic view of the aims of the Establishment Clause. The Framers were not concerned with the effects of certain incidental aids to individual worshippers which come about as by-products of general and nondiscriminatory welfare programs. If such benefits serve to make [303] easier or less expensive the practice of a particular creed, or of all religions, it can hardly be said that the purpose of the program is in any way religious, or that the consequence of its nondiscriminatory application is to create the forbidden degree of interdependence between secular and sectarian institutions. I cannot therefore accept the suggestion, which seems to me implicit in the argument outlined here, that every judicial or administrative construction which is designed to prevent a public welfare program from abridging the free exercise of religious beliefs, is for that reason *ipso facto* an establishment of religion.

F. Activities Which, Though Religious in Origin, Have Ceased to Have Religious Meaning.—As we noted in our *Sunday Law* decisions, nearly every criminal law on the books can be traced to some religious principle or inspiration. But that does not make the present enforcement of the criminal law in any sense an establishment of religion, simply because it accords with widely held religious principles. As we said in *McGowan v. Maryland*, 366 U.S. 420, 442, "the 'Establishment' Clause does not ban federal or state regulation of conduct whose reason or effect merely happens to coincide or harmonize with the tenets of some or all religions." This rationale suggests that the use of the motto "In God We Trust" on currency, on documents and public buildings and the like may not offend the clause. It is not that the use of those four words can be dismissed as "de minimis"—for I suspect there would be intense opposition to the abandonment of that motto. The truth is that we have simply interwoven the motto so deeply into the fabric of our civil polity that its present use may well not present that type of involvement which the First Amendment prohibits.

This general principle might also serve to insulate the various patriotic exercises and activities used in the public schools and elsewhere which, whatever may have been [304] their origins, no longer have a religious purpose or meaning. The reference to divinity in the revised pledge of allegiance, for example, may merely recognize the historical fact that our Nation was believed to have been founded "under God." Thus reciting the pledge may be no more of a religious exercise than the reading aloud of Lincoln's Gettysburg Address, which contains an allusion to the same historical fact.

The principles which we reaffirm and apply today can hardly be thought novel or radical. They are, in truth, as old as the Republic itself, and have always been as integral a part of the First Amendment as the very words of that charter of religious liberty. No less applicable today than they were when first pronounced a century ago, one year after the very first court decision involving religious exercises in the public schools, are the words of a distinguished Chief Justice of the Commonwealth of Pennsylvania, Jeremiah S. Black:

"The manifest object of the men who framed the institutions of this country, was to have a State without religion, and a Church without politics—that is to say, they meant that one should never be used as an engine for any purpose of the other, and that no man's rights in one should be tested by his opinions about the other. As the Church takes no note of men's political differences, so the State looks with equal eye on all the modes of religious faith. . . . Our fathers seem to have been perfectly sincere in their belief that the members of the Church would be more patriotic, and the citizens of the State more religious, by keeping their respective functions entirely separate." *Essay on Religious Liberty*, in Black, ed., *Essays and Speeches of Jeremiah S. Black* (1886), 53. . . .

[308] MR. JUSTICE STEWART, dissenting.

I think the records in the two cases before us are so fundamentally deficient as to make impossible an informed or responsible determination of the constitutional issues presented. Specifically, I cannot agree that on these records we can say that the Establishment Clause has necessarily been violated. But I think there exist serious questions under both that provision and the Free Exercise Clause—insofar as each is imbedded in the Fourteenth Amendment—which require the remand of these cases for the taking of additional evidence.

I

The First Amendment declares that "Congress shall make no law respecting an establishment of religion, or prohibiting the free exercise thereof. . . ." It is, I [309] think, a fallacious oversimplification to regard these two provisions as establishing a single constitutional standard of "separation of church and state," which can be mechanically applied in every case to delineate the required boundaries between government and religion. We err in the first place if we do not recognize, as a matter of history and as a matter of the imperatives of our free society, that religion and government must necessarily interact in countless ways. Secondly, the fact is that while in many contexts the Establishment Clause and the Free Exercise Clause fully complement each other, there are areas in which a doctrinaire reading of the Establishment Clause leads to irreconcilable conflict with the Free Exercise Clause.

A single obvious example should suffice to make the point. Spending federal funds to employ chaplains for the armed forces might be said to violate the Establishment Clause. Yet a lonely soldier stationed at some faraway outpost could surely complain that a government which did not provide him the opportunity for pastoral guidance was affirmatively prohibiting the free exercise of his religion. And such examples could readily be multiplied. The short of the matter is simply that the two relevant clauses of the First Amendment cannot accurately be reflected in a sterile metaphor which by its very nature may distort rather than illumine the problems involved in a particular case.

II

As a matter of history, the First Amendment was adopted solely as a limitation upon the newly created National Government. The events leading to its adoption strongly suggest that the Establishment Clause was primarily an attempt to insure that Congress not only would be powerless to establish a national church, but [310] would also be unable to interfere with existing state establishments. Each State was left free to go its own way and pursue its own policy with respect to religion. Thus Virginia from the beginning pursued a policy of disestablishmentarianism. Massachusetts, by contrast, had an established church until well into the nineteenth century.

So matters stood until the adoption of the Fourteenth Amendment, or more accurately, until this Court's decision in *Cantwell v. Connecticut*, in 1940. 310 U.S. 296. In that case the Court said: "The First Amendment declares that Congress shall make no law respecting an establishment of religion or prohibiting the free exercise thereof. The Fourteenth Amendment has rendered the legislatures of the states as incompetent as Congress to enact such laws."[2]

I accept without question that the liberty guaranteed by the Fourteenth Amendment against impairment by the States embraces in full the right of free exercise of religion protected by the First Amendment, and I yield to no one in my conception of the breadth of that freedom. I accept too the proposition that the Fourteenth Amendment has somehow absorbed the Establishment Clause, although it is not without irony that a constitutional provision evidently designed to leave the States free to go their own way should now have become a restriction upon their autonomy. But I cannot agree with what seems to me the insensitive definition of the Establishment Clause contained in the Court's opinion, nor with the different but, I think, equally mechanistic definitions contained in the separate opinions which have been filed.

[311] III

. . . Unlike other First Amendment guarantees, there is an inherent limitation upon the applicability of the Establishment Clause's ban on state support to religion. That limitation was succinctly put in *Everson v. Board of Education*, 330 U.S. 1, 18: "State power is no more to be used so as to handicap religions than it is to favor them." And in a later case, this Court recognized that the limitation was one which was itself compelled by the free exercise guarantee. "To hold that a state cannot consistently with the First and Fourteenth Amendments utilize its public school system to aid any or all religious faiths or sects in the dissemination of their doctrines and ideals does not . . . manifest a governmental hostility to religion or religious teachings. A manifestation of such hostility would be at war with our national tradition as embodied in the First Amendment's guaranty of the free [312] exercise of religion." *McCollum v. Board of Education*, 333 U.S. 203, 211–212.

That the central value embodied in the First Amendment—and, more particularly, in the guarantee of "liberty" contained in the Fourteenth—is the safeguarding of an individual's right to free exercise of his religion has been consistently recognized. . . .

It is this concept of constitutional protection embodied in our decisions which makes the cases before us such difficult ones for me. For there is involved in these cases a substantial free exercise claim on the part of those who affirmatively desire to have their children's school day open with the reading of passages from the Bible.

It has become accepted that the decision in *Pierce v. Society of Sisters* upholding the right of parents to send their children to nonpublic schools, was ultimately based upon

---

2. 310 U.S., at 303. The Court's statement as to the Establishment Clause in *Cantwell* was dictum. The case was decided on free exercise grounds.

the recognition of the validity of the free exercise claim involved in that situation. It might be argued here that parents who wanted their children to be exposed to religious influences in school could, under *Pierce*, send their children to private or parochial [313] schools. But the consideration which renders this contention too facile to be determinative has already been recognized by the Court: "Freedom of speech, freedom of the press, freedom of religion are available to all, not merely to those who can pay their own way." *Murdock v. Pennsylvania*, 319 U.S. 105, 111.

It might also be argued that parents who want their children exposed to religious influences can adequately fulfill that wish off school property and outside school time. With all its surface persuasiveness, however, this argument seriously misconceives the basic constitutional justification for permitting the exercises at issue in these cases. For a compulsory state educational system so structures a child's life that if religious exercises are held to be an impermissible activity in schools, religion is placed at an artificial and state-created disadvantage. Viewed in this light, permission of such exercises for those who want them is necessary if the schools are truly to be neutral in the matter of religion. And a refusal to permit religious exercises thus is seen, not as the realization of state neutrality, but rather as the establishment of a religion of secularism, or at the least, as government support of the beliefs of those who think that religious exercises should be conducted only in private.

What seems to me to be of paramount importance, then, is recognition of the fact that the claim advanced here in favor of Bible reading is sufficiently substantial to make simple reference to the constitutional phrase "establishment of religion" as inadequate an analysis of the cases before us as the ritualistic invocation of the nonconstitutional phrase "separation of church and state." What these cases compel, rather, is an analysis of just what the "neutrality" is which is required by the interplay of the Establishment and Free Exercise Clauses of the First Amendment, as imbedded in the Fourteenth.

[314] IV

Our decisions make clear that there is no constitutional bar to the use of government property for religious purposes. On the contrary, this Court has consistently held that the discriminatory barring of religious groups from public property is itself a violation of First and Fourteenth Amendment guarantees. *Fowler v. Rhode Island; Niemotko v. Maryland.* A different standard has been applied to public school property, because of the coercive effect which the use by religious sects of a compulsory school system would necessarily have upon the children involved. *McCollum v. Board of Education.* But insofar as the *McCollum* decision rests on the Establishment rather than the Free Exercise Clause, it is clear that its effect is limited to religious instruction—to government support of proselytizing activities of religious sects by throwing the weight of secular authority behind the dissemination of religious tenets.

The dangers both to government and to religion inherent in official support of instruction in the tenets of various religious sects are absent in the present cases, which involve only a reading from the Bible unaccompanied by comments which might otherwise constitute instruction. Indeed, since, from all that appears in either record, any teacher who does not wish to do so is free not to participate, it cannot even be contended that some [315] infinitesimal part of the salaries paid by the State are made contingent upon the performance of a religious function.

In the absence of evidence that the legislature or school board intended to prohibit local schools from substituting a different set of readings where parents requested such a change, we should not assume that the provisions before us—as actually administered—may not be construed simply as authorizing religious exercises, nor that the designations may not be treated simply as indications of the promulgating body's view as to the community's preference. We are under a duty to interpret these provisions so as to render them constitutional if reasonably possible. In the *Schempp* case there is evidence which indicates that variations were in fact permitted by the very school there involved, and that further variations were not introduced only because of the absence of requests from parents. And in the *Murray* case the Baltimore rule itself contains a provision permitting another version of the Bible to be substituted for the King James version.

If the provisions are not so construed, I think that their validity under the Establishment Clause would be extremely doubtful, because of the designation of a particular religious book and a denominational prayer. But since, even if the provisions are construed as I believe they must be, I think that the cases before us must be remanded for further evidence on other issues—thus affording the plaintiffs an opportunity to prove that local variations are not in fact permitted—I shall for the balance [316] of this dissenting opinion treat the provisions before us as making the variety and content of the exercises, as well as a choice as to their implementation, matters which ultimately reflect the consensus of each local school community. In the absence of coercion upon those who do not wish to participate—because they hold less strong beliefs, other beliefs, or no beliefs at all—such provisions cannot, in my view, be held to represent the type of support of religion barred by the Establishment Clause. For the only support which such rules provide for religion is the withholding of state hostility—a simple acknowledgment on the part of secular authorities that the Constitution does not require extirpation of all expression of religious belief.

V

I have said that these provisions authorizing religious exercises are properly to be regarded as measures making possible the free exercise of religion. But it is important to stress that, strictly speaking, what is at issue here is a privilege rather than a right. In other words, the question presented is not whether exercises such as those at issue here are constitutionally compelled, but rather whether they are constitutionally invalid. And that issue, in my view, turns on the question of coercion.

It is clear that the dangers of coercion involved in the holding of religious exercises in a schoolroom differ qualitatively from those presented by the use of similar exercises or affirmations in ceremonies attended by adults. Even as to children, however, the duty laid upon government in connection with religious exercises in the public schools is that of refraining from so structuring the school environment as to put any kind of pressure on a child to participate in those exercises; it is not that of providing an atmosphere in which children are kept scrupulously insulated from any awareness that some of their fellows [317] may want to open the school day with prayer, or of the fact that there exist in our pluralistic society differences of religious belief. . . .

[318] To be specific, it seems to me clear that certain types of exercises would present situations in which no possibility of coercion on the part of secular officials could be claimed to exist. Thus, if such exercises were held either before or after the official school day, or if the school schedule were such that participation were merely one among a number of desirable alternatives, it could hardly be contended that the exercises did anything more than to provide an opportunity for the voluntary expression of religious belief. On the other hand, a law which provided for religious exercises during the school

day and which contained no excusal provision would obviously be unconstitutionally coercive upon those who did not wish to participate. And even under a law containing an excusal provision, if the exercises were held during the school day, and no equally desirable alternative were provided by the school authorities, the likelihood that children might be under at least some psychological compulsion to participate would be great. In a case such as the latter, however, I think we would err if we assumed such coercion in the absence of any evidence.

[319] VI

Viewed in this light, it seems to me clear that the records in both of the cases before us are wholly inadequate to support an informed or responsible decision. Both cases involve provisions which explicitly permit any student who wishes, to be excused from participation in the exercises. There is no evidence in either case as to whether there would exist any coercion of any kind upon a student who did not want to participate. . . .

What our Constitution indispensably protects is the freedom of each of us, be he Jew or Agnostic, Christian or [320] Atheist, Buddhist or Freethinker, to believe or disbelieve, to worship or not worship, to pray or keep silent, according to his own conscience, uncoerced and unrestrained by government. It is conceivable that these school boards, or even all school boards, might eventually find it impossible to administer a system of religious exercises during school hours in such a way as to meet this constitutional standard—in such a way as completely to free from any kind of official coercion those who do not affirmatively want to participate. But I think we must not assume that school boards so lack the qualities of inventiveness and good will as to make impossible the achievement of that goal.

17

Sherbert v. Verner

374 U.S. 398 (1963)

Vote: 7—Warren, Black, Douglas, Clark, Brennan, Stewart, Goldberg
  2—Harlan, White

Opinion announcing the opinion of the Court: Brennan
Opinions concurring in the result: Douglas, Stewart
Dissenting opinion: Harlan

Adell Sherbert, a member of the Seventh-Day Adventist Church, was discharged by her South Carolina employer because she would not work on Saturdays, which she understood to be the sabbath. Sherbert was unable to obtain other employment because of her refusal to work on that day.

Sherbert filed a claim for unemployment compensation benefits under the South Carolina Unemployment Compensation Act. South Carolina law provided that to be eligible for benefits a claimant must be "able to work and . . . available for work" and, further, that a claimant was ineligible for unemployment compensation benefits if he or she "failed, without good cause . . . to accept available suitable work when offered . . . by the employment office or the employer." The South Carolina Employment Security Commission found that Sherbert's self-imposed restriction upon her availability for Saturday work brought her within the provision disqualifying for benefits insured workers who failed, without good cause, to accept "suitable work when offered . . . by the employment office or the employer." The employment commission, accordingly, denied Sherbert's application for unemployment compensation.

MR. JUSTICE BRENNAN delivered the opinion of the Court.

. . . [402] I

The door of the Free Exercise Clause stands tightly closed against any governmental regulation of religious beliefs as such, *Cantwell v. Connecticut*, 310 U.S. 296, 303. Government may neither compel affirmation of a repugnant belief, *Torcaso v. Watkins*; nor penalize or discriminate against individuals or groups because they hold religious views abhorrent to the authorities, *Fowler v. Rhode Island*; nor employ the taxing power to inhibit the dissemination of particular religious views, *Murdock v. Pennsylvania*; *Follett v.*

McCormick; cf. *Grosjean v. American Press Co.* On the other hand, [403] the Court has rejected challenges under the Free Exercise Clause to governmental regulation of certain overt acts prompted by religious beliefs or principles, for "even when the action is in accord with one's religious convictions, [it] is not totally free from legislative restrictions." *Braunfeld v. Brown,* 366 U.S. 599, 603. The conduct or actions so regulated have invariably posed some substantial threat to public safety, peace or order.

Plainly enough, appellant's conscientious objection to Saturday work constitutes no conduct prompted by religious principles of a kind within the reach of state legislation. If, therefore, the decision of the South Carolina Supreme Court is to withstand appellant's constitutional challenge, it must be either because her disqualification as a beneficiary represents no infringement by the State of her constitutional rights of free exercise, or because any incidental burden on the free exercise of appellant's religion may be justified by a "compelling state interest in the regulation of a subject within the State's constitutional power to regulate. . . ." *NAACP v. Button,* 371 U.S. 415, 438.

II

We turn first to the question whether the disqualification for benefits imposes any burden on the free exercise of appellant's religion. We think it is clear that it does. In a sense the consequences of such a disqualification to religious principles and practices may be only an indirect result of welfare legislation within the State's general competence to enact; it is true that no criminal sanctions directly compel appellant to work a six-day week. But this is only the beginning, not the end, of our [404] inquiry. For "[i]f the purpose or effect of a law is to impede the observance of one or all religions or is to discriminate invidiously between religions, that law is constitutionally invalid even though the burden may be characterized as being only indirect." *Braunfeld v. Brown,* at 607. Here not only is it apparent that appellant's declared ineligibility for benefits derives solely from the practice of her religion, but the pressure upon her to forego that practice is unmistakable. The ruling forces her to choose between following the precepts of her religion and forfeiting benefits, on the one hand, and abandoning one of the precepts of her religion in order to accept work, on the other hand. Governmental imposition of such a choice puts the same kind of burden upon the free exercise of religion as would a fine imposed against appellant for her Saturday worship.

Nor may the South Carolina court's construction of the statute be saved from constitutional infirmity on the ground that unemployment compensation benefits are not appellant's "right" but merely a "privilege." It is too late in the day to doubt that the liberties of religion and expression may be infringed by the denial of or placing of conditions upon a benefit or privilege. . . . [406] [T]o condition the availability of benefits upon this appellant's willingness to violate a cardinal principle of her religious faith effectively penalizes the free exercise of her constitutional liberties.

Significantly South Carolina expressly saves the Sunday worshipper from having to make the kind of choice which we here hold infringes the Sabbatarian's religious liberty. When in times of "national emergency" the textile plants are authorized by the State Commissioner of Labor to operate on Sunday, "no employee shall be required to work on Sunday . . . who is conscientiously opposed to Sunday work; and if any employee should refuse to work on Sunday on account of conscientious . . . objections he or she shall not jeopardize his or her seniority by such refusal or be discriminated against in any other manner." S. C. Code, 64-4. No question of the disqualification of a Sunday worshipper for benefits is likely to arise, since we cannot suppose that an employer will discharge him in violation of this statute. The unconstitutionality of the disqualification of the Sabbatarian is thus compounded by the religious discrimination which South Carolina's general statutory scheme necessarily effects.

III

We must next consider whether some compelling state interest enforced in the eligibility provisions of the South Carolina statute justifies the substantial infringement of appellant's First Amendment right. It is basic that no showing merely of a rational relationship to some colorable state interest would suffice; in this highly sensitive constitutional area, "[o]nly the gravest abuses, endangering paramount interests, give occasion for permissible limitation," *Thomas v. Collins*, 323 U.S. 516, 530. [407] No such abuse or danger has been advanced in the present case. The appellees suggest no more than a possibility that the filing of fraudulent claims by unscrupulous claimants feigning religious objections to Saturday work might not only dilute the unemployment compensation fund but also hinder the scheduling by employers of necessary Saturday work. But that possibility is not apposite here because no such objection appears to have been made before the South Carolina Supreme Court, and we are unwilling to assess the importance of an asserted state interest without the views of the state court. Nor, if the contention had been made below, would the record appear to sustain it; there is no proof whatever to warrant such fears of malingering or deceit as those which the respondents now advance. Even if consideration of such evidence is not foreclosed by the prohibition against judicial inquiry into the truth or falsity of religious beliefs—a question as to which we intimate no view since it is not before us—it is highly doubtful whether such evidence would be sufficient to warrant a substantial infringement of religious liberties. For even if the possibility of spurious claims did threaten to dilute the fund and disrupt the scheduling of work, it would plainly be incumbent upon the appellees to demonstrate that no alternative forms of regulation would combat such abuses without infringing First Amendment rights.

[408] In these respects, then, the state interest asserted in the present case is wholly dissimilar to the interests which were found to justify the less direct burden upon religious practices in *Braunfeld v. Brown*. The Court recognized that the Sunday closing law which that decision sustained undoubtedly served "to make the practice of [the Orthodox Jewish merchants'] . . . religious beliefs more expensive," 366 U.S., at 605. But the statute was nevertheless saved by a countervailing factor which finds no equivalent in the instant case—a strong state interest in providing one uniform day of rest for all workers. That secular objective could be achieved, the Court found, only by declaring Sunday to be that day of rest. Requiring exemptions for Sabbatarians, while theoretically possible, appeared to present an administrative [409] problem of such magnitude, or to afford the exempted class so great a competitive advantage, that such a requirement would have rendered the entire statutory scheme unworkable. In the present case no such justifications underlie the determination of the state court that appellant's religion makes her ineligible to receive benefits.

IV

In holding as we do, plainly we are not fostering the "establishment" of the Seventh-Day Adventist religion in South Carolina, for the extension of unemployment benefits to Sabbatarians in common with Sunday worshippers reflects nothing more than the governmental obligation of neutrality in the face of religious differences, and does not represent that involvement of religious with secular institutions which it is the object of the Establishment Clause to forestall. See *School District of Abington Township v. Schempp*, p. 203. Nor does the recognition of the appellant's right to unemployment benefits under the state statute serve to abridge any other person's religious liberties. Nor do we, by our decision today, declare the existence of a constitutional right to unemployment benefits on the part [410] of all persons whose religious convictions are the cause of their unemployment. This is not a case in which an employee's religious convictions serve to make him a nonproductive member of society. Finally, nothing we say today constrains the States to adopt any particular form or scheme of unemployment compensation. Our holding today is only that South Carolina may not constitutionally apply the eligibility provisions so as to constrain a worker to abandon his religious convictions respecting the day of rest. This holding but reaffirms a principle that we announced a decade and a half ago, namely that no State may "exclude individual Catholics, Lutherans, Mohammedans, Baptists, Jews, Methodists, Non-believers, Presbyterians, or the members of any other faith, because of their faith, or lack of it, from receiving the benefits of public welfare legislation." *Everson v. Board of Education*, 330 U.S. 1, 16. . . .

[413] MR. JUSTICE STEWART, concurring in the result.

Although fully agreeing with the result which the Court reaches in this case, I cannot join the Court's opinion. This case presents a double-barreled dilemma, which in all candor I think the Court's opinion has not succeeded in papering over. The dilemma ought to be resolved.

I

Twenty-three years ago in *Cantwell v. Connecticut*, 310 U.S. 296, 303, the Court said that both the Establishment Clause and the Free Exercise Clause of the First Amendment were made wholly applicable to the States by the Fourteenth Amendment. In the intervening years several cases involving claims of state abridgment of individual religious freedom have been decided here—most recently *Braunfeld v. Brown* and *Torcaso v. Watkins*. During the same period "cases dealing with the specific problems arising under the 'Establishment' Clause which have reached this Court are few in number." The most recent are last Term's *Engel v. Vitale* and this Term's *Schempp* and *Murray* cases, p. 203.

I am convinced that no liberty is more essential to the continued vitality of the free society which our Constitution guarantees than is the religious liberty protected by the Free Exercise Clause explicit in the First Amendment and imbedded in the Fourteenth. And I regret that on [414] occasion, and specifically in *Braunfeld v. Brown*, the Court has shown what has seemed to me a distressing insensitivity to the appropriate demands of this constitutional guarantee. By contrast I think that the Court's approach to the Establishment Clause has on occasion, and specifically in *Engel, Schempp* and *Murray*, been not only insensitive, but positively wooden, and that the Court has accorded to the Establishment Clause a meaning which neither the words, the history, nor the intention of the authors of that specific constitutional provision even remotely suggests.

But my views as to the correctness of the Court's decisions in these cases are beside the point here. The point is that the decisions are on the books. And the result is that there are many situations where legitimate claims under the Free Exercise Clause will run into head-on collision with the Court's insensitive and sterile construction of the Establishment Clause. The controversy now before us is clearly such a case.

Because the appellant refuses to accept available jobs which would require her to work on Saturdays, South Carolina has declined to pay unemployment compensation benefits to her. Her refusal to work on Saturdays is based on the tenets of her religious faith. The Court says that South Carolina cannot under these circumstances declare her to be not "available for work" within the meaning of its statute because to do so would violate her constitutional right to the free exercise of her religion.

Yet what this Court has said about the Establishment Clause must inevitably lead to a diametrically opposite result. If the appellant's refusal to work on Saturdays [415] were based on indolence, or on a compulsive desire to watch the Saturday television programs, no one would say that South Carolina could not hold that she was not "available for work" within the meaning of its statute. That being so, the Establishment Clause as construed by this Court not only permits but affirmatively requires South Carolina equally to deny the appellant's claim for unemployment compensation when her refusal to work on Saturdays is based upon her religious creed. For, as said in *Everson v. Board of Education*, 330 U.S. 1, 11, the Establishment Clause bespeaks "a government . . . stripped of all power . . . to support, or otherwise to assist any or all religions . . . ," and no State "can pass laws which aid one religion. . . ." *Id.*, at 15. In Mr. Justice Rutledge's words, adopted by the Court today in *Schempp*, p. 217, the Establishment Clause forbids "every form of public aid or support for religion." 330 U.S., at 32. In the words of the Court in *Engel v. Vitale*, 370 U.S., at 431, reaffirmed today in the *Schempp* case, p. 221, the Establishment Clause forbids the "financial support of government" to be "placed behind a particular religious belief."

To require South Carolina to so administer its laws as to pay public money to the appellant under the circumstances of this case is thus clearly to require the State to violate the Establishment Clause as construed by this Court. This poses no problem for me, because I think the Court's mechanistic concept of the Establishment Clause is historically unsound and constitutionally wrong. I think the process of constitutional decision in the area of the relationships between government and religion demands considerably more than the invocation of broadbrushed rhetoric of the kind I have quoted. And I think that the guarantee of religious liberty embodied in the Free Exercise Clause affirmatively requires government to create an atmosphere of hospitality and accommodation [416] to individual belief or disbelief. In short, I think our Constitution commands the positive protection by government of religious freedom—not only for a minority, however small—not only for the majority, however large—but for each of us.

South Carolina would deny unemployment benefits to a mother unavailable for work on Saturdays because she was unable to get a babysitter. Thus, we do not have before us a situation where a State provides unemployment compensation generally, and singles out for disqualification only those persons who are unavailable for work on religious grounds. This is not, in short, a scheme which operates so as to discriminate against religion as such. But the Court nevertheless holds that the State must prefer a religious over a secular ground for being unavailable for work—that state financial support of the appellant's religion is constitutionally required to carry out "the governmental obligation of neutrality in the face of religious differences. . . ."

Yet in cases decided under the Establishment Clause the Court has decreed otherwise. It has decreed that government must blind itself to the differing religious beliefs and traditions of the people. With all respect, I think it is the Court's duty to face up to the dilemma posed by the conflict between the Free Exercise Clause of the Constitution and the Establishment Clause as interpreted by the Court. It is a duty, I submit, which we owe to the people, the States, and the Nation, and a duty which we owe to ourselves. For so long as the resounding but fallacious fundamentalist rhetoric of some of our Establishment Clause opinions remains on our books, to be disregarded at will as in the present case, [417] or to be undiscriminatingly invoked as in the *Schempp* case, p. 203, so long will the possibility of consistent and perceptive decision in this most difficult and delicate area of constitutional law be impeded and impaired. And so long, I fear, will the guarantee of true religious freedom in our pluralistic society be uncertain and insecure. . . .

[418] MR. JUSTICE HARLAN, whom MR. JUSTICE WHITE joins, dissenting.

Today's decision is disturbing both in its rejection of existing precedent and in its implications for the future. The significance of the decision can best be understood after an examination of the state law applied in this case.

South Carolina's Unemployment Compensation Law was enacted in 1936 in response to the grave social and economic problems that arose during the depression of that period. As stated in the statute itself:

> "Economic insecurity due to unemployment is a serious menace to health, morals and welfare of the people of this State; *involuntary unemployment* is therefore a subject of general interest and concern . . . ; the achievement of social security requires protection against this greatest hazard of our economic life; this can be provided by encouraging the employers *to provide more stable employment and by the systematic accumulation of funds during periods of employment to provide benefits for periods of unemployment,* thus maintaining purchasing power and limiting the serious social consequences of poor relief assistance." § 68–38. (Emphasis added.)

[419] Thus the purpose of the legislature was to tide people over, and to avoid social and economic chaos, during periods when work was unavailable. But at the same time there was clearly no intent to provide relief for those who for purely personal reasons were or *became unavailable for work.* In accordance with this design, the legislature provided, in § 68-113, that "[a]n unemployed insured worker shall be eligible to receive benefits with respect to any week *only* if the Commission finds that . . . [h]e is able to work and is available for work. . . ." (Emphasis added.)

The South Carolina Supreme Court has uniformly applied this law in conformity with its clearly expressed purpose. It has consistently held that one is not "available for work" if his unemployment has resulted not from the inability of industry to provide a job but rather from personal circumstances, no matter how compelling. The reference to "involuntary unemployment" in the legislative statement of policy, whatever a sociologist, philosopher, or theologian might say, has been interpreted not to embrace such personal circumstances.

In the present case all that the state court has done is to apply these accepted principles. Since virtually all of the mills in the Spartanburg area were operating on a six-day week, the appellant was "unavailable for work," and thus ineligible for benefits, when personal considerations [420] prevented her from accepting employment on a fulltime basis in the industry and locality in which she had worked. The fact that these personal considerations sprang from her religious convictions was wholly without relevance to the state court's application of the law. Thus in no proper sense can it be said that the

State discriminated against the appellant on the basis of her religious beliefs or that she was denied benefits because she was a Seventh-Day Adventist. She was denied benefits just as any other claimant would be denied benefits who was not "available for work" for personal reasons.

With this background, this Court's decision comes into clearer focus. What the Court is holding is that if the State chooses to condition unemployment compensation on the applicant's availability for work, it is constitutionally compelled to carve out an exception—and to provide benefits—for those whose unavailability is due to their religious convictions. Such a holding has particular significance in two respects.

[421] First, despite the Court's protestations to the contrary, the decision necessarily overrules *Braunfeld v. Brown*, which held that it did not offend the "Free Exercise" Clause of the Constitution for a State to forbid a Sabbatarian to do business on Sunday. The secular purpose of the statute before us today is even clearer than that involved in *Braunfeld*. And just as in *Braunfeld*—where exceptions to the Sunday closing laws for Sabbatarians would have been inconsistent with the purpose to achieve a uniform day of rest and would have required case-by-case inquiry into religious beliefs—so here, an exception to the rules of eligibility based on religious convictions would necessitate judicial examination of those convictions and would be at odds with the limited purpose of the statute to smooth out the economy during periods of industrial instability. Finally, the indirect financial burden of the present law is far less than that involved in *Braunfeld*. Forcing a store owner to close his business on Sunday may well have the effect of depriving him of a satisfactory livelihood if his religious convictions require him to close on Saturday as well. Here we are dealing only with temporary benefits, amounting to a fraction of regular weekly wages and running for not more than 22 weeks. Clearly, any difference between this case and *Braunfeld* cut against the present appellant.

[422] Second, the implications of the present decision are far more troublesome than its apparently narrow dimensions would indicate at first glance. The meaning of today's holding, as already noted, is that the State must furnish unemployment benefits to one who is unavailable for work if the unavailability stems from the exercise of religious convictions. The State, in other words, must single out for financial assistance those whose behavior is religiously motivated, even though it denies such assistance to others whose identical behavior (in this case, inability to work on Saturdays) is not religiously motivated.

It has been suggested that such singling out of religious conduct for special treatment may violate the constitutional limitations on state action. My own view, however, is that at least under the circumstances of this case it would be a permissible accommodation of religion for the State, if it chose to do so, to create an exception to its eligibility requirements for persons like the appellant. The constitutional obligation of "neutrality," see *School District of Abington Township v. Schempp*, p. 222, is not so narrow a channel that the slightest deviation from an absolutely straight course leads to condemnation. There are too many instances in which no such course can be charted, too many areas in which the pervasive activities of the State justify some special provision for religion to prevent it from being submerged by an all-embracing secularism. The State violates its obligation of neutrality [423] when, for example, it mandates a daily religious exercise in its public schools, with all the attendant pressures on the school children that such an exercise entails. See *Engel v. Vitale; School District of Abington Township v. Schempp*. But there is, I believe, enough flexibility in the Constitution to permit a legislative judgment accommodating an unemployment compensation law to the exercise of religious beliefs such as appellant's.

For very much the same reasons, however, I cannot subscribe to the conclusion that the State is constitutionally compelled to carve out an exception to its general rule of eligibility in the present case. Those situations in which the Constitution may require special treatment on account of religion are, in my view, few and far between, and this view is amply supported by the course of constitutional litigation in this area. Such compulsion in the present case is particularly inappropriate in light of the indirect, remote, and insubstantial effect of the decision below on the exercise of appellant's religion and in light of the direct financial assistance to religion that today's decision requires.

For these reasons I respectfully dissent from the opinion and judgment of the Court.

United States v. Seeger*

380 U.S. 163 (1965)

Vote: 9—*Warren, Black, Douglas, Clark, Harlan, Brennan, Stewart, White, Goldberg*
  0

Opinion announcing the opinion of the Court: Clark
Concurring opinion: Douglas

This case, which was not decided under the First Amendment's Free Exercise Clause, involved the grounds on which one could receive conscientious objector status from military service under then existing federal law.

In his claim for conscientious objector status, Daniel Seeger declared that he was opposed to participation in war in any form by reason of his "religious" belief, but that he preferred to leave the question as to his belief in a Supreme Being open, "rather than answer 'yes' or 'no.'" He testified that his "skepticism or disbelief in the existence of God" did "not necessarily mean lack of faith in anything whatsoever" and that his was a "belief in and devotion to goodness and virtue for their own sakes, and a religious faith in a purely ethical creed." He cited Plato, Aristotle, and Spinoza for support of his ethical belief in intellectual and moral integrity "without belief in God, except in the remotest sense."

A local examining board found Seeger's beliefs to be sincere, honest, made in good faith, and based upon individual training and belief that included research in religious and cultural fields. His claim for conscientious objector status, however, was denied because it was not based upon a "belief in a relation to a Supreme Being" as required by § 6 (j) of the Universal Military Training and Service Act.

The origins of the Universal Military Training and Service Act can be traced to the Draft Act of 1917. That statute allowed conscientious objectors to perform noncombatant service in capacities designated by the president of the United States. Conscientious objector status was limited, however, to those affiliated with a "well-recognized religious sect or organization [then] organized and existing and whose existing creed or principles [forbade] its members to participate in war in any form." In the 1940 Selective Training and Service Act, Congress broadened the exemption by making it unnecessary for conscientious objectors to belong to a pacifist religious sect if the claimant's

---

*Together with No. 51, *United States v. Jakobson*, on certiorari to the same court, and No. 29, *Peter v. United States*, on certiorari to the U.S. Court of Appeals for the Ninth Circuit.

own opposition to war was based on "religious training and belief." In 1948, Congress sought to define the meaning of "religious training and belief." Section 6 (j) of the Universal Military Training and Service Act specified that "religious training and belief . . . means an individual's belief in a relation to a Supreme Being involving duties superior to those arising from any human relation, but does not include essentially political, sociological, or philosophical views or a merely personal moral code."

MR. JUSTICE CLARK delivered the opinion of the Court.

[164] These cases involve claims of conscientious objectors under § 6 (j) of the Universal Military Training and Service Act, which exempts from combatant training and service in the armed forces of the United States those persons who by [165] reason of their religious training and belief are conscientiously opposed to participation in war in any form. . . .

We have concluded that Congress, in using the expression "Supreme Being" rather than the designation "God," was merely clarifying the meaning of religious training and belief so as to embrace all religions and to exclude essentially political, sociological, or philosophical views. We believe that under this construction, the test of belief [166] "in a relation to a Supreme Being" is whether a given belief that is sincere and meaningful occupies a place in the life of its possessor parallel to that filled by the orthodox belief in God of one who clearly qualifies for the exemption. Where such beliefs have parallel positions in the lives of their respective holders we cannot say that one is "in a relation to a Supreme Being" and the other is not. We have concluded that the beliefs of the objectors in these cases meet these criteria. . . .

[173] INTERPRETATION OF § 6 (j).

1. The crux of the problem lies in the phrase "religious training and belief" which Congress has defined as "belief in a relation to a Supreme Being involving duties superior to those arising from any human relation." In assigning meaning to this statutory language we may narrow the inquiry by noting briefly those scruples expressly excepted from the definition. The section excludes those persons who, disavowing religious belief, decide on the basis of essentially political, sociological or economic considerations that war is wrong and that they will have no part of it. These judgments have historically been reserved for the Government, and in matters which can be said to fall within these areas the conviction of the individual has never been permitted to override that of the state. The statute further excludes those whose opposition to war stems from a "merely personal moral code," a phrase to which we shall have occasion to turn later in discussing the application of § 6 (j) to these cases. We also pause to take note of what is not involved in this litigation. No party claims to be an atheist or attacks the statute on this ground. The question is not, therefore, one between theistic and atheistic beliefs. We do not deal with [174] or intimate any decision on that situation in these cases. Nor do the parties claim the monotheistic belief that there is but one God; what they claim (with the possible exception of Seeger, who bases his position here not on factual but on purely constitutional grounds) is that they adhere to theism, which is the "Belief in the existence of a god or gods; . . . Belief in superhuman powers or spiritual agencies in one or many gods," as opposed to atheism. Our question, therefore, is the narrow one: Does the term "Supreme Being" as used in § 6 (j)

mean the orthodox God or the broader concept of a power or being, or a faith, "to which all else is subordinate or upon which all else is ultimately dependent"? *Webster's New International Dictionary* (Second Edition). In considering this question we resolve it solely in relation to the language of § 6 (j) and not otherwise.

2. Few would quarrel, we think, with the proposition that in no field of human endeavor has the tool of language proved so inadequate in the communication of ideas as it has in dealing with the fundamental questions of man's predicament in life, in death or in final judgment and retribution. This fact makes the task of discerning the intent of Congress in using the phrase "Supreme Being" a complex one. Nor is it made the easier by the richness and variety of spiritual life in our country. Over 250 sects inhabit our land. . . .

[175] In spite of the elusive nature of the inquiry, we are not without certain guidelines. In amending the 1940 Act, Congress adopted almost intact the language of Chief Justice Hughes in *United States v. Macintosh*:

> "The essence of religion is belief in a relation to *God* involving duties superior to those arising from any human relation." At 633–634. (Emphasis supplied.)

By comparing the statutory definition with those words, however, it becomes readily apparent that the Congress deliberately broadened them by substituting the phrase "Supreme Being" for the appellation "God." And in so doing it is also significant that Congress did not elaborate on the form or nature of this higher authority which it chose to designate as "Supreme Being." By so refraining it must have had in mind the admonitions of the Chief [176] Justice when he said in the same opinion that even the word "God" had myriad meanings for men of faith:

> "[P]utting aside dogmas with their particular conceptions of deity, freedom of conscience itself implies respect for an innate conviction of paramount duty. The battle for religious liberty has been fought and won with respect to religious beliefs and practices, which are not in conflict with good order, upon the very ground of the supremacy of conscience within its proper field." At 634.

Moreover, the Senate Report on the bill specifically states that § 6 (j) was intended to re-enact "substantially the same provisions as were found" in the 1940 Act. That statute, of course, refers to "religious training and belief" without more. Admittedly, all of the parties here purport to base their objection on religious belief. It appears, therefore, that we need only look to this clear statement of congressional intent as set out in the report. Under the 1940 Act it was necessary only to have a conviction based upon religious training and belief; we believe that is all that is required here. Within that phrase would come all sincere religious beliefs which are based upon a power or being, or upon a faith, to which all else is subordinate or upon which all else is ultimately dependent. The test might be stated in these words: A sincere and meaningful belief which occupies in the life of its possessor a place parallel to that filled by the God of those admittedly qualifying for the exemption comes within the statutory definition. This construction avoids imputing to Congress an intent to classify different religious beliefs, exempting some and excluding others, and is in accord with the well-established congressional policy of equal treatment for those whose opposition to service is grounded in their religious tenets. . . .

[183] 5. We recognize the difficulties that have always faced the trier of fact in these cases. We hope that the test that we lay down proves less onerous. The examiner is

furnished [184] a standard that permits consideration of criteria with which he has had considerable experience. While the applicant's words may differ, the test is simple of application. It is essentially an objective one, namely, does the claimed belief occupy the same place in the life of the objector as an orthodox belief in God holds in the life of one clearly qualified for exemption?

Moreover, it must be remembered that in resolving these exemption problems one deals with the beliefs of different individuals who will articulate them in a multitude of ways. In such an intensely personal area, of course, the claim of the registrant that his belief is an essential part of a religious faith must be given great weight. . . .

The validity of what he believes cannot be questioned. Some theologians, and indeed some examiners, might be tempted to question the existence of the registrant's "Supreme Being" or the truth of his concepts. But these are inquiries foreclosed to Government. As MR. JUSTICE DOUGLAS stated in *United States v. Ballard*, 322 U.S. 78, 86 (1944): "Men may believe what they cannot prove. They may not be put to the proof of their religious doctrines or beliefs. Religious experiences which are as real as life to some may be incomprehensible to others." Local [185] boards and courts in this sense are not free to reject beliefs because they consider them "incomprehensible." Their task is to decide whether the beliefs professed by a registrant are sincerely held and whether they are, in his own scheme of things, religious.

But we hasten to emphasize that while the "truth" of a belief is not open to question, there remains the significant question whether it is "truly held." This is the threshold question of sincerity which must be resolved in every case. It is, of course, a question of fact—a prime consideration to the validity of every claim for exemption as a conscientious objector. The Act provides a comprehensive scheme for assisting the Appeal Boards in making this determination, placing at their service the facilities of the Department of Justice, including the Federal Bureau of Investigation and hearing officers. . . .

APPLICATION OF § 6 (j) TO THE INSTANT CASES.

As we noted earlier, the statutory definition excepts those registrants whose beliefs are based on a "merely personal moral code." The records in these cases, however, [186] show that at no time did any one of the applicants suggest that his objection was based on a "merely personal moral code." Indeed at the outset each of them claimed in his application that his objection was based on a religious belief. We have construed the statutory definition broadly and it follows that any exception to it must be interpreted narrowly. The use by Congress of the words "merely personal" seems to us to restrict the exception to a moral code which is not only personal but which is the sole basis for the registrant's belief and is in no way related to a Supreme Being. It follows, therefore, that if the claimed religious beliefs of the respective registrants in these cases meet the test that we lay down then their objections cannot be based on a "merely personal" moral code.

In *Seeger*, No. 50, the Court of Appeals failed to find sufficient "externally compelled beliefs." However, it did find that "it would seem impossible to say with assurance that [Seeger] is not bowing to 'external commands' in virtually the same sense as is the objector who defers to the will of a supernatural power." 326 F.2d, at 853. It found little distinction between Jakobson's devotion to a mystical force of "Godness" and Seeger's compulsion to "goodness." Of course, as we have said, the statute does not distinguish between externally and internally derived beliefs. Such a determination would, as the Court of Appeals observed, prove impossible as a practical matter, and we have found that Congress intended no such distinction.

The Court of Appeals also found that there was no question of the applicant's sincerity. He was a product of a devout Roman Catholic home; he was a close student of Quaker beliefs from which he said "much of [his] thought is derived"; he approved of their opposition to war in any form; he devoted his spare hours to the American [187] Friends Service Committee and was assigned to hospital duty.

In summary, Seeger professed "religious belief" and "religious faith." He did not disavow any belief "in a relation to a Supreme Being"; indeed he stated that "the cosmic order does, perhaps, suggest a creative intelligence." He decried the tremendous "spiritual" price man must pay for his willingness to destroy human life. In light of his beliefs and the unquestioned sincerity with which he held them, we think the Board, had it applied the test we propose today, would have granted him the exemption. We think it clear that the beliefs which prompted his objection occupy the same place in his life as the belief in a traditional deity holds in the lives of his friends, the Quakers. We are reminded once more of Dr. Tillich's thoughts:

> "And if that word [God] has not much meaning for you, translate it, and speak of the depths of your life, of the source of your being, of your ultimate concern, *of what you take seriously without any reservation.* Perhaps, in order to do so, you must forget everything traditional that you have learned about God. . . ." Tillich, *The Shaking of the Foundations* 57 (1948). (Emphasis supplied.)

It may be that Seeger did not clearly demonstrate what his beliefs were with regard to the usual understanding of the term "Supreme Being." But as we have said, Congress did not intend that to be the test. . . .

Board of Education v. Allen

392 U.S. 236 (1968)

Vote: 6—Warren, Harlan, Brennan, Stewart, White, Marshall
    3—Black, Douglas, Fortas

Opinion announcing the opinion of the Court: White
Concurring opinion: Harlan
Dissenting opinions: Black, Douglas, Fortas

In 1965, the New York legislature amended state law to require local public school authorities to lend textbooks free of charge to all students in grades 7–12, including students in private religious schools. The state legislature found the "public welfare and safety require that the state and local communities give assistance to educational programs which are important to our national defense and the general welfare of the state."

Local school boards were required to purchase textbooks and lend them without charge "to all children residing in such district who are enrolled in grades seven to twelve of a public or private school which complies with the compulsory education law." The loaned books were to be "text-books which are designated for use in any public, elementary or secondary schools of the state or are approved by any boards of education" and which—according to a 1966 amendment—"a pupil is required to use as a text for a semester or more in a particular class in the school he legally attends."

MR. JUSTICE WHITE delivered the opinion of the Court.

[238] A law of the State of New York requires local public school authorities to lend textbooks free of charge to all students in grades seven through 12; students attending private schools are included. This case presents the question whether this statute is a "law respecting an establishment of religion, or prohibiting the free exercise thereof," and so in conflict with the First and Fourteenth Amendments to the Constitution, because it authorizes the loan of textbooks to students attending parochial schools. We hold that the law is not in violation of the Constitution. . . .

[241] *Everson v. Board of Education,* 330 U.S. 1 (1947), is the case decided by this Court that is most nearly in [242] point for today's problem. New Jersey reimbursed

parents for expenses incurred in busing their children to parochial schools. The Court stated that the Establishment Clause bars a State from passing "laws which aid one religion, aid all religions, or prefer one religion over another," and bars too any "tax in any amount, large or small . . . levied to support any religious activities or institutions, whatever they may be called, or whatever form they may adopt to teach or practice religion." 330 U.S., at 15–16. Nevertheless, said the Court, the Establishment Clause does not prevent a State from extending the benefits of state laws to all citizens without regard for their religious affiliation and does not prohibit "New Jersey from spending tax-raised funds to pay the bus fares of parochial school pupils as a part of a general program under which it pays the fares of pupils attending public and other schools." The statute was held to be valid even though one of its results was that "children are helped to get to church schools" and "some of the children might not be sent to the church schools if the parents were compelled to pay their children's bus fares out of their own pockets." 330 U.S., at 17. As with public provision of police and fire protection, sewage facilities, and streets and sidewalks, payment of bus fares was of some value to the religious school, but was nevertheless not such support of a religious institution as to be a prohibited establishment of religion within the meaning of the First Amendment.

Everson and later cases have shown that the line between state neutrality to religion and state support of religion is not easy to locate. "The constitutional standard is the separation of Church and State. The problem, like many problems in constitutional law, is one of degree." *Zorach v. Clauson,* 343 U.S. 306, 314 (1952). Based [243] on *Everson, Zorach, McGowan,* and other cases, *Abington School District v. Schempp,* 374 U.S. 203 (1963), fashioned a test subscribed to by eight Justices for distinguishing between forbidden involvements of the State with religion and those contacts which the Establishment Clause permits:

> "The test may be stated as follows: what are the purpose and the primary effect of the enactment? If either is the advancement or inhibition of religion then the enactment exceeds the scope of legislative power as circumscribed by the Constitution. That is to say that to withstand the strictures of the Establishment Clause there must be a secular legislative purpose and a primary effect that neither advances nor inhibits religion. *Everson v. Board of Education. . . ."* 374 U.S., at 222.

This test is not easy to apply, but the citation of *Everson* by the *Schempp* Court to support its general standard made clear how the *Schempp* rule would be applied to the facts of *Everson.* The statute upheld in *Everson* would be considered a law having "a secular legislative purpose and a primary effect that neither advances nor inhibits religion." We reach the same result with respect to the New York law requiring school books to be loaned free of charge to all students in specified grades. The express purpose of § 701 was stated by the New York Legislature to be furtherance of the educational opportunities available to the young. Appellants have shown us nothing about the necessary effects of the statute that is contrary to its stated purpose. The law merely makes available to all children the benefits of a general program to lend school books free of charge. Books are furnished at the request of the pupil and ownership remains, at least technically, in the State. Thus no funds or books are furnished [244] to parochial schools, and the financial benefit is to parents and children, not to schools. Perhaps free books make it more likely that some children choose to attend a sectarian school, but that was true of the state-paid bus fares in *Everson* and does not alone demonstrate an unconstitutional degree of support for a religious institution.

Of course books are different from buses. Most bus rides have no inherent religious significance, while religious books are common. However, the language of § 701 does not authorize the loan of religious books, and the State claims no right to distribute religious literature. Although the books loaned are those required by the parochial school for use in specific courses, each book [245] loaned must be approved by the public school authorities; only secular books may receive approval. The law was construed by the Court of Appeals of New York as "merely making available secular textbooks at the request of the individual student," *supra*, and the record contains no suggestion that religious books have been loaned. Absent evidence, we cannot assume that school authorities, who constantly face the same problem in selecting textbooks for use in the public schools, are unable to distinguish between secular and religious books or that they will not honestly discharge their duties under the law. In judging the validity of the statute on this record we must proceed on the assumption that books loaned to students are books that are not unsuitable for use in the public schools because of religious content.

The major reason offered by appellants for distinguishing free textbooks from free bus fares is that books, but not buses, are critical to the teaching process, and in a sectarian school that process is employed to teach religion. However this Court has long recognized that religious schools pursue two goals, religious instruction and secular education. . . .

[247] Underlying these cases, and underlying also the legislative judgments that have preceded the court decisions, has been a recognition that private education has played and is playing a significant and valuable role in raising national levels of knowledge, competence, and experience. Americans care about the quality of the secular education available to their children. They have considered high quality education to be an indispensable ingredient for achieving the kind of nation, and the kind of citizenry, that they have desired to create. Considering this attitude, the continued willingness to rely on private school systems, including parochial systems, strongly suggests [248] that a wide segment of informed opinion, legislative and otherwise, has found that those schools do an acceptable job of providing secular education to their students. This judgment is further evidence that parochial schools are performing, in addition to their sectarian function, the task of secular education.

Against this background of judgment and experience, unchallenged in the meager record before us in this case, we cannot agree with appellants either that all teaching in a sectarian school is religious or that the processes of secular and religious training are so intertwined that secular textbooks furnished to students by the public are in fact instrumental in the teaching of religion. This case comes to us after summary judgment entered on the pleadings. Nothing in this record supports the proposition that all textbooks, whether they deal with mathematics, physics, foreign languages, history, or literature, are used by the parochial schools to teach religion. No evidence has been offered about particular schools, particular courses, particular teachers, or particular books. We are unable to hold, based solely on judicial notice, that this statute results in unconstitutional involvement of the State with religious instruction or that § 701, for this or the other reasons urged, is a law respecting the establishment of religion within the meaning of the First Amendment. . . .

[250] MR. JUSTICE BLACK, dissenting.

The Court here affirms a judgment of the New York Court of Appeals which sustained the constitutionality of a New York law providing state tax-raised funds to supply school books for use by pupils in schools owned and operated by religious sects. I believe the New York law held valid is a flat, flagrant, open violation of the First and Fourteenth Amendments which together forbid Congress or state legislatures to enact any law "respecting an establishment of religion." For that reason I would reverse the New York Court of Appeals' judgment. This, I am confident, would be in keeping with the deliberate statement we made in *Everson v. Board of Education*, 330 U.S. 1, 15–16 (1947), and repeated in *McCollum v. Board of Education*, 333 U.S. 203, 210–211 (1948), that:

> "Neither a state nor the Federal Government can set up a church. Neither can pass laws which aid one religion, aid all religions, or prefer one religion over another. Neither can force nor influence a person to go to or to remain away from church against his will or force him to profess a belief or disbelief in any religion. No person can be punished for entertaining or professing religious beliefs or disbeliefs, for church attendance or non-attendance. No tax in any amount, large or small, can be levied to support any religious activities or institutions, whatever they may be called, or whatever form they may adopt to teach or practice religion. Neither a state nor the Federal Government can, openly or secretly, participate in the affairs of any religious [251] organizations or groups and vice versa. In the words of Jefferson, the clause against establishment of religion by law was intended to erect 'a wall of separation between church and State.'"

The *Everson* and *McCollum* cases plainly interpret the First and Fourteenth Amendments as protecting the taxpayers of a State from being compelled to pay taxes to their government to support the agencies of private religious organizations the taxpayers oppose. To authorize a State to tax its residents for such church purposes is to put the State squarely in the religious activities of certain religious groups that happen to be strong enough politically to write their own religious preferences and prejudices into the laws. This links state and churches together in controlling the lives and destinies of our citizenship—a citizenship composed of people of myriad religious faiths, some of them bitterly hostile to and completely intolerant of the others. It was to escape laws precisely like this that a large part of the Nation's early immigrants fled to this country. It was also to escape such laws and such consequences that the First Amendment was written in language strong and clear barring passage of any law "respecting an establishment of religion."

It is true, of course, that the New York law does not as yet formally adopt or establish a state religion. But it takes a great stride in that direction and coming events cast their shadows before them. The same powerful sectarian religious propagandists who have succeeded in securing passage of the present law to help religious schools carry on their sectarian religious purposes can and doubtless will continue their propaganda, looking toward complete domination and supremacy of their particular brand of religion. And it nearly always is [252] by insidious approaches that the citadels of liberty are most successfully attacked.

I know of no prior opinion of this Court upon which the majority here can rightfully rely to support its holding this New York law constitutional. In saying this, I am not unmindful of the fact that the New York Court of Appeals purported to follow *Everson v. Board of Education* in which this Court, in an opinion written by me, upheld a New Jersey law authorizing reimbursement to parents for the transportation of children attending sectarian schools. That law did not attempt to deny the benefit of its general terms to children of any faith going to any legally authorized school. Thus, it was treated in the same way as a general law paying the streetcar fare of all school children, or a law providing midday lunches for all children or all school children, or a law to provide police protection for children going to and from school, or general laws to provide police and fire protection for buildings, including, of course, churches and church school buildings as well as others.

As my Brother DOUGLAS so forcefully shows, in an argument with which I fully agree, upholding a State's power to pay bus or streetcar fares for school children cannot provide support for the validity of a state law using tax-raised funds to buy school books for a religious school. The First Amendment's bar to establishment of religion must preclude a State from using funds levied from all of its citizens to purchase books for use by sectarian schools, which, although "secular," realistically will in some way inevitably tend to propagate the religious views of the favored sect. Books are the most essential tool of education since they contain the resources of knowledge which the educational process is designed to exploit. In this sense it is not difficult [253] to distinguish books, which are the heart of any school, from bus fares, which provide a convenient and helpful general public transportation service. With respect to the former, state financial support actively and directly assists the teaching and propagation of sectarian religious viewpoints in clear conflict with the First Amendment's establishment bar; with respect to the latter, the State merely provides a general and nondiscriminatory transportation service in no way related to substantive religious views and beliefs.

This New York law, it may be said by some, makes but a small inroad and does not amount to complete state establishment of religion. But that is no excuse for upholding it. It requires no prophet to foresee that on the argument used to support this law others could be upheld providing for state or federal government funds to buy property on which to erect religious school buildings or to erect the buildings themselves, to pay the salaries of the religious school teachers, and finally to have the sectarian religious groups cease to rely on voluntary contributions of members of their sects while waiting for the Government to pick up all the bills for the religious schools. Arguments made in favor of this New York law point squarely in this direction, namely, that the fact that government has not heretofore aided religious schools with tax-raised funds amounts to a discrimination against those schools and against religion. And that there are already efforts to have government supply the money to erect buildings for sectarian religious schools is shown by a recent Act of Congress which apparently allows for precisely that. See Higher Education Facilities Act of 1963, 77 Stat. 363, 20 U.S.C. 701 *et seq.*

I still subscribe to the belief that tax-raised funds cannot constitutionally be used to support religious schools, buy their school books, erect their buildings, pay their [254] teachers, or pay any other of their maintenance expenses, even to the extent of one penny. The First Amendment's prohibition against governmental establishment of religion was written on the assumption that state aid to religion and religious schools generates discord, disharmony, hatred, and strife among our people, and that any government that supplies such aids is to that extent a tyranny. And I still believe that the only way to protect minority religious groups from majority groups in this country is to keep the wall of separation between church and state high and impregnable as the First and Fourteenth Amendments provide. The Court's affirmance here bodes nothing but evil to religious peace in this country.

MR. JUSTICE DOUGLAS, dissenting.

We have for review a statute which authorizes New York State to supply textbooks to students in parochial as well as in public schools. The New York Court of Appeals sustained the law on the grounds that it involves only "secular textbooks" and that that type of aid falls within *Everson v. Board of Education*, 330 U.S. 1, 1, where a divided Court upheld a state law which made bus service available to students in parochial schools as well as to students in public schools.

The statute on its face empowers each parochial school to determine for itself which textbooks will be eligible for loans to its students, for the Act provides that the [255] only text which the State may provide is "a book which a pupil is required to use as a text for a semester or more in a particular class in the school he legally attends." New York Education Law § 701, subd. 2. This initial and crucial selection is undoubtedly made by the parochial school's principal or its individual instructors, who are, in the case of Roman Catholic schools, normally priests or nuns.

The next step under the Act is an "individual request" for an eligible textbook (§ 701, subd. 3), but the State Education Department has ruled that a pupil may make his request to the local public board of education through a "private school official." Local boards have accordingly provided for those requests to be made by the individual or "by groups or classes." And forms for textbook requisitions to be filled out by the head of the private school are provided.

The role of the local public school board is to decide whether to veto the selection made by the parochial school. This is done by determining first whether the text has been or should be "approved" for use in public schools and second whether the text is "secular," "nonreligious," or "non-sectarian." The local boards apparently [256] have broad discretion in exercising this veto power.

Thus the statutory system provides that the parochial school will ask for the books that it wants. Can there be the slightest doubt that the head of the parochial school will select the book or books that best promote its sectarian creed?

If the board of education supinely submits by approving and supplying the sectarian or sectarian-oriented textbooks, the struggle to keep church and state separate has been lost. If the board resists, then the battle line between church and state will have been drawn and the contest will be on to keep the school board independent or to put it under church domination and control.

[257] Whatever may be said of *Everson*, there is nothing ideological about a bus. There is nothing ideological about a school lunch, or a public nurse, or a scholarship. The constitutionality of such public aid to students in parochial schools turns on considerations not present in this textbook case. The textbook goes to the very heart of education in a parochial school. It is the chief, although not solitary, instrumentality for propagating a particular religious creed or faith. How can we possibly approve such state aid to a religion? A parochial school textbook may contain many, many more seeds of creed and dogma than a prayer. Yet we struck down in *Engel v. Vitale*, 370 U.S. 421, an official New York prayer for its public schools, even though it was not plainly denominational. For we emphasized the violence done the Establishment Clause when the power was given religious-political groups "to write their own prayers into law." *Id.*, at 427. That risk is compounded here by giving parochial schools the initiative in selecting the textbooks they desire to be furnished at public expense. . . .

20

Epperson v. Arkansas

393 U.S. 97 (1968)

Vote: 9—Warren, Black, Douglas, Harlan, Brennan, Stewart, White, Fortas, Marshall
0

Opinion announcing the opinion of the Court: Fortas
Concurring opinions: Black, Harlan
Opinion concurring in the result: Stewart

A 1928 Arkansas law prohibited teachers in any state-supported school or university "to teach the theory or doctrine that mankind ascended or descended from a lower order of animals" or "to adopt or use in any such institution a textbook that teaches" this theory. Violation of the law was a misdemeanor and subjected the violator to dismissal from his or her position. No record existed of any prosecutions under the statute.

Litigation was commenced by Susan Epperson, an Arkansas public school biology teacher who was assigned to teach from a textbook that, she feared, violated the statute.

MR. JUSTICE FORTAS delivered the opinion of the Court.

I

. . . [99] The present case concerns the teaching of biology in a high school in Little Rock. According to the testimony, until the events here in litigation, the official textbook furnished for the high school biology course did not have a section on the Darwinian Theory. Then, for the academic year 1965–1966, the school administration, on recommendation of the teachers of biology in the school system, adopted and prescribed a textbook which contained a chapter setting forth "the theory about the origin . . . of man from a lower form of animal."

[100] Susan Epperson, a young woman who graduated from Arkansas' school system and then obtained her master's degree in zoology at the University of Illinois, was employed by the Little Rock school system in the fall of 1964 to teach 10th grade biology at Central High School. At the start of the next academic year, 1965, she was confronted by the new textbook (which one surmises from the record was not unwelcome to her). She faced at least a literal dilemma because she was supposed to use the new textbook

for classroom instruction and presumably to teach the statutorily condemned chapter; but to do so would be a criminal offense and subject her to dismissal. . . .

[101] Only Arkansas and Mississippi have such "anti-evolution" or "monkey" laws on their books. There is no record of any prosecutions in Arkansas [102] under its statute. It is possible that the statute is presently more of a curiosity than a vital fact of life in these States. Nevertheless, the present case was brought, the appeal as of right is properly here, and it is our duty to decide the issues presented.

II

At the outset, it is urged upon us that the challenged statute is vague and uncertain and therefore within the condemnation of the Due Process Clause of the Fourteenth Amendment. The contention that the Act is vague and uncertain is supported by language in the brief opinion of Arkansas' Supreme Court. That court, perhaps reflecting the discomfort which the statute's quixotic prohibition necessarily engenders in the modern mind, stated that it "expresses no opinion" as to whether the Act prohibits "explanation" of the theory of evolution or merely forbids "teaching that the theory is true." Regardless of this uncertainty, the court held that the statute is constitutional.

On the other hand, counsel for the State, in oral argument in this Court, candidly stated that, despite the State Supreme Court's equivocation, Arkansas would interpret the statute "to mean that to make a student aware of the theory . . . just to teach that there was [103] such a theory" would be grounds for dismissal and for prosecution under the statute; and he said "that the Supreme Court of Arkansas' opinion should be interpreted in that manner." He said: "If Mrs. Epperson would tell her students that 'Here is Darwin's theory, that man ascended or descended from a lower form of being,' then I think she would be under this statute liable for prosecution."

In any event, we do not rest our decision upon the asserted vagueness of the statute. On either interpretation of its language, Arkansas' statute cannot stand. It is of no moment whether the law is deemed to prohibit mention of Darwin's theory, or to forbid any or all of the infinite varieties of communication embraced within the term "teaching." Under either interpretation, the law must be stricken because of its conflict with the constitutional prohibition of state laws respecting an establishment of religion or prohibiting the free exercise thereof. The overriding fact is that Arkansas' law selects from the body of knowledge a particular segment which it proscribes for the sole reason that it is deemed to conflict with a particular religious doctrine; that is, with a particular interpretation of the Book of Genesis by a particular religious group.

III

The antecedents of today's decision are many and unmistakable. They are rooted in the foundation soil of our Nation. They are fundamental to freedom.

Government in our democracy, state and national, must be neutral in matters of religious theory, doctrine, [104] and practice. It may not be hostile to any religion or to the advocacy of no-religion; and it may not aid, foster, or promote one religion or religious theory against another or even against the militant opposite. The First Amendment mandates governmental neutrality between religion and religion, and between religion and nonreligion.

As early as 1872, this Court said: "The law knows no heresy, and is committed to the support of no dogma, the establishment of no sect." *Watson v. Jones*, 13 Wall. 679,

728. This has been the interpretation of the great First Amendment which this Court has applied in the many and subtle problems which the ferment of our national life has presented for decision within the Amendment's broad command. . . .

[106] There is and can be no doubt that the First Amendment does not permit the State to require that teaching and learning must be tailored to the principles or prohibitions of any religious sect or dogma. In *Everson v. Board of Education*, this Court, in upholding a state law to provide free bus service to school children, including those attending parochial schools, said: "Neither [a State nor the Federal Government] can pass laws which aid one religion, aid all religions, or prefer one religion over another." 330 U.S. 1, 15 (1947).

[107] The State's undoubted right to prescribe the curriculum for its public schools does not carry with it the right to prohibit, on pain of criminal penalty, the teaching of a scientific theory or doctrine where that prohibition is based upon reasons that violate the First Amendment. It is much too late to argue that the State may impose upon the teachers in its schools any conditions that it chooses, however restrictive they may be of constitutional guarantees.

In the present case, there can be no doubt that Arkansas has sought to prevent its teachers from discussing the theory of evolution because it is contrary to the belief of some that the Book of Genesis must be the exclusive source of doctrine as to the origin of man. No suggestion has been made that Arkansas' law may be justified by considerations of state policy other than the religious views of some of its citizens. It is clear [108] that fundamentalist sectarian conviction was and is the law's reason for existence. Its antecedent, Tennessee's "monkey law," candidly stated its purpose: to make it unlawful "to teach any theory that denies the story of the Divine Creation of man as taught in the Bible, and to teach instead that man has descended from a [109] lower order of animals." Perhaps the sensational publicity attendant upon the Scopes trial induced Arkansas to adopt less explicit language. It eliminated Tennessee's reference to "the story of the Divine Creation of man" as taught in the Bible, but there is no doubt that the motivation for the law was the same: to suppress the teaching of a theory which, it was thought, "denied" the divine creation of man.

Arkansas' law cannot be defended as an act of religious neutrality. Arkansas did not seek to excise from the curricula of its schools and universities all discussion of the origin of man. The law's effort was confined to an attempt to blot out a particular theory because of its supposed conflict with the Biblical account, literally read. Plainly, the law is contrary to the mandate of the First, and in violation of the Fourteenth, Amendment to the Constitution. . . .

MR. JUSTICE BLACK, concurring.

. . . [112] The Court, not content to strike down this Arkansas Act on the unchallengeable ground of its plain vagueness, chooses rather to invalidate it as a violation of the Establishment of Religion Clause of the First Amendment. I would not decide this case on such a sweeping ground for the following reasons, among others.

1. In the first place I find it difficult to agree with the Court's statement that "there can be no doubt that Arkansas has sought to prevent its teachers from discussing the theory of evolution because it is contrary to the belief of some that the Book of Genesis must be the exclusive source of doctrine as to the origin of man." It may

be instead that the people's motive was merely that it would be best to remove this controversial [113] subject from its schools; there is no reason I can imagine why a State is without power to withdraw from its curriculum any subject deemed too emotional and controversial for its public schools. And this Court has consistently held that it is not for us to invalidate a statute because of our views that the "motives" behind its passage were improper; it is simply too difficult to determine what those motives were.

2. A second question that arises for me is whether this Court's decision forbidding a State to exclude the subject of evolution from its schools infringes the religious freedom of those who consider evolution an anti-religious doctrine. If the theory is considered anti-religious, as the Court indicates, how can the State be bound by the Federal Constitution to permit its teachers to advocate such an "anti-religious" doctrine to schoolchildren? The very cases cited by the Court as supporting its conclusion hold that the State must be neutral, not favoring one religious or anti-religious view over another. The Darwinian theory is said to challenge the Bible's story of creation; so too have some of those who believe in the Bible, along with many others, challenged the Darwinian theory. Since there is no indication that the literal Biblical doctrine of the origin of man is included in the curriculum of Arkansas schools, does not the removal of the subject of evolution leave the State in a neutral position toward these supposedly competing religious and anti-religious doctrines? Unless this Court is prepared simply to write off as pure nonsense the views of those who consider evolution an anti-religious doctrine, then this issue presents problems under the Establishment Clause far more troublesome than are discussed in the Court's opinion.

3. I am also not ready to hold that a person hired to teach school children takes with him into the classroom a constitutional right to teach sociological, economic, [114] political, or religious subjects that the school's managers do not want discussed. This Court has said that the rights of free speech "while fundamental in our democratic society, still do not mean that everyone with opinions or beliefs to express may address a group at any public place and at any time." *Cox v. Louisiana*, 379 U.S. 536, 554. I question whether it is absolutely certain, as the Court's opinion indicates, that "academic freedom" permits a teacher to breach his contractual agreement to teach only the subjects designated by the school authorities who hired him.

Certainly the Darwinian theory, precisely like the Genesis story of the creation of man, is not above challenge. In fact the Darwinian theory has not merely been criticized by religionists but by scientists, and perhaps no scientist would be willing to take an oath and swear that everything announced in the Darwinian theory is unquestionably true. The Court, it seems to me, makes a serious mistake in bypassing the plain, unconstitutional vagueness of this statute in order to reach out and decide this troublesome, to me, First Amendment question. However wise this Court may be or may become hereafter, it is doubtful that, sitting in Washington, it can successfully supervise and censor the curriculum of every public school in every hamlet and city in the United States. I doubt that our wisdom is so nearly infallible.

I would either strike down the Arkansas Act as too vague to enforce, or remand to the State Supreme Court for clarification of its holding and opinion.

[115] MR. JUSTICE STEWART, concurring in the result.

The States are most assuredly free "to choose their own curriculums for their own schools." A State is entirely [116] free, for example, to decide that the only foreign language to be taught in its public school system shall be Spanish. But would a State be constitutionally free to punish a teacher for letting his students know that other languages are also spoken in the world? I think not.

It is one thing for a State to determine that "the subject of higher mathematics, or astronomy, or biology" shall or shall not be included in its public school curriculum. It is quite another thing for a State to make it a criminal offense for a public school teacher so much as to mention the very existence of an entire system of respected human thought. That kind of criminal law, I think, would clearly impinge upon the guarantees of free communication contained in the First Amendment, and made applicable to the States by the Fourteenth.

The Arkansas Supreme Court has said that the statute before us may or may not be just such a law. The result, as MR. JUSTICE BLACK points out, is that "a teacher cannot know whether he is forbidden to mention Darwin's theory at all." Since I believe that no State could constitutionally forbid a teacher "to mention Darwin's theory at all," and since Arkansas may, or may not, have done just that, I conclude that the statute before us is so vague as to be invalid under the Fourteenth Amendment.

21

Walz v. Tax Commission of the City of New York

397 U.S. 664 (1970)

Vote: 7—Burger, Black, Harlan, Brennan, Stewart, White, Marshall
     1—Douglas

Opinion announcing the opinion of the Court: Burger
Concurring opinions: Brennan, Harlan
Dissenting opinion: Douglas

Real property tax law in the state of New York included the following exemption:

> *Real property owned by a corporation or association organized exclusively for the moral or mental improvement of men and women, or for religious, bible, tract, charitable, benevolent, missionary, hospital, infirmary, educational, public playground, scientific, literary, bar association, medical society, library, patriotic, historical or cemetery purposes . . . and used exclusively for carrying out thereupon one or more of such purposes . . . shall be exempt from taxation as provided in this section.*

A property owner residing in Richmond County, New York, sought an injunction to prevent the New York City Tax Commission from granting property tax exemptions to religious organizations for religious properties used solely for religious worship.

MR. CHIEF JUSTICE BURGER delivered the opinion of the Court.

. . . [667] I

Prior opinions of this Court have discussed the development and historical background of the First Amendment in detail. It would therefore serve no useful purpose to review in detail the background of the Establishment and Free [668] Exercise Clauses of the First Amendment or to restate what the Court's opinions have reflected over the years.

It is sufficient to note that for the men who wrote the Religion Clauses of the First Amendment the "establishment" of a religion connoted sponsorship, financial support, and active involvement of the sovereign in religious activity. In England, and in some Colonies at the time of the separation in 1776, the Church of England was sponsored and supported by the Crown as a state, or established, church; in other countries "establishment" meant sponsorship by the sovereign of the Lutheran or Catholic Church. The exclusivity of established churches in the 17th and 18th centuries, of course, was often carried to prohibition of other forms of worship.

The Establishment and Free Exercise Clauses of the First Amendment are not the most precisely drawn portions of the Constitution. The sweep of the absolute prohibitions in the Religion Clauses may have been calculated; but the purpose was to state an objective, not to write a statute. In attempting to articulate the scope of the two Religion Clauses, the Court's opinions reflect the limitations inherent in formulating general principles on a case-by-case basis. The considerable internal inconsistency in the opinions of the Court derives from what, in retrospect, may have been too sweeping utterances on aspects of these clauses that seemed clear in relation to the particular cases but have limited meaning as general principles.

The Court has struggled to find a neutral course between the two Religion Clauses, both of which are cast in absolute terms, and either of which, if expanded to a [669] logical extreme, would tend to clash with the other. For example, in *Zorach v. Clauson*, 343 U.S. 306 (1952), MR. JUSTICE DOUGLAS, writing for the Court, noted:

> "The First Amendment, however, does not say that in every and all respects there shall be a separation of Church and State." *Id.*, at 312.
>
> "We sponsor an attitude on the part of government that shows no partiality to any one group and that lets each flourish according to the zeal of its adherents and the appeal of its dogma." *Id.*, at 313.

MR. JUSTICE HARLAN expressed something of this in his dissent in *Sherbert v. Verner*, 374 U.S. 398 (1963), saying that the constitutional neutrality imposed on us

> "is not so narrow a channel that the slightest deviation from an absolutely straight course leads to condemnation." *Id.*, at 422.

The course of constitutional neutrality in this area cannot be an absolutely straight line; rigidity could well defeat the basic purpose of these provisions, which is to insure that no religion be sponsored or favored, none commanded, and none inhibited. The general principle deducible from the First Amendment and all that has been said by the Court is this: that we will not tolerate either governmentally established religion or governmental interference with religion. Short of those expressly proscribed governmental acts there is room for play in the joints productive of a benevolent neutrality which will permit religious exercise to exist without sponsorship and without interference.

Each value judgment under the Religion Clauses must therefore turn on whether particular acts in question are intended to establish or interfere with religious beliefs and practices or have the effect of doing so. Adherence to the policy of neutrality that derives from an accommodation of the Establishment and Free Exercise Clauses [670] has prevented the kind of involvement that would tip the balance toward government control of churches or governmental restraint on religious practice.

Adherents of particular faiths and individual churches frequently take strong positions on public issues including, as this case reveals in the several briefs *amici*, vigorous advocacy of legal or constitutional positions. Of course, churches as much as secular bodies and private citizens have that right. No perfect or absolute separation is really possible; the very existence of the Religion Clauses is an involvement of sorts—one that seeks to mark boundaries to avoid excessive entanglement.

The hazards of placing too much weight on a few words or phrases of the Court is abundantly illustrated within the pages of the Court's opinion in *Everson*. MR. JUSTICE BLACK, writing for the Court's majority, said the First Amendment

"means at least this: Neither a state nor the Federal Government can . . . pass laws which aid one religion, aid all religions, or prefer one religion over another." 330 U.S., at 15.

Yet he had no difficulty in holding that:

"Measured by these standards, we cannot say that the First Amendment prohibits New Jersey from spending tax-raised funds to pay the bus fares of parochial school pupils as a part of a general program under which it pays the fares of pupils attending public and other schools. *It is undoubtedly true that children are helped to get to church schools. There is even a possibility that some of the children might not be sent to the church schools if the parents were compelled to pay their children's bus fares out of their own pockets. . . .*" *Id.*, at 17. (Emphasis added.)

[671] The Court did not regard such "aid" to schools teaching a particular religious faith as any more a violation of the Establishment Clause than providing "state-paid policemen, detailed to protect children . . . [at the schools] from the very real hazards of traffic. . . ." *Ibid.*

Mr. Justice Jackson, in perplexed dissent in *Everson*, noted that

"the undertones of the opinion, advocating complete and uncompromising separation . . . seem utterly discordant with its conclusion. . . ." *Id.*, at 19.

Perhaps so. One can sympathize with Mr. Justice Jackson's logical analysis but agree with the Court's eminently sensible and realistic application of the language of the Establishment Clause. In *Everson* the Court declined to construe the Religion Clauses with a literalness that would undermine the ultimate constitutional objective as illuminated by history. Surely, bus transportation and police protection to pupils who receive religious instruction "aid" that particular religion to maintain schools that plainly tend to assure future adherents to a particular faith by having control of their total education at an early age. No religious body that maintains schools would deny this as an affirmative if not dominant policy of church schools. But if as in *Everson* buses can be provided to carry and policemen to protect church school pupils, we fail to see how a broader range of police and fire protection given equally to all churches, along with nonprofit hospitals, art galleries, and libraries receiving the same tax exemption, is different for purposes of the Religion Clauses.

Similarly, making textbooks available to pupils in parochial schools in common with public schools was surely an "aid" to the sponsoring churches because it relieved those churches of an enormous aggregate cost [672] for those books. Supplying of costly teaching materials was not seen either as manifesting a legislative purpose to aid or as having a primary effect of aid contravening the First Amendment. *Board of Education v. Allen*, 392 U.S. 236 (1968). In so holding the Court was heeding both its own prior decisions and our religious tradition. MR. JUSTICE DOUGLAS, in *Zorach v. Clauson*, after recalling that we "are a religious people whose institutions presuppose a Supreme Being," went on to say:

"We make room for as wide a variety of beliefs and creeds as the spiritual needs of man deem necessary. . . . *When the state encourages religious instruction . . . it follows the best of our traditions.* For it then respects the religious nature of our people and accommodates the public service to their spiritual needs." 343 U.S., at 313–314. (Emphasis added.)

With all the risks inherent in programs that bring about administrative relationships between public education bodies and church-sponsored schools, we have been able to chart a course that preserved the autonomy and freedom of religious bodies while avoiding any semblance of established religion. This is a "tight rope" and one we have successfully traversed.

II

The legislative purpose of the property tax exemption is neither the advancement nor the inhibition of religion; it is neither sponsorship nor hostility. New York, in common with the other States, has determined that certain entities that exist in a harmonious relationship to the community at large, and that foster its "moral or mental improvement," should not be inhibited in their activities by property taxation or the hazard of loss of those properties for nonpayment of taxes. It [673] has not singled out one particular church or religious group or even churches as such; rather, it has granted exemption to all houses of religious worship within a broad class of property owned by nonprofit, quasi-public corporations which include hospitals, libraries, playgrounds, scientific, professional, historical, and patriotic groups. The State has an affirmative policy that considers these groups as beneficial and stabilizing influences in community life and finds this classification useful, desirable, and in the public interest. Qualification for tax exemption is not perpetual or immutable; some tax-exempt groups lose that status when their activities take them outside the classification and new entities can come into being and qualify for exemption.

Governments have not always been tolerant of religious activity, and hostility toward religion has taken many shapes and forms—economic, political, and sometimes harshly oppressive. Grants of exemption historically reflect the concern of authors of constitutions and statutes as to the latent dangers inherent in the imposition of property taxes; exemption constitutes a reasonable and balanced attempt to guard against those dangers. The limits of permissible state accommodation to religion are by no means coextensive with the noninterference mandated by the Free Exercise Clause. To equate the two would be to deny a national heritage with roots in the Revolution itself. We cannot read New York's statute as attempting to establish religion; it is simply sparing the exercise of religion from the burden of property taxation levied on private profit institutions.

[674] We find it unnecessary to justify the tax exemption on the social welfare services or "good works" that some churches perform for parishioners and others—family counseling, aid to the elderly and the infirm, and to children. Churches vary substantially in the scope of such services; programs expand or contract according to resources and need. As public-sponsored programs enlarge, private aid from the church sector may diminish. The extent of social services may vary, depending on whether the church serves an urban or rural, a rich or poor constituency. To give emphasis to so variable an aspect of the work of religious bodies would introduce an element of governmental evaluation and standards as to the worth of particular social welfare programs, thus producing a kind of continuing day-to-day relationship which the policy of neutrality seeks to minimize. Hence, the use of a social welfare yardstick as a significant element to qualify for tax exemption could conceivably give rise to confrontations that could escalate to constitutional dimensions.

Determining that the legislative purpose of tax exemption is not aimed at establishing, sponsoring, or supporting religion does not end the inquiry, however. We must also be sure that the end result—the effect—is not an excessive government entanglement with religion. The test is inescapably one of degree. Either course, taxation of churches or exemption, occasions some degree of involvement with religion. Elimination of exemption would tend to expand the involvement of government by giving rise to tax valuation of church property, tax liens, tax foreclosures, and the direct confrontations and conflicts that follow in the train of those legal processes. . . .

[677] It is significant that Congress, from its earliest days, has viewed the Religion Clauses of the Constitution as authorizing statutory real estate tax exemption to religious bodies. In 1802 the 7th Congress enacted a taxing statute for the County of Alexandria, adopting the 1800 Virginia statutory pattern which provided tax exemptions for churches. As early as 1813 the 12th Congress refunded import duties paid by religious societies on the importation of religious articles. During this period the City Council of Washington, D. C., acting under congressional authority enacted a series of real and personal property assessments that uniformly exempted church property. In 1870 the Congress specifically exempted all churches in the District of Columbia [678] and appurtenant grounds and property "from any and all taxes or assessments, national, municipal, or county." Act of June 17, 1870, 16 Stat. 153.

It is obviously correct that no one acquires a vested or protected right in violation of the Constitution by long use, even when that span of time covers our entire national existence and indeed predates it. Yet an unbroken practice of according the exemption to churches, openly and by affirmative state action, not covertly or by state inaction, is not something to be lightly cast aside. Nearly 50 years ago Mr. Justice Holmes stated:

"If a thing has been practised for two hundred years by common consent, it will need a strong case for the Fourteenth Amendment to affect it. . . ." *Jackman v. Rosenbaum Co.*, 260 U.S. 22, 31 (1922).

Nothing in this national attitude toward religious tolerance and two centuries of uninterrupted freedom from taxation has given the remotest sign of leading to an established church or religion and on the contrary it has operated affirmatively to help guarantee the free exercise of all forms of religious belief. Thus, it is hardly useful to suggest that tax exemption is but the "foot in the door" or the "nose of the camel in the tent" leading to an established church. If tax exemption can be seen as this first step toward "establishment" of religion, as MR. JUSTICE DOUGLAS fears, the second step has been long in coming. Any move that realistically "establishes" a church or tends to do so can be dealt with "while this Court sits." . . .

MR. JUSTICE BRENNAN, concurring.

[680] I concur for reasons expressed in my opinion in *Abington School Dist. v. Schempp*, 374 U.S. 203, 230 (1963). I adhere to the view there stated that to give concrete meaning to the Establishment Clause,

"the line we must draw between the permissible and the impermissible is one which accords with history and faithfully reflects the understanding of the Founding Fathers. It is a line which the Court has consistently sought to mark in its decisions expounding the religious guarantees of the First Amendment. What the Framers meant to foreclose, and what our decisions under the Establishment Clause have forbidden, are those involvements of religious with secular institutions which (a) serve the essentially religious activities of religious institutions; (b) employ the organs of government for essentially religious purposes; or (c) use essentially religious means to serve governmental ends, where secular means would suffice. When the secular and religious institutions become involved in such a manner, there inhere in the relationship precisely those [681] dangers—as much to church as to state—which the Framers feared would subvert religious liberty and the strength of a system of secular government. On the other hand, there may be myriad forms of involvements of government with religion which do not import such dangers and therefore should not, in my judgment, be deemed to violate the Establishment Clause." *Id.*, at 294–295.

Thus, in my view, the history, purpose, and operation of real property tax exemptions for religious organizations must be examined to determine whether the Establishment Clause is breached by such exemptions. See *id.*, at 293.

I

The existence from the beginning of the Nation's life of a practice, such as tax exemptions for religious organizations, is not conclusive of its constitutionality. But such practice is a fact of considerable import in the interpretation of abstract constitutional language. On its face, the Establishment Clause is reasonably susceptible of different interpretations regarding the exemptions. This Court's interpretation of the clause, accordingly, is appropriately influenced by the reading it has received in the practices of the Nation. As Mr. Justice Holmes observed in an analogous context, in resolving such questions of interpretation "a page of history is worth a volume of logic." *New York Trust Co. v. Eisner*, 256 U.S. 345, 349 (1921). The more longstanding and widely accepted a practice, the greater its impact upon constitutional interpretation. History is particularly compelling in the present case because of the undeviating acceptance given religious tax exemptions from our earliest days as a Nation. Rarely if ever has this Court considered the constitutionality of a practice for which the historical support is so overwhelming.

[682] The Establishment Clause, along with the other provisions of the Bill of Rights, was ratified by the States in 1791. Religious tax exemptions were not an issue in the petitions calling for the Bill of Rights, in the pertinent congressional debates, or in the debates preceding ratification by the States. The absence of concern about the exemptions could not have resulted from failure to foresee the possibility of their existence, for they were widespread during colonial days. Rather, it seems clear that the exemptions were not among the evils that the Framers and Ratifiers of the Establishment Clause sought to avoid. Significantly, within a decade after ratification, at least four States passed statutes exempting the property of religious organizations from taxation.[3] . . .

[684] Thomas Jefferson was President when tax exemption was first given Washington churches, and James Madison sat in sessions of the Virginia General Assembly that voted exemptions for churches in that Commonwealth. I have found no record of

---

3. 2 Del. Laws of 1700–1797, p. 1247 (Act of Feb. 9, 1796); 2 Md. Laws (1785–1799, Kilty), c. 89 (Act of Jan. 20, 1798); N. Y. Laws of 1797–1800, c. 72, at 414 (Act of April 1, 1799); 2 Va. Statutes at Large of 1792–1806 (Shepherd) 200 (Act of Jan. 23, 1800). See also 16 Penn. Statutes at Large of 1682–1801, at 379 (Act of April 11, 1799). . . .

their personal views on the respective Acts.⁵ The absence of such a record is itself [685] significant. It is unlikely that two men so concerned with the separation of church and state would have remained silent had they thought the exemptions established religion. And if they had not either approved the exemptions, or been mild in their opposition, it is probable that their views would be known to us today. Both Jefferson and Madison wrote prolifically about issues they felt important, and their opinions were well known to contemporary chroniclers. Much the same can be said of the other Framers and Ratifiers of the Bill of Rights who remained active in public affairs during the late 18th and early 19th centuries. The adoption of the early exemptions without controversy, in other words, strongly suggests that they were not thought incompatible with constitutional prohibitions against involvements of church and state.

The exemptions have continued uninterrupted to the present day. . . .

[686] Mr. Justice Holmes said that "if a thing has been practised for two hundred years by common consent, it will need a strong case for the Fourteenth Amendment to affect it. . . ." *Jackman v. Rosenbaum Co.*, 260 U.S. 22, 31 (1922). For almost 200 years the view expressed in the actions of legislatures and courts has been that tax exemptions for churches do not threaten "those consequences which the Framers deeply feared" or "tend to promote that type of interdependence between religion and state which the First Amendment was designed to prevent." *Schempp*, at 236 (BRENNAN, J., concurring). An examination both of the governmental purposes for granting the exemptions and of the type of [687] church-state relationship that has resulted from their existence makes clear that no "strong case" exists for holding unconstitutional this historic practice.⁷

II

Government has two basic secular purposes for granting real property tax exemptions to religious organizations. First, these organizations are exempted because they, among a range of other private, nonprofit organizations, contribute to the well-being of the community in a variety of nonreligious ways, and thereby bear burdens that would otherwise either have to be met by general taxation, or be left undone, to the detriment of the community. Thus, New York exempts "real property owned by a corporation or association [688] organized exclusively for the moral or mental improvement of men and women, or for religious, bible, tract, charitable, benevolent, missionary, hospital, infirmary, educational, public playground, scientific, literary, bar association, medical

---

5. In an essay written after he had left the presidency, Madison did argue against tax exemptions for churches, the incorporation of ecclesiastical bodies with the power of acquiring and holding property in perpetuity, the right of the Houses of Congress to choose chaplains who are paid out of public funds, the provision of chaplains in the Army and Navy, and presidential proclamations of days of thanksgiving or prayer—though he admitted proclaiming several such days at congressional request. See Fleet, *Madison's "Detatched [sic] Memoranda,"* 3 Wm. & Mary Q. (3d ser.) 534, 555–562 (1946). These arguments were advanced long after the passage of the Virginia exemption discussed in the text, *supra*, and even longer after the adoption of the Establishment Clause. They represent at most an extreme view of church-state relations, which Madison himself may have reached only late in life. He certainly expressed no such understanding of Establishment during the debates on the First Amendment. See 1 Annals of Cong. 434, 730–731, 755 (1789). And even if he privately held these views at that time, there is no evidence that they were shared by others among the Framers and Ratifiers of the Bill of Rights.

7. Compare the very different situation regarding prayers in public schools. The practice was not widespread at the time of the adoption of the First Amendment. Legislative authorization for the prayers came much later and then only in a relatively small number of States. Moreover, courts began to question the constitutionality of the practice by the late 19th century. The prayers were found unconstitutional by courts in six States and by state attorneys general in several others. See 374 U.S., at 270, 274–275.

society, library, patriotic, historical or cemetery purposes, for the enforcement of laws relating to children or animals, or for two or more such purposes. . . ." N. Y. Real Prop. Tax Law § 420, subd. 1 (Supp. 1969–1970).

Appellant seeks to avoid the force of this secular purpose of the exemptions by limiting his challenge to "exemptions from real property taxation to religious organizations on real property used exclusively for religious purposes." Appellant assumes, apparently, that church-owned property is used for exclusively religious purposes if it does not house a hospital, orphanage, weekday school, or the like. Any assumption that a church building itself is used for exclusively religious activities, however, rests on a simplistic view of ordinary church operations. As the appellee's brief cogently observes, "the public welfare activities and the sectarian activities of religious institutions are . . . intertwined. . . . Often a particular church will use the same personnel, facilities and source of funds to carry out both its secular and religious activities." Thus, the same people who gather in church facilities for religious worship and study may return to these facilities to participate in Boy Scout activities, to promote antipoverty causes, to discuss public issues, or to listen to chamber music. Accordingly, the funds used to maintain the facilities as a place for religious worship and study also maintain them as a place for secular activities beneficial to the community as a whole. Even during formal worship services, churches frequently collect the funds used to finance [689] their secular operations and make decisions regarding their nature.

Second, government grants exemptions to religious organizations because they uniquely contribute to the pluralism of American society by their religious activities. Government may properly include religious institutions among the variety of private, nonprofit groups that receive tax exemptions, for each group contributes to the diversity of association, viewpoint, and enterprise essential to a vigorous, pluralistic society. To this end, New York extends its exemptions not only to religious and social service organizations but also to scientific, literary, bar, library, patriotic, and historical groups, and generally to institutions "organized exclusively for the moral or mental improvement of men and women." The very breadth of this scheme of exemptions negates any suggestion that the State intends to single out religious organizations for special preference. The scheme is not designed to inject any religious activity into a nonreligious context, as was the case with school prayers. No particular activity of a religious organization—for example, the propagation of its beliefs—is specially promoted by the exemptions. They merely facilitate the existence of a broad range of private, nonprofit organizations, among them religious groups, by leaving each free to come into existence, then to flourish or wither, without being burdened by real property taxes.

III

Although governmental purposes for granting religious exemptions may be wholly secular, exemptions can nonetheless violate the Establishment Clause if they result in [690] extensive state involvement with religion. Accordingly, those who urge the exemptions' unconstitutionality argue that exemptions are the equivalent of governmental subsidy of churches. General subsidies of religious activities would, of course, constitute impermissible state involvement with religion.

Tax exemptions and general subsidies, however, are qualitatively different. Though both provide economic assistance, they do so in fundamentally different ways. A subsidy involves the direct transfer of public monies to the subsidized enterprise and uses resources exacted from taxpayers as a whole. An exemption, on the other hand, involves no such transfer. It assists the exempted enterprise only passively, by relieving a privately funded venture of the burden of paying taxes. . . .

[692] IV

Against the background of this survey of the history, purpose, and operation of religious tax exemptions, I must conclude that the exemptions do not "serve the essentially religious activities of religious institutions." Their principal effect is to carry out secular purposes—the encouragement of public service activities and of a pluralistic society. During their ordinary operations, most churches engage in activities of a secular nature [693] that benefit the community; and all churches by their existence contribute to the diversity of association, viewpoint, and enterprise so highly valued by all of us.

Nor do I find that the exemptions "employ the organs of government for essentially religious purposes." To the extent that the exemptions further secular ends, they do not advance "essentially religious purposes." To the extent that purely religious activities are benefited by the exemptions, the benefit is passive. Government does not affirmatively foster these activities by exempting religious organizations from taxes, as it would were it to subsidize them. The exemption simply leaves untouched that which adherents of the organization bring into being and maintain.

Finally, I do not think that the exemptions "use essentially religious means to serve governmental ends, where secular means would suffice." The means churches use to carry on their public service activities are not "essentially religious" in nature. They are the same means used by any purely secular organization—money, human time and skills, physical facilities. It is true that each church contributes to the pluralism of our society through its purely religious activities, but the state encourages these activities not because it champions religion *per se* but because it values religion among a variety of private, nonprofit enterprises that contribute to the diversity of the Nation. Viewed in this light, there is no nonreligious substitute for religion as an element in our societal mosaic, just as there is no nonliterary substitute for literary groups.

As I said in *Schempp*, the First Amendment does not invalidate "the propriety of certain tax . . . exemptions which incidentally benefit churches and religious institutions, along with many secular charities and nonprofit organizations. . . . Religious institutions simply share benefits which government makes generally available [694] to educational, charitable, and eleemosynary groups. There is no indication that taxing authorities have used such benefits in any way to subsidize worship or foster belief in God." 374 U.S., at 301.

Opinion of MR. JUSTICE HARLAN.

While I entirely subscribe to the result reached today and find myself in basic agreement with what THE CHIEF JUSTICE has written, I deem it appropriate, in view of the radiations of the issues involved, to state those considerations that are, for me, controlling in this case and lead me to conclude that New York's constitutional provision, as implemented by its real property law, does not offend the Establishment Clause. Preliminarily, I think it relevant to face up to the fact that it is far easier to agree on the purpose that underlies the First Amendment's Establishment and Free Exercise Clauses than to obtain agreement on the standards that should govern their application. What is at stake as a matter of policy is preventing that kind and degree of government involvement in religious life that, as history teaches us, is apt to lead to strife and frequently strain a political system to the breaking point.

I

Two requirements frequently articulated and applied in our cases for achieving this goal are "neutrality" and "voluntarism." These related and mutually reinforcing concepts are short-form for saying that the Government must neither legislate to accord benefits that favor religion over nonreligion, nor sponsor a particular sect, nor try to encourage participation in or abnegation of religion. Mr. Justice Goldberg's concurring opinion in [695] *Abington* which I joined set forth these principles: "The fullest realization of true religious liberty requires that government neither engage in nor compel religious practices, that it effect no favoritism among sects or between religion and nonreligion, and that it work deterrence of no religious belief." 374 U.S., at 305. The Court's holding in *Torcaso v. Watkins*, 367 U.S. 488, 495 (1961), is to the same effect: the State cannot "constitutionally pass laws or impose requirements which aid all religions as against non-believers, and neither can [it] aid those religions based on a belief in the existence of God as against those religions founded on different beliefs." In the vast majority of cases the inquiry, albeit an elusive one, can end at this point. Neutrality and voluntarism stand as barriers against the most egregious and hence divisive kinds of state involvement in religious matters.

While these concepts are at the "core" of the Religion Clauses, they may not suffice by themselves to achieve in all cases the purposes of the First Amendment. As Professor Freund has only recently pointed out in *Public Aid to Parochial Schools*, 82 Harv. L. Rev. 1680 (1969), governmental involvement, while neutral, may be so direct or in such degree as to engender a risk of politicizing religion. Thus, as the opinion of THE CHIEF JUSTICE notes, religious groups inevitably represent certain points of view and not infrequently assert them in the political arena, as evidenced by the continuing debate respecting birth control and abortion laws. Yet history cautions that political fragmentation on sectarian lines must be guarded against. Although the very fact of neutrality may limit the intensity of involvement, government participation in certain programs, whose very nature is apt to entangle the state in details of administration and planning, may escalate to the point of inviting undue fragmentation.

[696] II

This legislation neither encourages nor discourages participation in religious life and thus satisfies the voluntarism requirement of the First Amendment. Unlike the instances of school prayers, *Abington School Dist. v. Schempp* and *Engel v. Vitale*, or "released time" programs, *Zorach v. Clauson* and *McCollum v. Board of Education*, the State is not "utilizing the prestige, power, and influence" of a public institution to bring religion into the lives of citizens. 374 U.S., at 307 (Goldberg, J., concurring).

The statute also satisfies the requirement of neutrality. Neutrality in its application requires an equal protection mode of analysis. The Court must survey meticulously the circumstances of governmental categories to eliminate, as it were, religious gerrymanders. In any particular case the critical question is whether the circumference of legislation encircles a class so broad that it can be fairly concluded that religious institutions could be thought to fall within the natural perimeter.

The statute that implements New York's constitutional provision for tax exemptions to religious organizations has defined a class of nontaxable entities whose common denominator is their nonprofit pursuit of activities devoted to cultural and moral improvement and the doing of "good works" by performing certain social services in the community that might otherwise have to be assumed by government. Included are such broad and divergent groups as historical and literary societies and more generally associations "for the moral or mental [697] improvement of men." The statute by its terms grants this exemption in furtherance of moral and intellectual diversity and would appear not to omit any organization that could be reasonably thought to contribute to that goal.

To the extent that religious institutions sponsor the secular activities that this legislation is designed to promote, it is consistent with neutrality to grant them an exemption just as other organizations devoting resources to these projects receive exemptions. I think, moreover, in the context of a statute so broad as the one before us, churches may properly receive an exemption even though they do not themselves sponsor the secular-type activities mentioned in the statute but exist merely for the convenience of their interested members. As long as the breadth of exemption includes groups that pursue cultural, moral, or spiritual improvement in multifarious secular ways, including, I would suppose, groups whose avowed tenets may be antitheological, atheistic, or agnostic, I can see no lack of neutrality in extending the benefit of the exemption to organized religious groups. . . .

[700] MR. JUSTICE DOUGLAS, dissenting.

Petitioner is the owner of real property in New York and is a Christian. But he is not a member of any of the religious organizations, "rejecting them as hostile." The New York statute exempts from taxation real property "owned by a corporation or association organized exclusively for . . . religious . . . purposes" and used "exclusively for carrying out" such purposes. Yet non-believers who own realty are taxed at the usual rate. The question in the case therefore is whether believers—organized in church groups—can be made exempt from real estate taxes, merely because they are believers, while nonbelievers, whether organized or not, must pay the real estate taxes.

My Brother HARLAN says he "would suppose" that the tax exemption extends to "groups whose avowed tenets may be antitheological, atheistic, or agnostic." *Ante*, at 697. If it does, then the line between believers and nonbelievers has not been drawn. But, with all respect, there is not even a suggestion in the present record that the statute covers property used exclusively by organizations for "antitheological purposes," "atheistic purposes," or "agnostic purposes."

In *Torcaso v. Watkins*, 367 U.S. 488, we held that [701] a State could not bar an atheist from public office in light of the freedom of belief and religion guaranteed by the First and Fourteenth Amendments. Neither the State nor the Federal Government, we said, "can constitutionally pass laws or impose requirements which aid all religions as against non-believers, and neither can aid those religions based on a belief in the existence of God as against those religions founded on different beliefs." *Id.*, at 495.

That principle should govern this case.

There is a line between what a State may do in encouraging "religious" activities, *Zorach v. Clauson*, and what a State may not do by using its resources to promote "religious" activities, *McCollum v. Board of Education*, or bestowing benefits because of them. Yet that line may not always be clear. Closing public schools on Sunday is in the former category; subsidizing churches, in my view, is in the latter. Indeed I would suppose that in common understanding one of the best ways to "establish" one or more religions is to subsidize them, which a tax exemption does. The State may not do that any more than it may prefer "those who believe in no religion over those who do believe." *Zorach v. Clauson*, at 314. . . .

[710] Direct financial aid to churches or tax exemptions to the church *qua* church is not, in my view, even arguably permitted. Sectarian causes are certainly not antipublic and many would rate their own church or perhaps all churches as the highest form of welfare. The difficulty is that sectarian causes must remain in the private domain not subject to public control or subsidy. . . .

[711] The exemptions provided here insofar as welfare projects are concerned may have the ring of neutrality. But subsidies either through direct grant or tax exemption for sectarian causes, whether carried on by church *qua* church or by church *qua* welfare agency, must be treated differently, lest we in time allow the church *qua* church to be on the public payroll, which, I fear, is imminent. . . .

We should adhere to what we said in *Torcaso v. Watkins*, 367 U.S., at 495, that neither a State nor the Federal Government "can constitutionally pass laws or impose requirements *which aid all religions as against nonbelievers*, and neither can aid those religions based on a belief in the existence of God as against those religions founded on different beliefs." (Emphasis added.)

Unless we adhere to that principle, we do not give full support either to the Free Exercise Clause or to the Establishment Clause. . . .

[716] If believers are entitled to public financial support, so are nonbelievers. A believer and nonbeliever under the present law are treated differently because of the articles of their faith. Believers are doubtless comforted that the cause of religion is being fostered by this legislation. Yet one of the mandates of the First Amendment is to promote a viable, pluralistic society and to keep government neutral, not only between sects, but also between believers and nonbelievers. The present involvement of government in religion may seem *de minimis*. But it is, I fear, a long step down the Establishment path. Perhaps I have been misinformed. But as I have read the Constitution and its philosophy, I gathered that independence was the price of liberty.

I conclude that this tax exemption is unconstitutional.

22

Welsh v. United States

398 U.S. 333 (1970)

Vote: 5—Black, Douglas, Harlan, Brennan, Marshall
 3—Burger, Stewart, White

Opinion announcing the judgment of the Court: Black
Opinion concurring in the result: Harlan
Dissenting opinion: White
Not participating in the consideration or decision of the case: Blackmun

After his application for conscientious objector status was denied, Elliott Ashton Welsh II was convicted by a United States district court judge of refusing to submit to induction into the armed forces and sentenced to three years' imprisonment. As described in Justice Black's opinion below, Welsh was denied conscientious objector status because his pacifist beliefs were found to lack a religious basis. Welsh appealed his conviction, contending that the Supreme Court's decision in United States v. Seeger, 380 U.S. 163 *(1965), entitled him to conscientious objector status.*

MR. JUSTICE BLACK announced the judgment of the Court and delivered an opinion in which MR. JUSTICE DOUGLAS, MR. JUSTICE BRENNAN, and MR. JUSTICE MARSHALL join.

. . . [335] The controlling facts in this case are strikingly similar to those in *Seeger*. Both Seeger and Welsh were brought up in religious homes and attended church in their childhood, but in neither case was this church one which taught its members not to engage in war at any time for [336] any reason. Neither Seeger nor Welsh continued his childhood religious ties into his young manhood, and neither belonged to any religious group or adhered to the teachings of any organized religion during the period of his involvement with the Selective Service System. At the time of registration for the draft, neither had yet come to accept pacifist principles. Their views on war developed only in subsequent years, but when their ideas did fully mature both made application to their local draft boards for conscientious objector exemptions from military service under § 6 (j) of the Universal Military Training and Service Act. That section then provided, in part[2]:

---

2. 62 Stat. 612. An amendment to the Act in 1967, subsequent to the Court's decision in the *Seeger* case, deleted the reference to a "Supreme Being" but continued to provide that "religious training and belief" does

"Nothing contained in this title shall be construed to require any person to be subject to combatant training and service in the armed forces of the United States who, by reason of religious training and belief, is conscientiously opposed to participation in war in any form. Religious training and belief in this connection means an individual's belief in a relation to a Supreme Being involving duties superior to those arising from any human relation, but does not include essentially political, sociological, or philosophical views or a merely personal moral code."

In filling out their exemption applications both Seeger and Welsh were unable to sign the statement that, as printed in the Selective Service form, stated "I am, by reason of my religious training and belief, conscien- [337] tiously opposed to participation in war in any form." Seeger could sign only after striking the words "training and" and putting quotation marks around the word "religious." Welsh could sign only after striking the words "my religious training and." On those same applications, neither could definitely affirm or [sic] deny that he believed in a "Supreme Being," both stating that they preferred to leave the question open.[3] But both Seeger and Welsh affirmed on those applications that they held deep conscientious scruples against taking part in wars where people were killed. Both strongly believed that killing in war was wrong, unethical, and immoral, and their consciences forbade them to take part in such an evil practice. Their objection to participating in war in any form could not be said to come from a "still, small voice of conscience"; rather, for them that voice was so loud and insistent that both men preferred to go to jail rather than serve in the Armed Forces. There was never any question about the sincerity and depth of Seeger's convictions as a conscientious objector, and the same is true of Welsh. In this regard the Court of Appeals noted, "the government concedes that [Welsh's] beliefs are held with the strength of more traditional religious convictions." 404 F.2d, at 1081. But in both cases the Selective Service System concluded that the beliefs of these men were in some sense insufficiently "religious" to qualify them for conscientious objector exemptions under the terms of § 6 (j). Seeger's conscientious objector claim was denied "solely because it was not based upon a 'belief in a relation to a Supreme Being' as required by § 6 (j) of the Act," *United States v. Seeger*, 380 U.S. 163, 167 (1965), while Welsh was [338] denied the exemption because his Appeal Board and the Department of Justice hearing officer "could find no religious basis for the registrant's beliefs, opinions and convictions." Both Seeger and Welsh subsequently refused to submit to induction into the military and both were convicted of that offense.

In *Seeger* the Court was confronted, first, with the problem that § 6 (j) defined "religious training and belief" in terms of a "belief in a relation to a Supreme Being . . . ," a definition that arguably gave a preference to those who believed in a conventional God as opposed to those who did not. Noting the "vast panoply of beliefs" prevalent in our country, the Court construed the congressional intent as being in "keeping with its long-established policy of not picking and choosing among religious beliefs," *id.*, at 175, and accordingly interpreted "the meaning of religious training and belief so as to embrace *all* religions. . . ." *Id.*, at 165. (Emphasis added.) But, having decided that all religious conscientious objectors were entitled to the exemption, we faced the more serious problem of determining which beliefs were "religious" within the meaning of the statute. This

---

not include "essentially political, sociological, or philosophical views, or a merely personal moral code." 81 Stat. 104, 50 U.S.C. App. § 456 (j) (1964 ed., Supp. IV).

3. In his original application in April 1964, Welsh stated that he did not believe in a Supreme Being, but in a letter to his local board in June 1965, he requested that his original answer be stricken and the question left open.

question was particularly difficult in the case of Seeger himself. Seeger stated that his was a "belief in and devotion to goodness and virtue for their own sakes, and a religious faith in a purely ethical creed." 380 U.S., at 166. In a letter to his draft board, he wrote:

> "My decision arises from what I believe to be considerations of validity from the standpoint of the welfare of humanity and the preservation of the democratic values which we in the United States are struggling to maintain. I have concluded that war, from the practical standpoint, is futile and self-defeating, and that from the more important moral standpoint, it is unethical." 326 F.2d 846, 848 (1964).

[339] On the basis of these and similar assertions, the Government argued that Seeger's conscientious objection to war was not "religious" but stemmed from "essentially political, sociological, or philosophical views or a merely personal moral code."

In resolving the question whether Seeger and the other registrants in that case qualified for the exemption, the Court stated that "[the] task is to decide whether the beliefs professed by a registrant are sincerely held and whether they are, *in his own scheme of things*, religious." 380 U.S., at 185. (Emphasis added.) The reference to the registrant's "own scheme of things" was intended to indicate that the central consideration in determining whether the registrant's beliefs are religious is whether these beliefs play the role of a religion and function as a religion in the registrant's life. The Court's principal statement of its test for determining whether a conscientious objector's beliefs are religious within the meaning of § 6 (j) was as follows:

> "The test might be stated in these words: A sincere and meaningful belief which occupies in the life of its possessor a place parallel to that filled by the God of those admittedly qualifying for the exemption comes within the statutory definition." 380 U.S., at 176.

The Court made it clear that these sincere and meaningful beliefs that prompt the registrant's objection to all wars need not be confined in either source or content to traditional or parochial concepts of religion. It held that § 6 (j) "does not distinguish between externally and internally derived beliefs," *id.*, at 186, and also held that "intensely personal" convictions which some might find "incomprehensible" or "incorrect" come within the meaning of "religious belief" in the Act. *Id.*, at 184–185. What is necessary under *Seeger* for a registrant's conscientious [340] objection to all war to be "religious" within the meaning of § 6 (j) is that this opposition to war stem from the registrant's moral, ethical, or religious beliefs about what is right and wrong and that these beliefs be held with the strength of traditional religious convictions. Most of the great religions of today and of the past have embodied the idea of a Supreme Being or a Supreme Reality—a God—who communicates to man in some way a consciousness of what is right and should be done, of what is wrong and therefore should be shunned. If an individual deeply and sincerely holds beliefs that are purely ethical or moral in source and content but that nevertheless impose upon him a duty of conscience to refrain from participating in any war at any time, those beliefs certainly occupy in the life of that individual "a place parallel to that filled by . . . God" in traditionally religious persons. Because his beliefs function as a religion in his life, such an individual is as much entitled to a "religious" conscientious objector exemption under § 6 (j) as is someone who derives his conscientious opposition to war from traditional religious convictions.

Applying this standard to Seeger himself, the Court noted the "compulsion to 'goodness'" that shaped his total opposition to war, the undisputed sincerity with which he held his views, and the fact that Seeger had "decried the tremendous 'spiritual' price man must pay for his willingness to destroy human life." 380 U.S., at 186–187. The Court concluded:

"We think it clear that the beliefs which prompted his objection occupy the same place in his life as the belief in a traditional deity holds in the lives of his friends, the Quakers." 380 U.S., at 187.

Accordingly, the Court found that Seeger should be granted conscientious objector status.

In the case before us the Government seeks to distinguish our holding in *Seeger* on basically two grounds, [341] both of which were relied upon by the Court of Appeals in affirming Welsh's conviction. First, it is stressed that Welsh was far more insistent and explicit than Seeger in denying that his views were religious. For example, in filling out their conscientious objector applications, Seeger put quotation marks around the word "religious," but Welsh struck the word "religious" entirely and later characterized his beliefs as having been formed "by reading in the fields of history and sociology." The Court of Appeals found that Welsh had "denied that his objection to war was premised on religious belief" and concluded that "the Appeal Board was entitled to take him at his word." 404 F.2d, at 1082. We think this attempt to distinguish *Seeger* fails for the reason that it places undue emphasis on the registrant's interpretation of his own beliefs. The Court's statement in *Seeger* that a registrant's characterization of his own belief as "religious" should carry great weight, 380 U.S., at 184, does not imply that his declaration that his views are nonreligious should be treated similarly. When a registrant states that his objections to war are "religious," that information is highly relevant to the question of the function his beliefs have in his life. But very few registrants are fully aware of the broad scope of the word "religious" as used in § 6 (j), and accordingly a registrant's statement that his beliefs are nonreligious is a highly unreliable guide for those charged with administering the exemption. Welsh himself presents a case in point. Although he originally characterized his beliefs as nonreligious, he later upon reflection wrote a long and thoughtful letter to his Appeal Board in which he declared that his beliefs were "certainly religious in the ethical sense of the word." He explained:

"I believe I mentioned taking of life as not being, for me, a religious wrong. Again, I assumed Mr. [Brady (the Department of Justice hearing [342] officer)] was using the word 'religious' in the conventional sense, and, in order to be perfectly honest did not characterize my belief as 'religious.'"

The Government also seeks to distinguish *Seeger* on the ground that Welsh's views, unlike Seeger's, were "essentially political, sociological, or philosophical views or a merely personal moral code." As previously noted, the Government made the same argument about Seeger, and not without reason, for Seeger's views had a substantial political dimension. In this case, Welsh's conscientious objection to war was undeniably based in part on his perception of world politics. In a letter to his local board, he wrote:

"I can only act according to what I am and what I see. And I see that the military complex wastes both human and material resources, that it fosters disregard for (what I consider a paramount concern) human needs and ends; I see that the means we employ to 'defend' our 'way of life' profoundly change that way of life. I see that in our failure to recognize the political, social, and economic realities of the world, we, *as a nation*, fail our responsibility *as a nation*."

We certainly do not think that § 6 (j)'s exclusion of those persons with "essentially political, sociological, or philosophical views or a merely personal moral code" should be read to exclude those who hold strong beliefs about our domestic and foreign affairs or even those whose conscientious objection to participation in all wars is founded to a substantial extent upon considerations of public policy. The two groups of registrants that obviously do fall within these exclusions from the exemption are those whose beliefs are not deeply held and those whose objection to war does not rest at all upon moral, ethical, or religious principle but instead rests solely upon [343] considerations of policy, pragmatism, or expediency. In applying § 6 (j)'s exclusion of those whose views are "essentially political, sociological, or philosophical" or of those who have a "merely personal moral code," it should be remembered that these exclusions are definitional and do not therefore restrict the category of persons who are conscientious objectors by "religious training and belief." Once the Selective Service System has taken the first step and determined under the standards set out here and in *Seeger* that the registrant is a "religious" conscientious objector, it follows that his views cannot be "essentially political, sociological, or philosophical." Nor can they be a "merely personal moral code."

Welsh stated that he "believe[d] the taking of life—anyone's life—to be morally wrong." In his original conscientious objector application he wrote the following:

> "I believe that human life is valuable in and of itself; in its living; therefore I will not injure or kill another human being. This belief (and the corresponding 'duty' to abstain from violence toward another person) is not 'superior to those arising from any human relation.' On the contrary: *it is essential to every human relation*. I cannot, therefore, conscientiously comply with the Government's insistence that I assume duties which I feel are immoral and totally repugnant."

Welsh elaborated his beliefs in later communications with Selective Service officials. On the basis of these beliefs and the conclusion of the Court of Appeals that he held them "with the strength of more traditional religious convictions," 404 F.2d, at 1081, we think Welsh was clearly entitled to a conscientious objector exemption. Section [344] 6 (j) requires no more. That section exempts from military service all those whose consciences, spurred by deeply held moral, ethical, or religious beliefs, would give them no rest or peace if they allowed themselves to become a part of an instrument of war.

MR. JUSTICE HARLAN, concurring in the result.

Candor requires me to say that I joined the Court's opinion in *United States v. Seeger*, 380 U.S. 163 (1965), only with the gravest misgivings as to whether it was a legitimate exercise in statutory construction, and today's decision convinces me that in doing so I made a mistake which I should now acknowledge.

In *Seeger* the Court construed § 6 (j) of the Universal Military Training and Service Act so as to sustain a conscientious objector claim not founded on a theistic belief. The Court, in treating with the provision of the statute that limited conscientious objector claims to those stemming from belief in "a Supreme Being," there said: "Congress, in using the expression 'Supreme Being' rather than the designation 'God,' was merely clarifying the meaning of religious training and belief so as to embrace all religions and to exclude essentially political, sociological, or philosophical views," and held that the test of belief "'in a relation to a Supreme Being' is whether a given belief that is sincere and meaningful occupies a place in the life of its possessor parallel to that filled by the orthodox [345] belief in God of one who clearly qualifies for the exemption." 380 U.S., at 165–166. Today the prevailing opinion makes explicit its total elimination of the statutorily required religious content for a conscientious objector exemption. The prevailing opinion now says: "If an individual deeply and sincerely holds beliefs that are *purely ethical* or *moral* in source and content but that nevertheless impose upon him a duty of conscience to refrain from participating in any war at any time" (emphasis added), he qualifies for a § 6 (j) exemption.

In my opinion, the liberties taken with the statute both in *Seeger* and today's decision cannot be justified in the name of the familiar doctrine of construing federal statutes in a manner that will avoid possible constitutional infirmities in them. There are limits to the permissible application of that doctrine, and, as I will undertake to show in this opinion, those limits were crossed in *Seeger*, and even more apparently have been exceeded in the present case. I therefore find myself unable to escape facing the constitutional issue that this case squarely presents: whether § 6 (j) in limiting this draft exemption to those opposed to war in general because of theistic beliefs runs afoul of the religious clauses of the First Amendment. For reasons later appearing I believe it does, and on that basis I concur in the judgment reversing this conviction, and adopt the test announced by MR. JUSTICE BLACK, not as a matter of statutory construction, but as the touchstone for salvaging a congressional policy of long standing that would otherwise have to be nullified.

I

. . . [353] The Draft Act of 1917 conditioned conscientious objector status on membership in or affiliation with a "well-recognized religious sect or organization [then] organized and existing and whose existing creed or principles forb[ade] its members to participate in war in any form. . . ." That § 5 (g) of the 1940 Act eliminated the affiliation and membership requirement does not, in my view, mean as the Court, in effect, concluded in *Seeger* that Congress was embracing a secular definition of religion.[7]

[354] Unless we are to assume an Alice-in-Wonderland world where words have no meaning, I think it fair to say that Congress' choice of language cannot fail to convey to the discerning reader the very policy choice that the prevailing opinion today completely obliterates: that between conventional religions that usually have an organized and formal structure and dogma and a cohesive group identity, even when nontheistic, and cults that represent schools of thought and in the usual case are without formal structure or are, at most, loose and informal associations of individuals who share common ethical, moral, or intellectual views. . . .

---

7. The apparent purpose of the 1940 change in language was to eliminate membership as a decisive criterion in recognition of the fact that mere formal affiliation is no measure of the intensity of beliefs, and that many nominal adherents do not share or pursue the ethics of their church. That the focus was made the conscientiousness of the individual's own belief does not mean that Congress was indifferent to its source. Were this the case there would have been no occasion to allude to "religious training" in the 1940 enactment, and to contrast it with secular ethics in the 1948 statute. Yet the prevailing opinion today holds that "beliefs that are purely ethical," no matter how acquired, qualify the holder for § 6 (j) status if they are held with the requisite intensity.

However, even the prevailing opinion's ambulatory concept of "religion" does not suffice to embrace Welsh, since petitioner insisted that his beliefs had been formed "by reading in the fields of history and sociology" and "denied that his objection to war was premised on religious belief." That opinion not only establishes a definition of religion that amounts to "Newspeak" but it refuses to listen to petitioner who is speaking the same language.

[356] III

The constitutional question that must be faced in this case is whether a statute that defers to the individual's conscience only when his views emanate from adherence to theistic religious beliefs is within the power of Congress. Congress, of course, could, entirely consistently with the requirements of the Constitution, eliminate *all* exemptions for conscientious objectors. Such a course would be wholly "neutral" and, in my view, would not offend the Free Exercise Clause, for reasons set forth in my dissenting opinion in *Sherbert v. Verner*, 374 U.S. 398, 418 (1963). However, having chosen to exempt, it cannot draw the line between theistic or nontheistic religious beliefs on the one hand and secular beliefs on the other. Any such distinctions are not, in my view, compatible with the Establishment Clause of the First Amendment. [357] The implementation of the neutrality principle of these cases requires, in my view, as I stated in *Walz v. Tax Comm'n*, "an equal protection mode of analysis. The Court must survey meticulously the circumstances of governmental categories to eliminate, as it were, religious gerrymanders. In any particular case the critical question is whether the scope of legislation encircles a class so broad that it can be fairly concluded that [all groups that] could be thought to fall within the natural perimeter [are included]." 397 U.S., at 696.

The "radius" of this legislation is the conscientiousness with which an individual opposes war in general, yet the statute, as I think it must be construed, excludes from its "scope" individuals motivated by teachings of nontheistic religions, and individuals guided by an inner ethical voice that bespeaks secular and not "religious" reflection. It not only accords a preference to the "religious" but also disadvantages adherents of religions that do not worship a Supreme Being. The constitutional infirmity cannot be cured, moreover, even by an impermissible construction that eliminates the theistic requirement and simply draws the line between religious and nonreligious. This in my view offends the Establishment Clause and is that kind of classification [358] that this Court has condemned.

If the exemption is to be given application, it must encompass the class of individuals it purports to exclude, those whose beliefs emanate from a purely moral, ethical, or philosophical source. The common denominator must be the intensity of moral conviction with which a belief is held. Common experience teaches that among [359] "religious" individuals some are weak and others strong adherents to tenets and this is no less true of individuals whose lives are guided by personal ethical considerations. . . .

[361] IV

Where a statute is defective because of underinclusion there exist two remedial alternatives: a court may either declare it a nullity and order that its benefits not extend to the class that the legislature intended to benefit, or it may extend the coverage of the statute to include those who are aggrieved by exclusion.

[362] The appropriate disposition of this case, which is a prosecution for refusing to submit to induction and not an action for a declaratory judgment on the constitutionality of § 6 (j), is determined by the fact that at the time of Welsh's induction notice and prosecution the Selective Service was, as required by statute, exempting individuals whose beliefs were identical in all respects to those held by petitioner except that they derived from a religious source. Since this created a religious benefit not accorded to petitioner, it is clear to me that this conviction must be reversed under the Establishment Clause of the First Amendment unless Welsh is to go remediless. . . .

[365] The policy of exempting religious conscientious objectors is one of longstand-ing tradition in this country and accords recognition to what is, in a diverse and "open" society, the important value of reconciling individuality [366] of belief with practical exigencies whenever possible. It dates back to colonial times and has been perpetuated in state and federal conscription statutes. That it has been phrased in religious terms re-flects, I assume, the fact that ethics and morals, while the concern of secular philosophy, have traditionally been matters taught by organized religion and that for most individu-als spiritual and ethical nourishment is derived from that source. It further reflects, I would suppose, the assumption that beliefs emanating from a religious source are prob-ably held with great intensity.

When a policy has roots so deeply embedded in history, there is a compelling rea-son for a court to hazard the necessary statutory repairs if they can be made within the administrative framework of the statute and without impairing other legislative goals, even though they entail, not simply eliminating an offending section, but rather build-ing upon it. Thus I am prepared to accept the prevailing opinion's conscientious objector test, not as a reflection of congressional statutory intent but as patchwork [367] of judi-cial making that cures the defect of underinclusion in § 6 (j) and can be administered by local boards in the usual course of business. Like the prevailing opinion, I also conclude that petitioner's beliefs are held with the required intensity and consequently vote to reverse the judgment of conviction.

MR. JUSTICE WHITE, with whom THE CHIEF JUSTICE and MR. JUSTICE STEWART join, dissenting.

Whether or not *United States v. Seeger*, 380 U.S. 163 (1965), accurately reflected the intent of Congress in providing draft exemptions for religious conscientious objectors to war, I cannot join today's construction of § 6 (j) extending draft exemption to those who disclaim religious objections to war and whose views about war represent a purely personal code arising not from religious training and belief as the statute requires but from readings in philosophy, history, and sociology. Our obligation [368] in statutory construction cases is to enforce the will of Congress, not our own; and as MR. JUSTICE HARLAN has demonstrated, construing § 6 (j) to include Welsh exempts from the draft a class of persons to whom Congress has expressly denied an exemption.

For me that conclusion should end this case. Even if Welsh is quite right in asserting that exempting religious believers is an establishment of religion forbidden by the First Amendment, he nevertheless remains one of those persons whom Congress took pains not to relieve from military duty. Whether or not § 6 (j) is constitutional, Welsh had no First Amendment excuse for refusing to report for induction. If it is contrary to the express will of Congress to exempt Welsh, as I think it is, then there is no warrant for saving the religious exemption and the statute by redrafting it in this Court to include Welsh and all others like him.

If the Constitution expressly provided that aliens should not be exempt from the draft, but Congress purported to exempt them and no others, Welsh, a citizen, could hardly qualify for exemption by demonstrating that exempting aliens is unconstitu-tional. By the same token, if the Constitution prohibits Congress from exempting reli-gious believers, but Congress exempts them anyway, why should the invalidity of the exemption create a draft immunity for Welsh? Surely not just because he would otherwise go without a remedy along with all those others not qualifying for exemption under the statute. And not as a reward for seeking a declaration of the invalidity of § 6 (j); for as long as Welsh is among those from whom Congress expressly withheld the exemption, he has no standing to raise the establishment issue even if § 6 (j) would present no First Amendment problems if it had included Welsh and others like him. "One to whom application of a statute is constitutional will not be heard to attack the [369] statute on the ground that impliedly it might also be taken as applying to other persons or other situations in which its application might be unconstitutional." *United States v. Raines*, 362 U.S. 17, 21 (1960). Nothing in the First Amendment prohibits drafting Welsh and other nonreligious objectors to war. Saving § 6 (j) by extending it to include Welsh cannot be done in the name of a presumed congressional will but only by the Court's taking upon itself the power to make draft-exemption policy.

If I am wrong in thinking that Welsh cannot benefit from invalidation of § 6 (j) on Establishment Clause grounds, I would nevertheless affirm his conviction; for I cannot hold that Congress violated the Clause in exempting from the draft all those who oppose war by reason of religious training and belief. In exempting religious conscientious objectors, Congress was making one of two judgments, perhaps both. First, § 6 (j) may represent a purely practical judgment that religious objectors, however admirable, would be of no more use in combat than many others unqualified for military service. Exemption was not extended to them to further religious belief or practice but to limit military service to those who were prepared to undertake the fighting that the armed services have to do. On this basis, the exemption has neither the primary purpose nor the effect of furthering religion. As Mr. Justice Frankfurter, joined by MR. JUSTICE HARLAN, said in a separate opinion in the *Sunday Closing Law Cases*, 366 U.S. 420, 468 (1961), an establishment contention "can prevail only if the absence of any substantial legislative purpose other than a religious one is made to appear."

Second, Congress may have granted the exemption because otherwise religious objectors would be forced into conduct that their religions forbid and because [370] in the view of Congress to deny the exemption would violate the Free Exercise Clause or at least raise grave problems in this respect. True, this Court has more than once stated its unwillingness to construe the First Amendment, standing alone, as requiring draft exemptions for religious believers. *Hamilton v. Board of Regents*, 293 U.S. 245, 263–264 (1934); *United States v. Macintosh*, 283 U.S. 605, 623–624 (1931). But this Court is not alone in being obliged to construe the Constitution in the course of its work; nor does it even approach having a monopoly on the wisdom and insight appropriate to the task. Legislative exemptions for those with religious convictions against war date from colonial days. As Chief Justice Hughes explained in his dissent in *United States v. Macintosh*, at 633, the importance of giving immunity to those having conscientious scruples against bearing arms has consistently been emphasized in debates in Congress and such draft exemptions are "indicative of the actual operation of the principles of the Constitution." However this Court might construe the First Amendment, Congress has regularly steered clear of free exercise problems by granting exemptions to those who conscientiously oppose war on religious grounds.

If there were no statutory exemption for religious objectors to war and failure to provide it was held by this Court to impair the free exercise of religion contrary to the First Amendment, an exemption reflecting this constitutional command would be no more an establishment of religion than the exemption required for Sabbatarians in *Sherbert v. Verner*, 374 U.S. 398 (1963), or the exemption from the flat tax on book sellers held required for evangelists, *Follett v. McCormick*, 321 U.S. 573 (1944). Surely a statutory exemption for religionists required by the Free Exercise Clause is not an invalid establishment because it fails to include nonreligious believers as well; nor would it be any less an establishment [371] if camouflaged by granting additional exemptions for nonreligious, but "moral" objectors to war.

On the assumption, however, that the Free Exercise Clause of the First Amendment does not by its own force require exempting devout objectors from military service, it does not follow that § 6 (j) is a law respecting an establishment of religion within the meaning of the First Amendment. It is very likely that § 6 (j) is a recognition by Congress of free exercise values and its view of desirable or required policy in implementing the Free Exercise Clause. That judgment is entitled to respect. . . .

[373] The Establishment Clause as construed by this Court unquestionably has independent significance; its function is not wholly auxiliary to the Free Exercise Clause. It bans some involvements of the State with religion that [374] otherwise might be consistent with the Free Exercise Clause. But when in the rationally based judgment of Congress free exercise of religion calls for shielding religious objectors from compulsory combat duty, I am reluctant to frustrate the legislative will by striking down the statutory exemption because it does not also reach those to whom the Free Exercise Clause offers no protection whatsoever.

23

Lemon v. Kurtzman

403 U.S. 602 (1971)

Vote: 7/1—Burger, Black, Douglas, Harlan, Brennan, Stewart, White, Blackmun
  1/0—White

Opinion announcing the opinion of the Court: Burger
Concurring opinions: Douglas, Brennan
Opinion concurring in the judgment and dissenting in part: White
Not participating in the case: Marshall

In this decision, the Supreme Court rendered judgment on similar cases involving tax-payer funding of private religious schools in Rhode Island and Pennsylvania.

Rhode Island's 1969 Salary Supplement Act provided a 15 percent salary supplement to teachers employed at nonpublic schools where the average per-pupil expenditure on secular education was below the average in public schools. The act rested on the legislature's finding that the quality of education in Rhode Island's nonpublic elementary schools had been jeopardized by their inability to offer sufficient salaries to attract competent and dedicated teachers. Individuals eligible for salary supplements could only teach courses offered in the public schools, using only materials used in the public schools, and their salaries, after being supplemented, could not exceed the maximum paid to the state's public school teachers. To be eligible for a supplement, individuals also had to agree in writing not to teach courses in religion. At the time of litigation, about 25 percent of Rhode Island's elementary school students attended nonpublic schools, and about 95 percent of those students attended Roman Catholic schools. As implemented, around 250 teachers received salary supplements, all of whom taught at Roman Catholic schools.

Pennsylvania's 1968 Nonpublic Elementary and Secondary Education Act authorized the state superintendent of public instruction to "purchase" certain "secular educational services" from nonpublic schools. The act was passed in response to legislative findings that a crisis existed in the state's nonpublic schools on account of rapidly rising costs and that the state's educational aims could be appropriately fulfilled by financial support of "those purely secular educational objectives achieved through nonpublic education." Recipient nonpublic schools were directly reimbursed for teacher salaries, textbooks, and instructional materials. Reimbursements were restricted to courses in mathematics, modern foreign languages (excluding Latin, Hebrew, and classical

Greek), physical science, and physical education. Reimbursed textbooks and materials had to be approved by the superintendent, and no payment was to be made for any course containing "any subject matter expressing religious teaching, or the morals or forms of worship of any sect." Schools seeking reimbursements had to maintain prescribed accounting procedures, subject to state audit, that identified the separate costs of secular educational services. Most of the reimbursements under the program went to Catholic schools. At the time of litigation, more than 20 percent of elementary and secondary students in Pennsylvania attended Catholic schools.

BURGER, C. J., delivered the opinion of the Court, in which BLACK, DOUGLAS, HARLAN, STEWART, and BLACKMUN, JJ., joined.

. . . [612] The language of the Religion Clauses of the First Amendment is at best opaque, particularly when compared with other portions of the Amendment. Its authors did not simply prohibit the establishment of a state church or a state religion, an area history shows they regarded as very important and fraught with great dangers. Instead they commanded that there should be "no law respecting an establishment of religion." A law may be one "respecting" the forbidden objective while falling short of its total realization. A law "respecting" the proscribed result, that is, the establishment of religion, is not always easily identifiable as one violative of the Clause. A given law might not establish a state religion but nevertheless be one "respecting" that end in the sense of being a step that could lead to such establishment and hence offend the First Amendment.

In the absence of precisely stated constitutional prohibitions, we must draw lines with reference to the three main evils against which the Establishment Clause was intended to afford protection: "sponsorship, financial support, and active involvement of the sovereign in religious activity." *Walz v. Tax Commission*, 397 U.S. 664, 668 (1970).

Every analysis in this area must begin with consideration of the cumulative criteria developed by the Court over many years. Three such tests may be gleaned from our cases. First, the statute must have a secular legislative purpose; second, its principal or primary effect must be one that neither advances nor inhibits religion, *Board of Education v. Allen*, 392 U.S. 236, 243 (1968); [613] finally, the statute must not foster "an excessive government entanglement with religion." *Walz*, at 674.

Inquiry into the legislative purposes of the Pennsylvania and Rhode Island statutes affords no basis for a conclusion that the legislative intent was to advance religion. On the contrary, the statutes themselves clearly state that they are intended to enhance the quality of the secular education in all schools covered by the compulsory attendance laws. There is no reason to believe the legislatures meant anything else. A State always has a legitimate concern for maintaining minimum standards in all schools it allows to operate. As in *Allen*, we find nothing here that undermines the stated legislative intent; it must therefore be accorded appropriate deference.

In *Allen* the Court acknowledged that secular and religious teachings were not necessarily so intertwined that secular textbooks furnished to students by the State were in fact instrumental in the teaching of religion. 392 U.S., at 248. The legislatures of Rhode Island and Pennsylvania have concluded that secular and religious education are identifiable and separable. In the abstract we have no quarrel with this conclusion.

The two legislatures, however, have also recognized that church-related elementary and secondary schools have a significant religious mission and that a substantial portion of their activities is religiously oriented. They have therefore sought to create statutory restrictions designed to guarantee the separation between secular and religious educational functions and to ensure that State financial aid supports only the former. All these provisions are precautions taken in candid recognition that these programs approached, even if they did not intrude upon, the forbidden areas under the Religion Clauses. We need not decide whether these legislative precautions restrict the principal or primary effect of the programs to the point where they do not offend the Religion [614] Clauses, for we conclude that the cumulative impact of the entire relationship arising under the statutes in each State involves excessive entanglement between government and religion.

III

In *Walz v. Tax Commission, supra,* the Court upheld state tax exemptions for real property owned by religious organizations and used for religious worship. That holding, however, tended to confine rather than enlarge the area of permissible state involvement with religious institutions by calling for close scrutiny of the degree of entanglement involved in the relationship. The objective is to prevent, as far as possible, the intrusion of either into the precincts of the other.

Our prior holdings do not call for total separation between church and state; total separation is not possible in an absolute sense. Some relationship between government and religious organizations is inevitable. Fire inspections, building and zoning regulations, and state requirements under compulsory school-attendance laws are examples of necessary and permissible contacts. Indeed, under the statutory exemption before us in *Walz,* the State had a continuing burden to ascertain that the exempt property was in fact being used for religious worship. Judicial caveats against entanglement must recognize that the line of separation, far from being a "wall," is a blurred, indistinct, and variable barrier depending on all the circumstances of a particular relationship. . . .

[615] In order to determine whether the government entanglement with religion is excessive, we must examine the character and purposes of the institutions that are benefited, the nature of the aid that the State provides, and the resulting relationship between the government and the religious authority. MR. JUSTICE HARLAN, in a separate opinion in *Walz,* echoed the classic warning as to "programs, whose very nature is apt to entangle the state in details of administration . . ." at 695. Here we find that both statutes foster an impermissible degree of entanglement.

(a) Rhode Island Program

The District Court made extensive findings on the grave potential for excessive entanglement that inheres in the religious character and purpose of the Roman Catholic elementary schools of Rhode Island, to date the sole beneficiaries of the Rhode Island Salary Supplement Act.

The church schools involved in the program are located close to parish churches. This understandably permits convenient access for religious exercises since instruction in faith and morals is part of the total educational process. The school buildings contain identifying religious symbols such as crosses on the exterior and crucifixes, and religious paintings and statues either in the classrooms or hallways. Although only approximately 30 minutes a day are devoted to direct religious instruction, there are religiously oriented extracurricular activities. Approximately two-thirds of the teachers in these schools are nuns of various religious orders. Their dedicated efforts provide an atmosphere in which religious instruction and religious vocations are natural and proper parts of life in such schools. Indeed, as the District Court found, the role of teaching nuns in enhancing the religious atmosphere has led the parochial school authorities [616] to attempt to maintain a one-to-one ratio between nuns and lay teachers in all schools rather than to permit some to be staffed almost entirely by lay teachers.

On the basis of these findings the District Court concluded that the parochial schools constituted "an integral part of the religious mission of the Catholic Church." The various characteristics of the schools make them "a powerful vehicle for transmitting the Catholic faith to the next generation." This process of inculcating religious doctrine is, of course, enhanced by the impressionable age of the pupils, in primary schools particularly. In short, parochial schools involve substantial religious activity and purpose.

The substantial religious character of these church-related schools gives rise to entangling church-state relationships of the kind the Religion Clauses sought to avoid. Although the District Court found that concern for religious values did not inevitably or necessarily intrude into the content of secular subjects, the considerable religious activities of these schools led the legislature to provide for careful governmental controls and surveillance by state authorities in order to ensure that state aid supports only secular education.

The dangers and corresponding entanglements are enhanced by the particular form of aid that the Rhode Island Act provides. Our decisions from *Everson* to *Allen* have permitted the States to provide church-related schools with secular, neutral, or nonideological services, facilities, or materials. Bus transportation, school lunches, public health services, and secular textbooks supplied in common to all students were not [617] thought to offend the Establishment Clause. We note that the dissenters in *Allen* seemed chiefly concerned with the pragmatic difficulties involved in ensuring the truly secular content of the textbooks provided at state expense.

In *Allen* the Court refused to make assumptions, on a meager record, about the religious content of the textbooks that the State would be asked to provide. We cannot, however, refuse here to recognize that teachers have a substantially different ideological character from books. In terms of potential for involving some aspect of faith or morals in secular subjects, a textbook's content is ascertainable, but a teacher's handling of a subject is not. We cannot ignore the danger that a teacher under religious control and discipline poses to the separation of the religious from the purely secular aspects of precollege education. The conflict of functions inheres in the situation.

In our view the record shows these dangers are present to a substantial degree. The Rhode Island Roman Catholic elementary schools are under the general supervision of the Bishop of Providence and his appointed representative, the Diocesan Superintendent of Schools. In most cases, each individual parish, however, assumes the ultimate financial responsibility for the school, with the parish priest authorizing the allocation of parish funds. With only two exceptions, school principals are nuns appointed either by the Superintendent or the Mother Provincial of the order whose members staff the school. By 1969 lay teachers constituted more than a third of all teachers in the parochial elementary schools, and their number is growing. They are first interviewed by the superintendent's office and then by the school principal. The contracts are signed by the parish priest, and he retains some discretion in negotiating salary levels. Religious authority necessarily pervades the school system. . . .

[618] We need not and do not assume that teachers in parochial schools will be guilty of bad faith or any conscious design to evade the limitations imposed by the statute and the First Amendment. We simply recognize that a dedicated religious person, teaching in a school affiliated with his or her faith and operated to inculcate its tenets, will

inevitably experience great difficulty in remaining religiously neutral. Doctrines and faith are not inculcated or advanced by neutrals. With the best of intentions such a teacher would find it hard to make [619] a total separation between secular teaching and religious doctrine. What would appear to some to be essential to good citizenship might well for others border on or constitute instruction in religion. Further difficulties are inherent in the combination of religious discipline and the possibility of disagreement between teacher and religious authorities over the meaning of the statutory restrictions.

We do not assume, however, that parochial school teachers will be unsuccessful in their attempts to segregate their religious beliefs from their secular educational respon-sibilities. But the potential for impermissible fostering of religion is present. The Rhode Island Legislature has not, and could not, provide state aid on the basis of a mere as-sumption that secular teachers under religious discipline can avoid conflicts. The State must be certain, given the Religion Clauses, that subsidized teachers do not inculcate religion—indeed the State here has undertaken to do so. To ensure that no trespass oc-curs, the State has therefore carefully conditioned its aid with pervasive restrictions. An eligible recipient must teach only those courses that are offered in the public schools and use only those texts and materials that are found in the public schools. In addition the teacher must not engage in teaching any course in religion.

A comprehensive, discriminating, and continuing state surveillance will inevitably be required to ensure that these restrictions are obeyed and the First Amendment oth-erwise respected. Unlike a book, a teacher cannot be inspected once so as to determine the extent and intent of his or her personal beliefs and subjective acceptance of the limitations imposed by the First Amendment. These prophylactic contacts will involve excessive and enduring entanglement between state and church.

[620] There is another area of entanglement in the Rhode Island program that gives concern. The statute excludes teachers employed by nonpublic schools whose average per-pupil expenditures on secular education equal or exceed the comparable figures for public schools. In the event that the total expenditures of an otherwise eligible school exceed this norm, the program requires the government to examine the school's records in order to determine how much of the total expenditures is attributable to secular edu-cation and how much to religious activity. This kind of state inspection and evaluation of the religious content of a religious organization is fraught with the sort of entangle-ment that the Constitution forbids. It is a relationship pregnant with dangers of exces-sive government direction of church schools and hence of churches. The Court noted "the hazards of government supporting churches" in *Walz v. Tax Commission*, at 675, and we cannot ignore here the danger that pervasive modern governmental power will ultimately intrude on religion and thus conflict with the Religion Clauses.

(b) Pennsylvania Program

The Pennsylvania statute also provides state aid to church-related schools for teach-ers' salaries. The complaint describes an educational system that is very similar to the one existing in Rhode Island. According to the allegations, the church-related elemen-tary and secondary schools are controlled by religious organizations, have the purpose of propagating and promoting a particular religious faith, and conduct their operations to fulfill that purpose. Since this complaint was dismissed for failure to state a claim for relief, we must accept these allegations as true for purposes of our review.

As we noted earlier, the very restrictions and surveillance necessary to ensure that teachers play a strictly nonideological role give rise to entanglements between [621] church and state. The Pennsylvania statute, like that of Rhode Island, fosters this kind of relationship. Reimbursement is not only limited to courses offered in the public schools and materials approved by state officials, but the statute excludes "any subject matter expressing religious teaching, or the morals or forms of worship of any sect." In addition, schools seeking reimbursement must maintain accounting procedures that require the State to establish the cost of the secular as distinguished from the religious instruction.

The Pennsylvania statute, moreover, has the further defect of providing state financial aid directly to the church-related school. This factor distinguishes both *Everson* and *Allen*, for in both those cases the Court was careful to point out that state aid was provided to the student and his parents—not to the church-related school. *Board of Education v. Allen*, *supra*, at 243–244; *Everson v. Board of Education*, at 18. In *Walz v. Tax Commission*, at 675, the Court warned of the dangers of direct payments to religious organizations:

> "Obviously a direct money subsidy would be a relationship pregnant with involvement and, as with most governmental grant programs, could encompass sustained and detailed administrative relationships for enforcement of statutory or administrative standards. . . ."

The history of government grants of a continuing cash subsidy indicates that such programs have almost always been accompanied by varying measures of control and surveillance. The government cash grants before us now provide no basis for predicting that comprehensive measures of surveillance and controls will not follow. In particular the government's post-audit power to inspect and evaluate a church-related school's financial records and to determine which expenditures are religious and [622] which are secular creates an intimate and continuing relationship between church and state.

IV

A broader base of entanglement of yet a different character is presented by the divisive political potential of these state programs. In a community where such a large number of pupils are served by church-related schools, it can be assumed that state assistance will entail considerable political activity. Partisans of parochial schools, understandably concerned with rising costs and sincerely dedicated to both the religious and secular educational missions of their schools, will inevitably champion this cause and promote political action to achieve their goals. Those who oppose state aid, whether for constitutional, religious, or fiscal reasons, will inevitably respond and employ all of the usual political campaign techniques to prevail. Candidates will be forced to declare and voters to choose. It would be unrealistic to ignore the fact that many people confronted with issues of this kind will find their votes aligned with their faith.

Ordinarily political debate and division, however vigorous or even partisan, are normal and healthy manifestations of our democratic system of government, but political division along religious lines was one of the principal evils against which the First Amendment was intended to protect. Freund, *Comment, Public Aid to Parochial Schools*, 82 Harv. L. Rev. 1680, 1692 (1969). The potential divisiveness of such conflict is a threat to the normal political process. *Walz v. Tax Commission*, at 695 (separate opinion of HARLAN, J.). To have States or communities divide on the issues presented by state aid to parochial schools would tend to confuse [623] and obscure other issues of great urgency. We have an expanding array of vexing issues, local and national, domestic and international, to debate and divide on. It conflicts with our whole history and tradition to permit questions of the Religion Clauses to assume such importance in our legislatures and in our elections that they could divert attention from the myriad issues and problems that confront every level of government. The highways of church and state relationships are not likely to be one-way streets, and the Constitution's authors sought to protect religious worship from the pervasive power of government. The history of many countries attests to the hazards of religion's intruding into the political arena or of political power intruding into the legitimate and free exercise of religious belief.

Of course, as the Court noted in *Walz*, "[a]dherents of particular faiths and individual churches frequently take strong positions on public issues." *Walz v. Tax Commission*, at 670. We could not expect otherwise, for religious values pervade the fabric of our national life. But in *Walz* we dealt with a status under state tax laws for the benefit of all religious groups. Here we are confronted with successive and very likely permanent annual appropriations that benefit relatively few religious groups. Political fragmentation and divisiveness on religious lines are thus likely to be intensified.

The potential for political divisiveness related to religious belief and practice is aggravated in these two statutory programs by the need for continuing annual appropriations and the likelihood of larger and larger demands as costs and populations grow. The Rhode Island District Court found that the parochial school system's "monumental and deepening financial crisis" would "inescapably" require larger annual appropriations subsidizing greater percentages of the salaries of lay teachers. Although no facts have been developed in this respect [624] in the Pennsylvania case, it appears that such pressures for expanding aid have already required the state legislature to include a portion of the state revenues from cigarette taxes in the program.

V

In *Walz* it was argued that a tax exemption for places of religious worship would prove to be the first step in an inevitable progression leading to the establishment of state churches and state religion. That claim could not stand up against more than 200 years of virtually universal practice imbedded in our colonial experience and continuing into the present.

The progression argument, however, is more persuasive here. We have no long history of state aid to church-related educational institutions comparable to 200 years of tax exemption for churches. Indeed, the state programs before us today represent something of an innovation. We have already noted that modern governmental programs have self-perpetuating and self-expanding propensities. These internal pressures are only enhanced when the schemes involve institutions whose legitimate needs are growing and whose interests have substantial political support. Nor can we fail to see that in constitutional adjudication some steps, which when taken were thought to approach "the verge," have become the platform for yet further steps. A certain momentum develops in constitutional theory and it can be a "downhill thrust" easily set in motion but difficult to retard or stop. Development by momentum is not invariably bad; indeed, it is the way the common law has grown, but it is a force to be recognized and reckoned with. The dangers are increased by the difficulty of perceiving in advance exactly where the "verge" of the precipice lies. As well as constituting an independent evil against which the Religion Clauses were intended to protect, involvement [625] or entanglement between government and religion serves as a warning signal.

Finally, nothing we have said can be construed to disparage the role of church-related elementary and secondary schools in our national life. Their contribution has been and is enormous. Nor do we ignore their economic plight in a period of rising costs and expanding need. Taxpayers generally have been spared vast sums by the maintenance of these edu-cational institutions by religious organizations, largely by the gifts of faithful adherents.

The merit and benefits of these schools, however, are not the issue before us in these cases. The sole question is whether state aid to these schools can be squared with the dictates of the Religion Clauses. Under our system the choice has been made that gov-ernment is to be entirely excluded from the area of religious instruction and churches excluded from the affairs of government. The Constitution decrees that religion must be a private matter for the individual, the family, and the institutions of private choice, and that while some involvement and entanglement are inevitable, lines must be drawn. . . .

[661] MR. JUSTICE WHITE, concurring in part, dissenting in part.

It is our good fortune that the States of this country long ago recognized that instruc-tion of the young and old ranks high on the scale of proper governmental functions [662] and not only undertook secular education as a public responsibility but also required compulsory attendance at school by their young. Having recognized the value of edu-cated citizens and assumed the task of educating them, the States now before us assert a right to provide for the secular education of children whether they attend public schools or choose to enter private institutions, even when those institutions are church-related. The Federal Government also asserts that it is entitled, where requested, to contribute to the cost of secular education by furnishing buildings and facilities to all institutions of higher learning, public and private alike. Both the United States and the States urge that if parents choose to have their children receive instruction in the required secular subjects in a school where religion is also taught and a religious atmosphere may prevail, part or all of the cost of such secular instruction may be paid for by governmental grants to the religious institution conducting the school and seeking the grant. Those who chal-lenge this position would bar official contributions to secular education where the family prefers the parochial to both the public and nonsectarian private school.

The issue is fairly joined. It is precisely the kind of issue the Constitution contemplates this Court must ultimately decide. This is true although neither affirmance nor reversal of any of these cases follows automatically from the spare language of the First Amendment, from its history, or from the cases of this Court construing it and even though reasonable men can very easily and sensibly differ over the import of that language.

But, while the decision of the Court is legitimate, it is surely quite wrong in over-turning the Pennsylvania and Rhode Island statutes on the ground that they amount to an establishment of religion forbidden by the First Amendment.

[663] No one in these cases questions the constitutional right of parents to satisfy their state-imposed obligation to educate their children by sending them to private schools, sectarian or otherwise, as long as those schools meet minimum standards es-tablished for secular instruction. The States are not only permitted, but required by the Constitution, to free students attending private schools from any public school atten-dance obligation. *Pierce v. Society of Sisters* (1925). The States may also furnish transpor-tation for students, *Everson v. Board of Education* (1947), and books for teaching secular subjects to students attending parochial and other private as well as public schools, *Board of Education v. Allen* (1968); we have also upheld arrangements whereby students are released from public school classes so that they may attend religious instruction. *Zorach v. Clauson* (1952). Outside the field of education, we have upheld Sunday closing laws, *McGowan v. Maryland* (1961), state and federal laws exempting church property

and church activity from taxation, *Walz v. Tax Commission* (1970), and governmental grants to religious organizations for the purpose of financing improvements in the facilities of hospitals managed and controlled by religious orders. *Bradfield v. Roberts* (1899).

Our prior cases have recognized the dual role of parochial schools in American society: they perform both religious and secular functions. See *Board of Education v. Allen*, at 248. Our cases also recognize that legislation having a secular purpose and extending governmental assistance to sectarian schools in the performance of their secular functions does not constitute "law[s] respecting an establishment of religion" forbidden by the First Amendment merely because a secular program may incidentally benefit a church in fulfilling its religious mission. [664] That religion may indirectly benefit from governmental aid to the secular activities of churches does not convert that aid into an impermissible establishment of religion. . . .

It is enough for me that the States and the Federal Government are financing a separable secular function of overriding importance in order to sustain the legislation here challenged. That religion and private interests other than education may substantially benefit does not convert these laws into impermissible establishments of religion.

[665] The Court strikes down the Rhode Island statute on its face. No fault is found with the secular purpose of the program; there is no suggestion that the purpose of the program was aid to religion disguised in secular attire. Nor does the Court find that the primary effect of the program is to aid religion rather than to implement secular goals. The Court nevertheless finds [666] that impermissible "entanglement" will result from administration of the program. The reasoning is a curious and mystifying blend, but a critical factor appears to be an unwillingness to accept the District Court's express findings that on the evidence before it none of the teachers here involved mixed religious and secular instruction. Rather, the District Court struck down the Rhode Island statute because it concluded that activities outside the secular classroom would probably have a religious content and that support for religious education therefore necessarily resulted from the financial aid to the secular programs, since that aid generally strengthened the parochial schools and increased the number of their students.

In view of the decision in *Tilton*, however, where these same factors were found insufficient to invalidate the federal plan, the Court is forced to other considerations. Accepting the District Court's observation in *DiCenso* that education is an integral part of the religious mission of the Catholic church [sic]—an observation that should neither surprise nor alarm anyone, especially judges who have already approved substantial aid to parochial schools in various forms—the majority then interposes findings and conclusions that the District Court expressly abjured, namely, that nuns, clerics, and dedicated Catholic laymen unavoidably pose a grave risk in that they might not be able to put aside their religion in the secular classroom. Although stopping short of considering them untrustworthy, the Court concludes that for them the difficulties of avoiding teaching religion along with secular subjects would pose intolerable risks and would in any event entail an unacceptable enforcement regime. Thus, the potential for impermissible fostering of religion in secular classrooms—an untested assumption of the Court—paradoxically renders unacceptable the State's efforts at insuring that secular teachers under religious discipline successfully avoid conflicts between the religious mission [667] of the school and the secular purpose of the State's education program.

The difficulty with this is twofold. In the first place, it is contrary to the evidence and the District Court's findings in *DiCenso*. The Court points to nothing in this record indicating that any participating teacher had inserted religion into his secular teaching or had any difficulty in avoiding doing so. The testimony of the teachers was quite the contrary. . . .

Secondly, the Court accepts the model for the Catholic elementary and secondary schools that was rejected for the Catholic universities or colleges in the *Tilton* case. There it was urged that the Catholic condition of higher learning was an integral part of the religious mission of the church and that these institutions did everything they could to foster the faith. The Court's response was that on the record before it none of [668] the involved institutions was shown to have complied with the model and that it would not purport to pass on cases not before it. Here, however, the Court strikes down this Rhode Island statute based primarily on its own model and its own suppositions and unsupported views of what is likely to happen in Rhode Island parochial school classrooms, although on this record there is no indication that entanglement difficulties will accompany the salary supplement program.

The Court thus creates an insoluble paradox for the State and the parochial schools. The State cannot finance secular instruction if it permits religion to be taught in the same classroom; but if it exacts a promise that religion not be so taught—a promise the school and its teachers are quite willing and on this record able to give—and enforces it, it is then entangled in the "no entanglement" aspect of the Court's Establishment Clause jurisprudence.

[669] With respect to Pennsylvania, the Court, accepting as true the factual allegations of the complaint, as it must for purposes of a motion to dismiss, would reverse the dismissal of the complaint and invalidate the legislation. [670] The critical allegations, as paraphrased by the Court, are that "the church-related elementary and secondary schools are controlled by religious organizations, have the purpose of propagating and promoting a particular religious faith, and conduct their operations to fulfill that purpose." *Ante*, at 620. From these allegations the Court concludes that forbidden entanglements would follow from enforcing compliance with the secular purpose for which the state money is being paid.

I disagree. There is no specific allegation in the complaint that sectarian teaching does or would invade secular classes supported by state funds. That the schools are operated to promote a particular religion is quite consistent with the view that secular teaching devoid of religious instruction can successfully be maintained, for good secular instruction is, as Judge Coffin wrote for the District Court in the Rhode Island case, essential to the success of the religious mission of the parochial school. I would no more here than in the Rhode Island case substitute presumption for proof that religion is or would be taught in state-financed secular courses or assume that enforcement measures would be so extensive as to border on a free exercise violation. We should not forget that the Pennsylvania statute does not compel church schools to accept state funds. I cannot hold that the First Amendment forbids an agreement between the school and the State that the state funds would be used only to teach secular subjects.

I do agree, however, that the complaint should not have been dismissed for failure to state a cause of action. Although it did not specifically allege that the schools involved mixed religious teaching with secular subjects, the complaint did allege that the schools were operated to fulfill religious purposes and one of the legal theories stated in the complaint was that the Pennsylvania Act "finances and participates in the blending of sectarian [671] and secular instruction." At trial under this complaint, evidence showing such a blend in a course supported by state funds would appear to be admissible and, if credited, would establish financing of religious instruction by the State. Hence, I would reverse the judgment of the District Court and remand the case for trial, thereby holding the Pennsylvania legislation valid on its face but leaving open the question of its validity as applied to the particular facts of this case. . . .

Tilton v. Richardson

403 U.S. 672 (1971)

Vote: 5—Burger, Harlan, Stewart, White, Blackmun
    4—Black, Douglas, Brennan, Marshall

Opinion announcing the opinion of the Court: Burger
Opinion concurring in the judgment: White
Dissenting opinions: Douglas (in part), Brennan

This case resulted from a taxpayer challenge to expenditures made pursuant to Title I of the Higher Education Facilities Act of 1963. The federal law authorized grants and loans up to 50 percent of the cost for the construction of undergraduate academic facilities in both public and private colleges and universities. The act was passed in response to a nationwide demand for the expansion of college and university facilities to meet the sharply rising number of young people pursuing higher education.

A project was eligible for funding if construction would result "in an urgently needed substantial expansion of the institution's student enrollment capacity, capacity to provide needed health care to students or personnel of the institution, or capacity to carry out extension and continuing education programs on the campus of such institution." 20 U.S.C. § 716 (1964 ed., Supp. V). Academic facilities were defined as "structures suitable for use as classrooms, laboratories, libraries, and related facilities necessary or appropriate for instruction of students, or for research . . . programs." The act excluded for funding facilities that were "used or to be used for sectarian instruction or as a place for religious worship" or any facilities that were used "primarily in connection with any part of the program of a school or department of divinity." 20 U.S.C. § 751 (a) (1964 ed., Supp. V). Under the act, the government retained a twenty-year interest in financed facilities. If a financed facility was used for purposes other than as a secular academic facility during that twenty-year period, the United States was entitled to recover a proportionate part of the federal grant. During the twenty-year period, the statutory restrictions were to be enforced by the Office of Education, primarily by way of on-site inspections. At the end of the twenty-year period, the federal interest in the facility ceased, and the college was free to use it as it pleased.

The specific expenditures at issue in this case related to the construction of a library at Sacred Heart University; a music, drama, and arts building at Annhurst College; a library and a science building at Fairfield University; and a laboratory at Albertus

Magnus College. All four higher education institutions were Catholic in character and controlled by religious orders.

MR. CHIEF JUSTICE BURGER announced the judgment of the Court and an opinion in which MR. JUSTICE HARLAN, MR. JUSTICE STEWART, and MR. JUSTICE BLACKMUN join.

. . . [677] III

Numerous cases considered by the Court have noted the internal tension in the First Amendment between the Establishment Clause and the Free Exercise Clause. *Walz v. Tax Comm'n*, 397 U.S. 664 (1970), is the most recent decision seeking to define the boundaries of the neutral area between these two provisions within which the legislature may legitimately act. There, as in other decisions, the Court treated the three main concerns against which the Establishment Clause sought to protect: "sponsorship, financial support, and active involvement of the sovereign in religious activity." *Id.*, at 668.

Every analysis must begin with the candid acknowledgment that there is no single constitutional caliper that can be used to measure the precise degree to which these three factors are present or absent. Instead, our [678] analysis in this area must begin with a consideration of the cumulative criteria developed over many years and applying to a wide range of governmental action challenged as violative of the Establishment Clause.

There are always risks in treating criteria discussed by the Court from time to time as "tests" in any limiting sense of that term. Constitutional adjudication does not lend itself to the absolutes of the physical sciences or mathematics. The standards should rather be viewed as guidelines with which to identify instances in which the objectives of the Religion Clauses have been impaired. And, as we have noted in *Lemon v. Kurtzman* and *Earley v. DiCenso*, at 612, candor compels the acknowledgment that we can only dimly perceive the boundaries of permissible government activity in this sensitive area of constitutional adjudication.

Against this background we consider four questions: First, does the Act reflect a secular legislative purpose? Second, is the primary effect of the Act to advance or inhibit religion? Third, does the administration of the Act foster an excessive government entanglement with religion? Fourth, does the implementation of the Act inhibit the free exercise of religion?

(a)

The stated legislative purpose appears in the preamble where Congress found and declared that

> "the security and welfare of the United States require that this and future generations of American youth be assured ample opportunity for the fullest development of their intellectual capacities, and that this opportunity will be jeopardized unless the Nation's colleges and universities are encouraged and assisted in their efforts to accommodate rapidly growing numbers of youth who aspire to a higher education." 20 U.S.C. § 701.

[679] This expresses a legitimate secular objective entirely appropriate for governmental action.

The simplistic argument that every form of financial aid to church-sponsored activity violates the Religion Clauses was rejected long ago in *Bradfield v. Roberts*, 175 U.S. 291 (1899). There a federal construction grant to a hospital operated by a religious order was upheld. Here the Act is challenged on the ground that its primary effect is to aid the religious purposes of church-related colleges and universities. Construction grants surely aid these institutions in the sense that the construction of buildings will assist them to perform their various functions. But bus transportation, textbooks, and tax exemptions all gave aid in the sense that religious bodies would otherwise have been forced to find other sources from which to finance these services. Yet all of these forms of governmental assistance have been upheld. The crucial question is not whether some benefit accrues to a religious institution as a consequence of the legislative program, but whether its principal or primary effect advances religion.

A possibility always exists, of course, that the legitimate objectives of any law or legislative program may be subverted by conscious design or lax enforcement. There is nothing new in this argument. But judicial concern about these possibilities cannot, standing alone, warrant striking down a statute as unconstitutional. . . .

[682] (b)

Although we reject appellants' broad constitutional arguments we do perceive an aspect in which the statute's enforcement provisions are inadequate to ensure that the impact of the federal aid will not advance religion. If a recipient institution violates any of the statutory restrictions on the use of a federally financed facility, § 754 (b)(2) permits the Government to recover an amount equal to the proportion of the facility's present value that the federal grant bore to its original cost.

[683] This remedy, however, is available to the Government only if the statutory conditions are violated "within twenty years after completion of construction." This 20-year period is termed by the statute as "the period of Federal interest" and reflects Congress' finding that after 20 years "the public benefit accruing to the United States" from the use of the federally financed facility "will equal or exceed in value" the amount of the federal grant. 20 U.S.C. § 754 (a).

Under § 754 (b)(2), therefore, a recipient institution's obligation not to use the facility for sectarian instruction or religious worship would appear to expire at the end of 20 years. We note, for example, that under § 718 (b)(7)(C) (1964 ed., Supp. V), an institution applying for a federal grant is only required to provide assurances that the facility will not be used for sectarian instruction or religious worship "during at least the period of the Federal interest therein (as defined in section 754 of this title)."

Limiting the prohibition for religious use of the structure to 20 years obviously opens the facility to use for any purpose at the end of that period. It cannot be assumed that a substantial structure has no value after that period and hence the unrestricted use of a valuable property is in effect a contribution of some value to a religious body. Congress did not base the 20-year provision on any contrary conclusion. If, at the end of 20 years, the building is, for example, converted into a chapel or otherwise used to promote religious interests, the original federal grant will in part have the effect of advancing religion.

To this extent the Act therefore trespasses on the Religion Clauses. The restrictive obligations of a recipient institution under § 751 (a)(2) cannot, compatibly with the Religion Clauses, expire while the building has substantial value. This circumstance does not require us to [684] invalidate the entire Act, however. "The cardinal principle of statutory construction is to save and not to destroy." *NLRB v. Jones & Laughlin Steel Corp.*, 301 U.S. 1, 30 (1937). . . .

IV

We next turn to the question of whether excessive entanglements characterize the relationship between government and church under the Act. . . .

[685] There are generally significant differences between the religious aspects of church-related institutions of higher learning and parochial elementary and secondary schools. The "affirmative if not dominant policy" of the instruction in pre-college church schools is "to assure future [686] adherents to a particular faith by having control of their total education at an early age." *Walz v. Tax Comm'n, supra*, at 671. There is substance to the contention that college students are less impressionable and less susceptible to religious indoctrination. Common observation would seem to support that view, and Congress may well have entertained it. The skepticism of the college student is not an inconsiderable barrier to any attempt or tendency to subvert the congressional objectives and limitations. Furthermore, by their very nature, college and postgraduate courses tend to limit the opportunities for sectarian influence by virtue of their own internal disciplines. Many church-related colleges and universities are characterized by a high degree of academic freedom and seek to evoke free and critical responses from their students.

The record here would not support a conclusion that any of these four institutions departed from this general pattern. . . .

[687] Since religious indoctrination is not a substantial purpose or activity of these church-related colleges and universities, there is less likelihood than in primary and secondary schools that religion will permeate the area of secular education. This reduces the risk that government aid will in fact serve to support religious activities. Correspondingly, the necessity for intensive government surveillance is diminished and the resulting entanglements between government and religion lessened. Such inspection as may be necessary to ascertain that the facilities are devoted to secular education is minimal and indeed hardly more than the inspections that States impose over all private schools within the reach of compulsory education laws.

The entanglement between church and state is also lessened here by the nonideological character of the aid that the Government provides. Our cases from *Everson* to *Allen* have permitted church-related schools to receive government aid in the form of secular, neutral, or nonideological services, facilities, or materials that are supplied to all students regardless of the affiliation of the school that they attend. . . .

[688] Finally, government entanglements with religion are reduced by the circumstance that, unlike the direct and continuing payments under the Pennsylvania program, and all the incidents of regulation and surveillance, the Government aid here is a onetime, single-purpose construction grant. There are no continuing financial relationships or dependencies, no annual audits, and no government analysis of an institution's expenditures on secular as distinguished from religious activities. Inspection as to use is a minimal contact. . . .

We think that cumulatively these three factors also substantially lessen the potential for divisive religious fragmentation in the political arena. This conclusion is admittedly difficult to document, but neither have appellants pointed to any continuing religious aggravation on this matter in the political processes. Possibly this can be explained by the character and diversity of the recipient colleges and universities and the absence of any intimate continuing relationship or dependency between government and religiously af-filiated institutions. The [689] potential for divisiveness inherent in the essentially local problems of primary and secondary schools is significantly less with respect to a college or university whose student constituency is not local but diverse and widely dispersed.

V

Finally, we must consider whether the implementation of the Act inhibits the free exercise of religion in violation of the First Amendment. Appellants claim that the Free Exercise Clause is violated because they are compelled to pay taxes, the proceeds of which in part finance grants under the Act. Appellants, however, are unable to identify any coercion directed at the practice or exercise of their religious beliefs. Their share of the cost of the grants under the Act is not fundamentally distinguishable from the impact of the tax exemption sustained in *Walz* or the provision of textbooks upheld in *Allen*.

We conclude that the Act does not violate the Religion Clauses of the First Amendment except that part of § 754 (b)(2) providing a 20-year limitation on the religious use restrictions contained in § 751 (a)(2).

MR. JUSTICE DOUGLAS, with whom MR. JUSTICE BLACK and MR. JUSTICE MARSHALL concur, dissenting in part.

The correct constitutional principle for this case was stated by President Kennedy in 1961 when questioned as [690] to his policy respecting aid to private and parochial schools[1]:

> "The Constitution clearly prohibits aid to the school, to parochial schools. I don't think there is any doubt of that.
>
> The *Everson* case, which is probably the most celebrated case, provided only by a 5 to 4 decision was it possible for a local community to provide bus rides to nonpublic school children. But all through the majority and minority statements on that particular question there was a very clear prohibition against aid to the school direct. The Supreme Court made its decision in the *Everson* case by determining that the aid was to the child, not to the school. Aid to the school is—there isn't any room for debate on that subject. It is prohibited by the Constitution, and the Supreme Court has made that very clear. And therefore there would be no possibility of our recommending it." . . .

[692] The public purpose in secular education is, to be sure, furthered by the program. Yet the sectarian purpose is aided by making the parochial school system viable. The purpose is to increase "student enrollment" and the students obviously aimed at are those of the particular faith now financed by taxpayers' money. Parochial schools are not beamed at agnostics, atheists, or those of a competing sect. The more sophisticated institutions may admit minorities; but the dominant religious character is not changed.

The reversion of the facility to the parochial school[2] at the end of 20 years is an outright grant, measurable by the present discounted worth of the facility. A gift of taxpay-

---

1. Public Papers of the Presidents of the United States, John F. Kennedy, 1961, pp. 142–143, News Conference March 1, 1961.

2. "It should be clear to all that a Roman Catholic parochial school is an integral part of that church, as definitely so as is the service of worship. A parochial school is usually developed in connection with a church. In many cases the church and school monies are not even separated. Such a school is in no sense a public

ers' funds in that amount would plainly be unconstitutional. The Court properly bars it even though disguised in the form of a reversionary interest.

But the invalidation of this one clause cannot cure the constitutional infirmities of the statute as a whole. The Federal Government is giving religious schools a block grant to build certain facilities. The fact that money is [693] given once at the beginning of a program rather than apportioned annually as in *Lemon* and *DiCenso* is without constitutional significance. The First Amendment bars establishment of a religion. And as I noted today in *Lemon* and *DiCenso*, this bar has been consistently interpreted from *Everson v. Board of Education*, 330 U.S. 1, 16, through *Torcaso v. Watkins*, 367 U.S. 488, 493, as meaning: "No tax in any amount, large or small, can be levied to support any religious activities or institutions, whatever they may be called, or whatever form they may adopt to teach or practice religion." Thus it is hardly impressive that rather than giving a smaller amount of money annually over a long period of years, Congress instead gives a large amount all at once. The plurality's distinction is in effect that small violations of the First Amendment over a period of years are unconstitutional (see *Lemon* and *DiCenso*) while a huge violation occurring only once is *de minimis*. I cannot agree with such sophistry.

What I have said in *Lemon* and in the *DiCenso* cases decided today is relevant here. The facilities financed by taxpayers' funds are not to be used for "sectarian" purposes. Religious teaching and secular teaching are so enmeshed in parochial schools that only the strictest supervision and surveillance would insure compliance with the condition. Parochial schools may require religious exercises, even in the classroom. A parochial school operates on one budget. Money not spent for one purpose becomes available for other purposes. Thus the fact that there are no religious observances in federally financed facilities is not controlling because required religious observances will take place in other buildings. Our decision in *Engel v. Vitale* held that a requirement of a prayer in public schools violated the Establishment Clause. Once these schools become federally funded they become bound by federal standards [694] and accordingly adherence to *Engel* would require an end to required religious exercises. That kind of surveillance and control will certainly be obnoxious to the church authorities and if done will radically change the character of the parochial school. Yet if that surveillance is not searching and continuous, this federal financing is obnoxious under the Establishment and Free Exercise Clauses for the reasons stated in the companion cases.

In other words, surveillance creates an entanglement of government and religion which the First Amendment was designed to avoid. Yet after today's decision there will be a requirement of surveillance which will last for the useful life of the building and as we have previously noted, "[it] is hardly lack of due process for the Government to regulate that which it subsidizes." *Wickard v. Filburn*, 317 U.S. 111, 131. The price of the subsidy under the Act is violation of the Free Exercise Clause. Could a course in the History of Methodism be taught in a federally financed building? Would a religiously slanted version of the Reformation or Quebec politics under Duplessis be permissible? How can the Government know what is taught in the federally financed building without a continuous auditing of classroom instruction? Yet both the Free Exercise Clause

---

school, even though some children from other groups may be admitted to it. The buildings are not owned and controlled by a community of American people, not even by a community of American Roman Catholic *people*. The title of ownership in a public school is vested in the local community, in the elected officers of the school board or the city council. But the title of ownership in a parochial school is vested in the bishop as an individual, who is appointed by, who is under the direct control of, and who reports to the pope in Rome." L. Boettner, *Roman Catholicism* 375 (1962) (italics in original).

and academic freedom are violated when the Government agent must be present to determine whether the course content is satisfactory.

As I said in the *Lemon* and *DiCenso* cases, a parochial school is a unitary institution with subtle blending of sectarian and secular instruction. Thus the practices of religious schools are in no way affected by the minimal requirement that the government financed facility may [695] not "be used for sectarian instruction or as a place for religious worship." Money saved from one item in the budget is free to be used elsewhere. By conducting religious services in another building, the school has—rent free—a building for nonsectarian use. This is not called Establishment simply because the government retains a continuing interest in the building for its useful life, even though the religious schools need never pay a cent for the use of the building. . . .

[697] I dissent not because of any lack of respect for parochial schools but out of a feeling of despair that the respect which through history has been accorded the First Amendment is this day lost.

It should be remembered that in this case we deal with federal grants and with the command that "Congress shall make no law respecting an establishment of religion, or prohibiting the free exercise thereof." The million-dollar grants sustained today put Madison's miserable "three pence" to shame. But he even thought, as I do, that even a small amount coming out of the pocket of taxpayers and going into the coffers of a church was not in keeping with our constitutional ideal. . . .

25

Wisconsin v. Yoder

406 U.S. 205 (1972)

Vote: 6—Burger, Brennan, Stewart, White, Marshall, Blackmun
     1—Douglas

Opinion announcing the opinion of the Court: Burger
Concurring opinion: Stewart, White
Dissenting opinion: Douglas (in part)
Not participating in the case: Powell, Rehnquist

Respondents Jonas Yoder and Wallace Miller were members of the Old Order Amish religion and the Conservative Amish Mennonite religion. After declining to send their children to public or private school after the children had graduated from eighth grade, Yoder and Miller were fined $5 each as a result of their conviction for violating a Wisconsin compulsory school-attendance law. The law required all children in the state to attend school until the age of sixteen.

Trial testimony showed that Yoder and Miller believed, in accordance with the tenets of Old Order Amish communities in general, that their children's attendance at high school, public or private, was contrary to the Amish religion and way of life and that sending their children to high school would lead to censure by their church community. The county court found the respondents believed that to continue sending their children to school would endanger their own salvation and that of their children. The state stipulated that the respondents' religious beliefs were sincere. At trial, it was also demonstrated that the Amish provided informal vocational education to their children, which was designed to prepare them for life in the rural Amish community.

In its majority opinion, the Supreme Court discussed various aspects of the Amish religion: that, in general, Old Order Amish communities are devoted to a life in harmony with nature and the soil, as exemplified by the simple life of early Christians; that Amish beliefs require community members to make their living by farming or closely related activities; that Old Order Amish religion pervades and determines the entire mode of life of its adherents; that conduct is regulated in great detail by the Ordnung, or rules, of the church community; and that adult baptism, which occurs in late adolescence, is the time at which Amish young people voluntarily undertake heavy obligations to abide by the rules of the church community. The Court's opinion further explained that the Amish object to high school and higher education in general *because the values learned there are in marked variance with Amish values and the Amish way of life. The Amish, the Court reported, view secondary school education as an impermissible exposure of their children to a "worldly" influence (e.g., intellectual and scientific accomplishments, self-distinction, competitiveness, worldly success, and social life with other students) that lies in conflict with their beliefs in informal learning through doing; a life of "goodness," rather than a life of intellect; wisdom rather than technical knowledge; community welfare rather than competition; and separation from, rather than integration with, contemporary worldly society. According to the Supreme Court, Old Order Amish communities are characterized by a fundamental belief that salvation requires life in a church community separate and apart from the world and worldly influence and that this concept of life aloof from the world and its values is central to their faith.*

BURGER, C. J., delivered the opinion of the Court, in which BRENNAN, STEWART, WHITE, MARSHALL, and BLACKMUN, JJ., joined.

. . . [213] I

There is no doubt as to the power of a State, having a high responsibility for education of its citizens, to impose reasonable regulations for the control and duration of basic education. See, *e.g.*, *Pierce v. Society of Sisters*, 268 U.S. 510, 534 (1925). Providing public schools ranks at the very apex of the function of a State. Yet even this paramount responsibility was, in *Pierce*, made to yield to the right of parents to provide an equivalent education in a privately operated system. There the Court held that Oregon's statute compelling attendance in a public school from age eight to age 16 unreasonably interfered with the interest of parents in directing the rearing of their offspring, including their education in church-operated schools. As that case suggests, the values of parental direction of the religious upbringing [214] and education of their children in their early and formative years have a high place in our society. Thus, a State's interest in universal education, however highly we rank it, is not totally free from a balancing process when it impinges on fundamental rights and interests, such as those specifically protected by the Free Exercise Clause of the First Amendment, and the traditional interest of parents with respect to the religious upbringing of their children so long as they, in the words of *Pierce*, "prepare [them] for additional obligations." 268 U.S., at 535.

It follows that in order for Wisconsin to compel school attendance beyond the eighth grade against a claim that such attendance interferes with the practice of a legitimate religious belief, it must appear either that the State does not deny the free exercise of religious belief by its requirement, or that there is a state interest of sufficient magnitude to override the interest claiming protection under the Free Exercise Clause. . . .

[215] II

We come then to the quality of the claims of the respondents concerning the alleged encroachment of Wisconsin's compulsory school-attendance statute on their rights and the rights of their children to the free exercise of the religious beliefs they and their forebears have adhered to for almost three centuries. In evaluating those claims we must be careful to determine whether the Amish religious faith and their mode of life are, as they claim, inseparable and interdependent. A way of life, however virtuous and admirable, may not be interposed as a barrier to reasonable state regulation of education if it is based on purely secular considerations; to have the protection of the Religion Clauses, the claims must be rooted in religious belief. Although a determination of what is a "religious" belief or practice entitled to constitutional protection may present a most delicate question, the very concept of ordered liberty precludes [216] allowing every person to make his own standards on matters of conduct in which society as a whole has important interests. Thus, if the Amish asserted their claims because of their subjective evaluation and rejection of the contemporary secular values accepted by the majority, much as Thoreau rejected the social values of his time and isolated himself at Walden Pond, their claims would not rest on a religious basis. Thoreau's choice was philosophical and personal rather than religious, and such belief does not rise to the demands of the Religion Clauses.

Giving no weight to such secular considerations, however, we see that the record in this case abundantly supports the claim that the traditional way of life of the Amish is not merely a matter of personal preference, but one of deep religious conviction, shared by an organized group, and intimately related to daily living. That the Old Order Amish daily life and religious practice stem from their faith is shown by the fact that it is in response to their literal interpretation of the Biblical injunction from the Epistle of Paul to the Romans, "be not conformed to this world. . . ." This command is fundamental to the Amish faith. Moreover, for the Old Order Amish, religion is not simply a matter of theocratic belief. As the expert witnesses explained, the Old Order Amish religion pervades and determines virtually their entire way of life, regulating it with the detail of the Talmudic diet through the strictly enforced rules of the church community.

The record shows that the respondents' religious beliefs and attitude toward life, family, and home have remained constant—perhaps some would say static—in a period of unparalleled progress in human knowledge generally and great changes in education. The respondents [217] freely concede, and indeed assert as an article of faith, that their religious beliefs and what we would today call "life style" have not altered in fundamentals for centuries. Their way of life in a church-oriented community, separated from the outside world and "worldly" influences, their attachment to nature and the soil, is a way inherently simple and uncomplicated, albeit difficult to preserve against the pressure to conform. Their rejection of telephones, automobiles, radios, and television, their mode of dress, of speech, their habits of manual work do indeed set them apart from much of contemporary society; these customs are both symbolic and practical. . . .

As the record so strongly shows, the values and programs of the modern secondary school are in sharp conflict with the fundamental mode of life mandated by the Amish religion; modern laws requiring compulsory secondary education have accordingly engendered great concern and conflict. [218] The conclusion is inescapable that secondary schooling, by exposing Amish children to worldly influences in terms of attitudes, goals, and values contrary to beliefs, and by substantially interfering with the religious development of the Amish child and his integration into the way of life of the Amish faith community at the crucial adolescent stage of development, contravenes the basic religious tenets and practice of the Amish faith, both as to the parent and the child.

The impact of the compulsory-attendance law on respondents' practice of the Amish religion is not only severe, but inescapable, for the Wisconsin law affirmatively compels them, under threat of criminal sanction, to perform acts undeniably at odds with fundamental tenets of their religious beliefs. Nor is the impact of the compulsory-attendance law confined to grave interference with important Amish religious tenets from a subjective point of view. It carries with it precisely the kind of objective danger to the free exercise of religion that the First Amendment was designed to prevent. As the record shows, compulsory school attendance to age 16 for Amish children carries with it a very real threat of undermining the Amish community and religious practice as they exist today; they must either abandon belief and be assimilated into society at large, or be forced to migrate to some other and more tolerant region.

[219] In sum, the unchallenged testimony of acknowledged experts in education and religious history, almost 300 years of consistent practice, and strong evidence of a sustained faith pervading and regulating respondents' entire mode of life support the claim that enforcement of the State's requirement of compulsory formal education after the eighth grade would gravely endanger if not destroy the free exercise of respondents' religious beliefs.

III

Neither the findings of the trial court nor the Amish claims as to the nature of their faith are challenged in this Court by the State of Wisconsin. Its position is that the State's interest in universal compulsory formal secondary education to age 16 is so great that it is paramount to the undisputed claims of respondents that their mode of preparing their youth for Amish life, after the traditional elementary education, is an essential part of their religious belief and practice. Nor does the State undertake to meet the claim that the Amish mode of life and education is inseparable from and a part of the basic tenets of their religion—indeed, as much a part of their religious belief and practices as baptism, the confessional, or a sabbath may be for others. . . .

[220] Nor can this case be disposed of on the grounds that Wisconsin's requirement for school attendance to age 16 applies uniformly to all citizens of the State and does not, on its face, discriminate against religions or a particular religion, or that it is motivated by legitimate secular concerns. A regulation neutral on its face may, in its application, nonetheless offend the constitutional requirement for governmental neutrality if it unduly burdens the free exercise of religion. The Court must not ignore the danger that an exception [221] from a general obligation of citizenship on religious grounds may run afoul of the Establishment Clause, but that danger cannot be allowed to prevent any exception no matter how vital it may be to the protection of values promoted by the right of free exercise. By preserving doctrinal flexibility and recognizing the need for a sensible and realistic application of the Religion Clauses

> "we have been able to chart a course that preserved the autonomy and freedom of religious bodies while avoiding any semblance of established religion. This is a 'tight rope' and one we have successfully traversed." *Walz v. Tax Commission*, at 672.

We turn, then, to the State's broader contention that its interest in its system of compulsory education is so compelling that even the established religious practices of the Amish must give way. Where fundamental claims of religious freedom are at stake, however, we cannot accept such a sweeping claim; despite its admitted validity in the generality of cases, we must searchingly examine the interests that the State seeks to promote by its requirement for compulsory education to age 16, and the impediment to those objectives that would flow from recognizing the claimed Amish exemption.

The State advances two primary arguments in support of its system of compulsory education. It notes, as Thomas Jefferson pointed out early in our history, that some degree of education is necessary to prepare citizens to participate effectively and intelligently in our open political system if we are to preserve freedom and independence.

Further, education prepares individuals to be self-reliant and self-sufficient participants in society. We accept these propositions.

[222] However, the evidence adduced by the Amish in this case is persuasively to the effect that an additional one or two years of formal high school for Amish children in place of their long-established program of informal vocational education would do little to serve those interests. Respondents' experts testified at trial, without challenge, that the value of all education must be assessed in terms of its capacity to prepare the child for life. It is one thing to say that compulsory education for a year or two beyond the eighth grade may be necessary when its goal is the preparation of the child for life in modern society as the majority live, but it is quite another if the goal of education be viewed as the preparation of the child for life in the separated agrarian community that is the keystone of the Amish faith.

The State attacks respondents' position as one fostering "ignorance" from which the child must be protected by the State. No one can question the State's duty to protect children from ignorance but this argument does not square with the facts disclosed in the record. Whatever their idiosyncrasies as seen by the majority, this record strongly shows that the Amish community has been a highly successful social unit within our society, even if apart from the conventional "mainstream." Its members are productive and very law-abiding members of society; they reject public welfare in any of its usual modern forms. The Congress itself recognized their self-sufficiency by authorizing exemption of such groups as the Amish from the obligation to pay social security taxes. . . .

[224] The State, however, supports its interest in providing an additional one or two years of compulsory high school education to Amish children because of the possibility that some such children will choose to leave the Amish community, and that if this occurs they will be ill-equipped for life. The State argues that if Amish children leave their church they should not be in the position of making their way in the world without the education available in the one or two additional years the State requires. However, on this record, that argument is highly speculative. There is no specific evidence of the loss of Amish adherents by attrition, nor is there any showing that upon leaving the Amish community Amish children, with their practical agricultural training and habits of industry and self-reliance, would become burdens on society because of educational short-comings. . . .

[234] V

For the reasons stated we hold, with the Supreme Court of Wisconsin, that the First and Fourteenth Amendments prevent the State from compelling respondents to cause their children to attend formal high school to age 16. Our disposition of this case, however, in no way [235] alters our recognition of the obvious fact that courts are not school boards or legislatures, and are ill-equipped to determine the "necessity" of discrete aspects of a State's program of compulsory education. This should suggest that courts must move with great circumspection in performing the sensitive and delicate task of weighing a State's legitimate social concern when faced with religious claims for exemption from generally applicable educational requirements. It cannot be overemphasized that we are not dealing with a way of life and mode of education by a group claiming to have recently discovered some "progressive" or more enlightened process for rearing children for modern life.

Aided by a history of three centuries as an identifiable religious sect and a long history as a successful and self-sufficient segment of American society, the Amish in this case have convincingly demonstrated the sincerity of their religious beliefs, the interrelationship of belief with their mode of life, the vital role that belief and daily conduct play in the continued survival of Old Order Amish communities and their religious organization, and the hazards presented by the State's enforcement of a statute generally valid as to others. Beyond this, they have carried the even more difficult burden of demonstrating the adequacy of their alternative mode of continuing informal vocational education in terms of precisely those overall interests that the State advances in support of its program of compulsory high school education. In light of this convincing [236] showing, one that probably few other religious groups or sects could make, and weighing the minimal difference between what the State would require and what the Amish already accept, it was incumbent on the State to show with more particularity how its admittedly strong interest in compulsory education would be adversely affected by granting an exemption to the Amish. . . .

[241] MR. JUSTICE DOUGLAS, dissenting in part.

I agree with the Court that the religious scruples of the Amish are opposed to the education of their children beyond the grade schools, yet I disagree with the Court's conclusion that the matter is within the dispensation of parents alone. The Court's analysis assumes that the only interests at stake in the case are those of the Amish parents on the one hand, and those of the State on the other. The difficulty with this approach is that, despite the Court's claim, the parents are seeking to vindicate not only their own free exercise claims, but also those of their high-school-age children. . . .

[242] If the parents in this case are allowed a religious exemption, the inevitable effect is to impose the parents' notions of religious duty upon their children. Where the child is mature enough to express potentially conflicting desires, it would be an invasion of the child's rights to permit such an imposition without canvassing his views. As in *Prince v. Massachusetts*, it is an imposition resulting from this very litigation. As the child has no other effective forum, it is in this litigation that his rights should be considered. And, if an Amish child desires to attend high school, and is mature enough to have that desire respected, the State may well be able to override the parents' religiously motivated objections. . . .

[244] On this important and vital matter of education, I think the children should be entitled to be heard. While the parents, absent dissent, normally speak for the entire family, the education of the child is a matter on which the child will often have decided views. He may want to be a pianist or an astronaut or an oceanographer. [245] To do so he will have to break from the Amish tradition.

It is the future of the student, not the future of the parents, that is imperiled by today's decision. If a parent keeps his child out of school beyond the grade school, then the child will be forever barred from entry into the new and amazing world of diversity that we have today. The child may decide that that is the preferred course, or he may rebel. It is the student's judgment, not his parents', that is essential if we are to give full meaning to what we have said about the Bill of Rights and of the right of students to be masters of their own destiny. If he is harnessed to the Amish way of life [246] by those in authority over him and if his education is truncated, his entire life may be stunted and deformed. The child, therefore, should be given an opportunity to be heard before the State gives the exemption which we honor today.

The views of the two children in question were not canvassed by the Wisconsin courts. The matter should be explicitly reserved so that new hearings can be held on remand of the case. . . .

Committee for Public Education and Religious Liberty v. Nyquist

413 U.S. 756 (1973)

Vote: 6—Douglas, Brennan, Stewart, White, Blackmun, Powell
2—Burger, Rehnquist (concurring in part and dissenting in part)
1—White

Opinion announcing the opinion of the Court: Powell
Opinion concurring in part and dissenting in part: Burger
Opinion dissenting in part: Rehnquist
Dissenting opinion: White

In May 1972, the governor of New York signed into law several amendments to the state's education and tax laws. The first five sections of these amendments established three distinct financial aid programs for nonpublic elementary and secondary schools, including church-affiliated schools.

The first section provided for direct money grants to "qualifying" nonpublic schools to be used for "maintenance and repair" of facilities and equipment. A "qualifying" school was a nonpublic, nonprofit elementary or secondary school serving a high concentration of pupils from low-income families. The annual grant was $30 per pupil ($40 per pupil if the facilities were more than twenty-five years old). The grant could not exceed 50 percent of the average per-pupil cost for equivalent services in the public schools. The statute defined "maintenance and repair" to include "the provision of heat, light, water, ventilation and sanitary facilities; cleaning, janitorial and custodial services; snow removal; necessary upkeep and renovation of buildings, grounds and equipment; fire and accident protection; and such other items as the commissioner may deem necessary to ensure the health, welfare and safety of enrolled pupils." The law was adopted subsequent to legislative findings that the state "has a primary responsibility to ensure the health, welfare and safety of children attending . . . nonpublic schools"; that the "fiscal crisis in nonpublic education . . . has caused a diminution of proper maintenance and repair programs, threatening the health, welfare and safety of nonpublic school children" in low-income urban areas; and that "a healthy and safe school environment" contributes "to the stability of urban neighborhoods."

The second section established a tuition-reimbursement plan for parents of children attending nonpublic elementary or secondary schools. To qualify, a parent's annual taxable income had to be less than $5,000. The amount of reimbursement was $50 per *child in grade school and $100 per high school student so long as those amounts did not exceed 50 percent of actual tuition paid. Section 2 was prefaced by a series of legislative findings declaring that a "healthy competitive and diverse alternative to public education is not only desirable but indeed vital to a state and nation that have continually reaffirmed the value of individual differences." The findings further emphasized that the ability to select among alternative educational systems "is diminished or even denied to children of lower-income families, whose parents, of all groups, have the least options in determining where their children are to be educated." The findings also stated that any "precipitous decline in the number of nonpublic school pupils would cause a massive increase in public school enrollment and costs," an increase that would "aggravate an already serious fiscal crisis in public education" and would "seriously jeopardize quality education for all children." Repeating a declaration contained in § 1, the findings concluded that "such assistance is clearly secular, neutral and nonideological."*

The third program, contained in §§ 3, 4, and 5 of the challenged law, provided tax relief to parents failing to qualify for tuition reimbursement. Each eligible taxpayer-parent was entitled to deduct a stipulated sum from his adjusted gross income for each child attending a nonpublic school. The amount of the deduction was unrelated to the amount of tuition actually paid and decreased as the amount of taxable income increased. If the taxpayer's adjusted gross income was less than $9,000, the taxpayer could subtract $1,000 for each of as many as three dependents. If a taxpayer had an adjusted gross income of $15,000, the taxpayer could subtract only $400 per dependent. Once adjusted gross income surpassed $25,000, no deduction was allowed. The tax deductions were designed to begin at approximately the income level at which tuition reimbursement benefits ended. These sections were also prefaced by a series of legislative findings similar to those accompanying the previous sections.

At the time of legislation, almost 20 percent of New York's students (between seven and eight hundred thousand children) attended nonpublic schools, approximately 85 percent of which were church affiliated. While practically all the schools entitled to receive maintenance and repair grants were Catholic, institutions qualifying under the remainder of the statute included a substantial number of Jewish, Lutheran, Episcopal, Seventh-Day Adventist, and other church-affiliated schools.

POWELL, J., delivered the opinion of the Court, in which DOUGLAS, BRENNAN, STEWART, MARSHALL, and BLACKMUN, JJ., joined.

[759] These cases raise a challenge under the Establishment Clause of the First Amendment to the constitutionality of a recently enacted New York law which provides financial assistance, in several ways, to nonpublic elementary and secondary schools in that State. The cases involve an intertwining of societal and constitutional issues of the greatest importance. . . .

[770] II

The history of the Establishment Clause has been recounted frequently and need not be repeated here. [771] It is enough to note that it is now firmly established that a law may be one "respecting an establishment of religion" even though its consequence is not to promote a "state religion," *Lemon v. Kurtzman*, 403 U.S. 602, 612 (1971), and even though it does not aid one religion more than another but merely benefits all religions alike. It is equally well established, however, that not every law that confers an "indirect," "remote," or "incidental" benefit upon religious institutions is, for that reason alone, constitutionally invalid. [772] What our cases require is careful examination of any law challenged on establishment grounds with a view to ascertaining whether it furthers any of the evils against which that Clause protects. Primary among those evils have been "sponsorship, financial support, and active involvement of the sovereign in religious activity." *Walz v. Tax Comm'n*, at 668; *Lemon v. Kurtzman*, at 612.

Most of the cases coming to this Court raising Establishment Clause questions have involved the relationship between religion and education. Among these religion-education precedents, two general categories of cases may be identified: those dealing with religious activities within the public schools, and those involving public aid in varying forms to sectarian educational institutions. While the New York legislation places this case in the latter category, its resolution requires consideration not only of the several aid-to-sectarian-education cases, but also of our other education precedents and of several important noneducation cases. For the now well-defined three-part test that has emerged from our decisions is a product of considerations derived from the full sweep of the Establishment Clause cases. Taken together, [773] these decisions dictate that to pass muster under the Establishment Clause the law in question, first, must reflect a clearly secular legislative purpose, second, must have a primary effect that neither advances nor inhibits religion, and, third, must avoid excessive government entanglement with religion.

In applying these criteria to the three distinct forms of aid involved in this case, we need touch only briefly on the requirement of a "secular legislative purpose." As the recitation of legislative purposes appended to New York's law indicates, each measure is adequately supported by legitimate, nonsectarian state interests. We do not question the propriety, and fully secular content, of New York's interest in preserving a healthy and safe educational environment for all of its schoolchildren. And we do not doubt—indeed, we fully recognize—the validity of the State's interests in promoting pluralism and diversity among its public and nonpublic schools. Nor do we hesitate to acknowledge the reality of its concern for an already overburdened public school system that might suffer in the event that a significant percentage of children presently attending nonpublic schools should abandon those schools in favor of the public schools.

[774] But the propriety of a legislature's purposes may not immunize from further scrutiny a law which either has a primary effect that advances religion, or which fosters excessive entanglements between Church and State. Accordingly, we must weigh each of the three aid provisions challenged here against these criteria of effect and entanglement.

A

The "maintenance and repair" provisions of § 1 authorize direct payments to nonpublic schools, virtually all of which are Roman Catholic schools in low-income areas. The grants, totaling $30 or $40 per pupil depending on the age of the institution, are given largely without restriction on usage. So long as expenditures do not exceed 50% of comparable expenses in the public school system, it is possible for a sectarian elementary or secondary school to finance its entire "maintenance and repair" budget from state tax-raised funds. No attempt is made to restrict payments to those expenditures related to the upkeep of facilities used exclusively for secular purposes, nor do we think it possible within the context of these religion-oriented institutions to impose such restrictions. Nothing in the statute, for instance, bars a qualifying school from paying out of state funds the salaries of employees who maintain the school chapel, or the cost of renovating classrooms in which religion is taught, or the cost of heating and lighting those same facilities. Absent appropriate restrictions on expenditures for these and similar purposes, it simply cannot be denied that this section has a primary effect that advances religion in that it subsidizes directly the religious activities of sectarian elementary and secondary schools. . . .

[779] What we have said demonstrates that New York's maintenance and repair provisions violate the Establishment Clause because their effect, inevitably, is to subsidize and advance the religious mission of sectarian [780] schools. We have no occasion, therefore, to consider the further question whether those provisions as presently written would also fail to survive scrutiny under the administrative entanglement aspect of the three-part test because assuring the secular use of all funds requires too intrusive and continuing a relationship between Church and State.

B

New York's tuition reimbursement program also fails the "effect" test, for much the same reasons that govern its maintenance and repair grants. The state program is designed to allow direct, unrestricted grants of $50 to $100 per child (but no more than 50% of tuition actually paid) as reimbursement to parents in low-income brackets who send their children to nonpublic schools, the bulk of which is concededly sectarian in orientation. To qualify, a parent must have earned less than $5,000 in taxable income and must present a receipted tuition bill from a nonpublic school.

There can be no question that these grants could not, consistently with the Establishment Clause, be given directly to sectarian schools, since they would suffer from the same deficiency that renders invalid the grants for maintenance and repair. In the absence of an effective means of guaranteeing that the state aid derived from public funds will be used exclusively for secular, neutral, and nonideological purposes, it is clear from our cases that direct aid in whatever form is invalid. As Mr. Justice Black put it quite simply in *Everson*:

> "No tax in any amount, large or small, can be levied to support any religious activities or institutions, whatever they may be called, or whatever form they may adopt to teach or practice religion." 330 U.S., at 16.

[781] The controlling question here, then, is whether the fact that the grants are delivered to parents rather than schools is of such significance as to compel a contrary result. The State and intervenor-appellees rely on *Everson* and *Allen* for their claim that grants to parents, unlike grants to institutions, respect the "wall of separation" required by the Constitution. It is true that in those cases the Court upheld laws that provided benefits to children attending religious schools and to their parents: As noted above, in *Everson* parents were reimbursed for bus fares paid to send children to parochial schools, and in *Allen* textbooks were loaned directly to the children. But those decisions make clear that, far from providing a per se immunity from examination of the substance of the State's program, the fact that aid is disbursed to parents rather than to the schools is only one among many factors to be considered. . . .

[783] There has been no endeavor "to guarantee the separation between secular and religious educational functions and to ensure that State financial aid supports only the former." *Lemon v. Kurtzman*, at 613. Indeed, it is precisely the function of New York's

law to provide assistance to private schools, the great majority of which are sectarian. By reimbursing parents for a portion of their tuition bill, the State seeks to relieve their financial burdens sufficiently to assure that they continue to have the option to send their children to religion-oriented schools. And while the other purposes for that aid—to perpetuate a pluralistic educational environment and to protect the fiscal integrity of overburdened public schools—are certainly unexceptionable, the effect of the aid is unmistakably to provide desired financial support for nonpublic, sectarian institutions. . . .

[789] C

Sections 3, 4, and 5 establish a system for providing income tax benefits to parents of children attending New York's nonpublic schools. . . .

[792] Tax exemptions for church property enjoyed an apparently universal approval in this country both before and after the adoption of the First Amendment. The Court in *Walz* surveyed the history of tax exemptions and found that each of the 50 States has long provided for tax exemptions for places of worship, that Congress has exempted religious organizations from taxation for over three-quarters of a century, and that congressional enactments in 1802, 1813, and 1870 specifically exempted church property from taxation. In sum, the Court concluded that "few concepts are more deeply embedded in the fabric of our national life, beginning with pre-Revolutionary colonial times, than for the government to exercise at the very least this kind of benevolent neutrality toward churches and religious exercise generally." 397 U.S., at 676–677. We know of no historical precedent for New York's recently promulgated tax relief program. Indeed, it seems clear that tax benefits for parents whose children attend parochial schools are a recent innovation, occasioned by the growing financial plight of such nonpublic institutions and designed, albeit unsuccessfully, to tailor state aid in a manner not incompatible with the recent decisions of this Court.

But historical acceptance without more would not alone have sufficed, as "no one acquires a vested or protected right in violation of the Constitution by long use." *Walz*, 397 U.S., at 678. It was the reason underlying that long history of tolerance of tax exemptions for religion that proved controlling. A proper respect for both the Free Exercise and the Establishment Clauses compels the State [793] to pursue a course of "neutrality" toward religion. Yet governments have not always pursued such a course, and oppression has taken many forms, one of which has been taxation of religion. Thus, if taxation was regarded as a form of "hostility" toward religion, "exemption constitute[d] a reasonable and balanced attempt to guard against those dangers." *Id.*, at 673. Special tax benefits, however, cannot be squared with the principle of neutrality established by the decisions of this Court. To the contrary, insofar as such benefits render assistance to parents who send their children to sectarian schools, their purpose and inevitable effect are to aid and advance those religious institutions.

Apart from its historical foundations, *Walz* is a product of the same dilemma and inherent tension found in most government-aid-to-religion controversies. To be sure, the exemption of church property from taxation conferred a benefit, albeit an indirect and incidental one. Yet that "aid" was a product not of any purpose to support or to subsidize, but of a fiscal relationship designed to minimize involvement and entanglement between Church and State. "The exemption," the Court emphasized, "tends to complement and reinforce the desired separation insulating each from the other." *Id.*, at 676. Furthermore, "elimination of the exemption would tend to expand the involvement of government by giving rise to tax valuation of church property, tax liens, tax foreclosures, and the direct confrontations and conflicts that follow in the train of those legal processes." *Id.*, at 674. The granting of the tax benefits under the New York statute, unlike the extension of an exemption, would tend to increase rather than limit the involvement between Church and State.

One further difference between tax exemptions for church property and tax benefits for parents should be [794] noted. The exemption challenged in *Walz* was not restricted to a class composed exclusively or even predominantly of religious institutions. Instead, the exemption covered all property devoted to religious, educational, or charitable purposes. As the parties here must concede, tax reductions authorized by this law flow primarily to the parents of children attending sectarian, nonpublic schools. Without intimating whether this factor alone might have controlling significance in another context in some future case, it should be apparent that in terms of the potential divisiveness of any legislative measure the narrowness of the benefited class would be an important factor.

In conclusion, we find the *Walz* analogy unpersuasive, and in light of the practical similarity between New York's tax and tuition reimbursement programs, we hold that neither form of aid is sufficiently restricted to assure that it will not have the impermissible effect of advancing the sectarian activities of religious schools.

III

Because we have found that the challenged sections have the impermissible effect of advancing religion, we need not consider whether such aid would result in entanglement of the State with religion in the sense of "[a] comprehensive, discriminating, and continuing state surveillance." *Lemon v. Kurtzman*, 403 U.S., at 619. But the importance of the competing societal interests implicated here prompts us to make the further observation that, apart from any specific entanglement of the State in particular religious programs, assistance of the sort here involved carries grave potential for entanglement in the broader sense of continuing political strife over aid to religion. . . .

[795] One factor of recurring significance in this weighing process is the potentially divisive political effect of an aid program. As Mr. Justice Black's opinion in *Everson* [796] *v. Board of Education*, emphasizes, competition among religious sects for political and religious supremacy has occasioned considerable civil strife, "generated in large part" by competing efforts to gain or maintain the support of government. 330 U.S., at 8–9. As Mr. Justice Harlan put it, "what is at stake as a matter of policy [in Establishment Clause cases] is preventing that kind and degree of government involvement in religious life that, as history teaches us, is apt to lead to strife and frequently strain a political system to the breaking point." *Walz v. Tax Comm'n*, 397 U.S., at 694 (separate opinion).

The Court recently addressed this issue specifically and fully in *Lemon v. Kurtzman*. After describing the political activity and bitter differences likely to result from the state programs there involved, the Court said:

> "The potential for political divisiveness related to religious belief and practice is aggravated in these two statutory programs by the need for continuing annual appropriations and the likelihood of larger and larger demands as costs and populations grow." 403 U.S., at 623.

The language of the Court applies with peculiar force to the New York statute now before us. Section 1 (grants for maintenance) and § 2 (tuition grants) will require continuing annual appropriations. Sections 3, 4, and 5 (income tax relief) will not necessarily require [797] annual re-examination, but the pressure for frequent enlargement of the relief is predictable. All three of these programs start out at modest levels: the maintenance grant is not to exceed $40 per pupil per year in approved schools; the tuition grant provides parents not more than $50 a year for each child in the first eight grades and $100 for each child in the high school grades; and the tax benefit, though more difficult to compute, is equally modest. But we know from long experience with both Federal and State Governments that aid programs of any kind tend to become entrenched, to escalate in cost, and to generate their own aggressive constituencies. And the larger the class of recipients, the greater the pressure for accelerated increases. Moreover, the State itself, concededly anxious to avoid assuming the burden of educating children now in private and parochial schools, has a strong motivation for increasing this aid as public school costs rise and population increases. In this situation, where the underlying issue is the deeply emotional one of Church-State relationships, the potential for seriously divisive political consequences needs no elaboration. And while the prospect of such divisiveness [798] may not alone warrant the invalidation of state laws that otherwise survive the careful scrutiny required by the decisions of this Court, it is certainly a "warning signal" not to be ignored. 403 U.S., at 625.

Our examination of New York's aid provisions, in light of all relevant considerations, compels the judgment that each, as written, has a "primary effect that advances religion" and offends the constitutional prohibition against laws "respecting an establishment of religion." . . .

[805] MR. JUSTICE REHNQUIST, with whom THE CHIEF JUSTICE and MR. JUSTICE WHITE concur, dissenting in part.

Differences of opinion are undoubtedly to be expected when the Court turns to the task of interpreting the meaning of the Religion Clauses of the First Amendment, since our previous cases arising under these Clauses, as the Court notes, "have presented some of the most perplexing questions to come before this Court." *Ante*, [806] at 760. I dissent from those portions of the Court's opinion which strike down §§ 2 through 5, N. Y. Laws 1972, c. 414. Section 2 grants limited state aid to low-income parents sending their children to nonpublic schools and §§ 3 through 5 make roughly comparable benefits available to middle-income parents through the use of tax deductions. I find both the Court's reasoning and result all but impossible to reconcile with *Walz v. Tax Comm'n* (1970), decided only three years ago, and with *Board of Education v. Allen* (1968), and *Everson v. Board of Education* (1947).

I

The opinions in *Walz* make it clear that tax deductions and exemptions, even when directed to religious institutions, occupy quite a different constitutional status under the Religion Clauses of the First Amendment than do outright grants to such institutions. MR. CHIEF JUSTICE BURGER, speaking for the Court in *Walz*, said:

"The grant of a tax exemption is not sponsorship since the government does not transfer part of its revenue to churches but simply abstains from demanding that the church support the state. No one has ever suggested that tax exemption has converted libraries, art galleries, or hospitals into arms of the state or put employees 'on the public payroll.' *There is no genuine nexus between tax exemption and establishment of religion."* 397 U.S., at 675 (emphasis added).

MR. JUSTICE BRENNAN in his concurring opinion amplified the distinction between tax benefits and direct payments in these words:

"Tax exemptions and general subsidies, however, are qualitatively different. Though both provide [807] economic assistance, they do so in fundamentally different ways. A subsidy involves the direct transfer of public monies to the subsidized enterprise and uses resources exacted from taxpayers as a whole. An exemption, on the other hand, involves no such transfer. . . . Tax exemptions, accordingly, constitute mere passive state involvement with religion and not the affirmative involvement characteristic of outright governmental subsidy." *Id.,* at 690–691.

Here the effect of the tax benefit is trebly attenuated as compared with the outright exemption considered in *Walz.* There the result was a complete forgiveness of taxes, while here the result is merely a reduction in taxes. There the ultimate benefit was available to an actual house of worship, while here even the ultimate benefit redounds only to a religiously sponsored school. There the churches themselves received the direct reduction in the tax bill, while here it is only the parents of the children who are sent to religiously sponsored schools who receive the direct benefit. . . .

[810] II

In striking down both plans, the Court places controlling weight on the fact that the State has not purported [811] to restrict to secular purposes either the reimbursements or the money which it has not taxed. This factor assertedly serves to distinguish *Board of Education v. Allen,* and *Everson v. Board of Education,* and compels the result that inevitably the primary effect of the plans is to provide financial support for sectarian schools. . . .

[812] Both *Everson* and *Allen* gave significant recognition to the "benevolent neutrality" concept, and the Court was guided by the fact that any effect from state aid to parents has a necessarily attenuated impact on religious institutions when compared to direct aid to such institutions.

The reimbursement and tax benefit plans today struck down, no less than the plans in *Everson* and *Allen,* are consistent with the principle of neutrality. New York has recognized that parents who are sending their children to nonpublic schools are rendering the State a service by decreasing the costs of public education and by physically relieving an already overburdened public school system. Such parents are nonetheless compelled to support public school services unused by them and to pay for their own children's education. Rather than offering "an incentive to parents to send their children to sectarian schools," *ante,* at 786, as the majority suggests, New York is effectuating the secular purpose of the equalization of the cost of educating New York children that are borne by parents who send their children to nonpublic schools. As in *Everson* and *Allen,* the impact, if any, on religious [813] education from the aid granted is significantly diminished by the fact that the benefits go to the parents rather than to the institutions.

The increasing difficulties faced by private schools in our country are no reason at all for this Court to readjust the admittedly rough-hewn limits on governmental involvement with religion which are found in the First and Fourteenth Amendments. But, quite understandably, these difficulties can be expected to lead to efforts on the part of those who wish to keep alive pluralism in education to obtain through legislative channels forms of permissible public assistance which were not thought necessary a generation ago. Within the limits permitted by the Constitution, these decisions are quite rightly hammered out on the legislative anvil. If the Constitution does indeed allow for play in the legislative joints, *Walz*, at 669, the Court must distinguish between a new exercise of power within constitutional limits and an exercise of legislative power which transgresses those limits. I believe the Court has failed to make that distinction here, and I therefore dissent.

27

McDaniel v. Paty

435 U.S. 618 (1978)

Vote: 8—Burger, Brennan, Stewart, White, Marshall, Powell, Rehnquist, Stevens
0

Opinion announcing the judgment of the Court: Burger
Opinions concurring in the judgment: Brennan, Stewart, White
Not participating in the case: Blackmun

Article 8, § 1 of the Tennessee Constitution of 1796, the state's first constitution, held, "Whereas the ministers of the gospel are, by their professions, dedicated to God and the care of souls, and ought not to be diverted from the great duties of their functions; therefore no minister of the gospel, or priest of any denomination whatever, shall be eligible to a seat in either house of the legislature."

At the time of this case, the disqualifying provision had continued unchanged since its adoption and was found in Article 9, § 1 of the Tennessee State Constitution. The Tennessee state legislature applied this provision to candidates who sought to serve as delegates in the state's 1977 limited constitutional convention.

As explained in the Supreme Court opinion below, McDaniel, an ordained minister of a Baptist church in Chattanooga, filed as a candidate for delegate to the constitutional convention. An opposing candidate, Selma Cash Paty, sued in the chancery court for a declaratory judgment that McDaniel was disqualified from serving as a delegate and for a judgment striking his name from the ballot. The chancery court held that the minister exclusion violated the First and Fourteenth Amendments to the federal Constitution and declared McDaniel eligible for the office of delegate. In the ensuing election, McDaniel was elected.

The Tennessee Supreme Court, however, reversed the chancery court's ruling, holding that the clergy disqualification imposed no burden on "religious belief" and restricted "religious action . . . [only] in the law making process of government—where religious action is absolutely prohibited by the establishment clause." Pursuant to the Tennessee Supreme Court decision, McDaniel was found to be ineligible for election to the Tennessee constitutional convention.

MR. CHIEF JUSTICE BURGER announced the judgment of the Court and delivered an opinion in which MR. JUSTICE POWELL, MR. JUSTICE REHNQUIST, and MR. JUSTICE STEVENS joined.

[620] The question presented by this appeal is whether a Tennessee statute barring "Minister[s] of the Gospel, or priest[s] of any denomination whatever" from serving as delegates to the State's limited constitutional convention deprived appellant McDaniel, an ordained minister, of the right to the free exercise of religion guaranteed by the First Amendment and made applicable to the States by the Fourteenth Amendment. The First Amendment forbids all laws "prohibiting the free exercise" of religion. . . .

[622] II

A

The disqualification of ministers from legislative office was a practice carried from England by seven of the original States; later six new States similarly excluded clergymen from some political offices. In England the practice of excluding clergy from the House of Commons was justified on a variety of grounds: to prevent dual officeholding, that is, membership by a minister in both Parliament and Convocation; to insure that the priest or deacon devoted himself to his "sacred calling" rather than to "such mundane activities as were appropriate to a member of the House of Commons"; and to prevent ministers, who after 1533 were subject to the Crown's powers over the benefices of the clergy, from using membership in Commons to diminish its independence by increasing the influence of the King and the nobility.

The purpose of the several States in providing for disqualification was primarily to assure the success of a new political experiment, the separation of church and state. [623] Prior to 1776, most of the 13 Colonies had some form of an established, or government-sponsored, church. Even after ratification of the First Amendment, which prohibited the Federal Government from following such a course, some States continued pro-establishment provisions. Massachusetts, the last State to accept disestablishment, did so in 1833.

In light of this history and a widespread awareness during that period of undue and often dominant clerical influence in public and political affairs here, in England, and on the Continent, it is not surprising that strong views were held by some that one way to assure disestablishment was to keep clergymen out of public office. Indeed, some of the foremost political philosophers and statesmen of that period held such views regarding the clergy. Earlier, John Locke argued for confining the authority of the English clergy "within the bounds of the church, nor can it in any manner be extended to civil affairs; because the church itself is a thing absolutely separate and distinct from the commonwealth." Thomas Jefferson initially advocated such a position in his 1783 draft of a constitution for Virginia. James Madison, however, disagreed and vigorously [624] urged the position which in our view accurately reflects the spirit and purpose of the Religion Clauses of the First Amendment. Madison's response to Jefferson's position was:

"Does not The exclusion of Ministers of the Gospel as such violate a fundamental principle of liberty by punishing a religious profession with the privation of a civil right? does it

[not] violate another article of the plan itself which exempts religion from the cognizance of Civil power? does it not violate justice by at once taking away a right and prohibiting a compensation for it? does it not in fine violate impartiality by shutting the door [against] the Ministers of one Religion and leaving it open for those of every other." 5 *Writings of James Madison* 288 (G. Hunt ed. 1904).

Madison was not the only articulate opponent of clergy disqualification. When proposals were made earlier to prevent clergymen from holding public office, John Witherspoon, a Presbyterian minister, president of Princeton University, and the only clergyman to sign the Declaration of Independence, made a cogent protest and, with tongue in cheek, offered an amendment to a provision much like that challenged here:

"No clergyman, of any denomination, shall be capable of being elected a member of the Senate or House of Representatives, because (here insert the grounds of offensive disqualification, which I have not been able to discover) Provided always, and it is the true intent and meaning of this part of the constitution, that if at any time he shall be completely deprived of the clerical character by those by whom he was invested with it, as by deposition for cursing and swearing, drunkenness or uncleanness, he shall then be fully restored to all the privileges of a free [625] citizen; his offense [of being a clergyman] shall no more be remembered against him; but he may be chosen either to the Senate or House of Representatives, and shall be treated with all the respect due to his brethren, the other members of Assembly."

As the value of the disestablishment experiment was perceived, 11 of the 13 States disqualifying the clergy from some types of public office gradually abandoned that limitation. New York, for example, took that step in 1846 after delegates to the State's constitutional convention argued that the exclusion of clergymen from the legislature was an "odious distinction." Only Maryland and Tennessee continued their clergy-disqualification provisions into this century and, in 1974, a District Court held Maryland's provision violative of the First and Fourteenth Amendments' guarantees of the free exercise of religion. Today Tennessee remains the only State excluding ministers from certain public offices.

The essence of this aspect of our national history is that in all but a few States the selection or rejection of clergymen for public office soon came to be viewed as something safely left to the good sense and desires of the people.

B

This brief review of the history of clergy-disqualification provisions also amply demonstrates, however, that, at least during the early segment of our national life, those provisions enjoyed the support of responsible American statesmen and were accepted as having a rational basis. Against this background we do not lightly invalidate a statute enacted pursuant to a provision of a state constitution which has been sustained by its highest court. The challenged provision came to the Tennessee Supreme Court clothed with the presumption of validity to which that court was bound to give deference.

[626] However, the right to the free exercise of religion unquestionably encompasses the right to preach, proselyte, and perform other similar religious functions, or, in other words, to be a minister of the type McDaniel was found to be. Tennessee also acknowledges the right of its adult citizens generally to seek and hold office as legislators or delegates to the state constitutional convention. Yet under the clergy-disqualification

provision, McDaniel cannot exercise both rights simultaneously because the State has conditioned the exercise of one on the surrender of the other. Or, in James Madison's words, the State is "punishing a religious profession with the privation of a civil right." In so doing, Tennessee has encroached upon McDaniel's right to the free exercise of religion. "[T]o condition the availability of benefits [including access to the ballot] upon this appellant's willingness to violate a cardinal principle of [his] religious faith [by surrendering his religiously impelled ministry] effectively penalizes the free exercise of [his] constitutional liberties." *Sherbert v. Verner*, 374 U.S. 398, 406 (1963).

If the Tennessee disqualification provision were viewed as depriving the clergy of a civil right solely because of their religious beliefs, our inquiry would be at an end. The Free Exercise Clause categorically prohibits government from regulating, prohibiting, or rewarding religious beliefs as such. In *Torcaso v. Watkins* (1961), the Court reviewed the Maryland constitutional requirement that all holders of "any office of profit or trust in this State" declare their belief in the existence of God. In striking down the Maryland requirement, the Court did not evaluate the interests assertedly justifying it but rather held that it violated freedom of religious belief.

In our view, however, *Torcaso* does not govern. By its [627] terms, the Tennessee disqualification operates against McDaniel because of his status as a "minister" or "priest." The meaning of those words is, of course, a question of state law. And although the question has not been examined extensively in state-law sources, such authority as is available indicates that ministerial status is defined in terms of conduct and activity rather than in terms of belief. Because the Tennessee disqualification is directed primarily at status, acts, and conduct it is unlike the requirement in *Torcaso*, which focused on belief. Hence, the Free Exercise Clause's absolute prohibition of infringements on the "freedom to believe" is inapposite here.

This does not mean, of course, that the disqualification escapes judicial scrutiny or that McDaniel's activity does not enjoy significant First Amendment protection. The Court [628] recently declared in *Wisconsin v. Yoder*, 406 U.S. 205, 215 (1972):

"The essence of all that has been said and written on the subject is that only those interests of the highest order and those not otherwise served can overbalance legitimate claims to the free exercise of religion."

Tennessee asserts that its interest in preventing the establishment of a state religion is consistent with the Establishment Clause and thus of the highest order. The constitutional history of the several States reveals that generally the interest in preventing establishment prompted the adoption of clergy disqualification provisions. There is no occasion to inquire whether promoting such an interest is a permissible legislative goal, however, for Tennessee has failed to demonstrate that its views of the dangers of clergy participation in the political process have not lost whatever validity they may once have enjoyed. The essence of the rationale underlying the Tennessee restriction on ministers is that if elected to public office they will necessarily exercise [629] their powers and influence to promote the interests of one sect or thwart the interests of another, thus pitting one against the others, contrary to the anti-establishment principle with its command of neutrality. However widely that view may have been held in the 18th century by many, including enlightened statesmen of that day, the American experience provides no persuasive support for the fear that clergymen in public office will be less careful of anti-establishment interests or less faithful to their oaths of civil office than their unordained counterparts.

We hold that § 4 of ch. 848 violates McDaniel's First Amendment right to the free exercise of his religion made applicable to the States by the Fourteenth Amendment. Accordingly, the judgment of the Tennessee Supreme Court is reversed, and the case is remanded to that court for further proceedings not inconsistent with this opinion.

MR. JUSTICE BRENNAN, with whom MR. JUSTICE MARSHALL joins, concurring in the judgment.

I would hold that § 4 of the legislative call to the Tennessee constitutional convention, to the extent that it incorporates [630] Art. 9, § 1, of the Tennessee Constitution violates both the Free Exercise and Establishment Clauses of the First Amendment as applied to the States through the Fourteenth Amendment. I therefore concur in the reversal of the judgment of the Tennessee Supreme Court.

I

The Tennessee Supreme Court sustained Tennessee's exclusion on the ground that it "does not infringe upon religious belief or religious action within the protection of the free exercise clause[, and] that such indirect burden as may be imposed upon ministers and priests by excluding them from the lawmaking process of government is justified by the compelling state interest in maintaining the wall of separation between church and state." 547 S. W. 2d 897, 907 (1977). In reaching this conclusion, the state court relied on two interrelated propositions which are inconsistent with decisions of this Court. The first is that a distinction may be made between "religious belief or religious action" on the one hand, and the "career or calling" of the ministry on the other. The court stated that "[i]t is not religious belief, but the career or calling, by which one is identified as dedicated to the full time promotion of the religious objectives of a particular religious sect, that disqualifies." *Id.,* at 903. The second is that the disqualification provision does not interfere with the free exercise of religion because the practice of the ministry is left unimpaired; only candidacy for legislative office is proscribed.

[631] The characterization of the exclusion as one burdening appellant's "career or calling" and not religious belief cannot withstand analysis. Clearly freedom of belief protected by the Free Exercise Clause embraces freedom to profess or practice that belief, even including doing so to earn a livelihood. One's religious belief surely does not cease to enjoy the protection of the First Amendment when held with such depth of sincerity as to impel one to join the ministry.

Whether or not the provision discriminates among religions (and I accept for purposes of discussion the State Supreme [632] Court's construction that it does not), it establishes a religious classification—involvement in protected religious activity—governing the eligibility for office, which I believe is absolutely prohibited. The provision imposes a unique disability upon those who exhibit a defined level of intensity of involvement in protected religious activity. Such a classification as much imposes a test for office based on religious conviction as one based on denominational preference. A law which limits political participation to those who eschew prayer, public worship, or the ministry as much establishes a religious test as one which disqualifies Catholics, or Jews, or Protestants. Because the challenged provision establishes as a condition of office the willingness to eschew certain protected religious practices, *Torcaso v. Watkins,* 367 U.S. 488 (1961), compels the conclusion that it violates the Free Exercise Clause.

Torcaso struck down Maryland's requirement that an appointee to the office of notary public declare his belief in the existence of God, expressly disavowing "the historically and constitutionally discredited policy of probing religious beliefs by test oaths or limiting public offices to persons who have, or perhaps more properly profess to have, a belief in some particular kind [633] of religious concept." *Id.*, at 494. That principle equally condemns the religious qualification for elective office imposed by Tennessee.

The second proposition—that the law does not interfere with free exercise because it does not directly prohibit religious activity, but merely conditions eligibility for office on its abandonment—is also squarely rejected by precedent. In *Sherbert v. Verner* (1963), a state statute disqualifying from unemployment compensation benefits persons unwilling to work on Saturdays was held to violate the Free Exercise Clause as applied to a Sabbatarian whose religious faith forbade Saturday work. That decision turned upon the fact that "[t]he ruling forces her to choose between following the precepts of her religion and forfeiting benefits, on the one hand, and abandoning one of the precepts of her religion in order to accept work, on the other hand. Governmental imposition of such a choice puts the same kind of burden upon the free exercise of religion as would a fine imposed against appellant for her Saturday worship." *Id.*, at 404. Similarly, in "prohibiting legislative service because of a person's leadership role in a religious faith," 547 S. W. 2d, at 903, Tennessee's disqualification provision imposed an unconstitutional penalty upon appellant's exercise of his religious faith. . . .

[636] II

The State Supreme Court's justification of the prohibition, echoed here by the State, as intended to prevent those most intensely involved in religion from injecting sectarian goals and policies into the lawmaking process, and thus to avoid fomenting religious strife or the fusing of church with state affairs, itself raises the question whether the exclusion violates the Establishment Clause. As construed, the exclusion manifests patent hostility toward, not neutrality respecting, religion; forces or influences a minister or priest to abandon his ministry as the price of public office; and, in sum, has a primary effect which inhibits religion. . . .

[639] Tennessee nevertheless invokes the Establishment Clause to excuse the imposition of a civil disability upon those deemed [640] to be deeply involved in religion. In my view, that Clause will not permit, much less excuse or condone, the deprivation of religious liberty here involved.

Fundamental to the conception of religious liberty protected by the Religion Clauses is the idea that religious beliefs are a matter of voluntary choice by individuals and their associations, and that each sect is entitled to "flourish according to the zeal of its adherents and the appeal of its dogma." *Zorach v. Clauson*, 343 U.S. 306, 313 (1952). Accordingly, religious ideas, no less than any other, may be the subject of debate which is "uninhibited, robust, and wide-open. . . ." *New York Times Co. v. Sullivan*, 376 U.S. 254, 270 (1964). Government may not interfere with efforts to proselyte or worship in public places. *Kunz v. New York* (1951). It may not tax the dissemination of religious ideas. *Murdock v. Pennsylvania* (1943). It may not seek to shield its citizens from those who would solicit them with their religious beliefs. *Martin v. City of Struthers* (1943).

That public debate of religious ideas, like any other, may arouse emotion, may incite, may foment religious divisiveness and strife does not rob it of constitutional protection. The mere fact that a purpose of the Establishment Clause is to reduce or eliminate religious divisiveness or strife, does not place religious discussion, association, or political participation in a status less preferred than rights of discussion, association, and political participation generally. "Adherents of particular faiths and individual churches frequently take strong positions on public [641] issues including . . . vigorous advocacy of legal or constitutional positions. Of course, churches as much as secular bodies and private citizens have that right." *Walz v. Tax Comm'n*, 397 U.S. 664, 670 (1970).

The State's goal of preventing sectarian bickering and strife may not be accomplished by regulating religious speech and political association. The Establishment Clause does not license government to treat religion and those who teach or practice it, simply by virtue of their status as such, as subversive of American ideals and therefore subject to unique disabilities. Government may not inquire into the religious beliefs and motivations of officeholders—it may not remove them from office merely for making public statements regarding religion, or question whether their legislative actions stem from religious conviction.

In short, government may not as a goal promote "safe thinking" with respect to religion and fence out from political participation those, such as ministers, whom it regards as overinvolved in religion. Religionists no less than members of any other group enjoy the full measure of protection afforded speech, association, and political activity generally. The Establishment Clause, properly understood, is a shield against any attempt by government to inhibit religion as it has done here. It may not be used as a sword to justify repression of religion or its adherents from any aspect of public life.

[642] Our decisions under the Establishment Clause prevent government from supporting or involving itself in religion or from becoming drawn into ecclesiastical disputes. These prohibitions naturally tend, as they were designed to, to avoid channeling political activity along religious lines and to reduce any tendency toward religious divisiveness in society. Beyond enforcing these prohibitions, however, government may not go. The antidote which the Constitution provides against zealots who would inject sectarianism into the political process is to subject their ideas to refutation in the market-place of ideas and their platforms to rejection at the polls. With these safeguards, it is unlikely that they will succeed in inducing government to act along religiously divisive lines, and, with judicial enforcement of the Establishment Clause, any measure of success they achieve must be short-lived, at best.

28

Stone v. Graham

449 U.S. 39 (1980)

Vote: 5—Brennan, White, Marshall, Powell, Stevens
*   4—Burger, Stewart, Blackmun, Rehnquist*

Per curium opinion without argument
Dissenting opinion: Rehnquist

In 1978, the Kentucky state legislature mandated the posting of the Ten Command-
ments in each public school classroom. The statute (1978 Ky. Acts, ch. 436, 1 [effective
June 17, 1978], Ky. Rev. Stat. 158.178 [1980]) in its entirety provided as follows:

(1) It shall be the duty of the superintendent of public instruction, provided sufficient
funds are available as provided in subsection (3) of this Section, to ensure that a
durable, permanent copy of the Ten Commandments shall be displayed on a wall in
each public elementary and secondary school classroom in the Commonwealth. The
copy shall be sixteen (16) inches wide by twenty (20) inches high.

(2) In small print below the last commandment shall appear a notation concerning the
purpose of the display, as follows: "The secular application of the Ten Command-
ments is clearly seen in its adoption as the fundamental legal code of Western Civi-
lization and the Common Law of the United States."

(3) The copies required by this Act shall be purchased with funds made available through
voluntary contributions made to the state treasurer for the purposes of this Act.

PER CURIAM.

[40] . . . This Court has announced a three-part test for determining whether a challenged state statute is permissible under the Establishment Clause of the United States
Constitution:

"First, the statute must have a secular legislative purpose; second, its principal or primary
effect must be one that neither advances nor inhibits religion . . . ; finally the statute must
not foster 'an excessive government entanglement with religion.'" *Lemon v. Kurtzman,*
403 U.S. 602, 612–613 (1971).

If a statute violates any of these three principles, it must be [41] struck down under the Establishment Clause. We conclude that Kentucky's statute requiring the posting of the Ten Commandments in public school rooms has no secular legislative purpose, and is therefore unconstitutional.

The Commonwealth insists that the statute in question serves a secular legislative purpose, observing that the legislature required the following notation in small print at the bottom of each display of the Ten Commandments: "The secular application of the Ten Commandments is clearly seen in its adoption as the fundamental legal code of Western Civilization and the Common Law of the United States." 1978 Ky. Acts, ch. 436, 1 (effective June 17, 1978), Ky. Rev. Stat. 158.178 (1980). . . .

The pre-eminent purpose for posting the Ten Commandments on schoolroom walls is plainly religious in nature. The Ten Commandments are undeniably a sacred text in the Jewish and Christian faiths, and no legislative recitation of a supposed secular purpose can blind us to that fact. The Commandments do not confine themselves to arguably secular matters, such as honoring one's parents, killing or murder, [42] adultery, stealing, false witness, and covetousness. See Exodus 20: 12–17; Deuteronomy 5: 16–21. Rather, the first part of the Commandments concerns the religious duties of believers: worshipping the Lord God alone, avoiding idolatry, not using the Lord's name in vain, and observing the Sabbath Day. See Exodus 20: 1–11; Deuteronomy 5: 6–15.

This is not a case in which the Ten Commandments are integrated into the school curriculum, where the Bible may constitutionally be used in an appropriate study of history, civilization, ethics, comparative religion, or the like. Posting of religious texts on the wall serves no such educational function. If the posted copies of the Ten Commandments are to have any effect at all, it will be to induce the schoolchildren to read, meditate upon, perhaps to venerate and obey, the Commandments. However desirable this might be as a matter of private devotion, it is not a permissible state objective under the Establishment Clause.

It does not matter that the posted copies of the Ten Commandments are financed by voluntary private contributions, for the mere posting of the copies under the auspices of the legislature provides the "official support of the State . . . Government" that the Establishment Clause prohibits. 374 U.S., at 222; see *Engel v. Vitale*, 370 U.S. 421, 431 (1962). Nor is it significant that the Bible verses involved in this case are merely posted on the wall, rather than read aloud as in *Schempp* and *Engel*, for "it is no defense to urge that the religious practices here may be relatively minor encroachments on the First Amendment." *Abington School District v. Schempp*, at 225. We conclude that Ky. Rev. [43] Stat. 158.178 (1980) violates the first part of the *Lemon v. Kurtzman* test, and thus the Establishment Clause of the Constitution.

JUSTICE REHNQUIST, dissenting.

With no support beyond its own *ipse dixit*, the Court concludes that the Kentucky statute involved in this case "has *no* secular legislative purpose," *ante*, at 41 (emphasis supplied), and that "[t]he pre-eminent purpose for posting the Ten Commandments on schoolroom walls is plainly religious in nature," *ibid*. This even though, as the trial court found, "[t]he General Assembly thought the statute had a secular legislative purpose and specifically said so." The Court's summary rejection of a secular purpose articulated by the legislature and confirmed by the state court is without precedent in Establishment Clause jurisprudence. This Court regularly looks to legislative articulations of a statute's purpose in Establishment Clause cases [44] and accords such pronouncements the deference they are due. The fact that the asserted secular purpose may overlap with what some may see as a religious objective does not render it unconstitutional. As this Court stated in *McGowan v. Maryland*, 366 U.S. 420, 445 (1961), in upholding the validity of Sunday closing laws, "the present purpose and effect of most of [these laws] is to provide a uniform day of rest for all citizens; the fact that this day is Sunday, a day of particular significance for the dominant Christian sects, does not bar the state from achieving its secular goals." . . .

[45] The Court rejects the secular purpose articulated by the State because the Decalogue is "undeniably a sacred text," *ante*, at 41. It is equally undeniable, however, as the elected representatives of Kentucky determined, that the Ten Commandments have had a significant impact on the development of secular legal codes of the Western World. The trial court concluded that evidence submitted substantiated this determination. Certainly the State was permitted to conclude that a document with such secular significance should be placed before its students, with an appropriate statement of the document's secular import.

The Establishment Clause does not require that the public sector be insulated from all things which may have a religious [46] significance or origin. This Court has recognized that "religion has been closely identified with our history and government," *Abington School District*, at 212, and that "[t]he history of man is inseparable from the history of religion," *Engel v. Vitale*, 370 U.S. 421, 434 (1962). Kentucky has decided to make students aware of this fact by demonstrating the secular impact of the Ten Commandments. . . .

[47] I therefore dissent from what I cannot refrain from describing as a cavalier summary reversal, without benefit of oral argument or briefs on the merits, of the highest court of Kentucky.

Thomas v. Review Board of the Indiana Employment Security Division

450 U.S. 707 (1981)

Vote: 8—Burger, Brennan, Stewart, White, Marshall, Blackmun, Powell, Stevens
1—Rehnquist

Opinion announcing the opinion of the Court: Burger
Dissenting opinion: Rehnquist

This case commenced as a result of a decision by the Review Board of the Indiana Employment Security Division to deny Thomas unemployment compensation benefits under the Indiana Employment Security Act.

Thomas, a Jehovah's Witness, was initially hired by Blaw-Knox Foundry & Machinery Co. to work in the company's roll foundry, which fabricated sheet steel for a variety of industrial uses. On his application form, Thomas listed his membership in the Jehovah's Witnesses and noted that his hobbies were Bible study and Bible reading. He placed no conditions on his employment, and he did not describe his religious tenets in any detail on the form.

Approximately a year later, the roll foundry closed, and Blaw-Knox transferred Thomas to a department that fabricated turrets for military tanks. On his first day at his new job, Thomas realized that his work would be weapons related. He checked for other in-plant job openings but discovered that all of the remaining departments at Blaw-Knox were engaged directly in the production of weapons. Since a transfer to another department would not resolve his problem, Thomas requested a layoff. When that request was denied, he quit, asserting that he could not work on weapons without violating the principles of his religion. The trial record did not show that Thomas was offered any non-weapons-related work by Blaw-Knox or that any such work was available.

Upon leaving Blaw-Knox, Thomas applied for unemployment compensation benefits under the Indiana Employment Security Act. He testified at an administrative hearing that he believed that contributing to the production of arms violated his religion, although he could, in good conscience, engage indirectly in the production of materials that might be used ultimately to fabricate arms. The hearing referee reported, "Claimant continually searched for a transfer to another department which would not be so armament related; however, this did not materialize, and prior to the date of his leaving, claimant requested a layoff, which was denied; and on November 6, 1975, claimant did quit due to his religious convictions." The referee concluded nonetheless that

Thomas's termination was not based upon a "good cause [arising] in connection with [his] work" and, accordingly, that Thomas was not entitled to benefits under Indiana law. The review board adopted the referee's findings and conclusions and affirmed the denial of benefits.

BURGER, C. J., delivered the opinion of the Court, in which BRENNAN, STEWART, WHITE, MARSHALL, POWELL, and STEVENS, JJ., joined, and in Parts I, II, and III of which BLACKMUN, J., joined.

[713] II

Only beliefs rooted in religion are protected by the Free Exercise Clause, which, by its terms, gives special protection to the exercise of religion. [714] The determination of what is a "religious" belief or practice is more often than not a difficult and delicate task, as the division in the Indiana Supreme Court attests. However, the resolution of that question is not to turn upon a judicial perception of the particular belief or practice in question; religious beliefs need not be acceptable, logical, consistent, or comprehensible to others in order to merit First Amendment protection. . . .

[716] III

A

More than 30 years ago, the Court held that a person may not be compelled to choose between the exercise of a First Amendment right and participation in an otherwise available public program. A state may not

"exclude individual Catholics, Lutherans, Mohammedans, Baptists, Jews, Methodists, Non-believers, Presbyterians, or the members of any other faith, because of their faith, or lack of it, from receiving the benefits of public welfare legislation." *Everson v. Board of Education*, 330 U.S. 1, 16 (1947) (emphasis deleted).

Later, in *Sherbert* the Court examined South Carolina's attempt to deny unemployment compensation benefits to a Sabbatarian who declined to work on Saturday. In sustaining her right to receive benefits, the Court held:

"The ruling [disqualifying Mrs. Sherbert from benefits because of her refusal to work on Saturday in violation of her faith] forces her to choose between following the [717] precepts of her religion and forfeiting benefits, on the one hand, and abandoning one of the precepts of her religion in order to accept work, on the other hand. Governmental imposition of such a choice puts the same kind of burden upon the free exercise of religion as would a fine imposed against [her] for her Saturday worship." 374 U.S., at 404.

The respondent Review Board argues, and the Indiana Supreme Court held, that the burden upon religion here is only the indirect consequence of public welfare legislation that the State clearly has authority to enact. "Neutral objective standards must be met to qualify for compensation." 391 N. E. 2d, at 1130. Indiana requires applicants for unemployment compensation to show that they left work for "good cause in connection with the work." *Ibid.*

A similar argument was made and rejected in *Sherbert*, however. It is true that, as in *Sherbert*, the Indiana law does not compel a violation of conscience. But, "this is only the beginning, not the end, of our inquiry." 374 U.S., at 403–404. In a variety of ways we have said that "[a] regulation neutral on its face may, in its application, nonetheless offend the constitutional requirement for governmental neutrality if it unduly burdens the free exercise of religion." *Wisconsin v. Yoder*, 406 U.S., at 220.

Here, as in *Sherbert*, the employee was put to a choice between fidelity to religious belief or cessation of work; the coercive impact on Thomas is indistinguishable from *Sherbert*, where the Court held:

> "[N]ot only is it apparent that appellant's declared ineligibility for benefits derives solely from the practice of her religion, but the pressure upon her to forego that practice is un-mistakable." 374 U.S., at 404.

Where the state conditions receipt of an important benefit upon conduct proscribed by a religious faith, or where it denies [718] such a benefit because of conduct mandated by religious belief, thereby putting substantial pressure on an adherent to modify his behavior and to violate his beliefs, a burden upon religion exists. While the compulsion may be indirect, the infringement upon free exercise is nonetheless substantial.

The respondents also contend that *Sherbert* is inapposite because, in that case, the employee was dismissed by the employer's action. But we see that Mrs. Sherbert was dismissed because she refused to work on Saturdays after the plant went to a 6-day workweek. Had Thomas simply presented himself at the Blaw-Knox plant turret line but refused to perform any assigned work, it must be assumed that he, like Sherbert, would have been terminated by the employer's action, if no other work was available. In both cases, the termination flowed from the fact that the employment, once acceptable, became religiously objectionable because of changed conditions.

B

The mere fact that the petitioner's religious practice is burdened by a governmental program does not mean that an exemption accommodating his practice must be granted. The state may justify an inroad on religious liberty by showing that it is the least re-strictive means of achieving some compelling state interest. However, it is still true that "[t]he essence of all that has been said and written on the subject is that only those interests of the highest order . . . can overbalance legitimate claims to the free exercise of religion." *Wisconsin v. Yoder*, at 215.

The purposes urged to sustain the disqualifying provision of the Indiana unemploy-ment compensation scheme are two-fold: (1) to avoid the widespread unemployment and the consequent burden on the fund resulting if people were permitted to leave jobs for "personal" reasons; and (2) to [719] avoid a detailed probing by employers into job ap-plicants' religious beliefs. These are by no means unimportant considerations. When the focus of the inquiry is properly narrowed, however, we must conclude that the interests advanced by the State do not justify the burden placed on free exercise of religion.

There is no evidence in the record to indicate that the number of people who find themselves in the predicament of choosing between benefits and religious beliefs is large enough to create "widespread unemployment," or even to seriously affect unemploy-ment—and no such claim was advanced by the Review Board. Similarly, although detailed inquiry by employers into applicants' religious beliefs is undesirable, there is no evidence in the record to indicate that such inquiries will occur in Indiana, or that they have occurred in any of the states that extend benefits to people in the petitioner's position. Nor is there any reason to believe that the number of people terminating employment for religious reasons will be so great as to motivate employers to make such inquiries.

Neither of the interests advanced is sufficiently compelling to justify the burden upon Thomas' religious liberty. Accordingly, Thomas is entitled to receive benefits unless, as the respondents contend and the Indiana court held, such payment would violate the Establishment Clause.

IV

The respondents contend that to compel benefit payments to Thomas involves the State in fostering a religious faith. There is, in a sense, a "benefit" to Thomas deriving from his religious beliefs, but this manifests no more than the tension between the two Religious Clauses which the Court resolved in *Sherbert*:

> "In holding as we do, plainly we are not fostering the 'establishment' of the Seventh-Day Adventist religion [720] in South Carolina, for the extension of unemployment benefits to Sabbatarians in common with Sunday worshippers reflects nothing more than the governmental obligation of neutrality in the face of religious differences, and does not represent that involvement of religious with secular institutions which it is the object of the Establishment Clause to forestall." *Sherbert v. Verner*, 374 U.S., at 409.

Unless we are prepared to overrule *Sherbert*, Thomas cannot be denied the benefits due him on the basis of the findings of the referee, the Review Board, and the Indiana Court of Appeals that he terminated his employment because of his religious convictions.

JUSTICE REHNQUIST, dissenting.

The Court today holds that the State of Indiana is constitutionally required to provide direct financial assistance to a person solely on the basis of his religious beliefs. Because I believe that the decision today adds mud to the already muddied waters of First Amendment jurisprudence, I dissent.

I

The Court correctly acknowledges that there is a "tension" between the Free Exercise and Establishment Clauses of the First Amendment of the United States Constitution. Although the relationship of the two Clauses has been the subject of much commentary, the "tension" is of fairly recent [721] vintage, unknown at the time of the framing and adoption of the First Amendment. The causes of the tension, it seems to me, are threefold. First, the growth of social welfare legislation during the latter part of the 20th century has greatly magnified the potential for conflict between the two Clauses, since such legislation touches the individual at so many points in his life. Second, the decision by this Court that the First Amendment was "incorporated" into the Fourteenth Amendment and thereby made applicable against the States, *Stromberg v. California*, 283 U.S. 359 (1931); *Cantwell v. Connecticut*, 310 U.S. 296 (1940), similarly multiplied the number of instances in which the "tension" might arise. The third, and perhaps most important, cause of the tension is our overly expansive interpretation of both Clauses.

By broadly construing both Clauses, the Court has constantly narrowed the channel between the Scylla and Charybdis through which any state or federal action must pass in order to survive constitutional scrutiny.

None of these developments could have been foreseen by those who framed and adopted the First Amendment. The First Amendment was adopted well before the growth of much social welfare legislation and at a time when the Federal Government was in a real sense considered a government of limited delegated powers. Indeed, the principal argument against adopting the Constitution without a "Bill of Rights" was not that such an enactment would be undesirable, but that it was unnecessary because of the limited nature of the Federal Government. So long as the Government enacts little social welfare legislation, as was the case in 1791, there are few occasions in which the two Clauses may conflict. Moreover, as originally enacted, the First Amendment applied only to the Federal Government, not the government of the States. The Framers could hardly anticipate *Barron* being superseded by the "selective incorporation" doctrine adopted by the Court, a decision which greatly expanded the number of statutes [722] which would be subject to challenge under the First Amendment. Because those who drafted and adopted the First Amendment could not have foreseen either the growth of social welfare legislation or the incorporation of the First Amendment into the Fourteenth Amendment, we simply do not know how they would view the scope of the two Clauses.

II

The decision today illustrates how far astray the Court has gone in interpreting the Free Exercise and Establishment Clauses of the First Amendment. Although the Court holds that a State is constitutionally required to provide direct financial assistance to persons solely on the basis of their religious beliefs and recognizes the "tension" between the two Clauses, it does little to help resolve that tension or to offer meaningful guidance to other courts which must decide cases like this on a day-by-day basis. Instead, it simply asserts that there is no Establishment Clause violation here and leaves the tension between the two Religion Clauses to be resolved on a case-by-case basis. As suggested above, however, I believe that the "tension" is largely of this Court's own making, and would diminish almost to the vanishing point if the Clauses were properly interpreted.

Just as it did in *Sherbert v. Verner*, 374 U.S. 398 (1963), the Court today reads the Free Exercise Clause more broadly than is warranted. As to the proper interpretation of the Free Exercise Clause, I would accept the decision of *Braunfeld v. Brown*, 366 U.S. 599 (1961), and the dissent in *Sherbert*. In *Braunfeld*, we held that Sunday closing laws do not violate the First Amendment rights of Sabbatarians. Chief Justice Warren explained that the statute did not make unlawful any religious practices of appellants; it simply made the practice of their religious beliefs more expensive. We concluded that "[t]o strike down, without the most critical scrutiny, legislation which imposes only an indirect burden on the exercise of religion, i.e. legislation which does not [723] make unlawful the religious practice itself, would radically restrict the operating latitude of the legislature." 366 U.S., at 606. Likewise in this case, it cannot be said that the State discriminated against Thomas on the basis of his religious beliefs or that he was denied benefits because he was a Jehovah's Witness. Where, as here, a State has enacted a general statute, the purpose and effect of which is to advance the State's secular goals, the Free Exercise Clause does not in my view require the State to conform that statute to the dictates of religious conscience of any group. As Justice Harlan recognized in his dissent in *Sherbert v. Verner, supra*: "Those situations in which the Constitution may require special treatment on account of religion are . . . few and far between." *Id.*, at 423. Like him I believe that although a State could choose to grant exemptions to religious persons from state unemployment regulations, a State is not constitutionally compelled to do so. *Id.*, at 422–423.

[724] The Court's treatment of the Establishment Clause issue is equally unsatisfying. Although today's decision requires a State to provide direct financial assistance to persons solely on the basis of their religious beliefs, the Court nonetheless blandly assures us, just as it did in *Sherbert*, that its decision "plainly" does not foster the "establishment" of religion. *Ante*, at 719. I would agree that the Establishment Clause, properly interpreted, would not be violated if Indiana voluntarily [725] chose to grant unemployment benefits to those persons who left their jobs for religious reasons. But I also believe that the decision below is inconsistent with many of our prior Establishment Clause cases. Those cases, if faithfully applied, would require us to hold that such voluntary action by a State did violate the Establishment Clause.

JUSTICE STEWART noted this point in his concurring opinion in *Sherbert*, 374 U.S., at 414–417. He observed that decisions like *Sherbert*, and the one rendered today, squarely conflict with the more extreme language of many of our prior Establishment Clause cases. In *Everson v. Board of Education*, 330 U.S. 1 (1949), the Court stated that the Establishment Clause bespeaks a "government . . . stripped of all power . . . to support, or otherwise to assist any or all religions . . . ," and no State "can pass laws which aid one religion . . . [or] all religions." *Id.*, at 11, 15. In *Torcaso v. Watkins*, 367 U.S. 488, 495 (1961), the Court asserted that the government cannot "constitutionally pass laws or impose requirements which aid all religions as against non-believers." And in *Abington School District v. Schempp*, 374 U.S. 203, 217 (1963), the Court adopted Justice Rutledge's words in *Everson* that the Establishment Clause forbids "every form of public aid or support for religion."

In recent years the Court has moved away from the mechanistic "no-aid-to-religion" approach to the Establishment Clause and has stated a three-part test to determine the constitutionality of governmental aid to religion. First, the statute must serve a secular legislative purpose. Second, it must have a "primary effect" that neither advances nor inhibits religion. And third, the State and its administration must avoid excessive entanglement with religion. *Walz v. Tax Comm'n*, 397 U.S. 664 (1970).

[726] It is not surprising that the Court today makes no attempt to apply those principles to the facts of this case. If Indiana were to legislate what the Court today requires—an unemployment compensation law which permitted benefits to be granted to those persons who quit their jobs for religious reasons—the statute would "plainly" violate the Establishment Clause as interpreted in such cases as *Lemon* and *Nyquist*. First, although the unemployment statute as a whole would be enacted to serve a secular legislative purpose, the proviso would clearly serve only a religious purpose. It would grant financial benefits for the sole purpose of accommodating religious beliefs. Second, there can be little doubt that the primary effect of the proviso would be to "advance" religion by facilitating the exercise of religious belief. Third, any statute including such a proviso would surely "entangle" the State in religion far more than the mere grant of tax exemptions, as in *Walz*, or the award of tuition grants and tax credits, as in *Nyquist*. By granting financial benefits to persons solely on the basis of their religious beliefs, the State must necessarily inquire whether the claimant's belief is "religious" and whether it is sincerely held. Otherwise any dissatisfied employee may leave his job without cause and claim that he did so because his own particular beliefs required it.

It is unclear from the Court's opinion whether it has temporarily retreated from its expansive view of the Establishment Clause, or wholly abandoned it. I would welcome the latter. Just as I think that Justice Harlan in *Sherbert* correctly stated the proper approach to free exercise questions, I believe that JUSTICE STEWART, dissenting in *Abington School District v. Schempp*, accurately stated the reach of the Establishment Clause. He explained that the Establishment Clause is limited to "government support of proselytizing activities of religious sects by throwing the weight of secular authorit[ies] behind the dissemination of religious tenets." *Id.*, at 314. See *McCollum v. Board of Education*, 333 U.S. 203, 248 (1948) (Reed, J., dissenting) [727] (impermissible aid is only "purposeful assistance directly to the church itself or to some religious group . . . performing ecclesiastical functions"). Conversely, governmental assistance which does not have the effect of "inducing" religious belief, but instead merely "accommodates" or implements an independent religious choice, does not impermissibly involve the government in religious choices and therefore does not violate the Establishment Clause of the First Amendment. I would think that in this case, as in *Sherbert*, had the State voluntarily chosen to pay unemployment compensation benefits to persons who left their jobs for religious reasons, such aid would be constitutionally permissible because it redounds directly to the benefit of the individual.

In sum, my difficulty with today's decision is that it reads the Free Exercise Clause too broadly and it fails to squarely acknowledge that such a reading conflicts with many of our Establishment Clause cases. As such, the decision simply exacerbates the "tension" between the two Clauses. If the Court were to construe the Free Exercise Clause as it did in *Braunfeld* and the Establishment Clause as JUSTICE STEWART did in *Schempp*, the circumstances in which there would be a conflict between the two Clauses would be few and far between. Although I heartily agree with the Court's tacit abandonment of much of our rhetoric about the Establishment Clause, I regret that the Court cannot see its way clear to restore what was surely intended to have been a greater degree of flexibility to the Federal and State Governments in legislating consistently with the Free Exercise Clause. Accordingly, I would affirm the judgment of the Indiana Supreme Court.

30

Widmar v. Vincent

454 U.S. 263 (1981)

Vote: 8—Burger, Brennan, Marshall, Blackmun, Powell, Rehnquist, Stevens, O'Connor
1—White

Opinion announcing the opinion of the Court: Powell
Opinion concurring in the judgment: Stevens
Dissenting opinion: White

This case commenced as a result of a decision by the University of Missouri at Kansas City (UMKC) to deny use of its facilities to an organization of evangelical Christian students.

At the time of litigation, the University of Missouri at Kansas City, a state university, made its facilities generally available to registered student groups to further the university's stated policy of encouraging student organizations' activities. Students paid an activity fee of $41 per semester (1978–1979) to help defray the university's costs.

From 1973 until 1977, a registered religious group named Cornerstone regularly sought and received permission to conduct its on-campus meetings in classrooms and in the student center. These meetings were open to the public and attracted up to 125 students. A typical Cornerstone meeting included prayer, hymns, Bible commentary, and discussion of religious views and experiences. In 1977, the university informed the group that it no longer could meet in university buildings. The exclusion was based on a regulation adopted by the Board of Curators in 1972 that prohibited the use of university buildings or grounds "for purposes of religious worship of religious teaching."

POWELL, J., delivered the opinion of the Court, in which BURGER, C. J., and BRENNAN, MARSHALL, BLACKMUN, REHNQUIST, and O'CONNOR, JJ., joined.

. . . [267] II

Through its policy of accommodating their meetings, the University has created a forum generally open for use by student groups. Having done so, the University has assumed an obligation to justify its discriminations and exclusions under applicable constitutional norms. The Constitution [268] forbids a State to enforce certain exclusions from a forum generally open to the public, even if it was not required to create the forum in the first place.

The University's institutional mission, which it describes as providing a "secular education" to its students, does not exempt its actions from constitutional scrutiny. With respect to persons entitled to be there, our cases leave no doubt that the First Amendment [269] rights of speech and association extend to the campuses of state universities.

Here UMKC has discriminated against student groups and speakers based on their desire to use a generally open forum to engage in religious worship and discussion. These are forms of speech and association protected by the First Amendment.[6] In order to justify discriminatory [270] exclusion from a public forum based on the religious content of a group's intended speech, the University must therefore satisfy the standard of review appropriate to content-based exclusions. It must show that its regulation is necessary to serve a compelling state interest and that it is narrowly drawn to achieve that end.

III

In this case the University claims a compelling interest in maintaining strict separation of church and State. It derives this interest from the "Establishment Clauses" of both the Federal and Missouri Constitutions.

A

The University first argues that it cannot offer its facilities to religious groups and speakers on the terms available to [271] other groups without violating the Establishment Clause of the Constitution of the United States. We agree that the interest of the University in complying with its constitutional obligations may be characterized as compelling. It does not follow, however, that an "equal access" policy would be incompatible with this Court's Establishment Clause cases. Those cases hold that a policy

---

6. The dissent argues that "religious worship" is not speech generally protected by the "free speech" guarantee of the First Amendment and the "equal protection" guarantee of the Fourteenth Amendment. If "religious worship" were protected "speech," the dissent reasons, "the Religion Clauses would be emptied of any independent meaning in circumstances in which religious practice took the form of speech." *Post*, at 284. This is a novel argument. The dissent does not deny that speech about religion is speech entitled to the general protections of the First Amendment. See *post*, at 283–284, and n. 2, 286. It does not argue that descriptions of religious experiences fail to qualify as "speech." Nor does it repudiate last Term's decision in *Heffron v. International Society for Krishna Consciousness, Inc.*, which assumed that religious appeals to nonbelievers constituted protected "speech." Rather, the dissent seems to attempt a distinction between the kinds of religious speech explicitly protected by our cases and a new class of religious "speech act[s]," *post*, at 285, constituting "worship." There are at least three difficulties with this distinction.

First, the dissent fails to establish that the distinction has intelligible content. There is no indication when "singing hymns, reading scripture, and teaching biblical principles," *post*, at 283, cease to be "singing, teaching, and reading"—all apparently forms of "speech," despite their religious subject matter—and become unprotected "worship."

Second, even if the distinction drew an arguably principled line, it is highly doubtful that it would lie within the judicial competence to administer. Merely to draw the distinction would require the university—and ultimately the courts—to [270] inquire into the significance of words and practices to different religious faiths, and in varying circumstances by the same faith. Such inquiries would tend inevitably to entangle the State with religion in a manner forbidden by our cases.

Finally, the dissent fails to establish the relevance of the distinction on which it seeks to rely. The dissent apparently wishes to preserve the vitality of the Establishment Clause. See *post*, at 284–285. But it gives no reason why the Establishment Clause, or any other provision of the Constitution, would require different treatment for religious speech designed to win religious converts, see *Heffron, supra*, than for religious worship by persons already converted. It is far from clear that the State gives greater support in the latter case than in the former.

will not offend the Establishment Clause if it can pass a three-pronged test: "First, the [governmental policy] must have a secular legislative purpose; second, its principal or primary effect must be one that neither advances nor inhibits religion . . . ; finally, the [policy] must not foster 'an excessive government entanglement with religion.'" *Lemon v. Kurtzman*, 403 U.S. 602, 612–613 (1971).

In this case two prongs of the test are clearly met. Both the District Court and the Court of Appeals held that an open-forum policy, including nondiscrimination against religious speech, would have a secular purpose and would [272] avoid entanglement with religion. But the District Court concluded, and the University argues here, that allowing religious groups to share the limited public forum would have the "primary effect" of advancing religion.

[273] The University's argument misconceives the nature of this case. The question is not whether the creation of a religious forum would violate the Establishment Clause. The University has opened its facilities for use by student groups, and the question is whether it can now exclude groups because of the content of their speech. In this context we are unpersuaded that the primary effect of the public forum, open to all forms of discourse, would be to advance religion.

We are not oblivious to the range of an open forum's likely effects. It is possible—perhaps even foreseeable—that religious groups will benefit from access to University facilities. But this Court has explained that a religious organization's enjoyment of merely "incidental" benefits does not violate the prohibition against the "primary advancement" of religion. *Committee for Public Education v. Nyquist*, 413 U.S. 756, [274] 771 (1973).

We are satisfied that any religious benefits of an open forum at UMKC would be "incidental" within the meaning of our cases. Two factors are especially relevant.

First, an open forum in a public university does not confer any imprimatur of state approval on religious sects or practices. As the Court of Appeals quite aptly stated, such a policy "would no more commit the University . . . to religious goals" than it is "now committed to the goals of the Students for a Democratic Society, the Young Socialist Alliance," or any other group eligible to use its facilities.

Second, the forum is available to a broad class of nonreligious as well as religious speakers; there are over 100 recognized student groups at UMKC. The provision of benefits to so broad a spectrum of groups is an important index of secular effect. If the Establishment Clause barred the extension of general benefits to religious groups, "a church could not be protected by the police and fire departments [275] or have its public sidewalk kept in repair." *Roemer v. Maryland Public Works Bd.*, at 747 (plurality opinion). At least in the absence of empirical evidence that religious groups will dominate UMKC's open forum, we agree with the Court of Appeals that the advancement of religion would not be the forum's "primary effect." . . .

[276] IV

Our holding in this case in no way undermines the capacity of the University to establish reasonable time, place, and manner regulations. Nor do we question the right of the University to make academic judgments as to how best to allocate scarce resources or "to determine for itself on academic grounds who may teach, what may be taught, how it shall be taught, and who may be admitted to study." *Sweezy v. New Hampshire*, 354 U.S. 234, 263 (1957) (Frankfurter, J., concurring in result). Finally, [277] we affirm the continuing validity of cases, *e.g.*, *Healy v. James*, 408 U.S., at 188–189, that recognize a university's right to exclude even First Amendment activities that violate reasonable campus rules or substantially interfere with the opportunity of other students to obtain an education.

The basis for our decision is narrow. Having created a forum generally open to student groups, the University seeks to enforce a content-based exclusion of religious speech. Its exclusionary policy violates the fundamental principle that a state regulation of speech should be content-neutral, and the University is unable to justify this violation under applicable constitutional standards. . . .

[282] JUSTICE WHITE, dissenting.

In affirming the decision of the Court of Appeals, the majority rejects petitioners' argument that the Establishment Clause of the Constitution prohibits the use of university buildings for religious purposes. A state university may permit its property to be used for purely religious services without violating the First and Fourteenth Amendments. With this I agree. The Establishment Clause, however, sets limits only on what the State may do with respect to religious organizations; it does not establish what the State is required to do. I have long argued that Establishment Clause limits on state action which incidentally aids religion are not as strict as the Court has held. The step from the permissible to the necessary, however, is a long one. In my view, just as there is room under the Religion Clauses for state policies that may have some beneficial effect on religion, there is also room for state policies that may incidentally burden religion. In other words, I believe the State to be a good deal freer to formulate policies that affect religion in divergent ways than does the majority. The majority's position will inevitably lead to those contradictions and tensions between the Establishment and Free Exercise Clauses warned against by Justice Stewart in *Sherbert v. Verner*, at 416. . . .

[284] A large part of respondents' argument, accepted by the court below and accepted by the majority, is founded on the proposition that because religious worship uses speech, it is protected by the Free Speech Clause of the First Amendment. Not only is it protected, they argue, but religious worship *qua* speech is not different from any other variety of protected speech as a matter of constitutional principle. I believe that this proposition is plainly wrong. Were it right, the Religion Clauses would be emptied of any independent meaning in circumstances in which religious practice took the form of speech.

Although the majority describes this argument as "novel," *ante*, at 269, n. 6, I believe it to be clearly supported by our previous cases. Just last Term, the Court found it sufficiently [285] obvious that the Establishment Clause prohibited a State from posting a copy of the Ten Commandments on the classroom wall that a statute requiring such a posting was summarily struck down. *Stone v. Graham*, 449 U.S. 39 (1980). That case necessarily presumed that the State could not ignore the religious content of the written message, nor was it permitted to treat that content as it would, or must, treat other—secular—messages under the First Amendment's protection of speech. Similarly, the Court's decisions prohibiting prayer in the public schools rest on a content-based distinction between varieties of speech: as a speech act, apart from its content, a prayer is indistinguishable from a biology lesson. See *Abington School District v. Schempp*, 374 U.S. 203 (1963); *Engel v. Vitale*, 370 U.S. 421 (1962). Operation of the Free Exercise Clause is equally dependent, in certain circumstances, on recognition of a content-based distinction between religious and secular speech. Thus, in *Torcaso v. Watkins*, 367 U.S.

488 (1961), the Court struck down, as violative of the Free Exercise Clause, a state requirement that made a declaration of belief in God a condition of state employment. A declaration is again a speech act, but it was the content of the speech that brought the case within the scope of the Free Exercise Clause.

If the majority were right that no distinction may be drawn between verbal acts of worship and other verbal acts, all of these cases would have to be reconsidered. Although I agree that the line may be difficult to draw in many cases, surely the majority cannot seriously suggest that no line may ever be drawn. If that were the case, the majority would [286] have to uphold the University's right to offer a class entitled "Sunday Mass." Under the majority's view, such a class would be—as a matter of constitutional principle—indistinguishable from a class entitled "The History of the Catholic Church."

There may be instances in which a State's attempt to disentangle itself from religious worship would intrude upon secular speech about religion. In such a case, the State's action would be subject to challenge under the Free Speech Clause of the First Amendment. This is not such a case. This case involves religious worship only; the fact that that worship is accomplished through speech does not add anything to respondents' argument. That argument must rely upon the claim that the State's action impermissibly interferes with the free exercise of respondents' religious practices. Although this is a close question, I conclude that it does not.

Plausible analogies on either side suggest themselves. Respondents argue, and the majority agrees, that by permitting any student group to use its facilities for communicative purposes other than religious worship, the University has created a "public forum." *Ante*, at 267–268. With ample [287] support, they argue that the State may not make content-based distinctions as to what groups may use, or what messages may be conveyed in, such a forum. The right of the religious to nondiscriminatory access to the public forum is well established. See *Niemotko v. Maryland* (1951); *Murdock v. Pennsylvania* (1943). Moreover, it is clear that there are bounds beyond which the University could not go in enforcing its regulation: I do not suppose it could prevent students from saying grace before meals in the school cafeteria, or prevent distribution of religious literature on campus.

Petitioners, on the other hand, argue that allowing use of their facilities for religious worship is constitutionally indistinguishable from directly subsidizing such religious services: It would "fun[d] a specifically religious activity in an otherwise substantially secular setting." *Hunt v. McNair*, 413 U.S. 734, 743 (1973). They argue that the fact that secular student groups are entitled to the in-kind subsidy at issue here does not establish that a religious group is entitled to the same subsidy. They could convincingly argue, for example, that a state university that pays for basketballs for the basketball team is not thereby required to pay for Bibles for a group like Cornerstone.

[288] A third analogy suggests itself, one that falls between these two extremes. There are a variety of state policies which incidentally benefit religion that this Court has upheld without implying that they were constitutionally required of the State. See *Board of Education v. Allen* (1968) (state loan of textbooks to parochial school students); *Zorach v. Clauson* (1952) (release of students from public schools, during school hours, to perform religious activities away from the school grounds); *Everson v. Board of Education* (1947) (state provision of transportation to parochial school students). Provision of university facilities on a uniform basis to all student groups is not very different from provision of textbooks or transportation. From this perspective the issue is not whether the State must, or must not, open its facilities to religious worship; rather, it is whether the State may choose not to do so.

Each of these analogies is persuasive. Because they lead to different results, however, they are of limited help in reaching a decision here. They also demonstrate the difficulty in reconciling the various interests expressed in the Religion Clauses. In my view, therefore, resolution of this case is best achieved by returning to first principles. This requires an assessment of the burden on respondents' ability freely to exercise their religious beliefs and practices and of the State's interest in enforcing its regulation.

Respondents complain that compliance with the regulation would require them to meet "about a block and a half" from campus under conditions less comfortable than those previously available on campus. I view this burden on free exercise [289] as minimal. Because the burden is minimal, the State need do no more than demonstrate that the regulation furthers some permissible state end. The State's interest in avoiding claims that it is financing or otherwise supporting religious worship—in maintaining a definitive separation between church and State—is such an end. That the State truly does mean to act toward this end is amply supported by the treatment of religion in the State Constitution. Thus, I believe the interest of the State is sufficiently strong to justify the imposition of the minimal burden on respondents' ability freely to exercise their religious beliefs.

On these facts, therefore, I cannot find that the application of the regulation to prevent Cornerstone from holding religious worship services in University facilities violates the First and Fourteenth Amendments. I would not hold as the majority does that if a university permits students and others to use its property for secular purposes, it must also furnish facilities to religious groups for the purposes of worship and the practice of their religion. Accordingly, I would reverse the judgment of the Court of Appeals.

31

United States v. Lee

455 U.S. 252 (1982)

Vote: 9—Burger, Brennan, White, Marshall, Blackmun, Powell, Rehnquist, Stevens, O'Connor

0

Opinion announcing the opinion of the Court: Burger
Opinion concurring in the judgment: Stevens

A self-employed farmer and carpenter who was a member of the Old Order Amish religion filed this suit for a refund of the social security taxes he paid on account of his employment of other members of that religion on his farm and in his carpentry shop. He claimed that imposition of social security taxes violated his First Amendment free exercise rights and those of his employees.

Members of the Old Order Amish religion believe they have a religiously based obligation to provide for their fellow members the kind of assistance contemplated by the social security system, and, therefore, their religion prohibits acceptance of social security benefits and payment of social security taxes.

BURGER, C. J., delivered the opinion of the Court, in which BRENNAN, WHITE, MARSHALL, BLACKMUN, POWELL, REHNQUIST, and O'CONNOR, JJ., joined.

. . . [256] II

. . . A

The preliminary inquiry in determining the existence of a constitutionally required exemption is whether the payment [257] of social security taxes and the receipt of benefits interferes with the free exercise rights of the Amish. The Amish believe that there is a religiously based obligation to provide for their fellow members the kind of assistance contemplated by the social security system. Although the Government does not challenge the sincerity of this belief, the Government does contend that payment of social security taxes will not threaten the integrity of the Amish religious belief or observance. It is not within "the judicial function and judicial competence," however, to determine whether appellee or the Government has the proper interpretation of the Amish faith; "[courts] are not arbiters of scriptural interpretation." *Thomas v. Review Bd. of Indiana Employment Security Div.*, 450 U.S. 707, 716 (1981). We therefore accept appellee's contention that both payment and receipt of social security benefits is forbidden by the Amish faith. Because the payment of the taxes or receipt of benefits violates Amish religious beliefs, compulsory participation in the social security system interferes with their free exercise rights.

The conclusion that there is a conflict between the Amish faith and the obligations imposed by the social security system is only the beginning, however, and not the end of the inquiry. Not all burdens on religion are unconstitutional. The state may justify a limitation on religious liberty by showing that it is essential to accomplish an overriding governmental interest.

[258] B

Because the social security system is nationwide, the governmental interest is apparent. The social security system in the United States serves the public interest by providing a comprehensive insurance system with a variety of benefits available to all participants, with costs shared by employers and employees. The social security system is by far the largest domestic governmental program in the United States today, distributing approximately $11 billion monthly to 36 million Americans. The design of the system requires support by mandatory contributions from covered employers and employees. This mandatory participation is indispensable to the fiscal vitality of the social security system. "[Widespread] individual voluntary coverage under social security . . . would undermine the soundness of the social security program." S. Rep. No. 404, 89th Cong., 1st Sess., pt. 1, p. 116 (1965). Moreover, a comprehensive national social security system providing for voluntary participation would be almost a contradiction in terms and difficult, if not impossible, to administer. Thus, the Government's interest in assuring [259] mandatory and continuous participation in and contribution to the social security system is very high.

C

The remaining inquiry is whether accommodating the Amish belief will unduly interfere with fulfillment of the governmental interest. In *Braunfeld v. Brown*, 366 U.S. 599, 605 (1961), this Court noted that "to make accommodation between the religious action and an exercise of state authority is a particularly delicate task . . . because resolution in favor of the State results in the choice to the individual of either abandoning his religious principle or facing . . . prosecution." The difficulty in attempting to accommodate religious beliefs in the area of taxation is that "we are a cosmopolitan nation made up of people of almost every conceivable religious preference." *Braunfeld*, at 606. The Court has long recognized that balance must be struck between the values of the comprehensive social security system, which rests on a complex of actuarial factors, and the consequences of allowing religiously based exemptions. To maintain an organized society that guarantees religious freedom to a great variety of faiths requires that some religious practices yield to the common good. Religious beliefs can be accommodated, but there is a point at which accommodation would "radically restrict the operating latitude of the legislature." *Braunfeld*, at 606.

Unlike the situation presented in *Wisconsin v. Yoder*, it would be difficult to accommodate the comprehensive [260] social security system with myriad exceptions flowing from a wide variety of religious beliefs. The obligation to pay the social security tax initially is not fundamentally different from the obligation to pay income taxes; the difference—in theory at least—is that the social security tax revenues are segregated for use only in furtherance of the statutory program. There is no principled way, however, for purposes of this case, to distinguish between general taxes and those imposed under the Social Security Act. If, for example, a religious adherent believes war is a sin, and if a certain percentage of the federal budget can be identified as devoted to war-related activities, such individuals would have a similarly valid claim to be exempt from paying that percentage of the income tax. The tax system could not function if denominations were allowed to challenge the tax system because tax payments were spent in a manner that violates their religious belief. Because the broad public interest in maintaining a sound tax system is of such a high order, religious belief in conflict with the payment of taxes affords no basis for resisting the tax.

III

Congress has accommodated, to the extent compatible with a comprehensive national program, the practices of those who believe it a violation of their faith to participate in the social security system. In § 1402 (g) Congress granted an exemption, on religious grounds, to self-employed Amish and others. Confining the § 1402 (g) exemption to the self-employed [261] provided for a narrow category which was readily identifiable. Self-employed persons in a religious community having its own "welfare" system are distinguishable from the generality of wage earners employed by others.

Congress and the courts have been sensitive to the needs flowing from the Free Exercise Clause, but every person cannot be shielded from all the burdens incident to exercising every aspect of the right to practice religious beliefs. When followers of a particular sect enter into commercial activity as a matter of choice, the limits they accept on their own conduct as a matter of conscience and faith are not to be superimposed on the statutory schemes which are binding on others in that activity. Granting an exemption from social security taxes to an employer operates to impose the employer's religious faith on the employees. Congress drew a line in § 1402 (g), exempting the self-employed Amish but not all persons working for an Amish employer. The tax imposed on employers to support the social security system must be uniformly applicable to all, except as Congress provides explicitly otherwise. . . .

JUSTICE STEVENS, concurring in the judgment.

The clash between appellee's religious obligation and his civic obligation is irreconcilable. He must violate either an Amish belief or a federal statute. According to the Court, the religious duty must prevail unless the Government shows [262] that enforcement of the civic duty "is essential to accomplish an overriding governmental interest." *Ante*, at 257–258. That formulation of the constitutional standard suggests that the Government always bears a heavy burden of justifying the application of neutral general laws to individual conscientious objectors. In my opinion, it is the objector who must shoulder the burden of demonstrating that there is a unique reason for allowing him a special exemption from a valid law of general applicability.

Congress already has granted the Amish a limited exemption from social security taxes. As a matter of administration, it would be a relatively simple matter to extend the exemption to the taxes involved in this case. As a matter of fiscal policy, an enlarged exemption probably would benefit the social security system because the nonpayment of these taxes by the Amish would be more than offset by the elimination of their right to collect benefits. In view of the fact that the Amish have demonstrated their capacity to care for their own, the social cost of eliminating this relatively small group of dedicated believers would be minimal. Thus, if we confine the analysis to the Government's interest in rejecting the particular claim to an exemption at stake in this case, the constitutional standard as formulated by the Court has not been met.

The Court rejects the particular claim of this appellee, not because it presents any special problems, but rather because of the risk that a myriad of other claims would be too difficult to process. The Court overstates the magnitude of this risk because the Amish claim applies only to a small religious community with an established welfare system of its own. [263] Nevertheless, I agree with the Court's conclusion that the difficulties associated with processing other claims to tax exemption on religious grounds justify a rejection of this claim.[2] I believe, however, that this reasoning supports the adoption of a different constitutional standard than the Court purports to apply.

The Court's analysis supports a holding that there is virtually no room for a "constitutionally required exemption" on religious grounds from a valid tax law that is entirely neutral in its general application.[3] Because I agree with that holding, I concur in the judgment.

---

2. In my opinion, the principal reason for adopting a strong presumption against such claims is not a matter of administrative convenience. It is the overriding interest in keeping the government—whether it be the legislature or the courts—out of the business of evaluating the relative merits of differing religious claims. The risk that governmental approval of some and disapproval of others will be perceived as favoring one religion over another is an important risk the Establishment Clause was designed to preclude.

3. Today's holding is limited to a claim to a tax exemption. I believe, however, that a standard that places an almost insurmountable burden on any individual who objects to a valid and neutral law of general applicability on the ground that the law proscribes (or prescribes) conduct that his religion prescribes (or proscribes) better explains most of this Court's holdings than does the standard articulated by the Court today. The principal exception is *Wisconsin v. Yoder*, in which the Court granted the Amish an exemption from Wisconsin's compulsory school-attendance law by actually applying the subjective balancing approach it purports to apply today. The Court's attempt to distinguish *Yoder* is unconvincing because precisely the same religious interest is implicated in both cases, and Wisconsin's interest in requiring its children to attend school until they reach the age of 16 is surely not inferior to the federal interest in collecting these social security taxes.

There is also tension between this standard and the reasoning in *Thomas v. Review Bd. of Indiana Employment Security Div.* and *Sherbert v. Verner*. Arguably, however, laws intended to provide a benefit to a limited class of otherwise disadvantaged persons should be judged by a different standard than that appropriate for the enforcement of neutral laws of general applicability. A tax exemption entails no cost to the claimant; if tax exemptions were dispensed on religious grounds, every citizen would have an economic motivation to join the favored sects. No comparable economic motivation could explain the conduct of the employees in *Sherbert* and *Thomas*. In both of those cases changes in work requirements dictated by the employer forced the employees to surrender jobs that they would have preferred to retain rather than accept unemployment compensation. In each case the treatment of the religious objection to the new job requirements as though it were tantamount to a physical impairment that made it impossible for the employee to continue to work under changed circumstances could be viewed as a protection against unequal treatment rather than a grant of favored treatment for the members of the religious sect. In all events, the decision in *Thomas* was clearly compelled by *Sherbert*.

32

Bob Jones University v. United States*
461 U.S. 574 (1983)

Vote: 8—Burger, Brennan, White, Marshall, Blackmun, Powell, Stevens, O'Connor
   1—Rehnquist

Opinion announcing the opinion of the Court: Burger
Opinion concurring in part and concurring in the judgment: Powell
Dissenting opinion: Rehnquist

At the time of litigation, Bob Jones University enrolled approximately five thousand students from kindergarten through college and graduate school. Located in Greenville, South Carolina, the school was not affiliated with any religious denomination but was dedicated to the teaching and propagation of its fundamentalist Christian beliefs. Teachers were required to be devout Christians, all courses were taught according to the Bible, entering students' religious beliefs were screened, and student conduct was strictly regulated by standards promulgated by school officials. In its certificate of incorporation, the school stated its purpose as being "to conduct an institution of learning . . . giving special emphasis to the Christian religion and the ethics revealed in the Holy Scriptures."

School officials held that the Bible forbids interracial dating and marriage. To effectuate this view, black students were not admitted to the school prior to 1971. From 1971 to May 1975, the school accepted no applications from unmarried black students but did accept applications from black students married within their race. Following a 1975 Fourth Circuit Court of Appeals decision that prohibited racial exclusion from private schools, Bob Jones University revised its admission policy and began to enroll unmarried black students.

A school disciplinary rule, however, prohibited interracial dating and marriage. That rule stated,

> *There is to be no interracial dating.*
>
> 1. *Students who are partners in an interracial marriage will be expelled.*
> 2. *Students who are members of or affiliated with any group or organization which holds as one of its goals or advocates interracial marriage will be expelled.*

---

*Together with No. 81-1, *Goldsboro Christian Schools, Inc. v. United States*, also on certiorari to the same court.

3. *Students who date outside of their own race will be expelled.*
4. *Students who espouse, promote, or encourage others to violate the University's dating rules and regulations will be expelled.*

The school also continued to deny admission to applicants engaged in an interracial marriage or known to advocate interracial marriage or dating.

Until 1970, the Internal Revenue Service (IRS) extended tax-exempt status to Bob Jones University under § 501 (c)(3). On November 30, 1970, the IRS formally notified the school of a change in IRS policy and announced its intention to challenge the tax-exempt status of private schools practicing racial discrimination in their admissions policies. On January 19, 1976, after years of administrative hearings and legal action, the IRS officially revoked the university's tax-exempt status, effective as of December 1, 1970, the day after the school was formally notified of the change in IRS policy. The school then initiated a new legal action in an attempt to regain its tax-exempt status.

BURGER, C. J., delivered the opinion of the Court, in which BRENNAN, WHITE, MARSHALL, BLACKMUN, STEVENS, and O'CONNOR, JJ., joined, and in Part III of which POWELL, J., joined.

[577] We granted *certiorari* to decide whether petitioners, nonprofit private schools that prescribe and enforce racially discriminatory admissions standards on the basis of religious doctrine, qualify as tax-exempt organizations under § 501 (c)(3) of the Internal Revenue Code of 1954. . . .

[585] II

A

. . . [588] More than a century ago, this Court announced the caveat that is critical in this case:

"[It] has now become an established principle of American law, that courts of chancery will sustain and protect . . . a gift . . . to public charitable uses, *provided the same is consistent with local laws and public policy. . . .*" *Perin v. Carey*, 24 How. 465, 501 (1861) (emphasis added).

Soon after that, in 1877, the Court commented:

"A charitable use, *where neither law nor public policy forbids*, may be applied to almost any thing *that tends to promote the well-doing and well-being of social man.*" *Ould v. Washington Hospital for Foundlings*, 95 U.S. 303, 311 (emphasis added).

[589] In 1891, in a restatement of the English law of charity which has long been recognized as a leading authority in this country, Lord MacNaghten stated:

"'Charity' in its legal sense comprises four principal divisions: trusts for the relief of poverty; *trusts for the advancement of education;* trusts for the advancement of religion; and trusts for *other purposes beneficial to the community*, not falling under any of the preceding heads." *Commissioners v. Pemsel*, [1891] A. C. 531, 583 (emphasis added).

These statements clearly reveal the legal background against which Congress enacted the first charitable exemption statute in 1894: charities were to be given preferential treatment because they provide a benefit to society. . . .

[591] When the Government grants exemptions or allows deductions all taxpayers are affected; the very fact of the exemption or deduction for the donor means that other taxpayers can be said to be indirect and vicarious "donors." Charitable exemptions are justified on the basis that the exempt entity confers a public benefit—a benefit which the society or the community may not itself choose or be able to provide, or which supplements and advances the work of public institutions already supported by tax revenues. History buttresses [592] logic to make clear that, to warrant exemption under § 501 (c) (3), an institution must fall within a category specified in that section and must demonstrably serve and be in harmony with the public interest. The institution's purpose must not be so at odds with the common community conscience as to undermine any public benefit that might otherwise be conferred.

B

We are bound to approach these questions with full awareness that determinations of public benefit and public policy are sensitive matters with serious implications for the institutions affected; a declaration that a given institution is not "charitable" should be made only where there can be no doubt that the activity involved is contrary to a fundamental public policy. But there can no longer be any doubt that racial discrimination in education violates deeply and widely accepted views of elementary justice. . . .

[595] Few social or political issues in our history have been more vigorously debated and more extensively ventilated than the issue of racial discrimination, particularly in education. Given the stress and anguish of the history of efforts to escape from the shackles of the "separate but equal" doctrine of *Plessy v. Ferguson*, 163 U.S. 537 (1896), it cannot be said that educational institutions that, for whatever reasons, practice racial discrimination, are institutions exercising "beneficial and stabilizing influences in community life," *Walz v. Tax Comm'n*, 397 U.S. 664, 673 (1970), or should be encouraged by having all taxpayers share in their support by way of special tax status.

There can thus be no question that the interpretation of § 170 and § 501 (c)(3) announced by the IRS in 1970 was correct. That it may be seen as belated does not undermine its soundness. It would be wholly incompatible with the concepts underlying tax exemption to grant the benefit of tax-exempt status to racially discriminatory educational entities, which "[exert] a pervasive influence on the entire educational process." *Norwood v. Harrison*, at 469. Whatever may be the rationale for such private schools' policies, and however sincere the rationale may be, racial discrimination in education is contrary to public policy. Racially discriminatory educational institutions cannot be viewed as conferring a public benefit within the "charitable" concept discussed earlier, [596] or within the congressional intent underlying § 170 and § 501 (c)(3). . . .

[602] III

Petitioners contend that, even if the Commissioner's policy is valid as to nonreligious private schools, that policy cannot constitutionally be applied to schools that engage in racial discrimination on the basis of sincerely held religious beliefs. [603] As to such schools, it is argued that the IRS construction of § 170 and § 501 (c)(3) violates their free exercise rights under the Religion Clauses of the First Amendment. This contention presents claims not heretofore considered by this Court in precisely this context.

This Court has long held the Free Exercise Clause of the First Amendment to be an absolute prohibition against governmental regulation of religious beliefs. As interpreted by this Court, moreover, the Free Exercise Clause provides substantial protection for lawful conduct grounded in religious belief, see *Wisconsin v. Yoder*, at 220; *Thomas v. Review Board of Indiana Employment Security Div.*, 450 U.S. 707 (1981); *Sherbert v. Verner, supra*, at 402–403. However, "[not] all burdens on religion are unconstitutional. . . . The state may justify a limitation on religious liberty by showing that it is essential to accomplish an overriding governmental interest." *United States v. Lee*, 455 U.S. 252, 257–258 (1982).

On occasion this Court has found certain governmental interests so compelling as to allow even regulations prohibiting religiously based conduct. In *Prince v. Massachusetts*, 321 U.S. 158 (1944), for example, the Court held that neutrally cast child labor laws prohibiting sale of printed materials on public streets could be applied to prohibit children from dispensing religious literature. The Court found no constitutional infirmity in "excluding [Jehovah's Witness children] from doing there what no other children may do." *Id.*, at 171. Denial of tax benefits will inevitably have a substantial [604] impact on the operation of private religious schools, but will not prevent those schools from observing their religious tenets.

The governmental interest at stake here is compelling. As discussed in Part II-B, the Government has a fundamental, overriding interest in eradicating racial discrimination in education—discrimination that prevailed, with official approval, for the first 165 years of this Nation's constitutional history. That governmental interest substantially outweighs whatever burden denial of tax benefits places on petitioners' exercise of their religious beliefs. The interests asserted by petitioners cannot be accommodated with that compelling governmental interest, see *United States v. Lee*, at 259–260; and no "less restrictive means," see *Thomas v. Review Board of Indiana Employment Security Div.*, at 718, are available to achieve the governmental interest. . . .

[606] JUSTICE POWELL, concurring in part and concurring in the judgment.

I join the Court's judgment, along with Part III of its opinion holding that the denial of tax exemptions to petitioners does not violate the First Amendment. I write separately because I am troubled by the broader implications of the Court's opinion with respect to the authority of the Internal Revenue Service (IRS) and its construction of §§ 170 (c) and 501 (c)(3) of the Internal Revenue Code. . . .

[608] II

. . . With all respect, I am unconvinced that the critical question in determining tax-exempt status is whether an individual organization provides a clear "public benefit" as defined by the Court. Over 106,000 organizations filed § 501 (c)(3) returns in 1981. [609] I find it impossible to believe that all or even most of those organizations could prove that they "demonstrably serve and [are] in harmony with the public interest" or that they are "beneficial and stabilizing influences in community life." Nor am I prepared to say that petitioners, because of their racially discriminatory policies, necessarily contribute nothing of benefit to the community. It is clear from the substantially secular character of the curricula and degrees offered that petitioners provide educational benefits.

Even more troubling to me is the element of conformity that appears to inform the Court's analysis. The Court asserts that an exempt organization must "demonstrably serve and be in harmony with the public interest," must have a purpose that comports with "the common community conscience," and must not act in a manner "affirmatively at odds with [the] declared position of the whole Government." Taken together, these passages suggest that the primary function of a tax-exempt organization is to act on behalf of the Government in carrying out governmentally approved policies. In my opinion, such a view of § 501 (c)(3) ignores the important role played by tax exemptions in encouraging diverse, indeed often sharply conflicting, activities and viewpoints. As JUSTICE BRENNAN has observed, private, nonprofit groups receive tax exemptions because "each group contributes to the diversity of association, viewpoint, and enterprise essential to a vigorous, pluralistic society." *Walz*, at 689 (concurring opinion). Far from representing an effort to reinforce any perceived "common community conscience," the provision of tax exemptions to nonprofit groups is one indispensable means of limiting the influence of governmental orthodoxy on important areas of community life. . . .

[612] JUSTICE REHNQUIST, dissenting.

The Court points out that there is a strong national policy in this country against racial discrimination. To the extent that the Court states that Congress in furtherance of this policy could deny tax-exempt status to educational institutions that promote racial discrimination, I readily agree. But, unlike the Court, I am convinced that Congress simply has failed to take this action and, as this Court has said over and over again, regardless of our view on the propriety of Congress' failure to legislate we are not constitutionally empowered to act for it. . . .

[622] I have no disagreement with the Court's finding that there is a strong national policy in this country opposed to racial discrimination. I agree with the Court that Congress has the power to further this policy by denying § 501 (c)(3) status to organizations that practice racial discrimination.[3] But as of yet Congress has failed to do so. Whatever the reasons for the failure, this Court should not legislate for Congress.

[623] Petitioners are each organized for the "instruction or training of the individual for the purpose of improving or developing his capabilities," and thus are organized for "educational purposes" within the meaning of § 501 (c)(3). Petitioners' nonprofit status is uncontested. There is no indication that either petitioner has been involved in lobbying activities or political campaigns. Therefore, it is my view that unless and until Congress affirmatively amends § 501 (c)(3) to require more, the IRS is without authority to deny petitioners § 501 (c)(3) status. For this reason, I would reverse the Court of Appeals.

---

3. I agree with the Court that such a requirement would not infringe on petitioners' First Amendment rights.

33

Mueller v. Allen

463 U.S. 388 (1983)

Vote: 5—Burger, White, Powell, Rehnquist, O'Connor
4—Brennan, Marshall, Blackmun, Stevens

Opinion announcing the opinion of the Court: Rehnquist
Dissenting opinion: Marshall

Minnesota law allowed state taxpayers to deduct expenses incurred in providing "tuition, textbooks and transportation" for their children attending a nonprofit elementary or secondary school that fulfilled the state's compulsory-attendance laws. The statute specified that

> *"textbooks" shall mean and include books and other instructional materials and equipment used in elementary and secondary schools in teaching only those subjects legally and commonly taught in public elementary and secondary schools in this state and shall not include instructional books and materials used in the teaching of religious tenets, doctrines or worship, the purpose of which is to inculcate such tenets, doctrines or worship, nor shall it include such books or materials for, or transportation to, extra-curricular activities including sporting events, musical or dramatic events, speech activities, driver's education, or programs of a similar nature.*

At the time of litigation, approximately 820,000 students were enrolled in Minnesota's public elementary and secondary schools. Another ninety-one thousand elementary and secondary students attended some five hundred privately supported schools located in Minnesota. About 95 percent of these students attended sectarian schools.

REHNQUIST, J., delivered the opinion of the Court, in which BURGER, C. J., and WHITE, POWELL, and O'CONNOR, JJ., joined.

. . . [392] Today's case is no exception to our oft-repeated statement that the Establishment Clause presents especially difficult questions of interpretation and application. It is easy enough to quote the few words constituting that Clause—"Congress shall make no law respecting an establishment of [393] religion." It is not at all easy, however, to apply this Court's various decisions construing the Clause to governmental programs of financial assistance to sectarian schools and the parents of children attending those schools. Indeed, in many of these decisions we have expressly or implicitly acknowledged that "we can only dimly perceive the lines of demarcation in this extraordinarily sensitive area of constitutional law." *Lemon v. Kurtzman*, 403 U.S. 602, 612 (1971).

One fixed principle in this field is our consistent rejection of the argument that "any program which in some manner aids an institution with a religious affiliation" violates the Establishment Clause. *Hunt v. McNair*, 413 U.S. 734, 742 (1973). For example, it is now well established that a State may reimburse parents for expenses incurred in transporting their children to school, *Everson v. Board of Education* (1947), and that it may loan secular textbooks to all schoolchildren within the State, *Board of Education v. Allen* (1968).

Notwithstanding the repeated approval given programs such as those in *Allen* and *Everson*, our decisions also have struck down arrangements resembling, in many respects, these forms of assistance. See, *e.g.*, *Lemon v. Kurtzman*; *Levitt v. Committee for Public Education* (1973); *Meek v. Pittenger* (1975); *Wolman v. Walter*, 433 U.S. 229, 237–238 (1977). In this case we [394] are asked to decide whether Minnesota's tax deduction bears greater resemblance to those types of assistance to parochial schools we have approved, or to those we have struck down. Petitioners place particular reliance on our decision in *Committee for Public Education v. Nyquist* where we held invalid a New York statute providing public funds for the maintenance and repair of the physical facilities of private schools and granting thinly disguised "tax benefits," actually amounting to tuition grants, to the parents of children attending private schools. As explained below, we conclude that § 290.09, subd. 22, bears less resemblance to the arrangement struck down in *Nyquist* than it does to assistance programs upheld in our prior decisions and those discussed with approval in *Nyquist*.

The general nature of our inquiry in this area has been guided, since the decision in *Lemon v. Kurtzman*, by the "three-part" test laid down in that case:

> "First, the statute must have a secular legislative purpose; second, its principal or primary effect must be one that neither advances nor inhibits religion . . . ; finally, the statute must not foster 'an excessive government entanglement with religion.'" *Id.*, at 612–613.

While this principle is well settled, our cases have also emphasized that it provides "no more than [a] helpful [signpost]" in dealing with Establishment Clause challenges. *Hunt v. McNair*, at 741. With this caveat in mind, we turn to the specific challenges raised against § 290.09, subd. 22, under the *Lemon* framework.

Little time need be spent on the question of whether the Minnesota tax deduction has a secular purpose. Under our prior decisions, governmental assistance programs have consistently survived this inquiry even when they have run afoul of other aspects of the *Lemon* framework. This reflects, at least in part, our reluctance to attribute unconstitutional motives to the States, particularly when a plausible secular purpose [395] for the State's program may be discerned from the face of the statute.

A State's decision to defray the cost of educational expenses incurred by parents— regardless of the type of schools their children attend—evidences a purpose that is both secular and understandable. An educated populace is essential to the political and economic health of any community, and a State's efforts to assist parents in meeting the rising cost of educational expenses plainly serves this secular purpose of ensuring that the State's citizenry is well educated. Similarly, Minnesota, like other States, could conclude that there is a strong public interest in assuring the continued financial health of private schools, both sectarian and nonsectarian. By educating a substantial number of students such schools relieve public schools of a correspondingly great burden—to the benefit of all taxpayers. In addition, private schools may serve as a benchmark for public schools, in a manner analogous to the "TVA yardstick" for private power companies. As JUSTICE POWELL has remarked:

> "Parochial schools, quite apart from their sectarian purpose, have provided an educational alternative for millions of young Americans; they often afford wholesome competition with our public schools; and in some States they relieve substantially the tax burden incident to the operation of public schools. The State has, moreover, a legitimate interest in facilitating education of the highest quality for all children within its boundaries, whatever school their parents have chosen for them." *Wolman v. Walter*, at 262 (concurring in part, concurring in judgment in part, and dissenting in part).

All these justifications are readily available to support § 290.09, subd. 22, and each is sufficient to satisfy the secular purpose inquiry of *Lemon*.

[396] We turn therefore to the more difficult but related question whether the Minnesota statute has "the primary effect of advancing the sectarian aims of the nonpublic schools." In concluding that it does not, we find several features of the Minnesota tax deduction particularly significant. First, an essential feature of Minnesota's arrangement is the fact that § 290.09, subd. 22, is only one among many deductions—such as those for medical expenses, § 290.09, subd. 10, and charitable contributions, § 290.21, subd. 3— available under the Minnesota tax laws. Our decisions consistently have recognized that traditionally "[legislatures] have especially broad latitude in creating classifications and distinctions in tax statutes," *Regan v. Taxation with Representation of Wash.*, 461 U.S. 540, 547 (1983), in part because the "familiarity with local conditions" enjoyed by legislators especially enables them to "achieve an equitable distribution of the tax burden." *Madden v. Kentucky*, 309 U.S. 83, 88 (1940). Under our prior decisions, the Minnesota Legislature's judgment that a deduction for educational expenses fairly equalizes the tax burden of its citizens and encourages desirable expenditures for educational purposes is entitled to substantial deference.

[397] Other characteristics of § 290.09, subd. 22, argue equally strongly for the provision's constitutionality. Most importantly, the deduction is available for educational expenses incurred by all parents, including those whose children attend public schools and those whose children attend nonsectarian private schools or sectarian private schools. Just as in *Widmar v. Vincent*, 454 U.S. 263, 274 (1981), where we concluded that the State's provision of a forum neutrally "available to a broad class of nonreligious as well as religious speakers" does not "confer any imprimatur of state approval," *ibid.*, so here: "[the] provision of benefits to so broad a spectrum of groups is an important index of secular effect."

[398] In this respect, as well as others, this case is vitally different from the scheme struck down in *Nyquist*. There, public assistance amounting to tuition grants was provided only to parents of children in nonpublic schools. This fact had considerable bearing on our decision striking down the New York statute at issue; we explicitly distinguished both *Allen* and *Everson* on the grounds that "[in] both cases the class of beneficiaries included *all* schoolchildren, those in public as well as those in private schools." 413 U.S., at 782–783, n. 38 (emphasis in original). Moreover, we intimated that "public assistance (e.g., scholarships) made available generally without regard to the sectarian-nonsectarian or public-nonpublic nature of the institution benefited," *ibid.*, might not offend the Establishment Clause. We think the tax deduction adopted by Minnesota is more similar to this latter type of program than it is to the arrangement struck down in *Nyquist*. Un-

like the assistance at issue in *Nyquist*, § 290.09, subd. 22, permits all parents—whether their children attend public school or private—to deduct their children's educational expenses. As *Widmar* and our other decisions indicate, a program, like § 290.09, subd. 22, that neutrally provides [399] state assistance to a broad spectrum of citizens is not readily subject to challenge under the Establishment Clause.

We also agree with the Court of Appeals that, by channeling whatever assistance it may provide to parochial schools through individual parents, Minnesota has reduced the Establishment Clause objections to which its action is subject. It is true, of course, that financial assistance provided to parents ultimately has an economic effect comparable to that of aid given directly to the schools attended by their children. It is also true, however, that under Minnesota's arrangement public funds become available only as a result of numerous private choices of individual parents of school-age children. For these reasons, we recognized in *Nyquist* that the means by which state assistance flows to private schools is of some importance: we said that "the fact that aid is disbursed to parents rather than to . . . schools" is a material consideration in Establishment Clause analysis, albeit "only one among many factors to be considered." 413 U.S., at 781. It is noteworthy that all but one of our recent cases invalidating state aid to parochial schools have involved the direct transmission of assistance from the State to the schools themselves. The exception, of course, was *Nyquist*, which, as discussed previously, is distinguishable from this case on other grounds. Where, as here, aid to parochial schools is available only as a result of decisions of individual parents no "imprimatur of state approval," *Widmar*, at 274, can be deemed to have been conferred on any particular religion, or on religion generally.

We find it useful, in the light of the foregoing characteristics of § 290.09, subd. 22, to compare the attenuated financial benefits flowing to parochial schools from the section to the evils against which the Establishment Clause was designed to protect. These dangers are well described by our statement that "[what] is at stake as a matter of policy [in Establishment Clause cases] is preventing that kind and degree of government involvement in religious life that, as history [400] teaches us, is apt to lead to strife and frequently strain a political system to the breaking point." *Nyquist*, 413 U.S., at 796, quoting *Walz v. Tax Comm'n*, 397 U.S., at 694 (opinion of Harlan, J.). It is important, however, to "keep these issues in perspective":

> "At this point in the 20th century we are quite far removed from the dangers that prompted the Framers to include the Establishment Clause in the Bill of Rights. See *Walz v. Tax Comm'n*, 397 U.S. 664, 668 (1970). The risk of significant religious or denominational control over our democratic processes—or even of deep political division along religious lines—is remote, and when viewed against the positive contributions of sectarian schools, any such risk seems entirely tolerable in light of the continuing oversight of this Court." *Wolman*, 433 U.S., at 263 (POWELL, J., concurring in part, concurring in judgment in part, and dissenting in part).

The Establishment Clause of course extends beyond prohibition of a state church or payment of state funds to one or more churches. We do not think, however, that its prohibition extends to the type of tax deduction established by Minnesota. The historic purposes of the Clause simply do not encompass the sort of attenuated financial benefit, ultimately controlled by the private choices of individual parents, that eventually flows to parochial schools from the neutrally available tax benefit at issue in this case.

Petitioners argue that, notwithstanding the facial neutrality of § 290.09, subd. 22, in application the statute primarily benefits religious institutions. Petitioners rely, as they did [401] below, on a statistical analysis of the type of persons claiming the tax deduction. They contend that most parents of public school children incur no tuition expenses, see Minn. Stat. § 120.06 (1982), and that other expenses deductible under § 290.09, subd. 22, are negligible in value; moreover, they claim that 96% of the children in private schools in 1978–1979 attended religiously affiliated institutions. Because of all this, they reason, the bulk of deductions taken under § 290.09, subd. 22, will be claimed by parents of children in sectarian schools. Respondents reply that petitioners have failed to consider the impact of deductions for items such as transportation, summer school tuition, tuition paid by parents whose children attended schools outside the school districts in which they resided, rental or purchase costs for a variety of equipment, and tuition for certain types of instruction not ordinarily provided in public schools.

We need not consider these contentions in detail. We would be loath to adopt a rule grounding the constitutionality of a facially neutral law on annual reports reciting the extent to which various classes of private citizens claimed benefits under the law. Such an approach would scarcely provide the certainty that this field stands in need of, nor can we perceive principled standards by which such statistical evidence might be evaluated. Moreover, the fact that private persons fail in a particular year to claim the tax relief to which they are entitled—under a facially neutral statute—should be of little importance in determining the constitutionality of the statute permitting such relief.

Finally, private educational institutions, and parents paying for their children to attend these schools, make special contributions to the areas in which they operate. "Parochial [402] schools, quite apart from their sectarian purpose, have provided an educational alternative for millions of young Americans; they often afford wholesome competition with our public schools; and in some States they relieve substantially the tax burden incident to the operation of public schools." *Wolman*, at 262 (POWELL, J., concurring in part, concurring in judgment in part, and dissenting in part). If parents of children in private schools choose to take especial advantage of the relief provided by § 290.09, subd. 22, it is no doubt due to the fact that they bear a particularly great financial burden in educating their children. More fundamentally, whatever unequal effect may be attributed to the statutory classification can fairly be regarded as a rough return for the benefits, discussed above, provided to the State and all taxpayers by parents sending their children to parochial schools. In the light of all this, we believe it wiser to decline to engage in the type of empirical inquiry into those persons benefited by state law which petitioners urge.

Thus, we hold that the Minnesota tax deduction for educational expenses satisfies the primary effect inquiry of our Establishment Clause cases.

[403] Turning to the third part of the *Lemon* inquiry, we have no difficulty in concluding that the Minnesota statute does not "excessively entangle" the State in religion. The only plausible source of the "comprehensive, discriminating, and continuing state surveillance," 403 U.S., at 619, necessary to run afoul of this standard would lie in the fact that state officials must determine whether particular textbooks qualify for a deduction. In making this decision, state officials must disallow deductions taken for "instructional books and materials used in the teaching of religious tenets, doctrines or worship, the purpose of which is to inculcate such tenets, doctrines or worship." Minn. Stat. § 290.09, subd. 22 (1982). Making decisions such as this does not differ substantially from making the types of decisions approved in earlier opinions of this Court. In *Board of Education v. Allen* (1968), for example, the Court upheld the loan of secular textbooks to parents or children attending nonpublic schools; though state officials were required to determine whether particular books were or were not secular, the system was held not to violate the Establishment Clause. The same result follows in this case. . . .

[404] JUSTICE MARSHALL, with whom JUSTICE BRENNAN, JUSTICE BLACKMUN, and JUSTICE STEVENS join, dissenting.

The Establishment Clause of the First Amendment prohibits a State from subsidizing religious education, whether it does so directly or indirectly. In my view, this principle of neutrality forbids not only the tax benefits struck down in *Committee for Public Education v. Nyquist* (1973), but any tax benefit, including the tax deduction at issue here, which subsidizes tuition payments to sectarian schools. I also believe that the Establishment Clause prohibits the tax deductions that Minnesota authorizes for the cost of books and other instructional materials used for sectarian purposes.

I

The majority today does not question the continuing vitality of this Court's decision in *Nyquist*. That decision established that a State may not support religious education either through direct grants to parochial schools or through financial aid to parents of parochial school students. *Nyquist* also established that financial aid to parents of students attending parochial schools is no more permissible if it is provided in the form of a tax credit than if provided in the form of cash payments. Notwithstanding these accepted principles, [405] the Court today upholds a statute that provides a tax deduction for the tuition charged by religious schools. The Court concludes that the Minnesota statute is "vitally different" from the New York statute at issue in *Nyquist*. *Ante*, at 398. As demonstrated below, there is no significant difference between the two schemes. The Minnesota tax statute violates the Establishment Clause for precisely the same reason as the statute struck down in *Nyquist*: it has a direct and immediate effect of advancing religion.

A

In calculating their net income for state income tax purposes, Minnesota residents are permitted to deduct the cost of their children's tuition, subject to a ceiling of $500 or $700 per child. By taking this deduction, a taxpayer reduces his tax bill by a sum equal to the amount of tuition multiplied by his rate of tax. Although this tax benefit is available to any parents whose children attend schools which charge tuition, the vast majority of the taxpayers who are eligible to receive the benefit are parents whose children attend religious schools. In the 1978–1979 school year, 90,000 students were enrolled in nonpublic schools charging tuition; over 95% of those students attended sectarian schools. Although the statute also allows a deduction for the tuition expenses of children attending public schools, Minnesota public schools are generally prohibited by law from charging tuition. Minn. Stat. § 120.06 (1982). Public schools may assess tuition charges only for students accepted from outside the district. § 123.39, subd. 5. In the 1978–1979 school year, only 79 public school students fell into this category. The parents of the remaining 815,000 students who attended public schools were ineligible to receive this tax benefit.

Like the law involved in *Nyquist*, the Minnesota law can be said to serve a secular purpose: promoting pluralism and diversity among the State's public and nonpublic schools. But the Establishment Clause requires more than that legislation have a secular purpose. *Nyquist*, 413 U.S., at 773. "[The] [406] propriety of a legislature's purposes may not immunize from further scrutiny a law which . . . has a primary effect that advances religion." *Id.*, at 774. Moreover, even if one "'primary' effect [is] to promote some legitimate end under the State's police power," the legislation is not "immune from further examination to ascertain whether it also has the direct and immediate effect of advancing religion." *Id.*, at 783–784, n. 39.

As we recognized in *Nyquist*, direct government subsidization of parochial school tuition is impermissible because "the effect of the aid is unmistakably to provide desired financial support for nonpublic, sectarian institutions." 413 U.S., at 783. "[Aid] to the educational function of [parochial] schools . . . necessarily results in aid to the sectarian school enterprise as a whole" because "[the] very purpose of many of those schools is to provide an integrated secular and religious education." *Meek v. Pittenger*, at 366. For this reason, aid to sectarian schools must be restricted to ensure that it may be not used to further the religious mission of those schools. While "services such as police and fire protection, sewage disposal, highways, and sidewalks" may be provided to parochial schools in common with other institutions, because this type of assistance is clearly "marked off from the religious function" of those schools, *Nyquist*, at 781–782, quoting *Everson v. Board of Education*, 330 U.S. 1, 18 (1947), unrestricted financial assistance, such as grants for the maintenance and construction of parochial schools, may not be [407] provided. *Nyquist*, 413 U.S., at 774–780. "In the absence of an effective means of guaranteeing that the state aid derived from public funds will be used exclusively for secular, neutral, and nonideological purposes, it is clear from our cases that direct aid in whatever form is invalid." *Id.*, at 780.

Indirect assistance in the form of financial aid to parents for tuition payments is similarly impermissible because it is not "subject to . . . restrictions" which "guarantee the separation between secular and religious educational functions and . . . ensure that State financial aid supports only the former." *Id.*, at 783, quoting *Lemon v. Kurtzman*, 403 U.S. 602, 613 (1971). By ensuring that parents will be reimbursed for tuition payments they make, the Minnesota statute requires that taxpayers in general pay for the cost of parochial education and extends a financial "incentive to parents to send their children to sectarian schools." *Nyquist*, 413 U.S., at 786. As was true of the law struck down in *Nyquist*:

> "[It] is precisely the function of [Minnesota's] law to provide assistance to private schools, the great majority of which are sectarian. By reimbursing parents for a portion of their tuition bill, the State seeks to relieve their financial burdens sufficiently to assure that they continue to have the option to send their children to religion-oriented schools. And while the other purposes for that aid—to perpetuate a pluralistic educational environment and to protect the fiscal integrity of overburdened public schools—are certainly unexceptionable, the effect of the aid is unmistakably to provide desired financial support for nonpublic, sectarian institutions." *Id.*, at 783.

That parents receive a reduction of their tax liability, rather than a direct reimbursement, is of no greater significance here than it was in *Nyquist*. "[For] purposes of determining whether such aid has the effect of advancing religion," [408] it makes no difference whether the qualifying "parent receives an actual cash payment [or] is allowed to reduce . . . the sum he would otherwise be obliged to pay over to the State." *Id.*, at 790–791. It is equally irrelevant whether a reduction in taxes takes the form of a tax "credit," a tax "modification," or a tax "deduction." *Id.*, at 789–790. What is of controlling significance is not the form but the "substantive impact" of the financial aid. *Id.*, at 786. "[Insofar] as such benefits render assistance to parents who send their children to *sectarian* schools, their purpose and inevitable effect are to aid and advance those religious institutions." *Id.*, at 793 (emphasis added).

B

The majority attempts to distinguish *Nyquist* by pointing to two differences between the Minnesota tuition-assistance program and the program struck down in *Nyquist*. Neither of these distinctions can withstand scrutiny.

I

The majority first attempts to distinguish *Nyquist* on the ground that Minnesota makes all parents eligible to deduct up to $500 or $700 for each dependent, whereas the New York law allowed a deduction only for parents whose children attended nonpublic schools. Although Minnesota taxpayers who send their children to local public schools may not deduct tuition expenses because they incur none, they may deduct other expenses, such as the cost of gym clothes, pencils, and notebooks, which are shared by all parents of school-age children. This, in the majority's view, distinguishes the Minnesota scheme from the law at issue in *Nyquist*.

That the Minnesota statute makes some small benefit available to all parents cannot alter the fact that the most substantial benefit provided by the statute is available only to those parents who send their children to schools that charge tuition. It is simply undeniable that the single largest expense that may be deducted under the Minnesota statute is tuition. The statute is little more than a subsidy of tuition masquerading [409] as a subsidy of general educational expenses. The other deductible expenses are *de minimis* in comparison to tuition expenses.

Contrary to the majority's suggestion, *ante*, at 401, the bulk of the tax benefits afforded by the Minnesota scheme are enjoyed by parents of parochial school children not because parents of public school children fail to claim deductions to which they are entitled, but because the latter are simply unable to claim the largest tax deduction that Minnesota authorizes. Fewer than 100 of more than 900,000 school-age children in Minnesota attend public schools that charge a general tuition. Of the total number of taxpayers who are eligible for the tuition deduction, approximately 96% send their children to religious schools. Parents who send their children to free public schools are simply ineligible to obtain the full benefit of the deduction except in the unlikely event that they buy $700 worth of pencils, notebooks, and bus rides for their school-age children. Yet parents who pay at least $700 in tuition to nonpublic, sectarian schools can claim the full deduction even if they incur no other educational expenses.

That this deduction has a primary effect of promoting religion can easily be determined without any resort to the type of "statistical evidence" that the majority fears would lead to constitutional uncertainty. . . .

[411] In this case, it is undisputed that well over 90% of the children attending tuition-charging schools in Minnesota are enrolled in sectarian schools. History and experience likewise instruct us that any generally available financial assistance for elementary and secondary school tuition expenses mainly will further religious education because the majority of the schools which charge tuition are sectarian. Because Minnesota, like every other State, is committed to providing free public education, tax assistance for

tuition payments inevitably redounds to the benefit of nonpublic, sectarian schools and parents who send their children to those schools.

2

The majority also asserts that the Minnesota statute is distinguishable from the statute struck down in *Nyquist* in another respect: the tax benefit available under Minnesota law is a "genuine tax deduction," whereas the New York law provided a benefit which, while nominally a deduction, also had features of a "tax credit." *Ante*, at 396. Under the Minnesota law, the amount of the tax benefit varies directly with the amount of the expenditure. Under the New York law, the amount of deduction was not dependent upon the amount actually paid for tuition but was a predetermined amount which depended on the tax bracket of each taxpayer. The deduction was designed to yield roughly the same amount of tax "forgiveness" for each taxpayer.

This is a distinction without a difference. Our prior decisions have rejected the relevance of the majority's formalistic distinction between tax deductions and the tax benefit at issue in *Nyquist*. [412] The deduction afforded by Minnesota law was "designed to yield a [tax benefit] in exchange for performing a specific act which the State desires to encourage." *Nyquist*, at 789. Like the tax benefit held impermissible in *Nyquist*, the tax deduction at issue here concededly was designed to "[encourage] desirable expenditures for educational purposes." *Ante*, at 396. Of equal importance, as the majority also concedes, the "economic [consequence]" of these programs is the same, *ante*, at 397, n. 6, for in each case the "financial assistance provided to parents ultimately has an economic effect comparable to that of aid given directly to the schools." *Ante*, at 399. It was precisely the substantive impact of the financial support, and not its particular form, that rendered the programs in *Nyquist* and *Sloan* [413] v. *Lemon* unconstitutional. See *Nyquist*, at 790–791, 794; *Sloan v. Lemon*, 413 U.S., at 832. . . .

[414] II

In my view, Minnesota's tax deduction for the cost of textbooks and other instructional materials is also constitutionally infirm. The majority is simply mistaken in concluding that a tax deduction, unlike a tax credit or a direct grant to parents, promotes religious education in a manner that is only "attenuated." *Ante*, at 399, 400. A tax deduction has a primary effect that advances religion if it is provided to offset expenditures which are not restricted to the secular activities of parochial schools.

The instructional materials which are subsidized by the Minnesota tax deduction plainly may be used to inculcate religious values and belief. In *Meek v. Pittenger*, 421 U.S., at 366, we held that even the use of "wholly neutral, secular instructional material and equipment" by church-related schools contributes to religious instruction because "[the] secular education those schools provide goes hand in hand with the religious mission that is the only reason for the schools' existence." In *Wolman v. Walter*, 433 U.S., at 249–250, we concluded that precisely the same impermissible effect results when the instructional materials are loaned to the pupil or his parent, rather than directly to the schools. We stated that "it would exalt form over substance if this distinction were found to justify a result different from that in *Meek*." *Id.*, at 250. It follows that a tax deduction to offset the cost of purchasing instructional materials for use in sectarian schools, like a loan of such materials to parents, "necessarily results in aid to the sectarian school enterprise as a whole" and is therefore a "substantial advancement of religious activity" that "constitutes an impermissible establishment of religion." *Meek v. Pittenger*, at 366.

There is no reason to treat Minnesota's tax deduction for textbooks any differently. Secular textbooks, like other secular instructional materials, contribute to the religious mission of the parochial schools that use those books. Although this Court upheld the loan of secular textbooks to religious [415] schools in *Board of Education v. Allen*, the Court believed at that time that it lacked sufficient experience to determine "based solely on judicial notice" that "the processes of secular and religious training are so intertwined that secular textbooks furnished to students by the public [will always be] instrumental in the teaching of religion." 392 U.S., at 248. This basis for distinguishing secular instructional materials and secular textbooks is simply untenable, and is inconsistent with many of our more recent decisions concerning state aid to parochial schools.

In any event, the Court's assumption in *Allen* that the textbooks at issue there might be used only for secular education was based on the fact that those very books had been chosen by the State for use in the public schools. 392 U.S., at 244–245. In contrast, the Minnesota statute does not limit the tax deduction to those books which the State has approved for use in public schools. Rather, it permits a deduction for books that are chosen by the parochial schools themselves. Indeed, under the Minnesota statutory scheme, textbooks chosen by parochial schools but not used by public schools are likely to be precisely the ones purchased by parents for their children's use. Like the law upheld in *Board of Education v. Allen*, Minn. Stat. §§ 123.932 and 123.933 (1982) authorize the State Board of Education to provide textbooks used in public schools to nonpublic school students. Parents have little reason to purchase textbooks that can be borrowed under this provision.

[416] III

. . . In my view, the lines drawn in *Nyquist* were drawn on a reasoned basis with appropriate regard for the principles of neutrality embodied by the Establishment Clause. I do not believe that the same can be said of the lines drawn by the majority today. For the first time, the Court has upheld financial support for religious schools without any reason at all to assume that the support will be restricted to the secular functions of those schools and will not be used to support religious [417] instruction. This result is flatly at odds with the fundamental principle that a State may provide no financial support whatsoever to promote religion. As the Court stated in *Everson*, 330 U.S., at 16, and has often repeated, see, *e.g.*, *Meek v. Pittenger*, 421 U.S., at 359; *Nyquist*, 413 U.S., at 780:

> "No tax in any amount, large or small, can be levied to support any religious activities or institutions, whatever they may be called, or whatever form they may adopt to teach or practice religion."

I dissent.

34

Marsh v. Chambers

463 U.S. 783 (1983)

Vote: 6—Burger, White, Blackmun, Powell, Rehnquist, O'Connor
 3—Brennan, Marshall, Stevens

Opinion announcing the opinion of the Court: Burger
Dissenting opinions: Brennan, Stevens

The Nebraska state legislature began each of its sessions with a prayer offered by a chaplain chosen biennially by the Executive Board of the Legislative Council and paid with public funds. At the time of litigation, Robert E. Palmer, a Presbyterian minister, had served as chaplain since 1965 at a salary of $319.75 per month for each month the legislature was in session.

BURGER, C. J., delivered the opinion of the Court, in which WHITE, BLACKMUN, POWELL, REHNQUIST, and O'CONNOR, JJ., joined.

[784] The question presented is whether the Nebraska Legislature's practice of opening each legislative day with a prayer by a chaplain paid by the State violates the Establishment Clause of the First Amendment. . . .

[786] II

The opening of sessions of legislative and other deliberative public bodies with prayer is deeply embedded in the history and tradition of this country. From colonial times through the founding of the Republic and ever since, the practice of legislative prayer has coexisted with the principles of disestablishment and religious freedom. In the very courtrooms in which the United States District Judge and later three Circuit Judges heard and decided this case, the proceedings opened with an announcement that concluded, "God save the United States and this Honorable Court." The same invocation occurs at all sessions of this Court.

[787] The tradition in many of the Colonies was, of course, linked to an established church, but the Continental Congress, beginning in 1774, adopted the traditional procedure of opening its sessions with a prayer offered by a paid chaplain. Although prayers

were not offered during the Constitutional Convention, the First Congress, as one of [788] its early items of business, adopted the policy of selecting a chaplain to open each session with prayer. Thus, on April 7, 1789, the Senate appointed a committee "to take under consideration the manner of electing Chaplains." S. Jour., 1st Cong., 1st Sess., 10 (1820 ed.). On April 9, 1789, a similar committee was appointed by the House of Representatives. On April 25, 1789, the Senate elected its first chaplain, *id.*, at 16; the House followed suit on May 1, 1789, H. R. Jour., 1st Cong., 1st Sess., 26 (1826 ed.). A statute providing for the payment of these chaplains was enacted into law on September 22, 1789. 2 Annals of Cong. 2180; § 4, 1 Stat. 71.

On September 25, 1789, three days after Congress authorized the appointment of paid chaplains, final agreement was reached on the language of the Bill of Rights. Clearly the men who wrote the First Amendment Religion Clauses did not view paid legislative chaplains and opening prayers as a violation of that Amendment, for the practice of opening sessions with prayer has continued without interruption ever since that early session of Congress. It has also been followed consistently [789] in most of the states, including Nebraska, where the institution of opening legislative sessions with prayer was adopted even before the State attained statehood.

[790] Standing alone, historical patterns cannot justify contemporary violations of constitutional guarantees, but there is far more here than simply historical patterns. In this context, historical evidence sheds light not only on what the draftsmen intended the Establishment Clause to mean, but also on how they thought that Clause applied to the practice authorized by the First Congress—their actions reveal their intent. An Act

"passed by the first Congress assembled under the Constitution, many of whose members had taken part in framing that instrument, . . . is contemporaneous and weighty evidence of its true meaning." *Wisconsin v. Pelican Ins. Co.*, 127 U.S. 265, 297 (1888).

In *Walz v. Tax Comm'n*, 397 U.S. 664, 678 (1970), we considered the weight to be accorded to history:

"It is obviously correct that no one acquires a vested or protected right in violation of the Constitution by long use, even when that span of time covers our entire national existence and indeed predates it. Yet an unbroken practice . . . is not something to be lightly cast aside."

No more is Nebraska's practice of over a century, consistent with two centuries of national practice, to be cast aside. It can hardly be thought that in the same week Members of the First Congress voted to appoint and to pay a chaplain for each House and also voted to approve the draft of the First Amendment for submission to the states, they intended the Establishment Clause of the Amendment to forbid what they had just declared acceptable. In applying the First Amendment to the states through the Fourteenth Amendment, *Cantwell v. Connecticut* (1940), it would be incongruous to interpret that Clause as imposing more stringent [791] First Amendment limits on the states than the draftsmen imposed on the Federal Government.

This unique history leads us to accept the interpretation of the First Amendment draftsmen who saw no real threat to the Establishment Clause arising from a practice of prayer similar to that now challenged. We conclude that legislative prayer presents no more potential for establishment than the provision of school transportation, *Everson v. Board of Education* (1947), beneficial grants for higher education, *Tilton v. Richardson* (1971), or tax exemptions for religious organizations, *Walz*.

Respondent cites JUSTICE BRENNAN's concurring opinion in *Abington School Dist. v. Schempp*, 374 U.S. 203, 237 (1963), and argues that we should not rely too heavily on "the advice of the Founding Fathers" because the messages of history often tend to be ambiguous and not relevant to a society far more heterogeneous than that of the Framers, *id.*, at 240. Respondent also points out that John Jay and John Rutledge opposed the motion to begin the first session of the Continental Congress with prayer.

We do not agree that evidence of opposition to a measure weakens the force of the historical argument; indeed it infuses it with power by demonstrating that the subject was considered carefully and the action not taken thoughtlessly, by force of long tradition and without regard to the problems posed by a pluralistic society. Jay and Rutledge specifically grounded their objection on the fact that the delegates to the Congress "were so divided in religious sentiments . . . that [they] could not join in the same act of worship." Their objection [792] was met by Samuel Adams, who stated that "he was no bigot, and could hear a prayer from a gentleman of piety and virtue, who was at the same time a friend to his country."

This interchange emphasizes that the delegates did not consider opening prayers as a proselytizing activity or as symbolically placing the government's "official seal of approval on one religious view." Rather, the Founding Fathers looked at invocations as "conduct whose . . . effect . . . [harmonized] with the tenets of some or all religions." *McGowan v. Maryland*, 366 U.S. 420, 442 (1961). The Establishment Clause does not always bar a state from regulating conduct simply because it "harmonizes with religious canons." *Id.*, at 462 (Frankfurter, J., concurring). Here, the individual claiming injury by the practice is an adult, presumably not readily susceptible to "religious indoctrination," see *Tilton*, at 686, or peer pressure, compare *Abington*, at 290 (BRENNAN, J., concurring).

In light of the unambiguous and unbroken history of more than 200 years, there can be no doubt that the practice of opening legislative sessions with prayer has become part of the fabric of our society. To invoke Divine guidance on a public body entrusted with making the laws is not, in these circumstances, an "establishment" of religion or a step toward establishment; it is simply a tolerable acknowledgment of beliefs widely held among the people of this country. As Justice Douglas observed, "[we] are a religious people whose institutions presuppose a Supreme Being." *Zorach v. Clauson*, 343 U.S. 306, 313 (1952).

III

We turn then to the question of whether any features of the Nebraska practice violate the Establishment Clause. [793] Beyond the bare fact that a prayer is offered, three points have been made: first, that a clergyman of only one denomination—Presbyterian—has been selected for 16 years; second, that the chaplain is paid at public expense; and third, that the prayers are in the Judeo-Christian tradition. Weighed against the historical background, these factors do not serve to invalidate Nebraska's practice.

The Court of Appeals was concerned that Palmer's long tenure has the effect of giving preference to his religious views. We cannot, any more than Members of the Congresses of this century, perceive any suggestion that choosing a clergyman of one denomination advances the beliefs of a particular church. To the contrary, the evidence indicates that Palmer was reappointed because his performance and personal qualities were acceptable to the body appointing him. Palmer was not the only clergyman heard by the legislature; guest chaplains have officiated at the request of various legislators and as substitutes during Palmer's absences. Absent proof that the chaplain's reappointment stemmed from an impermissible motive, we conclude [794] that his long tenure does not in itself conflict with the Establishment Clause.

Nor is the compensation of the chaplain from public funds a reason to invalidate the Nebraska Legislature's chaplaincy; remuneration is grounded in historic practice initiated, as we noted earlier, *supra*, at 788, by the same Congress that drafted the Establishment Clause of the First Amendment. The Continental Congress paid its chaplain, as did some of the states. Currently, many state legislatures and the United States Congress provide compensation for their chaplains. Nebraska has paid its chaplain for well over a century. The content of the prayer is not of concern to judges where, as here, there is no indication that the prayer opportunity has been exploited to proselytize or advance any one, [795] or to disparage any other, faith or belief. That being so, it is not for us to embark on a sensitive evaluation or to parse the content of a particular prayer.

We do not doubt the sincerity of those, who like respondent, believe that to have prayer in this context risks the beginning of the establishment the Founding Fathers feared. But this concern is not well founded, for as Justice Goldberg aptly observed in his concurring opinion in *Abington*, 374 U.S., at 308:

> "It is of course true that great consequences can grow from small beginnings, but the measure of constitutional adjudication is the ability and willingness to distinguish between real threat and mere shadow."

The unbroken practice for two centuries in the National Congress and for more than a century in Nebraska and in many other states gives abundant assurance that there is no real threat "while this Court sits," *Panhandle Oil Co. v. Mississippi ex rel. Knox*, 277 U.S. 218, 223 (1928) (Holmes, J., dissenting).

JUSTICE BRENNAN, with whom JUSTICE MARSHALL joins, dissenting.

The Court today has written a narrow and, on the whole, careful opinion. In effect, the Court holds that officially sponsored legislative prayer, primarily on account of its "unique history," *ante*, at 791, is generally exempted from the First Amendment's prohibition against "an establishment of religion." The Court's opinion is consistent with dictum in at least one of our prior decisions,[1] and its limited rationale should pose little threat to the overall fate of the Establishment Clause. Moreover, disagreement with the Court [796] requires that I confront the fact that some 20 years ago, in a concurring opinion in one of the cases striking down official prayer and ceremonial Bible reading in the public schools, I came very close to endorsing essentially the result reached by the Court today.[2] Nevertheless, after much reflection, I have come to the conclusion that I was wrong then and that the Court is wrong today. I now believe that the practice of official invocational prayer, as it exists in Nebraska and most other state legislatures, is unconstitutional. It is contrary to the doctrine as well the underlying purposes of the Establishment Clause, and it is not saved either by its history or by any of the other considerations suggested in the Court's opinion.

I respectfully dissent.

---

1. See *Zorach v. Clauson*, 343 U.S. 306, 312–313 (1952); cf. *Abington School Dist. v. Schempp*, 374 U.S. 203, 213 (1963).

2. "The saying of invocational prayers in legislative chambers, state or federal, and the appointment of legislative chaplains, might well represent no involvements of the kind prohibited by the Establishment Clause. Legislators, federal and state, are mature adults who may presumably absent themselves from such public and ceremonial exercises without incurring any penalty, direct or indirect." *Schempp*, at 299–300 (BRENNAN, J., concurring).

I

The Court makes no pretense of subjecting Nebraska's practice of legislative prayer to any of the formal "tests" that have traditionally structured our inquiry under the Establishment Clause. That it fails to do so is, in a sense, a good thing, for it simply confirms that the Court is carving out an exception to the Establishment Clause rather than reshaping Establishment Clause doctrine to accommodate legislative prayer. For my purposes, however, I must begin by demonstrating what should be obvious: that, if the Court were to judge legislative prayer through the unsentimental eye of our settled doctrine, it would have to strike it down as a clear violation of the Establishment Clause.

The most commonly cited formulation of prevailing Establishment Clause doctrine is found in *Lemon v. Kurtzman*, 403 U.S. 602 (1971):

> [797] "Every analysis in this area must begin with consideration of the cumulative criteria developed by the Court over many years. Three such tests may be gleaned from our cases. First, the statute [at issue] must have a secular legislative purpose; second, its principal or primary effect must be one that neither advances nor inhibits religion; finally, the statute must not foster 'an excessive government entanglement with religion.'" *Id.*, at 612–613.

That the "purpose" of legislative prayer is pre-eminently religious rather than secular seems to me to be self-evident. "To invoke Divine guidance on a public body entrusted with making the laws," *ante*, at 792, is nothing but a religious act. Moreover, whatever secular functions legislative prayer might play—formally opening the legislative session, getting the members of the body to quiet down, and imbuing them with a sense of seriousness and high purpose—could so plainly be performed in a purely nonreligious fashion that to claim a secular purpose for the prayer is an insult to the perfectly [798] honorable individuals who instituted and continue the practice.

As Reverend Palmer put the matter: "I would say that I strive to relate the Senators and their helpers to the divine." "[My] purpose is to provide an opportunity for Senators to be drawn closer to their understanding of God as they understand God. In order that the divine wisdom might be theirs as they conduct their business for the day."

The "primary effect" of legislative prayer is also clearly religious. As we said in the context of officially sponsored prayers in the public schools, "prescribing a particular form of religious worship," even if the individuals involved have the choice not to participate, places "indirect coercive pressure upon religious minorities to conform to the prevailing officially approved religion. . . ." *Engel v. Vitale*, 370 U.S. 421, 431 (1962). More importantly, invocations in Nebraska's legislative halls explicitly link religious belief and observance to the power and prestige of the State. "[The] mere appearance of a joint exercise of legislative authority by Church and State provides a significant symbolic benefit to religion in the minds of some by reason of the power conferred."

Finally, there can be no doubt that the practice of legislative prayer leads to excessive "entanglement" between the State and religion. *Lemon* pointed out that "entanglement" can take two forms: First, a state statute or program might involve the state impermissibly in monitoring and overseeing [799] religious affairs. 403 U.S., at 614–622. In the case of legislative prayer, the process of choosing a "suitable" chaplain, whether on a permanent or rotating basis, and insuring that the chaplain limits himself or herself to "suitable" prayers, involves precisely the sort of supervision that agencies of government should if at all possible avoid.

Second, excessive "entanglement" might arise out of "the divisive political potential" of a state statute or program. 403 U.S., at 622.

"Ordinarily political debate and division, however vigorous or even partisan, are normal and healthy manifestations of our democratic system of government, but political division along religious lines was one of the principal evils against which the First Amendment was intended to protect. The potential divisiveness of such conflict is a threat to the normal political process." *Ibid.*

In this case, this second aspect of entanglement is also clear. The controversy between Senator Chambers and his colleagues, which had reached the stage of difficulty and rancor long before this lawsuit was brought, has split the Nebraska [800] Legislature precisely on issues of religion and religious conformity. The record in this case also reports a series of instances, involving legislators other than Senator Chambers, in which invocations by Reverend Palmer and others led to controversy along religious lines. And in general, the history of legislative prayer has been far more eventful—and divisive—than a hasty reading of the Court's opinion might indicate. . . .

In sum, I have no doubt that, if any group of law students were asked to apply the principles of *Lemon* to the question [801] of legislative prayer, they would nearly unanimously find the practice to be unconstitutional.

II

The path of formal doctrine, however, can only imperfectly capture the nature and importance of the issues at stake in this case. A more adequate analysis must therefore take [802] into account the underlying function of the Establishment Clause, and the forces that have shaped its doctrine.

A

Most of the provisions of the Bill of Rights, even if they are not generally enforceable in the absence of state action, nevertheless arise out of moral intuitions applicable to individuals as well as governments. The Establishment Clause, however, is quite different. It is, to its core, nothing less and nothing more than a statement about the proper role of government in the society that we have shaped for ourselves in this land.

The Establishment Clause embodies a judgment, born of a long and turbulent history, that, in our society, religion "must be a private matter for the individual, the family, and the institutions of private choice. . . ." *Lemon v. Kurtzman*, 403 U.S., at 625.

"Government in our democracy, state and national, must be neutral in matters of religious theory, doctrine, and practice. It may not be hostile to any religion or to the advocacy of no-religion; and it may not aid, foster, or promote one religion or religious theory against another or even against the militant opposite. The First Amendment mandates governmental neutrality between religion and religion, and between religion and non-religion." *Epperson v. Arkansas*, 393 U.S. 97, 103–104 (1968).

"In the words of Jefferson, the clause against establishment of religion by law was intended to erect 'a wall of separation between church and State.'" *Everson v. Board of Education*, 330 U.S. 1, 16 (1947), quoting *Reynolds v. United States*, 98 U.S. 145, 164 (1879).

[803] The principles of "separation" and "neutrality" implicit in the Establishment Clause serve many purposes. Four of these are particularly relevant here.

The first, which is most closely related to the more general conceptions of liberty found in the remainder of the First Amendment, is to guarantee the individual right to conscience. The right to conscience, in the religious sphere, is not only implicated when the government engages in direct or indirect coercion. It is also implicated when the government requires individuals to support the practices of a faith with which they do not agree.

> "[To] compel a man to furnish contributions of money for the propagation of [religious] opinions which he disbelieves, is sinful and tyrannical; . . . even . . . forcing him to support this or that teacher of his own religious persuasion, is depriving him of the comfortable liberty of giving his contributions to the particular pastor, whose morals he would make his pattern. . . ." *Everson v. Board of Education*, at 13, quoting Virginia Bill for Religious Liberty.

The second purpose of separation and neutrality is to keep the state from interfering in the essential autonomy of religious life, either by taking upon itself the decision of religious [804] issues, or by unduly involving itself in the supervision of religious institutions or officials.

This and the remaining purposes that I discuss cannot be reduced simply to a question of individual liberty. A court, for example, will refuse to decide an essentially religious issue even if the issue is otherwise properly before the court, and even if it is asked to decide it.

The third purpose of separation and neutrality is to prevent the trivialization and degradation of religion by too close an attachment to the organs of government. The Establishment Clause "stands as an expression of principle on the part of the Founders of our Constitution that religion is too personal, too sacred, too holy, to permit its 'unhallowed perversion' by a civil magistrate." *Engel v. Vitale*, 370 U.S., at 432, quoting *Memorial and Remonstrance against Religious Assessments*.

[805] Finally, the principles of separation and neutrality help assure that essentially religious issues, precisely because of their importance and sensitivity, not become the occasion for battle in the political arena. See *Lemon*, 403 U.S., at 622–624; *Board of Education v. Allen*, 392 U.S. 236, 249 (Harlan, J., concurring); *Engel*, at 429–430. With regard to most issues, the government may be influenced by partisan argument and may act as a partisan itself. In each case, there will be winners and losers in the political battle, and the losers' most common recourse is the right to dissent and the right to fight the battle again another day. With regard to matters that are essentially religious, however, the Establishment Clause seeks that there should be no political battles, and that no American should at any point feel alienated [806] from his government because that government has declared or acted upon some "official" or "authorized" point of view on a matter of religion. . . .

[808] C

Legislative prayer clearly violates the principles of neutrality and separation that are embedded within the Establishment Clause. It is contrary to the fundamental message of *Engel* and *Schempp*. It intrudes on the right to conscience by forcing some legislators either to participate in a "prayer opportunity," *ante*, at 794, with which they are in basic disagreement, or to make their disagreement a matter of public comment by declining to participate. It forces all residents of the State to support a religious exercise that may be contrary to their own beliefs. It requires the State to commit itself on fundamental theological issues. It has the potential for degrading religion by allowing a religious call to worship to be intermeshed with a secular call to order. And it injects religion into the political sphere by creating the potential that each and every selection of a chaplain, or consideration of a particular prayer, or even reconsideration of the practice itself, will provoke a political battle along religious lines and ultimately alienate some religiously identified group of citizens. . . .

[813] The Court's main argument for carving out an exception sustaining legislative prayer is historical. The Court cannot—and does not—purport to find a pattern of "undeviating acceptance," *Walz*, at 681 (BRENNAN, J., concurring), of legislative prayer. See *ante*, at 791. It also disclaims exclusive reliance on the mere longevity of legislative prayer. *Ante*, at 790. The Court does, however, point out that, only three days before the First Congress reached agreement on the final wording of the Bill of Rights, it authorized the appointment of paid chaplains for [814] its own proceedings, *ante*, at 788, and the Court argues that in light of this "unique history," *ante*, at 791, the actions of Congress reveal its intent as to the meaning of the Establishment Clause, *ante*, at 788–790. I agree that historical practice is "of considerable import in the interpretation of abstract constitutional language," *Walz*, 397 U.S., at 681 (BRENNAN, J., concurring). This is a case, however, in which—absent the Court's invocation of history—there would be no question that the practice at issue was unconstitutional. And despite the surface appeal of the Court's argument, there are at least three reasons why specific historical practice should not in this case override that clear constitutional imperative.

First, it is significant that the Court's historical argument does not rely on the legislative history of the Establishment Clause itself. Indeed, that formal history is profoundly unilluminating on this and most other subjects. Rather, the Court assumes that the Framers of the Establishment Clause would not have themselves authorized a practice that they thought violated the guarantees contained in the Clause. *Ante*, at 790. This assumption, however, is questionable. Legislators, influenced by the passions and exigencies of the moment, the pressure of constituents and colleagues, and the press of business, do not always pass sober constitutional judgment on every piece of legislation they enact, and this [815] must be assumed to be as true of the Members of the First Congress as any other. Indeed, the fact that James Madison, who voted for the bill authorizing the payment of the first congressional chaplains, later expressed the view that the practice was unconstitutional is instructive on precisely this point. Madison's later views may not have represented so much a change of mind as a change of role, from a Member of Congress engaged in the hurly-burly of legislative activity to a detached observer engaged in unpressured reflection. Since the latter role is precisely the one with which this Court is charged, I am not at all sure that Madison's later writings should be any less influential in our deliberations than his earlier vote.

One commentator has pointed out that the chaplaincy established by the First Congress was "a carry-over from the days of the Continental Congress, which . . . exercised plenary jurisdiction in matters of religion; and ceremonial practices such as [this] are not easily dislodged after becoming so firmly established."

Second, the Court's analysis treats the First Amendment simply as an Act of Congress, as to whose meaning the intent of Congress is the single touchstone. Both the Constitution and its Amendments, however, became supreme law only by virtue of their ratification by the States, and the understanding of the States should be as relevant to our analysis as the understanding of Congress. This observation is especially compelling in considering [816] the meaning of the Bill of Rights. The first 10 Amendments were not enacted because the Members of the First Congress came up with a bright idea one morning; rather, their enactment was forced upon Congress by a number of the States as a condition for their ratification of the original Constitution. To treat any practice authorized by the First Congress as presumptively consistent with the Bill of Rights is therefore somewhat akin to treating any action of a party to a contract as presumptively consistent with the terms of the contract. The latter proposition, if it were accepted, would of course resolve many of the heretofore perplexing issues in contract law.

Finally, and most importantly, the argument tendered by the Court is misguided because the Constitution is not a static document whose meaning on every detail is fixed for all time by the life experience of the Framers. We have recognized in a wide variety of constitutional contexts that the practices that were in place at the time any particular guarantee was enacted into the Constitution do not necessarily fix forever the meaning of that guarantee. To be truly faithful to the Framers, "our use of the history of their time must limit itself to broad purposes, not specific practices." *Abington School Dist. v. Schempp*, 374 U.S., at 241 (BRENNAN, J., concurring). Our primary task must be to translate "the majestic generalities of the Bill of Rights, conceived as part of the pattern of liberal government in the eighteenth century, into concrete restraints on officials dealing with the [817] problems of the twentieth century. . . ." *West Virginia Bd. of Education v. Barnette*, 319 U.S. 624, 639 (1943).

The inherent adaptability of the Constitution and its amendments is particularly important with respect to the Establishment Clause. "[Our] religious composition makes us a vastly more diverse people than were our forefathers. . . . In the face of such profound changes, practices which may have been objectionable to no one in the time of Jefferson and Madison may today be highly offensive to many persons, the deeply devout and the nonbelievers alike." *Schempp*, at 240–241 (BRENNAN, J., concurring). Cf. *McDaniel v. Paty*, 435 U.S. 618, 628 (1978) (plurality opinion). President John Adams issued during his Presidency a number of official proclamations calling on all Americans to engage in Christian prayer. Justice Story, in his treatise on the Constitution, contended that the "real object" of the First Amendment "was, not to countenance, much less to advance Mahometanism, or Judaism, or infidelity, by prostrating Christianity; but to exclude all rivalry among Christian sects. . . ." Whatever deference Adams' actions and Story's views might once have deserved in this Court, the Establishment Clause must now be read in a very different light. Similarly, the Members of the First Congress should be treated, not as sacred figures whose every action must be emulated, but as the authors of a document meant to last for the ages. Indeed, a proper respect for the Framers themselves forbids us to give so static and lifeless a meaning to their work. To my mind, the Court's focus here on a narrow piece of history is, in a fundamental sense, a betrayal of the lessons of history. . . .

Lynch v. Donnelly

465 U.S. 668 (1984)

Vote: 5—Burger, White, Powell, Rehnquist, O'Connor
4—Brennan, Marshall, Blackmun, Stevens

Opinion announcing the opinion of the Court: Burger
Concurring opinion: O'Connor
Dissenting opinions: Brennan, Blackmun

The city of Pawtucket, Rhode Island, in cooperation with the downtown retail merchants' association, annually erected a Christmas display in a park owned by a nonprofit organization and located in the heart of the city's shopping district. The display included many of the figures and decorations conventionally associated with Christmas, including, among other things, a Santa Claus house; reindeer pulling Santa's sleigh; candy-striped poles; a Christmas tree; carolers; cutout figures representing such characters as a clown, an elephant, and a teddy bear; hundreds of colored lights; and a large banner that read "Seasons Greetings." For forty years or more, the display also included a crèche, or nativity scene, consisting of such traditional figures as the infant Jesus, Mary and Joseph, angels, shepherds, kings, and animals.

In 1973, the city spent $1,365 to acquire the crèche that was being used at the time of litigation. The erection and dismantling of the crèche figures, which ranged from five feet to five inches, cost the city about $20 per year. Nominal expenses were incurred in lighting the crèche. No city money had been expended for maintenance for the crèche for several years prior to litigation.

BURGER, C. J., delivered the opinion of the Court, in which WHITE, POWELL, REHNQUIST, and O'CONNOR, JJ., joined.

. . . [672] This Court has explained that the purpose of the Establishment and Free Exercise Clauses of the First Amendment is

> "to prevent, as far as possible, the intrusion of either [the church or the state] into the precincts of the other." *Lemon v. Kurtzman*, 403 U.S. 602, 614 (1971).

At the same time, however, the Court has recognized that

"total separation is not possible in an absolute sense. Some relationship between government and religious organizations is inevitable." *Ibid.*

In every Establishment Clause case, we must reconcile the inescapable tension between the objective of preventing unnecessary intrusion of either the church or the state
upon the other, and the reality that, as the Court has so often noted, total separation of
the two is not possible.

[673] The Court has sometimes described the Religion Clauses as erecting a "wall"
between church and state, see, *e.g., Everson v. Board of Education*, 330 U.S. 1, 18 (1947).
The concept of a "wall" of separation is a useful figure of speech probably deriving from
views of Thomas Jefferson. The metaphor has served as a reminder that the Establishment Clause forbids an established church or anything approaching it. But the metaphor
itself is not a wholly accurate description of the practical aspects of the relationship that
in fact exists between church and state.

No significant segment of our society and no institution within it can exist in a
vacuum or in total or absolute isolation from all the other parts, much less from government. "It has never been thought either possible or desirable to enforce a regime of total
separation. . . ." *Committee for Public Education & Religious Liberty v. Nyquist*, 413
U.S. 756, 760 (1973). Nor does the Constitution require complete separation of church
and state; it affirmatively mandates accommodation, not merely tolerance, of all religions, and forbids hostility toward any. Anything less would require the "callous indifference" we have said was never intended by the Establishment Clause. *Zorach*, at 314.
Indeed, we have observed, such hostility would bring us into "war with our national tradition as embodied in the First Amendment's guaranty of the free exercise of religion."
McCollum, at 211–212. . . .

[678] In each case, the inquiry calls for line-drawing; no fixed, *per se* rule can be
framed. The Establishment Clause like the Due Process Clauses is not a precise, detailed
provision in a legal code capable of ready application. The purpose of the Establishment
Clause "was to state an objective, not to write a statute." *Walz*, at 668. The line between
permissible relationships and those barred by the Clause can no [679] more be straight
and unwavering than due process can be defined in a single stroke or phrase or test. The
Clause erects a "blurred, indistinct, and variable barrier depending on all the circumstances of a particular relationship." *Lemon*, 403 U.S., at 614.

In the line-drawing process we have often found it useful to inquire whether the challenged law or conduct has a secular purpose, whether its principal or primary effect is to
advance or inhibit religion, and whether it creates an excessive entanglement of government with religion. But, we have repeatedly emphasized our unwillingness to be confined to any single test or criterion in this sensitive area. In two cases, the Court did not
even apply the *Lemon* "test." We did not, for example, consider that analysis relevant in
Marsh v. Chambers (1983). Nor did we find *Lemon* useful in *Larson v. Valente* (1982),
where there was substantial evidence of overt discrimination against a particular church.

In this case, the focus of our inquiry must be on the crèche in the context of the
Christmas season. . . .

[680] The District Court inferred from the religious nature of the crèche that the
city has no secular purpose for the display. In so doing, it rejected the city's claim that
its reasons for including the crèche are essentially the same as its reasons for sponsoring
the display as a whole. The District Court plainly erred by focusing almost exclusively

on the crèche. When viewed in the proper context of the Christmas Holiday season, it is apparent that, on this record, there is insufficient evidence to establish that the inclusion of the crèche is a purposeful or surreptitious effort to express some kind of subtle governmental advocacy of a particular religious message. In a pluralistic society a variety of motives and purposes are implicated. The city, like the Congresses and Presidents, however, has principally taken note of a significant historical religious event long celebrated in the Western World. The crèche in the display depicts the historical origins of this traditional event long recognized as a National Holiday.

[681] The narrow question is whether there is a secular purpose for Pawtucket's display of the crèche. The display is sponsored by the city to celebrate the Holiday and to depict the origins of that Holiday. These are legitimate secular purposes. The District Court's inference, drawn from the religious nature of the crèche, that the city has no secular purpose was, on this record, clearly erroneous.

The District Court found that the primary effect of including the crèche is to confer a substantial and impermissible benefit on religion in general and on the Christian faith in particular. Comparisons of the relative benefits to religion of different forms of governmental support are elusive and difficult to make. But to conclude that the primary effect of including the crèche is to advance religion in violation of the Establishment Clause would require that we view it as more beneficial to and more an endorsement of religion, for example, than expenditure of large sums of public money for textbooks supplied throughout the country to students attending church-sponsored schools, *Board of Education v. Allen*; expenditure of public funds for transportation of [682] students to church-sponsored schools, *Everson v. Board of Education*; federal grants for college buildings of church-sponsored institutions of higher education combining secular and religious education, *Tilton v. Richardson* (1971); noncategorical grants to church-sponsored colleges and universities, *Roemer v. Board of Public Works* (1976); and the tax exemptions for church properties sanctioned in *Walz v. Tax Comm'n* (1970). It would also require that we view it as more of an endorsement of religion than the Sunday Closing Laws upheld in *McGowan v. Maryland* (1961); the release time program for religious training in *Zorach v. Clauson* (1952); and the legislative prayers upheld in *Marsh v. Chambers* (1983).

We are unable to discern a greater aid to religion deriving from inclusion of the crèche than from these benefits and endorsements previously held not violative of the Establishment Clause. What was said about the legislative prayers in *Marsh*, at 792, and implied about the Sunday Closing Laws in *McGowan* is true of the city's inclusion of the crèche: its "reason or effect merely happens to coincide or harmonize with the tenets of some . . . religions." See *McGowan*, at 442. . . .

[683] The dissent asserts some observers may perceive that the city has aligned itself with the Christian faith by including a Christian symbol in its display and that this serves to advance religion. We can assume, *arguendo*, that the display advances religion in a sense; but our precedents plainly contemplate that on occasion some advancement of religion will result from governmental action. The Court has made it abundantly clear, however, that "not every law that confers an 'indirect,' 'remote,' or 'incidental' benefit upon [religion] is, for that reason alone, constitutionally invalid." *Nyquist*, 413 U.S., at 771; see also *Widmar v. Vincent*, 454 U.S. 263, 273 (1981). Here, whatever benefit there is to one faith or religion or to all religions, is indirect, remote, and incidental; display of the crèche is no more an advancement or endorsement of religion than the Congressional and Executive recognition of the origins of the Holiday itself as "Christ's Mass," or the exhibition of literally hundreds of religious paintings in governmentally supported museums.

The District Court found that there had been no administrative entanglement between religion and state resulting from the city's ownership and use of the crèche. But it went on to hold that some political divisiveness was engendered by this litigation. Coupled with its finding of an impermissible sectarian purpose and effect, this persuaded the court that there was "excessive entanglement." The Court of Appeals expressly declined to [684] accept the District Court's finding that inclusion of the crèche has caused political divisiveness along religious lines, and noted that this Court has never held that political divisiveness alone was sufficient to invalidate government conduct.

Entanglement is a question of kind and degree. In this case, however, there is no reason to disturb the District Court's finding on the absence of administrative entanglement. There is no evidence of contact with church authorities concerning the content or design of the exhibit prior to or since Pawtucket's purchase of the crèche. No expenditures for maintenance of the crèche have been necessary; and since the city owns the crèche, now valued at $200, the tangible material it contributes is *de minimis*. In many respects the display requires far less ongoing, day-to-day interaction between church and state than religious paintings in public galleries. There is nothing here, of course, like the "comprehensive, discriminating, and continuing state surveillance" or the "enduring entanglement" present in *Lemon*, 403 U.S., at 619–622.

The Court of Appeals correctly observed that this Court has not held that political divisiveness alone can serve to invalidate otherwise permissible conduct. And we decline to so hold today. This case does not involve a direct subsidy to church-sponsored schools or colleges, or other religious institutions, and hence no inquiry into potential political divisiveness is even called for, *Mueller v. Allen*, 463 U.S. 388, 403–404, n. 11 (1983). In any event, apart from this litigation there is no evidence of political friction or divisiveness over the crèche in the 40-year history of Pawtucket's Christmas celebration. The District Court stated that the inclusion of the crèche for the 40 years has been "marked by no apparent dissension" and that the display has had a "calm history." Curiously, it went on to hold that the political divisiveness engendered by this lawsuit was evidence of excessive entanglement. A litigant cannot, by the very act of commencing a lawsuit, however, create the appearance [685] of divisiveness and then exploit it as evidence of entanglement.

We are satisfied that the city has a secular purpose for including the crèche, that the city has not impermissibly advanced religion, and that including the crèche does not create excessive entanglement between religion and government. . . .

[687] We hold that, notwithstanding the religious significance of the crèche, the city of Pawtucket has not violated the Establishment Clause of the First Amendment.

JUSTICE O'CONNOR, concurring.

I concur in the opinion of the Court. I write separately to suggest a clarification of our Establishment Clause doctrine. The suggested approach leads to the same result in this case as that taken by the Court, and the Court's opinion, as I read it, is consistent with my analysis.

I

The Establishment Clause prohibits government from making adherence to a religion relevant in any way to a person's standing in the political community. Government can run afoul of that prohibition in two principal ways. One is excessive [688] entanglement with religious institutions, which may interfere with the independence of the institutions, give the institutions access to government or governmental powers not fully shared by nonadherents of the religion, and foster the creation of political constituencies defined along religious lines. The second and more direct infringement is government endorsement or disapproval of religion. Endorsement sends a message to nonadherents that they are outsiders, not full members of the political community, and an accompanying message to adherents that they are insiders, favored members of the political community. Disapproval sends the opposite message. . . .

Our prior cases have used the three-part test articulated in *Lemon v. Kurtzman*, 403 U.S. 602, 612–613 (1971), as a guide to detecting these two forms of unconstitutional government action. It has never been entirely clear, however, [689] how the three parts of the test relate to the principles enshrined in the Establishment Clause. Focusing on institutional entanglement and on endorsement or disapproval of religion clarifies the *Lemon* test as an analytical device. . . .

II

In this case, as even the District Court found, there is no institutional entanglement. Nevertheless, the respondents contend that the political divisiveness caused by Pawtucket's display of its crèche violates the excessive-entanglement prong of the *Lemon* test. The Court's opinion follows the suggestion in *Mueller v. Allen*, 463 U.S. 388, 403–404, n. 11 (1983), and concludes that "no inquiry into potential political divisiveness is even called for" in this case. *Ante*, at 684. In my view, political divisiveness along religious lines should not be an independent test of constitutionality.

Although several of our cases have discussed political divisiveness under the entanglement prong of *Lemon*, we have never relied on divisiveness as an independent ground for holding a government practice unconstitutional. Guessing the potential for political divisiveness inherent in a government practice is simply too speculative an enterprise, in part because the existence of the litigation, as this case illustrates, itself may affect the political response to the government practice. Political divisiveness is admittedly an evil addressed by the Establishment Clause. Its existence may be evidence that institutional entanglement is excessive or that a government practice is perceived as an endorsement of religion. But the constitutional inquiry should focus ultimately on the character of the government activity that might cause such divisiveness, not on the divisiveness itself. The entanglement prong of the *Lemon* test is properly limited to institutional entanglement.

[690] III

The central issue in this case is whether Pawtucket has endorsed Christianity by its display of the crèche. To answer that question, we must examine both what Pawtucket intended to communicate in displaying the crèche and what message the city's display actually conveyed. The purpose and effect prongs of the *Lemon* test represent these two aspects of the meaning of the city's action.

The meaning of a statement to its audience depends both on the intention of the speaker and on the "objective" meaning of the statement in the community. Some listeners need not rely solely on the words themselves in discerning the speaker's intent: they can judge the intent by, for example, examining the context of the statement or asking questions of the speaker. Other listeners do not have or will not seek access to such evidence of intent. They will rely instead on the words themselves; for them the message actually conveyed may be something not actually intended. If the audience is large, as it always is when government "speaks" by word or deed, some portion of the audience will inevitably receive a message determined by the "objective" content of the statement, and some portion will inevitably receive the intended message. Examination of both the subjective and the objective components of the message communicated by a government action is therefore necessary to determine whether the action carries a forbidden meaning.

The purpose prong of the *Lemon* test asks whether government's actual purpose is to endorse or disapprove of religion. The effect prong asks whether, irrespective of government's actual purpose, the practice under review in fact conveys a message of endorsement or disapproval. An affirmative answer to either question should render the challenged practice invalid.

A

The purpose prong of the *Lemon* test requires that a government activity have a secular purpose. That requirement [691] is not satisfied, however, by the mere existence of some secular purpose, however dominated by religious purposes. In *Stone v. Graham* (1980), for example, the Court held that posting copies of the Ten Commandments in schools violated the purpose prong of the *Lemon* test, yet the State plainly had some secular objectives, such as instilling most of the values of the Ten Commandments and illustrating their connection to our legal system, but see 449 U.S., at 41. The proper inquiry under the purpose prong of *Lemon*, I submit, is whether the government intends to convey a message of endorsement or disapproval of religion.

Applying that formulation to this case, I would find that Pawtucket did not intend to convey any message of endorsement of Christianity or disapproval of non-Christian religions. The evident purpose of including the crèche in the larger display was not promotion of the religious content of the crèche but celebration of the public holiday through its traditional symbols. Celebration of public holidays, which have cultural significance even if they also have religious aspects, is a legitimate secular purpose. . . .

B

Focusing on the evil of government endorsement or disapproval of religion makes clear that the effect prong of the *Lemon* test is properly interpreted not to require invalidation of a government practice merely because it in fact causes, [692] even as a primary effect, advancement or inhibition of religion. The laws upheld in *Walz v. Tax Comm'n* (1970) (tax exemption for religious, educational, and charitable organizations), in *McGowan v. Maryland* (1961) (mandatory Sunday closing law), and in *Zorach v. Clauson* (1952) (released time from school for off-campus religious instruction) had such effects, but they did not violate the Establishment Clause. What is crucial is that a government practice not have the effect of communicating a message of government endorsement or disapproval of religion. It is only practices having that effect, whether intentionally or unintentionally, that make religion relevant, in reality or public perception, to status in the political community.

Pawtucket's display of its crèche, I believe, does not communicate a message that the government intends to endorse the Christian beliefs represented by the crèche. Although the religious and indeed sectarian significance of the crèche, as the District Court found, is not neutralized by the setting, the overall holiday setting changes what viewers may fairly understand to be the purpose of the display—as a typical museum setting, though not neutralizing the religious content of a religious painting, negates any message of endorsement of that content. The display celebrates a public holiday, and no one contends that declaration of that holiday is understood to be an endorsement of religion. The holiday itself has very strong secular components and traditions. Government celebration of the holiday, which is extremely common, generally is not understood to endorse the religious content of the holiday, just as government celebration of Thanksgiving is not so understood. The crèche is a traditional symbol of the holiday that is very commonly displayed along with purely secular symbols, as it was in Pawtucket.

These features combine to make the government's display of the crèche in this particular physical setting no more an endorsement of religion than such governmental "acknowledgments" [693] of religion as legislative prayers of the type approved in *Marsh v. Chambers* (1983), government declaration of Thanksgiving as a public holiday, printing of "In God We Trust" on coins, and opening court sessions with "God save the United States and this honorable court." Those government acknowledgments of religion serve, in the only ways reasonably possible in our culture, the legitimate secular purposes of solemnizing public occasions, expressing confidence in the future, and encouraging the recognition of what is worthy of appreciation in society. For that reason, and because of their history and ubiquity, those practices are not understood as conveying government approval of particular religious beliefs. The display of the crèche likewise serves a secular purpose—celebration of a public holiday with traditional symbols. It cannot fairly be understood to convey a message of government endorsement of religion. It is significant in this regard that the crèche display apparently caused no political divisiveness prior to the filing of this lawsuit, although Pawtucket had incorporated the crèche in its annual Christmas display for some years. For these reasons, I conclude that Pawtucket's display of the crèche does not have the effect of communicating endorsement of Christianity. . . .

[694] IV

Every government practice must be judged in its unique circumstances to determine whether it constitutes an endorsement or disapproval of religion. In making that determination, courts must keep in mind both the fundamental place held by the Establishment Clause in our constitutional scheme and the myriad, subtle ways in which Establishment Clause values can be eroded. Government practices that purport to celebrate or acknowledge events with religious significance must be subjected to careful judicial scrutiny.

The city of Pawtucket is alleged to have violated the Establishment Clause by endorsing the Christian beliefs represented by the crèche included in its Christmas display. Giving the challenged practice the careful scrutiny it deserves, I cannot say that the particular crèche display at issue in this case was intended to endorse or had the effect of endorsing Christianity. I agree with the Court that the judgment below must be reversed.

JUSTICE BRENNAN, with whom JUSTICE MARSHALL, JUSTICE BLACKMUN, and JUSTICE STEVENS join, dissenting.

The principles announced in the compact phrases of the Religion Clauses have, as the Court today reminds us, *ante*, at 678–679, proved difficult to apply. Faced with that uncertainty, the Court properly looks for guidance to the settled test announced in *Lemon v. Kurtzman* (1971), for assessing whether a challenged governmental practice involves an impermissible step toward the establishment of religion. Applying that test to this case, the [695] Court reaches an essentially narrow result which turns largely upon the particular holiday context in which the city of Pawtucket's nativity scene appeared. The Court's decision implicitly leaves open questions concerning the constitutionality of the public display on public property of a crèche standing alone, or the public display of other distinctively religious symbols such as a cross. Despite the narrow contours of the Court's opinion, our precedents in my view compel the holding that Pawtucket's inclusion of a life-sized display depicting the biblical description of the birth of Christ as part of its annual Christmas celebration is unconstitutional. Nothing in the history of such practices or the setting in which the city's crèche is presented obscures or diminishes the plain fact that Pawtucket's action amounts to an impermissible governmental endorsement of a particular faith.

Last Term, I expressed the hope that the Court's decision in *Marsh v. Chambers* (1983) would prove to be only a single, aberrant departure from our settled method [696] of analyzing Establishment Clause cases. *Id.*, at 796 (BRENNAN, J., dissenting). That the Court today returns to the settled analysis of our prior cases gratifies that hope. At the same time, the Court's less-than-vigorous application of the *Lemon* test suggests that its commitment to those standards may only be superficial. After reviewing the Court's opinion, I am convinced that this case appears hard not because the principles of decision are obscure, but because the Christmas holiday seems so familiar and agreeable. Although the [697] Court's reluctance to disturb a community's chosen method of celebrating such an agreeable holiday is understandable, that cannot justify the Court's departure from controlling precedent. In my view, Pawtucket's maintenance and display at public expense of a symbol as distinctively sectarian as a crèche simply cannot be squared with our prior cases. And it is plainly contrary to the purposes and values of the Establishment Clause to pretend, as the Court does, that the otherwise secular setting of Pawtucket's nativity scene dilutes in some fashion the crèche's singular religiosity, or that the city's annual display reflects nothing more than an "acknowledgment" of our shared national heritage. Neither the character of the Christmas holiday itself, nor our heritage of religious expression supports this result. Indeed, our remarkable and precious religious diversity as a Nation, which the Establishment Clause seeks to protect, runs directly counter to today's decision. . . .

[698] Applying the three-part [*Lemon*] test to Pawtucket's crèche, I am persuaded that the city's inclusion of the crèche in its Christmas display simply does not reflect a "clearly secular . . . purpose." *Nyquist*, at 773. Unlike the typical case in which the record reveals some contemporaneous expression of a clear purpose to advance religion, or, conversely, a clear secular purpose, [699] here we have no explicit statement of purpose by Pawtucket's municipal government accompanying its decision to purchase, display, and maintain the crèche. Governmental purpose may nevertheless be inferred. For instance, in *Stone v. Graham*, 449 U.S. 39, 41 (1980) (*per curiam*), this Court found, despite the State's avowed purpose of reminding schoolchildren of the secular application of the commands of the Decalogue, that the "pre-eminent purpose for posting the Ten Commandments on schoolroom walls is plainly religious in nature." In the present case, the city claims that its purposes were exclusively secular. Pawtucket sought, according to this view, only to participate in the celebration of a national holiday and to attract people to the downtown area in order to promote pre-Christmas retail sales and to help engender the spirit of goodwill and neighborliness commonly associated with the Christmas season.

Despite these assertions, two compelling aspects of this case indicate that our generally prudent "reluctance to attribute unconstitutional motives" to a governmental body, *Mueller v. Allen*, 463 U.S. 388, 394 (1983), should be overcome. First, as was true in *Larkin v. Grendel's Den, Inc.*, 459 U.S. 116, 123–124 (1982), all of Pawtucket's "valid secular objectives can be readily accomplished by other means." Plainly, the city's interest in celebrating the holiday and in promoting both retail sales and goodwill are fully served by the elaborate display of Santa Claus, reindeer, and wishing wells that are already a part of Pawtucket's annual Christmas [700] display. More importantly, the nativity scene, unlike every other element of the Hodgson Park display, reflects a sectarian exclusivity that the avowed purposes of celebrating the holiday season and promoting retail commerce simply do not encompass. To be found constitutional, Pawtucket's seasonal celebration must at least be nondenominational and not serve to promote religion. The inclusion of a distinctively religious element like the crèche, however, demonstrates that a narrower sectarian purpose lay behind the decision to include a nativity scene. That the crèche retained this religious character for the people and municipal government of Pawtucket is suggested by the Mayor's testimony at trial in which he stated that for him, as well as others in the city, the effort to eliminate the nativity scene from Pawtucket's Christmas celebration "is a step towards establishing another religion, nonreligion that it may be." Plainly, the city and its leaders understood that the inclusion of the crèche in its display would serve the wholly religious purpose [701] of "[keeping] 'Christ in Christmas.'" From this record, therefore, it is impossible to say with the kind of confidence that was possible in *McGowan v. Maryland*, 366 U.S. 420, 445 (1961), that a wholly secular goal predominates.

The "primary effect" of including a nativity scene in the city's display is, as the District Court found, to place the government's imprimatur of approval on the particular religious beliefs exemplified by the crèche. Those who believe in the message of the nativity receive the unique and exclusive benefit of public recognition and approval of their views. For many, the city's decision to include the crèche as part of its extensive and costly efforts to celebrate Christmas can only mean that the prestige of the government has been conferred on the beliefs associated with the crèche, thereby providing "a significant symbolic benefit to religion. . . ." *Larkin v. Grendel's Den, Inc.*, at 125–126. The effect on minority religious groups, as well as on those who may reject all religion, is to convey the message that their views are not similarly worthy of public recognition nor entitled to public support. It was precisely this sort of religious chauvinism that the Establishment Clause was intended forever to prohibit. . . .

[702] Finally, it is evident that Pawtucket's inclusion of a crèche as part of its annual Christmas display does pose a significant threat of fostering "excessive entanglement." As the Court notes, *ante*, at 683, the District Court found no administrative entanglement in this case, primarily because the city had been able to administer the annual display without extensive consultation with religious officials. Of course, there is no reason to disturb that finding, but it is worth noting that after today's decision, administrative entanglements may well develop. Jews and other non-Christian groups, prompted perhaps by the Mayor's remark that he will include a Menorah in future displays, can be expected to press government for inclusion of their symbols, and faced with such requests, government will have to become involved in accommodating the various demands. More importantly, although no political divisiveness was apparent in Pawtucket [703] prior to the filing of respondents' lawsuit, that act, as the District Court found, unleashed powerful emotional reactions which divided the city along religious lines. The

fact that calm had prevailed prior to this suit does not immediately suggest the absence of any division on the point for, as the District Court observed, the quiescence of those opposed to the crèche may have reflected nothing more than their sense of futility in opposing the majority. Of course, the Court is correct to note that we have never held that the potential for divisiveness alone is sufficient to invalidate a challenged governmental practice; we have, nevertheless, repeatedly emphasized that "too close a proximity" between religious and civil authorities, *Schempp*, 374 U.S., at 259 (BRENNAN, J., concurring), may represent a "warning signal" that the values embodied in the Establishment Clause are at risk. Furthermore, the Court should not blind itself to the fact that because communities [704] differ in religious composition, the controversy over whether local governments may adopt religious symbols will continue to fester. In many communities, non-Christian groups can be expected to combat practices similar to Pawtucket's; this will be so especially in areas where there are substantial non-Christian minorities.

In sum, considering the District Court's careful findings of fact under the three-part analysis called for by our prior cases, I have no difficulty concluding that Pawtucket's display of the crèche is unconstitutional. . . .

[726] JUSTICE BLACKMUN, with whom JUSTICE STEVENS joins, dissenting.

As JUSTICE BRENNAN points out, the logic of the Court's decision in *Lemon v. Kurtzman*, 403 U.S. 602, 612–613 (1971) (which THE CHIEF JUSTICE would say has been applied by this Court "often," *ante*, at 679, but which JUSTICE O'CONNOR acknowledges with the words, "Our prior cases have used the three-part test articulated in *Lemon*," *ante*, at 688), compels an affirmance here. If that case and its guidelines mean anything, the presence of Pawtucket's crèche in a municipally sponsored display must be held to be a violation of the First Amendment.

Not only does the Court's resolution of this controversy make light of our precedents, but also, ironically, the majority does an injustice to the crèche and the message it manifests. While certain persons, including the Mayor of Pawtucket, undertook a crusade to "keep 'Christ' in Christmas," the Court today has declared that presence virtually irrelevant. The majority urges that the display, "with or without a crèche," "[recalls] the religious nature of the Holiday," and "engenders a friendly community spirit of goodwill in keeping with the season." *Ante*, at 685. Before the District Court, an expert witness for the city made [727] a similar, though perhaps more candid, point, stating that Pawtucket's display invites people "to participate in the Christmas spirit, brotherhood, peace, and let loose with their money." The crèche has been relegated to the role of a neutral harbinger of the holiday season, useful for commercial purposes, but devoid of any inherent meaning and incapable of enhancing the religious tenor of a display of which it is an integral part. The city has its victory—but it is a Pyrrhic one indeed.

The import of the Court's decision is to encourage use of the crèche in a municipally sponsored display, a setting where Christians feel constrained in acknowledging its symbolic meaning and non-Christians feel alienated by its presence. Surely, this is a misuse of a sacred symbol. Because I cannot join the Court in denying either the force of our precedents or the sacred message that is at the core of the crèche, I dissent and join JUSTICE BRENNAN's opinion.

36

Wallace v. Jaffree

472 U.S. 38 (1985)

Vote: 6—Brennan, Marshall, Blackmun, Powell, Stevens, O'Connor
*   3—Burger, White, Rehnquist*

Opinion announcing the opinion of the Court: Stevens
Concurring opinion: Powell
Opinion concurring in the judgment: O'Connor
Dissenting opinions: Burger, White, Rehnquist

In 1978, subsequent to Supreme Court decisions finding prayer in public schools un-
constitutional, the state of Alabama passed legislation authorizing a one-minute period
of silence in public elementary schools "for meditation." The 1978 statute (§ 16-1-20)
specified, "At the commencement of the first class each day in the first through the
sixth grades in all public schools, the teacher in charge of the room in which each such
class is held shall announce that a period of silence, not to exceed one minute in du-
ration, shall be observed for meditation, and during any such period silence shall be
maintained and no activities engaged in."

*   In 1981, the Alabama state legislature amended § 16-1-20 to authorize a period of*
silence "for meditation or voluntary prayer" in all grades. The 1981 statute (§ 16-1-20.1)
specified, "At the commencement of the first class of each day in all grades in all public
schools the teacher in charge of the room in which each class is held may announce that
a period of silence not to exceed one minute in duration shall be observed for meditation
or voluntary prayer, and during any such period no other activities shall be engaged in."

*   In 1982, the Alabama state legislature further amended its moment-of-silence law*
to authorize public school teachers to lead "willing students" in a prescribed prayer.
The 1982 amendment (§ 16-1-20.2) specified:

> *From henceforth, any teacher or professor in any public educational institution within*
> *the state of Alabama, recognizing that the Lord God is one, at the beginning of any*
> *homeroom or any class, may pray, may lead willing students in prayer, or may lead the*
> *willing students in the following prayer to God:*
>
> *   "Almighty God, You alone are our God. We acknowledge You as the Creator and Su-*
> *preme Judge of the world. May Your justice, Your truth, and Your peace abound this day*
> *in the hearts of our countrymen, in the counsels of our government, in the sanctity of our*
> *homes and in the classrooms of our schools in the name of our Lord. Amen."*

The federal district court opinion in this case was particularly notable. After a four-day trial in 1982 that pertained primarily to activities that occurred during the 1981–1982 academic year and the 1981 Alabama statute (§ 16-1-20.1) authorizing a moment of silence for "meditation or voluntary prayer," federal district court judge W. Brevard Hand concluded that "the establishment clause of the first amendment to the United States Constitution does not prohibit the state from establishing a religion." Jaffree v. Board of Commissioners of Mobile County, 554 F. Supp. 1104, 1128 (S.D. Ala. 1983). Citing the legislative history surrounding the adoption of both the First Amendment and the Fourteenth Amendment and the plain language of those amendments, Judge Hand found that the Constitution established a federal arrangement on matters of establishment of religion, restricting only the national government from establishing a religion.

The Eleventh Circuit Court of Appeals reversed the district court opinion, holding that both § 16-1-20.1 and § 16-1-20.2 violated the Establishment Clause. The Supreme Court reviewed the circuit court's decision concerning § 16-1-20.1, the "for meditation or voluntary prayer" provision.

STEVENS, J., delivered the opinion of the Court, in which BRENNAN, MARSHALL, BLACKMUN, and POWELL, JJ., joined.

. . . [55] When the Court has been called upon to construe the breadth of the Establishment Clause, it has examined the criteria developed over a period of many years. Thus, in *Lemon v. Kurtzman*, 403 U.S. 602, 612–613 (1971), we wrote:

"Every analysis in this area must begin with consideration of the cumulative criteria developed by the Court over many years. Three such tests may be gleaned from our cases. First, the statute must have a secular legislative purpose; second, its principal or primary effect must be one that neither advances nor inhibits religion; finally, the statute must not foster 'an excessive [56] government entanglement with religion.'"

It is the first of these three criteria that is most plainly implicated by this case. As the District Court correctly recognized, no consideration of the second or third criteria is necessary if a statute does not have a clearly secular purpose. For even though a statute that is motivated in part by a religious purpose may satisfy the first criterion, the First Amendment requires that a statute must be invalidated if it is entirely motivated by a purpose to advance religion.

In applying the purpose test, it is appropriate to ask "whether government's actual purpose is to endorse or disapprove of religion." In this case, the answer to that question is dispositive. For the record not only provides us with an unambiguous affirmative answer, but it also reveals that the enactment of § 16-1-20.1 was not motivated by any clearly secular purpose—indeed, the statute had no secular purpose.

The sponsor of the bill that became § 16-1-20.1, Senator Donald Holmes, inserted into the legislative record—apparently [57] without dissent—a statement indicating that the legislation was an "effort to return voluntary prayer" to the public schools.[43] Later

---

43. The statement indicated, in pertinent part:

Gentlemen, by passage of this bill by the Alabama Legislature our children in this state will have the opportunity of sharing in the spiritual heritage of this state and this country. The United States as well as the State of Alabama was founded by people who believe in God. *I believe this effort to return voluntary prayer* to our public schools for its return to us to the original position of the writers of the

Senator Holmes confirmed this purpose before the District Court. In response to the question whether he had any purpose for the legislation other than returning voluntary prayer to public schools, he stated: "No, I did not have no other purpose in mind." The State did not present evidence of any secular purpose.

[58] The unrebutted evidence of legislative intent contained in the legislative record and in the testimony of the sponsor of § 16-1-20.1 is confirmed by a consideration of the relationship between this statute and the two other measures that were considered in this case. The District Court found that the 1981 statute and its 1982 sequel had a common, nonsecular purpose. The wholly religious character of the later enactment is plainly evident from its text. When the differences between § 16-1-20.1 and its 1978 predecessor, § 16-1-20, are examined, it is equally clear that the 1981 statute has the same wholly religious character.

There are only three textual differences between § 16-1-20.1 and § 16-1-20: (1) the earlier statute applies only to grades one through six, whereas § 16-1-20.1 applies to all grades; (2) the earlier statute uses the word "shall" whereas § 16-1-20.1 uses the word "may"; (3) the earlier statute refers [59] only to "meditation" whereas § 16-1-20.1 refers to "meditation or voluntary prayer." The first difference is of no relevance in this litigation because the minor appellees were in kindergarten or second grade during the 1981–1982 academic year. The second difference would also have no impact on this litigation because the mandatory language of § 16-1-20 continued to apply to grades one through six. Thus, the only significant textual difference is the addition of the words "or voluntary prayer."

The legislative intent to return prayer to the public schools is, of course, quite different from merely protecting every student's right to engage in voluntary prayer during an appropriate moment of silence during the schoolday. The 1978 statute already protected that right, containing nothing that prevented any student from engaging in voluntary prayer during a silent minute of meditation. Appellants have not identified any secular purpose that was not fully served by § 16-1-20 before the enactment of § 16-1-20.1. Thus, only two conclusions are consistent with the text of § 16-1-20.1: (1) the statute was enacted to convey a message of state endorsement and promotion of prayer; or (2) the statute was enacted for no purpose. No one suggests that the statute was nothing but a meaningless or irrational act.

We must, therefore, conclude that the Alabama Legislature intended to change existing law and that it was motivated [60] by the same purpose that the Governor's answer to the second amended complaint expressly admitted; that the statement inserted in the legislative history revealed; and that Senator Holmes' testimony frankly described. The legislature enacted § 16-1-20.1, despite the existence of § 16-1-20 for the sole purpose of expressing the State's endorsement of prayer activities for one minute at the beginning of each schoolday. The addition of "or voluntary prayer" indicates that the State intended to characterize prayer as a favored practice. Such an endorsement is not consistent with the established principle that the government must pursue a course of complete neutrality toward religion.

The importance of that principle does not permit us to treat this as an inconsequential case involving nothing more than a few words of symbolic speech on behalf of the political majority. For whenever the State itself speaks on a religious [61] subject, one of

---

Constitution, this local philosophies and beliefs hundreds of Alabamians have urged my continuous support for permitting school prayer. Since coming to the Alabama Senate I have worked hard *on this legislation to accomplish the return of voluntary prayer in our public schools and return to the basic moral fiber.* (Emphasis added.)

the questions that we must ask is "whether the government intends to convey a message of endorsement or disapproval of religion." The well-supported concurrent findings of the District Court and the Court of Appeals—that § 16-1-20.1 was intended to convey a message of state approval of prayer activities in the public schools—make it unnecessary, and indeed inappropriate, to evaluate the practical significance of the addition of the words "or voluntary prayer" to the statute. Keeping in mind, as we must, "both the fundamental place held by the Establishment Clause in our constitutional scheme and the myriad, subtle ways in which Establishment Clause values can be eroded," we conclude that § 16-1-20.1 violates the First Amendment. . . .

[67] JUSTICE O'CONNOR, concurring in the judgment.

Nothing in the United States Constitution as interpreted by this Court or in the laws of the State of Alabama prohibits public school students from voluntarily praying at any time before, during, or after the schoolday. Alabama has facilitated voluntary silent prayers of students who are so inclined by enacting Ala. Code § 16-1-20 (Supp. 1984), which provides a moment of silence in appellees' schools each day. The parties to these proceedings concede the validity of this enactment. At issue in these appeals is the constitutional validity of an additional and subsequent Alabama statute, Ala. Code § 16-1-20.1 (Supp. 1984), which both the District Court and the Court of Appeals concluded was enacted solely to officially encourage prayer during the moment of silence. I agree with the judgment of the Court that, in light of the findings of the courts below and the history of its enactment, § 16-1-20.1 of the Alabama Code violates the Establishment Clause of the First Amendment. In my view, there can be little doubt that the purpose and likely effect of this subsequent enactment is to endorse and sponsor voluntary prayer in the public schools. I write separately to identify the peculiar features of the Alabama law that render it invalid, and to explain why moment of silence laws in other States do not necessarily manifest the same infirmity. I also write to explain why neither history nor the Free Exercise Clause of the First Amendment validates the Alabama law struck down by the Court today.

I

The Religion Clauses of the First Amendment, coupled with the Fourteenth Amendment's guarantee of ordered liberty, preclude both the Nation and the States from making any law respecting an establishment of religion or prohibiting [68] the free exercise thereof. Although a distinct jurisprudence has enveloped each of these Clauses, their common purpose is to secure religious liberty. On these principles the Court has been and remains unanimous.

As these cases once again demonstrate, however, "it is far easier to agree on the purpose that underlies the First Amendment's Establishment and Free Exercise Clauses than to obtain agreement on the standards that should govern their application." *Walz v. Tax Comm'n*, 397 U.S. 664, 694 (1970) (opinion of Harlan, J.). It once appeared that the Court had developed a workable standard by which to identify impermissible government establishments of religion. Under the now familiar *Lemon* test, statutes must have both a secular legislative purpose and a principal or primary effect that neither advances nor inhibits religion, and in addition they must not foster excessive government entanglement with religion. Despite its initial promise, the *Lemon* test has proved problematic. The required inquiry into "entanglement" has been modified and questioned, see *Mueller v. Allen*, 463 U.S. 388, 403, n. 11 (1983), and in one case we have upheld state action against an Establishment Clause challenge without applying the *Lemon* test at all. *Marsh v. Chambers* (1983). The author of *Lemon* himself apparently questions the test's general applicability. See *Lynch v. Donnelly*, 465 U.S. 668, 679 (1984). JUSTICE REHNQUIST today suggests that we abandon *Lemon* entirely, and in the process limit the reach of the Establishment Clause to state discrimination between sects and government designation of a particular church as a "state" or "national" one. *Post*, at 108–113.

Perhaps because I am new to the struggle, I am not ready to abandon all aspects of the *Lemon* test. I do believe, however, that the standards announced in *Lemon* should be [69] reexamined and refined in order to make them more useful in achieving the underlying purpose of the First Amendment. We must strive to do more than erect a constitutional "signpost," to be followed or ignored in a particular case as our predilections may dictate. Instead, our goal should be "to frame a principle for constitutional adjudication that is not only grounded in the history and language of the first amendment, but one that is also capable of consistent application to the relevant problems." Choper, *Religion in the Public Schools: A Proposed Constitutional Standard*, 47 Minn. L. Rev. 329, 332–333 (1963). Last Term, I proposed a refinement of the *Lemon* test with this goal in mind. *Lynch v. Donnelly*, 465 U.S., at 687–689 (concurring opinion).

The *Lynch* concurrence suggested that the religious liberty protected by the Establishment Clause is infringed when the government makes adherence to religion relevant to a person's standing in the political community. Direct government action endorsing religion or a particular religious practice is invalid under this approach because it "sends a message to nonadherents that they are outsiders, not full members of the political community, and an accompanying message to adherents that they are insiders, favored members of the political community." Under this view, *Lemon*'s inquiry as to the purpose and effect of a statute requires courts to examine whether government's purpose is to endorse religion and whether the statute actually conveys a message of endorsement.

The endorsement test is useful because of the analytic content it gives to the *Lemon*-mandated inquiry into legislative purpose and effect. In this country, church and state must necessarily operate within the same community. Because of this coexistence, it is inevitable that the secular interests of government and the religious interests of various sects and their adherents will frequently intersect, conflict, and combine. A statute that ostensibly promotes a secular interest [70] often has an incidental or even a primary effect of helping or hindering a sectarian belief. Chaos would ensue if every such statute were invalid under the Establishment Clause. For example, the State could not criminalize murder for fear that it would thereby promote the Biblical command against killing. The task for the Court is to sort out those statutes and government practices whose purpose and effect go against the grain of religious liberty protected by the First Amendment.

The endorsement test does not preclude government from acknowledging religion or from taking religion into account in making law and policy. It does preclude government from conveying or attempting to convey a message that religion or a particular religious belief is favored or preferred. Such an endorsement infringes the religious liberty of the nonadherent, for "[when] the power, prestige and financial support of government is placed behind a particular religious belief, the indirect coercive pressure upon religious minorities to conform to the prevailing officially approved religion is plain." *Engel v. Vitale*, at 431. At issue today is whether state moment of silence statutes in general, and Alabama's moment of silence statute in particular, embody an impermissible endorsement of prayer in public schools.

A

Twenty-five states permit or require public school teachers to have students observe a moment of silence in their classrooms. . . .

[72] A state-sponsored moment of silence in the public schools is different from state-sponsored vocal prayer or Bible reading. First, a moment of silence is not inherently religious. Silence, unlike prayer or Bible reading, need not be associated with a religious exercise. Second, a pupil who participates in a moment of silence need not compromise his or her beliefs. During a moment of silence, a student who objects to prayer is left to his or her own thoughts, and is not compelled to listen to the prayers or thoughts of others. For these simple reasons, a moment of silence statute does not stand or fall under the Establishment Clause according to how the Court regards vocal prayer or Bible reading. Scholars and at least one Member of this Court have recognized the distinction and suggested that a moment of silence in public schools would be constitutional. See *Abington*, at 281 (BRENNAN, J., concurring) ("[The] observance of a moment [73] of reverent silence at the opening of class" may serve "the solely secular purposes of the devotional activities without jeopardizing either the religious liberties of any members of the community or the proper degree of separation between the spheres of religion and government"). As a general matter, I agree. It is difficult to discern a serious threat to religious liberty from a room of silent, thoughtful schoolchildren.

By mandating a moment of silence, a State does not necessarily endorse any activity that might occur during the period. Even if a statute specifies that a student may choose to pray silently during a quiet moment, the State has not thereby encouraged prayer over other specified alternatives. Nonetheless, it is also possible that a moment of silence statute, either as drafted or as actually implemented, could effectively favor the child who prays over the child who does not. For example, the message of endorsement would seem inescapable if the teacher exhorts children to use the designated time to pray. Similarly, the face of the statute or its legislative history may clearly establish that it seeks to encourage or promote voluntary prayer over other alternatives, rather than merely provide a quiet moment that may be dedicated to prayer by those so inclined. The crucial question is whether the State has conveyed or attempted to convey the message that children should use the moment of silence for prayer. [74] This question cannot be answered in the abstract, but instead requires courts to examine the history, language, and administration of a particular statute to determine whether it operates as an endorsement of religion.

Before reviewing Alabama's moment of silence law to determine whether it endorses prayer, some general observations on the proper scope of the inquiry are in order. First, the inquiry into the purpose of the legislature in enacting a moment of silence law should be deferential and limited. In determining whether the government intends a moment of silence statute to convey a message of endorsement or disapproval of religion, a court has no license to psychoanalyze the legislators. If a legislature expresses a plausible secular purpose for a moment of silence statute in either the text or the legislative history, or if the statute disclaims an intent to encourage prayer over alternatives during a moment of silence, then courts should generally [75] defer to that stated intent. It is particularly troublesome to denigrate an expressed secular purpose due to postenactment testimony by particular legislators or by interested persons who witnessed the drafting of the statute. Even if the text and official history of a statute express no secular purpose, the statute should be held to have an improper purpose only if it is beyond purview that endorsement of religion or a religious belief "was and is the law's reason for existence."

Epperson v. Arkansas, 393 U.S. 97, 108 (1968). Since there is arguably a secular peda-gogical value to a moment of silence in public schools, courts should find an improper purpose behind such a statute only if the statute on its face, in its official legislative his-tory, or in its interpretation by a responsible administrative agency suggests it has the primary purpose of endorsing prayer.

JUSTICE REHNQUIST suggests that this sort of deferential inquiry into legislative purpose "means little," because "it only requires the legislature to express any secular purpose and omit all sectarian references." *Post*, at 108. It is not a trivial matter, how-ever, to require that the legislature manifest a secular purpose and omit all sectarian endorsements from its laws. That requirement is precisely tailored to the Establishment Clause's purpose of assuring that government not intentionally endorse religion or a re-ligious practice. It is of course possible that a legislature will enunciate a sham secular purpose for a statute. I have little doubt that our courts are capable of distinguishing a sham secular purpose from a sincere one, or that the *Lemon* inquiry into the effect of an enactment would help decide those close cases where the validity of an expressed secular purpose is in doubt. While the secular purpose requirement alone may rarely be determinative in striking down a statute, it nevertheless serves an important function. It reminds government that [76] when it acts it should do so without endorsing a particular religious belief or practice that all citizens do not share. In this sense the secular purpose requirement is squarely based in the text of the Establishment Clause it helps to enforce.

Second, the *Lynch* concurrence suggested that the effect of a moment of silence law is not entirely a question of fact:

"[Whether] a government activity communicates endorsement of religion is not a ques-tion of simple historical fact. Although evidentiary submissions may help answer it, the question is, like the question whether racial or sex-based classifications communicate an invidious message, in large part a legal question to be answered on the basis of judicial interpretation of social facts." 465 U.S., at 693–694.

The relevant issue is whether an objective observer, acquainted with the text, legisla-tive history, and implementation of the statute, would perceive it as a state endorsement of prayer in public schools. A moment of silence law that is clearly drafted and imple-mented so as to permit prayer, meditation, and reflection within the prescribed period, without endorsing one alternative over the others, should pass this test.

B

The analysis above suggests that moment of silence laws in many States should pass Establishment Clause scrutiny because they do not favor the child who chooses to pray during a moment of silence over the child who chooses to meditate [77] or reflect. Alabama Code § 16-1-20.1 (Supp. 1984) does not stand on the same footing. However deferentially one examines its text and legislative history, however objectively one views the message attempted to be conveyed to the public, the conclusion is unavoidable that the purpose of the statute is to endorse prayer in public schools. I accordingly agree with the Court of Appeals that the Alabama statute has a purpose which is in violation of the Establishment Clause, and cannot be upheld.

In finding that the purpose of § 16-1-20.1 is to endorse voluntary prayer during a moment of silence, the Court relies on testimony elicited from State Senator Donald G. Holmes during a preliminary injunction hearing. Senator Holmes testified that the sole purpose of the statute was to return voluntary prayer to the public schools. For the reasons expressed above, I would give little, if any, weight to this sort of evidence of legislative intent. Nevertheless, the text of the statute in light of its official legislative history leaves little doubt that the purpose of this statute corresponds to the purpose expressed by Senator Holmes at the preliminary injunction hearing.

First, it is notable that Alabama already had a moment of silence statute before it enacted § 16-1-20.1. See Ala. Code § 16-1-20 (Supp. 1984). Appellees do not challenge this statute—indeed, they concede its validity. The only significant addition made by § 16-1-20.1 is to specify expressly that voluntary prayer is one of the authorized activities during a moment of silence. Any doubt as to the legislative purpose of that addition is removed by the official legislative history. The sole purpose reflected in the official history is "to return voluntary prayer to our public schools." Nor does anything in the legislative history contradict an intent to encourage children to choose prayer over other alternatives during the moment of silence. Given this legislative history, it is not surprising that the State of Alabama conceded in the [78] courts below that the purpose of the statute was to make prayer part of daily classroom activity, and that both the District Court and the Court of Appeals concluded that the law's purpose was to encourage religious activity. In light of the legislative history and the findings of the courts below, I agree with the Court that the State intended § 16-1-20.1 to convey a message that prayer was the endorsed activity during the state-prescribed moment of silence.[5] While it is therefore unnecessary also to determine the effect of the statute, it also seems likely that the message actually conveyed to objective observers by § 16-1-20.1 is approval of the child who selects prayer over other alternatives during a moment of silence.

I also disagree with THE CHIEF JUSTICE's suggestion that the Court's opinion invalidates any moment of silence statute that includes the word "prayer." *Post*, at 85. As noted *supra*, at 73, "[even] if a statute specifies that a student may choose to pray silently during a quiet moment, the State has not thereby encouraged prayer over other specified alternatives."

Given this evidence in the record, candor requires us to admit that this Alabama statute was intended to convey a message of state encouragement and endorsement of religion. In *Walz v. Tax Comm'n*, 397 U.S., at 669, the Court stated that the Religion Clauses of the First Amendment are flexible enough to "permit religious exercise to exist without sponsorship and without interference." Alabama Code § 16-1-20.1 (Supp. 1984) does more than permit prayer to occur during a moment of silence "without interference." It [79] endorses the decision to pray during a moment of silence, and accordingly sponsors a religious exercise. For that reason, I concur in the judgment of the Court. . . .

CHIEF JUSTICE BURGER, dissenting.

[84] Some who trouble to read the opinions in these cases will find it ironic—perhaps even bizarre—that on the very day we heard arguments in the cases, the Court's session opened with an invocation for Divine protection. Across the park a few hundred yards

---

5. THE CHIEF JUSTICE suggests that one consequence of the Court's emphasis on the difference between § 16-1-20.1 and its predecessor statute might be to render the Pledge of Allegiance unconstitutional because Congress amended it in 1954 to add the words "under God." *Post*, at 88. I disagree. In my view, the words "under God" in the Pledge, as codified at 36 U.S.C. § 172, serve as an acknowledgment of religion with "the legitimate secular purposes of solemnizing public occasions, [and] expressing confidence in the future." *Lynch v. Donnelly*, 465 U.S. 668, 693 (1984) (concurring opinion).

away, the House of Representatives and [85] the Senate regularly open each session with a prayer. These legislative prayers are not just one minute in duration, but are extended, thoughtful invocations and prayers for Divine guidance. They are given, as they have been since 1789, by clergy appointed as official chaplains and paid from the Treasury of the United States. Congress has also provided chapels in the Capitol, at public expense, where Members and others may pause for prayer, meditation—or a moment of silence.

Inevitably some wag is bound to say that the Court's holding today reflects a belief that the historic practice of the Congress and this Court is justified because members of the Judiciary and Congress are more in need of Divine guidance than are schoolchildren. Still others will say that all this controversy is "much ado about nothing," since no power on earth—including this Court and Congress—can stop any teacher from opening the schoolday with a moment of silence for pupils to meditate, to plan their day—or to pray if they voluntarily elect to do so.

I make several points about today's curious holding.

(a) It makes no sense to say that Alabama has "endorsed prayer" by merely enacting a new statute "to specify expressly that voluntary prayer is *one* of the authorized activities during a moment of silence," *ante*, at 77 (O'CONNOR, J., concurring in judgment) (emphasis added). To suggest that a moment-of-silence statute that includes the word "prayer" unconstitutionally endorses religion, while one that simply provides for a moment of silence does not, manifests not neutrality but hostility toward religion. For decades our opinions have stated that hostility toward any religion or toward all religions is as much forbidden by the Constitution as is an official establishment of religion. The Alabama Legislature has no more "endorsed" religion than a state or the Congress does when it provides for legislative chaplains, or than this Court does when it opens each session with an invocation to [86] God. Today's decision recalls the observations of Justice Goldberg:

> "[Untutored] devotion to the concept of neutrality can lead to invocation or approval of results which partake not simply of that noninterference and noninvolvement with the religious which the Constitution commands, but of a brooding and pervasive dedication to the secular and a passive, or even active, hostility to the religious. Such results are not only not compelled by the Constitution, but, it seems to me, are prohibited by it." *Abington School District v. Schempp*, 374 U.S. 203, 306 (1963) (concurring opinion).

(b) The inexplicable aspect of the foregoing opinions, however, is what they advance as support for the holding concerning the purpose of the Alabama Legislature. Rather than determining legislative purpose from the face of the statute as a whole, the opinions rely on three factors in concluding that the Alabama Legislature had a "wholly religious" purpose for enacting the statute under review, Ala. Code § 16-1-20.1 (Supp. 1984): (i) statements of the statute's sponsor, (ii) admissions in Governor James' answer to the second amended complaint, and (iii) the difference between § 16-1-20.1 and its predecessor statute.

Curiously, the opinions do not mention that all of the sponsor's statements relied upon—including the statement "inserted" into the Senate Journal—were made after the legislature had passed the statute; indeed, the testimony that the Court finds critical was given well over a year after the statute was enacted. As even the appellees concede there is not a shred of evidence that [87] the legislature as a whole shared the sponsor's motive or that a majority in either house was even aware of the sponsor's view of the bill when it was passed. The sole relevance of the sponsor's statements, therefore, is that they reflect the personal, subjective motives of a single legislator. No case in the 195-year history of this Court supports the disconcerting idea that postenactment statements by individual legislators are relevant in determining the constitutionality of legislation.

Even if an individual legislator's after-the-fact statements could rationally be considered relevant, all of the opinions fail to mention that the sponsor also testified that one of his purposes in drafting and sponsoring the moment-of-silence bill was to clear up a widespread misunderstanding that a schoolchild is legally prohibited from engaging in silent, individual prayer once he steps inside a public school building. That testimony is at least as important as the statements the Court relies upon, and surely that testimony manifests a permissible purpose.

The Court also relies on the admissions of Governor James' answer to the second amended complaint. Strangely, however, the Court neglects to mention that there was no trial bearing on the constitutionality of the Alabama statutes; trial became unnecessary when the District Court held that the Establishment Clause does not apply to the states. The absence of a trial on the issue of the constitutionality of § 16-1-20.1 is significant because the answer filed by the State Board and Superintendent of Education did not make the same admissions that the Governor's answer made. The Court cannot know whether, if these cases had been tried, those state officials would have offered evidence to contravene appellees' allegations concerning legislative purpose. Thus, it is completely inappropriate to accord any relevance to the admissions in the Governor's answer.

[88] The several preceding opinions conclude that the principal difference between § 16-1-20.1 and its predecessor statute proves that the sole purpose behind the inclusion of the phrase "or voluntary prayer" in § 16-1-20.1 was to endorse and promote prayer. This reasoning is simply a subtle way of focusing exclusively on the religious component of the statute rather than examining the statute as a whole. Such logic—if it can be called that—would lead the Court to hold, for example, that a state may enact a statute that provides reimbursement for bus transportation to the parents of all schoolchildren, but may not add parents of parochial school students to an existing program providing reimbursement for parents of public school students. Congress amended the statutory Pledge of Allegiance 31 years ago to add the words "under God." Act of June 14, 1954, Pub. L. 396, 68 Stat. 249. Do the several opinions in support of the judgment today render the Pledge unconstitutional? That would be the consequence of their method of focusing on the difference between § 16-1-20.1 and its predecessor statute rather than examining § 16-1-20.1 as a whole.[3] Any such holding would of course make a mockery of our decisionmaking in Establishment Clause cases. And even were the Court's method correct, the inclusion of the words "or voluntary prayer" in § 16-1-20.1 is wholly consistent with the clearly permissible purpose of clarifying that silent, voluntary prayer is not forbidden in the public school building.

[89] (c) The Court's extended treatment of the "test" of *Lemon v. Kurtzman* (1971) suggests a naive preoccupation with an easy, bright-line approach for addressing constitutional issues. We have repeatedly cautioned that *Lemon* did not establish a rigid caliper capable of resolving every Establishment Clause issue, but that it sought only to provide "signposts." "In each [Establishment Clause] case, the inquiry calls for line-drawing; no fixed, per se rule can be framed." *Lynch v. Donnelly*, 465 U.S. 668, 678 (1984). In any event, our responsibility is not to apply tidy formulas by rote; our duty is to determine whether

---

3. The House Report on the legislation amending the Pledge states that the purpose of the amendment was to affirm the principle that "our people and our Government [are dependent] upon the moral directions of the Creator." H. R. Rep. No. 1693, 83d Cong., 2d Sess., 2 (1954). If this is simply "acknowledgment," not "endorsement," of religion, see *ante*, at 78, n. 5 (O'CONNOR, J., concurring in judgment), the distinction is far too infinitesimal for me to grasp.

the statute or practice at issue is a step toward establishing a state religion. Given today's decision, however, perhaps it is understandable that the opinions in support of the judgment all but ignore the Establishment Clause itself and the concerns that underlie it.

(d) The notion that the Alabama statute is a step toward creating an established church borders on, if it does not trespass into, the ridiculous. The statute does not remotely threaten religious liberty; it affirmatively furthers the values of religious freedom and tolerance that the Establishment Clause was designed to protect. Without pressuring those who do not wish to pray, the statute simply creates an opportunity to think, to plan, or to pray if one wishes—as Congress does by providing chaplains and chapels. It accommodates the purely private, voluntary religious choices of the individual pupils who wish to pray while at the same time creating a time for nonreligious reflection for those who do not choose to pray. The statute also provides a meaningful opportunity for schoolchildren to appreciate the absolute constitutional right of each individual to worship and believe as the individual wishes. The statute "endorses" only the view that the religious observances of others should be tolerated and, [90] where possible, accommodated. If the government may not accommodate religious needs when it does so in a wholly neutral and noncoercive manner, the "benevolent neutrality" that we have long considered the correct constitutional standard will quickly translate into the "callous indifference" that the Court has consistently held the Establishment Clause does not require.

The Court today has ignored the wise admonition of Justice Goldberg that "the measure of constitutional adjudication is the ability and willingness to distinguish between real threat and mere shadow." *Abington School District v. Schempp*, 374 U.S., at 308 (concurring opinion). The innocuous statute that the Court strikes down does not even rise to the level of "mere shadow." JUSTICE O'CONNOR paradoxically acknowledges: "It is difficult to discern a serious threat to religious liberty from a room of silent, thoughtful schoolchildren." *Ante*, at 73. I would add to that, "even if they choose to pray."

The mountains have labored and brought forth a mouse.[6]

[91] JUSTICE REHNQUIST, dissenting.

Thirty-eight years ago this Court, in *Everson v. Board of Education*, 330 U.S. 1, 16 (1947), summarized its exegesis of Establishment Clause doctrine thus:

"In the words of Jefferson, the clause against establishment of religion by law was intended to erect 'a wall of separation between church and State.' *Reynolds v. United States*, [98 U.S. 145, 164 (1879)]."

This language from *Reynolds*, a case involving the Free Exercise Clause of the First Amendment rather than the Establishment Clause, quoted from Thomas Jefferson's letter to the Danbury Baptist Association the phrase "I contemplate with sovereign reverence that act of the whole American people which declared that their legislature should 'make no law respecting an establishment of religion, or prohibiting the free exercise thereof,' thus building a wall of separation [92] between church and State."[1]

It is impossible to build sound constitutional doctrine upon a mistaken understanding of constitutional history, but unfortunately the Establishment Clause has been

---

6. Horace, *Epistles*, bk. III (*Ars Poetica*), line 139.
1. *Reynolds* is the only authority cited as direct precedent for the "wall of separation theory." 330 U.S., at 16. *Reynolds* is truly inapt; it dealt with a Mormon's Free Exercise Clause challenge to a federal polygamy law.

expressly freighted with Jefferson's misleading metaphor for nearly 40 years. Thomas Jefferson was of course in France at the time the constitutional Amendments known as the Bill of Rights were passed by Congress and ratified by the States. His letter to the Danbury Baptist Association was a short note of courtesy, written 14 years after the Amendments were passed by Congress. He would seem to any detached observer as a less than ideal source of contemporary history as to the meaning of the Religion Clauses of the First Amendment.

Jefferson's fellow Virginian, James Madison, with whom he was joined in the battle for the enactment of the Virginia Statute of Religious Liberty of 1786, did play as large a part as anyone in the drafting of the Bill of Rights. He had two advantages over Jefferson in this regard: he was present in the United States, and he was a leading Member of the First Congress. But when we turn to the record of the proceedings in the First Congress leading up to the adoption of the Establishment Clause of the Constitution, including Madison's significant contributions thereto, we see a far different picture of its purpose than the highly simplified "wall of separation between church and State."

During the debates in the Thirteen Colonies over ratification of the Constitution, one of the arguments frequently used by opponents of ratification was that without a Bill of Rights guaranteeing individual liberty the new general Government [93] carried with it a potential for tyranny. The typical response to this argument on the part of those who favored ratification was that the general Government established by the Constitution had only delegated powers, and that these delegated powers were so limited that the Government would have no occasion to violate individual liberties. This response satisfied some, but not others, and of the 11 Colonies which ratified the Constitution by early 1789, 5 proposed one or another amendments guaranteeing individual liberty. Three—New Hampshire, New York, and Virginia—included in one form or another a declaration of religious freedom. Rhode Island and North Carolina flatly refused to ratify the Constitution in the absence of amendments in the nature of a Bill of Rights. Virginia and North Carolina proposed identical guarantees of religious freedom:

> "[All] men have an equal, natural and unalienable right to the free exercise of religion, according to the dictates of conscience, and . . . no particular religious sect or society ought to be favored or established, by law, in preference to others."[2]

On June 8, 1789, James Madison rose in the House of Representatives and "reminded the House that this was the day that he had heretofore named for bringing forward amendments to the Constitution." 1 Annals of Cong. 424. Madison's subsequent remarks in urging the House to adopt his drafts of the proposed amendments were less those of a dedicated advocate of the wisdom of such measures than those of a prudent statesman seeking the enactment of measures [94] sought by a number of his fellow citizens which could surely do no harm and might do a great deal of good. He said, *inter alia*:

> "It appears to me that this House is bound by every motive of prudence, not to let the first session pass over without proposing to the State Legislatures, some things to be incorporated into the Constitution, that will render it as acceptable to the whole people of the United States, as it has been found acceptable to a majority of them. I wish, among other reasons why something should be done, that those who had been friendly to the adoption of this Constitution may have the opportunity of proving to those who were opposed to

---

2. The New York and Rhode Island proposals were quite similar. They stated that no particular "religious sect or society ought to be favored or established by law in preference to others."

it that they were as sincerely devoted to liberty and a Republican Government, as those who charged them with wishing the adoption of this Constitution in order to lay the foundation of an aristocracy or despotism. It will be a desirable thing to extinguish from the bosom of every member of the community, any apprehensions that there are those among his countrymen who wish to deprive them of the liberty for which they valiantly fought and honorably bled. And if there are amendments desired of such a nature as will not injure the Constitution, and they can be ingrafted so as to give satisfaction to the doubting part of our fellow-citizens, the friends of the Federal Government will evince that spirit of deference and concession for which they have hitherto been distinguished." *Id.*, at 431–432.

The language Madison proposed for what ultimately became the Religion Clauses of the First Amendment was this:

"The civil rights of none shall be abridged on account of religious belief or worship, nor shall any national religion be established, nor shall the full and equal rights of conscience be in any manner, or on any pretext, infringed." *Id.*, at 434.

[95] On the same day that Madison proposed them, the amendments which formed the basis for the Bill of Rights were referred by the House to a Committee of the Whole, and after several weeks' delay were then referred to a Select Committee consisting of Madison and 10 others. The Committee revised Madison's proposal regarding the establishment of religion to read:

"[No] religion shall be established by law, nor shall the equal rights of conscience be infringed." *Id.*, at 729.

The Committee's proposed revisions were debated in the House on August 15, 1789. The entire debate on the Religion Clauses is contained in two full columns of the "Annals," and does not seem particularly illuminating. See *id.*, at 729–731. Representative Peter Sylvester of New York expressed his dislike for the revised version, because it might have a tendency "to abolish religion altogether." Representative John Vining suggested that the two parts of the sentence be transposed; Representative Elbridge Gerry thought the language should be changed to read "that no religious doctrine shall be established by law." *Id.*, at 729. Roger Sherman of Connecticut had the traditional reason for opposing provisions of a Bill of Rights—that Congress had no delegated authority to "make religious establishments"—and therefore he opposed the adoption of the amendment. Representative Daniel Carroll of Maryland thought it desirable to adopt the words proposed, saying "[he] would not contend with gentlemen about the phraseology, his object was to secure the substance in such a manner as to satisfy the wishes of the honest part of the community."

Madison then spoke, and said that "he apprehended the meaning of the words to be, that Congress should not establish a religion, and enforce the legal observation of it by law, nor compel men to worship God in any manner contrary to their conscience." *Id.*, at 730. He said that some of the state conventions had thought that Congress might rely on [96] the Necessary and Proper Clause to infringe the rights of conscience or to establish a national religion, and "to prevent these effects he presumed the amendment was intended, and he thought it as well expressed as the nature of the language would admit." *Ibid.*

Representative Benjamin Huntington then expressed the view that the Committee's language might "be taken in such latitude as to be extremely hurtful to the cause of religion. He understood the amendment to mean what had been expressed by the gentleman from Virginia; but others might find it convenient to put another construction upon it." Huntington, from Connecticut, was concerned that in the New England States, where state-established religions were the rule rather than the exception, the federal courts might not be able to entertain claims based upon an obligation under the bylaws of a religious organization to contribute to the support of a minister or the building of a place of worship. He hoped that "the amendment would be made in such a way as to secure the rights of conscience, and a free exercise of the rights of religion, but not to patronise those who professed no religion at all." *Id.*, at 730–731.

Madison responded that the insertion of the word "national" before the word "religion" in the Committee version should satisfy the minds of those who had criticized the language. "He believed that the people feared one sect might obtain a pre-eminence, or two combine together, and establish a religion to which they would compel others to conform. He thought that if the word 'national' was introduced, it would point the amendment directly to the object it was intended to prevent." *Id.*, at 731. Representative Samuel Livermore expressed himself as dissatisfied with Madison's proposed amendment, and thought it would be better if the Committee language were altered to read that "Congress shall make no laws touching religion, or infringing the rights of conscience." *Ibid.*

Representative Gerry spoke in opposition to the use of the word "national" because of strong feelings expressed during [97] the ratification debates that a federal government, not a national government, was created by the Constitution. Madison thereby withdrew his proposal but insisted that his reference to a "national religion" only referred to a national establishment and did not mean that the Government was a national one. The question was taken on Representative Livermore's motion, which passed by a vote of 31 for and 20 against. *Ibid.*

The following week, without any apparent debate, the House voted to alter the language of the Religion Clauses to read "Congress shall make no law establishing religion, or to prevent the free exercise thereof, or to infringe the rights of conscience." *Id.*, at 766. The floor debates in the Senate were secret, and therefore not reported in the Annals. The Senate on September 3, 1789, considered several different forms of the Religion Amendment, and reported this language back to the House:

> "Congress shall make no law establishing articles of faith or a mode of worship, or prohibiting the free exercise of religion." C. Antieau, A. Downey, & E. Roberts, *Freedom from Federal Establishment* 130 (1964).

The House refused to accept the Senate's changes in the Bill of Rights and asked for a conference; the version which emerged from the conference was that which ultimately found its way into the Constitution as a part of the First Amendment.

> "Congress shall make no law respecting an establishment of religion, or prohibiting the free exercise thereof."

The House and the Senate both accepted this language on successive days, and the Amendment was proposed in this form.

On the basis of the record of these proceedings in the House of Representatives, James Madison was undoubtedly the most important architect among the Members of the [98] House of the Amendments which became the Bill of Rights, but it was James Madison speaking as an advocate of sensible legislative compromise, not as an advocate of incorporating the Virginia Statute of Religious Liberty into the United States Constitution. During the ratification debate in the Virginia Convention, Madison had actually opposed the idea of any Bill of Rights. His sponsorship of the Amendments in the House was obviously not that of a zealous believer in the necessity of the Religion Clauses, but of one who felt it might do some good, could do no harm, and would satisfy those who had ratified the Constitution on the condition that Congress propose a Bill of Rights.[3] His original language "nor shall any national religion be established" obviously does not conform to the "wall of separation" between church and State idea which latter-day commentators have ascribed to him. His explanation on the floor of the meaning of his language—"that Congress should not establish a religion, and enforce the legal observation of it by law"—is of the same ilk. When he replied to Huntington in the debate over the proposal which came from the Select Committee of the House, he urged that the language "no religion shall be established by law" should be amended by inserting the word "national" in front of the word "religion."

It seems indisputable from these glimpses of Madison's thinking, as reflected by actions on the floor of the House in 1789, that he saw the Amendment as designed to prohibit the establishment of a national religion, and perhaps to prevent discrimination among sects. He did not see it as requiring neutrality on the part of government between religion and irreligion. Thus the Court's opinion in *Everson*—while correct in bracketing Madison and Jefferson together in their exertions in their home State leading to the enactment of the [99] Virginia Statute of Religious Liberty—is totally incorrect in suggesting that Madison carried these views onto the floor of the United States House of Representatives when he proposed the language which would ultimately become the Bill of Rights.

The repetition of this error in the Court's opinion in *Illinois ex rel. McCollum v. Board of Education* (1948), and, *inter alia, Engel v. Vitale* (1962), does not make it any sounder historically. Finally, in *Abington School District v. Schempp*, 374 U.S. 203, 214 (1963), the Court made the truly remarkable statement that "the views of Madison and Jefferson, preceded by Roger Williams, came to be incorporated not only in the Federal Constitution but likewise in those of most of our States." On the basis of what evidence we have, this statement is demonstrably incorrect as a matter of history.[4] And its repetition in varying forms in succeeding opinions of the Court can give it no more authority than it possesses as a matter of fact; *stare decisis* may bind courts as to matters of law, but it cannot bind them as to matters of history.

None of the other Members of Congress who spoke during the August 15th debate expressed the slightest indication that they thought the language before them from the Select Committee, or the evil to be aimed at, would require that the Government be absolutely neutral as between religion and irreligion. The evil to be aimed at, so far as those who spoke were concerned, appears to have been the establishment of a national church, and perhaps the preference of one religious sect over another; but it was definitely not concerned about whether the Government might aid all religions evenhandedly. If one were to follow the advice of JUSTICE BRENNAN, concurring in *Abington School District v. Schempp*, at 236, and construe the Amendment in the light of what particular [100] "practices . . . challenged threaten those consequences which the Framers deeply

---

3. In a letter he sent to Jefferson in France, Madison stated that he did not see much importance in a Bill of Rights but he planned to support it because it was "anxiously desired by others . . . [and] it might be of use, and if properly executed could not be of disservice." 5 *Writings of James Madison* 271 (G. Hunt ed. 1904).

4. State establishments were prevalent throughout the late 18th and early 19th centuries. See Mass. Const. of 1780, Part 1, Art. III; N. H. Const. of 1784, Art. VI; Md. Declaration of Rights of 1776, Art. XXXIII; R. I. Charter of 1633 (superseded 1842).

feared; whether, in short, they tend to promote that type of interdependence between religion and state which the First Amendment was designed to prevent," one would have to say that the First Amendment Establishment Clause should be read no more broadly than to prevent the establishment of a national religion or the governmental preference of one religious sect over another.

The actions of the First Congress, which reenacted the Northwest Ordinance for the governance of the Northwest Territory in 1789, confirm the view that Congress did not mean that the Government should be neutral between religion and irreligion. The House of Representatives took up the Northwest Ordinance on the same day as Madison introduced his proposed amendments which became the Bill of Rights; while at that time the Federal Government was of course not bound by draft amendments to the Constitution which had not yet been proposed by Congress, say nothing of ratified by the States, it seems highly unlikely that the House of Representatives would simultaneously consider proposed amendments to the Constitution and enact an important piece of territorial legislation which conflicted with the intent of those proposals. The Northwest Ordinance, 1 Stat. 50, reenacted the Northwest Ordinance of 1787 and provided that "[religion], morality, and knowledge, being necessary to good government and the happiness of mankind, schools and the means of education shall forever be encouraged." Id., at 52, n. (a). Land grants for schools in the Northwest Territory were not limited to public schools. It was not until 1845 that Congress limited land grants in the new States and Territories to nonsectarian schools.

On the day after the House of Representatives voted to adopt the form of the First Amendment Religion Clauses which was ultimately proposed and ratified, Representative [101] Elias Boudinot proposed a resolution asking President George Washington to issue a Thanksgiving Day proclamation. Boudinot said he "could not think of letting the session pass over without offering an opportunity to all the citizens of the United States of joining with one voice, in returning to Almighty God their sincere thanks for the many blessings he had poured down upon them." 1 Annals of Cong. 914 (1789). Representative Aedanas Burke objected to the resolution because he did not like "this mimicking of European customs"; Representative Thomas Tucker objected that whether or not the people had reason to be satisfied with the Constitution was something that the States knew better than the Congress, and in any event "it is a religious matter, and, as such, is proscribed to us." Id., at 915. Representative Sherman supported the resolution "not only as a laudable one in itself, but as warranted by a number of precedents in Holy Writ: for instance, the solemn thanksgivings and rejoicings which took place in the time of Solomon, after the building of the temple, was a case in point. This example, he thought, worthy of Christian imitation on the present occasion. . . ." Ibid.

Boudinot's resolution was carried in the affirmative on September 25, 1789. Boudinot and Sherman, who favored the Thanksgiving Proclamation, voted in favor of the adoption of the proposed amendments to the Constitution, including the Religion Clauses; Tucker, who opposed the Thanksgiving Proclamation, voted against the adoption of the amendments which became the Bill of Rights.

Within two weeks of this action by the House, George Washington responded to the Joint Resolution which by now had been changed to include the language that the President "recommend to the people of the United States a day of public thanksgiving and prayer, to be observed by acknowledging with grateful hearts the many and signal favors of Almighty God, especially by affording them an opportunity peaceably to establish a form of government for their safety and happiness." 1 J. Richardson, Messages and

Papers of [102] *the Presidents, 1789–1897*, p. 64 (1897). The Presidential Proclamation was couched in these words:

> "Now, therefore, I do recommend and assign Thursday, the 26th day of November next, to be devoted by the people of these States to the service of that great and glorious Being who is the beneficent author of all the good that was, that is, or that will be; that we may then all unite in rendering unto Him our sincere and humble thanks for His kind care and protection of the people of this country previous to their becoming a nation; for the signal and manifold mercies and the favorable interpositions of His providence in the course and conclusion of the late war; for the great degree of tranquillity, union, and plenty which we have since enjoyed; for the peaceable and rational manner in which we have been enabled to establish constitutions of government for our safety and happiness, and particularly the national one now lately instituted; for the civil and religious liberty with which we are blessed, and the means we have of acquiring and diffusing useful knowledge; and, in general, for all the great and various favors which He has been pleased to confer upon us.
>
> And also that we may then unite in most humbly offering our prayers and supplications to the great Lord and Ruler of Nations, and beseech Him to pardon our national and other transgressions; to enable us all, whether in public or private stations, to perform our several and relative duties properly and punctually; to render our National Government a blessing to all the people by constantly being a Government of wise, just, and constitutional laws, discreetly and faithfully executed and obeyed; to protect and guide all sovereigns and nations (especially such as have shown kindness to us), and to bless them with good governments, peace, and concord; to promote the knowledge and practice of true religion and virtue, and the increase of science among them and [103] us; and, generally, to grant unto all mankind such a degree of temporal prosperity as He alone knows to be best." *Ibid.*

George Washington, John Adams, and James Madison all issued Thanksgiving Proclamations; Thomas Jefferson did not, saying:

> "Fasting and prayer are religious exercises; the enjoining them an act of discipline. Every religious society has a right to determine for itself the times for these exercises, and the objects proper for them, according to their own particular tenets; and this right can never be safer than in their own hands, where the Constitution has deposited it." 11 *Writings of Thomas Jefferson* 429 (A. Lipscomb ed. 1904).

As the United States moved from the 18th into the 19th century, Congress appropriated time and again public moneys in support of sectarian Indian education carried on by religious organizations. Typical of these was Jefferson's treaty with the Kaskaskia Indians, which provided annual cash support for the Tribe's Roman Catholic priest and church. It was not until 1897, when aid to sectarian education [104] for Indians had reached $500,000 annually, that Congress decided thereafter to cease appropriating money for education in sectarian schools. See generally R. Cord, *Separation of Church and State* 61–82 (1982). This history shows the fallacy of the notion found in *Everson* that "no tax in any amount" may be levied for religious activities in any form. 330 U.S., at 15–16.

From 1789 to 1823 the United States Congress had provided a trust endowment of up to 12,000 acres of land "for the Society of the United Brethren, for propagating the Gospel among the Heathen." See, *e.g.*, ch. 46, 1 Stat. 490. The Act creating this endowment was renewed periodically and the renewals were signed into law by Washington, Adams, and Jefferson.

Congressional grants for the aid of religion were not limited to Indians. In 1787 Congress provided land to the Ohio Company, including acreage for the support of religion. This grant was reauthorized in 1792. See 1 Stat. 257. In 1833 Congress authorized the State of Ohio to sell the land set aside for religion and use the proceeds "for the support of religion . . . and for no other use or purpose whatsoever. . . ." 4 Stat. 618–619.

Joseph Story, a Member of this Court from 1811 to 1845, and during much of that time a professor at the Harvard Law School, published by far the most comprehensive treatise on the United States Constitution that had then appeared. Volume 2 of Story's *Commentaries on the Constitution of the United States* 630–632 (5th ed. 1891) discussed the meaning of the Establishment Clause of the First Amendment this way:

"Probably at the time of the adoption of the Constitution, and of the amendment to it now under consideration [First Amendment], the general if not the universal sentiment in America was, that Christianity ought to receive encouragement from the State so far as was not incompatible with the private rights of conscience and the freedom of religious worship. An attempt to level all religions, and to make it a matter of state policy to hold all in utter indifference, would have created universal disapprobation, if not universal indignation. . . .

The real object of the [First] [Amendment] was not to countenance, much less to advance, Mahometanism, or Judaism, or infidelity, by prostrating Christianity; but to exclude all rivalry among Christian sects, and to prevent [105] any national ecclesiastical establishment which should give to a hierarchy the exclusive patronage of the national government. It thus cut off the means of religious persecution (the vice and pest of former ages), and of the subversion of the rights of conscience in matters of religion, which had been trampled upon almost from the days of the Apostles to the present age. . . ."

Thomas Cooley's eminence as a legal authority rivaled that of Story. Cooley stated in his treatise entitled *Constitutional Limitations* that aid to a particular religious sect was prohibited by the United States Constitution, but he went on to say:

"But while thus careful to establish, protect, and defend religious freedom and equality, the American constitutions contain no provisions which prohibit the authorities from such solemn recognition of a superintending Providence in public transactions and exercises as the general religious sentiment of mankind inspires, and as seems meet and proper in finite and dependent beings. Whatever may be the shades of religious belief, all must acknowledge the fitness of recognizing in important human affairs the superintending care and control of the Great Governor of the Universe, and of acknowledging with thanksgiving his boundless favors, or bowing in contrition when visited with the penalties of his broken laws. No principle of constitutional law is violated when thanksgiving or fast days are appointed; when chaplains are designated for the army and navy; when legislative sessions are opened with prayer or the reading of the Scriptures, or when religious teaching is encouraged by a general exemption of the houses of religious worship from taxation for the support of State government. Undoubtedly the spirit of the Constitution will require, in all these cases, that care be taken to avoid discrimination [106] in favor of or against any one religious denomination or sect; but the power to do any of these things does not become unconstitutional simply because of its susceptibility to abuse. . . ." *Id.*, at *470–*471.

Cooley added that

"[this] public recognition of religious worship, however, is not based entirely, perhaps not even mainly, upon a sense of what is due to the Supreme Being himself as the author of all good and of all law; but the same reasons of state policy which induce the government to aid institutions of charity and seminaries of instruction will incline it also to foster religious worship and religious institutions, as conservators of the public morals and valuable, if not indispensable, assistants to the preservation of the public order." *Id.*, at *470.

It would seem from this evidence that the Establishment Clause of the First Amendment had acquired a well-accepted meaning: it forbade establishment of a national religion, and forbade preference among religious sects or denominations. Indeed, the first American dictionary defined the word "establishment" as "the act of establishing, founding, ratifying or ordaining," such as in "[the] episcopal form of religion, so called, in England." 1 N. Webster, *American Dictionary of the English Language* (1st ed. 1828). The Establishment Clause did not require government neutrality between religion and irreligion nor did it prohibit the Federal Government from providing nondiscriminatory aid to religion. There is simply no historical foundation for the proposition that the Framers intended to build the "wall of separation" that was constitutionalized in *Everson*.

Notwithstanding the absence of a historical basis for this theory of rigid separation, the wall idea might well have served as a useful albeit misguided analytical concept, had it led this Court to unified and principled results in Establishment Clause cases. The opposite, unfortunately, has been [107] true; in the 38 years since *Everson* our Establishment Clause cases have been neither principled nor unified. Our recent opinions, many of them hopelessly divided pluralities, have with embarrassing candor conceded that the "wall of separation" is merely a "blurred, indistinct, and variable barrier," which "is not wholly accurate" and can only be "dimly perceived." *Lemon v. Kurtzman*, 403 U.S. 602, 614 (1971); *Tilton v. Richardson*, 403 U.S. 672, 677–678 (1971); *Wolman v. Walter*, 433 U.S. 229, 236 (1977); *Lynch v. Donnelly*, 465 U.S. 668, 673 (1984).

Many of our other Establishment Clause cases have been decided by bare 5–4 majorities. *Committee for Public Education & Religious Liberty v. Regan* (1980); *Larson v. Valente* (1982); *Mueller v. Allen* (1983); *Lynch v. Donnelly* (1984); cf. *Levitt v. Committee for Public Education & Religious Liberty* (1973).

Whether due to its lack of historical support or its practical unworkability, the *Everson* "wall" has proved all but useless as a guide to sound constitutional adjudication. It illustrates only too well the wisdom of Benjamin Cardozo's observation that "[metaphors] in law are to be narrowly watched, for starting as devices to liberate thought, they end often by enslaving it." *Berkey v. Third Avenue R. Co.*, 244 N. Y. 84, 94, 155 N. E. 58, 61 (1926).

But the greatest injury of the "wall" notion is its mischievous diversion of judges from the actual intentions of the drafters of the Bill of Rights. The "crucible of litigation," *ante*, at 52, is well adapted to adjudicating factual disputes on the basis of testimony presented in court, but no amount of repetition of historical errors in judicial opinions can make the errors true. The "wall of separation between church and State" is a metaphor based on bad history, a metaphor which has proved useless as a guide to judging. It should be frankly and explicitly abandoned.

[108] The Court has more recently attempted to add some mortar to *Everson*'s wall through the three-part test of *Lemon v. Kurtzman*, at 614–615, which served at first to offer a more useful test for purposes of the Establishment Clause than did the "wall" metaphor. Generally stated, the *Lemon* test proscribes state action that has a sectarian purpose or effect, or causes an impermissible governmental entanglement with religion.

Lemon cited *Board of Education v. Allen*, 392 U.S. 236, 243 (1968), as the source of the "purpose" and "effect" prongs of the three-part test. The *Allen* opinion explains, however, how it inherited the purpose and effect elements from *Schempp* and *Everson*, both of which contain the historical errors described above. See *Allen*, at 243. Thus the purpose and effect prongs have the same historical deficiencies as the wall concept itself: they are in no way based on either the language or intent of the drafters.

The secular purpose prong has proved mercurial in application because it has never been fully defined, and we have never fully stated how the test is to operate. If the purpose prong is intended to void those aids to sectarian institutions accompanied by a stated legislative purpose to aid religion, the prong will condemn nothing so long as the legislature utters a secular purpose and says nothing about aiding religion. Thus the constitutionality of a statute may depend upon what the legislators put into the legislative history and, more importantly, what they leave out. The purpose prong means little if it only requires the legislature to express any secular purpose and omit all sectarian references, because legislators might do just that. Faced with a valid legislative secular purpose, we could not properly ignore that purpose without a factual basis for doing so.

However, if the purpose prong is aimed to void all statutes enacted with the intent to aid sectarian institutions, whether stated or not, then most statutes providing any aid, such as [109] textbooks or bus rides for sectarian school children, will fail because one of the purposes behind every statute, whether stated or not, is to aid the target of its largesse. In other words, if the purpose prong requires an absence of any intent to aid sectarian institutions, whether or not expressed, few state laws in this area could pass the test, and we would be required to void some state aids to religion which we have already upheld. *E.g., Allen, supra.*

The entanglement prong of the *Lemon* test came from *Walz v. Tax Comm'n*, 397 U.S. 664, 674 (1970). *Walz* involved a constitutional challenge to New York's time-honored practice of providing state property tax exemptions to church property used in worship. The *Walz* opinion refused to "undermine the ultimate constitutional objective [of the Establishment Clause] as illuminated by history," *id.,* at 671, and upheld the tax exemption. The Court examined the historical relationship between the State and church when church property was in issue, and determined that the challenged tax exemption did not so entangle New York with the church as to cause an intrusion or interference with religion. Interferences with religion should arguably be dealt with under the Free Exercise Clause, but the entanglement inquiry in *Walz* was consistent with that case's broad survey of the relationship between state taxation and religious property.

We have not always followed *Walz'* reflective inquiry into entanglement, however. *E.g., Wolman,* at 254. One of the difficulties with the entanglement prong is that, when divorced from the logic of *Walz,* it creates an "insoluable paradox" in school aid cases: we have required aid to parochial schools to be closely watched lest it be put to sectarian use, yet this close supervision itself will create an entanglement. For example, in *Wolman,* the Court in part struck the State's nondiscriminatory provision of buses for parochial school field trips, because the state supervision [110] of sectarian officials in charge of field trips would be too onerous. This type of self-defeating result is certainly not required to ensure that States do not establish religions.

The entanglement test as applied in cases like *Wolman* also ignores the myriad state administrative regulations properly placed upon sectarian institutions such as curriculum, attendance, and certification requirements for sectarian schools, or fire and safety regulations for churches. Avoiding entanglement between church and State may be an important consideration in a case like *Walz,* but if the entanglement prong were applied to all state and church relations in the automatic manner in which it has been applied to school aid cases, the State could hardly require anything of church-related institutions as a condition for receipt of financial assistance.

These difficulties arise because the *Lemon* test has no more grounding in the history of the First Amendment than does the wall theory upon which it rests. The three-part test represents a determined effort to craft a workable rule from a historically faulty doctrine; but the rule can only be as sound as the doctrine it attempts to service. The three-part test has simply not provided adequate standards for deciding Establishment Clause cases, as this Court has slowly come to realize. Even worse, the *Lemon* test has caused this Court to fracture into unworkable plurality opinions depending upon how each of the three factors applies to a certain state action. The results from our school services cases show the difficulty we have encountered in making the *Lemon* test yield principled results.

For example, a State may lend to parochial school children geography textbooks[7] that contain maps of the United States, but the State may not lend maps of the United States for use in geography class.[8] A State may lend textbooks on American colonial history, but it may not lend a film on [111] George Washington, or a film projector to show it in history class. A State may lend classroom workbooks, but may not lend workbooks in which the parochial school children write, thus rendering them nonreusable.[9] A State may pay for bus transportation to religious schools[10] but may not pay for bus transportation from the parochial school to the public zoo or natural history museum for a field trip.[11] A State may pay for diagnostic services conducted in the parochial school but therapeutic services must be given in a different building; speech and hearing "services" conducted by the State inside the sectarian school are forbidden, *Meek v. Pittenger*, 421 U.S. 349, 367, 371 (1975), but the State may conduct speech and hearing diagnostic testing inside the sectarian school. *Wolman*, 433 U.S., at 241. Exceptional parochial school students may receive counseling, but it must take place outside of the parochial school,[12] such as in a trailer parked down the street. *Id.*, at 245. A State may give cash to a parochial school to pay for the administration of state-written tests and state-ordered reporting services,[13] but it may not provide funds for teacher-prepared tests on secular subjects.[14] Religious instruction may not be given in public school,[15] but the public school may release students during the day for religion classes elsewhere, and may enforce attendance at those classes with its truancy laws.[16]

These results violate the historically sound principle "that the Establishment Clause does not forbid governments . . . to [provide] general welfare under which benefits are distributed to private individuals, even though many of those individuals [112] may elect to use those benefits in ways that 'aid' religious instruction or worship." *Committee for Public Education & Religious Liberty v. Nyquist*, 413 U.S. 756, 799 (1973) (BURGER, C. J., concurring in part and dissenting in part). It is not surprising in the light of this record that our most recent opinions have expressed doubt on the usefulness of the *Lemon* test.

Although the test initially provided helpful assistance, *e.g.*, *Tilton v. Richardson* (1971), we soon began describing the test as only a "guideline," *Committee for Public*

---

7. *Board of Education v. Allen*, 392 U.S. 236 (1968).

8. *Meek*, 421 U.S., at 362–366. A science book is permissible, a science kit is not. See *Wolman*, 433 U.S., at 249.

9. See *Meek, supra*, at 354–355, nn. 3, 4, 362–366.

10. *Everson v. Board of Education*, 330 U.S. 1 (1947).

11. *Wolman*, at 252–255.

12. *Wolman*, at 241–248; *Meek*, at 352, n. 2, 367–373.

13. *Regan*, 444 U.S., at 648, 657–659.

14. *Levitt*, 413 U.S., at 479–482.

15. *Illinois ex rel. McCollum v. Board of Education*, 333 U.S. 203 (1948).

16. *Zorach v. Clauson*, 343 U.S. 306 (1952).

Education & Religious Liberty v. Nyquist, and lately we have described it as "no more than [a] useful [signpost]." *Mueller v. Allen,* 463 U.S. 388, 394 (1983), citing *Hunt v. Mc-Nair,* 413 U.S. 734, 741 (1973); *Larkin v. Grendel's Den, Inc.* (1982). We have noted that the *Lemon* test is "not easily applied," *Meek,* at 358, and as JUSTICE WHITE noted in *Committee for Public Education & Religious Liberty v. Regan* (1980), under the *Lemon* test we have "[sacrificed] clarity and predictability for flexibility." 444 U.S., at 662. In *Lynch* we reiterated that the *Lemon* test has never been binding on the Court, and we cited two cases where we had declined to apply it. 465 U.S., at 679, citing *Marsh v. Chambers* (1983); *Larson v. Valente* (1982).

If a constitutional theory has no basis in the history of the amendment it seeks to interpret, is difficult to apply and yields unprincipled results, I see little use in it. The "crucible of litigation," *ante,* at 52, has produced only consistent unpredictability, and today's effort is just a continuation of "the sisyphean task of trying to patch together the 'blurred, indistinct and variable barrier' described in *Lemon v. Kurtzman.*" *Regan,* at 671 (STEVENS, J., dissenting). We have done much straining since 1947, but still we admit that we can only "dimly perceive" the *Everson* wall. *Tilton, supra.* Our perception has been clouded not by the Constitution but by the mists of an unnecessary metaphor.

[113] The true meaning of the Establishment Clause can only be seen in its history. As drafters of our Bill of Rights, the Framers inscribed the principles that control today. Any deviation from their intentions frustrates the permanence of that Charter and will only lead to the type of unprincipled decisionmaking that has plagued our Establishment Clause cases since *Everson.*

The Framers intended the Establishment Clause to prohibit the designation of any church as a "national" one. The Clause was also designed to stop the Federal Government from asserting a preference for one religious denomination or sect over others. Given the "incorporation" of the Establishment Clause as against the States via the Fourteenth Amendment in *Everson,* States are prohibited as well from establishing a religion or discriminating between sects. As its history abundantly shows, however, nothing in the Establishment Clause requires government to be strictly neutral between religion and irreligion, nor does that Clause prohibit Congress or the States from pursuing legitimate secular ends through nondiscriminatory sectarian means.

The Court strikes down the Alabama statute because the State wished to "characterize prayer as a favored practice." *Ante,* at 60. It would come as much of a shock to those who drafted the Bill of Rights as it will to a large number of thoughtful Americans today to learn that the Constitution, as construed by the majority, prohibits the Alabama Legislature from "endorsing" prayer. George Washington himself, at the request of the very Congress which passed the Bill of Rights, proclaimed a day of "public thanksgiving and prayer, to be observed by acknowledging with grateful hearts the many and signal favors of Almighty God." History must judge whether it was the Father of his Country in 1789, or a majority of the Court today, which has strayed from the meaning of the Establishment Clause.

The State surely has a secular interest in regulating the manner in which public schools are conducted. Nothing in [114] the Establishment Clause of the First Amendment, properly understood, prohibits any such generalized "endorsement" of prayer. I would therefore reverse the judgment of the Court of Appeals.

37

Witters v. Washington Department of Services for the Blind

474 U.S. 481 (1986)

Vote: 9—Burger, Brennan, White, Marshall, Blackmun, Powell, Rehnquist, Stevens, O'Connor

   0

Opinion announcing the opinion of the Court: Marshall
Concurring opinions: White, Powell
Opinion concurring in part and concurring in the judgment: O'Connor

On account of his eye condition, Larry Witters applied for vocational rehabilitation assistance under a state statute that authorized the Washington Commission for the Blind to "[provide] for special education and/or training in the professions, business or trades" so as to "assist visually handicapped persons to overcome vocational handicaps and to obtain the maximum degree of self-support and self-care." Witters attended Inland Empire School of the Bible, a private Christian college in Spokane, Washington, where he was studying the Bible, ethics, speech, and church administration in order to equip himself for a career as a pastor, missionary, or youth director.

The Washington Commission for the Blind denied Witters aid, relying on an earlier determination embodied in a commission policy statement that "[the] Washington State constitution forbids the use of public funds to assist an individual in the pursuit of a career or degree in theology or related areas" and on its conclusion that Witters's training was "religious instruction" subject to that ban. The commission's ruling was affirmed by a state hearings examiner, who held that the commission was precluded from funding Witters's training "in light of the Washington State Constitution's prohibition against the state directly or indirectly supporting a religion." The hearings examiner cited two provisions in the Washington state constitution: "no public money or property shall be appropriated for or applied to any religious worship, exercise or instruction, or the support of any religious establishment" (Art. I, § 11), and "[all] schools maintained or supported wholly or in part by the public funds shall be forever free from sectarian control or influence" (Art. IX, § 4). The hearings examiner's ruling was upheld in an internal administrative appeal.

MARSHALL, J., delivered the opinion of the Court, in which BURGER, C. J., and BRENNAN, WHITE, BLACKMUN, POWELL, REHNQUIST, and STEVENS, JJ., joined, and in Parts I and III of which O'CONNOR, J., joined.

. . . [485] II

The Establishment Clause of the First Amendment has consistently presented this Court with difficult questions of interpretation and application. We acknowledged in *Lemon v. Kurtzman*, 403 U.S. 602 (1971), that "we can only dimly perceive the lines of demarcation in this extraordinarily sensitive area of constitutional law." *Id.*, at 612. Nonetheless, the Court's opinions in this area have at least clarified "the broad contours of our inquiry," *Committee for Public Education and Religious Liberty v. Nyquist*, 413 U.S. 756, 761 (1973), and are sufficient to dispose of this case.

We are guided, as was the court below, by the three-part test set out by this Court in *Lemon*. Our analysis relating to the first prong of that test is simple: all parties concede the unmistakably secular purpose of the Washington program. That program was designed to promote the well-being of the visually handicapped through the provision of vocational rehabilitation [486] services, and no more than a minuscule amount of the aid awarded under the program is likely to flow to religious education. No party suggests that the State's "actual purpose" in creating the program was to endorse religion, *Wallace v. Jaffree*, 472 U.S. 38, 74 (1985), quoting *Lynch v. Donnelly*, 465 U.S. 668, 690 (1984) (O'CONNOR, J., concurring), or that the secular purpose articulated by the legislature is merely "sham." *Wallace*, at 64 (POWELL, J., concurring).

The answer to the question posed by the second prong of the *Lemon* test is more difficult. We conclude, however, that extension of aid to petitioner is not barred on that ground either. It is well settled that the Establishment Clause is not violated every time money previously in the possession of a State is conveyed to a religious institution. For example, a State may issue a paycheck to one of its employees, [487] who may then donate all or part of that paycheck to a religious institution, all without constitutional barrier; and the State may do so even knowing that the employee so intends to dispose of his salary. It is equally well settled, on the other hand, that the State may not grant aid to a religious school, whether cash or in kind, where the effect of the aid is "that of a direct subsidy to the religious school" from the State. *Grand Rapids School District v. Ball*, 473 U.S., at 394. Aid may have that effect even though it takes the form of aid to students or parents. The question presented is whether, on the facts as they appear in the record before us, extension of aid to petitioner and the use of that aid by petitioner to support his religious education is a permissible transfer similar to the hypothetical salary donation described above, or is an impermissible "direct subsidy."

Certain aspects of Washington's program are central to our inquiry. As far as the record shows, vocational assistance provided under the Washington program is paid directly to the student, who transmits it to the educational institution of his or her choice. Any aid provided under Washington's program that ultimately flows to religious institutions does so only as a result of the genuinely independent and private choices of aid recipients. Washington's program is "made available generally without regard to the sectarian-nonsectarian, or public-nonpublic nature of the institution benefited," *Committee for Public Education and Religious* [488] *Liberty v. Nyquist*, 413 U.S., at 782–783, n. 38, and is in no way skewed towards religion. It is not one of "the ingenious plans for channeling state aid to sectarian schools that periodically reach this Court," *id.*, at 785. It creates no financial incentive for students to undertake sectarian education, see *id.*, at

785–786. It does not tend to provide greater or broader benefits for recipients who apply their aid to religious education, nor are the full benefits of the program limited, in large part or in whole, to students at sectarian institutions. On the contrary, aid recipients have full opportunity to expend vocational rehabilitation aid on wholly secular education, and as a practical matter have rather greater prospects to do so. Aid recipients' choices are made among a huge variety of possible careers, of which only a small handful are sectarian. In this case, the fact that aid goes to individuals means that the decision to support religious education is made by the individual, not by the State.

Further, and importantly, nothing in the record indicates that, if petitioner succeeds, any significant portion of the aid expended under the Washington program as a whole will end up flowing to religious education. The function of the Washington program is hardly "to provide desired financial support for nonpublic, sectarian institutions." *Id.*, at 783. The program, providing vocational assistance to the visually handicapped, does not seem well suited to serve as the vehicle for such a subsidy. No evidence has been presented indicating that any other person has ever sought to finance religious education or activity pursuant to the State's program. The combination of these factors, we think, makes the link between the State and the school petitioner wishes to attend a highly attenuated one.

On the facts we have set out, it does not seem appropriate to view any aid ultimately flowing to the Inland Empire School of the Bible as resulting from a *state* action sponsoring or subsidizing religion. Nor does the mere circumstance [489] that petitioner has chosen to use neutrally available state aid to help pay for his religious education confer any message of state endorsement of religion. Thus, while *amici* supporting respondent are correct in pointing out that aid to a religious institution unrestricted in its potential uses, if properly attributable to the State, is "clearly prohibited under the Establishment Clause," *Grand Rapids*, at 395, because it may subsidize the religious functions of that institution, that observation is not apposite to this case. On the facts present here, we think the Washington program works no state support of religion prohibited by the Establishment Clause. . . .

38

Goldman v. Weinberger

475 U.S. 503 (1986)

Vote: 5—Burger, White, Powell, Rehnquist, Stevens
  4—Brennan, Marshall, Blackmun, O'Connor

Opinion announcing the opinion of the Court: Rehnquist
Concurring opinion: Stevens
Dissenting opinions: Brennan, Blackmun, O'Connor

At the time of this case, a United States Air Force uniform regulation prohibited the wearing of headgear while indoors, except for headgear for armed security police in the performance of their duties. Air Force officer S. Simcha Goldman, an Orthodox Jew and an ordained rabbi, ran afoul of the dress regulation, which led him to file this lawsuit challenging it.

A clinical psychologist serving at a mental health clinic on March Air Force Base in Riverside, California, Goldman was not prevented from wearing his yarmulke on the base for a time. He avoided controversy by remaining close to his duty station in the health clinic and by wearing his service cap over the yarmulke when out of doors. In April 1981, after he testified as a defense witness at a court-martial hearing wearing his yarmulke but not his service cap, opposing counsel lodged a complaint with the hospital commander. The complaint contended that Goldman's practice of wearing his yarmulke was in violation of Air Force Regulation (AFR) 35-10, which stated in its relevant part, "[Headgear] will not be worn . . . [while] indoors except by armed security police in the performance of their duties."

Goldman was ordered by his hospital commander to discontinue wearing a yarmulke while on duty indoors and warned that failure to obey the regulation could subject him to a court-martial. Goldman sued the secretary of defense and others, claiming that the application of AFR 35-10 to prevent him from wearing his yarmulke infringed upon his First Amendment freedom to exercise his religious beliefs.

REHNQUIST, J., delivered the opinion of the Court, in which BURGER, C. J., and WHITE, POWELL, and STEVENS, JJ., joined.

. . . [507] Our review of military regulations challenged on First Amendment grounds is far more deferential than constitutional review of similar laws or regulations designed for civilian society. The military need not encourage debate or tolerate protest to the extent that such tolerance is required of the civilian state by the First Amendment; to accomplish its mission the military must foster instinctive obedience, unity, commitment, and esprit de corps. The essence of military service "is the subordination of the desires and interests of the individual to the needs of the service." *Orloff v. Willoughby*, at 92.

These aspects of military life do not, of course, render entirely nugatory in the military context the guarantees of the First Amendment. But "within the military community there is simply not the same [individual] autonomy as there is in the larger civilian community." *Parker v. Levy*, at 751. In the context of the present case, when evaluating whether military needs justify a particular restriction on religiously motivated conduct, courts must give great deference to the professional judgment of military authorities concerning the relative importance of a particular military interest. Not only are courts "ill-equipped to determine the impact upon discipline that any particular intrusion upon military authority might have," *Chappell v. Wallace*, [508] at 305, quoting Warren, *The Bill of Rights and the Military*, 37 N. Y. U. L. Rev. 181, 187 (1962), but the military authorities have been charged by the Executive and Legislative Branches with carrying out our Nation's military policy. "[Judicial] deference . . . is at its apogee when legislative action under the congressional authority to raise and support armies and make rules and regulations for their governance is challenged." *Rostker v. Goldberg*, 453 U.S. 57, 70 (1981).

The considered professional judgment of the Air Force is that the traditional outfitting of personnel in standardized uniforms encourages the subordination of personal preferences and identities in favor of the overall group mission. Uniforms encourage a sense of hierarchical unity by tending to eliminate outward individual distinctions except for those of rank. The Air Force considers them as vital during peacetime as during war because its personnel must be ready to provide an effective defense on a moment's notice; the necessary habits of discipline and unity must be developed in advance of trouble. We have acknowledged that "[the] inescapable demands of military discipline and obedience to orders cannot be taught on battlefields; the habit of immediate compliance with military procedures and orders must be virtually reflex with no time for debate or reflection." *Chappell v. Wallace*, at 300.

To this end, the Air Force promulgated AFR 35-10, a 190-page document, which states that "Air Force members will wear the Air Force uniform while performing their military duties, except when authorized to wear civilian clothes on duty." The rest of the document describes in minute detail all of the various items of apparel that must be worn as part of the Air Force uniform. It authorizes a few individualized options with respect to certain pieces of jewelry and hairstyle, but even these are subject to severe limitations. In general, authorized headgear may [509] be worn only out of doors. Indoors, "[headgear] [may] not be worn . . . except by armed security police in the performance of their duties." AFR 35-10, para. 1-6.h (2)(f) (1980). A narrow exception to this rule exists for headgear worn during indoor religious ceremonies. In addition, military commanders may in their discretion permit visible religious headgear and other such apparel in designated living quarters and nonvisible items generally.

Petitioner Goldman contends that the Free Exercise Clause of the First Amendment requires the Air Force to make an exception to its uniform dress requirements for religious apparel unless the accouterments create a "clear danger" of undermining discipline and esprit de corps. He asserts that in general, visible but "unobtrusive" apparel will not create such a danger and must therefore be accommodated. He argues that the Air Force failed to prove that a specific exception for his practice of wearing an unobtrusive yarmulke would threaten discipline. He contends that the Air Force's assertion to the contrary is mere *ipse dixit*, with no support from actual experience or a scientific study in the record, and is contradicted by expert testimony that religious exceptions to AFR 35-10 are in fact desirable and will increase morale by making the Air Force a more humane place.

But whether or not expert witnesses may feel that religious exceptions to AFR 35-10 are desirable is quite beside the point. The desirability of dress regulations in the military is decided by the appropriate military officials, and they are under no constitutional mandate to abandon their considered professional judgment. Quite obviously, to the extent the regulations do not permit the wearing of religious apparel such as a yarmulke, a practice described by petitioner as silent devotion akin to prayer, military life may be more objectionable for petitioner and probably others. But the First Amendment does not require the military to accommodate [510] such practices in the face of its view that they would detract from the uniformity sought by the dress regulations. The Air Force has drawn the line essentially between religious apparel that is visible and that which is not, and we hold that those portions of the regulations challenged here reasonably and evenhandedly regulate dress in the interest of the military's perceived need for uniformity. The First Amendment therefore does not prohibit them from being applied to petitioner even though their effect is to restrict the wearing of the headgear required by his religious beliefs. . . .

[513] JUSTICE BRENNAN, with whom JUSTICE MARSHALL joins, dissenting.

Simcha Goldman invokes this Court's protection of his First Amendment right to fulfill one of the traditional religious obligations of a male Orthodox Jew—to cover his head before an omnipresent God. The Court's response to Goldman's [514] request is to abdicate its role as principal expositor of the Constitution and protector of individual liberties in favor of credulous deference to unsupported assertions of military necessity. I dissent.

I . . .

[516] B

I

The Government maintains in its brief that discipline is jeopardized whenever exceptions to military regulations are granted. Service personnel must be trained to obey even the most arbitrary command reflexively. Non-Jewish personnel will perceive the wearing of a yarmulke by an Orthodox Jew as an unauthorized departure from the rules and will begin to question the principle of unswerving obedience. Thus shall our fighting forces slip down the treacherous slope [517] toward unkempt appearance, anarchy, and, ultimately, defeat at the hands of our enemies.

The contention that the discipline of the Armed Forces will be subverted if Orthodox Jews are allowed to wear yarmulkes with their uniforms surpasses belief. It lacks support in the record of this case, and the Air Force offers no basis for it as a general proposition. While the perilous slope permits the services arbitrarily to refuse exceptions requested to satisfy mere personal preferences, before the Air Force may burden free exercise rights it must advance, at the *very least*, a rational reason for doing so.

Furthermore, the Air Force cannot logically defend the content of its rule by insisting that discipline depends upon absolute adherence to whatever rule is established. If, as General Usher admitted at trial, the dress code codified religious exemptions from the "no-headgear-indoors" regulation, then the wearing of a yarmulke would be sanctioned by the code and could not be considered an unauthorized deviation from the rules.

2

The Government also argues that the services have an important interest in uniform dress, because such dress establishes the preeminence of group identity, thus fostering esprit de corps and loyalty to the service that transcends individual bonds. In its brief, the Government characterizes the yarmulke as an assertion of individuality and as a badge of religious and ethnic identity, strongly suggesting that, as such, it could drive a wedge of divisiveness between members of the services.

First, the purported interests of the Air Force in complete uniformity of dress and in elimination of individuality or visible identification with any group other than itself are belied by the service's own regulations. The dress code expressly abjures the need for total uniformity:

> [518] "(1) The American public and its elected representatives draw certain conclusions on military effectiveness based on what they see; that is, the image the Air Force presents. The image must instill public confidence and leave no doubt that the service member lives by a common standard and responds to military order and discipline.
>
> (2) Appearance in uniform is an important part of this image. . . . Neither the Air Force nor the public expects absolute uniformity of appearance. Each member has the right, within limits, to express individuality through his or her appearance. However, the image of a disciplined service member who can be relied on to do his or her job excludes the extreme, the unusual, and the fad." AFR 35-10, paras. 1-12a (1) and (2) (1978).

It cannot be seriously contended that a serviceman in a yarmulke presents so extreme, so unusual, or so faddish an image that public confidence in his ability to perform his duties will be destroyed. Under the Air Force's own standards, then, Dr. Goldman should have and could have been granted an exception to wear his yarmulke.

The dress code also allows men to wear up to three rings and one identification bracelet of "neat and conservative," but nonuniform, design. AFR 35-10, para. 1-12b (1) (b) (1978). This jewelry is apparently permitted even if, as is often the case with rings, it associates the wearer with a denominational school or a religious or secular fraternal organization. If these emblems of religious, social, and ethnic identity are not deemed to be unacceptably divisive, the Air Force cannot rationally justify its bar against yarmulkes on that basis.

Moreover, the services allow, and rightly so, other manifestations of religious diversity. It is clear to all service personnel that some members attend Jewish services, some [519] Christian, some Islamic, and some yet other religious services. Barracks mates see Mormons wearing temple garments, Orthodox Jews wearing tzitzit, and Catholics wearing crosses and scapulars. That they come from different faiths and ethnic backgrounds is not a secret that can or should be kept from them.

I find totally implausible the suggestion that the overarching group identity of the Air Force would be threatened if Orthodox Jews were allowed to wear yarmulkes with their uniforms. To the contrary, a yarmulke worn with a United States military uniform is an eloquent reminder that the shared and proud identity of United States serviceman embraces and unites religious and ethnic pluralism.

Finally, the Air Force argues that while Dr. Goldman describes his yarmulke as an "unobtrusive" addition to his uniform, obtrusiveness is a purely relative, standardless judgment. The Government notes that while a yarmulke might not seem obtrusive to a Jew, neither does a turban to a Sikh, a saffron robe to a Satchidananda Ashram-Integral Yogi, nor dreadlocks to a Rastafarian. If the Court were to require the Air Force to permit yarmulkes, the service must also allow all of these other forms of dress and grooming.

The Government dangles before the Court a classic parade of horribles, the specter of a brightly-colored, "rag-tag band of soldiers." Although turbans, saffron robes, and dreadlocks are not before us in this case and must each be evaluated against the reasons a service branch offers for prohibiting personnel from wearing them while in uniform, a reviewing court could legitimately give deference to dress and grooming rules that have a *reasoned* basis in, for example, functional utility, health and safety considerations, and the goal of a polished, professional appearance. AFR 35-10, paras. 1-12a and 1-12a (1) (1978) [520] (identifying neatness, cleanliness, safety, and military image as the four elements of the dress code's "high standard of dress and personal appearance"). It is the lack of any reasoned basis for prohibiting yarmulkes that is so striking here.

Furthermore, contrary to its intimations, the Air Force has available to it a familiar standard for determining whether a particular style of yarmulke is consistent with a polished, professional military appearance—the "neat and conservative" standard by which the service judges jewelry. No rational reason exists why yarmulkes cannot be judged by the same criterion. Indeed, at argument Dr. Goldman declared himself willing to wear whatever style and color yarmulke the Air Force believes best comports with its uniform. . . .

[523] III

. . . It is not the province of the federal courts to second-guess the professional judgments of the military services, but we are bound by the Constitution to assure ourselves that there exists a rational foundation for assertions of military necessity when they interfere with the free exercise of religion. "The concept of military necessity is seductively broad," *Glines*, 444 U.S., at 369 (BRENNAN, J., dissenting), and military decisionmakers themselves are as likely to succumb to its allure as are the courts and the general public. Definitions of necessity are influenced by decisionmakers' experiences and values. As a consequence, in pluralistic societies such as ours, institutions dominated by a majority are inevitably, if inadvertently, insensitive to the needs and values of minorities when these needs and values differ from those [524] of the majority. The military, with its strong ethic of conformity and unquestioning obedience, may be particularly impervious to minority needs and values. A critical function of the Religion Clauses of the First Amendment is to protect the rights of members of minority religions against quiet erosion by majoritarian social institutions that dismiss minority beliefs and practices as unimportant, because unfamiliar. It is the constitutional role of this Court to ensure that this purpose of the First Amendment be realized.

The Court and the military services have presented patriotic Orthodox Jews with a painful dilemma—the choice between fulfilling a religious obligation and serving their country. Should the draft be reinstated, compulsion will replace choice. Although the pain the services inflict on Orthodox Jewish servicemen is clearly the result of insensitivity rather than design, it is unworthy of our military because it is unnecessary. The Court and the military have refused these servicemen their constitutional rights; we must hope that Congress will correct this wrong.

JUSTICE BLACKMUN, dissenting.

I would reverse the judgment of the Court of Appeals, but for reasons somewhat different from those respectively enunciated by JUSTICE BRENNAN and JUSTICE O'CONNOR. I feel that the Air Force is justified in considering not only the costs of allowing Captain Goldman to cover his head indoors, but also the cumulative costs of accommodating constitutionally indistinguishable requests for religious exemptions. Because, however, the Government has failed to make any [525] meaningful showing that either set of costs is significant, I dissent from the Court's rejection of Goldman's claim. . . .

[526] In my view, this case does not require us to determine the extent to which the ordinary test for inroads on religious freedom must be modified in the military context, because the Air Force has failed to produce even a minimally credible explanation for its refusal to allow Goldman to keep his head covered indoors. I agree with the Court that deference is due the considered judgment of military professionals that, as a general matter, standardized dress serves to promote discipline and esprit de corps. But Goldman's modest supplement to the Air Force uniform clearly poses by itself no threat to the Nation's military readiness. Indeed, the District Court specifically found that Goldman has worn a yarmulke on base for years without any adverse effect on his performance, any disruption of operations at the base, or any complaints from other personnel.

The Air Force argues that it has no way of distinguishing fairly between Goldman's request for an exemption and the potential requests of others whose religious practices may conflict with the appearance code, perhaps in more conspicuous ways. . . .

[527] The problem with this argument, it seems to me, is not doctrinal but empirical. The Air Force simply has not shown any reason to fear that a significant number of enlisted personnel and officers would request religious exemptions that could not be denied on neutral grounds such as safety, let alone that granting these requests would noticeably impair the overall image of the service. The Air Force contends that the potential for such disruption was demonstrated at trial through the introduction of an Army publication discussing the beliefs and practices of a variety of religious denominations, some of which have traditions or requirements involving attire. But that publication provides no indication whatsoever as to how many soldiers belong to the denominations it describes, or as to how many are likely to seek religious exemptions from the dress code.

In these circumstances, deference seems unwarranted. Reasoned military judgments, of course, are entitled to respect, but the military has failed to show that this particular judgment with respect to Captain Goldman is a reasoned one. If, in the future, the Air Force is besieged with requests for [528] religious exemptions from the dress code, and those requests cannot be distinguished on functional grounds from Goldman's, the service may be able to argue credibly that circumstances warrant a flat rule against any visible religious apparel. That, however, would be a case different from the one at hand.

39

Edwards v. Aguillard

482 U.S. 578 (1987)

Vote: 7—Brennan, White, Marshall, Blackmun, Powell, Stevens, O'Connor
2—Rehnquist, Scalia

Opinion announcing the opinion of the Court: Brennan
Concurring opinion: Powell
Opinion concurring in the judgment: White
Dissenting opinion: Scalia

In order to protect academic freedom, the state of Louisiana adopted the Creationism Act in 1981. The act required the state's public schools to give "balanced treatment" to "creation science" and "evolution science." It defined these as the scientific evidences for creation and evolution and inferences from those scientific evidences, but the statute did not define "creation" or "evolution." The law did not require a school to teach either creation science or evolution science; rather, it provided that if either one was taught, the other must also be taught. Under the statute, "creation scientists" were to develop and supply curriculum guides and research services for creation science. The statute also forbade school boards to discriminate against creation scientists and those who taught "creationism."

BRENNAN, J., delivered the opinion of the Court, in which MARSHALL, BLACKMUN, POWELL, and STEVENS, JJ., joined, and in all but Part II of which O'CONNOR, J., joined.

. . . [582] II

The Establishment Clause forbids the enactment of any law "respecting an establishment of religion." The Court [583] has applied a three-pronged test to determine whether legislation comports with the Establishment Clause. First, the legislature must have adopted the law with a secular purpose. Second, the statute's principal or primary effect must be one that neither advances nor inhibits religion. Third, the statute must not result in an excessive entanglement of government with religion. *Lemon v. Kurtzman,*

403 U.S. 602, 612–613 (1971).[4] State action violates the Establishment Clause if it fails to satisfy any of these prongs.

In this case, the Court must determine whether the Establishment Clause was violated in the special context of the public elementary and secondary school system. States and local school boards are generally afforded considerable discretion in operating public schools. "At the same time . . . we have necessarily recognized that the discretion of the States and local school boards in matters of education must be exercised in a manner that comports with the transcendent imperatives of the First Amendment." *Board of Education, Island Trees Union Free School Dist. No. 26 v. Pico*, 457 U.S. 853, 864 (1982).

The Court has been particularly vigilant in monitoring compliance with the Establishment Clause in elementary and [584] secondary schools. Families entrust public schools with the education of their children, but condition their trust on the understanding that the classroom will not purposely be used to advance religious views that may conflict with the private beliefs of the student and his or her family. Students in such institutions are impressionable and their attendance is involuntary. The State exerts great authority and coercive power through mandatory attendance requirements, and because of the students' emulation of teachers as role models and the children's susceptibility to peer pressure.[5] Furthermore, "the public school is at once the symbol of our democracy and the most pervasive means for promoting our common destiny. In no activity of the State is it more vital to keep out divisive forces than in its schools. . . ." *Illinois ex rel. McCollum v. Board of Education*, 333 U.S. 203, 231 (1948) (opinion of Frankfurter, J.). . . .

[585] III

Lemon's first prong focuses on the purpose that animated adoption of the Act. "The purpose prong of the *Lemon* test asks whether government's actual purpose is to endorse or disapprove of religion." *Lynch v. Donnelly*, 465 U.S. 668, 690 (1984) (O'CONNOR, J., concurring). A governmental intention to promote religion is clear when the State enacts a law to serve a religious purpose. This intention may be evidenced by promotion of religion in general, see *Wallace v. Jaffree*, at 52–53 (Establishment Clause protects individual freedom of conscience "to select any religious faith or none at all"), or by advancement of a particular religious belief, *e.g.*, *Stone v. Graham*, at 41 (invalidating requirement to post Ten Commandments, which are "undeniably a sacred text in the Jewish and Christian faiths"); *Epperson v. Arkansas*, at 106 (holding that banning the teaching of evolution in public schools violates the First Amendment since "teaching and learning" must not "be tailored to the principles or prohibitions of any religious sect or dogma"). If the law was enacted for the purpose of endorsing religion, "no consideration of the second or third criteria [of *Lemon*] is necessary." *Wallace v. Jaffree*, at 56. In this case, appellants have identified no clear secular purpose for the Louisiana Act.

---

4. The *Lemon* test has been applied in all cases since its adoption in 1971, except in *Marsh v. Chambers* (1983), where the Court held that the Nebraska Legislature's practice of opening a session with a prayer by a chaplain paid by the State did not violate the Establishment Clause. The Court based its conclusion in that case on the historical acceptance of the practice. Such a historical approach is not useful in determining the proper roles of church and state in public schools, since free public education was virtually nonexistent at the time the Constitution was adopted.

5. The potential for undue influence is far less significant with regard to college students who voluntarily enroll in courses. "This distinction warrants a difference in constitutional results." *Abington School Dist. v. Schempp*, at 253 (BRENNAN, J., concurring). Thus, for instance, the Court has not questioned the authority of state colleges and universities to offer courses on religion or theology.

[586] True, the Act's stated purpose is to protect academic freedom. This phrase might, in common parlance, be understood as referring to enhancing the freedom of teachers to teach what they will. The Court of Appeals, however, correctly concluded that the Act was not designed to further that goal. We find no merit in the State's argument that the "legislature may not [have] used the terms 'academic freedom' in the correct legal sense. They might have [had] in mind, instead, a basic concept of fairness; teaching all of the evidence." Even if "academic freedom" is read to mean "teaching all of the evidence" with respect to the origin of human beings, the Act does not further this purpose. The goal of providing a more comprehensive science curriculum is not furthered either by outlawing the teaching of evolution or by requiring the teaching of creation science.

A

While the Court is normally deferential to a State's articulation of a secular purpose, it is required that the statement [587] of such purpose be sincere and not a sham.

It is clear from the legislative history that the purpose of the legislative sponsor, Senator Bill Keith, was to narrow the science curriculum. During the legislative hearings, Senator Keith stated: "My preference would be that neither [creationism nor evolution] be taught." Such a ban on teaching does not promote—indeed, it undermines—the provision of a comprehensive scientific education.

It is equally clear that requiring schools to teach creation science with evolution does not advance academic freedom. The Act does not grant teachers a flexibility that they did not already possess to supplant the present science curriculum with the presentation of theories, besides evolution, about the origin of life. Indeed, the Court of Appeals found that no law prohibited Louisiana public school teachers from teaching any scientific theory. As the president of the Louisiana Science Teachers Association testified, "any scientific concept that's based on established fact can be included in our curriculum already, and no legislation allowing this is necessary." The Act provides Louisiana schoolteachers with no new authority. Thus the stated purpose is not furthered by it. . . .

[588] If the Louisiana Legislature's purpose was solely to maximize the comprehensiveness and effectiveness of science instruction, it would have encouraged the teaching of all scientific theories about the origins of humankind.[8] But under [589] the Act's requirements, teachers who were once free to teach any and all facets of this subject are now unable to do so. Moreover, the Act fails even to ensure that creation science will be taught, but instead requires the teaching of this theory only when the theory of evolution is taught. Thus we agree with the Court of Appeals' conclusion that the Act does not serve to protect academic freedom, but has the distinctly different purpose of discrediting "evolution by counterbalancing its teaching at every turn with the teaching of creationism. . . ." 765 F.2d, at 1257.

---

8. The dissent concludes that the Act's purpose was to protect the academic freedom of students, and not that of teachers. *Post*, at 628. Such a view is not at odds with our conclusion that if the Act's purpose was to provide comprehensive scientific education (a concern shared by students and teachers, as well as parents), that purpose was not advanced by the statute's provisions. *Supra*, at 587.

Moreover, it is astonishing that the dissent, to prove its assertion, relies on a section of the legislation that was eventually deleted by the legislature. Compare § 3702 in 1 App. E-292 (text of section prior to amendment) with La. Rev. Stat. Ann. § 17:286.2 (West 1982). The dissent contends that this deleted section—which was explicitly rejected by the Louisiana Legislature—reveals the legislature's "obviously intended meaning of the statutory terms 'academic freedom.'" *Post*, at 628. Quite to the contrary, Boudreaux, the main expert relied on by the sponsor of the Act, cautioned the legislature that the words "academic freedom" meant "freedom to teach science." His testimony was given at the time the legislature was deciding whether to delete this section of the Act.

B

. . . [591] The preeminent purpose of the Louisiana Legislature was clearly to advance the religious viewpoint that a supernatural being created humankind. The term "creation science" was defined as embracing this particular religious doctrine by those responsible for the passage of the Creationism Act. Senator Keith's leading expert on creation science, Edward Boudreaux, testified at the legislative hearings that the theory of creation science included belief in the existence of a supernatural creator. Senator Keith also cited testimony from other experts to support the creation-science view that "a creator [was] responsible for the universe and everything in it." The legislative history [592] therefore reveals that the term "creation science," as contemplated by the legislature that adopted this Act, embodies the religious belief that a supernatural creator was responsible for the creation of humankind.

Furthermore, it is not happenstance that the legislature required the teaching of a theory that coincided with this religious view. The legislative history documents that the Act's primary purpose was to change the science curriculum of public schools in order to provide persuasive advantage to a particular religious doctrine that rejects the factual basis of evolution in its entirety. The sponsor of the Creationism Act, Senator Keith, explained during the legislative hearings that his disdain for the theory of evolution resulted from the support that evolution supplied to views contrary to his own religious beliefs. According to Senator Keith, the theory of evolution was consonant with the "cardinal principle[s] of religious humanism, secular humanism, theological liberalism, aetheistism [*sic*]." The state senator repeatedly stated that scientific evidence supporting his religious views should be included in the public school curriculum to redress the fact that the theory of evolution incidentally coincided with what he characterized as religious beliefs antithetical to his own. The [593] legislation therefore sought to alter the science curriculum to reflect endorsement of a religious view that is antagonistic to the theory of evolution.

In this case, the purpose of the Creationism Act was to restructure the science curriculum to conform with a particular religious viewpoint. Out of many possible science subjects taught in the public schools, the legislature chose to affect the teaching of the one scientific theory that historically has been opposed by certain religious sects. As in *Epperson*, the legislature passed the Act to give preference to those religious groups which have as one of their tenets the creation of humankind by a divine creator. The "overriding fact" that confronted the Court in *Epperson* was "that Arkansas' law selects from the body of knowledge a particular segment which it proscribes for the sole reason that it is deemed to conflict with . . . a particular interpretation of the Book of Genesis by a particular religious group." 393 U.S., at 103. Similarly, the Creationism Act is designed *either* to promote the theory of creation science which embodies a particular religious tenet by requiring that creation science be taught whenever evolution is taught *or* to prohibit the teaching of a scientific theory disfavored by certain religious sects by forbidding the teaching of evolution when creation science is not also taught. The Establishment Clause, however, "forbids *alike* the preference of a religious doctrine *or* the prohibition of theory which is deemed antagonistic to a particular dogma." *Id.*, at 106–107 (emphasis added). Because the primary purpose of the Creationism Act is to advance a particular religious belief, the Act endorses religion in violation of the First Amendment.

We do not imply that a legislature could never require that scientific critiques of prevailing scientific theories be taught. Indeed, the Court acknowledged in *Stone* that its decision [594] forbidding the posting of the Ten Commandments did not mean that no use could ever be made of the Ten Commandments, or that the Ten Commandments played an exclusively religious role in the history of Western Civilization. In a similar way, teaching a variety of scientific theories about the origins of humankind to schoolchildren might be validly done with the clear secular intent of enhancing the effectiveness of science instruction. But because the primary purpose of the Creationism Act is to endorse a particular religious doctrine, the Act furthers religion in violation of the Establishment Clause. . . .

[610] JUSTICE SCALIA, with whom THE CHIEF JUSTICE joins, dissenting.

Even if I agreed with the questionable premise that legislation can be invalidated under the Establishment Clause on the basis of its motivation alone, without regard to its effects, I would still find no justification for today's decision. The Louisiana legislators who passed the "Balanced Treatment for Creation-Science and Evolution-Science Act" (Balanced Treatment Act), each of whom had sworn to support the Constitution, were well aware of the potential Establishment Clause problems and considered that aspect of the legislation with great care. After seven hearings and several months of study, resulting in substantial revision of the original proposal, they approved the Act overwhelmingly and specifically articulated the secular purpose they meant it to serve. Although the record contains abundant evidence of the sincerity of that purpose (the only issue pertinent to this case), the Court today holds, essentially on the basis of "its visceral knowledge regarding what *must* have motivated the legislators," 778 F.2d 225, 227 (CA5 1985) (Gee, J., dissenting) (emphasis added), that the members of the Louisiana Legislature knowingly violated their oaths and then lied about it. I dissent. Had requirements of the Balanced Treatment Act that [611] are not apparent on its face been clarified by an interpretation of the Louisiana Supreme Court, or by the manner of its implementation, the Act might well be found unconstitutional; but the question of its constitutionality cannot rightly be disposed of on the gallop, by impugning the motives of its supporters.

I

. . . [612] Like the Court of Appeals, the Court finds it necessary to consider only the motives of the legislators who supported the Balanced Treatment Act. After examining the statute, its legislative history, and its historical and social context, the Court holds that the Louisiana Legislature acted without "a secular legislative purpose" and that the Act therefore fails the "purpose" prong of the three-part test set forth in *Lemon v. Kurtzman* (1971). As I explain below, [613] I doubt whether that "purpose" requirement of *Lemon* is a proper interpretation of the Constitution; but even if it were, I could not agree with the Court's assessment that the requirement was not satisfied here.

This Court has said little about the first component of the *Lemon* test. Almost invariably, we have effortlessly discovered a secular purpose for measures challenged under the Establishment Clause, typically devoting no more than a sentence or two to the matter. In fact, only once before deciding *Lemon*, and twice since, have we invalidated a law for lack of a secular purpose. See *Wallace v. Jaffree* (1985); *Stone v. Graham* (1980); *Epperson v. Arkansas* (1968).

Nevertheless, a few principles have emerged from our cases, principles which should, but to an unfortunately large extent do not, guide the Court's application of *Lemon* today. It is clear, first of all, that regardless of what "legislative purpose" may mean in other contexts, for the purpose of the *Lemon* test it means the "actual" motives of those responsible for the challenged action. The Court recognizes this, see *ante*, at 585, as it has in the past, see, *e.g.*, *Witters v. Washington Dept. of Services for Blind*, at 486; *Wallace v. Jaffree*, at 56. [614] Thus, if those legislators who supported the Balanced Treatment Act *in fact* acted with a "sincere" secular purpose, *ante*, at 587, the Act survives the first component of the *Lemon* test, regardless of whether that purpose is likely to be achieved by the provisions they enacted.

Our cases have also confirmed that when the *Lemon* Court referred to "a secular . . . purpose," 403 U.S., at 612, it meant "*a* secular purpose." The author of *Lemon*, writing for the Court, has said that invalidation under the purpose prong is appropriate when "there [is] *no question* that the statute or activity was motivated *wholly* by religious considerations." *Lynch v. Donnelly*, 465 U.S. 668, 680 (1984) (Burger, C. J.) (emphasis added). In all three cases in which we struck down laws under the Establishment Clause for lack of a secular purpose, we found that the legislature's sole motive was to promote religion. Thus, the majority's invalidation of the Balanced Treatment Act is defensible only if the record indicates that the Louisiana Legislature had *no* secular purpose.

It is important to stress that the purpose forbidden by *Lemon* is the purpose to "advance religion." 403 U.S., at 613. [615] Our cases in no way imply that the Establishment Clause forbids legislators merely to act upon their religious convictions. We surely would not strike down a law providing money to feed the hungry or shelter the homeless if it could be demonstrated that, but for the religious beliefs of the legislators, the funds would not have been approved. Also, political activism by the religiously motivated is part of our heritage. Notwithstanding the majority's implication to the contrary, *ante*, at 589–591, we do not presume that the sole purpose of a law is to advance religion merely because it was supported strongly by organized religions or by adherents of particular faiths. To do so would deprive religious men and women of their right to participate in the political process. Today's religious activism may give us the Balanced Treatment Act, but yesterday's resulted in the abolition of slavery, and tomorrow's may bring relief for famine victims.

Similarly, we will not presume that a law's purpose is to advance religion merely because it "happens to coincide or harmonize with the tenets of some or all religions," *Harris v. McRae*, at 319 (quoting *McGowan v. Maryland*, 366 U.S. 420, 442 [1961]), or because it benefits religion, even substantially. We have, for example, turned back Establishment Clause challenges to restrictions on abortion funding, *Harris v. McRae*, and to Sunday closing laws, *McGowan v. Maryland*, despite the fact that both "agre[e] with the dictates of [some] Judaeo-Christian religions," *id.*, at 442. . . . [616] Thus, the fact that creation science coincides with the beliefs of certain religions, a fact upon which the majority relies heavily, does not itself justify invalidation of the Act.

Finally, our cases indicate that even certain kinds of governmental actions undertaken with the specific intention of improving the position of religion do not "advance religion" as that term is used in *Lemon*. 403 U.S., at 613. Rather, we have said that in at least two circumstances government *must* act to advance religion, and that in a third it *may* do so.

First, since we have consistently described the Establishment Clause as forbidding not only state action motivated by the desire to *advance* religion, but also that intended to "disapprove," "inhibit," or evince "hostility" toward religion; and since we have said that governmental "neutrality" toward religion is the preeminent goal of the First Amendment, [617] a State which discovers that its employees are inhibiting religion must take steps to prevent them from doing so, even though its purpose would clearly be to advance religion. Thus, if the Louisiana Legislature sincerely believed that the State's science teachers were being hostile to religion, our cases indicate that it could act to eliminate that hostility without running afoul of *Lemon*'s purpose test.

Second, we have held that intentional governmental advancement of religion is sometimes required by the Free Exercise Clause. For example, in *Hobbie v. Unemployment Appeals Comm'n of Fla.* (1987); *Thomas v. Review Bd., Indiana Employment Security Div.* (1981); *Wisconsin v. Yoder* (1972); and *Sherbert v. Verner* (1963), we held that in some circumstances States must accommodate the beliefs of religious citizens by exempting them from generally applicable regulations. We have not yet come close to reconciling *Lemon* and our Free Exercise cases, and typically we do not really try. It is clear, however, that members of the Louisiana Legislature were not impermissibly motivated for purposes of the *Lemon* test if they believed that approval of the Balanced Treatment Act was *required* by the Free Exercise Clause.

We have also held that in some circumstances government may act to accommodate religion, even if that action is not required by the First Amendment. It is well established that "the limits of permissible state accommodation to religion are by no means co-extensive with the noninterference mandated by the Free Exercise Clause." *Walz v. Tax Comm'n of New York City*, at 673. [618] We have implied that voluntary governmental accommodation of religion is not only permissible, but desirable. Thus, few would contend that Title VII of the Civil Rights Act of 1964, which both forbids religious discrimination by private-sector employers and requires them reasonably to accommodate the religious practices of their employees violates the Establishment Clause, even though its "purpose" is, of course, to advance religion, and even though it is almost certainly not required by the Free Exercise Clause. While we have warned that at some point, accommodation may devolve into "an unlawful fostering of religion," *Hobbie v. Unemployment Appeals Comm'n of Fla.*, at 145, we have not suggested precisely (or even roughly) where that point might be. It is possible, then, that even if the sole motive of those voting for the Balanced Treatment Act was to advance religion, and its passage was not actually required, or even believed to be required, by either the Free Exercise or Establishment Clauses, the Act would nonetheless survive scrutiny under *Lemon*'s purpose test. . . .

[619] With the foregoing in mind, I now turn to the purposes underlying adoption of the Balanced Treatment Act.

II . . .

[626] B

. . . [628] As originally introduced, the "purpose" section of the Balanced Treatment Act read: "This Chapter is enacted for the purposes of protecting academic freedom . . . *of students* . . . and assisting *students* in their search for truth" (emphasis added). Among the proposed findings of fact contained in the original version of the bill was the following: "Public school instruction in only evolution-science . . . *violates the principle of academic freedom because it denies students a choice between scientific models and instead indoctrinates them in evolution science alone*" (emphasis added).[5] Senator Keith unquestionably understood "academic freedom" to mean "freedom from indoctrination."

---

5. The majority finds it "astonishing" that I would cite a portion of Senator Keith's original bill that was later deleted as evidence of the legislature's understanding of the phrase "academic freedom." *Ante*, at 589, n. 8. What is astonishing is the majority's implication that the deletion of that section deprives it of value as a clear indication of what the phrase meant—there and in the other, retained, sections of the bill. The Senate Committee on Education deleted most of the lengthy "purpose" section of the bill (with Senator Keith's consent) because it resembled legislative "findings of fact," which, committee members felt, should generally not be incorporated in legislation. The deletion had absolutely nothing to do with the manner in which the section described "academic freedom."

If one adopts the obviously intended meaning of the statutory term "academic freedom," there is no basis whatever for concluding that the purpose they express is a "sham." *Ante*, [629] at 587. To the contrary, the Act pursues that purpose plainly and consistently. . . .

The Act's reference to "creation" is not convincing evidence of religious purpose. The Act defines creation science as "*scientific evidenc[e]*" (emphasis added), and Senator Keith and his witnesses repeatedly stressed that the subject can and should be presented without religious content. We have no basis on the record to conclude that creation science need be anything other than a collection of scientific data supporting the theory that life abruptly appeared on earth. Creation science, its proponents insist, no more must explain *whence* life came than evolution must explain whence came the inanimate materials from which it says life evolved. But even if that were not so, to posit a past creator is not to posit the eternal and personal God who is the object of religious veneration. [630] Indeed, it is not even to posit the "*unmoved* mover" hypothesized by Aristotle and other notably nonfundamentalist philosophers. Senator Keith suggested this when he referred to "a creator *however you define a creator*" (emphasis added). . . .

[633] In sum, even if one concedes, for the sake of argument, that a majority of the Louisiana Legislature voted for the Balanced Treatment Act partly in order to foster (rather [634] than merely eliminate discrimination against) Christian fundamentalist beliefs, our cases establish that that alone would not suffice to invalidate the Act, so long as there was a genuine secular purpose as well. We have, moreover, no adequate basis for disbelieving the secular purpose set forth in the Act itself, or for concluding that it is a sham enacted to conceal the legislators' violation of their oaths of office. I am astonished by the Court's unprecedented readiness to reach such a conclusion, which I can only attribute to an intellectual predisposition created by the facts and the legend of *Scopes v. State*, 154 Tenn. 105 (1927)—an instinctive reaction that any governmentally imposed requirements bearing upon the teaching of evolution must be a manifestation of Christian fundamentalist repression. In this case, however, it seems to me the Court's position is the repressive one. The people of Louisiana, including those who are Christian fundamentalists, are quite entitled, as a secular matter, to have whatever scientific evidence there may be against evolution presented in their schools, just as Mr. Scopes was entitled to present whatever scientific evidence there was for it. Perhaps what the Louisiana Legislature has done is unconstitutional because there *is* no such evidence, and the scheme they have established will amount to no more than a presentation of the Book of Genesis. But we cannot say that on the evidence before us in this summary judgment context, which includes ample uncontradicted testimony that "creation science" is a body of scientific knowledge rather than revealed belief. *Infinitely less* can we say (or should we say) that the scientific evidence for evolution is so conclusive that no one could be gullible enough to believe that there is any real scientific evidence to the contrary, so that the legislation's stated purpose must be a lie. Yet that illiberal judgment, that *Scopes*-in-reverse, is ultimately the basis on which the Court's facile rejection of the Louisiana Legislature's purpose must rest. . . .

[636] Because I believe that the Balanced Treatment Act had a secular purpose, which is all the first component of the *Lemon* test requires, I would reverse the judgment of the Court of Appeals and remand for further consideration.

III

. . . I have to this point assumed the validity of the *Lemon* "purpose" test. In fact, however, I think the pessimistic evaluation that THE CHIEF JUSTICE made of the totality of *Lemon* is particularly applicable to the "purpose" prong: it is "a constitutional theory [that] has no basis in the history of the amendment it seeks to interpret, is difficult to apply and yields unprincipled results. . . ." *Wallace v. Jaffree*, 472 U.S., at 112 (REHNQUIST, J., dissenting).

Our cases interpreting and applying the purpose test have made such a maze of the Establishment Clause that even the most conscientious governmental officials can only guess what motives will be held unconstitutional. We have said essentially the following: Government may not act with the purpose of advancing religion, except when forced to do so by the Free Exercise Clause (which is now and then); or when eliminating existing governmental hostility to religion (which exists sometimes); or even when merely accommodating governmentally uninhibited religious practices, except that at some point (it is unclear where) intentional accommodation results in the fostering of religion, which is of course unconstitutional.

But the difficulty of knowing what vitiating purpose one is looking for is as nothing compared with the difficulty of knowing how or where to find it. For while it is possible to discern the objective "purpose" of a statute (i.e., the public good at which its provisions appear to be directed), or even the formal motivation for a statute where that is explicitly set forth (as it was, to no avail, here), discerning the subjective motivation of those enacting the statute is, to be honest, almost always an impossible task. The number of possible [637] motivations, to begin with, is not binary, or indeed even finite. In the present case, for example, a particular legislator need not have voted for the Act either because he wanted to foster religion or because he wanted to improve education. He may have thought the bill would provide jobs for his district, or may have wanted to make amends with a faction of his party he had alienated on another vote, or he may have been a close friend of the bill's sponsor, or he may have been repaying a favor he owed the Majority Leader, or he may have hoped the Governor would appreciate his vote and make a fundraising appearance for him, or he may have been pressured to vote for a bill he disliked by a wealthy contributor or by a flood of constituent mail, or he may have been seeking favorable publicity, or he may have been reluctant to hurt the feelings of a loyal staff member who worked on the bill, or he may have been settling an old score with a legislator who opposed the bill, or he may have been mad at his wife who opposed the bill, or he may have been intoxicated and utterly *un*motivated when the vote was called, or he may have accidentally voted "yes" instead of "no," or, of course, he may have had (and very likely did have) a combination of some of the above and many other motivations. To look for *the sole purpose* of even a single legislator is probably to look for something that does not exist.

Putting that problem aside, however, where ought we to look for the individual legislator's purpose? We cannot of course assume that every member present (if, as is unlikely, we know who or even how many they were) agreed with the motivation expressed in a particular legislator's preenactment floor or committee statement. Quite obviously, "what motivates one legislator to make a speech about a statute is not necessarily what motivates scores of others to enact it." *United States v. O'Brien*, 391 U.S. 367, 384 (1968). Can we assume, then, that they all agree with the motivation expressed in the staff-prepared committee reports they might have read—even though we are unwilling to [638] assume that they agreed with the motivation expressed in the very statute that they voted for? Should we consider postenactment floor statements? Or postenactment testimony from legislators, obtained expressly for the lawsuit? Should we consider media reports on the realities of the legislative bargaining? All of these sources, of course, are eminently manipulable. Legislative histories can be contrived and sanitized, favorable media coverage orchestrated, and postenactment recollections conveniently distorted. Perhaps most valuable of all would be more objective indications—for example, evidence regarding the individual legislators' religious affiliations. And if that, why not evidence regarding the fervor or tepidity of their beliefs?

Having achieved, through these simple means, an assessment of what individual legislators intended, we must still confront the question (yet to be addressed in any of our cases) how *many* of them must have the invalidating intent. If a state senate approves a bill by vote of 26 to 25, and only one of the 26 intended solely to advance religion, is the law unconstitutional? What if 13 of the 26 had that intent? What if 3 of the 26 had the impermissible intent, but 3 of the 25 voting against the bill were motivated by religious hostility or were simply attempting to "balance" the votes of their impermissibly motivated colleagues? Or is it possible that the intent of the bill's sponsor is alone enough to invalidate it—on a theory, perhaps, that even though everyone else's intent was pure, what they produced was the fruit of a forbidden tree?

Because there are no good answers to these questions, this Court has recognized from Chief Justice Marshall, see *Fletcher v. Peck*, 6 Cranch 87, 130 (1810), to Chief Justice Warren, *United States v. O'Brien*, at 383–384, that determining the subjective intent of legislators is a perilous enterprise. It is perilous, I might note, not just for the judges who will very likely reach the wrong result, [639] but also for the legislators who find that they must assess the validity of proposed legislation—and risk the condemnation of having voted for an unconstitutional measure—not on the basis of what the legislation contains, nor even on the basis of what they themselves intend, but on the basis of what *others* have in mind.

Given the many hazards involved in assessing the subjective intent of governmental decisionmakers, the first prong of *Lemon* is defensible, I think, only if the text of the Establishment Clause demands it. That is surely not the case. The Clause states that "Congress shall make no law respecting an establishment of religion." One could argue, I suppose, that any time Congress acts with the *intent* of advancing religion, it has enacted a "law respecting an establishment of religion"; but far from being an unavoidable reading, it is quite an unnatural one. I doubt, for example, that the Clayton Act as amended could reasonably be described as a "law respecting an establishment of religion" if bizarre new historical evidence revealed that it lacked a secular purpose, even though it has no discernible nonsecular effect. It is, in short, far from an inevitable reading of the Establishment Clause that it forbids all governmental action intended to advance religion; and if not inevitable, any reading with such untoward consequences must be wrong.

In the past we have attempted to justify our embarrassing Establishment Clause jurisprudence on the ground that it [640] "sacrifices clarity and predictability for flexibility." *Committee for Public Education & Religious Liberty v. Regan*, 444 U.S., at 662. One commentator has aptly characterized this as "a euphemism . . . for . . . the absence of any principled rationale."* I think it time that we sacrifice some "flexibility" for "clarity and predictability." Abandoning *Lemon*'s purpose test—a test which exacerbates the tension between the Free Exercise and Establishment Clauses, has no basis in the language or history of the Amendment, and, as today's decision shows, has wonderfully flexible consequences—would be a good place to start.

---

*Scalia's reference is to Jesse Choper, *The Religion Clauses of the First Amendment: Reconciling the Conflict*, 41 U. Pitt. L. Rev. 673, 681 (1980).

40

Corporation of the Presiding Bishop of the Church of Jesus Christ of Latter-Day Saints v. Amos

483 U.S. 327 (1987)

Vote: 9—Rehnquist, Brennan, White, Marshall, Blackmun, Powell, Stevens, O'Connor, Scalia

0

Opinion announcing the opinion of the Court: White
Opinions concurring in the judgment: Brennan, Blackmun, O'Connor

Arthur Frank Mayson worked at the Deseret Gymnasium in Salt Lake City, Utah, for sixteen years as an assistant building engineer and then as building engineer. The gymnasium was a nonprofit facility, open to the public, run by the Corporation of the Presiding Bishop of the Church of Jesus Christ of Latter-Day Saints (CPB) and the Corporation of the President of the Church of Jesus Christ of Latter-Day Saints (COP). The CPB and the COP were "corporations sole" organized under Utah law to perform various activities on behalf of the Church of Jesus Christ of Latter-Day Saints (Church), an unincorporated religious association sometimes called the Mormon or LDS Church.

Mayson was fired his job in 1981 because he failed to qualify for a "temple recommend." Temple recommends are issued only to individuals who observe the LDS Church's standards in matters such as regular church attendance, tithing, and abstinence from coffee, tea, alcohol, and tobacco. They certify that an individual is a member of the LDS Church and eligible to attend its temples.

Mayson brought legal action against the CPB and the COP, alleging, among other things, discrimination on the basis of religion in violation of § 703 of the Civil Rights Act of 1964. The corporations moved to dismiss the claim on the ground that they were shielded from liability under § 702 of the act, which exempts religious organizations from the prohibition of § 703. Section 702 provides in relevant part:

> *This subchapter [prohibiting religious discrimination in employment] shall not apply . . . to a religious corporation, association, educational institution, or society with respect to the employment of individuals of a particular religion to perform work connected with the carrying on by such corporation, association, educational institution, or society of its activities.*

JUSTICE WHITE delivered the opinion of the Court, in which REHNQUIST, C. J., and POWELL, STEVENS, and SCALIA, JJ., joined.

[329] Section 702 of the Civil Rights Act of 1964, 78 Stat. 255, as amended, 42 U.S.C. § 2000e-1, exempts religious organizations from Title VII's prohibition against discrimination in employment on the basis of religion. The question presented [330] is whether applying the § 702 exemption to the secular nonprofit activities of religious organizations violates the Establishment Clause of the First Amendment. The District Court held that it does, and these cases are here on direct appeal pursuant to 28 U.S.C. § 1252. We reverse. . . .

[334] II

"This Court has long recognized that the government may (and sometimes must) accommodate religious practices and that it may do so without violating the Establishment Clause." *Hobbie v. Unemployment Appeals Comm'n of Fla.*, 480 U.S. 136, 144–145 (1987). It is well established, too, that "the limits of permissible state accommodation to religion are by no means co-extensive with the noninterference mandated by the Free Exercise Clause." *Walz v. Tax Comm'n*, 397 U.S. 664, 673 (1970). There is ample room under the Establishment Clause for "benevolent neutrality which will permit religious exercise to exist without sponsorship and without interference." *Id.*, at 669. At some point, accommodation may devolve into "an unlawful [335] fostering of religion," *Hobbie*, at 145, but these are not such cases, in our view.

The private appellants contend that we should not apply the three-part *Lemon* approach, which is assertedly unsuited to judging the constitutionality of exemption statutes such as § 702. The argument is that an exemption statute will always have the effect of advancing religion and hence be invalid under the second (effects) part of the *Lemon* test, a result claimed to be inconsistent with cases such as *Walz v. Tax Comm'n*, which upheld property tax exemptions for religious organizations. The first two of the three *Lemon* factors, however, were directly taken from pre-*Walz* decisions, 403 U.S., at 612–613, and *Walz* did not purport to depart from prior Establishment Clause cases, except by adding a consideration that became the third element of the *Lemon* test. 403 U.S., at 613. In any event, we need not reexamine *Lemon* as applied in this context, for the exemption involved here is in no way questionable under the *Lemon* analysis.

Lemon requires first that the law at issue serve a "secular legislative purpose." *Id.*, at 612. This does not mean that the law's purpose must be unrelated to religion—that would amount to a requirement "that the government show a callous indifference to religious groups," *Zorach v. Clauson*, 343 U.S. 306, 314 (1952), and the Establishment Clause has never been so interpreted. Rather, *Lemon*'s "purpose" requirement aims at preventing the relevant governmental decisionmaker—in this case, Congress—from abandoning neutrality and acting with the intent of promoting a particular point of view in religious matters.

Under the *Lemon* analysis, it is a permissible legislative purpose to alleviate significant governmental interference with the ability of religious organizations to define and carry out their religious missions. Appellees argue that there is no such purpose here because § 702 provided adequate protection for religious employers prior to the 1972 amendment, [336] when it exempted only the religious activities of such employers from the statutory ban on religious discrimination. We may assume for the sake of argument that the pre-1972 exemption was adequate in the sense that the Free Exercise Clause required no more. Nonetheless, it is a significant burden on a religious organization to require it, on pain of substantial liability, to predict which of its activities a secular court will consider religious. The line is hardly a bright one, and an organization might understandably be concerned that a judge would not understand its religious tenets and sense of mission. Fear of potential liability might affect the way an organization carried out what it understood to be its religious mission.

After a detailed examination of the legislative history of the 1972 amendment, the District Court concluded that Congress' purpose was to minimize governmental "interfer[ence] with the decision-making process in religions." We agree with the District Court that this purpose does not violate the Establishment Clause.

The second requirement under *Lemon* is that the law in question have "a principal or primary effect . . . that neither advances nor inhibits religion." 403 U.S., at 612. Undoubtedly, religious organizations are better able now to advance their purposes than they were prior to the 1972 amendment to § 702. But religious groups have been better able to advance their purposes on account of many laws that have passed constitutional muster: for example, the property tax exemption at issue in *Walz v. Tax Comm'n*, or the loans of schoolbooks to schoolchildren, including parochial school students, upheld in *Board of Education v. Allen*, [337] (1968). A law is not unconstitutional simply because it *allows* churches to advance religion, which is their very purpose. For a law to have forbidden "effects" under *Lemon*, it must be fair to say that the *government itself* has advanced religion through its own activities and influence. As the Court observed in *Walz*, "for the men who wrote the Religion Clauses of the First Amendment the 'establishment' of a religion connoted sponsorship, financial support, and active involvement of the sovereign in religious activity." 397 U.S., at 668. Accord, *Lemon*, 403 U.S., at 612.

The District Court appeared to fear that sustaining the exemption would permit churches with financial resources impermissibly to extend their influence and propagate their faith by entering the commercial, profit-making world. The cases before us, however, involve a nonprofit activity instituted over 75 years ago in the hope that "all who assemble here, and who come for the benefit of their health, and for physical blessings, [may] feel that they are in a house dedicated to the Lord." *Dedicatory Prayer for the Gymnasium.* These cases therefore do not implicate the apparent concerns of the District Court. Moreover, we find no persuasive evidence in the record before us that the Church's ability to propagate its religious doctrine through the Gymnasium is any greater now than it was prior to the passage of the Civil Rights Act in 1964. In such circumstances, we do not see how any advancement of religion achieved by the Gymnasium can be fairly attributed to the Government, as opposed to the Church.

[338] We find unpersuasive the District Court's reliance on the fact that § 702 singles out religious entities for a benefit. Although the Court has given weight to this consideration in its past decisions, it has never indicated that statutes that give special consideration to religious groups are *per se* invalid. That would run contrary to the teaching of our cases that there is ample room for accommodation of religion under the Establishment Clause. Where, as here, government acts with the proper purpose of lifting a regulation that burdens the exercise of religion, we see no reason to require that the exemption come packaged with benefits to secular entities. . . .

[339] It cannot be seriously contended that § 702 impermissibly entangles church and state; the statute effectuates a more complete separation of the two and avoids the

kind of intrusive inquiry into religious belief that the District Court engaged in in this case. The statute easily passes muster under the third part of the *Lemon* test.[17] . . .

JUSTICE BRENNAN, with whom JUSTICE MARSHALL joins, concurring in the judgment.

[340] I write separately to emphasize that my concurrence in the judgment rests on the fact that these cases involve a challenge to the application of § 702's categorical exemption to the activities of a *nonprofit* organization. I believe that the particular character of nonprofit activity makes inappropriate a case-by-case determination whether its nature is religious or secular.

These cases present a confrontation between the rights of religious organizations and those of individuals. Any exemption from Title VII's proscription on religious discrimination necessarily has the effect of burdening the religious liberty of prospective and current employees. An exemption says that a person may be put to the choice of either conforming to certain religious tenets or losing a job opportunity, a promotion, or, as in these cases, employment itself. [341] The potential for coercion created by such a provision is in serious tension with our commitment to individual freedom of conscience in matters of religious belief.

At the same time, religious organizations have an interest in autonomy in ordering their internal affairs, so that they may be free to:

"select their own leaders, define their own doctrines, resolve their own disputes, and run their own institutions. Religion includes important communal elements for most believers. They exercise their religion through religious organizations, and these organizations must be protected by the [Free Exercise] Clause." Laycock, *Towards a General Theory of Religion Clauses: The [342] Case of Church Labor Relations and the Right to Church Autonomy*, 81 Colum. L. Rev. 1373, 1389 (1981).

For many individuals, religious activity derives meaning in large measure from participation in a larger religious community. Such a community represents an ongoing tradition of shared beliefs, an organic entity not reducible to a mere aggregation of individuals. Determining that certain activities are in furtherance of an organization's religious mission, and that only those committed to that mission should conduct them, is thus a means by which a religious community defines itself. Solicitude for a church's ability to do so reflects the idea that furtherance of the autonomy of religious organizations often furthers individual religious freedom as well.

The authority to engage in this process of self-definition inevitably involves what we normally regard as infringement on free exercise rights, since a religious organization is able to condition employment in certain activities on subscription to particular religious tenets. We are willing to countenance the imposition of such a condition because we deem it vital that, if certain activities constitute part of a religious community's practice, then a religious organization should be able to [343] require that only members of its community perform those activities.

This rationale suggests that, ideally, religious organizations should be able to discriminate on the basis of religion *only* with respect to religious activities, so that a determina-

---

17. We have no occasion to pass on the argument of the COP and the CPB that the exemption to which they are entitled under § 702 is required by the Free Exercise Clause. . . .

tion should be made in each case whether an activity is religious or secular. This is because the infringement on religious liberty that results from conditioning performance of *secular* activity upon religious belief cannot be defended as necessary for the community's self-definition. Furthermore, the authorization of discrimination in such circumstances is not an accommodation that simply enables a church to gain members by the normal means of prescribing the terms of membership for those who seek to participate in furthering the mission of the community. Rather, it puts at the disposal of religion the added advantages of economic leverage in the secular realm. As a result, the authorization of religious discrimination with respect to nonreligious activities goes beyond reasonable accommodation, and has the effect of furthering religion in violation of the Establishment Clause.

What makes the application of a religious-secular distinction difficult is that the character of an activity is not self-evident. As a result, determining whether an activity is religious or secular requires a searching case-by-case analysis. This results in considerable ongoing government entanglement in religious affairs. Furthermore, this prospect of government intrusion raises concern that a religious organization may be chilled in its free exercise activity. While a church may regard the conduct of certain functions as integral to its mission, a court may disagree. A religious organization therefore would have an incentive to characterize as religious only those activities about which there likely would be no dispute, even if it genuinely believed that religious commitment was important in performing other tasks as well. As a result, the community's process [344] of self-definition would be shaped in part by the prospects of litigation. A case-by-case analysis for all activities therefore would both produce excessive government entanglement with religion and create the danger of chilling religious activity.

The risk of chilling religious organizations is most likely to arise with respect to *nonprofit* activities. The fact that an operation is not organized as a profit-making commercial enterprise makes colorable a claim that it is not purely secular in orientation. In contrast to a for-profit corporation, a nonprofit organization must utilize its earnings to finance the continued provision of the goods or services it furnishes, and may not distribute any surplus to the owners. This makes plausible a church's contention that an entity is not operated simply in order to generate revenues for the church, but that the activities themselves are infused with a religious purpose. Furthermore, unlike for-profit corporations, nonprofits historically have been organized specifically to provide certain community services, not simply to engage in commerce. Churches often regard the provision of such services as a means of fulfilling religious duty and of providing an example of the way of life a church seeks to foster.

[345] Nonprofit activities therefore are most likely to present cases in which characterization of the activity as religious or secular will be a close question. If there is a danger that a religious organization will be deterred from classifying as religious those activities it actually regards as religious, it is likely to be in this domain. This substantial potential for chilling religious activity makes inappropriate a case-by-case determination of the character of a nonprofit organization, and justifies a categorical exemption for nonprofit activities. Such an exemption demarcates a sphere of deference with respect to those activities most likely to be religious. It permits infringement on employee free exercise rights in those instances in which discrimination is most likely to reflect a religious community's self-definition. While not every nonprofit activity may be operated for religious purposes, the likelihood that many are makes a categorical rule a suitable means to avoid chilling the exercise of religion.[6]

---

6. It is also conceivable that some for-profit activities could have a religious character, so that religious discrimination with respect to these activities would be justified in some cases. The cases before us, how-

Sensitivity to individual religious freedom dictates that religious discrimination be permitted only with respect to employment in religious activities. Concern for the autonomy of religious organizations demands that we avoid the entanglement and the chill on religious expression that a case-by-case determination would produce. We cannot escape the fact that these aims are in tension. Because of the nature of nonprofit activities, I believe that a categorical exemption for [346] such enterprises appropriately balances these competing concerns. As a result, I concur in the Court's judgment that the nonprofit Deseret Gymnasium may avail itself of an automatic exemption from Title VII's proscription on religious discrimination.

JUSTICE BLACKMUN, concurring in the judgment.

Essentially for the reasons set forth in JUSTICE O'CONNOR's opinion, particularly the third and final paragraphs thereof, I, too, concur in the judgment of the Court. I fully agree that the distinction drawn by the Court seems "to obscure far more than to enlighten," as JUSTICE O'CONNOR states, *post*, at 347, and that, surely, the "question of the constitutionality of the § 702 exemption as applied to for-profit activities of religious organizations remains open," *post*, at 349.

JUSTICE O'CONNOR, concurring in the judgment.

Although I agree with the judgment of the Court, I write separately to note that this action once again illustrates certain difficulties inherent in the Court's use of the test articulated in *Lemon v. Kurtzman*, 403 U.S. 602, 612–613 (1971). As a result of this problematic analysis, while the holding of the opinion for the Court extends only to nonprofit organizations, its reasoning fails to acknowledge that the amended § 702, 42 U.S.C. § 2000e-1, raises different questions as it is applied to profit and nonprofit organizations.

In *Wallace v. Jaffree*, I noted a tension in the Court's use of the *Lemon* test to evaluate an Establishment Clause challenge to government efforts to accommodate the free exercise of religion:

> "On the one hand, a rigid application of the *Lemon* test would invalidate legislation exempting religious observers from generally applicable government obligations. [347] By definition, such legislation has a religious purpose and effect in promoting the free exercise of religion. On the other hand, judicial deference to all legislation that purports to facilitate the free exercise of religion would completely vitiate the Establishment Clause. Any statute pertaining to religion can be viewed as an 'accommodation' of free exercise rights." *Wallace v. Jaffree*, at 82.

In my view, the opinion for the Court leans toward the second of the two unacceptable options described above. While acknowledging that "undoubtedly, religious organizations are better able now to advance their purposes than they were prior to the 1972 amendment to § 702," the Court seems to suggest that the "effects" prong of the *Lemon* test is not at all implicated as long as the government action can be characterized as "allowing" religious organizations to advance religion, in contrast to government action

---

ever, involve a nonprofit organization; I believe that a *categorical* exemption authorizing discrimination is particularly appropriate for such entities, because claims that they possess a religious dimension will be especially colorable.

directly advancing religion. *Ante*, at 337. This distinction seems to me to obscure far more than to enlighten. Almost any government benefit to religion could be recharacterized as simply "allowing" a religion to better advance itself, unless perhaps it involved actual proselytization by government agents. In nearly every case of a government benefit to religion, the religious mission would not be advanced if the religion did not take advantage of the benefit; even a direct financial subsidy to a religious organization would not advance religion if for some reason the organization failed to make any use of the funds. It is for this same reason that there is little significance to the Court's observation that it was the Church rather than the Government that penalized Mayson's refusal to adhere to Church doctrine. The Church had the power to put Mayson to a choice of qualifying for a temple recommend or losing his job because *the Government* had lifted from religious organizations the general regulatory burden imposed by § 702.

[348] The necessary first step in evaluating an Establishment Clause challenge to a government action lifting from religious organizations a generally applicable regulatory burden is to recognize that such government action *does* have the effect of advancing religion. The necessary second step is to separate those benefits to religion that constitutionally accommodate the free exercise of religion from those that provide unjustifiable awards of assistance to religious organizations. As I have suggested in earlier opinions, the inquiry framed by the *Lemon* test should be "whether government's purpose is to endorse religion and whether the statute actually conveys a message of endorsement." *Wallace*, 472 U.S., at 69. To ascertain whether the statute conveys a message of endorsement, the relevant issue is how it would be perceived by an objective observer, acquainted with the text, legislative history, and implementation of the statute. *Id.*, at 76. Of course, in order to perceive the government action as a permissible accommodation of religion, there must in fact be an identifiable burden *on the exercise of religion* that can be said to be lifted by the government action. The determination whether the objective observer will perceive an endorsement of religion "is not a question of simple historical fact. Although evidentiary submissions may help answer it, the question is, like the question whether racial or sex-based classifications communicate an invidious message, in large part a legal question to be answered on the basis of judicial interpretation of social facts." *Lynch v. Donnelly*, at 693–694.

The above framework, I believe, helps clarify why the amended § 702 raises different questions as it is applied to nonprofit and for-profit organizations. As JUSTICE BRENNAN observes in his concurrence: "The fact that an operation is not organized as a profit-making commercial enterprise makes colorable a claim that it is not purely secular in orientation." *Ante*, at 344 (opinion concurring in judgment). These cases involve a Government decision to lift from a nonprofit [349] activity of a religious organization the burden of demonstrating that the particular nonprofit activity is religious as well as the burden of refraining from discriminating on the basis of religion. Because there is a probability that a nonprofit activity of a religious organization will itself be involved in the organization's religious mission, in my view the objective observer should perceive the Government action as an accommodation of the exercise of religion rather than as a Government endorsement of religion.

It is not clear, however, that activities conducted by religious organizations solely as profit-making enterprises will be as likely to be directly involved in the religious mission of the organization. While I express no opinion on the issue, I emphasize that under the holding of the Court, and under my view of the appropriate Establishment Clause analysis, the question of the constitutionality of the § 702 exemption as applied to for-profit activities of religious organizations remains open.

41

Lyng v. Northwest Indian Cemetery Protective Association

485 U.S. 439 (1988)

Vote: 5—Rehnquist, White, Stevens, O'Connor, Scalia
   3—Brennan, Marshall, Blackmun

Opinion announcing the judgment of the Court: O'Connor
Dissenting opinion: Brennan
Not participating in the consideration or decision of the case: Kennedy

As part of a project to create a paved seventy-five-mile road linking the California towns of Gasquet and Orleans, the U.S. Forest Service planned to construct a six-mile paved road through federal land, including the Chimney Rock area of the Six Rivers National Forest. The Forest Service commissioned two studies—one in 1977 on the environmental impact of the proposed project and another in 1979 on American Indian cultural and religious sites in the affected area—that found that the Yurok, Karok, and Tolowa Indians historically had used the area for religious rituals. The 1979 report found that the entire area was "significant as an integral and indispensible [sic] part of Indian religious conceptualization and practice." Particular sites were used for certain rituals, and "successful use of the [area] is dependent upon and facilitated by certain qualities of the physical environment, the most important of which are privacy, silence, and an undisturbed natural setting." It concluded that constructing a road along any of the available routes "would cause serious and irreparable damage to the sacred areas which are an integral and necessary part of the belief systems and lifeway of Northwest California Indian peoples." Accordingly, the 1979 report recommended that the six-mile road not be completed.

 In 1982, the Forest Service decided not to adopt this recommendation and prepared a final environmental-impact statement for construction of the road. The Regional Forester's Office selected a route that avoided archeological sites and was as far removed as possible from the sites used by Native Americans for specific spiritual activities. Alternative routes that would have avoided the Chimney Rock area altogether were rejected because they would have required acquisition of private land, had serious soil-stability problems, and would still have traversed areas of ritualistic value to Native Americans. At about the same time, the Forest Service adopted a management plan allowing for the harvesting of significant amounts of timber in this area of the forest. The management plan also provided for one-half-mile protective zones around all the religious sites identified in the report that had been commissioned in connection with the road.

After exhausting their administrative remedies, respondents—a Native American organization, individual Native Americans, nature organizations and individual members of those organizations, and the state of California—challenged both the road-building and the timber-harvesting decisions. They contended, among other things, that the Forest Service's decisions violated the Free Exercise Clause of the First Amendment.

O'CONNOR, J., delivered the opinion of the Court, in which REHNQUIST, C. J., and WHITE, STEVENS, and SCALIA, JJ., joined.

[441] This case requires us to consider whether the First Amendment's Free Exercise Clause forbids the Government from permitting timber harvesting in, or constructing a road through, a portion of a National Forest that has traditionally [442] been used for religious purposes by members of three American Indian tribes in northwestern California. We conclude that it does not. . . .

[447] III

A

The Free Exercise Clause of the First Amendment provides that "Congress shall make no law . . . prohibiting the free exercise [of religion]." It is undisputed that the Indian respondents' beliefs are sincere and that the Government's proposed actions will have severe adverse effects on the practice of their religion. Respondents contend that the burden on their religious practices is heavy enough to violate the Free Exercise Clause unless the Government can demonstrate a compelling need to complete the G-O road or to engage in timber harvesting in the Chimney Rock area. We disagree.

[448] In *Bowen v. Roy* (1986), we considered a challenge to a federal statute that required the States to use Social Security numbers in administering certain welfare programs. Two applicants for benefits under these programs contended that their religious beliefs prevented them from acceding to the use of a Social Security number for their two-year-old daughter because the use of a numerical identifier would "'rob the spirit' of [their] daughter and prevent her from attaining greater spiritual power." *Id.*, at 696. Similarly, in this case, it is said that disruption of the natural environment caused by the G-O road will diminish the sacredness of the area in question and create distractions that will interfere with "training and ongoing religious experience of individuals using [sites within] the area for personal medicine and growth . . . and as integrated parts of a system of religious belief and practice which correlates ascending degrees of personal power with a geographic hierarchy of power." The Court rejected this kind of challenge in *Roy*:

> "The Free Exercise Clause simply cannot be understood to require the Government to conduct its own internal affairs in ways that comport with the religious beliefs of particular citizens. Just as the Government may not insist that [the Roys] engage in any set form of religious observance, so [they] may not demand that the Government join in their chosen religious practices by refraining from using a number to identify their daughter. . . .
> . . . The Free Exercise Clause affords an individual protection from certain forms of governmental compulsion; it does not afford an individual a right to dictate the conduct of the Government's internal procedures." 476 U.S., at 699–700.

[449] The building of a road or the harvesting of timber on publicly owned land cannot meaningfully be distinguished from the use of a Social Security number in *Roy*. In both cases, the challenged government action would interfere significantly with private persons' ability to pursue spiritual fulfillment according to their own religious beliefs. In neither case, however, would the affected individuals be coerced by the Government's action into violating their religious beliefs; nor would either governmental action penalize religious activity by denying any person an equal share of the rights, benefits, and privileges enjoyed by other citizens. . . .

[450] It is true that this Court has repeatedly held that indirect coercion or penalties on the free exercise of religion, not just outright prohibitions, are subject to scrutiny under the First Amendment. Thus, for example, ineligibility for unemployment benefits, based solely on a refusal to violate the Sabbath, has been analogized to a fine imposed on Sabbath worship. *Sherbert*, at 404. This does not and cannot imply that incidental effects of government programs, which may make it more difficult to practice certain religions but which have no tendency to coerce individuals into acting contrary to their religious beliefs, require government to bring forward a compelling justification [451] for its otherwise lawful actions. The crucial word in the constitutional text is "prohibit": "For the Free Exercise Clause is written in terms of what the government cannot do to the individual, not in terms of what the individual can exact from the government." *Sherbert*, at 412 (Douglas, J., concurring).

Whatever may be the exact line between unconstitutional prohibitions on the free exercise of religion and the legitimate conduct by government of its own affairs, the location of the line cannot depend on measuring the effects of a governmental action on a religious objector's spiritual development. The Government does not dispute, and we have no reason to doubt, that the logging and road-building projects at issue in this case could have devastating effects on traditional Indian religious practices. Those practices are intimately and inextricably bound up with the unique features of the Chimney Rock area, which is known to the Indians as the "high country." Individual practitioners use this area for personal spiritual development; some of their activities are believed to be critically important in advancing the welfare of the tribe, and indeed, of mankind itself. The Indians use this area, as they have used it for a very long time, to conduct a wide variety of specific rituals that aim to accomplish their religious goals. According to their beliefs, the rituals would not be efficacious if conducted at other sites than the ones traditionally used, and too much disturbance of the area's natural state would clearly render any meaningful continuation of traditional practices impossible. To be sure, the Indians themselves were far from unanimous in opposing the G-O road, and it seems less than certain that construction of the road will be so disruptive that it will doom their religion. Nevertheless, we can assume that the threat to the efficacy of at least some religious practices is extremely grave.

Even if we assume that we should accept the Ninth Circuit's prediction, according to which the G-O road will "virtually destroy the Indians' ability to practice their religion," 795 F.2d, at 693 [452] (opinion below), the Constitution simply does not provide a principle that could justify upholding respondents' legal claims. However much we might wish that it were otherwise, government simply could not operate if it were required to satisfy every citizen's religious needs and desires. A broad range of government activities—from social welfare programs to foreign aid to conservation projects—will always be considered essential to the spiritual well-being of some citizens, often on the basis of sincerely held religious beliefs. Others will find the very same activities deeply offensive, and perhaps incompatible with their own search for spiritual fulfillment and with the tenets of their religion. The First Amendment must apply to all citizens alike, and it can give to none of them a veto over public programs that do not prohibit the free exercise of religion. The Constitution does not, and courts cannot, offer to reconcile the various competing demands on government, many of them rooted in sincere religious belief, that inevitably arise in so diverse a society as ours. That task, to the extent that it is feasible, is for the legislatures and other institutions. Cf. *The Federalist* No. 10 (suggesting that the effects of religious factionalism are best restrained through competition among a multiplicity of religious sects). . . .

[453] The Constitution does not permit government to discriminate against religions that treat particular physical sites as sacred, and a law forbidding the Indian respondents from visiting the Chimney Rock area would raise a different set of constitutional questions. Whatever rights the Indians may have to the use of the area, however, those rights do not divest the Government of its right to use what is, after all, its land. . . .

[456] C

The dissent proposes an approach to the First Amendment that is fundamentally inconsistent with the principles on which our decision rests. Notwithstanding the sympathy that we all must feel for the plight of the Indian respondents, it is plain that the approach taken by the dissent cannot withstand analysis. On the contrary, the path towards which it points us is incompatible with the text of the Constitution, with the precedents of this Court, and with a responsible sense of our own institutional role.

The dissent begins by asserting that the "constitutional guarantee we interpret today . . . is directed against *any* form of government action that frustrates or inhibits religious practice." *Post*, at 459 (emphasis added). The Constitution, however, says no such thing. Rather, it states: "Congress shall make no law . . . *prohibiting* the free exercise [of religion]" (emphasis added). . . .

[457] Perceiving a "stress point in the longstanding conflict between two disparate cultures," the dissent attacks us for declining to "balance these competing and potentially irreconcilable interests, choosing instead to turn this difficult task over to the federal legislature." *Post*, at 473. Seeing the Court as the arbiter, the dissent proposes a legal test under which it would decide which public lands are "central" or "indispensable" to which religions, and by implication which are "dispensable" or "peripheral," and would then decide which government programs are "compelling" enough to justify "infringement of those practices." *Post*, at 475. We would accordingly be required to weigh the value of every religious belief and practice that is said to be threatened by any government program. Unless a "showing of 'centrality,'" *post*, at 474, is nothing but an assertion of centrality, see *post*, at 475, the dissent thus offers us the prospect of this Court holding that some sincerely held religious beliefs and practices are not "central" to certain religions, despite protestations to the contrary from the religious objectors who brought the lawsuit. In other words, the dissent's approach would [458] require us to rule that some religious adherents misunderstand their own religious beliefs. We think such an approach cannot be squared with the Constitution or with our precedents, and that it would cast the judiciary in a role that we were never intended to play. . . .

JUSTICE BRENNAN, with whom JUSTICE MARSHALL and JUSTICE BLACKMUN join, dissenting.

"The Free Exercise Clause," the Court explains today, "is written in terms of what the government cannot do to the individual, not in terms of what the individual can exact from the government." *Ante,* at 451 (quoting *Sherbert v. Verner,* 374 U.S. 398, 412 [1963] [Douglas, J., concurring]). Pledging fidelity to this unremarkable constitutional principle, the Court nevertheless concludes that even where the Government uses federal land in a manner that threatens the very existence of a Native American religion, the Government is simply not "doing" anything to the practitioners of that faith. Instead, the Court believes that Native Americans who request that the Government refrain from destroying their religion effectively seek to exact from the Government de facto beneficial ownership of federal property. These two astonishing conclusions follow naturally from the Court's determination [459] that federal land-use decisions that render the practice of a given religion impossible do not burden that religion in a manner cognizable under the Free Exercise Clause, because such decisions neither coerce conduct inconsistent with religious belief nor penalize religious activity. The constitutional guarantee we interpret today, however, draws no such fine distinctions between types of restraints on religious exercise, but rather is directed against any form of governmental action that frustrates or inhibits religious practice. Because the Court today refuses even to acknowledge the constitutional injury respondents will suffer, and because this refusal essentially leaves Native Americans with absolutely no constitutional protection against perhaps the gravest threat to their religious practices, I dissent.

I

For at least 200 years and probably much longer, the Yurok, Karok, and Tolowa Indians have held sacred an approximately 25-square-mile area of land situated in what is today the Blue Creek Unit of Six Rivers National Forest in northwestern California. As the Government readily concedes, regular visits to this area, known to respondent Indians as the "high country," have played and continue to play a "critical" role in the religious practices and rituals of these tribes. Those beliefs, only briefly described in the Court's opinion, are crucial to a proper understanding of respondents' claims.

As the Forest Service's commissioned study, the Theodoratus Report, explains, for Native Americans religion is not a discrete sphere of activity separate from all others, and any attempt to isolate the religious aspects of Indian life "is in reality an exercise which forces Indian concepts into non-Indian categories." D. Theodoratus, *Cultural Resources of the Chimney Rock Section, Gasquet-Orleans Road, Six Rivers National Forest* (1979). Thus, for most Native Americans, "the area of worship cannot be delineated from [460] social, political, cultural and other areas of Indian lifestyle." American Indian Religious Freedom, Hearings on S. J. Res. 102 before the Select Committee on Indian Affairs, 95th Cong., 2d Sess., 86 (statement of Barney Old Coyote, Crow Tribe). A pervasive feature of this lifestyle is the individual's relationship with the natural world; this relationship, which can accurately though somewhat incompletely be characterized as one of stewardship, forms the core of what might be called, for want of a better nomenclature, the Indian religious experience. While traditional western religions view creation as the work of a deity "who institutes natural laws which then govern the operation of physical nature," tribal religions regard creation as an ongoing process in which they are morally and religiously obligated to participate. U.S. Federal Agencies Task Force, American Indian Religious Freedom Act Report 11 (1979) (Task Force Report). Native Americans fulfill this duty through ceremonies and rituals designed to preserve and stabilize the earth and to protect humankind from disease and other catastrophes. Failure to conduct these ceremonies in the manner and place specified, adherents believe, will result in great harm to the earth and to the people whose welfare depends upon it.

In marked contrast to traditional western religions, the belief systems of Native Americans do not rely on doctrines, creeds, or dogmas. Established or universal truths—the mainstay of western religions—play no part in Indian faith. Ceremonies are communal efforts undertaken for specific purposes in accordance with instructions handed down from generation to generation. Commentaries on or interpretations of the rituals themselves are deemed absolute violations of the ceremonies, whose value lies not in their ability to explain the natural world or to enlighten individual believers but in their efficacy as protectors and enhancers of tribal existence. Where dogma lies at the heart of western religions, Native American faith is inextricably [461] bound to the use of land. The site-specific nature of Indian religious practice derives from the Native American perception that land is itself a sacred, living being. Rituals are performed in prescribed locations not merely as a matter of traditional orthodoxy, but because land, like all other living things, is unique, and specific sites possess different spiritual properties and significance. Within this belief system, therefore, land is not fungible; indeed, at the time of the Spanish colonization of the American southwest, "all . . . Indians held in some form a belief in a sacred and indissoluble bond between themselves and the land in which their settlements were located." E. Spicer, *Cycle of Conquest: The Impact of Spain, Mexico, and the United States on the Indians of the United States* 576 (1962).

For respondent Indians, the most sacred of lands is the high country where, they believe, pre-human spirits moved with the coming of humans to the earth. Because these spirits are seen as the source of religious power, or "medicine," many of the tribes' rituals and practices require frequent journeys to the area. Thus, for example, religious leaders preparing for the complex of ceremonies that underlie the tribes' World Renewal efforts must travel to specific sites in the high country in order to attain the medicine necessary for successful renewal. Similarly, individual tribe members may seek curative powers for the healing of the sick, or personal medicine for particular purposes such as good luck in singing, hunting, or love. A period of preparation generally precedes such visits, and individuals must select trails in the sacred area according to the medicine they seek and their abilities, gradually moving to increasingly more powerful sites, which are typically located at higher altitudes. Among the most powerful of sites are Chimney Rock, Doctor Rock, and Peak 8, all of which are elevated rock outcroppings.

[462] According to the Theodoratus Report, the qualities "of silence, the aesthetic perspective, and the physical attributes, are an extension of the sacredness of [each] particular site." The act of medicine making is akin to meditation: the individual must integrate physical, mental and vocal actions in order to communicate with the pre-human spirits. As a result, "successful use of the high country is dependent upon and facilitated by certain qualities of the physical environment, the most important of which are privacy, silence, and an undisturbed natural setting." *Id.*, at 181. Although few tribe members actually make medicine at the most powerful sites, the entire tribe's welfare hinges on the success of the individual practitioners. . . .

[465] II

The Court does not for a moment suggest that the interests served by the G-O road are in any way compelling, or that they outweigh the destructive effect construction of the road will have on respondents' religious practices. Instead, the Court embraces the Government's contention that its prerogative as landowner should always take precedence over a claim that a particular use of federal property infringes religious practices. Attempting to justify this rule, the Court argues that the First Amendment bars only outright prohibitions, indirect coercion, and penalties on the free exercise of religion. All other "incidental effects of government programs," it concludes, even those "which may make it more difficult to practice certain religions but which have no tendency to coerce individuals into acting contrary to their religious beliefs," simply do not give rise to constitutional concerns. See *ante*, at 450. Since our recognition nearly half a century ago that restraints on religious conduct implicate the concerns of the Free Exercise Clause, see *Prince v. Massachusetts* (1944), we have never suggested that the protections of the guarantee are limited to so narrow a range of governmental burdens. The land-use decision challenged here will restrain respondents from practicing their religion as surely and as completely as any of the governmental actions we have struck down in the past, and the Court's efforts simply to define away respondents' injury [466] as nonconstitutional is both unjustified and ultimately unpersuasive.

A

. . . [467] Respondents here have demonstrated that construction of the G-O road will completely frustrate the practice of their religion, for as the lower courts found, the proposed logging and construction activities will virtually destroy [468] respondents' religion, and will therefore necessarily force them into abandoning those practices altogether. Indeed, the Government's proposed activities will restrain religious practice to a far greater degree here than in any of the cases cited by the Court today. None of the religious adherents in *Hobbie, Thomas*, and *Sherbert*, for example, claimed or could have claimed that the denial of unemployment benefits rendered the practice of their religions impossible; at most, the challenged laws made those practices more expensive. Here, in stark contrast, respondents have claimed—and proved—that the desecration of the high country will prevent religious leaders from attaining the religious power or medicine indispensable to the success of virtually all their rituals and ceremonies. Similarly, in *Yoder* the compulsory school law threatened to "undermine the Amish community and religious practice," and thus to force adherents to "abandon belief . . . or . . . to migrate to some other and more tolerant religion." 406 U.S., at 218. Here the threat posed by the desecration of sacred lands that are indisputably essential to respondents' religious practices is both more direct and more substantial than that raised by a compulsory school law that simply exposed Amish children to an alien value system. And of course respondents here do not even have the option, however unattractive it might be, of migrating to more hospitable locales; the site-specific nature of their belief system renders it non-transportable.

Ultimately, the Court's coercion test turns on a distinction between governmental actions that compel affirmative conduct inconsistent with religious belief, and those governmental actions that prevent conduct consistent with religious belief. In my view, such a distinction is without constitutional significance. The crucial word in the constitutional text, as the Court itself acknowledges, is "prohibit," see *ante*, at 451, a comprehensive term that in no way suggests that the intended protection is aimed only at governmental actions that coerce affirmative conduct.[4] Nor does the Court's distinction

---

4. The Court is apparently of the view that the term "prohibit" in the Free Exercise Clause somehow limits the constitutional protection such that it cannot possibly be understood to reach "*any* form of government action that frustrates or inhibits religious practice." *Ante*, at 456 (quoting, at 459) (emphasis added by majority). Although the dictionary is hardly the final word on the meaning of constitutional language, it is noteworthy that Webster's includes, as one of the two accepted definitions of "prohibit," "to prevent from doing something." *Webster's Ninth New Collegiate Dictionary* 940 (1983). Government action that frustrates or inhibits religious practice fits far more comfortably within this definition than does the Court's affirmative compulsion test.

comport with the principles animating the constitutional guarantee: religious freedom is threatened no less by governmental action that makes the practice of one's chosen faith impossible than by governmental programs that pressure one to engage in conduct inconsistent with religious beliefs. The Court attempts to explain the line it draws by arguing that the protections of the Free Exercise Clause "cannot depend on measuring the effects of a governmental action on a religious objector's spiritual development," *ibid.*, [469] for in a society as diverse as ours, the Government cannot help but offend the "religious needs and desires" of some citizens. *Ante*, at 452. While I agree that governmental action that simply offends religious sensibilities may not be challenged under the Clause, we have recognized that laws that affect spiritual development by impeding the integration of children into the religious community or by increasing the expense of adherence to religious principles—in short, laws that frustrate or inhibit religious practice—trigger the protections of the constitutional guarantee. Both common sense and our prior cases teach us, therefore, that governmental action that makes the practice of a given faith more difficult necessarily penalizes that practice and thereby tends to prevent adherence to religious belief. The harm to the practitioners is the same regardless of the manner in which the Government restrains their religious expression, and the Court's fear that an "effects" test will permit religious adherents to challenge governmental actions they merely find "offensive" in no way justifies its refusal to recognize the constitutional injury citizens suffer when governmental action not only offends but actually restrains their religious practices. Here, respondents have demonstrated that the Government's proposed activities will completely prevent them from practicing their religion, and such a showing, no less than those made out in *Hobbie, Thomas, Sherbert,* and *Yoder,* entitles them to the protections of the Free Exercise Clause.

B

Nor can I agree with the Court's assertion that respondents' constitutional claim is foreclosed by our decision in *Bowen v. Roy* (1986). There, applicants for certain welfare benefits objected to the use of a Social Security number in connection with the administration of their two year old daughter's application for benefits, contending that such use would "rob the [child's] spirit" and thus interfere with her spiritual development. In rejecting that challenge, [470] we stated that "the Free Exercise Clause simply cannot be understood to require the Government to conduct its own *internal affairs* in ways that comport with the religious beliefs of particular citizens." *Id.*, at 699 (emphasis added). . . .

Today the Court professes an inability to differentiate *Roy* from the present case, suggesting that "the building of a road or the harvesting of timber on publicly owned land cannot be meaningfully distinguished from the use of a Social Security number." *Ante*, at 449. I find this inability altogether remarkable. In *Roy*, we repeatedly stressed the "internal" nature of the Government practice at issue: noting that *Roy* objected to "the widespread use of the social security number by the federal or state governments *in their computer systems*," at 697 (emphasis added), we likened the use of such recordkeeping numbers to decisions concerning the purchase of office equipment. When the Government processes information, of course, it acts in a purely internal manner, and any free exercise challenge to such internal recordkeeping in effect seeks to dictate how the Government conducts its own affairs.

Federal land-use decisions, by contrast, are likely to have substantial external effects that government decisions concerning [471] office furniture and information storage obviously will not, and they are correspondingly subject to public scrutiny and public challenge in a host of ways that office equipment purchases are not. . . .

[473] C

In the final analysis, the Court's refusal to recognize the constitutional dimension of respondents' injuries stems from its concern that acceptance of respondents' claim could potentially strip the Government of its ability to manage and use vast tracts of federal property. See *ante*, at 452–453. In addition, the nature of respondents' site-specific religious practices raises the specter of future suits in which Native Americans seek to exclude all human activity from such areas. These concededly legitimate concerns lie at the very heart of this case, which represents yet another stress point in the longstanding conflict between two disparate cultures—the dominant western culture, which views land in terms of ownership and use, and that of Native Americans, in which concepts of private property are not only alien, but contrary to a belief system that holds land sacred. Rather than address this conflict in any meaningful fashion, however, the Court disclaims all responsibility for balancing these competing and potentially irreconcilable interests, choosing instead to turn this difficult task over to the federal legislature. Such an abdication is more than merely indefensible as an institutional matter: by defining respondents' injury as "non-constitutional," the Court has effectively bestowed on one party to this conflict the unilateral authority to resolve all future disputes in its favor, subject only to the Court's toothless exhortation to be "sensitive" to affected religions. In my view, however, Native Americans deserve—and the Constitution demands—more than this. . . .

[475] [I]n my view, while Native Americans need not demonstrate, as respondents did here, that the Government's land-use decision will assuredly eradicate their faith, I do not think it is enough to allege simply that the land in question is held sacred. Rather, adherents challenging a proposed use of federal land should be required to show that the decision poses a substantial and realistic threat of frustrating their religious practices. Once such a showing is made, the burden should shift to the Government to come forward with a compelling state interest sufficient to justify the infringement of those practices.

The Court today suggests that such an approach would place courts in the untenable position of deciding which practices and beliefs are "central" to a given faith and which are not, and invites the prospect of judges advising some religious adherents that they "misunderstand their own religious beliefs." *Ante*, at 458. In fact, however, courts need not undertake any such inquiries: like all other religious adherents, Native Americans would be the arbiters of which practices are central to their faith, subject only to the normal requirement that their claims be genuine and sincere. The question for the courts, then, is not whether the Native American claimants understand their own religion, but rather, whether they have discharged their burden of demonstrating, as the Amish did with respect to the compulsory school law in *Yoder*, that the land-use decision poses a substantial and realistic threat of undermining or frustrating their religious practices. Ironically, the Court's apparent solicitude for the integrity of religious belief and its desire to forestall the possibility that courts might second-guess the [476] claims of religious adherents leads to far greater inequities than those the Court postulates: today's ruling sacrifices a religion at least as old as the Nation itself, along with the spiritual well-being of its approximately 5,000 adherents, so that the Forest Service can build a six-mile segment of road that two lower courts found had only the most marginal and speculative utility, both to the Government itself and to the private lumber interests that might conceivably use it. . . .

42

Texas Monthly, Inc. v. Bullock

489 U.S. 1 (1989)

Vote: 6—Brennan, White, Marshall, Blackmun, Stevens, O'Connor
    3—Rehnquist, Scalia, Kennedy

Opinion announcing the judgment of the Court: Brennan
Opinions concurring in the judgment: White, Blackmun
Dissenting opinion: Scalia

Texas law exempted from sales and use taxes "periodicals . . . published or distributed by a religious faith . . . consist[ing] wholly of writings promulgating the teachings of the faith and books . . . consist[ing] wholly of writings sacred to a religious faith." In 1985, Texas Monthly, Inc., a nonreligious publisher of a general interest magazine that did not qualify for an exemption, filed suit claiming that the exemption, among other things, violated the Establishment Clause as made applicable to the state of Texas through the Fourteenth Amendment.

JUSTICE BRENNAN announced the judgment of the Court and delivered an opinion, in which JUSTICE MARSHALL and JUSTICE STEVENS join.

[5] Texas exempts from its sales tax "[p]eriodicals that are published or distributed by a religious faith and that consist wholly of writings promulgating the teaching of the faith and books that consist wholly of writings sacred to a religious faith." The question presented is whether this exemption violates the Establishment Clause or the Free Press Clause of the First Amendment when the State denies a like exemption for other publications. We hold that, when confined exclusively to publications advancing the tenets of a religious faith, the exemption runs afoul of the Establishment Clause; accordingly, we need not reach the question whether it contravenes the Free Press Clause as well. . . .

[8] III

In proscribing all laws "respecting an establishment of religion," the Constitution prohibits, at the very least, legislation that constitutes an endorsement of one or another set of religious beliefs or of religion generally. It is part of our settled jurisprudence that "the Establishment Clause prohibits government from abandoning secular purposes in order to put an imprimatur on one religion, or on religion as such, or [9] to favor the adherents of any sect or religious organization." *Gillette v. United States*, 401 U.S. 437, 450 (1971). The core notion animating the requirement that a statute possess "a secular legislative purpose" and that "its principal or primary effect . . . be one that neither advances nor inhibits religion," *Lemon v. Kurtzman*, 403 U.S., at 612, is not only that government may not be overtly hostile to religion but also that it may not place its prestige, coercive authority, or resources behind a single religious faith or behind religious belief in general, compelling nonadherents to support the practices or proselytizing of favored religious organizations and conveying the message that those who do not contribute gladly are less than full members of the community.

[10] It does not follow, of course, that government policies with secular objectives may not incidentally benefit religion. The nonsectarian aims of government and the interests of religious groups often overlap, and this Court has never required that public authorities refrain from implementing reasonable measures to advance legitimate secular goals merely because they would thereby relieve religious groups of costs they would otherwise incur. Nor have we required that legislative categories make no explicit reference to religion. Government need not resign itself to ineffectual diffidence because of exaggerated fears of contagion of or by religion, so long as neither intrudes unduly into the affairs of the other. . . .

[14] Texas' sales tax exemption for periodicals published or distributed by a religious faith and consisting wholly of writings promulgating the teaching of the faith lacks sufficient breadth to pass scrutiny under the Establishment Clause. Every tax exemption constitutes a subsidy that affects nonqualifying taxpayers, forcing them to become "indirect and vicarious 'donors.'" *Bob Jones University v. United States*, 461 U.S. 574, 591 (1983). Insofar as that subsidy is conferred upon a wide array of nonsectarian groups as well as religious organizations in pursuit of some legitimate secular end,[4] the fact that religious groups [15] benefit incidentally does not deprive the subsidy of the secular purpose and primary effect mandated by the Establishment Clause. However, when government directs a subsidy exclusively to religious organizations that is not required by the Free Exercise Clause and that either burdens nonbeneficiaries markedly or cannot reasonably be seen as removing a significant state-imposed deterrent to the free exercise of religion, as Texas has done, it "provide[s] unjustifiable awards of assistance to religious organizations" and cannot but "conve[y] a message of endorsement" to slighted members of the community. *Corporation of Presiding Bishop of Church of Jesus Christ of Latter-Day Saints v. Amos*, 483 U.S. 327, 348 (1987) (O'Connor, J., concurring in judgment). This is particularly true where, as here, the subsidy is targeted at writings that *promulgate* the teachings of religious faiths. It is difficult to view Texas' narrow exemption as anything but state sponsorship of religious belief, regardless of whether one adopts the perspective of beneficiaries or of uncompensated contributors.

How expansive the class of exempt organizations or activities must be to withstand constitutional assault depends upon the State's secular aim in granting a tax exemption.

---

4. The fact that Texas grants other sales tax exemptions (e.g., for sales of food, agricultural items, and property used in the manufacture of articles for ultimate sale) for *different* purposes does not rescue the exemption for religious periodicals from invalidation. What is crucial is that any subsidy afforded religious organizations be warranted by some overarching secular purpose that justifies like benefits for nonreligious groups. There is no evidence in the record, and Texas does not argue in its brief to this Court, that the exemption for religious periodicals was grounded in some secular legislative policy that motivated similar tax breaks for nonreligious activities. It certainly appears that the exemption was intended to benefit religion alone.

If the State chose to subsidize, by means of a tax exemption, all groups that contributed to the community's cultural, intellectual, and moral betterment, then the exemption for religious publications could be retained, provided that the exemption swept as widely as the property tax exemption we upheld in [16] *Walz*. By contrast, if Texas sought to promote reflection and discussion about questions of ultimate value and the contours of a good or meaningful life, then a tax exemption would have to be available to an extended range of associations whose publications were substantially devoted to such matters; the exemption could not be reserved for publications dealing solely with religious issues, let alone restricted to publications advocating rather than criticizing religious belief or activity, without signaling an endorsement of religion that is offensive to the principles informing the Establishment Clause. . . .

[25] JUSTICE WHITE, concurring in the judgment.

The Texas law at issue here discriminates on the basis of the content of publications: it provides that "[p]eriodicals . . . that consist wholly of writings promulgating the teaching of [a religious faith] . . . are exempted" from the burdens of the sales tax law. Thus, [26] the content of a publication determines whether its publisher is exempt or nonexempt. Appellant is subject to the tax, but other publications are not because of the message they carry. This is plainly forbidden by the Press Clause of the First Amendment. *Arkansas Writers' Project, Inc. v. Ragland* (1987), our most recent decision to this effect, is directly applicable here, and is the proper basis for reversing the judgment below.

JUSTICE BLACKMUN, with whom JUSTICE O'CONNOR joins, concurring in the judgment.

The Texas statute at issue touches upon values that underlie three different Clauses of the First Amendment: the Free Exercise Clause, the Establishment Clause, and the Press Clause. As indicated by the number of opinions issued in this case today, harmonizing these several values is not an easy task.

The Free Exercise Clause value suggests that a State may not impose a tax on spreading the gospel. See *Follett v. McCormick* (1944) and *Murdock v. Pennsylvania* (1943). The Establishment Clause value suggests that a State may not give a tax break to those who spread the gospel that it does not also give to others who actively might advocate disbelief in religion. See *Torcaso v. Watkins*, 367 U.S. 488, 495 (1961); *Everson v. Board of Education of Ewing*, 330 U.S. 1, 15–16 (1947). The Press Clause value suggests that a State may not tax the sale of some publications, but not others, based on their content, absent a compelling reason for doing so. See *Arkansas Writers' Project, Inc. v. Ragland*, 481 U.S. 221, 231 (1987).

It perhaps is fairly easy to reconcile the Free Exercise and Press Clause values. If the Free Exercise Clause suggests that a State may not tax the sale of religious literature by a religious organization, this fact alone would give a State a compelling reason to exclude this category of sales from an otherwise general sales tax. In this respect, I agree generally [27] with what Justice Scalia says in Part II of his dissenting opinion.

I find it more difficult to reconcile in this case the Free Exercise and Establishment Clause values. The Free Exercise Clause suggests that a special exemption for religious books is required. The Establishment Clause suggests that a special exemption for religious books is forbidden. This tension between mandated and prohibited religious exemptions is well recognized. Of course, identifying the problem does not resolve it. . . .

Perhaps it is a vain desire, but I would like to decide the present case without necessarily sacrificing either the Free Exercise Clause value or the Establishment Clause value. It is possible for a State to write a tax-exemption statute consistent with both values: for example, a state statute might exempt the sale not only of religious literature distributed by a religious organization but also of philosophical literature distributed by nonreligious organizations devoted to such matters of conscience as life and death, good and evil, being [28] and nonbeing, right and wrong. Such a statute, moreover, should survive Press Clause scrutiny because its exemption would be narrowly tailored to meet the compelling interests that underlie both the Free Exercise and Establishment Clauses.

To recognize this possible reconciliation of the competing First Amendment considerations is one thing; to impose it upon a State as its only legislative choice is something else. Justice Scalia rightly points out, *post*, at 42, that the Free Exercise and Establishment Clauses often appear like Scylla and Charybdis, leaving a State little room to maneuver between them. The Press Clause adds yet a third hazard to a State's safe passage through the legislative waters concerning the taxation of books and journals. We in the Judiciary must be wary of interpreting these three constitutional Clauses in a manner that negates the legislative role altogether.

I believe we can avoid most of these difficulties with a narrow resolution of the case before us. We need not decide today the extent to which the Free Exercise Clause requires a tax exemption for the sale of religious literature by a religious organization; in other words, defining the ultimate scope of *Follett* and *Murdock* may be left for another day. We need decide here only whether a tax exemption *limited to* the sale of religious literature by religious organizations violates the Establishment Clause. I conclude that it does.

In this case, by confining the tax exemption exclusively to the sale of religious publications, Texas engaged in preferential support for the communication of religious messages. Although some forms of accommodating religion are constitutionally permissible, this one surely is not. A statutory preference for the dissemination of religious ideas offends our most basic understanding of what the Establishment Clause is all about and hence is constitutionally intolerable. [29] Accordingly, whether or not *Follett* and *Murdock* prohibit taxing the sale of religious literature, the Establishment Clause prohibits a tax exemption limited to the sale of religious literature. . . .

JUSTICE SCALIA, with whom THE CHIEF JUSTICE and JUSTICE KENNEDY join, dissenting.

As a judicial demolition project, today's decision is impressive. The machinery employed by the opinions of Justice Brennan and Justice Blackmun is no more substantial than the antinomy that accommodation of religion may be required but not permitted, and the bold but unsupportable assertion (given such realities as the text of the Declaration of Independence, the national Thanksgiving Day proclaimed by every President since Lincoln, the inscriptions on our coins, the words of our Pledge of Allegiance, the invocation with [30] which sessions of our Court are opened and, come to think of it, the discriminatory protection of freedom of religion in the Constitution) that government may not "convey a message of endorsement of religion." With this frail equipment, the Court topples an exemption for religious publications of a sort that expressly appears in the laws of at least 15 of the 45 States that have sales and use taxes—States from Maine to Texas, from Idaho to New Jersey. In practice, a similar [31] exemption may well exist in even more States than that, since until today our case law has suggested that it is not only permissible but perhaps required. I expect, for example, that even in States without express exemptions many churches, and many tax assessors, have thought sales taxes inapplicable to the religious literature typically offered for sale in church foyers.

When one expands the inquiry to sales taxes on items other than publications and to other types of taxes such as property, income, amusement, and motor vehicle taxes—all of which are likewise affected by today's holding—the Court's accomplishment is even more impressive. At least 45 States provide exemptions for religious groups without analogous exemptions for other types of nonprofit institutions. For [32] over half a century the federal Internal Revenue Code has allowed "minister[s] of the gospel" (a term interpreted broadly enough to include cantors and rabbis) to exclude from gross [33] income the rental value of their parsonages. In short, religious tax exemptions of the type the Court invalidates today permeate the state and federal codes, and have done so for many years.

I dissent because I find no basis in the text of the Constitution, the decisions of this Court, or the traditions of our people for disapproving this longstanding and widespread practice.

I

... [35] We recognized in *Walz* that the exemption of religion from various taxes had existed without challenge in the law of all 50 States and the National Government before, during, and after the framing of the First Amendment's Religion Clauses, and had achieved "undeviating acceptance" throughout the 200-year history of our Nation. "Few concepts," we said, "are more deeply embedded in the fabric of our national life, beginning with pre-Revolutionary colonial times, than for the government to exercise at the very least this kind of benevolent neutrality toward churches and religious exercise generally so long as none was favored over others and none suffered interference." *Id.*, at 676–677.

[36] It should be apparent from this discussion that *Walz*, which we have reaffirmed on numerous occasions in the last two decades, is utterly dispositive of the Establishment Clause claim before us here. The Court invalidates § 151.312 of the Texas Tax Code only by distorting the holding of that case and radically altering the well-settled Establishment Clause jurisprudence which that case represents. ...

[38] Today's opinions go beyond misdescribing *Walz*, however. In repudiating what *Walz* in fact approved, they achieve a revolution in our Establishment Clause jurisprudence, effectively overruling other cases that were based, as *Walz* was, on the "accommodation of religion" rationale. According to Justice Brennan's opinion, no law is constitutional whose "benefits [are] confined to religious organizations," *ante*, at 11—except, of course, those laws that are unconstitutional *unless* they contain benefits confined to religious organizations, see *ante*, at 17–18. See also Justice Blackmun's opinion, *ante*, at 28. Our jurisprudence affords no support for this unlikely proposition. *Walz* is just one of a long line of cases in which we have recognized that "the government may (and sometimes must) accommodate religious practices and that it may do so without violating the Establishment Clause." *Hobbie v. Unemployment Appeals Comm'n of Fla.*, 480 U.S. 136, 144–145 (1987). In such cases as *Sherbert v. Verner* (1963), *Wisconsin v. Yoder* (1972), *Thomas v. Review Bd. of Ind. Employment Security Div.*, (1981), and *Hobbie v. Unemployment Appeals Comm'n of Fla.*, we held that the Free Exercise Clause of the First Amendment *required* religious beliefs to be accom-

modated by granting religion-specific exemptions from otherwise applicable laws. We have often made clear, however, that "[t]he limits of permissible state accommodation to religion are by no means coextensive with the noninterference mandated by the Free Exercise Clause." *Walz*, 397 U.S., at 673. . . .

[40] It is not always easy to determine when accommodation slides over into promotion, and neutrality into favoritism, but the withholding of a tax upon the dissemination of religious materials is not even a close case. The subjects of the exemption before us consist exclusively of "writings promulgating the teaching of the faith" and "writings sacred to a religious [41] faith." If there is any close question, it is not whether the exemption is permitted, but whether it is constitutionally compelled in order to avoid "interference with the dissemination of religious ideas." *Gillette*, 401 U.S., at 462. In *Murdock v. Pennsylvania* (1943), we held that it was unconstitutional to apply a municipal license tax on door-to-door solicitation to sellers of religious books and pamphlets. One Term later, in *Follett v. McCormick* (1944), we held that it was unconstitutional to apply to such persons a municipal license tax on "[a]gents selling books." Those cases are not as readily distinguishable as Justice Brennan suggests. . . .

I am willing to acknowledge, however, that *Murdock* and *Follett* are narrowly distinguishable. But what follows from that is not the facile conclusion that therefore the State has no "compelling interest in avoiding violations of the Free Exercise [42] and Establishment Clauses," *ante*, at 17, and thus the exemption is invalid. This analysis is yet another expression of Justice Brennan's repudiation of the accommodation principle—which, as described earlier, consists of recognition that "[t]he limits of permissible state accommodation to religion are by no means co-extensive with the noninterference mandated by the Free Exercise Clause." *Walz*, 397 U.S., at 673. By saying that what is not required cannot be allowed, Justice Brennan would completely block off the already narrow "channel between the Scylla [of what the Free Exercise Clause demands] and the Charybdis [of what the Establishment Clause forbids] through which any state or federal action must pass in order to survive constitutional scrutiny." *Thomas*, 450 U.S., at 721 (Rehnquist, J., dissenting). The proper lesson to be drawn from the narrow distinguishing of *Murdock* and *Follett* is quite different: If the exemption comes so close to being a constitutionally required accommodation, there is no doubt that it is at least a permissible one. . . .

[45] * * *

Today's decision introduces a new strain of irrationality in our Religion Clause jurisprudence. I have no idea how to reconcile it with *Zorach* (which seems a much harder case of accommodation), with *Walz* (which seems precisely in point), and with *Corporation of Presiding Bishop* (on which the ink is hardly dry). It is not right—it is not constitutionally healthy—that this Court should feel authorized to refashion anew our civil society's relationship with religion, adopting a theory of church and state that is contradicted by current practice, tradition, and even our own case law. I dissent.

43

County of Allegheny v. American Civil Liberties Union, Greater Pittsburgh Chapter

492 U.S. 573 (1989)

Vote:
Crèche Display
> *5—Brennan, Marshall, Blackmun, Stevens, O'Connor*
> *4—Rehnquist, White, Scalia, Kennedy*

Menorah Display
> *6—Rehnquist, White, Blackmun, O'Connor, Scalia, Kennedy*
> *3—Brennan, Marshall, Stevens*

Opinion announcing the judgment of the Court: Blackmun
Opinion concurring in part and concurring in the judgment: O'Connor
Opinions concurring in part and dissenting in part: Brennan, Stevens
Opinion concurring in the judgment in part and dissenting in part: Kennedy

This case involved Establishment Clause challenges to two recurring holiday displays located on public property in downtown Pittsburgh, Pennsylvania.

The first display, a crèche depicting the Christian Nativity scene, was placed on the Grand Staircase of the Allegheny County Courthouse, a county-owned building. At trial, the staircase was described as the "main," "most beautiful," and "most public" part of the courthouse. The crèche depicted the manger scene in Bethlehem shortly after the birth of Jesus as described in the Gospels of Luke and Matthew. It included figures of the infant Jesus, Mary, Joseph, farm animals, shepherds, and Wise Men, all placed in or before a wooden representation of a manger, which had at its crest an angel bearing a banner that proclaimed "Gloria in Excelsis Deo!" ("Glory to God in the Highest!"). The crèche, donated to the county by the Holy Name Society, a Roman Catholic group, was first displayed in 1981.

During the 1986–1987 holiday season, the crèche was on display on the Grand Staircase from November 26 to January 9. It had a wooden fence on three sides and bore a plaque stating, "This Display Donated by the Holy Name Society." Sometime during the week of December 2, the county placed red and white poinsettia plants around the fence. The county also placed a small evergreen tree, decorated with a red bow, behind each of the two endposts of the fence. These trees stood alongside the manger backdrop and were slightly shorter than it was. The angel thus was at the apex of the crèche display. Altogether, the crèche, the fence, the poinsettias, and the trees occupied a substantial amount of space on the Grand Staircase. No figures of Santa Claus or other decorations appeared on the Grand Staircase.

The county used the crèche as the setting for its annual Christmas-carol program. During the 1986 season, the county invited high school choirs and other musical groups to perform during weekday lunch hours from December 3 through December 23. The county dedicated this program to world peace and to the families of prisoners of war and of persons missing in action in Southeast Asia. Near the Grand Staircase was an area known as the "gallery forum," which was used for art and other cultural exhibits. According to the trial record, the crèche, with its fence-and-floral frame, was distinct from and not connected with any exhibit in the gallery forum. Other departments and offices within the county courthouse had their own Christmas decorations, but those were not visible from the Grand Staircase.

The second display at issue was an eighteen-foot Chanukah menorah, or candelabra, which was placed just outside the City-County Building next to the city's forty-five-foot decorated Christmas tree. The City-County Building is separate and a block removed from the county courthouse, and, as the name implies, it is jointly owned by the city of Pittsburgh and Allegheny County. The city's portion of the building houses the city's principal offices, including the mayor's. The city is responsible for the building's Grant Street entrance, which has three rounded arches supported by columns.

Following a practice that had been in place for a number of years, city employees on November 17, 1986, erected a forty-five-foot tree under the middle arch and decorated it with lights and ornaments. A few days later, the city placed at the foot of the tree a sign bearing the mayor's name and titled "Salute to Liberty." Beneath the title, the sign stated, "During this holiday season, the city of Pittsburgh salutes liberty. Let these festive lights remind us that we are the keepers of the flame of liberty and our legacy of freedom."

At least since 1982, the city had expanded its Grant Street holiday display to include a symbolic representation of Chanukah, an eight-day Jewish holiday that begins on the twenty-fifth day of the Jewish lunar month of Kislev. The twenty-fifth day of Kislev usually occurs in December, and thus Chanukah is the annual Jewish holiday that falls closest to Christmas Day each year. In 1986, Chanukah began at sundown on December 26.

According to Jewish tradition, on the twenty-fifth day of Kislev in 164 BCE, the Maccabees rededicated the Temple of Jerusalem after recapturing it from the Greek-influenced Seleucid Empire in the course of a political rebellion. Chanukah celebrates that event. The celebration's early history remains unclear; it appears that the holiday's central ritual, the lighting of lamps, was well established long before a single explanation of that ritual took hold.

On December 22, 1986, the city placed at the Grant Street entrance to the City-County Building an eighteen-foot Chanukah menorah of an abstract tree-and-branch design. The menorah was placed next to the city's forty-five-foot Christmas tree, against one of the columns that supports the arch into which the tree was set. The tree, the sign, and the menorah were all removed on January 13, 1987.

JUSTICE BLACKMUN announced the judgment of the Court and delivered the opinion of the Court with respect to Parts III-A, IV, and V, an opinion with respect to Parts I and II, in which JUSTICE STEVENS and JUSTICE O'CONNOR join, an opinion with respect to Part III-B, in which JUSTICE STEVENS joins, an opinion with respect to Part VII, in which JUSTICE O'CONNOR joins, and an opinion with respect to Part VI.

[578] This litigation concerns the constitutionality of two recurring holiday displays located on public property in downtown Pittsburgh. The first is a creche placed on the Grand Staircase of the Allegheny County Courthouse. The second is a Chanukah menorah placed just outside the City-County Building, next to a Christmas tree and a sign saluting liberty. The Court of Appeals for the Third Circuit ruled that each display violates the Establishment Clause of the First Amendment because each has the impermissible effect of endorsing religion. [579] We agree that the creche display has that unconstitutional effect but reverse the Court of Appeals' judgment regarding the menorah display. . . .

[III. B]

. . . [597] Since *Lynch*, the Court has made clear that, when evaluating the effect of government conduct under the Establishment Clause, we must ascertain whether "the challenged governmental action is sufficiently likely to be perceived by adherents of the controlling denominations as an endorsement, and by the nonadherents as a disapproval, of their individual religious choices." *Grand Rapids*, 473 U.S., at 390. Accordingly, our present task is to determine whether the display of the creche and the menorah, in their respective "particular physical settings," has the effect of endorsing or disapproving religious beliefs.

[598] IV

We turn first to the county's creche display. There is no doubt, of course, that the creche itself is capable of communicating a religious message. Indeed, the creche in this lawsuit uses words, as well as the picture of the Nativity scene, to make its religious meaning unmistakably clear. "Glory to God in the Highest!" says the angel in the creche—Glory to God because of the birth of Jesus. This praise to God in Christian terms is indisputably religious—indeed sectarian—just as it is when said in the Gospel or in a church service.

Under the Court's holding in *Lynch*, the effect of a creche display turns on its setting. Here, unlike in *Lynch*, nothing in the context of the display detracts from the creche's religious message. The *Lynch* display comprised a series of figures and objects, each group of which had its own focal point. Santa's house and his reindeer were objects of attention separate from the creche, and had their specific visual story to tell. Similarly, whatever a "talking" wishing well may be, it obviously was a center of attention separate from the creche. Here, in contrast, the creche stands alone: it is the single element of the display on the Grand Staircase.

[599] The floral decoration surrounding the creche cannot be viewed as somehow equivalent to the secular symbols in the overall *Lynch* display. The floral frame, like all

good frames, serves only to draw one's attention to the message inside the frame. The floral decoration surrounding the creche contributes to, rather than detracts from, the endorsement of religion conveyed by the creche. It is as if the county had allowed the Holy Name Society to display a cross on the Grand Staircase at Easter, and the county had surrounded the cross with Easter lilies. The county could not say that surrounding the cross with traditional flowers of the season would negate the endorsement of Christianity conveyed by the cross on the Grand Staircase. Its contention that the traditional Christmas greens negate the endorsement effect of the creche fares no better.

Nor does the fact that the creche was the setting for the county's annual Christmas-carol program diminish its religious meaning. First, the carol program in 1986 lasted only from December 3 to December 23 and occupied at most one hour a day. The effect of the creche on those who viewed it when the choirs were not singing—the vast majority of the time—cannot be negated by the presence of the choir program. Second, because some of the carols performed at the site of the creche were religious in nature, those carols were more likely to augment the religious quality of the scene than to secularize it.

Furthermore, the creche sits on the Grand Staircase, the "main" and "most beautiful part" of the building that is the seat of county government. No viewer could reasonably think that it occupies this location without the [600] support and approval of the government. Thus, by permitting the "display of the creche in this particular physical setting," *Lynch*, 465 U.S., at 692 (O'Connor, J., concurring), the county sends an unmistakable message that it supports and promotes the Christian praise to God that is the creche's religious message.

The fact that the creche bears a sign disclosing its ownership by a Roman Catholic organization does not alter this conclusion. On the contrary, the sign simply demonstrates that the government is endorsing the religious message of that organization, rather than communicating a message of its own. But the Establishment Clause does not limit only the religious content of the government's own communications. It also prohibits the government's support and promotion of religious communications by religious organizations. Indeed, the very concept of "endorsement" conveys [601] the sense of promoting someone else's message. Thus, by prohibiting government endorsement of religion, the Establishment Clause prohibits precisely what occurred here: the government's lending its support to the communication of a religious organization's religious message.

Finally, the county argues that it is sufficient to validate the display of the creche on the Grand Staircase that the display celebrates Christmas, and Christmas is a national holiday. This argument obviously proves too much. It would allow the celebration of the Eucharist inside a courthouse on Christmas Eve. While the county may have doubts about the constitutional status of celebrating the Eucharist inside the courthouse under the government's auspices, this Court does not. The government may acknowledge Christmas as a cultural phenomenon, but under the First Amendment it may not observe it as a Christian holy day by suggesting that people praise God for the birth of Jesus.

In sum, *Lynch* teaches that government may celebrate Christmas in some manner and form, but not in a way that endorses Christian doctrine. Here, Allegheny County has transgressed this line. It has chosen to celebrate Christmas in a way that has the effect of endorsing a patently Christian message: Glory to God for the birth of Jesus Christ. Under *Lynch*, and the rest of our cases, nothing more is required to [602] demonstrate a violation of the Establishment Clause. The display of the creche in this context, therefore, must be permanently enjoined.

V

Justice Kennedy and the three Justices who join him would find the display of the creche consistent with the Establishment Clause. He argues that this conclusion necessarily follows from the Court's decision in *Marsh v. Chambers* (1983), which sustained the constitutionality of legislative prayer. *Post*, at 665. He also asserts that the creche, even in this setting, poses "no realistic risk" of "represent[ing] an effort to proselytize," *post*, at 664, having repudiated the Court's endorsement inquiry in favor of a "proselytization" approach. The Court's analysis of the creche, he contends, "reflects an unjustified hostility toward religion." *Post*, at 655.

Justice Kennedy's reasons for permitting the creche on the Grand Staircase and his condemnation of the Court's reasons for deciding otherwise are so far reaching in their implications that they require a response in some depth.

A

. . . [604] Justice Kennedy's reading of *Marsh* would gut the core of the Establishment Clause, as this Court understands it. The history of this Nation, it is perhaps sad to say, contains numerous examples of official acts that endorsed Christianity specifically. Some of these examples date back to the Founding of the Republic, but this heritage of official discrimination [605] against non-Christians has no place in the jurisprudence of the Establishment Clause. Whatever else the Establishment Clause may mean (and we have held it to mean no official preference even for religion over nonreligion), it certainly means at the very least that government may not demonstrate a preference for one particular sect or creed (including a preference for Christianity over other religions). "The clearest command of the Establishment Clause is that one religious denomination cannot be officially preferred over another." *Larson v. Valente*, 456 U.S. 228, 244 (1982). There have been breaches of this command throughout this Nation's history, but they cannot diminish in any way the force of the command.

B

Although Justice Kennedy's misreading of *Marsh* is predicated on a failure to recognize the bedrock Establishment Clause principle that, regardless of history, government may not demonstrate a preference for a particular faith, even he is forced to acknowledge that some instances of such favoritism are constitutionally intolerable. *Post*, at 664–665, n. 3. He concedes also that the term "endorsement" long has been another way of defining a forbidden "preference" for [606] a particular sect, *post*, at 668–669, but he would repudiate the Court's endorsement inquiry as a "jurisprudence of minutiae," *post*, at 674, because it examines the particular contexts in which the government employs religious symbols. . . .

It is perhaps unfortunate, but nonetheless inevitable, that the broad language of many clauses within the Bill of Rights must be translated into adjudicatory principles that realize their full meaning only after their application to a series of concrete cases.

Indeed, not even under Justice Kennedy's preferred approach can the Establishment Clause be transformed into an exception to this rule. The Justice would substitute the term "proselytization" for "endorsement," *post*, at 659–660, 661, 664, but his "proselytization" test suffers from the same "defect," if one must call it that, of requiring close factual analysis. Justice Kennedy has no doubt, "for example, that the [Establishment] Clause forbids a city to permit the permanent erection of a large Latin cross on the roof of city hall . . . because such an obtrusive year-round religious display [607] would place the government's weight behind an obvious effort to proselytize on behalf of a particular religion." *Post*, at 661. He also suggests that a city would demonstrate an unconstitutional preference for Christianity if it displayed a Christian symbol during every major Christian holiday but did not display the religious symbols of other faiths during other religious holidays. *Post*, at 664–665, n. 3. But, for Justice Kennedy, would it be enough of a preference for Christianity if that city each year displayed a creche for 40 days during the Christmas season and a cross for 40 days during Lent (and never the symbols of other religions)? If so, then what if there were no cross but the 40-day creche display contained a sign exhorting the city's citizens "to offer up their devotions to God their Creator, and his Son Jesus Christ, the Redeemer of the world"?

The point of these rhetorical questions is obvious. In order to define precisely what government could and could not do under Justice Kennedy's "proselytization" test, the Court would have to decide a series of cases with particular fact patterns that fall along the spectrum of government references to religion (from the permanent display of a cross atop city hall to a passing reference to divine Providence in an official address). If one wished to be "uncharitable" to Justice Kennedy, see *post*, at 675, one could say that his methodology requires counting the number of days during which the government displays Christian symbols and subtracting from this the number of days during which non-Christian symbols are displayed, divided by the number of different non-Christian religions represented in these displays, and then somehow factoring into this equation the prominence of the display's location and the degree to which each symbol possesses an inherently proselytizing quality. Justice Kennedy, of course, could defend his position by pointing to the inevitably fact-specific nature of the question whether a particular governmental practice signals the government's [608] unconstitutional preference for a specific religious faith. But because Justice Kennedy's formulation of this essential Establishment Clause inquiry is no less fact intensive than the "endorsement" formulation adopted by the Court, Justice Kennedy should be wary of accusing the Court's formulation as "using little more than intuition and a tape measure," *post*, at 675, lest he find his own formulation convicted on an identical charge.

Indeed, perhaps the only real distinction between Justice Kennedy's "proselytization" test and the Court's "endorsement" inquiry is a burden of "unmistakable" clarity that Justice Kennedy apparently would require of government favoritism for specific sects in order to hold the favoritism in violation of the Establishment Clause. *Post*, at 664–665, n. 3. The question whether a particular practice "would place the government's weight behind an obvious effort to proselytize for a particular religion," *post*, at 661, is much the same as whether the practice demonstrates the government's support, promotion, or "endorsement" of the particular creed of a particular sect—except to the extent that it requires an "obvious" allegiance between the government and the sect. . . .

[610] C

Although Justice Kennedy repeatedly accuses the Court of harboring a "latent hostility" or "callous indifference" toward religion, *post*, at 657, 664, nothing could be further from the truth, and the accusations could be said to be as offensive as they are absurd. Justice Kennedy apparently has misperceived a respect for religious pluralism, a respect commanded by the Constitution, as hostility or indifference to religion. No misperception could be more antithetical to the values embodied in the Establishment Clause.

Justice Kennedy's accusations are shot from a weapon triggered by the following proposition: if government may celebrate the secular aspects of Christmas, then it must be allowed to celebrate the religious aspects as well because, otherwise, the government would be discriminating against citizens who celebrate Christmas as a religious, and not just a secular, holiday. *Post*, at 663–664. This proposition, however, is flawed at its foundation. The government does not discriminate against any citizen on the basis of the citizen's religious faith if the government is secular in its functions and operations. On the contrary, the Constitution mandates that the government remain secular, rather than affiliate itself with religious beliefs or institutions, precisely in order to avoid discriminating among citizens on the basis of their religious faiths.

A secular state, it must be remembered, is not the same as an atheistic or antireligious state. A secular state establishes neither atheism nor religion as its official creed. Justice Kennedy thus has it exactly backwards when he says that enforcing the Constitution's requirement that government [611] remain secular is a prescription of orthodoxy. *Post*, at 678. It follows directly from the Constitution's proscription against government affiliation with religious beliefs or institutions that there is no orthodoxy on religious matters in the secular state. Although Justice Kennedy accuses the Court of "an Orwellian rewriting of history," *ibid.*, perhaps it is Justice Kennedy himself who has slipped into a form of Orwellian newspeak when he equates the constitutional command of secular government with a prescribed orthodoxy.

To be sure, in a pluralistic society there may be some would-be theocrats, who wish that their religion were an established creed, and some of them perhaps may be even audacious enough to claim that the lack of established religion discriminates against their preferences. But this claim gets no relief, for it contradicts the fundamental premise of the Establishment Clause itself. The antidiscrimination principle inherent in the Establishment Clause necessarily means that would-be discriminators on the basis of religion cannot prevail.

For this reason, the claim that prohibiting government from celebrating Christmas as a religious holiday discriminates against Christians in favor of nonadherents must fail. Celebrating Christmas as a religious, as opposed to a secular, holiday necessarily entails professing, proclaiming, or believing that Jesus of Nazareth, born in a manger in Bethlehem, is the Christ, the Messiah. If the government celebrates Christmas as a religious holiday (for example, by issuing an official proclamation saying: "We rejoice in the glory of Christ's birth!"), it means that the government really is declaring Jesus to be the Messiah, a specifically Christian belief. In contrast, confining the government's own celebration of Christmas to the holiday's secular aspects does not favor the religious beliefs of non-Christians over those of Christians. Rather, it simply permits the government to acknowledge the holiday without expressing an allegiance to [612] Christian beliefs, an allegiance that would truly favor Christians over non-Christians. To be sure, some Christians may wish to see the government proclaim its allegiance to Christianity in a religious celebration of Christmas, but the Constitution does not permit the gratification of that desire, which would contradict the "the logic of secular liberty" it is the purpose of the Establishment Clause to protect. . . .

[613] VI

The display of the Chanukah menorah in front of the City-County Building may well present a closer constitutional question. The menorah, one must recognize, is a religious symbol: it serves to commemorate the miracle of the oil as described in the Talmud. But the menorah's message is not exclusively religious. The menorah is the primary visual [614] symbol for a holiday that, like Christmas, has both religious and secular dimensions. . . .

Moreover, the menorah here stands next to a Christmas tree and a sign saluting liberty. While no challenge has been made here to the display of the tree and the sign, their presence is obviously relevant in determining the effect of the menorah's display. The necessary result of placing a menorah next to a Christmas tree is to create an "overall holiday setting" that represents both Christmas and Chanukah—two holidays, not one.

The mere fact that Pittsburgh displays symbols of both Christmas and Chanukah does not end the constitutional inquiry. If the city celebrates both Christmas and Chanukah as religious holidays, then it violates the Establishment Clause. [615] The simultaneous endorsement of Judaism and Christianity is no less constitutionally infirm than the endorsement of Christianity alone.

Conversely, if the city celebrates both Christmas and Chanukah as secular holidays, then its conduct is beyond the reach of the Establishment Clause. Because government may celebrate Christmas as a secular holiday, it follows that government may also acknowledge Chanukah as a secular holiday. Simply put, it would be a form of discrimination against Jews to allow Pittsburgh to celebrate Christmas as a cultural tradition while simultaneously disallowing the city's acknowledgment of Chanukah as a contemporaneous cultural tradition. . . .

[616] Accordingly, the relevant question for Establishment Clause purposes is whether the combined display of the tree, the sign, and the menorah has the effect of endorsing both Christian and Jewish faiths, or rather simply recognizes that both Christmas and Chanukah are part of the same winter-holiday season, which has attained a secular status in our society. Of the two interpretations of this particular display, the latter seems far more plausible and is also in line with *Lynch*. . . .

The Christmas tree, unlike the menorah, is not itself a religious symbol. Although Christmas trees once carried religious connotations, today they typify the secular celebration of Christmas. Numerous Americans place [617] Christmas trees in their homes without subscribing to Christian religious beliefs, and when the city's tree stands alone in front of the City-County Building, it is not considered an endorsement of Christian faith. Indeed, a 40-foot Christmas tree was one of the objects that validated the creche in *Lynch*. The widely accepted view of the Christmas tree as the preeminent secular symbol of the Christmas holiday season serves to emphasize the secular component of the message communicated by other elements of an accompanying holiday display, including the Chanukah menorah.

The tree, moreover, is clearly the predominant element in the city's display. The 45-foot tree occupies the central position beneath the middle archway in front of the Grant Street entrance to the City-County Building; the 18-foot menorah is positioned to one side. Given this configuration, it is much more sensible to interpret the meaning of the menorah in light of the tree, rather than vice versa. In the shadow of the tree, the menorah is readily understood as simply a recognition that Christmas is not the only traditional way of observing the winter-holiday season. In these circumstances, then, the combination of the tree and the menorah communicates, not a simultaneous endorsement of both the Christian [618] and Jewish faiths, but instead, a secular celebration of Christmas coupled with an acknowledgment of Chanukah as a contemporaneous alternative tradition.

Although the city has used a symbol with religious meaning as its representation of Chanukah, this is not a case in which the city has reasonable alternatives that are less religious in nature. It is difficult to imagine a predominantly secular symbol of Chanukah that the city could place next to its Christmas tree. An 18-foot dreidel would look out of place and might be interpreted by some as mocking the celebration of Chanukah. The absence of a more secular alternative symbol is itself part of the context in which the city's actions must be judged in determining the likely effect of its use of the menorah. Where the government's secular message can be conveyed by two symbols, only one of which carries religious meaning, an observer reasonably might infer from the fact that the government has chosen to use the religious symbol that the government means to promote religious faith. But where, as here, no such choice has been made, this inference of endorsement is not present.

Thus, the menorah retains its religious significance even in this display, but it does not follow that the city has endorsed religious belief over nonbelief. In displaying the menorah next to the tree, the city has demonstrated no preference for the religious celebration of the holiday season. This conclusion, however, would be untenable had the city substituted a creche for its Christmas tree or if the city had failed to substitute for the menorah an alternative, more secular, representation of Chanukah.

[619] The mayor's sign further diminishes the possibility that the tree and the menorah will be interpreted as a dual endorsement of Christianity and Judaism. The sign states that during the holiday season the city salutes liberty. Moreover, the sign draws upon the theme of light, common to both Chanukah and Christmas as winter festivals, and links that theme with this Nation's legacy of freedom, which allows an American to celebrate the holiday season in whatever way he wishes, religiously or otherwise. While no sign can disclaim an overwhelming message of endorsement, an "explanatory plaque" may confirm that in particular contexts the government's association with a religious symbol does not represent the government's sponsorship of religious beliefs. Here, the mayor's sign serves to confirm what the context already reveals: that the display of the menorah is not an endorsement of religious faith but simply a recognition of cultural diversity.

[620] Given all these considerations, it is not "sufficiently likely" that residents of Pittsburgh will perceive the combined display of the tree, the sign, and the menorah as an "endorsement" or "disapproval . . . of their individual religious choices." While an adjudication of the display's effect must take into account the perspective of one who is neither Christian nor Jewish, as well as of those who adhere to either of these religions, *ibid.*, the constitutionality of its effect must also be judged according to the standard of a "reasonable observer." When measured against this standard, the menorah need not be excluded from this particular display. The Christmas tree alone in the Pittsburgh location does not endorse Christian belief; and, on the facts before us, the addition of the menorah "cannot fairly be understood to" result in the simultaneous endorsement of Christian and Jewish faiths. On the contrary, for purposes of the Establishment Clause, the city's overall display must be understood as conveying the city's secular recognition of different traditions for celebrating the winter-holiday season. . . .

[621] *Lynch v. Donnelly* confirms, and in no way repudiates, the longstanding constitutional principle that government may not engage in a practice that has the effect of promoting or endorsing religious beliefs. The display of the creche in the county courthouse has this unconstitutional effect. The display of the menorah in front of the City-County Building, however, does not have this effect, given its "particular physical setting." . . .

[623] JUSTICE O'CONNOR, with whom JUSTICE BRENNAN and JUSTICE STEVENS join as to Part II, concurring in part and concurring in the judgment.

I

. . . [626] For the reasons stated in Part IV of the Court's opinion in these cases, I agree that the creche displayed on the Grand Staircase of the Allegheny County Courthouse, the seat of county government, conveys a message to nonadherents of Christianity that they are not full members of the political community, and a corresponding message to Christians that they are favored members of the political community. In contrast to the creche in *Lynch*, which was displayed in a private park in the city's commercial district as part of a broader display of traditional secular symbols of the holiday season, this creche stands alone in the county courthouse. The display of religious symbols in public areas of core government buildings runs a special risk of "mak[ing] religion relevant, in reality or public perception, to status in the political community." *Lynch*, at 692 (concurring opinion). [627] The Court correctly concludes that placement of the central religious symbol of the Christmas holiday season at the Allegheny County Courthouse has the unconstitutional effect of conveying a government endorsement of Christianity.

II

In his separate opinion, Justice Kennedy asserts that the endorsement test "is flawed in its fundamentals and unworkable in practice." *Post*, at 669 (opinion concurring in judgment in part and dissenting in part). In my view, neither criticism is persuasive. As a theoretical matter, the endorsement test captures the essential command of the Establishment Clause, namely, that government must not make a person's religious beliefs relevant to his or her standing in the political community by conveying a message "that religion or a particular religious belief is favored or preferred." We live in a pluralistic society. Our citizens come from diverse religious traditions or adhere to no particular religious beliefs at all. If government is to be neutral in matters of religion, rather than showing either favoritism or disapproval towards citizens based on their personal religious choices, government cannot endorse the religious practices and beliefs of some citizens without sending a clear message to nonadherents that they are outsiders or less than full members of the political community.

An Establishment Clause standard that prohibits only "coercive" practices or overt efforts at government proselytization, *post*, at 659–662, 664–665, but fails to take account of the numerous more subtle ways that government can show favoritism [628] to particular beliefs or convey a message of disapproval to others, would not, in my view, adequately protect the religious liberty or respect the religious diversity of the members of our pluralistic political community. Thus, this Court has never relied on coercion alone as the touchstone of Establishment Clause analysis. To require a showing of coercion, even indirect coercion, as an essential element of an Establishment Clause violation would make the Free Exercise Clause a redundancy. Moreover, as even Justice Kennedy recognizes, any Establishment Clause test limited to "direct coercion" clearly would fail to account for forms of "[s]ymbolic recognition or accommodation of religious faith" that may violate the Establishment Clause. *Post*, at 661. . . .

[630] Justice Kennedy submits that the endorsement test is inconsistent with our precedents and traditions because, in his words, if it were "applied without artificial exceptions for historical practice," it would invalidate many traditional practices recognizing the role of religion in our society. *Post*, at 670. This criticism shortchanges both the endorsement test itself and my explanation of the reason why certain longstanding government acknowledgments of religion do not, under that test, convey a message of endorsement. Practices such as legislative prayers or opening Court sessions with "God save the United States and this honorable Court" serve the secular purposes of "solemnizing public occasions" and "expressing confidence in the future." These examples of ceremonial deism do not survive Establishment Clause scrutiny simply by virtue of their historical longevity alone. Historical acceptance of a practice does not in itself validate that practice under the Establishment Clause if the practice violates the values protected by that Clause, just as historical acceptance of racial or gender based discrimination does not immunize such practices from scrutiny under the Fourteenth Amendment. As we recognized in *Walz v. Tax Comm'n of New York City*, 397 U.S. 664, 678 (1970): "[N]o one acquires a vested or protected right in violation of the Constitution by long use, even when that span of time covers our entire national existence and indeed predates it."

Under the endorsement test, the "history and ubiquity" of a practice is relevant not because it creates an "artificial exception" from that test. On the contrary, the "history and ubiquity" of a practice is relevant because it provides part of the context in which a reasonable observer evaluates whether a challenged governmental practice conveys a message of endorsement of religion. It is the combination of the [631] longstanding existence of practices such as opening legislative sessions with legislative prayers or opening Court sessions with "God save the United States and this honorable Court," as well as their nonsectarian nature, that leads me to the conclusion that those particular practices, despite their religious roots, do not convey a message of endorsement of particular religious beliefs. Similarly, the celebration of Thanksgiving as a public holiday, despite its religious origins, is now generally understood as a celebration of patriotic values rather than particular religious beliefs. The question under endorsement analysis, in short, is whether a reasonable observer would view such longstanding practices as a disapproval of his or her particular religious choices, in light of the fact that they serve a secular purpose rather than a sectarian one and have largely lost their religious significance over time. Although the endorsement test requires careful and often difficult linedrawing and is highly context specific, no alternative test has been suggested that captures the essential mandate of the Establishment Clause as well as the endorsement test does, and it warrants continued application and refinement.

Contrary to Justice Kennedy's assertions, neither the endorsement test nor its application in these cases reflects "an unjustified hostility toward religion." *Post*, at 655. See also *post*, at 663, 667–678. Instead, the endorsement standard recognizes that the religious liberty so precious to the citizens who make up our diverse country is protected, not impeded, when government avoids endorsing religion or favoring particular beliefs over others. Clearly, the government can acknowledge the role of religion in our society in numerous ways that do not amount to an endorsement. Moreover, the government can accommodate religion by lifting government-imposed burdens on religion. [632] Indeed, the Free Exercise Clause may mandate that it do so in particular cases. In cases involving the lifting of government burdens on the free exercise of religion, a reasonable observer would take into account the values underlying the Free Exercise Clause in assessing whether the challenged practice conveyed a message of endorsement. By "build[ing] on the concerns at the core of nonestablishment doctrine and recogniz[ing] the role of accommodations in furthering free exercise," the endorsement test "provides a standard capable of consistent application and avoids the criticism levelled against the *Lemon* test." The cases before the Court today, however, do not involve lifting a governmental burden on the free exercise of religion. By repeatedly using the terms "acknowledgment" of religion and "accommodation" of religion interchangeably, however, *post*, at 662–664, 670, 678, Justice Kennedy obscures the fact that the displays at issue in these cases were not placed at city hall in order to remove a government-imposed burden on the free exercise of religion. Christians remain free to display their creches at their homes and churches. Allegheny County has neither placed nor removed a governmental burden on the free exercise of religion but rather, for the reasons stated in Part IV of the Court's opinion, has conveyed a message of governmental endorsement of Christian beliefs. This the Establishment Clause does not permit.

III

For reasons which differ somewhat from those set forth in Part VI of Justice Blackmun's opinion, I also conclude that the city of Pittsburgh's combined holiday display of a Chanukah menorah, a Christmas tree, and a sign saluting liberty does not have the effect of conveying an endorsement of religion. . . .

[634] In my view, the relevant question for Establishment Clause purposes is whether the city of Pittsburgh's display of the menorah, the religious symbol of a religious holiday, next to a Christmas tree and a sign saluting liberty sends a message of government endorsement of Judaism or whether it sends a message of pluralism and freedom to choose one's own beliefs. . . .

[635] In setting up its holiday display, which included the lighted tree and the menorah, the city of Pittsburgh stressed the theme of liberty and pluralism by accompanying the exhibit with a sign bearing the following message: "During this holiday season, the city of Pittsburgh salutes liberty. Let these festive lights remind us that we are the keepers of the flame of liberty and our legacy of freedom." This sign indicates that the city intended to convey its own distinctive message of pluralism and freedom. By accompanying its display of a Christmas tree—a secular symbol of the Christmas holiday season—with a salute to liberty, and by adding a religious symbol from a Jewish holiday also celebrated at roughly the same time of year, I conclude that the city did not endorse Judaism or religion in general, but rather conveyed a message of pluralism and freedom of belief during the holiday season. "Although the religious and indeed sectarian significance" of the menorah "is not neutralized by the setting," *Lynch*, 465 U.S., at 692 (concurring opinion), this particular physical setting "changes what viewers may fairly understand to be the purpose of the display—as a typical museum setting, though not neutralizing the religious content of a religious painting, negates any message of endorsement of that content." . . .

[636] My conclusion does not depend on whether or not the city had "a more secular alternative symbol" of Chanukah, *ante*, at 618, just as the Court's decision in *Lynch* clearly did not turn on whether the city of Pawtucket could have conveyed its tribute to the Christmas holiday season by using a "less religious" alternative to the creche symbol in its display of traditional holiday symbols. In my view, Justice Blackmun's new rule, *ante*, at 618, that an inference of endorsement arises every time government uses a symbol with religious meaning if a "more secular alternative" is available is too blunt an instrument for Establishment Clause analysis, which depends on sensitivity to the context and circumstances presented by each case. Indeed, the opinion appears to recognize the importance of this contextual sensitivity by creating an exception to its new rule in the very case announcing it: the opinion acknowledges that "a purely secular symbol" of Chanukah is available, namely, a dreidel or four-sided top, but rejects the use of such a

symbol because it "might be interpreted by some as mocking the celebration of Chanukah." This recognition that the more religious [637] alternative may, depending on the circumstances, convey a message that is least likely to implicate Establishment Clause concerns is an excellent example of the need to focus on the specific practice in question in its particular physical setting and context in determining whether government has conveyed or attempted to convey a message that religion or a particular religious belief is favored or preferred.

In sum, I conclude that the city of Pittsburgh's combined holiday display had neither the purpose nor the effect of endorsing religion, but that Allegheny County's creche display had such an effect. . . .

JUSTICE BRENNAN, with whom JUSTICE MARSHALL and JUSTICE STEVENS join, concurring in part and dissenting in part.

I have previously explained at some length my views on the relationship between the Establishment Clause and government-sponsored celebrations of the Christmas holiday. See *Lynch v. Donnelly*, 465 U.S. 668, 694–726 (1984) (dissenting opinion). I continue to believe that the display of an object that "retains a specifically Christian [or other] religious meaning," *id.*, at 708, is incompatible with the separation of church and state demanded by our Constitution. I therefore agree with the Court that Allegheny County's display of a creche at the county courthouse signals an endorsement of the Christian faith in violation of the Establishment Clause, and join Parts III-A, IV, and V of the Court's opinion. I cannot agree, however, that the city's display of a 45-foot Christmas tree and an 18-foot Chanukah menorah at the entrance to the building housing the mayor's office shows no favoritism towards Christianity, Judaism, or both. Indeed, I should have thought that the answer as to the first display supplied the answer to the second.

According to the Court, the creche display sends a message endorsing Christianity because the creche itself bears a [638] religious meaning, because an angel in the display carries a banner declaring "Glory to God in the highest!," and because the floral decorations surrounding the creche highlight it rather than secularize it. The display of a Christmas tree and Chanukah menorah, in contrast, is said to show no endorsement of a particular faith or faiths, or of religion in general, because the Christmas tree is a secular symbol which brings out the secular elements of the menorah. *Ante*, at 616–617. And, Justice Blackmun concludes, even though the menorah has religious aspects, its display reveals no endorsement of religion because no other symbol could have been used to represent the secular aspects of the holiday of Chanukah without mocking its celebration. *Ante*, at 618. Rather than endorsing religion, therefore, the display merely demonstrates that "Christmas is not the only traditional way of observing the winter-holiday season," and confirms our "cultural diversity." *Ante*, at 617, 619.

Thus, the decision as to the menorah rests on three premises: the Christmas tree is a secular symbol; Chanukah is a holiday with secular dimensions, symbolized by the menorah; and the government may promote pluralism by sponsoring or condoning displays having strong religious associations on its property. None of these is sound.

I

. . . [639] The notion that the Christmas tree is necessarily secular is, indeed, so shaky that, despite superficial acceptance of the idea, Justice O'Connor does not really take it seriously. While conceding that the "menorah standing alone at city hall may well send" a message of endorsement of the Jewish faith, she nevertheless concludes: "By accompanying its display of a Christmas tree—a secular symbol of the Christmas holiday season—with a salute to liberty, and by adding a religious symbol from a Jewish holiday also celebrated at roughly the same time of year, I conclude that the city did not endorse Judaism or religion in general, but rather conveyed a message [640] of pluralism and freedom of belief during the holiday season." *Ante*, at 635. But the "pluralism" to which Justice O'Connor refers is religious pluralism, and the "freedom of belief" she emphasizes is freedom of religious belief. The display of the tree and the menorah will symbolize such pluralism and freedom only if more than one religion is represented; if only Judaism is represented, the scene is about Judaism, not about pluralism. Thus, the pluralistic message Justice O'Connor stresses depends on the tree's possessing some religious significance. . . .

[643] II

The second premise on which today's decision rests is the notion that Chanukah is a partly secular holiday, for which the menorah can serve as a secular symbol. It is no surprise and no anomaly that Chanukah has historical and societal roots that range beyond the purely religious. I would venture that most, if not all, major religious holidays have beginnings and enjoy histories studded with figures, events, and practices that are not strictly religious. It does not seem to me that the mere fact that Chanukah shares this kind of background makes it a secular holiday in any meaningful sense. The menorah is indisputably a religious symbol, used ritually in a celebration that has deep religious significance. That, in my view, is all that need be said. Whatever secular practices the holiday of Chanukah has taken on in its contemporary observance are beside the point. . . .

[644] III

Justice Blackmun, in his acceptance of the city's message of "diversity," *ante*, at 619, and, even more so, Justice O'Connor, in her approval of the "message of pluralism and freedom to choose one's own beliefs," *ante*, at 634, appear to believe that, where seasonal displays are concerned, more is better. Whereas a display might be constitutionally problematic if it showcased the holiday of just one religion, those problems vaporize as soon as more than one religion is included. I know of no principle under the Establishment Clause, however, that permits us to conclude that governmental promotion of religion is acceptable so long as one religion is not favored. We have, on the contrary, interpreted that Clause to require neutrality, not just among religions, but between religion and nonreligion. . . .

JUSTICE STEVENS, with whom JUSTICE BRENNAN and JUSTICE MARSHALL join, concurring in part and dissenting in part.

. . . [650] In my opinion the Establishment Clause should be construed to create a strong presumption against the display of religious symbols on public property. There is always a [651] risk that such symbols will offend nonmembers of the faith being advertised as well as adherents who consider the particular advertisement disrespectful. Some devout Christians believe that the creche should be placed only in reverential settings, such as a church or perhaps a private home; they do not countenance its use as an aid to commercialization of Christ's birthday. In this very suit, members of the Jewish faith firmly opposed the use to which the menorah was put by the particular sect that sponsored the display at Pittsburgh's City-County Building. Even though "[p]assersby who disagree with the message conveyed by these displays are free to ignore them, or even to turn their backs," see *post*, at 664 (Kennedy, J., concurring in judgment in part and dissenting in part), displays of this kind inevitably have a greater tendency to emphasize sincere and deeply felt differences among individuals than to achieve an ecumenical goal. The Establishment Clause does not allow public bodies to foment such disagreement.

[652] Application of a strong presumption against the public use of religious symbols scarcely will "require a relentless extirpation of all contact between government and religion," see *post*, at 657 (Kennedy, J., concurring in judgment in part and dissenting in part), for it will prohibit a display only when its message, evaluated in the context in which it is presented, is nonsecular. For example, a carving of Moses holding the Ten Commandments, if that is the only adornment on a courtroom wall, conveys an equivocal message, perhaps of respect for Judaism, for religion in general, or for law. The addition of carvings depicting Confucius and Mohammed may honor religion, or particular religions, to an extent that the First Amendment does not tolerate any more than it does "the permanent erection of a large Latin cross on the roof of city hall." See *post*, at 661 (Kennedy, J., concurring in judgment in part and dissenting in part). Placement of secular figures such as Caesar Augustus, William Blackstone, Napoleon Bonaparte, and John Marshall alongside these three religious leaders, however, signals respect not [653] for great proselytizers but for great lawgivers. It would be absurd to exclude such a fitting message from a courtroom, as it would to exclude religious paintings by Italian Renaissance masters from a public museum. Far from "border[ing] on latent hostility toward religion," see *post*, at 657 (Kennedy, J., concurring in judgment in part and dissenting in part), this careful consideration of context gives due regard to religious and nonreligious members of our society. . . .

[654] I cannot agree with the Court's conclusion that the display at Pittsburgh's City-County Building was constitutional. Standing alone in front of a governmental headquarters, a lighted, 45-foot evergreen tree might convey holiday greetings linked too tenuously to Christianity to have constitutional moment. Juxtaposition of this tree with an 18-foot menorah does not make the latter secular, as Justice Blackmun contends, *ante*, at 616. Rather, the presence of the Chanukah menorah, unquestionably a religious symbol, gives religious significance to the Christmas tree. The overall display thus manifests governmental approval of the Jewish and Christian religions. [655] Although it conceivably might be interpreted as sending "a message of pluralism and freedom to choose one's own beliefs," *ante*, at 634 (O'Connor, J., concurring in part and concurring in judgment); accord, *ante*, at 617–618 (opinion of Blackmun, J.), the message is not sufficiently clear to overcome the strong presumption that the display, respecting two religions to the exclusion of all others, is the very kind of double establishment that the First Amendment was designed to outlaw. . . .

JUSTICE KENNEDY, with whom THE CHIEF JUSTICE, JUSTICE WHITE, and JUSTICE SCALIA join, concurring in the judgment in part and dissenting in part.

The majority holds that the County of Allegheny violated the Establishment Clause by displaying a creche in the county courthouse, because the "principal or primary effect" of the display is to advance religion within the meaning of *Lemon v. Kurtzman*, 403 U.S.

602, 612–613 (1971). This view of the Establishment Clause reflects an unjustified hostility toward religion, a hostility inconsistent with our history and our precedents, and I dissent from this holding. The creche display is constitutional, and, for the same reasons, the display of a menorah by the city of Pittsburgh is permissible as well. On this latter point, I concur in the result, but not the reasoning, of Part VI of Justice Blackmun's opinion.

I

In keeping with the usual fashion of recent years, the majority applies the *Lemon* test to judge the constitutionality of the holiday displays here in question. I am content for present purposes to remain within the *Lemon* framework, but do not wish to be seen as advocating, let alone adopting, that test as our primary guide in this difficult area. Persuasive criticism of *Lemon* has emerged. [656] Our cases often question its utility in providing concrete answers to Establishment Clause questions, calling it but a "helpful signpos[t]" or "guidelin[e]" to assist our deliberations rather than a comprehensive test. *Mueller v. Allen*, 463 U.S. 388, 394 (1983) (quoting *Hunt v. McNair*, 413 U.S. 734, 741 [1973]); *Committee for Public Education & Religious Liberty v. Nyquist*, 413 U.S. 756, 773, n. 31 (1973) (quoting *Tilton v. Richardson*, 403 U.S. 672, 677–678 [1971]); see *Lynch v. Donnelly*, 465 U.S. 668, 679 (1984) ("[W]e have repeatedly emphasized our unwillingness to be confined to any single test or criterion in this sensitive area"). Substantial revision of our Establishment Clause doctrine may be in order; but it is unnecessary to undertake that task today, for even the *Lemon* test, when applied with proper sensitivity to our traditions and our case law, supports the conclusion that both the creche and the menorah are permissible displays in the context of the holiday season.

The only *Lemon* factor implicated in these cases directs us to inquire whether the "principal or primary effect" of the challenged government practice is "one that neither advances nor inhibits religion." . . .

[657] Rather than requiring government to avoid any action that acknowledges or aids religion, the Establishment Clause permits government some latitude in recognizing and accommodating the central role religion plays in our society. Any approach less sensitive to our heritage would border on latent hostility toward religion, as it would require government in all its multifaceted roles to acknowledge only the secular, to the exclusion and so to the detriment of the religious. A categorical approach would install federal courts as jealous guardians of an absolute "wall of separation," sending a clear message of disapproval. In this century, as the modern administrative state expands to touch the lives of its citizens in such diverse ways and redirects [658] their financial choices through programs of its own, it is difficult to maintain the fiction that requiring government to avoid all assistance to religion can in fairness be viewed as serving the goal of neutrality. . . .

[659] The ability of the organized community to recognize and accommodate religion in a society with a pervasive public sector requires diligent observance of the border between accommodation and establishment. Our cases disclose two limiting principles: government may not coerce anyone to support or participate in any religion or its exercise; and it may not, in the guise of avoiding hostility or callous indifference, give direct benefits to religion in such a degree that it in fact "establishes a [state] religion or religious faith, or tends to do so." These two principles, while distinct, are not unrelated, for it would be difficult indeed to establish a religion without some measure of more or less subtle coercion, be it in the form of taxation to supply the substantial benefits that would sustain [660] a state-established faith, direct compulsion to observance, or governmental exhortation to religiosity that amounts in fact to proselytizing.

It is no surprise that without exception we have invalidated actions that further the interests of religion through the coercive power of government. Forbidden involvements include compelling or coercing participation or attendance at a religious activity, requiring religious oaths to obtain government office or benefits, or delegating government power to religious groups. The freedom to worship as one pleases without government interference or oppression is the great object of both the Establishment and the Free Exercise Clauses. Barring all attempts to aid religion through government coercion goes far toward attainment of this object.

As Justice Blackmun observes, *ante*, at 597–598, n. 47, some of our recent cases reject the view that coercion is the sole touchstone of an Establishment Clause violation. That may be true if by "coercion" is meant [661] direct coercion in the classic sense of an establishment of religion that the Framers knew. But coercion need not be a direct tax in aid of religion or a test oath. Symbolic recognition or accommodation of religious faith may violate the Clause in an extreme case. I doubt not, for example, that the Clause forbids a city to permit the permanent erection of a large Latin cross on the roof of city hall. This is not because government speech about religion is per se suspect, as the majority would have it, but because such an obtrusive year-round religious display would place the government's weight behind an obvious effort to proselytize on behalf of a particular religion. Speech may coerce in some circumstances, but this does not justify a ban on all government recognition of religion. As Chief Justice Burger wrote for the Court in *Walz*:

> "The general principle deducible from the First Amendment and all that has been said by the Court is this: that we will not tolerate either governmentally established religion or governmental interference with religion. Short of those expressly proscribed governmental acts there is room for play in the joints productive of a benevolent neutrality which will permit religious exercise to exist [662] without sponsorship and without interference." 397 U.S., at 669.

This is most evident where the government's act of recognition or accommodation is passive and symbolic, for in that instance any intangible benefit to religion is unlikely to present a realistic risk of establishment. Absent coercion, the risk of infringement of religious liberty by passive or symbolic accommodation is minimal. Our cases reflect this reality by requiring a showing that the symbolic recognition or accommodation advances religion to such a degree that it actually "establishes a religion or religious faith, or tends to do so." *Lynch*, 465 U.S., at 678.

In determining whether there exists an establishment, or a tendency toward one, we refer to the other types of church-state contacts that have existed unchallenged throughout our history, or that have been found permissible in our case law. In *Lynch*, for example, we upheld the city of Pawtucket's holiday display of a creche, despite the fact that "the display advance[d] religion in a sense." *Id.*, at 683. We held that the creche conferred no greater benefit on religion than did governmental support for religious education, legislative chaplains, "recognition of the origins of the [Christmas] Holiday itself as 'Christ's Mass,'" or many other forms of symbolic or tangible governmental assistance to religious faiths that are ensconced in the safety of national tradition. *Id.*, at 681, 683. And in *Marsh v. Chambers*, we found that Nebraska's practice of employing a legislative chaplain did not violate the Establishment Clause, because "legislative prayer presents no more potential for establishment than the provision of school transportation, beneficial grants for higher education, or tax exemptions for religious organizations." 463 U.S., at 791. Noncoercive government action within the realm of flexible accommodation or passive acknowledgment of existing symbols does not violate the Establishment Clause unless it benefits religion in a way [663] more direct and more substantial than practices that are accepted in our national heritage.

II

These principles are not difficult to apply to the facts of the cases before us. In permitting the displays on government property of the menorah and the creche, the city and county sought to do no more than "celebrate the season," and to acknowledge, along with many of their citizens, the historical background and the religious, as well as secular, nature of the Chanukah and Christmas holidays. This interest falls well within the tradition of government accommodation and acknowledgment of religion that has marked our history from the beginning. It cannot be disputed that government, if it chooses, may participate in sharing with its citizens the joy of the holiday season, by declaring public holidays, installing or permitting festive displays, sponsoring celebrations and parades, and providing holiday vacations for its employees. All levels of our government do precisely that. As we said in *Lynch,* "Government has long recognized—indeed it has subsidized—holidays with religious significance." 465 U.S., at 676.

If government is to participate in its citizens' celebration of a holiday that contains both a secular and a religious component, enforced recognition of only the secular aspect would [664] signify the callous indifference toward religious faith that our cases and traditions do not require; for by commemorating the holiday only as it is celebrated by nonadherents, the government would be refusing to acknowledge the plain fact, and the historical reality, that many of its citizens celebrate its religious aspects as well. Judicial invalidation of government's attempts to recognize the religious underpinnings of the holiday would signal not neutrality but a pervasive intent to insulate government from all things religious. The Religion Clauses do not require government to acknowledge these holidays or their religious component; but our strong tradition of government accommodation and acknowledgment permits government to do so.

There is no suggestion here that the government's power to coerce has been used to further the interests of Christianity or Judaism in any way. No one was compelled to observe or participate in any religious ceremony or activity. Neither the city nor the county contributed significant amounts of tax money to serve the cause of one religious faith. The creche and the menorah are purely passive symbols of religious holidays. Passersby who disagree with the message conveyed by these displays are free to ignore them, or even to turn their backs, just as they are free to do when they disagree with any other form of government speech.

There is no realistic risk that the creche and the menorah represent an effort to proselytize or are otherwise the first step down the road to an establishment of religion. *Lynch* [665] is dispositive of this claim with respect to the creche, and I find no reason for reaching a different result with respect to the menorah. Both are the traditional symbols of religious holidays that over time have acquired a secular component. *Ante,* at 579, and n. 3, 585, and n. 29. Without ambiguity, *Lynch* instructs that "the focus of our inquiry must be on the [religious symbol] in the context of the [holiday] season," 465 U.S., at 679. In that context, religious displays that serve "to celebrate the Holiday and to depict the origins of that Holiday" give rise to no Establishment Clause concern. *Id.,* at 681. If Congress and the state legislatures do not run afoul of the Establishment Clause when they begin each day with a state-sponsored prayer for divine guidance offered by a chaplain whose salary is paid at government expense, I cannot comprehend how a menorah or a creche, displayed in the limited context of the holiday season, can be invalid. . . .

[668] III

. . . Even if *Lynch* did not control, I would not commit this Court to the test applied by the majority today. The notion that cases arising under the Establishment Clause should be decided by an inquiry into whether a "reasonable observer" may "fairly understand" government action to "sen[d] a message to nonadherents that they are outsiders, not full members of the political community," is a recent, and in my view most unwelcome, addition to our tangled Establishment Clause jurisprudence. . . . [669] For the reasons expressed below, I submit that the endorsement test is flawed in its fundamentals and unworkable in practice. The uncritical adoption of this standard is every bit as troubling as the bizarre result it produces in the cases before us.

A

I take it as settled law that, whatever standard the Court applies to Establishment Clause claims, it must at least suggest results consistent with our precedents and the historical practices that, by tradition, have informed our First Amendment jurisprudence. It is true that, for reasons quite unrelated to the First Amendment, displays commemorating religious holidays were not commonplace in 1791. But the relevance of history is not confined to the inquiry into whether the challenged practice itself is a part of our accepted traditions dating back to the Founding.

Our decision in *Marsh v. Chambers* illustrates this proposition. The dissent in that case sought to characterize the decision as "carving out an exception to the Establishment [670] Clause rather than reshaping Establishment Clause doctrine to accommodate legislative prayer," 463 U.S., at 796 (Brennan, J., dissenting), but the majority rejected the suggestion that "historical patterns ca[n] justify contemporary violations of constitutional guarantees," *id.*, at 790. *Marsh* stands for the proposition, not that specific practices common in 1791 are an exception to the otherwise broad sweep of the Establishment Clause, but rather that the meaning of the Clause is to be determined by reference to historical practices and understandings. Whatever test we choose to apply must permit not only legitimate practices two centuries old but also any other practices with no greater potential for an establishment of religion. The First Amendment is a rule, not a digest or compendium. A test for implementing the protections of the Establishment Clause that, if applied with consistency, would invalidate longstanding traditions cannot be a proper reading of the Clause.

If the endorsement test, applied without artificial exceptions for historical practice, reached results consistent with history, my objections to it would have less force. But, as I understand that test, the touchstone of an Establishment Clause violation is whether nonadherents would be made to feel like "outsiders" by government recognition or accommodation of religion. Few of our traditional practices recognizing the part religion plays in our society can withstand scrutiny under a faithful application of this formula.

[671] Some examples suffice to make plain my concerns. Since the Founding of our Republic, American Presidents have issued Thanksgiving Proclamations establishing a national day of celebration and prayer. The first such proclamation was issued by President Washington at the request of the First Congress, and "recommend[ed] and assign[ed]" a day "to be devoted by the people of these States to the service of that great and glorious Being who is the beneficent author of all the good that was, that is, or that will be," so that "we may then unite in most humbly offering our prayers and supplications to the great Lord and Ruler of Nations, and beseech Him to . . . promote the knowledge and

practice of true religion and virtue. . . ." 1 J. Richardson, *A Compilation of Messages and Papers of the Presidents, 1789–1897*, p. 64 (1899). Most of President Washington's successors have followed suit, and the forthrightly religious nature of these proclamations has not waned with the years. President Franklin D. Roosevelt went so far as to "suggest a nationwide reading of the Holy Scriptures during the period from Thanksgiving Day to Christmas" so that "we may bear more earnest witness to our gratitude to Almighty God." Presidential Proclamation No. 2629, 58 Stat. 1160. It requires little imagination to conclude that these proclamations would cause nonadherents to feel excluded, yet they have been a part of our national heritage from the beginning.

[672] The Executive has not been the only Branch of our Government to recognize the central role of religion in our society. The fact that this Court opens its sessions with the request that "God save the United States and this honorable Court" has been noted elsewhere. The Legislature has gone much further, not only employing legislative chaplains, but also setting aside a special prayer room in the Capitol for use by Members of the House and Senate. The room is decorated with a large stained glass panel that depicts President Washington kneeling in prayer; around him is etched the first verse of the 16th Psalm: "Preserve me, O God, for in Thee do I put my trust." Beneath the panel is a rostrum on which a Bible is placed; next to the rostrum is an American Flag. Some endorsement is inherent in these reasonable accommodations, yet the Establishment Clause does not forbid them.

The United States Code itself contains religious references that would be suspect under the endorsement test. Congress has directed the President to "set aside and proclaim a suitable day each year . . . as a National Day of Prayer, on which the people of the United States may turn to God in prayer and meditation at churches, in groups, and as individuals." This statute does not require anyone to pray, of course, but it is a straightforward endorsement of the concept of "turn[ing] to God in prayer." Also by statute, the Pledge of Allegiance to the Flag describes the United States as "one Nation under God." 36 U.S.C. § 172. [673] To be sure, no one is obligated to recite this phrase, but it borders on sophistry to suggest that the "reasonable" atheist would not feel less than a "full membe[r] of the political community" every time his fellow Americans recited, as part of their expression of patriotism and love for country, a phrase he believed to be false. Likewise, our national motto, "In God we trust," 36 U.S.C. § 186, which is prominently engraved in the wall above the Speaker's dias in the Chamber of the House of Representatives and is reproduced on every coin minted and every dollar printed by the Federal Government, 31 U.S.C. §§ 5112 (d)(1), 5114 (b), must have the same effect.

If the intent of the Establishment Clause is to protect individuals from mere feelings of exclusion, then legislative prayer cannot escape invalidation. It has been argued that "[these] government acknowledgments of religion serve, in the only ways reasonably possible in our culture, the legitimate secular purposes of solemnizing public occasions, expressing confidence in the future, and encouraging the recognition of what is worthy of appreciation in society." *Lynch*, at 693 (O'Connor, J., concurring). I fail to see why prayer is the only way to convey these messages; appeals to patriotism, moments of silence, and any number of other approaches would be as effective, were the only purposes at issue the ones described by the *Lynch* concurrence. Nor is it clear to me why "encouraging the recognition of what is worthy of appreciation in society" can be characterized as a purely secular purpose, if it can be achieved only through religious prayer. No doubt prayer is "worthy of appreciation," but that is most assuredly not because it is secular. Even accepting the secular-solemnization explanation at face value, moreover, it seems incredible to suggest that the average observer of legislative prayer who either believes in no religion or whose faith rejects the concept of God would not receive the clear message that his faith is out of step with the [674] political norm. Either the endorsement test must invalidate scores of traditional practices recognizing the place religion holds in our culture, or it must be twisted and stretched to avoid inconsistency with practices we know to have been permitted in the past, while condemning similar practices with no greater endorsement effect simply by reason of their lack of historical antecedent. Neither result is acceptable.

B

In addition to disregarding precedent and historical fact, the majority's approach to government use of religious symbolism threatens to trivialize constitutional adjudication. By mischaracterizing the Court's opinion in *Lynch* as an endorsement-in-context test, *ante*, at 597, Justice Blackmun embraces a jurisprudence of minutiae. A reviewing court must consider whether the city has included Santas, talking wishing wells, reindeer, or other secular symbols as "a center of attention separate from the creche." *Ante*, at 598. After determining whether these centers of attention are sufficiently "separate" that each "had their specific visual story to tell," the court must then measure their proximity to the creche. *Ante*, at 598, and n. 48. A community that wishes to construct a constitutional display must also [675] take care to avoid floral frames or other devices that might insulate the creche from the sanitizing effect of the secular portions of the display. *Ibid.* The majority also notes the presence of evergreens near the creche that are identical to two small evergreens placed near official county signs. *Ante*, at 600, n. 50. After today's decision, municipal greenery must be used with care.

Another important factor will be the prominence of the setting in which the display is placed. In this case, the Grand Staircase of the county courthouse proved too resplendent. Indeed, the Court finds that this location itself conveyed an "unmistakable message that [the county] supports and promotes the Christian praise to God that is the creche's religious message." *Ante*, at 600.

My description of the majority's test, though perhaps uncharitable, is intended to illustrate the inevitable difficulties with its application. This test could provide workable guidance to the lower courts, if ever, only after this Court has decided a long series of holiday display cases, using little more than intuition and a tape measure. Deciding cases on [676] the basis of such an unguided examination of marginalia is irreconcilable with the imperative of applying neutral principles in constitutional adjudication. "It would be appalling to conduct litigation under the Establishment Clause as if it were a trademark case, with experts testifying about whether one display is really like another, and witnesses testifying they were offended—but would have been less so were the creche five feet closer to the jumbo candy cane." . . .

[677] The result the Court reaches in these cases is perhaps the clearest illustration of the unwisdom of the endorsement test. Although Justice O'Connor disavows Justice Blackmun's suggestion that the minority or majority status of a religion is relevant to the question whether government recognition constitutes a forbidden endorsement, *ante*, at 634 (O'Connor, J., concurring in part and concurring in judgment), the very nature of the endorsement test, with its emphasis on the feelings of the objective observer, easily lends itself to this type of inquiry. If there be such a person as the "reasonable observer," I am quite certain that he or she will take away a salient message from our holding in these cases: the Supreme Court of the United States has concluded

that the First Amendment creates classes of religions based on the relative numbers of their adherents. Those religions enjoying the largest following must be consigned to the status of least favored faiths so as to avoid any possible risk of offending members of minority religions. I would be the first to admit that many questions arising under the Establishment Clause do not admit of easy answers, but whatever the Clause requires, it is not the result reached by the Court today.

IV

The approach adopted by the majority contradicts important values embodied in the Clause. Obsessive, implacable resistance to all but the most carefully scripted and secularized [678] forms of accommodation requires this Court to act as a censor, issuing national decrees as to what is orthodox and what is not. What is orthodox, in this context, means what is secular; the only Christmas the State can acknowledge is one in which references to religion have been held to a minimum. The Court thus lends its assistance to an Orwellian rewriting of history as many understand it. I can conceive of no judicial function more antithetical to the First Amendment.

A further contradiction arises from the majority's approach, for the Court also assumes the difficult and inappropriate task of saying what every religious symbol means. Before studying these cases, I had not known the full history of the menorah, and I suspect the same was true of my colleagues. More important, this history was, and is, likely unknown to the vast majority of people of all faiths who saw the symbol displayed in Pittsburgh. Even if the majority is quite right about the history of the menorah, it hardly follows that this same history informed the observers' view of the symbol and the reason for its presence. This Court is ill equipped to sit as a national theology board, and I question both the wisdom and the constitutionality of its doing so. Indeed, were I required to choose between the approach taken by the majority and a strict separationist view, I would have to respect the consistency of the latter.

The suit before us is admittedly a troubling one. It must be conceded that, however neutral the purpose of the city and county, the eager proselytizer may seek to use these symbols for his own ends. The urge to use them to teach or to taunt is always present. It is also true that some devout adherents of Judaism or Christianity may be as offended by the holiday display as are nonbelievers, if not more so. To place these religious symbols in a common hallway or sidewalk, where they may be ignored or even insulted, must be distasteful to many who cherish their meaning.

[679] For these reasons, I might have voted against installation of these particular displays were I a local legislative official. But we have no jurisdiction over matters of taste within the realm of constitutionally permissible discretion. Our role is enforcement of a written Constitution. In my view, the principles of the Establishment Clause and our Nation's historic traditions of diversity and pluralism allow communities to make reasonable judgments respecting the accommodation or acknowledgment of holidays with both cultural and religious aspects. No constitutional violation occurs when they do so by displaying a symbol of the holiday's religious origins.

Employment Division, Department of Human Resources of Oregon v. Smith

494 U.S. 872 (1990)

Vote: 6—Rehnquist, White, Stevens, O'Connor, Scalia, Kennedy
3—Brennan, Marshall, Blackmun

Opinion announcing the opinion of the Court: Scalia
Opinion concurring in the judgment: O'Connor
Dissenting opinion: Blackmun

In response to their denial of unemployment insurance by the state of Oregon, respondents Alfred Smith and Galen Black filed this suit claiming an abridgement of their First Amendment rights under the Free Exercise Clause.

Smith and Black were employed as drug-rehabilitation counselors with a private corporation. Both were fired from their jobs for having ingested peyote, a hallucinogenic drug. State officials denied their subsequent applications for unemployment compensation because peyote use was criminal under Oregon law, making their discharges work-related "misconduct." Smith and Black's use of peyote occurred in the context of a Native American Church ceremony. The Native American Church traditionally uses peyote in a religious manner.

The Supreme Court's opinion below reflects its second consideration of the case. In 1988, the Supreme Court concluded that "if a State has prohibited through its criminal laws certain kinds of religiously motivated conduct without violating the First Amendment, it certainly follows that it may impose the lesser burden of denying unemployment compensation benefits to persons who engage in that conduct." Employment Div., Dept. of Human Resources of Oregon v. Smith, *485 U.S. 660, 670 (1988). The Supreme Court noted, however, that the Oregon Supreme Court had not decided whether respondents' sacramental use of peyote was in fact proscribed by Oregon's controlled-substance law and that the issue was a matter of dispute between the parties. Being uncertain about the legality of the religious use of peyote in Oregon, the Supreme Court vacated the initial judgment of the Oregon Supreme Court and remanded the case for further proceedings. On remand, the Oregon Supreme Court held that respondents' religiously inspired use of peyote fell within the prohibition of the Oregon statute, which made no exception for the sacramental use of the drug. It then considered whether that prohibition was valid under the First Amendment's Free Exercise Clause and concluded that it was not. The Oregon Supreme Court therefore reaffirmed its previous ruling that the state could not deny unemployment benefits to respondents for having engaged in that practice. The U.S. Supreme Court was petitioned to review the Oregon Supreme Court's decision, which led to the case coming before the Supreme Court a second time and to the decision below.*

SCALIA, J., delivered the opinion of the Court, in which REHNQUIST, C. J., and WHITE, STEVENS, and KENNEDY, JJ., joined.

[874] This case requires us to decide whether the Free Exercise Clause of the First Amendment permits the State of Oregon to include religiously inspired peyote use within the reach of its general criminal prohibition on use of that drug, and thus permits the State to deny unemployment benefits to persons dismissed from their jobs because of such religiously inspired use. . . .

[876] The Free Exercise Clause of the First Amendment, which has been made applicable to the States by incorporation into [877] the Fourteenth Amendment, see *Cantwell v. Connecticut*, 310 U.S. 296, 303 (1940), provides that "Congress shall make no law respecting an establishment of religion, or *prohibiting the free exercise thereof . . .*" (emphasis added). The free exercise of religion means, first and foremost, the right to believe and profess whatever religious doctrine one desires. Thus, the First Amendment obviously excludes all "governmental regulation of religious beliefs as such." *Sherbert v. Verner*, at 402. The government may not compel affirmation of religious belief, see *Torcaso v. Watkins* (1961), punish the expression of religious doctrines it believes to be false, *United States v. Ballard*, 322 U.S. 78, 86–88 (1944), impose special disabilities on the basis of religious views or religious status, see *McDaniel v. Paty* (1978); *Fowler v. Rhode Island*, 345 U.S. 67, 69 (1953); cf. *Larson v. Valente*, 456 U.S. 228, 245 (1982), or lend its power to one or the other side in controversies over religious authority or dogma, see *Presbyterian Church in U.S. v. Mary Elizabeth Blue Hull Memorial Presbyterian Church*, 393 U.S. 440, 445–452 (1969); *Kedroff v. St. Nicholas Cathedral*, 344 U.S. 94, 95–119 (1952); *Serbian Eastern Orthodox Diocese v. Milivojevich*, 426 U.S. 696, 708–725 (1976).

But the "exercise of religion" often involves not only belief and profession but the performance of (or abstention from) physical acts: assembling with others for a worship service, participating in sacramental use of bread and wine, proselytizing, abstaining from certain foods or certain modes of transportation. It would be true, we think (though no case of ours has involved the point), that a State would be "prohibiting the free exercise [of religion]" if it sought to ban such acts or abstentions only when they are engaged in for religious reasons, or only because of the religious belief that they display. It would doubtless be unconstitutional, for example, to ban the casting of "statues that are to be used [878] for worship purposes," or to prohibit bowing down before a golden calf.

Respondents in the present case, however, seek to carry the meaning of "prohibiting the free exercise [of religion]" one large step further. They contend that their religious motivation for using peyote places them beyond the reach of a criminal law that is not specifically directed at their religious practice, and that is concededly constitutional as applied to those who use the drug for other reasons. They assert, in other words, that "prohibiting the free exercise [of religion]" includes requiring any individual to observe a generally applicable law that requires (or forbids) the performance of an act that his religious belief forbids (or requires). As a textual matter, we do not think the words must be given that meaning. It is no more necessary to regard the collection of a general tax, for example, as "prohibiting the free exercise [of religion]" by those citizens who believe support of organized government to be sinful, than it is to regard the same tax as "abridging the freedom . . . of the press" of those publishing companies that must pay the tax as a condition of staying in business. It is a permissible reading of the text, in the one case as in the other, to say that if prohibiting the exercise of religion (or burdening the activity of printing) is not the object of the tax but merely the incidental effect of a generally applicable and otherwise valid provision, the First Amendment has not been offended.

Our decisions reveal that the latter reading is the correct one. We have never held that an individual's religious beliefs [879] excuse him from compliance with an otherwise valid law prohibiting conduct that the State is free to regulate. On the contrary, the record of more than a century of our free exercise jurisprudence contradicts that proposition. As described succinctly by Justice Frankfurter in *Minersville School Dist. Bd. of Ed. v. Gobitis*, 310 U.S. 586, 594–595 (1940): "Conscientious scruples have not, in the course of the long struggle for religious toleration, relieved the individual from obedience to a general law not aimed at the promotion or restriction of religious beliefs. The mere possession of religious convictions which contradict the relevant concerns of a political society does not relieve the citizen from the discharge of political responsibilities." We first had occasion to assert that principle in *Reynolds v. United States* (1879), where we rejected the claim that criminal laws against polygamy could not be constitutionally applied to those whose religion commanded the practice. "Laws," we said, "are made for the government of actions, and while they cannot interfere with mere religious belief and opinions, they may with practices. . . . Can a man excuse his practices to the contrary because of his religious belief? To permit this would be to make the professed doctrines of religious belief superior to the law of the land, and in effect to permit every citizen to become a law unto himself." *Id.,* at 166–167.

Subsequent decisions have consistently held that the right of free exercise does not relieve an individual of the obligation to comply with a "valid and neutral law of general applicability on the ground that the law proscribes (or prescribes) conduct that his religion prescribes (or proscribes)." *United States v. Lee*, 455 U.S. 252, 263, n. 3 (1982) (Stevens, J., concurring in judgment). . . .

[880] Our most recent decision involving a neutral, generally applicable regulatory law that compelled activity forbidden by an individual's religion was *United States v. Lee*, 455 U.S., at 258–261. There, an Amish employer, on behalf of himself and his employees, sought exemption from collection and payment of Social Security taxes on the ground that the Amish faith prohibited participation in governmental support programs. We rejected the claim that an exemption was constitutionally required. There would be no way, we observed, to distinguish the Amish believer's objection to Social Security taxes from the religious objections that others might have to the collection or use of other taxes. "If, for example, a religious adherent believes war is a sin, and if a certain percentage of the federal budget can be identified as devoted to war-related activities, such individuals would have a similarly valid claim to be exempt from paying that percentage of the income tax. The tax system could not function if denominations were allowed to challenge the tax system because tax payments were spent in a manner that violates their religious belief." *Id.,* at 260.

[881] The only decisions in which we have held that the First Amendment bars application of a neutral, generally applicable law to religiously motivated action have involved not the Free Exercise Clause alone, but the Free Exercise Clause in conjunction with other constitutional protections, such as freedom of speech and of the press, see *Cantwell v. Connecticut*, 310 U.S., at 304–307 (invalidating a licensing system for religious and charitable solicitations under which the administrator had discretion to

deny a license to any cause he deemed nonreligious); *Murdock v. Pennsylvania* (1943) (invalidating a flat tax on solicitation as applied to the dissemination of religious ideas); *Follett v. McCormick* (1944) (same), or the right of parents, acknowledged in *Pierce v. Society of Sisters* (1925), to direct the education of their children, see *Wisconsin v. Yoder* (1972) (invalidating compulsory school-attendance laws as applied to Amish parents who refused on religious grounds to send their children to school). . . .

[882] The present case does not present such a hybrid situation, but a free exercise claim unconnected with any communicative activity or parental right. Respondents urge us to hold, quite simply, that when otherwise prohibitable conduct is accompanied by religious convictions, not only the convictions but the conduct itself must be free from governmental regulation. We have never held that, and decline to do so now. There being no contention that Oregon's drug law represents an attempt to regulate religious beliefs, the communication of religious beliefs, or the raising of one's children in those beliefs, the rule to which we have adhered ever since *Reynolds* plainly controls. "Our cases do not at their farthest reach support the proposition that a stance of conscientious opposition relieves an objector from any colliding duty fixed by a democratic government." *Gillette v. United States*, at 461.

Respondents argue that even though exemption from generally applicable criminal laws need not automatically be extended to religiously motivated actors, at least the claim for a [883] religious exemption must be evaluated under the balancing test set forth in *Sherbert v. Verner* (1963). Under the *Sherbert* test, governmental actions that substantially burden a religious practice must be justified by a compelling governmental interest. Applying that test we have, on three occasions, invalidated state unemployment compensation rules that conditioned the availability of benefits upon an applicant's willingness to work under conditions forbidden by his religion. See *Sherbert v. Verner; Thomas v. Review Bd. of Indiana Employment Security Div.* (1981); *Hobbie v. Unemployment Appeals Comm'n of Florida* (1987). We have never invalidated any governmental action on the basis of the *Sherbert* test except the denial of unemployment compensation. Although we have sometimes purported to apply the *Sherbert* test in contexts other than that, we have always found the test satisfied, see *United States v. Lee* (1982); *Gillette v. United States* (1971). In recent years we have abstained from applying the *Sherbert* test (outside the unemployment compensation field) at all. . . .

[884] Even if we were inclined to breathe into *Sherbert* some life beyond the unemployment compensation field, we would not apply it to require exemptions from a generally applicable criminal law. The *Sherbert* test, it must be recalled, was developed in a context that lent itself to individualized governmental assessment of the reasons for the relevant conduct. As a plurality of the Court noted in *Roy*, a distinctive feature of unemployment compensation programs is that their eligibility criteria invite consideration of the particular circumstances behind an applicant's unemployment: "The statutory conditions [in *Sherbert* and *Thomas*] provided that a person was not eligible for unemployment compensation benefits if, 'without good cause,' he had quit work or refused available work. The 'good cause' standard created a mechanism for individualized exemptions." *Bowen v. Roy*, at 708 (opinion of Burger, C. J., joined by Powell and Rehnquist, JJ.). See also *Sherbert*, at 401, n. 4 (reading state unemployment compensation law as allowing benefits for unemployment caused by at least some "personal reasons"). As the plurality pointed out in *Roy*, our decisions in the unemployment cases stand for the proposition that where the State has in place a system of individual exemptions, it may not refuse to extend that system to cases of "religious hardship" without compelling reason. *Bowen v. Roy*, at 708.

Whether or not the decisions are that limited, they at least have nothing to do with an across-the-board criminal prohibition on a particular form of conduct. Although, as noted earlier, we have sometimes used the *Sherbert* test to analyze free exercise challenges to such laws, see *United States v.* [885] *Lee*, at 257–260; *Gillette v. United States*, at 462, we have never applied the test to invalidate one. We conclude today that the sounder approach, and the approach in accord with the vast majority of our precedents, is to hold the test inapplicable to such challenges. The government's ability to enforce generally applicable prohibitions of socially harmful conduct, like its ability to carry out other aspects of public policy, "cannot depend on measuring the effects of a governmental action on a religious objector's spiritual development." *Lyng*, at 451. To make an individual's obligation to obey such a law contingent upon the law's coincidence with his religious beliefs, except where the State's interest is "compelling"—permitting him, by virtue of his beliefs, "to become a law unto himself," *Reynolds v. United States*, 98 U.S., at 167—contradicts both constitutional tradition and common sense.

The "compelling government interest" requirement seems benign, because it is familiar from other fields. But using it as the standard that must be met before the government may accord different treatment on the basis of race, see, *e.g.*, [886] *Palmore v. Sidoti*, 466 U.S. 429, 432 (1984), or before the government may regulate the content of speech, see, *e.g.*, *Sable Communications of California v. FCC*, 492 U.S. 115, 126 (1989), is not remotely comparable to using it for the purpose asserted here. What it produces in those other fields—equality of treatment and an unrestricted flow of contending speech—are constitutional norms; what it would produce here—a private right to ignore generally applicable laws—is a constitutional anomaly. . . .

Nor is it possible to limit the impact of respondents' proposal by requiring a "compelling state interest" only when the conduct prohibited is "central" to the individual's religion. It is no [887] more appropriate for judges to determine the "centrality" of religious beliefs before applying a "compelling interest" test in the free exercise field, than it would be for them to determine the "importance" of ideas before applying the "compelling interest" test in the free speech field. What principle of law or logic can be brought to bear to contradict a believer's assertion that a particular act is "central" to his personal faith? Judging the centrality of different religious practices is akin to the unacceptable "business of evaluating the relative merits of differing religious claims." *United States v. Lee*, 455 U.S., at 263 n. 2 (Stevens, J., concurring). As we reaffirmed only last Term, "[i]t is not within the judicial ken to question the centrality of particular beliefs or practices to a faith, or the validity of particular litigants' interpretations of those creeds." *Hernandez v. Commissioner*, 490 U.S., at 699. Repeatedly and in many different contexts, we have warned that courts must not presume to determine the place of a particular belief in a religion or the plausibility of a religious claim.[4]

---

4. While arguing that we should apply the compelling interest test in this case, Justice O'Connor nonetheless agrees that "our determination of the constitutionality of Oregon's general criminal prohibition cannot, and should not, turn on the centrality of the particular religious practice at issue," *post*, at 906–907 (opinion concurring in judgment). This means, presumably, that compelling-interest scrutiny must be applied to generally applicable laws that regulate or prohibit any religiously motivated activity, no matter how unimportant to the claimant's religion. Earlier in her opinion, however, Justice O'Connor appears to contradict this, saying that the proper approach is "to determine whether the burden on the specific plaintiffs before us is constitutionally significant and whether the particular criminal interest asserted by the State before us is compelling." *Post*, at 899. "Constitutionally significant burden" would seem to be "centrality" under another name. In any case, dispensing with a "centrality" inquiry is utterly unworkable. It would require, for example, the same degree of "compelling state interest" to impede the practice of throwing rice at church weddings as to impede the practice of getting married in church. There is no way out of the difficulty that, if general laws are to be subjected

[888] If the "compelling interest" test is to be applied at all, then, it must be applied across the board, to all actions thought to be religiously commanded. Moreover, if "compelling interest" really means what it says (and watering it down here would subvert its rigor in the other fields where it is applied), many laws will not meet the test. Any society adopting such a system would be courting anarchy, but that danger increases in direct proportion to the society's diversity of religious beliefs, and its determination to coerce or suppress none of them. Precisely because "we are a cosmopolitan nation made up of people of almost every conceivable religious preference," *Braunfeld v. Brown*, 366 U.S., at 606, and precisely because we value and protect that religious divergence, we cannot afford the luxury of deeming presumptively invalid, as applied to the religious objector, every regulation of conduct that does not protect an interest of the highest order. The rule respondents favor would open the prospect of constitutionally required religious exemptions from civic obligations of almost every conceivable kind—ranging from [889] compulsory military service, see, *e.g., Gillette v. United States* (1971), to the payment of taxes, see, *e.g., United States v. Lee*; to health and safety regulation such as manslaughter and child neglect laws, see, *e.g., Funkhouser v. State* (Okla. Crim. App. 1988), compulsory vaccination laws, see, *e.g., Cude v. State*, 237 Ark. 927, 377 S. W. 2d 816 (1964), drug laws, see, *e.g., Olsen v. Drug Enforcement Administration*, 279 U.S. App. D. C. 1, 878 F.2d 1458 (1989), and traffic laws, see *Cox v. New Hampshire* (1941); to social welfare legislation such as minimum wage laws, see *Tony and Susan Alamo Foundation v. Secretary of Labor* (1985), child labor laws, see *Prince v. Massachusetts* (1944), animal cruelty laws, see, *e.g., Church of the Lukumi Babalu Aye, Inc. v. City of Hialeah*, 723 F. Supp. 1467 (SD Fla. 1989), cf. *State v. Massey*, 229 N. C. 734, 51 S. E. 2d 179, appeal dism'd, 336 U.S. 942 (1949), environmental protection laws, see *United States v. Little*, 638 F. Supp. 337 (Mont. 1986), and laws providing for equality of opportunity for the races, see, *e.g., Bob Jones University v. United States*, 461 U.S. 574, 603–604 (1983). The First Amendment's protection of religious liberty does not require this.[5]

[890] Values that are protected against government interference through enshrinement in the Bill of Rights are not thereby banished from the political process. Just as a society that believes in the negative protection accorded to the press by the First Amendment is likely to enact laws that affirmatively foster the dissemination of the printed word, so also a society that believes in the negative protection accorded to religious be-

---

to a "religious practice" exception, both the importance of the law at issue and the centrality of the practice at issue must reasonably be considered.

Nor is this difficulty avoided by Justice Blackmun's assertion that "although . . . courts should refrain from delving into questions whether, as a matter of religious doctrine, a particular practice is 'central' to the religion, . . . I do not think this means that the courts must turn a blind eye to the severe impact of a State's restrictions on the adherents of a minority religion." *Post*, at 919 (dissenting opinion). As Justice Blackmun's opinion proceeds to make clear, inquiry into "severe impact" is no different from inquiry into centrality. He has merely substituted for the question "How important is X to the religious adherent?" the question "How great will be the harm to the religious adherent if X is taken away?" There is no material difference.

5. Justice O'Connor contends that the "parade of horribles" in the text only "demonstrates . . . that courts have been quite capable of . . . strik[ing] sensible balances between religious liberty and competing state interests." *Post*, at 902 (opinion concurring in judgment). But the cases we cite have struck "sensible balances" only because they have all applied the general laws, despite the claims for religious exemption. In any event, Justice O'Connor mistakes the purpose of our parade: it is not to suggest that courts would necessarily permit harmful exemptions from these laws (though they might), but to suggest that courts would constantly be in the business of determining whether the "severe impact" of various laws on religious practice (to use Justice Blackmun's terminology, *post*, at 919) or the "constitutiona[l] significan[ce]" of the "burden on the specific plaintiffs" (to use Justice O'Connor's terminology, *post*, at 899) suffices to permit us to confer an exemption. It is a parade of horribles because it is horrible to contemplate that federal judges will regularly balance against the importance of general laws the significance of religious practice.

lief can be expected to be solicitous of that value in its legislation as well. It is therefore not surprising that a number of States have made an exception to their drug laws for sacramental peyote use. But to say that a nondiscriminatory religious-practice exemption is permitted, or even that it is desirable, is not to say that it is constitutionally required, and that the appropriate occasions for its creation can be discerned by the courts. It may fairly be said that leaving accommodation to the political process will place at a relative disadvantage those religious practices that are not widely engaged in; but that unavoidable consequence of democratic government must be preferred to a system in which each conscience is a law unto itself or in which judges weigh the social importance of all laws against the centrality of all religious beliefs.

* * *

Because respondents' ingestion of peyote was prohibited under Oregon law, and because that prohibition is constitutional, Oregon may, consistent with the Free Exercise Clause, deny respondents unemployment compensation when their dismissal results from use of the drug. . . .

[891] JUSTICE O'CONNOR, with whom JUSTICE BRENNAN, JUSTICE MARSHALL, and JUSTICE BLACKMUN join as to Parts I and II, concurring in the judgment.*

Although I agree with the result the Court reaches in this case, I cannot join its opinion. In my view, today's holding dramatically departs from well-settled First Amendment jurisprudence, appears unnecessary to resolve the question presented, and is incompatible with our Nation's fundamental commitment to individual religious liberty. . . .

[892] II

The Court today extracts from our long history of free exercise precedents the single categorical rule that "if prohibiting the exercise of religion . . . is . . . merely the incidental effect of a generally applicable and otherwise valid provision, the First Amendment has not been offended." *Ante*, at 878. Indeed, the Court holds that where the law is a generally applicable criminal prohibition, our usual free exercise jurisprudence does not even apply. To reach this sweeping result, however, the Court must not only give a strained reading of the First Amendment but must also disregard our consistent application of free exercise doctrine to cases involving generally applicable regulations that burden religious conduct.

[893] A

The Free Exercise Clause of the First Amendment commands that "Congress shall make no law . . . prohibiting the free exercise [of religion]." In *Cantwell v. Connecticut* (1940), we held that this prohibition applies to the States by incorporation into the Fourteenth Amendment and that it categorically forbids government regulation of religious

---

*Although Justices Brennan, Marshall, and Blackmun join parts I and II of this opinion, they do not concur in the judgment.

beliefs. As the Court recognizes, however, the "free exercise" of religion often, if not invariably, requires the performance of (or abstention from) certain acts. *Ante*, at 877; cf. 3 *A New English Dictionary on Historical Principles* 401–402 (J. Murray ed. 1897) (defining "exercise" to include "[t]he practice and performance of rites and ceremonies, worship, etc.; the right or permission to celebrate the observances (of a religion)" and religious observances such as acts of public and private worship, preaching, and prophesying). "[B]elief and action cannot be neatly confined in logic-tight compartments." *Wisconsin v. Yoder*, 406 U.S. 205, 220 (1972). Because the First Amendment does not distinguish between religious belief and religious conduct, conduct motivated by sincere religious belief, like the belief itself, must be at least presumptively protected by the Free Exercise Clause.

The Court today, however, interprets the Clause to permit the government to prohibit, without justification, conduct mandated by an individual's religious beliefs, so long as that prohibition is generally applicable. But a law that prohibits certain conduct—conduct that happens to be an act of worship for someone—manifestly does prohibit that person's free exercise of his religion. A person who is barred from engaging in religiously motivated conduct is barred from freely exercising his religion. Moreover, that person is barred from freely exercising his religion regardless of whether the law prohibits the conduct only when engaged in for religious reasons, only by members of that religion, or by all persons. It is difficult to deny that a law that prohibits [894] religiously motivated conduct, even if the law is generally applicable, does not at least implicate First Amendment concerns.

The Court responds that generally applicable laws are "one large step" removed from laws aimed at specific religious practices. The First Amendment, however, does not distinguish between laws that are generally applicable and laws that target particular religious practices. Indeed, few States would be so naive as to enact a law directly prohibiting or burdening a religious practice as such. Our free exercise cases have all concerned generally applicable laws that had the effect of significantly burdening a religious practice. If the First Amendment is to have any vitality, it ought not be construed to cover only the extreme and hypothetical situation in which a State directly targets a religious practice. As we have noted in a slightly different context, "[s]uch a test has no basis in precedent and relegates a serious First Amendment value to the barest level of minimum scrutiny that the Equal Protection Clause already provides." *Hobbie v. Unemployment Appeals Comm'n of Florida*, 480 U.S. 136, 141–142 (1987) (quoting *Bowen v. Roy*, 476 U.S. 693, 727 [1986] [O'Connor, J., concurring in part and dissenting in part]).

To say that a person's right to free exercise has been burdened, of course, does not mean that he has an absolute right to engage in the conduct. Under our established First Amendment jurisprudence, we have recognized that the freedom to act, unlike the freedom to believe, cannot be absolute. Instead, we have respected both the First Amendment's express textual mandate and the governmental interest in regulation of conduct by requiring the government to justify any substantial burden on religiously motivated conduct by a compelling state interest and by means narrowly tailored to achieve that interest. [895] The compelling interest test effectuates the First Amendment's command that religious liberty is an independent liberty, that it occupies a preferred position, and that the Court will not permit encroachments upon this liberty, whether direct or indirect, unless required by clear and compelling governmental interests "of the highest order," *Yoder*, at 215. "Only an especially important governmental interest pursued by narrowly tailored means can justify exacting a sacrifice of First Amendment freedoms as the price for an equal share of the rights, benefits, and privileges enjoyed by other citizens." *Roy*, at 728 (opinion concurring in part and dissenting in part).

The Court attempts to support its narrow reading of the Clause by claiming that "[w]e have never held that an individual's religious beliefs excuse him from compliance with an otherwise valid law prohibiting conduct that the State is free to regulate." *Ante*, at 878–879. But as the Court later notes, as it must, in cases such as *Cantwell* and *Yoder* we have in fact interpreted the Free Exercise Clause to forbid application of a generally applicable prohibition to religiously motivated conduct. Indeed, in *Yoder* we expressly rejected the interpretation the Court now adopts:

> "[O]ur decisions have rejected the idea that religiously grounded conduct is always outside the protection of the Free Exercise Clause. It is true that activities of individuals, even when religiously based, are often subject [896] to regulation by the States in the exercise of their undoubted power to promote the health, safety, and general welfare, or the Federal Government in the exercise of its delegated powers. But to agree that religiously grounded conduct must often be subject to the broad police power of the State is not to deny that there are areas of conduct protected by the Free Exercise Clause of the First Amendment and thus beyond the power of the State to control, even under regulations of general applicability. . . .
>
> . . . A regulation neutral on its face may, in its application, nonetheless offend the constitutional requirement for government neutrality if it unduly burdens the free exercise of religion," at 219–220.

The Court endeavors to escape from our decisions in *Cantwell* and *Yoder* by labeling them "hybrid" decisions, but there is no denying that both cases expressly relied on the Free Exercise Clause, and that we have consistently regarded those cases as part of the mainstream of our free exercise jurisprudence. Moreover, in each of the other cases cited by the Court to support its categorical rule, we rejected the particular constitutional claims before us only after carefully weighing the competing interests. That we rejected the free exercise [897] claims in those cases hardly calls into question the applicability of First Amendment doctrine in the first place. Indeed, it is surely unusual to judge the vitality of a constitutional doctrine by looking to the win-loss record of the plaintiffs who happen to come before us.

B

 . . . In my view, however, the essence of a free exercise claim is relief from a burden imposed by government on religious practices or beliefs, whether the burden is imposed directly through laws that prohibit or compel specific religious practices, or indirectly through laws that, in effect, make abandonment of one's own religion or conformity to the religious beliefs of others the price of an equal place in the civil community. As we explained in *Thomas*:

> "Where the state conditions receipt of an important benefit upon conduct proscribed by a religious faith, or where it denies such a benefit because of conduct mandated by religious belief, thereby putting substantial pressure on an adherent to modify his behavior and to violate his beliefs, a burden upon religion exists." 450 U.S., at 717–718.

[898] A State that makes criminal an individual's religiously motivated conduct burdens that individual's free exercise of religion in the severest manner possible, for it "results in the choice to the individual of either abandoning his religious principle or facing criminal prosecution." *Braunfeld*, at 605. I would have thought it beyond argument that such laws implicate free exercise concerns.

Indeed, we have never distinguished between cases in which a State conditions receipt of a benefit on conduct prohibited by religious beliefs and cases in which a State affirmatively prohibits such conduct. The *Sherbert* compelling interest test applies in both kinds of cases. . . .

I would reaffirm that principle today: A neutral criminal law prohibiting conduct that a State may legitimately regulate is, if anything, more burdensome than a neutral civil [899] statute placing legitimate conditions on the award of a state benefit.

Legislatures, of course, have always been "left free to reach actions which were in violation of social duties or subversive of good order." *Reynolds*, 98 U.S., at 164. Yet because of the close relationship between conduct and religious belief, "[i]n every case the power to regulate must be so exercised as not, in attaining a permissible end, unduly to infringe the protected freedom." *Cantwell*, 310 U.S., at 304. Once it has been shown that a government regulation or criminal prohibition burdens the free exercise of religion, we have consistently asked the government to demonstrate that unbending application of its regulation to the religious objector "is essential to accomplish an overriding governmental interest," *Lee*, at 257–258, or represents "the least restrictive means of achieving some compelling state interest," *Thomas*, at 718. To me, the sounder approach—the approach more consistent with our role as judges to decide each case on its individual merits—is to apply this test in each case to determine whether the burden on the specific plaintiffs before us is constitutionally significant and whether the particular criminal interest asserted by the State before us is compelling. Even if, as an empirical matter, a government's criminal laws might usually serve a compelling interest in health, safety, or public order, the First Amendment at least requires a case-by-case determination of the question, sensitive to the facts of each particular claim. Given the range of conduct that a State might legitimately make [900] criminal, we cannot assume, merely because a law carries criminal sanctions and is generally applicable, that the First Amendment never requires the State to grant a limited exemption for religiously motivated conduct. . . .

[901] The Court today gives no convincing reason to depart from settled First Amendment jurisprudence. There is nothing talismanic about neutral laws of general applicability or general criminal prohibitions, for laws neutral toward religion can coerce a person to violate his religious conscience or intrude upon his religious duties just as effectively as laws aimed at religion. Although the Court suggests that the compelling interest test, as applied to generally applicable laws, would result in a "constitutional anomaly," *ante*, at 886, the First Amendment unequivocally makes freedom of religion, like freedom from race discrimination and freedom of speech, a "constitutional nor[m]," not an "anomaly." . . . [902] The Court's parade of horribles not only fails as a reason for discarding the compelling interest test, it instead demonstrates just the opposite: that courts have been quite capable of applying our free exercise jurisprudence to strike sensible balances between religious liberty and competing state interests.

Finally, the Court today suggests that the disfavoring of minority religions is an "unavoidable consequence" under our system of government and that accommodation of such religions must be left to the political process. *Ante*, at 890. In my view, however, the First Amendment was enacted precisely to protect the rights of those whose religious practices are not shared by the majority and may be viewed with hostility. The history of our free exercise doctrine amply demonstrates the harsh impact majoritarian rule has had on unpopular or emerging religious groups such as the Jehovah's Witnesses and the Amish. Indeed, the words of Justice Jackson in *West Virginia State Bd. of Ed. v. Barnette* (overruling *Minersville School Dist. v. Gobitis* [1940]) are apt:

[903] "The very purpose of a Bill of Rights was to withdraw certain subjects from the vicissitudes of political controversy, to place them beyond the reach of majorities and officials and to establish them as legal principles to be applied by the courts. One's right to life, liberty, and property, to free speech, a free press, freedom of worship and assembly, and other fundamental rights may not be submitted to vote; they depend on the outcome of no elections." 319 U.S., at 638.

The compelling interest test reflects the First Amendment's mandate of preserving religious liberty to the fullest extent possible in a pluralistic society. For the Court to deem this command a "luxury," *ante*, at 888, is to denigrate "[t]he very purpose of a Bill of Rights."

III

The Court's holding today not only misreads settled First Amendment precedent; it appears to be unnecessary to this case. I would reach the same result applying our established free exercise jurisprudence.

A

There is no dispute that Oregon's criminal prohibition of peyote places a severe burden on the ability of respondents to freely exercise their religion. Peyote is a sacrament of the Native American Church and is regarded as vital to respondents' ability to practice their religion. [904] As we noted in *Smith I*, the Oregon Supreme Court concluded that "the Native American Church is a recognized religion, that peyote is a sacrament of that church, and that respondent's beliefs were sincerely held." 485 U.S., at 667. Under Oregon law, as construed by that State's highest court, members of the Native American Church must choose between carrying out the ritual embodying their religious beliefs and avoidance of criminal prosecution. That choice is, in my view, more than sufficient to trigger First Amendment scrutiny.

There is also no dispute that Oregon has a significant interest in enforcing laws that control the possession and use of controlled substances by its citizens. As we recently noted, drug abuse is "one of the greatest problems affecting the health and welfare of our population" and thus "one of the most serious problems confronting our society today." *Treasury Employees v. Von Raab*, 489 U.S. 656, 668, 674 (1989). Indeed, under federal law (incorporated by Oregon law in relevant part, see Ore. Rev. Stat. § 475.005[6] [1987]), peyote is specifically regulated as a Schedule I controlled substance, which means that Congress has found that it has a high potential for abuse, that there is no currently accepted medical use, and that there is a lack of accepted safety for use of the drug under medical supervision. In light of our recent decisions holding that the governmental [905] interests in the collection of income tax, *Hernandez*, 490 U.S., at 699–700, a comprehensive Social Security system, see *Lee*, 455 U.S., at 258–259, and military conscription, see *Gillette*, 401 U.S., at 460, are compelling, respondents do not seriously dispute that Oregon has a compelling interest in prohibiting the possession of peyote by its citizens.

B

Thus, the critical question in this case is whether exempting respondents from the State's general criminal prohibition "will unduly interfere with fulfillment of the governmental interest." *Lee*, at 259. Although the question is close, I would conclude that uniform application of Oregon's criminal prohibition is "essential to accomplish," *Lee*, at 257, its overriding interest in preventing the physical harm caused by the use of a Schedule I controlled substance. Oregon's criminal prohibition represents that State's judgment that the possession and use of controlled substances, even by only one person, is inherently harmful and dangerous. Because the health effects caused by the use of controlled substances exist regardless of the motivation of the user, the use of such substances, even for religious purposes, violates the very purpose of the laws that prohibit them. Moreover, in view of the societal interest in preventing trafficking in controlled substances, uniform application of the criminal prohibition at issue is essential to the effectiveness of Oregon's stated interest in preventing any possession of peyote.

[906] For these reasons, I believe that granting a selective exemption in this case would seriously impair Oregon's compelling interest in prohibiting possession of peyote by its citizens. Under such circumstances, the Free Exercise Clause does not require the State to accommodate respondents' religiously motivated conduct. Unlike in *Yoder*, where we noted that "[t]he record strongly indicates that accommodating the religious objections of the Amish by forgoing one, or at most two, additional years of compulsory education will not impair the physical or mental health of the child, or result in an inability to be self-supporting or to discharge the duties and responsibilities of citizenship, or in any other way materially detract from the welfare of society," 406 U.S., at 234; a religious exemption in this case would be incompatible with the State's interest in controlling use and possession of illegal drugs.

Respondents contend that any incompatibility is belied by the fact that the Federal Government and several States provide exemptions for the religious use of peyote. But other governments may surely choose to grant an exemption without Oregon, with its specific asserted interest in uniform application of its drug laws, being required to do so by the First Amendment. Respondents also note that the sacramental use of peyote is central to the tenets of the Native American Church, but I agree with the Court, *ante*, at 886–887, that because "[i]t is not within the judicial ken to question the centrality of particular beliefs or practices to a faith," quoting *Hernandez*, at 699, our determination of the constitutionality of Oregon's general criminal prohibition cannot, and should not, turn on the centrality of the particular [907] religious practice at issue. This does not mean, of course, that courts may not make factual findings as to whether a claimant holds a sincerely held religious belief that conflicts with, and thus is burdened by, the challenged law. The distinction between questions of centrality and questions of sincerity and burden is admittedly fine, but it is one that is an established part of our free exercise doctrine and one that courts are capable of making.

I would therefore adhere to our established free exercise jurisprudence and hold that the State in this case has a compelling interest in regulating peyote use by its citizens and that accommodating respondents' religiously motivated conduct "will unduly interfere with fulfillment of the governmental interest." *Lee, supra*, at 259. Accordingly, I concur in the judgment of the Court.

JUSTICE BLACKMUN, with whom JUSTICE BRENNAN and JUSTICE MARSHALL join, dissenting.

. . . [909] In weighing the clear interest of respondents Smith and Black (hereinafter respondents] in the free exercise of their religion against Oregon's asserted interest in enforcing its drug laws, it is important to articulate in precise terms the state interest involved. It is not the State's broad interest [910] in fighting the critical "war on drugs" that must be weighed against respondents' claim, but the State's narrow interest in refusing to make an exception for the religious, ceremonial use of peyote. Failure to reduce the competing interests to the same plane of generality tends to distort the weighing process in the State's favor.

The State's interest in enforcing its prohibition, in order to be sufficiently compelling to outweigh a free exercise claim, [911] cannot be merely abstract or symbolic. The State cannot plausibly assert that unbending application of a criminal prohibition is essential to fulfill any compelling interest, if it does not, in fact, attempt to enforce that prohibition. In this case, the State actually has not evinced any concrete interest in enforcing its drug laws against religious users of peyote. Oregon has never sought to prosecute respondents, and does not claim that it has made significant enforcement efforts against other religious users of peyote. The State's asserted interest thus amounts only to the symbolic preservation of an unenforced prohibition. But a government interest in "symbolism, even symbolism for so worthy a cause as the abolition of unlawful drugs," *Treasury Employees v. Von Raab*, 489 U.S. 656, 687 (1989) (Scalia, J., dissenting), cannot suffice to abrogate the constitutional rights of individuals.

Similarly, this Court's prior decisions have not allowed a government to rely on mere speculation about potential harms, but have demanded evidentiary support for a refusal to allow a religious exception. In this case, the State's justification for refusing to recognize an exception to its criminal laws for religious peyote use is entirely speculative.

The State proclaims an interest in protecting the health and safety of its citizens from the dangers of unlawful drugs. It offers, however, no evidence that the religious use of peyote [912] has ever harmed anyone. The factual findings of other courts cast doubt on the State's assumption that religious use of peyote is harmful.

The fact that peyote is classified as a Schedule I controlled substance does not, by itself, show that any and all uses of peyote, in any circumstance, are inherently harmful and dangerous. The Federal Government, which created the classifications of unlawful drugs from which Oregon's drug laws are derived, apparently does not find peyote so dangerous as to preclude an exemption for religious use. Moreover, [913] other Schedule I drugs have lawful uses.

The carefully circumscribed ritual context in which respondents used peyote is far removed from the irresponsible and unrestricted recreational use of unlawful drugs. The Native American Church's internal restrictions on, and supervision of, its members' use of peyote substantially obviate the State's health and safety concerns.

[914] Moreover, just as in *Yoder*, the values and interests of those seeking a religious exemption in this case are congruent, to a great degree, with those the State seeks to promote through its drug laws. Not only does the church's doctrine forbid nonreligious use of peyote; it also generally advocates self-reliance, familial responsibility, and abstinence from alcohol. [915] There is considerable evidence that the spiritual and social support provided by the church has been effective in combating the tragic effects of alcoholism on the Native American population. Two noted experts on peyotism, Dr. Omer C. Stewart and Dr. Robert Bergman, testified by affidavit to this effect on behalf of respondent Smith before the Employment Appeal Board. Far from promoting the lawless and irresponsible use of drugs, Native American Church members' spiritual [916] code exemplifies values that Oregon's drug laws are presumably intended to foster.

The State also seeks to support its refusal to make an exception for religious use of peyote by invoking its interest in abolishing drug trafficking. There is, however, practically no illegal traffic in peyote. See *Olsen,* 279 U.S. App. D. C., at 6, 7, 878 F.2d, at 1463, 1467 (quoting DEA Final Order to the effect that total amount of peyote seized and analyzed by federal authorities between 1980 and 1987 was 19.4 pounds; in contrast, total amount of marijuana seized during that period was over 15 million pounds). Also, the availability of peyote for religious use, even if Oregon were to allow an exemption from its criminal laws, would still be strictly controlled by federal regulations and by the State of Texas, the only State in which peyote grows in significant quantities. Peyote simply is not a popular drug; its distribution for use in religious rituals has nothing to do with the vast and violent traffic in illegal narcotics that plagues this country.

Finally, the State argues that granting an exception for religious peyote use would erode its interest in the uniform, fair, and certain enforcement of its drug laws. The State fears that, if it grants an exemption for religious peyote use, a flood of other claims to religious exemptions will follow. It would then be placed in a dilemma, it says, between allowing a patchwork of exemptions that would hinder its law enforcement efforts, and risking a violation of the Establishment Clause by arbitrarily limiting its religious exemptions. This [917] argument, however, could be made in almost any free exercise case. This Court, however, consistently has rejected similar arguments in past free exercise cases, and it should do so here as well.

The State's apprehension of a flood of other religious claims is purely speculative. Almost half the States, and the Federal Government, have maintained an exemption for religious peyote use for many years, and apparently have not found themselves overwhelmed by claims to other religious exemptions. Allowing an exemption for religious peyote use [918] would not necessarily oblige the State to grant a similar exemption to other religious groups. The unusual circumstances that make the religious use of peyote compatible with the State's interests in health and safety and in preventing drug trafficking would not apply to other religious claims. Some religions, for example, might not restrict drug use to a limited ceremonial context, as does the Native American Church. See, *e.g., Olsen,* 279 U.S. App. D. C., at 7, 878 F.2d, at 1464 ("[T]he Ethiopian Zion Coptic Church . . . teaches that marijuana is properly smoked 'continually all day'"). Some religious claims involve drugs such as marijuana and heroin, in which there is significant illegal traffic, with its attendant greed and violence, so that it would be difficult to grant a religious exemption without seriously compromising law enforcement efforts. That the State might grant an exemption for religious peyote use, but deny other religious claims arising in different circumstances, would not violate the Establishment Clause. Though the State must treat all religions equally, and not favor one over another, this obligation is fulfilled by the uniform application of the "compelling interest" test to all free exercise claims, not by reaching uniform results as to all claims. A showing that religious peyote use does not unduly interfere with the State's interests is "one that probably few other religious groups or sects could make," *Yoder,* 406 U.S., at 236; this does not mean that an exemption limited to peyote use is tantamount to an establishment of religion.

[919] II

Finally, although I agree with Justice O'Connor that courts should refrain from delving into questions whether, as a matter of religious doctrine, a particular practice is "central" to the religion, *ante,* at 906–907, I do not think this means that the courts must turn a blind eye to the severe impact of a State's restrictions on the adherents of a minority religion.

Respondents believe, and their sincerity has never been at issue, that the peyote plant embodies their deity, and eating it is an act of worship and communion. Without peyote, they could not enact the essential ritual of their religion.

[920] If Oregon can constitutionally prosecute them for this act of worship, they, like the Amish, may be "forced to migrate to some other and more tolerant region." *Yoder*, 406 U.S., at 218. This potentially devastating impact must be viewed in light of the federal policy—reached in reaction to many years of religious persecution and intolerance—of protecting the religious freedom of Native Americans. See American Indian Religious Freedom Act, 92 Stat. 469, 42 U.S.C. § 1996 (1982 ed.) ("[I]t shall be the policy of the United States to protect and preserve for American Indians their inherent right of freedom to believe, express, and exercise the traditional religions . . . , including but not limited to access to sites, use and possession of sacred objects, and the freedom to worship through ceremonials and traditional rites"). Congress recognized that certain substances, such as peyote,

> "have religious significance because they are sacred, they have power, they heal, they are necessary to the exercise of [921] the rites of the religion, they are necessary to the cultural integrity of the tribe, and, therefore, religious survival." H. R. Rep. No. 95-1308, p. 2 (1978).

The American Indian Religious Freedom Act, in itself, may not create rights enforceable against government action restricting religious freedom, but this Court must scrupulously apply its free exercise analysis to the religious claims of Native Americans, however unorthodox they may be. Otherwise, both the First Amendment and the stated policy of Congress will offer to Native Americans merely an unfulfilled and hollow promise.

III

For these reasons, I conclude that Oregon's interest in enforcing its drug laws against religious use of peyote is not sufficiently compelling to outweigh respondents' right to the free exercise of their religion. Since the State could not constitutionally enforce its criminal prohibition against respondents, the interests underlying the State's drug laws cannot justify its denial of unemployment benefits. Absent such justification, the State's regulatory interest in denying benefits for religiously motivated "misconduct," see *ante*, at 874, is indistinguishable from the state interests this Court has rejected in *Frazee*, *Hobbie*, *Thomas*, and *Sherbert*. The State of Oregon cannot, consistently with the Free Exercise Clause, deny respondents unemployment benefits.

I dissent.

45

Board of Education of the Westside Community Schools v. Mergens

496 U.S. 226 (1990)

Vote: 8—Rehnquist, Brennan, White, Marshall, Blackmun, O'Connor, Scalia, Kennedy
   1—Stevens

Opinion announcing the judgment of the Court: O'Connor
Opinion concurring in part and concurring in the judgment: Kennedy
Opinion concurring in the judgment: Marshall
Dissenting opinion: Stevens

This case resulted from the rejection by public school officials of an application by students to form a Christian student group at a public high school.

   Westside Community Schools School Board policy permitted its students to join recognized groups and clubs. Recognized clubs met after school hours on school premises. At the time the suit was filed, approximately thirty such groups existed at Westside, a public secondary school in Omaha, Nebraska. The school enrolled about 1,450 students, included grades 10–12, and received federal funds, making it subject to the federal Equal Access Act, the significance of which is described in the majority opinion below.

   School Board Policy 5610, which concerned student clubs and organizations, recognized student clubs as a "vital part of the total education program as a means of developing citizenship, wholesome attitudes, good human relations, knowledge and skills." It required each club to have faculty sponsorship and provided that "clubs and organizations shall not be sponsored by any political or religious organization, or by any organization which denies membership on the basis of race, color, creed, sex or political belief." Board Policy 6180, which pertained to recognition of religious beliefs and customs, required that "students adhering to a specific set of religious beliefs or holding to little or no belief shall be alike respected." In addition, Board Policy 5450 recognized its students' freedom of expression, consistent with the authority of the board.

   No written school board policy existed concerning the formation of student clubs. Students wishing to form a club presented their request to a school official who determined whether the proposed club's goals and objectives were consistent with school board policies and with the school district's "Mission and Goals"—a broadly worded "blueprint" that expressed the district's commitment to teaching academic, physical, civic, and personal skills and values.

In January 1985, Bridget Mergens, a senior at Westside High, met with the school's principal, Dr. James Findley, and requested permission to form a Christian club. The proposed club would have had the same privileges and met on the same terms and conditions as other Westside student groups, except that it would not have had a faculty sponsor. According to the students' testimony at trial, the club's purpose would have been, among other things, to permit the students to read and discuss the Bible, to have fellowship, and to pray together. Membership would have been voluntary and open to all students regardless of religious affiliation.

Principal Findley denied the request, as did more senior school administrators. School officials explained that school policy required all student clubs to have a faculty sponsor, which the proposed religious club would not or could not have, and that a religious club at the school would violate the Establishment Clause. Mergens appealed the denial of her request to the Board of Education, but the board upheld the denial.

O'CONNOR, J., announced the judgment of the Court and delivered the opinion of the Court with respect to Parts I, II-A, II-B, and II-C, in which REHNQUIST, C. J., and WHITE, BLACKMUN, SCALIA, and KENNEDY, JJ., joined, and an opinion with respect to Part III, in which REHNQUIST, C. J., and WHITE and BLACKMUN, JJ., joined.

[231] This case requires us to decide whether the Equal Access Act prohibits Westside High School from denying a student religious group permission to meet on school premises during noninstructional time, and if so, whether the Act, so construed, violates the Establishment Clause of the First Amendment. . . .

[234] II

A

In *Widmar v. Vincent* (1981), we invalidated, on free speech grounds, a state university regulation that prohibited [235] student use of school facilities "for purposes of religious worship or religious teaching." *Id.*, at 265. In doing so, we held that an "equal access" policy would not violate the Establishment Clause under our decision in *Lemon v. Kurtzman*, 403 U.S. 602, 612–613 (1971). In particular, we held that such a policy would have a secular purpose, would not have the primary effect of advancing religion, and would not result in excessive entanglement between government and religion. We noted, however, that "university students are, of course, young adults. They are less impressionable than younger students and should be able to appreciate that the University's policy is one of neutrality toward religion." *Id.*, at 274, n. 14.

In 1984, Congress extended the reasoning of *Widmar* to public secondary schools. Under the Equal Access Act, a public secondary school with a "limited open forum" is prohibited from discriminating against students who wish to conduct a meeting within that forum on the basis of the "religious, political, philosophical, or other content of the speech at such meetings." 20 U.S.C. §§ 4071 (a) and (b). Specifically, the Act provides:

"It shall be unlawful for any public secondary school which receives Federal financial assistance and which has a limited open forum to deny equal access or a fair opportunity to, or discriminate against, any students who wish to conduct a meeting within that limited open forum on the basis of the religious, political, philosophical, or other content of the speech at such meetings." 20 U.S.C. § 4071 (a).

A "limited open forum" exists whenever a public secondary school "grants an offering to or opportunity for one or more noncurriculum related student groups to meet on school premises during noninstructional time." § 4071 (b). "Meeting" is defined to include "those activities of student groups which are permitted under a school's limited open forum and are not directly related to the school curriculum." § 4072 (3). [236] "Noninstructional time" is defined to mean "time set aside by the school before actual classroom instruction begins or after actual classroom instruction ends." § 4072 (4). Thus, even if a public secondary school allows only one "noncurriculum related student group" to meet, the Act's obligations are triggered and the school may not deny other clubs, on the basis of the content of their speech, equal access to meet on school premises during noninstructional time.

The Act further specifies that "schools shall be deemed to offer a fair opportunity to students who wish to conduct a meeting within its limited open forum" if the school uniformly provides that the meetings are voluntary and student-initiated; are not sponsored by the school, the government, or its agents or employees; do not materially and substantially interfere with the orderly conduct of education activities within the school; and are not directed, controlled, conducted, or regularly attended by "nonschool persons." §§ 4071 (c)(1), (2), (4), and (5). "Sponsorship" is defined to mean "the acting of promoting, leading, or participating in a meeting. The assignment of a teacher, administrator, or other school employee to a meeting for custodial purposes does not constitute sponsorship of the meeting." § 4072 (2). If the meetings are religious, employees or agents of the school or government may attend only in a "nonparticipatory capacity." § 4071 (c) (3). Moreover, a State may not influence the form of any religious activity, require any person to participate in such activity, or compel any school agent or employee to attend a meeting if the content of the speech at the meeting is contrary to that person's beliefs. §§ 4071 (d)(1), (2), and (3).

Finally, the Act does not "authorize the United States to deny or withhold Federal financial assistance to any school," § 4071 (e), or "limit the authority of the school, its agents or employees, to maintain order and discipline on school premises, to protect the well-being of students and faculty, and to [237] assure that attendance of students at the meetings is voluntary," § 4071 (f). . . .

[247] III

Petitioners contend that even if Westside has created a limited open forum within the meaning of the Act, its denial of official recognition to the proposed Christian club must nevertheless stand because the Act violates the Establishment Clause of the First Amendment, as applied to the States through the Fourteenth Amendment. Specifically, petitioners maintain that because the school's recognized student activities are an integral part of its educational mission, official recognition of respondents' proposed club would effectively incorporate religious activities into the school's official program, endorse participation in the religious club, and provide [248] the club with an official platform to proselytize other students.

We disagree. In *Widmar*, we applied the three-part *Lemon* test to hold that an "equal access" policy, at the university level, does not violate the Establishment Clause, 454 U.S., at 271–275. We concluded that "an open-forum policy including nondiscrimination against religious speech, would have a secular purpose," 454 U.S., at 271, and would in fact avoid entanglement with religion. See *id.*, at 272, n. 11 ("The University would risk greater 'entanglement' by attempting to enforce its exclusion of 'religious worship' and 'religious speech'"). We also found that although incidental benefits accrued to religious groups who used university facilities, this result did not amount to an establishment of religion. First, we stated that a university's forum does not "confer any imprimatur of state approval on religious sects or practices." *Id.*, at 274. Indeed, the message is one of neutrality rather than endorsement; if a State refused to let religious groups use facilities open to others, then it would demonstrate not neutrality but hostility toward religion. "The Establishment Clause does not license government to treat religion and those who teach or practice it, simply by virtue of their status as such, as subversive of American ideals and therefore subject to unique disabilities." *McDaniel v. Paty*, 435 U.S. 618, 641 (1978) (BRENNAN, J., concurring in judgment). Second, we noted that "the [University's] provision of benefits to [a] broad . . . spectrum of groups"—both nonreligious and religious speakers—was "an important index of secular effect." 454 U.S., at 274.

We think the logic of *Widmar* applies with equal force to the Equal Access Act. As an initial matter, the Act's prohibition of discrimination on the basis of "political, philosophical, or other" speech as well as religious speech is a sufficient basis for meeting the secular purpose prong of the *Lemon* test. [249] Congress' avowed purpose—to prevent discrimination against religious and other types of speech—is undeniably secular. Even if some legislators were motivated by a conviction that religious speech in particular was valuable and worthy of protection, that alone would not invalidate the Act, because what is relevant is the legislative purpose of the statute, not the possibly religious motives of the legislators who enacted the law. Because the Act on its face grants equal access to both secular and religious speech, we think it clear that the Act's purpose was not to "endorse or disapprove of religion," *Wallace v. Jaffree*, 472 U.S. 38, 56 (1985).

Petitioners' principal contention is that the Act has the primary effect of advancing religion. Specifically, petitioners urge that, because the student religious meetings are held under school aegis, and because the state's compulsory attendance laws bring the students together (and thereby provide a ready-made audience for student evangelists), an objective observer in the position of a secondary school student will perceive official school support for such religious meetings.

[250] We disagree. First, although we have invalidated the use of public funds to pay for teaching state-required subjects at parochial schools, in part because of the risk of creating "a crucial symbolic link between government and religion, thereby enlisting—at least in the eyes of impressionable youngsters—the powers of government to the support of the religious denomination operating the school," *Grand Rapids School Dist. v. Ball*, 473 U.S. 373, 385 (1985), there is a crucial difference between government speech endorsing religion, which the Establishment Clause forbids, and private speech endorsing religion, which the Free Speech and Free Exercise Clauses protect. We think that secondary school students are mature enough and are likely to understand that a school does not endorse or support student speech that it merely permits on a nondiscriminatory basis. The proposition that schools do not endorse everything they fail to censor is not complicated. "Particularly in this age of massive media information . . . the few years difference in age between high school and college students [does not] justify departing from *Widmar*." *Bender v. Williamsport Area School Dist.*, 475 U.S. 534, 556 (1986) (Powell, J. dissenting). . . .

[251] Second, we note the Act expressly limits participation by school officials at meetings of student religious groups, and that any such meetings must be held during

"noninstructional time." The Act therefore avoids the problems of "the students' emulation of teachers as role models" and "mandatory attendance requirements," *Edwards v.
Aguillard*, 482 U.S., at 584. . . .

[252] Third, the broad spectrum of officially recognized student clubs at Westside,
and the fact that Westside students are free to initiate and organize additional student
clubs counteract any possible message of official endorsement of or preference for religion or a particular religious belief. Although a school may not itself lead or direct a
religious club, a school that permits a student-initiated and student-led religious club
to meet after school, just as it permits any other student group to do, does not convey
a message of state approval or endorsement of the particular religion. Under the Act, a
school with a limited open forum may not lawfully deny access to a Jewish students'
club, a Young Democrats club, or a philosophy club devoted to the study of Nietzsche.
To the extent that a religious club is merely one of many different student-initiated
voluntary clubs, students should perceive no message of government endorsement of
religion. Thus, we conclude that the Act does not, at least on its face and as applied to
Westside, have the primary effect of advancing religion.

Petitioners' final argument is that by complying with the Act's requirement, the
school risks excessive entanglement between government and religion. The proposed
club, petitioners urge, would be required to have a faculty sponsor who would be charged
with actively directing the activities of the group, guiding its leaders, and ensuring balance in the presentation of controversial ideas. Petitioners claim that this influence over
the club's religious program would entangle the government in day-to-day surveillance
of religion of the type forbidden by the Establishment Clause.

[253] Under the Act, however, faculty monitors may not participate in any religious
meetings, and nonschool persons may not direct, control, or regularly attend activities of
student groups. Moreover, the Act prohibits school "sponsorship" of any religious meetings, which means that school officials may not promote, lead, or participate in any such
meeting. Although the Act permits "the assignment of a teacher, administrator, or other
school employee to the meeting for custodial purposes," *ibid.*, such custodial oversight
of the student-initiated religious group, merely to ensure order and good behavior, does
not impermissibly entangle government in the day-to-day surveillance or administration
of religious activities. Indeed, as the Court noted in *Widmar*, a denial of equal access to
religious speech might well create greater entanglement problems in the form of invasive
monitoring to prevent religious speech at meetings at which such speech might occur.

Accordingly, we hold that the Equal Access Act does not on its face contravene the
Establishment Clause. Because we hold that petitioners have violated the Act, we do
not decide respondents' claims under the Free Speech and Free Exercise Clauses. For the
foregoing reasons, the judgment of the Court of Appeals is affirmed. . . .

JUSTICE KENNEDY, with whom JUSTICE SCALIA joins, concurring in part and concurring in the judgment.

. . . [260] II

I agree with the plurality that a school complying with the statute by satisfying the
criteria in § 4071 (c) does not violate the Establishment Clause. The accommodation
of religion mandated by the Act is a neutral one, and in the context of this case it suffices to inquire whether the Act violates either one of two principles. The first is that

the government cannot "give direct benefits to religion in such a degree that it in fact 'establishes a [state] religion or religious faith, or tends to do so.'" *County of Allegheny v. American Civil Liberties Union, Greater Pittsburgh Chapter* (1989) (KENNEDY, J., concurring in judgment in part and dissenting in part). Any incidental benefits that accompany official recognition of a religious club under the criteria set forth in the § 4071 (c) do not lead to the establishment of religion under this standard. The second principle controlling the case now before us, in my view, is that the government cannot coerce any student to participate in a religious activity. The Act is consistent with this standard [261] as well. Nothing on the face of the Act or in the facts of the case as here presented demonstrate that enforcement of the statute will result in the coercion of any student to participate in a religious activity. The Act does not authorize school authorities to require, or even to encourage, students to become members of a religious club or to attend a club's meetings; the meetings take place while school is not in session; and the Act does not compel any school employee to participate in, or to attend, a club's meetings or activities.

The plurality uses a different test, one which asks whether school officials, by complying with the Act, have endorsed religion. It is true that when government gives impermissible assistance to a religion it can be said to have "endorsed" religion; but endorsement cannot be the test. The word endorsement has insufficient content to be dispositive. And for reasons I have explained elsewhere, see *Allegheny County*, its literal application may result in neutrality in name but hostility in fact when the question is the government's proper relation to those who express some religious preference.

I should think it inevitable that a public high school "endorses" a religious club, in a common-sense use of the term, if the club happens to be one of many activities that the school permits students to choose in order to further the development of their intellect and character in an extracurricular setting. But no constitutional violation occurs if the school's action is based upon a recognition of the fact that membership in a religious club is one of many permissible ways for a student to further his or her own personal enrichment. The inquiry with respect to coercion must be whether the government imposes pressure upon a student to participate in a religious activity. This inquiry, of course, must be undertaken with sensitivity to the special circumstances that exist in a secondary school where the line between voluntary and [262] coerced participation may be difficult to draw. No such coercion, however, has been shown to exist as a necessary result of this statute, either on its face or as respondents seek to invoke it on the facts of this case.

For these reasons, I join Parts I and II of the Court's opinion, and concur in the judgment.

JUSTICE MARSHALL, with whom JUSTICE BRENNAN joins, concurring in the judgment.

I agree with the majority that "noncurriculum" must be construed broadly to "prohibit schools from discriminating on the basis of the content of a student group's speech." As the majority demonstrates, such a construction "is consistent with Congress' intent to provide a low threshold for triggering the Act's requirements." In addition, to the extent that Congress intended the Act to track this Court's free speech jurisprudence, as the dissent argues, the majority's construction is faithful to our commitment to nondiscriminatory access to open fora in public schools. When a school allows student-initiated clubs not directly tied to the school's curriculum to use school facilities, it has "created a forum generally open to student groups" and is therefore constitutionally prohibited from enforcing a "content-based exclusion" of other student speech. In this respect, the Act as construed by the majority simply codifies in statute what is already constitutionally mandated: schools may not discriminate among student-initiated groups that seek access to school facilities for expressive purposes not directly related to the school's curriculum.

The Act's low threshold for triggering equal access, however, raises serious Establishment Clause concerns where secondary schools with fora that differ substantially from the forum in *Widmar* are required to grant access to student religious groups. Indeed, as applied in the present case, the Act mandates a religious group's access to a forum that is dedicated to promoting fundamental values and citizenship as [263] defined by the school. The Establishment Clause does not forbid the operation of the Act in such circumstances, but it does require schools to change their relationship to their fora so as to disassociate themselves effectively from religious clubs' speech. Thus, although I agree with the plurality that the Act as applied to Westside could withstand Establishment Clause scrutiny, I write separately to emphasize the steps Westside must take to avoid appearing to endorse the Christian Club's goals. The plurality's Establishment Clause analysis pays inadequate attention to the differences between this case and *Widmar* and dismisses too lightly the distinctive pressures created by Westside's highly structured environment.

I

A

This case involves the intersection of two First Amendment guarantees—the Free Speech Clause and the Establishment Clause. We have long regarded free and open debate over matters of controversy as necessary to the functioning of our constitutional system. That the Constitution requires toleration of speech over its suppression is no less true in our Nation's schools.

But the Constitution also demands that the State not take action that has the primary effect of advancing religion. [264] The introduction of religious speech into the public schools reveals the tension between these two constitutional commitments, because the failure of a school to stand apart from religious speech can convey a message that the school endorses rather than merely tolerates that speech. Recognizing the potential dangers of school-endorsed religious practice, we have shown particular "vigilance in monitoring compliance with the Establishment Clause in elementary and secondary schools." *Edwards v. Aguillard*, 482 U.S. 578, 583–584 (1987). This vigilance must extend to our monitoring of the actual effects of an "equal access" policy. If public schools are perceived as conferring the imprimatur of the State on religious doctrine or practice as a result of such a policy, the nominally "neutral" character of the policy will not save it from running afoul of the Establishment Clause.

B

. . . [265] Westside currently does not recognize any student club that advocates a controversial viewpoint. Indeed, the clubs at Westside that trigger the Act involve scuba diving, chess, and counseling for special education students. As a matter of school policy,

Westside encourages student participation in clubs based on a broad conception of its educational mission. That mission comports with the Court's acknowledgment "that public schools are vitally important 'in the preparation of individuals for participation as citizens,' and as vehicles for 'inculcating fundamental values necessary to the maintenance of a democratic political system.'" *Board of Education, Island Trees Union Free School Dist. No. 26 v. Pico*, 457 U.S. 853, 864 (1982) (plurality). Given the nature and function of student clubs at Westside, the school makes no effort to disassociate itself from the activities and goals of its student clubs.

The entry of religious clubs into such a realm poses a real danger that those clubs will be viewed as part of the school's effort to inculcate fundamental values. The school's message with respect to its existing clubs is not one of toleration but one of endorsement. As the majority concedes, the program is part of the "district's commitment to teaching academic, physical, civic, and personal skills and values." But although a school may permissibly encourage its students to become well-rounded as student-athletes, student-musicians, and student-tutors, the Constitution forbids [266] schools to encourage students to become well-rounded as student-worshippers. Neutrality toward religion, as required by the Constitution, is not advanced by requiring a school that endorses the goals of some noncontroversial secular organizations to endorse the goals of religious organizations as well.

The fact that the Act, when triggered, provides access to political as well as religious speech does not ameliorate the potential threat of endorsement. The breadth of beneficiaries under the Act does suggest that the Act may satisfy the "secular purpose" requirement of the Establishment Clause inquiry we identified in *Lemon*, 403 U.S., at 612–613. But the crucial question is how the Act affects each school. If a school already houses numerous ideological organizations, then the addition of a religion club will most likely not violate the Establishment Clause because the risk that students will erroneously attribute the views of the religion club to the school is minimal. To the extent a school tolerates speech by a wide range of ideological clubs, students cannot reasonably understand the school to endorse all of the groups' divergent and contradictory views. But if the religion club is the sole advocacy-oriented group in the forum, or one of a very limited number, and the school continues to promote its student-club program as instrumental to citizenship, then the school's failure to disassociate itself from the religious activity will reasonably be understood as an endorsement of that activity. That political and other advocacy-oriented groups are permitted to participate in a forum that, through school support and encouragement, is devoted to fostering a student's civic identity does not ameliorate the appearance of school endorsement unless the invitation is accepted and the forum is transformed into a forum like that in *Widmar*.

For this reason, the plurality's reliance on *Widmar* is misplaced. The University of Missouri took concrete steps to ensure "that the University's name will not 'be identified in [267] any way with the aims, policies, programs, products, or opinions of any organization or its members,'" 454 U.S., at 274, n. 14. Westside, in contrast, explicitly promotes its student clubs "as a vital part of the total education program [and] as a means of developing citizenship." And while the University of Missouri recognized such clubs as the Young Socialist alliance and the Young Democrats, Westside has recognized no such political clubs. . . .

[268] The comprehensiveness of the access afforded by the Act further highlights the Establishment Clause dangers posed by the Act's application to fora such as Westside's. The Court holds that "official recognition allows student clubs to be part of the student activities program and carries with it access to the school newspaper, bulletin boards,

the public address system, and the annual Club Fair." Students would be alerted to the meetings of the religion club over the public address system; they would see religion club material posted on the official school bulletin board and club notices in the school newspaper, they would be recruited to join the religion club at the school-sponsored Club Fair. If a school has a variety of ideological clubs, as in *Widmar*, I agree with the plurality that a student is likely to understand that "a school does not endorse or support student speech that it merely permits on a nondiscriminatory basis." When a school has a religion club but no other political or ideological organizations, however, that relatively fine distinction may be lost.

Moreover, in the absence of a truly robust forum that includes the participation of more than one advocacy-oriented group, the presence of a religious club could provide a fertile ground for peer pressure, especially if the club commanded support from a substantial portion of the student body. Indeed, it is precisely in a school without such a forum that intolerance for different religious and other views would be most dangerous and that a student who does not share the religious beliefs of his classmates would perceive "that religion or a particular religious belief is favored or preferred." [269] *Wallace v. Jaffree*, 472 U.S. 38, 70 (1985) (O'CONNOR, J., concurring in judgment).

The plurality concedes that there is a "possibility of student peer pressure," but maintains that this does not amount to "official state endorsement." This dismissal is too facile. We must remain sensitive, especially in the public schools, to "the numerous more subtle ways that government can show favoritism to particular beliefs or convey a message of disapproval to others." *County of Allegheny v. ACLU*, 492 U.S. 573 (1989) (O'CONNOR, J., concurring in part and in judgment). When the government, through mandatory attendance laws, brings students together in a highly controlled environment every day for the better part of their waking hours and regulates virtually every aspect of their existence during that time, we should not be so quick to dismiss the problem of peer pressure as if the school environment had nothing to do with creating and fostering it. The State has structured an environment in which students holding mainstream views may be able to coerce adherents of minority religions to attend club meetings or to adhere to club beliefs. Thus, the State cannot disclaim its responsibility for those resulting pressures.

II

Given these substantial risks posed by the inclusion of the proposed Christian Club within Westside's present forum, Westside must redefine its relationship to its club program. The plurality recognizes that such redefinition is necessary to avoid the risk of endorsement and construes the Act accordingly. The plurality holds that the Act "limits participation by school officials at meetings of student religious groups" (citing § 4071[c] [2] and [3]), and requires religious club meetings to be held during noninstructional time (citing § 4071[b]). It also holds that schools may not sponsor any religious meetings. (citing § 4072[2]). Finally, [270] and perhaps most importantly, the plurality states that schools bear the responsibility for taking whatever further steps are necessary to make clear that their recognition of a religious club does not reflect their endorsement of the views of the club's participants.

Westside thus must do more than merely prohibit faculty members from actively participating in the Christian Club's meetings. It must fully disassociate itself from the Club's religious speech and avoid appearing to sponsor or endorse the Club's goals. It could, for example, entirely discontinue encouraging student participation in clubs and clarify that the clubs are not instrumentally related to the school's overall mission. Or, if the school sought to continue its general endorsement of those student clubs that did not engage in controversial speech, it could do so if it also affirmatively disclaimed any endorsement of the Christian Club.

III

The inclusion of the Christian Club in the type of forum presently established at Westside, without more, will not assure government neutrality toward religion. Rather, because the school endorses the extracurricular program as part of its educational mission, the inclusion of the Christian Club in that program will convey to students the school-sanctioned message that involvement in religion develops "citizenship, wholesome attitudes, good human relations, knowledge and skills." We need not question the value of that message to affirm that it is not the place of schools to issue it. Accordingly, schools such as Westside must be responsive not only to the broad terms of the Act's coverage, but also to this Court's mandate that they effectively disassociate themselves from the religious speech that now may become commonplace in their facilities.

46

Lee v. Weisman

505 U.S. 577 (1992)

Vote: 5—Blackmun, Stevens, O'Connor, Kennedy, Souter
      4—Rehnquist, White, Scalia, Thomas

Opinion announcing the opinion of the Court: Kennedy
Concurring opinions: Blackmun, Souter
Dissenting opinion: Scalia

The city of Providence, Rhode Island, had a policy of permitting its public high school and middle school principals to invite members of the clergy to offer invocation and benediction prayers as part of the schools' formal graduation ceremonies. A challenge to that policy resulted in the decision below.

Robert E. Lee, principal of Nathan Bishop Middle School, a public school in Providence, invited a Jewish rabbi to deliver a prayer at the 1989 graduation ceremony. The principal gave the rabbi a pamphlet titled "Guidelines for Civic Occasions," which had been prepared by the National Conference of Christians and Jews. He instructed the rabbi that the prayer should be nonsectarian. The pamphlet recommended that public prayers at nonsectarian civic ceremonies be composed with "inclusiveness and sensitivity."

Four days before graduation, the father of a graduating student sought a temporary restraining order to prohibit school officials from including an invocation or benediction in the ceremony. A federal district court denied the request. The student and her family attended the graduation, where the prayers below were recited. After the ceremony, the father sought a permanent injunction barring Lee and other Providence public school officials from inviting clergy to deliver invocations and benedictions at future graduations. To justify his standing before the court, he cited the likelihood that similar prayers would be at his daughter's public high school graduation.

Rabbi Gutterman's prayers at the middle school graduation were as follows:

INVOCATION
God of the Free, Hope of the Brave:
   For the legacy of America where diversity is celebrated and the rights of minorities are protected, we thank You. May these young men and women grow up to enrich it.
   For the liberty of America, we thank You. May these new graduates grow up to guard it.
   For the political process of America in which all its citizens may participate, for its court system where all may seek justice, we thank You. May those we honor this morning always turn to it in trust.

For the destiny of America, we thank You. May the graduates of Nathan Bishop Middle School so live that they might help to share it.

May our aspirations for our country and for these young people, who are our hope for the future, be richly fulfilled.

AMEN

BENEDICTION

O God, we are grateful to You for having endowed us with the capacity for learning which we have celebrated on this joyous commencement.

Happy families give thanks for seeing their children achieve an important milestone. Send Your blessings upon the teachers and administrators who helped prepare them.

The graduates now need strength and guidance for the future, help them to understand that we are not complete with academic knowledge alone. We must each strive to fulfill what You require of us all: To do justly, to love mercy, to walk humbly.

We give thanks to You, Lord, for keeping us alive, sustaining us and allowing us to reach this special, happy occasion.

AMEN

KENNEDY, J., delivered the opinion of the Court, in which BLACKMUN, STEVENS, O'CONNOR, and SOUTER, JJ., joined.

[580] School principals in the public school system of the city of Providence, Rhode Island, are permitted to invite members of the clergy to offer invocation and benediction prayers as part of the formal graduation ceremonies for middle schools and for high schools. The question before us is whether including clerical members who offer prayers as part of the official school graduation ceremony is consistent with the Religion Clauses of the First Amendment, provisions the Fourteenth Amendment makes applicable with full force to the States and their school districts. . . .

[586] These dominant facts mark and control the confines of our decision: State officials direct the performance of a formal religious exercise at promotional and graduation ceremonies for secondary schools. Even for those students who object to the religious exercise, their attendance and participation in the state-sponsored religious activity are in a fair and real sense obligatory, though the school district does not require attendance as a condition for receipt of the diploma. . . .

[587] The government involvement with religious activity in this case is pervasive, to the point of creating a state-sponsored and state-directed religious exercise in a public school. Conducting this formal religious observance conflicts with settled rules pertaining to prayer exercises for students, and that suffices to determine the question before us.

The principle that government may accommodate the free exercise of religion does not supersede the fundamental limitations imposed by the Establishment Clause. It is beyond dispute that, at a minimum, the Constitution guarantees that government may not coerce anyone to support or participate in religion or its exercise, or otherwise act in a way which "establishes a [state] religion or religious faith, or tends to do so." *Lynch*, at 678. The State's involvement in the school prayers challenged today violates these central principles.

That involvement is as troubling as it is undenied. A school official, the principal, decided that an invocation and a benediction should be given; this is a choice attributable to the State, and from a constitutional perspective it is as if a state statute decreed that the prayers must occur. The principal chose the religious participant, here a rabbi, and that choice is also attributable to the State. The reason for the choice of a rabbi is not disclosed by the record, but the potential for divisiveness over the choice of a particular member of the clergy to conduct the ceremony is apparent.

Divisiveness, of course, can attend any state decision respecting religions, and neither its existence nor its potential [588] necessarily invalidates the State's attempts to accommodate religion in all cases. The potential for divisiveness is of particular relevance here though, because it centers around an overt religious exercise in a secondary school environment where, as we discuss below, subtle coercive pressures exist and where the student had no real alternative which would have allowed her to avoid the fact or appearance of participation.

The State's role did not end with the decision to include a prayer and with the choice of a clergyman. Principal Lee provided Rabbi Gutterman with a copy of the "Guidelines for Civic Occasions," and advised him that his prayers should be nonsectarian. Through these means the principal directed and controlled the content of the prayers. Even if the only sanction for ignoring the instructions were that the rabbi would not be invited back, we think no religious representative who valued his or her continued reputation and effectiveness in the community would incur the State's displeasure in this regard. It is a cornerstone principle of our Establishment Clause jurisprudence that "it is no part of the business of government to compose official prayers for any group of the American people to recite as a part of a religious program carried on by government," *Engel v. Vitale*, 370 U.S. 421, 425 (1962), and that is what the school officials attempted to do. . . .

[589] The First Amendment's Religion Clauses mean that religious beliefs and religious expression are too precious to be either proscribed or prescribed by the State. The design of the Constitution is that preservation and transmission of religious beliefs and worship is a responsibility and a choice committed to the private sphere, which itself is promised freedom to pursue that mission. It must not be forgotten then, that while concern must be given to define the protection granted to an objector or a dissenting nonbeliever, these same Clauses exist to protect religion from government interference. [590] James Madison, the principal author of the Bill of Rights, did not rest his opposition to a religious establishment on the sole ground of its effect on the minority. A principal ground for his view was: "Experience witnesseth that ecclesiastical establishments, instead of maintaining the purity and efficacy of Religion, have had a contrary operation." *Memorial and Remonstrance against Religious Assessments* (1785).

These concerns have particular application in the case of school officials, whose effort to monitor prayer will be perceived by the students as inducing a participation they might otherwise reject. Though the efforts of the school officials in this case to find common ground appear to have been a good-faith attempt to recognize the common aspects of religions and not the divisive ones, our precedents do not permit school officials to assist in composing prayers as an incident to a formal exercise for their students. And these same precedents caution us to measure the idea of a civic religion against the central meaning of the Religion Clauses of the First Amendment, which is that all creeds must be tolerated and none favored. The suggestion that government may establish an official or civic religion as a means of avoiding the establishment of a religion with more specific creeds strikes us as a contradiction that cannot be accepted.

The degree of school involvement here made it clear that the graduation prayers bore the imprint of the State and thus put school-age children who objected in an untenable position. We turn our attention now to consider the position of the students, both those who desired the prayer and she who did not.

To endure the speech of false ideas or offensive content and then to counter it is part of learning how to live in a pluralistic society, a society which insists upon open discourse towards the end of a tolerant citizenry. And tolerance [591] presupposes some mutuality of obligation. It is argued that our constitutional vision of a free society requires confidence in our own ability to accept or reject ideas of which we do not approve, and that prayer at a high school graduation does nothing more than offer a choice. By the time they are seniors, high school students no doubt have been required to attend classes and assemblies and to complete assignments exposing them to ideas they find distasteful or immoral or absurd or all of these. Against this background, students may consider it an odd measure of justice to be subjected during the course of their educations to ideas deemed offensive and irreligious, but to be denied a brief, formal prayer ceremony that the school offers in return. This argument cannot prevail, however. It overlooks a fundamental dynamic of the Constitution.

The First Amendment protects speech and religion by quite different mechanisms. Speech is protected by ensuring its full expression even when the government participates, for the very object of some of our most important speech is to persuade the government to adopt an idea as its own. The method for protecting freedom of worship and freedom of conscience in religious matters is quite the reverse. In religious debate or expression the government is not a prime participant, for the Framers deemed religious establishment antithetical to the freedom of all. The Free Exercise Clause embraces a freedom of conscience and worship that has close parallels in the speech provisions of the First Amendment, but the Establishment Clause is a specific prohibition on forms of state intervention in religious affairs with no precise counterpart in the speech provisions. The explanation lies in the lesson of history that was and is the inspiration for the Establishment Clause, the lesson that in [592] the hands of government what might begin as a tolerant expression of religious views may end in a policy to indoctrinate and coerce. A state-created orthodoxy puts at grave risk that freedom of belief and conscience which are the sole assurance that religious faith is real, not imposed.

The lessons of the First Amendment are as urgent in the modern world as in the 18th century when it was written. One timeless lesson is that if citizens are subjected to state-sponsored religious exercises, the State disavows its own duty to guard and respect that sphere of inviolable conscience and belief which is the mark of a free people. To compromise that principle today would be to deny our own tradition and forfeit our standing to urge others to secure the protections of that tradition for themselves.

As we have observed before, there are heightened concerns with protecting freedom of conscience from subtle coercive pressure in the elementary and secondary public schools. Our decisions in *Engel v. Vitale* and *School Dist. of Abington* recognize, among other things, that prayer exercises in public schools carry a particular risk of indirect coercion. The concern may not be limited to the context of schools, but it is most pronounced there. What to most believers may seem nothing more than a reasonable request that the nonbeliever respect their religious practices, in a school context may appear to the nonbeliever or dissenter to be an attempt to employ the machinery of the State to enforce a religious orthodoxy.

[593] We need not look beyond the circumstances of this case to see the phenomenon at work. The undeniable fact is that the school district's supervision and control of a high school graduation ceremony places public pressure, as well as peer pressure, on attending students to stand as a group or, at least, maintain respectful silence during the invocation and benediction. This pressure, though subtle and indirect, can be as real as any overt compulsion. Of course, in our culture standing or remaining silent can signify adherence

to a view or simple respect for the views of others. And no doubt some persons who have no desire to join a prayer have little objection to standing as a sign of respect for those who do. But for the dissenter of high school age, who has a reasonable perception that she is being forced by the State to pray in a manner her conscience will not allow, the injury is no less real. There can be no doubt that for many, if not most, of the students at the graduation, the act of standing or remaining silent was an expression of participation in the rabbi's prayer. That was the very point of the religious exercise. It is of little comfort to a dissenter, then, to be told that for her the act of standing or remaining in silence signifies mere respect, rather than participation. What matters is that, given our social conventions, a reasonable dissenter in this milieu could believe that the group exercise signified her own participation or approval of it.

Finding no violation under these circumstances would place objectors in the dilemma of participating, with all that implies, or protesting. We do not address whether that choice is acceptable if the affected citizens are mature adults, but we think the State may not, consistent with the Establishment Clause, place primary and secondary school children in this position. Research in psychology supports the common assumption that adolescents are often susceptible to pressure from their peers towards conformity, and that the influence is strongest in matters of social convention. [594] To recognize that the choice imposed by the State constitutes an unacceptable constraint only acknowledges that the government may no more use social pressure to enforce orthodoxy than it may use more direct means. . . .

There was a stipulation in the District Court that attendance at graduation and promotional ceremonies is voluntary. Petitioners and [595] the United States, as *amicus*, made this a center point of the case, arguing that the option of not attending the graduation excuses any inducement or coercion in the ceremony itself. The argument lacks all persuasion. Law reaches past formalism. And to say a teenage student has a real choice not to attend her high school graduation is formalistic in the extreme. True, Deborah could elect not to attend commencement without renouncing her diploma; but we shall not allow the case to turn on this point. Everyone knows that in our society and in our culture high school graduation is one of life's most significant occasions. A school rule which excuses attendance is beside the point. Attendance may not be required by official decree, yet it is apparent that a student is not free to absent herself from the graduation exercise in any real sense of the term "voluntary," for absence would require forfeiture of those intangible benefits which have motivated the student through youth and all her high school years. Graduation is a time for family and those closest to the student to celebrate success and express mutual wishes of gratitude and respect, all to the end of impressing upon the young person the role that it is his or her right and duty to assume in the community and all of its diverse parts. . . .

[596] The Constitution forbids the State to exact religious conformity from a student as the price of attending her own high school graduation. This is the calculus the Constitution commands. . . .

[597] We do not hold that every state action implicating religion is invalid if one or a few citizens find it offensive. People may take offense at all manner of religious as well as nonreligious messages, but offense alone does not in every case show a violation. We know too that sometimes to endure [598] social isolation or even anger may be the price of conscience or nonconformity. But, by any reading of our cases, the conformity required of the student in this case was too high an exaction to withstand the test of the Establishment Clause. The prayer exercises in this case are especially improper because the State has in every practical sense compelled attendance and participation in an

explicit religious exercise at an event of singular importance to every student, one the objecting student had no real alternative to avoid. . . .

Our society would be less than true to its heritage if it lacked abiding concern for the values of its young people, and we acknowledge the profound belief of adherents to many faiths that there must be a place in the student's life for precepts of a morality higher even than the law we today enforce. We express no hostility to those aspirations, nor would our oath permit us to do so. A relentless and all-pervasive attempt to exclude religion from every aspect of public life could itself become inconsistent with the Constitution. We recognize that, at graduation time and throughout the course of the educational process, there will [599] be instances when religious values, religious practices, and religious persons will have some interaction with the public schools and their students. But these matters, often questions of accommodation of religion, are not before us. The sole question presented is whether a religious exercise may be conducted at a graduation ceremony in circumstances where, as we have found, young graduates who object are induced to conform. No holding by this Court suggests that a school can persuade or compel a student to participate in a religious exercise. That is being done here, and it is forbidden by the Establishment Clause of the First Amendment. . . .

[609] JUSTICE SOUTER, with whom JUSTICE STEVENS and JUSTICE O'CONNOR join, concurring.

I join the whole of the Court's opinion, and fully agree that prayers at public school graduation ceremonies indirectly coerce religious observance. I write separately nonetheless on two issues of Establishment Clause analysis that underlie my independent resolution of this case: whether the Clause applies to governmental practices that do not favor one religion or denomination over others, and whether state coercion of religious conformity, over and above state endorsement of religious exercise or belief, is a necessary element of an Establishment Clause violation.

I

Forty-five years ago, this Court announced a basic principle of constitutional law from which it has not strayed: the [610] Establishment Clause forbids not only state practices that "aid one religion . . . or prefer one religion over another," but also those that "aid all religions." *Everson v. Board of Ed. of Ewing*, 330 U.S. 1, 15 (1947). Today we reaffirm that principle, holding that the Establishment Clause forbids state-sponsored prayers in public school settings no matter how nondenominational the prayers may be. In barring the State from sponsoring generically theistic prayers where it could not sponsor sectarian ones, we hold true to a line of precedent from which there is no adequate historical case to depart. . . .

[612] Some have challenged this precedent by reading the Establishment Clause to permit "nonpreferential" state promotion of religion. The challengers argue that, as originally understood by the Framers, "the Establishment Clause did not require government neutrality between religion and irreligion nor did it prohibit the Federal Government from providing nondiscriminatory aid to religion." *Wallace*, at 106 (REHNQUIST, J., dissenting). While a case has been made for this position, it is not so convincing as to warrant reconsideration of our settled law; indeed, I find in the history

of the Clause's textual development a more powerful argument supporting the Court's jurisprudence following *Everson.*

When James Madison arrived at the First Congress with a series of proposals to amend the National Constitution, one of the provisions read that "the civil rights of none shall be abridged on account of religious belief or worship, nor shall any national religion be established, nor shall the full and equal rights of conscience be in any manner, or on any pretext, infringed." Madison's language did not last long. It was sent to a Select Committee of the House, which, without explanation, changed it to read that "no religion shall be established by law, nor shall the equal rights of conscience be infringed." Thence the proposal went to the Committee of the Whole, which was in turn dissatisfied with the Select Committee's language and adopted an alternative proposed by Samuel Livermore of New Hampshire: "Congress shall make no laws touching religion, or infringing the rights of conscience." Livermore's proposal would have forbidden laws having anything to do with religion and was thus not [613] only far broader than Madison's version, but broader even than the scope of the Establishment Clause as we now understand it.

The House rewrote the amendment once more before sending it to the Senate, this time adopting, without recorded debate, language derived from a proposal by Fisher Ames of Massachusetts: "Congress shall make no law establishing Religion, or prohibiting the free exercise thereof, nor shall the rights of conscience be infringed." Perhaps, on further reflection, the Representatives had thought Livermore's proposal too expansive, or perhaps, as one historian has suggested, they had simply worried that his language would not "satisfy the demands of those who wanted something said specifically against establishments of religion." L. Levy, *The Establishment Clause* 81 (1986). We do not know; what we do know is that the House rejected the Select Committee's version, which arguably ensured only that "no religion" enjoyed an official preference over others, and deliberately chose instead a prohibition extending to laws establishing "religion" in general.

The sequence of the Senate's treatment of this House proposal, and the House's response to the Senate, confirm that the Framers meant the Establishment Clause's prohibition to encompass nonpreferential aid to religion. In September 1789, the Senate considered a number of provisions that would have permitted such aid, and ultimately it adopted one of them. First, it briefly entertained this language: "Congress shall make no law establishing One Religious Sect or Society in preference to others, nor shall the rights of conscience be infringed." [614] After rejecting two minor amendments to that proposal, the Senate dropped it altogether and chose a provision identical to the House's proposal, but without the clause protecting the "rights of conscience." With no record of the Senate debates, we cannot know what prompted these changes, but the record does tell us that, six days later, the Senate went half circle and adopted its narrowest language yet: "Congress shall make no law establishing articles of faith or a mode of worship, or prohibiting the free exercise of religion." The Senate sent this proposal to the House along with its versions of the other constitutional amendments proposed.

Though it accepted much of the Senate's work on the Bill of Rights, the House rejected the Senate's version of the Establishment Clause and called for a joint conference committee, to which the Senate agreed. The House conferees ultimately won out, persuading the Senate to accept this as the final text of the Religion Clauses: "Congress shall make no law respecting an establishment of religion, or prohibiting the free exercise thereof." What is remarkable is that, unlike the earliest House drafts or the final Senate proposal, the prevailing language is not limited to laws respecting an establishment of "a religion," "a national religion," "one religious sect," or specific "articles of faith." The Framers repeatedly [615] considered and deliberately rejected such narrow language and instead extended their prohibition to state support for "religion" in general.

Implicit in their choice is the distinction between preferential and nonpreferential establishments, which the weight of evidence suggests the Framers appreciated. Of particular note, the Framers were vividly familiar with efforts in the Colonies and, later, the States to impose general, nondenominational assessments and other incidents of ostensibly ecumenical establishments. The Virginia statute for religious freedom, written by Jefferson and sponsored by Madison, captured the separationist response to such measures. Condemning all establishments, however nonpreferentialist, the statute broadly guaranteed that "no man shall be compelled to frequent or support any religious worship, place, or ministry whatsoever," including his own. Forcing a citizen to support even his own church would, among other things, deny "the ministry those temporary rewards, which proceeding from an approbation of their personal conduct, are an additional incitement to earnest and unremitting labours for the instruction of mankind." In general, Madison later added, "religion & Govt. will both exist in greater purity, the less they are mixed together." Letter from J. Madison to E. Livingston (July 10, 1822).

What we thus know of the Framers' experience underscores the observation of one prominent commentator, that confining the Establishment Clause to a prohibition on preferential aid "requires a premise that the Framers were extraordinarily bad drafters—that they believed one thing but adopted language that said something substantially different, and that they did so after repeatedly attending to the [616] choice of language." Laycock, *"Nonpreferential" Aid* 882–883. We must presume, since there is no conclusive evidence to the contrary, that the Framers embraced the significance of their textual judgment.[3] Thus, on balance, history neither contradicts nor warrants reconsideration of the settled principle that the Establishment Clause forbids support for religion in general no less than support for one religion or some.

While these considerations are, for me, sufficient to reject the nonpreferentialist position, one further concern animates my judgment. In many contexts, including this one, nonpreferentialism requires some distinction between "sectarian" religious practices and those that would be, by some measure, ecumenical enough to pass Establishment Clause muster. Simply by requiring the enquiry, nonpreferentialists invite the courts to engage in comparative theology. I can hardly imagine a subject less amenable to the competence [617] of the federal judiciary, or more deliberately to be avoided where possible.

This case is nicely in point. Since the nonpreferentiality of a prayer must be judged by its text, JUSTICE BLACKMUN pertinently observes that Rabbi Gutterman drew his exhortation "to do justly, to love mercy, to walk humbly" straight from the King James version of Micah, ch. 6, v. 8. At some undefinable point, the similarities between a state-sponsored prayer and the sacred text of a specific religion would so closely identify the former with the latter that even a nonpreferentialist would have to concede a breach of

---

3. In his dissent in *Wallace v. Jaffree*, THE CHIEF JUSTICE rested his nonpreferentialist interpretation partly on the post-ratification actions of the early National Government. Aside from the willingness of some (but not all) early Presidents to issue ceremonial religious proclamations, which were at worst trivial breaches of the Establishment Clause, he cited such seemingly preferential aid as a treaty provision, signed by Jefferson, authorizing federal subsidization of a Roman Catholic priest and church for the Kaskaskia Indians. 472 U.S. at 103. But this proves too much, for if the Establishment Clause permits a special appropriation of tax money for the religious activities of a particular sect, it forbids virtually nothing. See Laycock, *"Nonpreferential" Aid* 915. Although evidence of historical practice can indeed furnish valuable aid in the interpretation of contemporary language, acts like the one in question prove only that public officials, no matter when they serve, can turn a blind eye to constitutional principle.

the Establishment Clause. And even if Micah's thought is sufficiently generic for most believers, it still embodies a straightforwardly theistic premise, and so does the rabbi's prayer. Many Americans who consider themselves religious are not theistic; some, like several of the Framers, are deists who would question Rabbi Gutterman's plea for divine advancement of the country's political and moral good. Thus, a nonpreferentialist who would condemn subjecting public school graduates to, say, the Anglican liturgy would still need to explain why the government's preference for theistic over nontheistic religion is constitutional.

Nor does it solve the problem to say that the State should promote a "diversity" of religious views; that position would necessarily compel the government and, inevitably, the courts to make wholly inappropriate judgments about the number of religions the State should sponsor and the relative frequency with which it should sponsor each. In fact, the prospect would be even worse than that. As Madison observed in criticizing religious Presidential proclamations, the practice of sponsoring religious messages tends, over time, "to narrow the recommendation to the standard of the predominant sect." Madison's "Detached Memoranda." We have not changed much since the days of Madison, and the judiciary should not [618] willingly enter the political arena to battle the centripetal force leading from religious pluralism to official preference for the faith with the most votes.

II

Petitioners rest most of their argument on a theory that, whether or not the Establishment Clause permits extensive nonsectarian support for religion, it does not forbid the state to sponsor affirmations of religious belief that coerce neither support for religion nor participation in religious observance. I appreciate the force of some of the arguments supporting a "coercion" analysis of the Clause. But we could not adopt that reading without abandoning our settled law, a course that, in my view, the text of the Clause would not readily permit. Nor does the extratextual evidence of original meaning stand so unequivocally at odds with the textual premise inherent in existing precedent that we should fundamentally reconsider our course. . . .

[620] Like the provisions about "due" process and "unreasonable" searches and seizures, the constitutional language forbidding laws "respecting an establishment of religion" is not pellucid. But virtually everyone acknowledges that the Clause bans more than formal establishments of religion in the traditional sense, that is, massive state support for religion through, among other means, comprehensive schemes of taxation. This much follows from the Framers' explicit rejection of simpler provisions prohibiting either the establishment of a religion or laws "establishing religion" in favor of the broader ban on laws "respecting an establishment of religion."

While some argue that the Framers added the word "respecting" simply to foreclose federal interference with state establishments of religion, the language sweeps more broadly than that. In Madison's words, the Clause in its final form forbids "everything like" a national religious establishment, see Madison's "Detached Memoranda" 558, and, after incorporation, it forbids "everything like" a state religious establishment. The sweep is broad enough that Madison himself characterized congressional provisions for legislative and military chaplains as unconstitutional "establishments." Madison's "Detached Memoranda."

[621] While petitioners insist that the prohibition extends only to the "coercive" features and incidents of establishment, they cannot easily square that claim with the

constitutional text. The First Amendment forbids not just laws "respecting an establishment of religion," but also those "prohibiting the free exercise thereof." Yet laws that coerce nonadherents to "support or participate in any religion or its exercise," *County of Allegheny*, at 659–660 (opinion of KENNEDY, J.), would virtually by definition violate their right to religious free exercise. Thus, a literal application of the coercion test would render the Establishment Clause a virtual nullity, as petitioners' counsel essentially conceded at oral argument.

Our cases presuppose as much; as we said in *School Dist. of Abington*, "the distinction between the two clauses is apparent—a violation of the Free Exercise Clause is predicated on coercion while the Establishment Clause violation need not be so attended." 374 U.S. at 223. While one may argue that the Framers meant the Establishment Clause simply to ornament the First Amendment, that must be a reading of last resort. Without compelling evidence to the contrary, we should presume that the Framers meant the Clause to stand for something more than petitioners attribute to it.

[622] Petitioners argue from the political setting in which the Establishment Clause was framed, and from the Framers' own political practices following ratification, that government may constitutionally endorse religion so long as it does not coerce religious conformity. The setting and the practices warrant canvassing, but while they yield some evidence for petitioners' argument, they do not reveal the degree of consensus in early constitutional thought that would raise a threat to stare decisis by challenging the presumption that the Establishment Clause adds something to the Free Exercise Clause that follows it.

The Framers adopted the Religion Clauses in response to a long tradition of coercive state support for religion, particularly in the form of tax assessments, but their special antipathy to religious coercion did not exhaust their hostility to the features and incidents of establishment. Indeed, Jefferson and Madison opposed any political appropriation of religion, and, even when challenging the hated assessments, they did not always temper their rhetoric with distinctions between coercive and noncoercive state action. When, for example, Madison criticized Virginia's general assessment bill, he invoked principles antithetical to all state efforts to promote religion. An assessment, he wrote, is improper not simply because it forces people to donate "three pence" to religion, but, more broadly, because "it is itself a signal of persecution. It degrades from the equal rank of Citizens all those whose opinions in Religion do not bend to those of the Legislative authority." J. Madison, *Memorial and Remonstrance against Religious Assessments* (1785). Madison saw that, even without the tax collector's participation, an official endorsement of religion can impair religious liberty.

Petitioners contend that because the early Presidents included religious messages in their inaugural and Thanksgiving Day addresses, the Framers could not have meant the [623] Establishment Clause to forbid noncoercive state endorsement of religion. The argument ignores the fact, however, that Americans today find such proclamations less controversial than did the founding generation, whose published thoughts on the matter belie petitioners' claim. President Jefferson, for example, steadfastly refused to issue Thanksgiving proclamations of any kind, in part because he thought they violated the Religion Clauses. Letter from Thomas Jefferson to Rev. S. Miller (Jan. 23, 1808). In explaining his views to the Reverend Samuel Miller, Jefferson effectively anticipated, and rejected, petitioners' position:

"It is only proposed that I should *recommend*, not prescribe a day of fasting & prayer. That is, that I should *indirectly* assume to the U.S. an authority over religious exercises which the Constitution has directly precluded from them. It must be meant too that this recommendation is to carry some authority, and to be sanctioned by some penalty on those who disregard it; not indeed of fine and imprisonment, but of some degree of proscription perhaps in public opinion." *Id.*, at 98–99 (emphasis in original).

By condemning such noncoercive state practices that, in "recommending" the majority faith, demean religious dissenters "in public opinion," Jefferson necessarily condemned what, in modern terms, we call official endorsement of religion. He accordingly construed the Establishment Clause to forbid not simply state coercion, but also state endorsement, of religious belief and observance.[5] And if he opposed [624] impersonal Presidential addresses for inflicting "proscription in public opinion," all the more would he have condemned less diffuse expressions of official endorsement.

During his first three years in office, James Madison also refused to call for days of thanksgiving and prayer, though later, amid the political turmoil of the War of 1812, he did so on four separate occasions. See Madison's "Detached Memoranda" 562, and n.54. Upon retirement, in an essay condemning as an unconstitutional "establishment" the use of public money to support congressional and military chaplains, *id.*, at 558–560, he concluded that "religious proclamations [625] by the Executive recommending thanksgivings & fasts are shoots from the same root with the legislative acts reviewed. Altho' recommendations only, they imply a religious agency, making no part of the trust delegated to political rulers." *Id.*, at 560. Explaining that "the members of a Govt . . . can in no sense, be regarded as possessing an advisory trust from their Constituents in their religious capacities," *ibid.*, he further observed that the state necessarily freights all of its religious messages with political ones: "the idea of policy [is] associated with religion, whatever be the mode or the occasion, when a function of the latter is assumed by those in power." *Id.*, at 562.

Madison's failure to keep pace with his principles in the face of congressional pressure cannot erase the principles. He admitted to backsliding, and explained that he had made the content of his wartime proclamations inconsequential enough to mitigate much of their impropriety. While his writings suggest mild variations in his interpretation of the Establishment Clause, Madison was no different in that respect from the rest of his political generation. That he expressed so much doubt about the constitutionality of religious proclamations, however, suggests a brand of separationism stronger even than that embodied in our traditional jurisprudence. So too does his characterization of public subsidies for legislative and military chaplains as unconstitutional "establishments," for the federal courts, however expansive their general view of the Establishment Clause, have upheld both practices.

[626] To be sure, the leaders of the young Republic engaged in some of the practices that separationists like Jefferson and Madison criticized. The First Congress did hire institutional chaplains, and Presidents Washington and Adams unapologetically marked days of "public thanksgiving and prayer." Yet in the face of the separationist dissent,

---

5. . . . Petitioners also seek comfort in a different passage of the same letter. Jefferson argued that Presidential religious proclamations violate not just the Establishment Clause, but also the Tenth Amendment, for "what might be a right in a state government, was a violation of that right when assumed by another." Letter from Thomas Jefferson to Rev. S. Miller (Jan. 23, 1808). Jefferson did not, however, restrict himself to the Tenth Amendment in condemning such proclamations by a national officer. I do not, in any event, understand petitioners to be arguing that the Establishment Clause is exclusively a structural provision mediating the respective powers of the State and National Governments. Such a position would entail the argument, which petitioners do not make, and which we would almost certainly reject, that incorporation of the Establishment Clause under the Fourteenth Amendment was erroneous.

those practices prove, at best, that the Framers simply did not share a common understanding of the Establishment Clause, and, at worst, that they, like other politicians,
could raise constitutional ideals one day and turn their backs on them the next. "Indeed,
by 1787 the provisions of the state bills of rights had become what Madison called mere
'paper parchments'—expressions of the most laudable sentiments, observed as much in
the breach as in practice." Kurland, *The Origins of the Religion Clauses of the Constitution*, 27 Wm. & Mary L. Rev. 839, 852 (1986). Sometimes the National Constitution
fared no better. Ten years after proposing the First Amendment, Congress passed the
Alien and Sedition Acts, measures patently unconstitutional by modern standards. If the
early Congress's political actions were determinative, and not merely relevant, evidence
of constitutional meaning, we would have to gut our current First Amendment doctrine
to make room for political censorship.

While we may be unable to know for certain what the Framers meant by the Clause,
we do know that, around the time of its ratification, a respectable body of opinion
supported a considerably broader reading than petitioners urge upon us. This consistency
with the textual considerations is enough to preclude fundamentally reexamining our
settled law. . . .

[631] JUSTICE SCALIA, with whom THE CHIEF JUSTICE, JUSTICE WHITE, and JUSTICE THOMAS join, dissenting.

Three Terms ago, I joined an opinion recognizing that the Establishment Clause
must be construed in light of the "government policies of accommodation, acknowledgment, and support for religion [that] are an accepted part of our political and cultural
heritage." That opinion affirmed that "the meaning of the Clause is to be determined by
reference to historical practices and understandings." It said that "[a] test for implementing the protections of the Establishment Clause that, if applied with consistency, would
invalidate longstanding traditions cannot be a proper reading of the Clause." *County of
Allegheny v. American Civil Liberties Union, Greater Pittsburgh Chapter*, 492 U.S. 573,
657, 670 (1989) (KENNEDY, J., concurring in judgment in part and dissenting in part).

These views of course prevent me from joining today's opinion, which is conspicuously bereft of any reference to history. In holding that the Establishment Clause prohibits invocations and benedictions at public school graduation ceremonies, the Court—
with nary a mention that it is doing [632] so—lays waste a tradition that is as old as
public school graduation ceremonies themselves, and that is a component of an even
more longstanding American tradition of nonsectarian prayer to God at public celebrations generally. As its instrument of destruction, the bulldozer of its social engineering,
the Court invents a boundless, and boundlessly manipulable, test of psychological coercion, which promises to do for the Establishment Clause what the Durham rule did for
the insanity defense. Today's opinion shows more forcefully than volumes of argumentation why our Nation's protection, that fortress which is our Constitution, cannot possibly rest upon the changeable philosophical predilections of the Justices of this Court,
but must have deep foundations in the historic practices of our people.

Justice Holmes' aphorism that "a page of history is worth a volume of logic," *New
York Trust Co. v. Eisner*, 256 U.S. 345, 349 (1921), applies with particular force to our
Establishment Clause jurisprudence. As we have recognized, our interpretation of the
Establishment Clause should "comport with what history reveals was the contempo-
raneous understanding of its guarantees." *Lynch v. Donnelly*, 465 U.S. 668, 673 (1984).

"The line we must draw between the permissible and the impermissible is one which accords with history and faithfully reflects the understanding of the Founding Fathers." *School Dist. of Abington v. Schempp*, 374 U.S. 203, 294 (1963) (Brennan, J., concurring). "Historical evidence sheds light not only on what the draftsmen intended the Establishment Clause to mean, but also on how they thought that Clause applied" to contemporaneous practices. *Marsh v. Chambers*, 463 U.S. 783, 790 (1983). Thus, "the existence from the beginning of the Nation's life of a practice, [while] not conclusive of its constitutionality . . . [,] is a fact of considerable import in the interpretation" of the [633] Establishment Clause. *Walz v. Tax Comm'n of New York City*, 397 U.S. 664, 681 (1970) (Brennan, J., concurring).

The history and tradition of our Nation are replete with public ceremonies featuring prayers of thanksgiving and petition. Illustrations of this point have been amply provided in our prior opinions, but since the Court is so oblivious to our history as to suggest that the Constitution restricts "preservation and transmission of religious beliefs . . . to the private sphere," *ante*, 505 U.S. at 589, it appears necessary to provide another brief account.

From our Nation's origin, prayer has been a prominent part of governmental ceremonies and proclamations. The Declaration of Independence, the document marking our birth as a separate people, "appealed to the Supreme Judge of the world for the rectitude of our intentions" and avowed "a firm reliance on the protection of divine Providence." In his first inaugural address, after swearing his oath of office on a Bible, George Washington deliberately made a prayer a part of his first official act as President:

> "It would be peculiarly improper to omit in this first official act my fervent supplications to that Almighty Being who rules over the universe, who presides in the councils of nations, and whose providential aids can supply every human defect, that His benediction may consecrate to the liberties and happiness of the people of the United States a Government instituted by themselves for these essential purposes." *Inaugural Addresses of the Presidents of the United States*, S. Doc. 101-10, p. 2 (1989).

Such supplications have been a characteristic feature of inaugural addresses ever since. Thomas Jefferson, for example, [634] prayed in his first inaugural address: "May that Infinite Power which rules the destinies of the universe lead our councils to what is best, and give them a favorable issue for your peace and prosperity." In his second inaugural address, Jefferson acknowledged his need for divine guidance and invited his audience to join his prayer:

> "I shall need, too, the favor of that Being in whose hands we are, who led our fathers, as Israel of old, from their native land and planted them in a country flowing with all the necessaries and comforts of life; who has covered our infancy with His providence and our riper years with His wisdom and power, and to whose goodness I ask you to join in supplications with me that He will so enlighten the minds of your servants, guide their councils, and prosper their measures that whatsoever they do shall result in your good, and shall secure to you the peace, friendship, and approbation of all nations." *Id.*, at 22–23.

Similarly, James Madison, in his first inaugural address, placed his confidence

> "in the guardianship and guidance of that Almighty Being whose power regulates the destiny of nations, whose blessings have been so conspicuously dispensed to this rising Republic, and to whom we are bound to address our devout gratitude for the past, as well as our fervent supplications and best hopes for the future." *Id.*, at 28.

. . . [635] The other two branches of the Federal Government also have a long-established practice of prayer at public events. As we detailed in *Marsh*, congressional sessions have opened with a chaplain's prayer ever since the First Congress. And this Court's own sessions have opened with the invocation "God save the United States and this Honorable Court" since the days of Chief Justice Marshall.

In addition to this general tradition of prayer at public ceremonies, there exists a more specific tradition of invocations and benedictions at public school graduation exercises. By one account, the first public high school graduation ceremony took place in Connecticut in July 1868—the very month, as it happens, that the Fourteenth Amendment (the vehicle by which the Establishment Clause has been applied against the States) was ratified—when "15 seniors from the Norwich Free Academy marched in their best Sunday suits and dresses into a church hall and waited through majestic music and long prayers." [636] As the Court obliquely acknowledges in describing the "customary features" of high school graduations, *ante*, 505 U.S. at 583, and as respondents do not contest, the invocation and benediction have long been recognized to be "as traditional as any other parts of the [school] graduation program and are widely established."

II

The Court presumably would separate graduation invocations and benedictions from other instances of public "preservation and transmission of religious beliefs" on the ground that they involve "psychological coercion." I find it a sufficient embarrassment that our Establishment Clause jurisprudence regarding holiday displays has come to "require scrutiny more commonly associated with interior decorators than with the judiciary." *American Jewish Congress v. Chicago*, 827 F.2d 120, 129 (CA7 1987) (Easterbrook, J., dissenting). But interior decorating is a rock-hard science compared to psychology practiced by amateurs. A few citations of "research in psychology" that have no particular bearing upon the precise issue here cannot disguise the fact that the Court has gone beyond the realm where judges know what they are doing. The Court's argument that state officials have "coerced" students to take part in the invocation and benediction at graduation ceremonies is, not to put too fine a point on it, incoherent.

The Court identifies two "dominant facts" that it says dictate its ruling that invocations and benedictions at public school graduation ceremonies violate the Establishment Clause. Neither of them is in any relevant sense true.

[637] A

The Court declares that students' "attendance and participation in the [invocation and benediction] are in a fair and real sense obligatory." But what exactly is this "fair and real sense"? According to the Court, students at graduation who want "to avoid the fact or appearance of participation," *ante*, 505 U.S. at 588, in the invocation and benediction are psychologically obligated by "public pressure, as well as peer pressure, . . . to stand as a group or, at least, maintain respectful silence" during those prayers. *Ante*, 505 U.S. at 593. This assertion—the very linchpin of the Court's opinion—is almost as intriguing for what it does not say as for what it says. It does not say, for example, that students are psychologically coerced to bow their heads, place their hands in a Durer-like prayer position, pay attention to the prayers, utter "Amen," or in fact pray. (Perhaps further intensive psychological research remains to be done on these matters.) It claims only that students are psychologically coerced "to stand . . . *or*, at least, maintain respectful silence." *Ibid.* (emphasis added). Both halves of this disjunctive (both of which must amount to the fact or appearance of participation in prayer if the Court's analysis is to survive on its own terms) merit particular attention.

To begin with the latter: The Court's notion that a student who simply *sits* in "respectful silence" during the invocation and benediction (when all others are standing) has somehow joined—or would somehow be perceived as having joined—in the prayers is nothing short of ludicrous. We indeed live in a vulgar age. But surely "our social conventions," *ibid.*, have not coarsened to the point that anyone who does not stand on his chair and shout obscenities can reasonably be deemed to have assented to everything said in his presence. Since the Court does not dispute that students exposed to prayer at graduation ceremonies retain (despite "subtle coercive pressures," *ante*, 505 U.S. at 588) the free will to sit, there is absolutely no basis for the Court's [638] decision. It is fanciful enough to say that "a reasonable dissenter," standing head erect in a class of bowed heads, "could believe that the group exercise signified her own participation or approval of it," *ibid*. It is beyond the absurd to say that she could entertain such a belief while pointedly declining to rise.

But let us assume the very worst, that the nonparticipating graduate is "subtly coerced" . . . to stand! Even that half of the disjunctive does not remotely establish a "participation" (or an "appearance of participation") in a religious exercise. The Court acknowledges that "in our culture standing . . . can signify adherence to a view or simple respect for the views of others." *Ibid.* (Much more often the latter than the former, I think, except perhaps in the proverbial town meeting, where one votes by standing.) But if it is a permissible inference that one who is standing is doing so simply out of respect for the prayers of others that are in progress, then how can it possibly be said that a "reasonable dissenter . . . could believe that the group exercise signified her own participation or approval"? Quite obviously, it cannot. I may add, moreover, that maintaining respect for the religious observances of others is a fundamental civic virtue that government (including the public schools) can and should cultivate—so that even if it were the case that the displaying of such respect might be mistaken for taking part in the prayer, I would deny that the dissenter's interest in avoiding even the false appearance of participation constitutionally trumps the government's interest in fostering respect for religion generally.

The opinion manifests that the Court itself has not given careful consideration to its test of psychological coercion. For if it had, how could it observe, with no hint of concern or disapproval, that students stood for the Pledge of Allegiance, which immediately preceded Rabbi Gutterman's invocation? The government can, of course, no more coerce political orthodoxy than religious orthodoxy. [639] Moreover, since the Pledge of Allegiance has been revised since *Barnette* to include the phrase "under God," recital of the Pledge would appear to raise the same Establishment Clause issue as the invocation and benediction. If students were psychologically coerced to remain standing during the invocation, they must also have been psychologically coerced, moments before, to stand for (and thereby, in the Court's view, take part in or appear to take part in) the Pledge. Must the Pledge therefore be barred from the public schools (both from graduation ceremonies and from the classroom)? In *Barnette* we held that a public school student could not be compelled to recite the Pledge; we did not even hint that she could not be compelled to observe respectful silence—indeed, even to stand in respectful silence—when those who wished to recite it did so. Logically, that ought to be the next project for the Court's bulldozer.

I also find it odd that the Court concludes that high school graduates may not be subjected to this supposed psychological coercion, yet refrains from addressing whether "mature adults" may. I had thought that the reason graduation from high school is regarded as so significant an event is that it is generally associated with transition from adolescence to young adulthood. Many graduating seniors, of course, are old enough to vote. Why, then, does the Court treat them as though they were first-graders? Will we soon have a jurisprudence that distinguishes between mature and immature adults?

B

The other "dominant fact" identified by the Court is that "state officials direct the performance of a formal religious exercise" at school graduation ceremonies. *Ante,* 505 U.S. at 586. "Directing the performance of a formal religious exercise" has a sound of liturgy to it, summoning up images of the principal directing acolytes where to carry the cross, or showing the rabbi where to unroll the Torah. A Court professing to be [640] engaged in a "delicate and fact-sensitive" line-drawing, *ante,* 505 U.S. at 597, would better describe what it means as "prescribing the content of an invocation and benediction." But even that would be false. All the record shows is that principals of the Providence public schools, acting within their delegated authority, have invited clergy to deliver invocations and benedictions at graduations; and that Principal Lee invited Rabbi Gutterman, provided him a two-page pamphlet, prepared by the National Conference of Christians and Jews, giving general advice on inclusive prayer for civic occasions, and advised him that his prayers at graduation should be nonsectarian. How these facts can fairly be transformed into the charges that Principal Lee "directed and controlled the content of [Rabbi Gutterman's] prayer," *ante,* 505 U.S. at 588, that school officials "monitor prayer," *ante,* 505 U.S. at 590, and attempted to "compose official prayers," *ante,* 505 U.S. at 588, and that the "government involvement with religious activity in this case is pervasive," *ante,* 505 U.S. at 587, is difficult to fathom. The Court identifies nothing in the record remotely suggesting that school officials have ever drafted, edited, screened, or censored graduation prayers, or that Rabbi Gutterman was a mouthpiece of the school officials.

These distortions of the record are, of course, not harmless error: without them the Court's solemn assertion that the school officials could reasonably be perceived to be "enforcing a religious orthodoxy," *ante,* 505 U.S. at 592, would ring as hollow as it ought.

III

The deeper flaw in the Court's opinion does not lie in its wrong answer to the question whether there was state-induced "peer-pressure" coercion; it lies, rather, in the Court's making violation of the Establishment Clause hinge on such a precious question. The coercion that was a hallmark of historical establishments of religion was coercion of religious orthodoxy and of financial support by force of law and threat of penalty. Typically, attendance at the state [641] church was required; only clergy of the official church could lawfully perform sacraments; and dissenters, if tolerated, faced an array of civil disabilities. Thus, for example, in the Colony of Virginia, where the Church of England had been established, ministers were required by law to conform to the doctrine and rites of the Church of England; and all persons were required to attend church and observe the Sabbath, were tithed for the public support of Anglican ministers, and were taxed for the costs of building and repairing churches.

The Establishment Clause was adopted to prohibit such an establishment of religion at the federal level (and to protect state establishments of religion from federal interference). I will further acknowledge for the sake of argument that, as some scholars have argued, by 1790 the term "establishment" had acquired an additional meaning—"financial support of religion generally, by public taxation"—that reflected the development of "general or multiple" establishments, not limited to a single church. But that would still be an establishment coerced by force of law. And I will further concede that our constitutional tradition, from the Declaration of Independence and the first inaugural address of Washington, quoted earlier, down to the present day, has, with a few aberrations, ruled out of order government-sponsored endorsement of religion—even when no legal coercion is present, and indeed even when no ersatz, "peer-pressure" psycho-coercion is present—where the endorsement is sectarian, in the sense of specifying details upon which men and women who believe in a benevolent, omnipotent Creator and Ruler of the world are known to differ (for example, the divinity of Christ). But there is simply no support for the proposition that the officially sponsored nondenominational invocation and benediction read by Rabbi Gutterman—with no one legally coerced to recite [642] them—violated the Constitution of the United States. To the contrary, they are so characteristically American they could have come from the pen of George Washington or Abraham Lincoln himself.

Thus, while I have no quarrel with the Court's general proposition that the Establishment Clause "guarantees that government may not coerce anyone to support or participate in religion or its exercise," *ante*, 505 U.S. at 587, I see no warrant for expanding the concept of coercion beyond acts backed by threat of penalty—a brand of coercion that, happily, is readily discernible to those of us who have made a career of reading the disciples of Blackstone rather than of Freud. The Framers were indeed opposed to coercion of religious worship by the National Government; but, as their own sponsorship of nonsectarian prayer in public events demonstrates, they understood that "speech is not coercive; the listener may do as he likes." *American Jewish Congress v. Chicago*, 827 F.2d at 132 (Easterbrook, J., dissenting). . . .

[645] The reader has been told much in this case about the personal interest of Mr. Weisman and his daughter, and very little about the personal interests on the other side. They are not inconsequential. Church and state would not be such a difficult subject if religion were, as the Court apparently thinks it to be, some purely personal avocation that can be indulged entirely in secret, like pornography, in the privacy of one's room. For most believers it is not that, and has never been. Religious men and women of almost all denominations have felt it necessary to acknowledge and beseech the blessing of God as a people, and not just as individuals, because they believe in the "protection of divine Providence," as the Declaration of Independence put it, not just for individuals but for societies; because they believe God to be, as Washington's first Thanksgiving Proclamation put it, the "Great Lord and Ruler of Nations." One can believe in the effectiveness of such public worship, or one can deprecate and deride it. But the longstanding American tradition of prayer at official ceremonies displays with unmistakable clarity that the Establishment Clause does not forbid the government to accommodate it.

The narrow context of the present case involves a community's celebration of one of the milestones in its young citizens' [646] lives, and it is a bold step for this Court to seek to banish from that occasion, and from thousands of similar celebrations throughout this land, the expression of gratitude to God that a majority of the community wishes to make. The issue before us today is not the abstract philosophical question whether the alternative of frustrating this desire of a religious majority is to be preferred over the alternative of imposing "psychological coercion," or a feeling of exclusion, upon non-believers. Rather, the question is whether a mandatory choice in favor of the former has been imposed by the United States Constitution. As the age-old practices of our people show, the answer to that question is not at all in doubt.

I must add one final observation: The Founders of our Republic knew the fearsome potential of sectarian religious belief to generate civil dissension and civil strife. And they also knew that nothing, absolutely nothing, is so inclined to foster among religious believers of various faiths a toleration—no, an affection—for one another than voluntarily joining in prayer together, to the God whom they all worship and seek. Needless to say, no one should be compelled to do that, but it is a shame to deprive our public culture of the opportunity, and indeed the encouragement, for people to do it voluntarily. The Baptist or Catholic who heard and joined in the simple and inspiring prayers of Rabbi Gutterman on this official and patriotic occasion was inoculated from religious bigotry and prejudice in a manner that cannot be replicated. To deprive our society of that important unifying mechanism, in order to spare the nonbeliever what seems to me the minimal inconvenience of standing or even sitting in respectful nonparticipation, is as senseless in policy as it is unsupported in law.

For the foregoing reasons, I dissent.

47

Lamb's Chapel and John Steigerwald v. Center Moriches Union Free School District

508 U.S. 384 (1993)

Vote: 9—Rehnquist, White, Blackmun, Stevens, O'Connor, Scalia, Kennedy, Souter, Thomas

0

Opinion announcing the opinion of the Court: White
Opinion concurring in part and concurring in the judgment: Kennedy
Opinion concurring in the judgment: Scalia

Lamb's Chapel, an evangelical church, and its pastor, John Steigerwald, applied to the Center Moriches Union Free School District for permission to use school facilities after hours to show a six-part film series containing lectures by Dr. James Dobson. A brochure provided by request of the school district identified Dr. Dobson as a licensed psychologist, former associate clinical professor of pediatrics at the University of Southern California, best-selling author, and radio commentator. The brochure, which described the contents of the six-part series, stated that the series would present Dr. Dobson's views on how to counterbalance media influences by instilling in children traditional, Christian family values at an early age. The school district denied the application, finding that "this film does appear to be church related and therefore your request must be refused."

Lamb's Chapel then applied to use school premises after hours a second time. The second application was to screen a "Family oriented movie—from a Christian perspective." The application was also denied by the school district. The second rejection letter used identical language to that of the first letter.

WHITE, J., delivered the opinion of the Court, in which REHNQUIST, C. J., and BLACKMUN, STEVENS, O'CONNOR, and SOUTER, JJ., joined.

[386] New York Educ. Law § 414 authorizes local school boards to adopt reasonable regulations for the use of school property for 10 specified purposes when the property is not in use for school purposes. Among the permitted uses is the holding of "social, civic and recreational meetings and entertainments, and other uses pertaining to the welfare

of the community; but such meetings, entertainment and uses shall be non-exclusive and shall be open to the general public." § 414 (c). The list of permitted uses does not include meetings for religious purposes, and a New York appellate court in *Trietley v. Board of Ed. of Buffalo*, 65 A.D.2d 1, 409 N.Y.S.2d 912, 915 (App. Div. 1978), ruled that local boards could not allow student bible clubs to meet [387] on school property because "religious purposes are not included in the enumerated purposes for which a school may be used under section 414." . . .

Pursuant to § 414's empowerment of local school districts, the Board of Center Moriches Union Free School District (District) has issued rules and regulations with respect to the use of school property when not in use for school purposes. The rules allow only 2 of the 10 purposes authorized by § 414: social, civic, or recreational uses (Rule 10) and use by political organizations if secured in compliance with § 414 (Rule 8). Rule 7, however, consistent with the judicial interpretation of state law, provides that "the school premises shall not be used by any group for religious purposes."

The issue in this case is whether, against this background of state law, it violates the Free Speech Clause of the First Amendment, made applicable to the States by the Fourteenth Amendment, to deny a church access to school premises to exhibit for public viewing and for assertedly religious purposes, a film series dealing with family and child-rearing issues faced by parents today. . . .

[390] II

There is no question that the District, like the private owner of property, may legally preserve the property under its control for the use to which it is dedicated. [391] It is also common ground that the District need not have permitted after-hours use of its property for any of the uses permitted by N. Y. Educ. Law § 414. The District, however, did open its property for 2 of the 10 uses permitted by § 414. . . .

[392] With respect to public property that is not a designated public forum open for indiscriminate public use for communicative purposes, we have said that "control over access to a nonpublic forum can be based on subject matter and speaker identity so long as the distinctions drawn are reasonable in [393] light of the purpose served by the forum and are viewpoint neutral." *Cornelius*, 473 U.S. at 806, citing *Perry Education Assn.*, at 49. The Court of Appeals appeared to recognize that the total ban on using District property for religious purposes could survive First Amendment challenge only if excluding this category of speech was reasonable and viewpoint neutral. The court's conclusion in this case was that Rule 7 met this test. We cannot agree with this holding, for Rule 7 was unconstitutionally applied in this case.

The Court of Appeals thought that the application of Rule 7 in this case was viewpoint neutral because it had been, and would be, applied in the same way to all uses of school property for religious purposes. That all religions and all uses for religious purposes are treated alike under Rule 7, however, does not answer the critical question whether it discriminates on the basis of viewpoint to permit school property to be used for the presentation of all views about family issues and child rearing except those dealing with the subject matter from a religious standpoint.

There is no suggestion from the courts below or from the District or the State that a lecture or film about child rearing and family values would not be a use for social or civic purposes otherwise permitted by Rule 10. That subject matter is not one that the District has placed off limits to any and all speakers. Nor is there any indication in the record before us that the application to exhibit the particular film series involved here was, or would have been, denied for any reason other than the fact that the presentation would have [394] been from a religious perspective. In our view, denial on that basis was plainly invalid under our holding in *Cornelius*, at 806, that

> "although a speaker may be excluded from a nonpublic forum if he wishes to address a topic not encompassed within the purpose of the forum . . . or if he is not a member of the class of speakers for whose especial benefit the forum was created . . . , the government violates the First Amendment when it denies access to a speaker solely to suppress the point of view he espouses on an otherwise includible subject."

The film series involved here no doubt dealt with a subject otherwise permissible under Rule 10, and its exhibition was denied solely because the series dealt with the subject from a religious standpoint. The principle that has emerged from our cases "is that the First Amendment forbids the government to regulate speech in ways that favor some viewpoints or ideas at the expense of others." *City Council of Los Angeles v. Taxpayers for Vincent*, 466 U.S. 789, 804 (1984). That principle applies in the circumstances of this case; as Judge Posner said for the Court of Appeals for the Seventh Circuit, to discriminate "against a particular point of view . . . would . . . flunk the test . . . [of] *Cornelius*, provided that the defendants have no defense based on the establishment clause." *May v. Evansville-Vanderburgh School Corp.*, 787 F.2d 1105, 1114 (1986).

The District, as a respondent, would save its judgment below on the ground that to permit its property to be used for religious purposes would be an establishment of religion forbidden by the First Amendment. This Court suggested in *Widmar v. Vincent*, 454 U.S. 263, 271 (1981), that the interest of the State in avoiding an Establishment Clause violation "may be [a] compelling" one justifying an abridgment of free speech otherwise protected by the First Amendment; but the Court went on to hold that permitting use of university [395] property for religious purposes under the open access policy involved there would not be incompatible with the Court's Establishment Clause cases.

We have no more trouble than did the *Widmar* Court in disposing of the claimed defense on the ground that the posited fears of an Establishment Clause violation are unfounded. The showing of this film series would not have been during school hours, would not have been sponsored by the school, and would have been open to the public, not just to church members. The District property had repeatedly been used by a wide variety of private organizations. Under these circumstances, as in *Widmar*, there would have been no realistic danger that the community would think that the District was endorsing religion or any particular creed, and any benefit to religion or to the Church would have been no more than incidental. As in *Widmar*, at 271–272, permitting District property to be used to exhibit the film series involved in this case would not have been an establishment of religion under the three-part test articulated in *Lemon v. Kurtzman*, 403 U.S. 602 (1971): The challenged governmental action has a secular purpose, does not have the principal or primary effect of advancing or inhibiting religion, and does not foster an excessive entanglement with religion.[7]

---

7. While we are somewhat diverted by JUSTICE SCALIA'S evening at the cinema, at 398–399, we return to the reality that there is a proper way to inter an established decision and *Lemon*, however frightening it might be to some, has not been overruled. This case, like *Corporation of Presiding Bishop of Church of Jesus Christ of Latter-Day Saints v. Amos*, 483 U.S. 327 (1987), presents no occasion to do so. JUSTICE SCALIA apparently was less haunted by the ghosts of the living when he joined the opinion of the Court in that case.

The District also submits that it justifiably denied use of its property to a "radical" church for the purpose of proselytizing, since to do so would lead to threats of public unrest and even violence. There is nothing in the record to support such a justification, which in any event would be difficult to defend as a reason to deny the presentation of a religious point of view about a subject the District otherwise opens to discussion on District property. . . .

JUSTICE SCALIA, with whom JUSTICE THOMAS joins, concurring in the judgment.

[397] I join the Court's conclusion that the District's refusal to allow use of school facilities for petitioners' film viewing, while generally opening the schools for community activities, violates petitioners' First Amendment free-speech rights (as does N. Y. Educ. Law § 414 [McKinney 1988 and Supp. 1993], to the extent it compelled the District's denial, at 386–387). I also agree with the Court that allowing Lamb's Chapel to use school facilities poses "no realistic danger" of a violation of the Establishment Clause, *ante,* at [398] 395, but I cannot accept most of its reasoning in this regard. The Court explains that the showing of petitioners' film on school property after school hours would not cause the community to "think that the District was endorsing religion or any particular creed," and further notes that access to school property would not violate the three-part test articulated in *Lemon v. Kurtzman* (1971).

As to the Court's invocation of the *Lemon* test: Like some ghoul in a late-night horror movie that repeatedly sits up in its grave and shuffles abroad, after being repeatedly killed and buried, *Lemon* stalks our Establishment Clause jurisprudence once again, frightening the little children and school attorneys of Center Moriches Union Free School District. Its most recent burial, only last Term, was, to be sure, not fully six feet under: Our decision in *Lee v. Weisman,* 505 U.S. 577, 586–587 (1992), conspicuously avoided using the supposed "test" but also declined the invitation to repudiate it. Over the years, however, no fewer than five of the currently sitting Justices have, in their own opinions, personally driven pencils through the creature's heart (the author of today's opinion repeatedly), and a sixth has joined an opinion doing so. See, *e.g., Weisman,* at 644 (SCALIA, J., joined by, *inter alios,* THOMAS, J., dissenting); *Allegheny County v. American Civil Liberties Union, Greater Pittsburgh Chapter,* 492 U.S. 573, 655–657 (1989) (KENNEDY, J., concurring in judgment in part and dissenting in part); *Corporation of Presiding Bishop of Church of Jesus Christ of Latter-Day Saints v. Amos,* 483 U.S. 327, 346–349 (1987) (O'CONNOR, J., concurring in judgment); *Wallace v. Jaffree,* 472 U.S. 38, 107–113 (1985) (REHNQUIST, J., dissenting); *id.,* at 90–91 (WHITE, J., dissenting); *School Dist. of Grand Rapids v. Ball,* 473 U.S. 373, 400 (1985) (WHITE, J., dissenting); *Widmar v. Vincent,* 454 U.S. 263, 282 (1981) (WHITE, J., dissenting); *New York v. Cathedral Academy,* 434 U.S. 125, 134–135 (1977) [399] (WHITE, J., dissenting); *Roemer v. Board of Pub. Works of Md.,* 426 U.S. 736, 768 (1976) (WHITE, J., concurring in judgment); *Committee for Public Ed. & Religious Liberty v. Nyquist,* 413 U.S. 756, 820 (1973) (WHITE, J., dissenting).

The secret of the *Lemon* test's survival, I think, is that it is so easy to kill. It is there to scare us (and our audience) when we wish it to do so, but we can command it to return to the tomb at will. See, *e.g., Lynch v. Donnelly,* 465 U.S. 668, 679 (1984) (noting instances in which Court has not applied *Lemon* test). When we wish to strike down a practice it forbids, we invoke it, see, *e.g., Aguilar v. Felton* (1985) (striking down state remedial education program administered in part in parochial schools); when we wish to uphold a practice it forbids, we ignore it entirely, see *Marsh v. Chambers* (1983) (upholding state legislative chaplains). Sometimes, we take a middle course, calling its three prongs "no more than helpful signposts," *Hunt v. McNair*, 413 U.S. 734, 741 (1973). Such a docile and useful monster is worth keeping around, at least in a somnolent state; one never knows when one might need him.

For my part, I agree with the long list of constitutional scholars who have criticized *Lemon* and bemoaned the strange Establishment Clause geometry of crooked lines and wavering shapes its intermittent use has produced. I will decline to apply *Lemon*—whether it validates [400] or invalidates the government action in question—and therefore cannot join the opinion of the Court today.*

I cannot join for yet another reason: the Court's statement that the proposed use of the school's facilities is constitutional because (among other things) it would not signal endorsement of religion in general. What a strange notion, that a Constitution which *itself* gives "religion in general" preferential treatment (I refer to the Free Exercise Clause) forbids endorsement of religion in general. The attorney general of New York not only agrees with that strange notion, he has an explanation for it: "Religious advocacy," he writes, "serves the community only in the eyes of its adherents and yields a benefit only to those who already believe." That was *not* the view of those who adopted our Constitution, who believed that the public virtues inculcated by religion are a public good. It suffices to point out that during the summer of 1789, when it was in the process of drafting the First Amendment, Congress enacted the Northwest Territory Ordinance that the Confederation Congress had adopted in 1787—Article III of which provides: "Religion, morality, and knowledge, *being necessary to good government and the happiness of mankind*, schools and the means of education shall forever be encouraged." Unsurprisingly, then, indifference to "religion in general" is *not* what our cases, both old and recent, demand.

[401] ✶ ✶ ✶

For the reasons given by the Court, I agree that the Free Speech Clause of the First Amendment forbids what respondents have done here. As for the asserted Establishment Clause justification, I would hold, simply and clearly, that giving Lamb's Chapel nondiscriminatory access to school facilities cannot violate that provision because it does not signify state or local embrace of a particular religious sect.

---

　*[Editor note: The asterisk was used in the original.] The Court correctly notes, at 395, n. 7, that I joined the opinion in *Corporation of Presiding Bishop of Church of Jesus Christ of Latter-Day Saints v. Amos* (1987), which considered the *Lemon* test. Lacking a majority at that time to abandon *Lemon*, we necessarily focused on that test, which had been the exclusive basis for the lower court's judgment. Here, of course, the lower court did not mention *Lemon*, and indeed did not even address any Establishment Clause argument on behalf of respondents. Thus, the Court is ultimately correct that *Presiding Bishop* provides a useful comparison: It was as impossible to avoid *Lemon* there as it is unnecessary to inject *Lemon* here.

48

Church of the Lukumi Babalu Aye, Inc. v. City of Hialeah

508 U.S. 520 (1993)

Vote: 9—Rehnquist, White, Blackmun, Stevens, O'Connor, Scalia, Kennedy, Souter, Thomas

    0

Opinion announcing the opinion of the Court: Kennedy*
Opinions concurring in part and concurring in the judgment: Scalia, Souter
Opinion concurring in the judgment: Blackmun

This case resulted from challenges to a Florida city council's ordinances that restricted the practice of Santeria.

    Santeria ("the way of the saints") emerged in the nineteenth century when Yoruba slaves brought to Cuba from Africa infused their traditional religion with elements of Catholicism. It teaches that every individual has a destiny from God that is fulfilled with the aid and energy of spirits, called orishas. The basis of the religion is the nurturing of a personal relationship with the orishas, and one of the principal forms of devotion is an animal sacrifice. According to Santeria teaching, the orishas are powerful but not immortal, and they depend on the sacrifice for survival. Sacrifices are performed at birth, marriage, and death rites, for the cure of the sick, for the initiation of new members and priests, and during an annual celebration. The animals sacrificed—which include chickens, pigeons, doves, ducks, guinea pigs, goats, sheep, and turtles—are killed by the cutting of the carotid arteries in the neck. The sacrificed animal is then cooked and eaten, except after healing and death rituals.

    In April 1987, the Church of the Lukumi Babalu Aye, a Santeria church, announced plans to open a house of worship, school, cultural center, and museum in Hialeah, Florida. The church's president, Ernesto Pichardo, said the church's goal was to bring the practice of the Santeria faith, including its ritual of animal sacrifice, into the open. The church leased land and obtained the necessary licensing, inspection, and zoning approvals needed for its plans by August 1987. At the time of the initial trial, the federal district court estimated that there were at least fifty thousand Santeria practitioners in South Florida.

    The prospect of a Santeria church in their midst prompted the members of the Hialeah city council to hold an emergency public session on June 9, 1987. At that meeting,

---

*Justice Kennedy delivered the opinion of the Court, except as to part II-A-2.

the city council adopted Resolution 87-66, which noted the "concern" expressed by residents of the city "that certain religions may propose to engage in practices which are inconsistent with public morals, peace or safety" and declared that "the City reiterates its commitment to a prohibition against any and all acts of any and all religious groups which are inconsistent with public morals, peace or safety." The council also approved an emergency ordinance, Ordinance 87-40, which incorporated in full, except as to penalty, Florida's animal-cruelty laws. Among other things, the incorporated state law subjected to criminal punishment "whoever . . . unnecessarily or cruelly . . . kills any animal."

In September 1987, the city council adopted the following three substantive ordinances to address the issue of religious animal sacrifice. Ordinance 87-52 defined "to sacrifice" as "to unnecessarily kill, torment, torture, or mutilate an animal in a public or private ritual or ceremony not for the primary purpose of food consumption" and prohibited owning or possessing an animal "intending to use such animal for food purposes." It restricted application of this prohibition to any individual or group that "kills, slaughters or sacrifices animals for any type of ritual, regardless of whether or not the flesh or blood of the animal is to be consumed." The ordinance contained an exemption for slaughtering by "licensed establishment[s]" of animals "specifically raised for food purposes."

Ordinance 87-71 adopted the definition of "to sacrifice" set forth in Ordinance 87-52 and provided that "it shall be unlawful for any person, persons, corporations or associations to sacrifice any animal within the corporate limits of the City of Hialeah, Florida." The ordinance stated that the city council "has determined that the sacrificing of animals within the city limits is contrary to the public health, safety, welfare and morals of the community."

Ordinance 87-72 defined "slaughter" as "the killing of animals for food" and prohibited slaughter outside areas zoned for slaughterhouse use. The ordinance provided an exemption for the slaughter or processing for sale of "small numbers of hogs and/or cattle per week in accordance with an exemption provided by state law."

All three ordinances and resolutions passed the city council by unanimous vote. Violations of each ordinance were punishable by fines not exceeding $500 or imprisonment not exceeding sixty days, or both.

KENNEDY, J., delivered the opinion of the Court with respect to Parts I, III, and IV, in which REHNQUIST, C. J., and WHITE, STEVENS, SCALIA, SOUTER, and THOMAS, JJ., joined, the opinion of the Court with respect to Part II-B, in which REHNQUIST, C. J., and WHITE, STEVENS, SCALIA, and THOMAS, JJ., joined, the opinion of the Court with respect to Parts II-A-1 and II-A-3, in which REHNQUIST, C. J., and STEVENS, SCALIA, and THOMAS, JJ., joined, and an opinion with respect to Part II-A-2, in which STEVENS, J., joined.

[523] The principle that government may not enact laws that suppress religious belief or practice is so well understood that few violations are recorded in our opinions. Concerned that this fundamental nonpersecution principle of the First Amendment was implicated here, however, we granted *certiorari*.

[524] Our review confirms that the laws in question were enacted by officials who did not understand, failed to perceive, or chose to ignore the fact that their official actions

violated the Nation's essential commitment to religious freedom. The challenged laws had an impermissible object; and in all events the principle of general applicability was violated because the secular ends asserted in defense of the laws were pursued only with respect to conduct motivated by religious beliefs. We invalidate the challenged enactments and reverse the judgment of the Court of Appeals. . . .

[531] II

The Free Exercise Clause of the First Amendment, which has been applied to the States through the Fourteenth Amendment, provides that "Congress shall make no law respecting an establishment of religion, or *prohibiting the free exercise thereof.* . . ." (Emphasis added.) The city does not argue that Santeria is not a "religion" within the meaning of the First Amendment. Nor could it. Although the practice of animal sacrifice may seem abhorrent to some, "religious beliefs need not be acceptable, logical, consistent, or comprehensible to others in order to merit First Amendment protection." *Thomas v. Review Bd. of Indiana Employment Security Div.*, 450 U.S. 707, 714 (1981). Given the historical association between animal sacrifice and religious worship, petitioners' assertion that animal sacrifice is an integral part of their religion "cannot be deemed bizarre or incredible." *Frazee v. Illinois Dept. of Employment Security*, 489 U.S. 829, 834, n. 2 (1989). Neither the city nor the courts below, moreover, have questioned the sincerity of petitioners' professed desire to conduct animal sacrifices for religious reasons. We must consider petitioners' First Amendment claim.

In addressing the constitutional protection for free exercise of religion, our cases establish the general proposition that a law that is neutral and of general applicability need not be justified by a compelling governmental interest even if the law has the incidental effect of burdening a particular religious practice. *Employment Div., Dept. of Human Resources of Ore. v. Smith.* Neutrality and general applicability are interrelated, and, as becomes apparent in this case, failure to satisfy one requirement is a likely indication that the other has not been satisfied. A law failing to satisfy these requirements must be justified by a compelling governmental interest and must be narrowly tailored to advance [532] that interest. These ordinances fail to satisfy the *Smith* requirements. We begin by discussing neutrality.

A . . .

[533] I

Although a law targeting religious beliefs as such is never permissible, if the object of a law is to infringe upon or restrict practices because of their religious motivation, the law is not neutral; and it is invalid unless it is justified by a compelling interest and is narrowly tailored to advance that interest. There are, of course, many ways of demonstrating that the object or purpose of a law is the suppression of religion or religious conduct. To determine the object of a law, we must begin with its text, for the minimum requirement of neutrality is that a law not discriminate on its face. A law lacks facial neutrality if it refers to a religious practice without a secular meaning discernible from the language or context. Petitioners contend that three of the ordinances fail this test of facial neutrality because they use the words [534] "sacrifice" and "ritual," words with strong religious connotations. We agree that these words are consistent with the claim of facial discrimination, but the argument is not conclusive.

The words "sacrifice" and "ritual" have a religious origin, but current use admits also of secular meanings. The ordinances, furthermore, define "sacrifice" in secular terms, without referring to religious practices.

We reject the contention advanced by the city that our inquiry must end with the text of the laws at issue. Facial neutrality is not determinative. The Free Exercise Clause, like the Establishment Clause, extends beyond facial discrimination. The Clause "forbids subtle departures from neutrality," *Gillette v. United States*, 401 U.S. 437, 452 (1971), and "covert suppression of particular religious beliefs," *Bowen v. Roy*, at 703 (opinion of Burger, C. J.). Official action that targets religious conduct for distinctive treatment cannot be shielded by mere compliance with the requirement of facial neutrality. The Free Exercise Clause protects against governmental hostility which is masked as well as overt. "The Court must survey meticulously the circumstances of governmental categories to eliminate, as it were, religious gerrymanders." *Walz v. Tax Comm'n of New York City*, 397 U.S. 664, 696 (1970) (Harlan, J., concurring).

The record in this case compels the conclusion that suppression of the central element of the Santeria worship service was the object of the ordinances. First, though use of the words "sacrifice" and "ritual" does not compel a finding of improper targeting of the Santeria religion, the choice of these words is support for our conclusion. There are further respects in which the text of the city council's enactments discloses the improper attempt to target Santeria. [535] Resolution 87-66, adopted June 9, 1987, recited that "residents and citizens of the City of Hialeah have expressed their concern that certain religions may propose to engage in practices which are inconsistent with public morals, peace or safety," and "reiterate[d]" the city's commitment to prohibit "any and all [such] acts of any and all religious groups." No one suggests, and on this record it cannot be maintained, that city officials had in mind a religion other than Santeria.

It becomes evident that these ordinances target Santeria sacrifice when the ordinances' operation is considered. Apart from the text, the effect of a law in its real operation is strong evidence of its object. To be sure, adverse impact will not always lead to a finding of impermissible targeting. For example, a social harm may have been a legitimate concern of government for reasons quite apart from discrimination. The subject at hand does implicate, of course, multiple concerns unrelated to religious animosity, for example, the suffering or mistreatment visited upon the sacrificed animals and health hazards from improper disposal. But the ordinances when considered together disclose an object remote from these legitimate concerns. The design of these laws accomplishes instead a "religious gerrymander," *Walz v. Tax Comm'n of New York City*, at 696 (Harlan, J., concurring), an impermissible attempt to target petitioners and their religious practices.

It is a necessary conclusion that almost the only conduct subject to Ordinances 87-40, 87-52, and 87-71 is the religious exercise of Santeria church members. The texts show that they were drafted in tandem to achieve this result. . . .

[538] We also find significant evidence of the ordinances' improper targeting of Santeria sacrifice in the fact that they proscribe more religious conduct than is necessary to achieve their stated ends. It is not unreasonable to infer, at least when there are no persuasive indications to the contrary, that a law which visits "gratuitous restrictions" on religious conduct, *McGowan v. Maryland*, 366 U.S. at 520 (opinion of Frankfurter, J.), seeks not to effectuate the stated governmental interests, but to suppress the conduct because of its religious motivation.

The legitimate governmental interests in protecting the public health and preventing cruelty to animals could be addressed by restrictions stopping far short of a flat prohibition of all Santeria sacrificial practice. If improper disposal, not the sacrifice itself, is the harm to be prevented, the city could have imposed a general regulation on the disposal of organic garbage. It did not do so. Indeed, counsel for the city conceded at oral argument that, under the ordinances, Santeria sacrifices would be illegal even if they occurred in licensed, inspected, and zoned slaughterhouses. Thus, these broad ordinances prohibit Santeria sacrifice even when it does not threaten the city's [539] interest in the public health. The District Court accepted the argument that narrower regulation would be unenforceable because of the secrecy in the Santeria rituals and the lack of any central religious authority to require compliance with secular disposal regulations. It is difficult to understand, however, how a prohibition of the sacrifices themselves, which occur in private, is enforceable if a ban on improper disposal, which occurs in public, is not. The neutrality of a law is suspect if First Amendment freedoms are curtailed to prevent isolated collateral harms not themselves prohibited by direct regulation. . . .

[542] 3

In sum, the neutrality inquiry leads to one conclusion: The ordinances had as their object the suppression of religion. The pattern we have recited discloses animosity to Santeria adherents and their religious practices; the ordinances by their own terms target this religious exercise; the texts of the ordinances were gerrymandered with care to proscribe religious killings of animals but to exclude almost all secular killings; and the ordinances suppress much more religious conduct than is necessary in order to achieve the legitimate ends asserted in their defense. These ordinances are not neutral, and the court below committed clear error in failing to reach this conclusion. . . .

[546] III

A law burdening religious practice that is not neutral or not of general application must undergo the most rigorous of scrutiny. To satisfy the commands of the First Amendment, a law restrictive of religious practice must advance "interests of the highest order" and must be narrowly tailored in pursuit of those interests. The compelling interest standard that we apply once a law fails to meet the *Smith* requirements is not "water[ed] . . . down" but "really means what it says." *Employment Div., Dept. of Human Resources of Ore. v. Smith*, 494 U.S. at 888. A law that targets religious conduct for distinctive treatment or advances legitimate governmental interests only against conduct with a religious motivation will survive strict scrutiny only in rare cases. It follows from what we have already said that these ordinances cannot withstand this scrutiny. . . .

49

Zobrest v. Catalina Foothills School District

509 U.S. 1 (1993)

Vote: 5—Rehnquist, White, Scalia, Kennedy, Thomas
4—Blackmun, Stevens, O'Connor, Souter

Opinion announcing the opinion of the Court: Rehnquist
Dissenting opinions: Blackmun, O'Connor

Pursuant to the federal Individuals with Disabilities Education Act (IDEA) and its Arizona counterpart, James Zobrest asked the Catalina Foothills School District to provide a sign-language interpreter to accompany him to classes at his Roman Catholic high school. The school district acknowledged that Zobrest's disability (he was born deaf) made him eligible for the requested aid and that it would have paid for an interpreter if he attended a public school or a nonreligious private school. But citing the counsel the school district received from the county attorney and the Arizona attorney general, both of whom concluded that providing the requested aid would violate the Establishment Clause, the school district denied Zobrest's request. Zobrest and his parents then commenced legal action against the school district.

REHNQUIST, C. J., delivered the opinion of the Court, in which WHITE, SCALIA, KENNEDY, and THOMAS, JJ., joined.

[3] Petitioner James Zobrest, who has been deaf since birth, asked respondent school district to provide a sign-language interpreter to accompany him to classes at a Roman Catholic high school in Tucson, Arizona, pursuant to the Individuals with Disabilities Education Act (IDEA) and its Arizona counterpart. The United States Court of Appeals for the Ninth Circuit decided, however, that provision of such a publicly employed interpreter would violate the Establishment Clause of the First Amendment. We hold that the Establishment Clause does not bar the school district from providing the requested interpreter. . . .

[8] We have never said that "religious institutions are disabled by the First Amendment from participating in publicly sponsored social welfare programs." *Bowen v. Kendrick*, 487 U.S. 589, 609 (1988). For if the Establishment Clause did bar religious groups from receiving general government benefits, then "a church could not be protected by

the police and fire departments, or have its public sidewalk kept in repair." *Widmar v. Vincent*, 454 U.S. 263, 274–275 (1981). Given that a contrary rule would lead to such absurd results, we have consistently held that government programs that neutrally provide benefits to a broad class of citizens defined without reference to religion are not readily subject to an Establishment Clause challenge just because sectarian institutions may also receive an attenuated financial benefit. Nowhere have we stated this principle more clearly than in *Mueller v. Allen* (1983), and *Witters v. Washington Dept. of Services for Blind* (1986), two cases dealing specifically [9] with government programs offering general educational assistance.

In *Mueller*, we rejected an Establishment Clause challenge to a Minnesota law allowing taxpayers to deduct certain educational expenses in computing their state income tax, even though the vast majority of those deductions (perhaps over 90%) went to parents whose children attended sectarian schools. Two factors, aside from States' traditionally broad taxing authority, informed our decision. We noted that the law "permits *all* parents—whether their children attend public school or private—to deduct their children's educational expenses." 463 U.S. at 398 (emphasis in original). We also pointed out that under Minnesota's scheme, public funds become available to sectarian schools "only as a result of numerous private choices of individual parents of school-age children," thus distinguishing *Mueller* from our other cases involving "the direct transmission of assistance from the State to the schools themselves." 463 U.S. at 399.

Witters was premised on virtually identical reasoning. . . .

[10] That same reasoning applies with equal force here. The service at issue in this case is part of a general government program that distributes benefits neutrally to any child qualifying as "handicapped" under the IDEA, without regard to the "sectarian-nonsectarian, or public-nonpublic nature" of the school the child attends. By according parents freedom to select a school of their choice, the statute ensures that a government-paid interpreter will be present in a sectarian school only as a result of the private decision of individual parents. In other words, because the IDEA creates no financial incentive for parents to choose a sectarian school, an interpreter's presence there cannot be attributed to state decisionmaking. Viewed against the backdrop of *Mueller* and *Witters*, then, the Court of Appeals erred in its decision. When the government offers a neutral service on the premises of a sectarian school as part of a general program that "is in no way skewed towards religion," *Witters*, at 488, it follows under our prior decisions that provision of that service does not offend the Establishment Clause. Indeed, this is an even easier case than *Mueller* and *Witters* in the sense that, under the IDEA, no funds traceable to the government ever find their way into sectarian schools' coffers. The only indirect economic benefit a sectarian school might receive by dint of the IDEA is the handicapped child's tuition—and that is, [11] of course, assuming that the school makes a profit on each student; that, without an IDEA interpreter, the child would have gone to school elsewhere; and that the school, then, would have been unable to fill that child's spot.

Respondent contends, however, that this case differs from *Mueller* and *Witters*, in that petitioners seek to have a public employee physically present in a sectarian school to assist in James' religious education. . . .

[12] Respondent's reliance on *Meek* and *Ball* is misplaced for two reasons. First, the programs in *Meek* and *Ball*—through direct grants of government aid—relieved sectarian schools of costs they otherwise would have borne in educating their students. For example, the religious schools in *Meek* received teaching material and equipment from the State, relieving them of an otherwise necessary cost of performing their educational

function. 421 U.S. at 365–366. "Substantial aid to the educational function of such schools," we explained, "necessarily results in aid to the sectarian school enterprise as a whole," and therefore brings about "the direct and substantial advancement of religious activity." *Id.*, at 366. So, too, was the case in *Ball*: The programs challenged there, which provided teachers in addition to instructional equipment and material, "in effect subsidized the religious functions of the parochial schools by taking over a substantial portion of their responsibility for teaching secular subjects." 473 U.S. at 397. "This kind of direct aid," we determined, "is indistinguishable from the provision of a direct cash subsidy to the religious school." *Id.*, at 395. The extension of aid to petitioners, however, does not amount to "an impermissible 'direct subsidy'" of Salpointe. *Witters*, 474 U.S. at 487. For Salpointe is not relieved of an expense that it otherwise would have assumed in educating its students. And, as we noted above, any attenuated financial benefit that parochial schools do ultimately receive from the IDEA is attributable to "the private choices of individual parents." *Mueller*, 463 U.S. at 400. Handicapped children, not sectarian schools, are the primary beneficiaries of the IDEA; to the extent sectarian schools benefit at all from the IDEA, they are only incidental beneficiaries. Thus, the function of the IDEA is hardly "to provide desired financial [13] support for nonpublic, sectarian institutions." *Id.*, at 488.

Second, the task of a sign-language interpreter seems to us quite different from that of a teacher or guidance counselor. Notwithstanding the Court of Appeals' intimations to the contrary, see 963 F.2d at 1195, the Establishment Clause lays down no absolute bar to the placing of a public employee in a sectarian school. Such a flat rule, smacking of antiquated notions of "taint," would indeed exalt form over substance. Nothing in this record suggests that a sign-language interpreter would do more than accurately interpret whatever material is presented to the class as a whole. In fact, ethical guidelines require interpreters to "transmit everything that is said in exactly the same way it was intended." James' parents have chosen of their own free will to place him in a pervasively sectarian environment. The sign-language interpreter they have requested will neither add to nor subtract from that environment, and hence the provision of such assistance is not barred by the Establishment Clause.

The IDEA creates a neutral government program dispensing aid not to schools but to individual handicapped children. If a handicapped child chooses to enroll in a sectarian school, [14] we hold that the Establishment Clause does not prevent the school district from furnishing him with a sign-language interpreter there in order to facilitate his education.

JUSTICE BLACKMUN, with whom JUSTICE SOUTER joins, and with whom JUSTICE STEVENS and JUSTICE O'CONNOR join as to Part I, dissenting.

. . . [18] II

. . . Until now, the Court never has authorized a public employee to participate directly in religious indoctrination. Yet that is the consequence of today's decision.

Let us be clear about exactly what is going on here. The parties have stipulated to the following facts. Petitioner requested the State to supply him with a sign-language interpreter at Salpointe High School, a private Roman Catholic school operated by the Carmelite Order of the Catholic Church. Salpointe is a "pervasively religious" institution where "the two functions of secular education and advancement of religious values or beliefs are inextricably intertwined." Salpointe's overriding "objective" is to "instill a sense of Christian values." Its "distinguishing purpose" is "the inculcation in its students of the faith and morals of the Roman Catholic Church." Religion is a required subject at Salpointe, and Catholic students are "strongly encouraged" to attend daily Mass each morning. Salpointe's teachers must sign a Faculty Employment Agreement which requires them to promote the relationship among the religious, the academic, and the extracurricular. They are encouraged to do so by "assisting students in experiencing how the presence of God is manifest in nature, human history, in the struggles for economic and political justice, and other secular areas of the curriculum." The Agreement also sets forth detailed rules of [19] conduct teachers must follow in order to advance the school's Christian mission.

At Salpointe, where the secular and the sectarian are "inextricably intertwined," governmental assistance to the educational function of the school necessarily entails governmental participation in the school's inculcation of religion. A state-employed sign-language interpreter would be required to communicate the material covered in religion class, the nominally secular subjects that are taught from a religious perspective, and the daily Masses at which Salpointe encourages attendance for Catholic students. In an environment so pervaded by discussions of the divine, the interpreter's every gesture would be infused with religious significance. Indeed, petitioners willingly concede this point: "That the interpreter conveys religious messages is a given in the case." By this concession, petitioners would seem to surrender their constitutional claim.

The majority attempts to elude the impact of the record by offering three reasons why this sort of aid to petitioners survives Establishment Clause scrutiny. First, the majority observes that provision of a sign-language interpreter [20] occurs as "part of a general government program that distributes benefits neutrally to any child qualifying as 'handicapped' under the IDEA, without regard to the 'sectarian-nonsectarian, or public-nonpublic' nature of the school the child attends." *Ante*, at 8. Second, the majority finds significant the fact that aid is provided to pupils and their parents, rather than directly to sectarian schools. As a result, "any aid . . . that ultimately flows to religious institutions does so only as a result of the genuinely independent and private choices of aid recipients." *Ante*, at 7, quoting *Witters v. Washington Department of Services for the Blind*, 474 U.S. 481, 487 (1986). And, finally, the majority opines that "the task of a sign-language interpreter seems to us quite different from that of a teacher or guidance counselor." *Ante*, at 11.

But the majority's arguments are unavailing. As to the first two, even a general welfare program may have specific applications that are constitutionally forbidden under the Establishment Clause. For example, a general program granting remedial assistance to disadvantaged schoolchildren attending public and private, secular and sectarian schools alike would clearly offend the Establishment Clause insofar as it authorized the provision of teachers. Such a program would not be saved simply because it supplied teachers to secular as well as sectarian schools. Nor would the fact that teachers were furnished to pupils and their parents, rather than directly to sectarian schools, immunize such a program from Establishment Clause scrutiny. [21] The majority's decision must turn, then, upon the distinction between a teacher and a sign-language interpreter.

"Although Establishment Clause jurisprudence is characterized by few absolutes," at a minimum "the Clause does absolutely prohibit government-financed or government-sponsored indoctrination into the beliefs of a particular religious faith." *Grand Rapids*, 473 U.S. at 385. In keeping with this restriction, our cases consistently have rejected the provision by government of any resource capable of advancing a school's religious mission. Although the Court generally has permitted the provision of "secular and non-ideological services unrelated to the primary, religion-oriented educational function of the sectarian school," *Meek*, 421 U.S. at 364, it has always proscribed the provision of benefits that afford even "the opportunity for the transmission of sectarian views," *Wolman*, 433 U.S. at 244.

Thus, the Court has upheld the use of public school buses to transport children to and from school, *Everson v. Board of Education*, 330 U.S. 1 (1947), while striking down the [22] employment of publicly funded buses for field trips controlled by parochial school teachers, *Wolman*, 433 U.S. at 254. Similarly, the Court has permitted the provision of secular textbooks whose content is immutable and can be ascertained in advance, *Board of Education v. Allen* (1968), while prohibiting the provision of any instructional materials or equipment that could be used to convey a religious message, such as slide projectors, tape recorders, record players, and the like, *Wolman*, 433 U.S. at 249. State-paid speech and hearing therapists have been allowed to administer diagnostic testing on the premises of parochial schools, *Wolman*, 433 U.S. at 241–242, whereas state-paid remedial teachers and counselors have not been authorized to offer their services because of the risk that they may inculcate religious beliefs, *Meek*, 421 U.S. at 371.

These distinctions perhaps are somewhat fine, but "lines must be drawn." *Grand Rapids*, 473 U.S. at 398. And our cases make clear that government crosses the boundary when it furnishes the medium for communication of a religious message. . . .

[23] III

The Establishment Clause "rests upon the premise that both religion and government can best work to achieve their lofty aims if each is left free from the other within its respective sphere." *McCollum v. Board of Education*, [24] 333 U.S. 203, 212 (1948). To this end, our cases have strived to "chart a course that preserves the autonomy and freedom of religious bodies while avoiding any semblance of established religion." *Walz v. Tax Commission*, 397 U.S. 664, 672 (1970). I would not stray, as the Court does today, from the course set by nearly five decades of Establishment Clause jurisprudence. Accordingly, I dissent.

50

Capitol Square Review and Advisory Board v. Pinette

515 U.S. 753 (1995)

Vote: 7—Rehnquist, O'Connor, Scalia, Kennedy, Souter, Thomas, Breyer
*   2—Stevens, Ginsburg*

Opinion announcing the judgment of the Court: Scalia
Concurring opinion: Thomas
Opinions concurring in part and concurring in the judgment: O'Connor, Souter
Dissenting opinions: Stevens, Ginsburg

Ohio law made Capitol Square, a ten-acre, state-owned square surrounding the state-house in Columbus, a forum for discussion of public questions and for public activities. The Capitol Square Review and Advisory Board regulated access to the square. To use the square, a group had to complete an official application form and meet several speech-neutral criteria.

As explained in the majority opinion below, the Capitol Square Review and Advisory Board denied the application of members of the Ku Klux Klan (KKK) to display a cross in Capitol Square. Members of the KKK initiated legal action in response to the board's denial.

JUSTICE SCALIA announced the judgment of the Court and delivered the opinion of the Court with respect to Parts I, II, and III, and an opinion with respect to Part IV, in which THE CHIEF JUSTICE, JUSTICE KENNEDY, and JUSTICE THOMAS join.

[757] The Establishment Clause of the First Amendment, made binding upon the States through the Fourteenth Amendment, provides that government "shall make no law respecting an establishment of religion." The question in this case is whether a State violates the Establishment Clause when, pursuant to a religiously neutral state policy, it permits a private party to display an unattended religious symbol in a traditional public forum located next to its seat of government.

I

Capitol Square is a 10-acre, state-owned plaza surrounding the statehouse in Columbus, Ohio. For over a century the square has been used for public speeches, gatherings, and festivals advocating and celebrating a variety of causes, both secular and religious. Ohio Admin. Code Ann. § 128-4-02 (A) (1994) makes the square available "for use by the public . . . for free discussion of public questions, or for activities of a broad public purpose," and Ohio Rev. Code Ann. § 105.41 (1994) gives the Capitol Square Review and Advisory Board (Board) responsibility for regulating public access. To use the square, a group must simply fill out an official application [758] form and meet several criteria, which concern primarily safety, sanitation, and noninterference with other uses of the square, and which are neutral as to the speech content of the proposed event.

It has been the Board's policy "to allow a broad range of speakers and other gatherings of people to conduct events on the Capitol Square." Such diverse groups as homosexual rights organizations, the Ku Klux Klan, and the United Way have held rallies. The Board has also permitted a variety of unattended displays on Capitol Square: a state-sponsored lighted tree during the Christmas season, a privately sponsored menorah during Chanukah, a display showing the progress of a United Way fundraising campaign, and booths and exhibits during an arts festival. Although there was some dispute in this litigation regarding the frequency of unattended displays, the District Court found, with ample justification, that there was no policy against them.

In November 1993, after reversing an initial decision to ban unattended holiday displays from the square during December 1993, the Board authorized the State to put up its annual Christmas tree. On November 29, 1993, the Board granted a rabbi's application to erect a menorah. That same day, the Board received an application from respondent Donnie Carr, an officer of the Ohio Ku Klux Klan, to place a cross on the square from December 8, 1993, to December 24, 1993. The Board denied that application on December 3, informing the Klan by letter that the decision to deny "was made upon the advice of counsel, in a good faith attempt to comply with the Ohio and United States Constitutions, as they have been interpreted in relevant decisions by the Federal and State Courts." . . .

II

. . . [760] Respondents' religious display in Capitol Square was private expression. Our precedent establishes that private religious speech, far from being a First Amendment orphan, is as fully protected under the Free Speech Clause as secular private expression. Indeed, in Anglo-American history, at least, government suppression of speech has so commonly been directed precisely at religious speech that a free-speech clause without religion would be Hamlet without the prince. Accordingly, we have not excluded from free-speech protections religious proselytizing, *Heffron*, at 647, or even acts of worship, *Widmar*, at 269, n. 6. Petitioners do not dispute that respondents, in displaying their cross, were engaging in constitutionally protected expression. They do contend that the constitutional protection [761] does not extend to the length of permitting that expression to be made on Capitol Square.

It is undeniable, of course, that speech which is constitutionally protected against state suppression is not thereby accorded a guaranteed forum on all property owned by the State. The right to use government property for one's private expression depends upon whether the property has by law or tradition been given the status of a public forum, or rather has been reserved for specific official uses. If the former, a State's right to limit protected expressive activity is sharply circumscribed: It may impose reasonable, content-neutral time, place, and manner restrictions (a ban on all unattended displays, which did not exist here, might be one such), but it may regulate expressive content only if such a restriction is necessary, and narrowly drawn, to serve a compelling state interest. These strict standards apply here, since the District Court and the Court of Appeals found that Capitol Square was a traditional public forum.

Petitioners do not claim that their denial of respondents' application was based upon a content-neutral time, place, or manner restriction. To the contrary, they concede—indeed it is the essence of their case—that the Board rejected the display precisely because its content was religious. Petitioners advance a single justification for closing Capitol Square to respondents' cross: the State's interest in avoiding official endorsement of Christianity, as required by the Establishment Clause.

III

There is no doubt that compliance with the Establishment Clause is a state interest sufficiently compelling to justify [762] content-based restrictions on speech. Whether that interest is implicated here, however, is a different question. And we do not write on a blank slate in answering it. We have twice previously addressed the combination of private religious expression, a forum available for public use, content-based regulation, and a State's interest in complying with the Establishment Clause. Both times, we have struck down the restriction on religious content. *Lamb's Chapel; Widmar.* . . .

[763] Quite obviously, the factors that we considered determinative in *Lamb's Chapel* and *Widmar* exist here as well. The State did not sponsor respondents' expression, the expression was made on government property that had been opened to the public for speech, and permission was requested through the same application process and on the same terms required of other private groups.

IV

Petitioners argue that one feature of the present case distinguishes it from *Lamb's Chapel* and *Widmar*: the forum's proximity to the seat of government, which, they contend, may produce the perception that the cross bears the State's approval. They urge us to apply the so-called "endorsement test," and to find that, because an observer might mistake private expression for officially endorsed religious expression, the State's content-based restriction is constitutional. . . .

[766] Of course, giving sectarian religious speech preferential access to a forum close to the seat of government (or anywhere else for that matter) would violate the Establishment Clause (as well as the Free Speech Clause, since it would involve content discrimination). And one can conceive of a case in which a governmental entity manipulates its administration of a public forum close to the seat of government (or within a government building) in such a manner that only certain religious groups take advantage of it, creating an impression of endorsement that is in fact accurate. But those situations, which involve governmental favoritism, do not exist here. Capitol Square is a genuinely public forum, is known to be a public forum, and has been widely used as a public forum for many, many years. Private religious speech cannot be subject to veto by those who see favoritism where there is none.

The contrary view, most strongly espoused by JUSTICE STEVENS, *post*, at 806–807, but endorsed by JUSTICE SOUTER and JUSTICE O'CONNOR as well, exiles private religious speech to a realm of less-protected expression heretofore [767] inhabited only by sexually explicit displays and commercial speech. It will be a sad day when this Court casts piety in with pornography, and finds the First Amendment more hospitable to private expletives, see *Cohen v. California*, 403 U.S. 15, 26 (1971), than to private prayers. This would be merely bizarre were religious speech simply as protected by the Constitution as other forms of private speech; but it is outright perverse when one considers that private religious expression receives preferential treatment under the Free Exercise Clause. It is no answer to say that the Establishment Clause tempers religious speech. By its terms that Clause applies only to the words and acts of government. It was never meant, and has never been read by this Court, to serve as an impediment to purely private religious speech connected to the State only through its occurrence in a public forum.

Since petitioners' "transferred endorsement" principle cannot possibly be restricted to squares in front of state capitols, the Establishment Clause regime that it would usher in is most unappealing. To require (and permit) access by a religious group in *Lamb's Chapel*, it was sufficient that the group's activity was not in fact government sponsored, that the event was open to the public, and that the benefit of the facilities was shared by various organizations. Petitioners' rule would require school districts adopting similar policies in the future to guess whether some undetermined critical mass of the community might nonetheless perceive the district to be advocating a religious viewpoint. Similarly, state universities would be forced to reassess our statement that "an open forum in a public university does not confer any imprimatur of state approval on religious sects or practices." *Widmar*, 454 U.S. at 274. Whether it does would henceforth depend upon immediate appearances. Policymakers [768] would find themselves in a vise between the Establishment Clause on one side and the Free Speech and Free Exercise Clauses on the other. Every proposed act of private, religious expression in a public forum would force officials to weigh a host of imponderables. How close to government is too close? What kind of building, and in what context, symbolizes state authority? If the State guessed wrong in one direction, it would be guilty of an Establishment Clause violation; if in the other, it would be liable for suppressing free exercise or free speech (a risk not run when the State restrains only its own expression).

The "transferred endorsement" test would also disrupt the settled principle that policies providing incidental benefits to religion do not contravene the Establishment Clause. That principle is the basis for the constitutionality of a broad range of laws, not merely those that implicate free-speech issues. It has radical implications for our public policy to suggest that neutral laws are invalid whenever hypothetical observers may— even reasonably—confuse an incidental benefit to religion with state endorsement.[3]

---

3. If it is true, as JUSTICE O'CONNOR suggests, *post*, at 775, that she would not "be likely to come to a different result from the plurality where truly private speech is allowed on equal terms in a vigorous public forum that the government has administered properly," then she is extending the "endorsement test" to private speech to cover an eventuality that is "not likely" to occur. Before doing that, it would seem desirable to explore the precise degree of the unlikelihood (is it perhaps 100%?)—for as we point out in text, the extension to private speech has considerable costs. Contrary to what JUSTICE O'CONNOR, JUSTICE SOUTER, and JUSTICE STEVENS argue, the endorsement test does not supply an appropriate standard for the inquiry before us. It supplies no standard whatsoever. The lower federal courts that JUSTICE O'CONNOR's concurrence identifies as having "applied the endorsement test in precisely the context before us today," *ibid.*, have reached precisely differing results—which is what led the Court to take this case. And if further proof of the invited chaos is required, one need only follow the debate between the concurrence and JUSTICE STEVENS' dissent as to whether the hypothetical beholder who will be the determinant of "endorsement" should be any beholder (no matter how unknowledgeable), or the average beholder, or (what JUSTICE STEVENS accuses the concurrence of favoring) the "ultrareasonable" beholder. See *post*, at 778–782 (O'CONNOR, J., concurring in part and concurring in judgment); *post*, at 807–808 (STEVENS, J., dissenting). And, of course, even when one achieves agreement upon that question, it will be unrealistic to expect different judges (or should it be juries?) to reach consistent answers as to what any beholder, the average beholder, or the ultrareasonable beholder (as the case may be) would think. It is irresponsible to make the Nation's legislators walk this minefield.

[769] If Ohio is concerned about misperceptions, nothing prevents it from requiring all private displays in the square to be identified as such. That would be a content-neutral "manner" restriction that is assuredly constitutional. But the State may not, on the claim of misperception of official endorsement, ban all private religious speech from the public square, or discriminate against it by requiring religious speech alone to disclaim public sponsorship.

[770] * * *

Religious expression cannot violate the Establishment Clause where it (1) is purely private and (2) occurs in a traditional or designated public forum, publicly announced and open to all on equal terms. Those conditions are satisfied here, and therefore the State may not bar respondents' cross from Capitol Square.

JUSTICE O'CONNOR, with whom JUSTICE SOUTER and JUSTICE BREYER join, concurring in part and concurring in the judgment.

. . . [776] Our agreement as to the outcome of this case, however, cannot mask the fact that I part company with the plurality on a fundamental point: I disagree that "it has radical implications for our public policy to suggest that neutral laws are invalid whenever hypothetical observers may—even reasonably—confuse an incidental benefit to religion with state [777] endorsement." *Ante,* at 768. On the contrary, when the reasonable observer would view a government practice as endorsing religion, I believe that it is our duty to hold the practice invalid. The plurality today takes an exceedingly narrow view of the Establishment Clause that is out of step both with the Court's prior cases and with well-established notions of what the Constitution requires. The Clause is more than a negative prohibition against certain narrowly defined forms of government favoritism, see *ante,* at 766; it also imposes affirmative obligations that may require a State, in some situations, to take steps to avoid being perceived as supporting or endorsing a private religious message. That is, the Establishment Clause forbids a State from hiding behind the application of formally neutral criteria and remaining studiously oblivious to the effects of its actions. Governmental intent cannot control, and not all state policies are permissible under the Religion Clauses simply because they are neutral in form.

Where the government's operation of a public forum has the effect of endorsing religion, even if the governmental actor neither intends nor actively encourages that result, see *Lynch,* 465 U.S. at 690 (O'CONNOR, J., concurring), the Establishment Clause is violated. This is so not because of "transferred endorsement," *ante,* at 764, or mistaken attribution of private speech to the State, but because the State's own actions (operating the forum in a particular manner and permitting the religious expression to take place therein), and their relationship to the private speech at issue, actually convey a message of endorsement. At some point, for example, a private religious group may so dominate a public forum that a formal policy of equal access is transformed into a demonstration of approval. [778] Other circumstances may produce the same effect—whether because of the fortuity of geography, the nature of the particular public space, or the character of the religious speech at issue, among others. Our Establishment Clause jurisprudence should remain flexible enough to handle such situations when they arise.

In the end, I would recognize that the Establishment Clause inquiry cannot be distilled into a fixed, *per se* rule. Thus, "every government practice must be judged in its unique circumstances to determine whether it constitutes an endorsement or disapproval of religion." *Lynch*, 465 U.S. at 694 (O'CONNOR, J., concurring). And this question cannot be answered in the abstract, but instead requires courts to examine the history and administration of a particular practice to determine whether it operates as such an endorsement. I continue to believe that government practices relating to speech on religious topics "must be subjected to careful judicial scrutiny," *ibid.*, and that the endorsement test supplies an appropriate standard for that inquiry.

[779] II

. . . Because an Establishment Clause violation must be moored in government action of some sort, and because our concern is with the political community writ large, see *Allegheny*, at 627 (O'CONNOR, J., concurring in part and concurring in judgment); *Lynch*, at 690, the endorsement inquiry is not about the perceptions of particular individuals or saving isolated nonadherents from the discomfort of viewing symbols of a faith to which they do not subscribe. Indeed, to avoid "entirely sweeping away all government recognition and acknowledgment of the role of religion in the lives of our citizens," *Allegheny*, at 623 (O'CONNOR, J., concurring in part and concurring in judgment), our Establishment Clause jurisprudence must seek to identify the point at which the government becomes responsible, whether due to favoritism toward or disregard for the evident effect of religious speech, for the injection of religion into the political life of the citizenry.

I therefore disagree that the endorsement test should focus on the actual perception of individual observers, who naturally have differing degrees of knowledge. Under such an approach, a religious display is necessarily precluded so long as some passersby would perceive a governmental endorsement thereof. In my view, however, the endorsement test creates a more collective standard to gauge "the 'objective' meaning of the [government's] statement in the community," *Lynch*, at 690 (O'CONNOR, J., concurring). In this respect, the applicable observer is similar to the "reasonable person" in tort law, who "is not to be identified with any ordinary individual, who might occasionally do unreasonable [780] things," but is "rather a personification of a community ideal of reasonable behavior, determined by the [collective] social judgment." Thus, "we do not ask whether there is any person who could find an endorsement of religion, whether some people may be offended by the display, or whether some reasonable person might think [the State] endorses religion." Saying that the endorsement inquiry should be conducted from the perspective of a hypothetical observer who is presumed to possess a certain level of information that all citizens might not share neither chooses the perceptions of the majority over those of a "reasonable non-adherent," nor invites disregard for the values the Establishment Clause was intended to protect. It simply recognizes the fundamental difficulty inherent in focusing on actual people: There is always someone who, with a particular quantum of knowledge, reasonably might perceive a particular action as an endorsement of religion. A State has not made religion relevant to standing in the political community simply because a particular viewer of a display might feel uncomfortable.

It is for this reason that the reasonable observer in the endorsement inquiry must be deemed aware of the history and context of the community and forum in which the religious display appears. As I explained in *Allegheny*, "the 'history and ubiquity' of a practice is relevant because it provides part of the context in which a reasonable observer evaluates whether a challenged governmental practice conveys a message of endorsement of religion." 492 U.S. at 630. Nor can the knowledge attributed to the reasonable observer be limited to the information gleaned simply from viewing the challenged display. Today's proponents of the endorsement test all agree that we should attribute to the observer knowledge that the cross is a religious symbol, that [781] Capitol Square is owned by the State, and that the large building nearby is the seat of state government. In my view, our hypothetical observer also should know the general history of the place in which the cross is displayed. Indeed, the fact that Capitol Square is a public park that has been used over time by private speakers of various types is as much a part of the display's context as its proximity to the Ohio Statehouse. This approach does not require us to assume an "'ultrareasonable observer' who understands the vagaries of this Court's First Amendment jurisprudence," *post*, at 807 (STEVENS, J., dissenting). An informed member of the community will know how the public space in question has been used in the past—and it is that fact, not that the space may meet the legal definition of a public forum, which is relevant to the endorsement inquiry. . . .

[782] In this case, I believe, the reasonable observer would view the Klan's cross display fully aware that Capitol Square is a public space in which a multiplicity of groups, both secular and religious, engage in expressive conduct. It is precisely this type of knowledge that we presumed in *Lamb's Chapel*, 508 U.S. at 395, and in *Mergens*, 496 U.S. at 250 (plurality opinion). Moreover, this observer would certainly be able to read and understand an adequate disclaimer, which the Klan had informed the State it would include in the display at the time it applied for the permit and the content of which the Board could have defined as it deemed necessary as a condition of granting the Klan's application. On the facts of this case, therefore, I conclude that the reasonable observer would not interpret the State's tolerance of the Klan's private religious display in Capitol Square as an endorsement of religion. . . .

[797] JUSTICE STEVENS, dissenting.

The Establishment Clause should be construed to create a strong presumption against the installation of unattended religious symbols on public property. Although the State of Ohio has allowed Capitol Square, the area around the seat of its government, to be used as a public forum, and although it has occasionally allowed private groups to erect other sectarian displays there, neither fact provides a sufficient basis for rebutting that presumption. On the contrary, the sequence of sectarian displays disclosed by the record in this case illustrates the importance of rebuilding the "wall of separation between church and State" that Jefferson envisioned.

I

At issue in this case is an unadorned Latin cross, which the Ku Klux Klan placed, and left unattended, on the lawn in front of the Ohio State Capitol. The Court decides this case on the assumption that the cross was a religious symbol. I agree with that assumption notwithstanding the hybrid character of this particular object. The record indicates that the "Grand Titan of the Knights of the Ku Klux Klan for the Realm of Ohio" applied for a permit to place a cross in front of the state capitol because "the Jews" were placing a "symbol for the Jewish belief" in the Square. Some observers, unaware of who had sponsored the cross, or unfamiliar with the history of the Klan and its reaction to the menorah, might interpret the Klan's cross as an inspirational symbol of the crucifixion and resurrection of Jesus Christ. [798] More knowledgeable observers might regard it, given the context, as an antisemitic symbol of bigotry and disrespect for a particular religious sect. Under the first interpretation, the cross is plainly a religious symbol. Under the second, an icon of intolerance expressing an anticlerical message should also be treated as a religious symbol because the Establishment Clause must prohibit official sponsorship of irreligious as well as religious messages. This principle is no less binding if the antireligious message is also a bigoted message.

Thus, while this unattended, freestanding wooden cross was unquestionably a religious symbol, observers may well have received completely different messages from that symbol. Some might have perceived it as a message of love, others as a message of hate, still others as a message of exclusion—a statehouse sign calling powerfully to mind their outsider status. In any event, it was a message that the State of Ohio may not communicate to its citizens without violating the Establishment Clause. . . .

51

Rosenberger v. Rector and Visitors of the University of Virginia

515 U.S. 819 (1995)

Vote: 5—*Rehnquist, O'Connor, Scalia, Kennedy, Thomas*
    4—*Stevens, Souter, Ginsburg, Breyer*

Opinion announcing the opinion of the Court: Kennedy
Concurring opinions: O'Connor, Thomas
Dissenting opinion: Souter

Under a policy set by the University of Virginia, a public university founded by Thomas Jefferson, some student groups were eligible to receive funding through the university's Student Activity Fund (SAF). This case resulted from the university's denial of a Christian student group's SAF funding application.

Funded by a mandatory $14-per-semester fee assessed to each full-time student, the University of Virginia established the SAF to support a broad range of extracurricular activities. A student council, elected by the student body, had initial authority to disburse SAF funds, but its actions were subject to review by a faculty body chaired by a designee of the vice president for student affairs. Guidelines governing the SAF required that it be administered "in a manner consistent with the educational purpose of the University as well as with state and federal law."

University guidelines established that student groups with the status of contracted independent organization (CIO) were permitted to request payments from the SAF for some specific purposes. With the exception of "religious organizations," CIO status was available to any group that had full-time students as its managing officers and a majority student membership. A CIO had to file its constitution with the university, pledge not to discriminate in its membership, and include in dealings with third parties and in all written materials a disclaimer stating that the CIO was independent of the university and that the university was not responsible for the CIO. CIOs enjoyed access to university facilities, including meeting rooms and computer terminals. A standard agreement signed between each CIO and the university provided that the benefits and opportunities afforded to CIOs "should not be misinterpreted as meaning that those organizations are part of or controlled by the University, that the University is responsible for the organizations' contracts or other acts or omissions, or that the University approves of the organizations' goals or activities." As noted, "religious organizations" were ineligible for CIO status. They were defined as "an organization whose purpose is to practice a devotion to an acknowledged ultimate reality or deity."

University guidelines established eleven categories of CIO student groups that could seek SAF payments to third-party contractors because their activities were "related to the educational purpose of the University of Virginia." One category was "student news, information, opinion, entertainment, or academic communications media groups." The guidelines specified, however, that certain activities were ineligible for SAF funding, including religious activities, philanthropic contributions and activities, political activities, activities that would jeopardize the university's tax-exempt status, those involving payment of honoraria or similar fees, and social entertainment or related expenses. A "religious activity" was defined as any activity that "primarily promotes or manifests a particular belief in or about a deity or an ultimate reality." The prohibition on "political activities" was defined only to limit electioneering and lobbying. It also specified that "these restrictions on funding political activities are not intended to preclude funding of any otherwise eligible student organization which . . . espouses particular positions or ideological viewpoints, including those that may be unpopular or are not generally accepted."

Organizations that sought SAF support submitted their bills to the student council, which then paid the organization's creditors upon determining that the expenses were appropriate. No direct payments were made to the student groups. During the 1990–1991 academic year, 343 student groups qualified as CIOs. Of 135 groups that applied for support from the SAF, 118 received funding. Fifteen of the groups were funded as "student news, information, opinion, entertainment, or academic communications media groups."

In 1990 Ronald Rosenberger and other UVA undergraduates formed Wide Awake Productions (WAP), established "to publish a magazine of philosophical and religious expression," "to facilitate discussion which fosters an atmosphere of sensitivity to and tolerance of Christian viewpoints," and "to provide a unifying focus for Christians of multicultural backgrounds." WAP published Wide Awake: A Christian Perspective at the University of Virginia. *In the paper's first issue, the editors wrote that the journal "offers a Christian perspective on both personal and community issues, especially those relevant to college students at the University of Virginia." The editors committed the paper to a two-fold mission: "to challenge Christians to live, in word and deed, according to the faith they proclaim and to encourage students to consider what a personal relationship with Jesus Christ means." The advertisements in* Wide Awake *were, for the most part, for churches, centers for Christian study, or Christian bookstores. By June 1992, WAP had distributed about five thousand copies of* Wide Awake *to university students, free of charge.*

WAP acquired CIO status soon after it was organized. At no point during its dispute with the university did the university contend that WAP was a "religious organization" and thus ineligible for CIO status. A few months after being granted CIO status, WAP requested that the SAF pay its printer $5,862 for the costs of printing its newspaper. The student council's Appropriations Committee denied WAP's request on the ground that Wide Awake *was a "religious activity" within the meaning of the guidelines—that is, that the newspaper "promoted or manifested a particular belief in or about a deity or an ultimate reality." It made its determination after examining the first issue of* Wide Awake. *WAP appealed the denial to the full student council, contending that WAP met*

all the applicable guidelines and that denial of SAF support on the basis of the maga-
zine's religious perspective violated the Constitution. The appeal was denied without
further comment. WAP then appealed to the Student Activities Committee. In a letter
signed by the dean of students, the committee sustained the denial of funding. Having
no further recourse within the university, WAP, Wide Awake, and three of its editors
and members filed suit in federal court.

KENNEDY, J., delivered the opinion of the Court, in which REHNQUIST, C. J., and O'CONNOR, SCALIA, and THOMAS, JJ., joined.

[822] The University of Virginia, an instrumentality of the Commonwealth for which it is named and thus bound by the First and Fourteenth Amendments, authorizes the payment of outside contractors for the printing costs of a variety of student publications. It withheld any authorization for payments on behalf of petitioners for the sole reason that their student [823] paper "primarily promotes or manifests a particular belief in or about a deity or an ultimate reality." That the paper did promote or manifest views within the defined exclusion seems plain enough. The challenge is to the University's regulation and its denial of authorization, the case raising issues under the Speech and Establishment Clauses of the First Amendment. . . .

[828] II

It is axiomatic that the government may not regulate speech based on its substantive content or the message it conveys. Other principles follow from this precept. In the realm of private speech or expression, government regulation may not favor one speaker over another. Discrimination against speech because of its message is presumed to be unconstitutional. These rules informed our determination that the government offends the First Amendment when it imposes financial burdens on certain speakers based on the content of their expression. [829] When the government targets not subject matter, but particular views taken by speakers on a subject, the violation of the First Amendment is all the more blatant. Viewpoint discrimination is thus an egregious form of content discrimination. The government must abstain from regulating speech when the specific motivating ideology or the opinion or perspective of the speaker is the rationale for the restriction.

These principles provide the framework forbidding the State from exercising viewpoint discrimination, even when the limited public forum is one of its own creation. In a case involving a school district's provision of school facilities for private uses, we declared that "there is no question that the District, like the private owner of property, may legally preserve the property under its control for the use to which it is dedicated." *Lamb's Chapel v. Center Moriches Union Free School Dist.*, 508 U.S. 384, 390 (1993). The necessities of confining a forum to the limited and legitimate purposes for which it was created may justify the State in reserving it for certain groups or for the discussion of certain topics. Once it has opened a limited forum, however, the State must respect the lawful boundaries it has itself set. The State may not exclude speech where its distinction is not "reasonable in light of the purpose served by the forum," nor may it discriminate against speech on the basis of its viewpoint. Thus, in determining whether the State is acting to preserve the limits of the forum it has created so that the exclusion of a class of speech is legitimate, we have observed a distinction between, [830] on the one hand, content discrimination, which may be permissible if it preserves the purposes of that limited forum, and, on the other hand, viewpoint discrimination, which is presumed impermissible when directed against speech otherwise within the forum's limitations. . . .

The University does acknowledge (as it must in light of our precedents) that "ideologically driven attempts to suppress a particular point of view are presumptively unconstitutional in funding, as in other contexts," but insists that this case does not present that issue because the Guidelines draw lines based on content, not viewpoint. As we have noted, discrimination against one set of [831] views or ideas is but a subset or particular instance of the more general phenomenon of content discrimination. And, it must be acknowledged, the distinction is not a precise one. It is, in a sense, something of an understatement to speak of religious thought and discussion as just a viewpoint, as distinct from a comprehensive body of thought. The nature of our origins and destiny and their dependence upon the existence of a divine being have been subjects of philosophic inquiry throughout human history. We conclude, nonetheless, that here, as in *Lamb's Chapel*, viewpoint discrimination is the proper way to interpret the University's objections to *Wide Awake*. By the very terms of the SAF prohibition, the University does not exclude religion as a subject matter but selects for disfavored treatment those student journalistic efforts with religious editorial viewpoints. Religion may be a vast area of inquiry, but it also provides, as it did here, a specific premise, a perspective, a standpoint from which a variety of subjects may be discussed and considered. The prohibited perspective, not the general subject matter, resulted in the refusal to make third-party payments, for the subjects discussed were otherwise within the approved category of publications. . . .

[835] Vital First Amendment speech principles are at stake here. The first danger to liberty lies in granting the State the power to examine publications to determine whether or not they are based on some ultimate idea and, if so, for the State to classify them. The second, and corollary, danger is to speech from the chilling of individual thought and expression. That danger is especially real in the University setting, where the State acts against a background and tradition of thought and experiment that is at the center of our intellectual and philosophic tradition. [836] In ancient Athens, and, as Europe entered into a new period of intellectual awakening, in places like Bologna, Oxford, and Paris, universities began as voluntary and spontaneous assemblages or concourses for students to speak and to write and to learn. The quality and creative power of student intellectual life to this day remains a vital measure of a school's influence and attainment. For the University, by regulation, to cast disapproval on particular viewpoints of its students risks the suppression of free speech and creative inquiry in one of the vital centers for the Nation's intellectual life, its college and university campuses.

The Guideline invoked by the University to deny third-party contractor payments on behalf of WAP effects a sweeping restriction on student thought and student inquiry in the context of University sponsored publications. The prohibition on funding on behalf of publications that "primarily promote or manifest a particular belief in or about a deity or an ultimate reality," in its ordinary and common-sense meaning, has a vast potential reach. The term "promotes" as used here would comprehend any writing advocating a philosophic position that rests upon a belief in a deity or ultimate reality. And the term "manifests" would bring within the scope of the prohibition any writing that is explicable as resting upon a premise that presupposes the existence of a deity or ultimate reality. Were the prohibition applied with much vigor at all, it would bar funding of essays by hypothetical student contributors named Plato, Spinoza, and Descartes. And if the regulation covers, as the University [837] says it does, those student journalistic efforts that primarily manifest or promote a belief that there is no deity and no ultimate reality, then undergraduates named Karl Marx, Bertrand Russell, and Jean-Paul Sartre would likewise have some of their major essays excluded from student publications. If any manifestation of beliefs in first principles disqualifies the writing, as seems to be the case, it is indeed difficult to name renowned thinkers whose writings would be accepted, save perhaps for articles disclaiming all connection to their ultimate philosophy. Plato could contrive perhaps to submit an acceptable essay on making pasta or peanut butter cookies, provided he did not point out their (necessary) imperfections.

Based on the principles we have discussed, we hold that the regulation invoked to deny SAF support, both in its terms and in its application to these petitioners, is a denial of their right of free speech guaranteed by the First Amendment. It remains to be considered whether the violation following from the University's action is excused by the necessity of complying with the Constitution's prohibition against state establishment of religion. We turn to that question.

III

. . . [839] A central lesson of our decisions is that a significant factor in upholding governmental programs in the face of Establishment Clause attack is their neutrality towards religion. We have decided a series of cases addressing the receipt of government benefits where religion or religious views are implicated in some degree. The first case in our modern Establishment Clause jurisprudence was *Everson v. Board of Ed. of Ewing* (1947). There we cautioned that in enforcing the prohibition against laws respecting establishment of religion, we must "be sure that we do not inadvertently prohibit [the government] from extending its general state law benefits to all its citizens without regard to their religious belief." *Id.*, at 16. We have held that the guarantee of neutrality is respected, not offended, when the government, following neutral criteria and even-handed policies, extends benefits to recipients whose ideologies and viewpoints, including religious ones, are broad and diverse. More than once have we rejected the position that the Establishment Clause even justifies, much less requires, a refusal to extend free speech rights to religious speakers who participate in broad-reaching government programs neutral in design.

[840] The governmental program here is neutral toward religion. There is no suggestion that the University created it to advance religion or adopted some ingenious device with the purpose of aiding a religious cause. The object of the SAF is to open a forum for speech and to support various student enterprises, including the publication of newspapers, in recognition of the diversity and creativity of student life. The University's SAF Guidelines have a separate classification for, and do not make third-party payments on behalf of, "religious organizations," which are those "whose purpose is to practice a devotion to an acknowledged ultimate reality or deity." The category of support here is for "student news, information, opinion, entertainment, or academic communications media groups," of which *Wide Awake* was 1 of 15 in the 1990 school year. WAP did not seek a subsidy because of its Christian editorial viewpoint; it sought funding as a student journal, which it was.

The neutrality of the program distinguishes the student fees from a tax levied for the direct support of a church or group of churches. A tax of that sort, of course, would run contrary to Establishment Clause concerns dating from the earliest days of the Republic. The apprehensions of our predecessors involved the levying of taxes upon the public for the sole and exclusive purpose of establishing and supporting specific sects. The exaction here, by contrast, is a student activity fee designed to reflect the reality that student life in its many dimensions includes the necessity of wide-ranging speech and inquiry and that student expression is an integral part of the University's educational mission. . . .

[841] Government neutrality is apparent in the State's overall scheme in a further meaningful respect. The program respects the critical difference "between government speech endorsing religion, which the Establishment Clause forbids, and private speech endorsing religion, which the Free Speech and Free Exercise Clauses protect." *Mergens*, at 250 (opinion of O'CONNOR, J.). In this case, "the government has not fostered or encouraged" any mistaken impression that the student newspapers speak for the University. *Capitol Square Review and Advisory Bd. v. Pinette*, at 766. The University has taken pains to disassociate itself from the private speech involved in this case. The Court of Appeals' apparent concern that *Wide Awake*'s religious orientation would be attributed to the University is not a plausible fear, and there is no real likelihood that the [842] speech in question is being either endorsed or coerced by the State. . . .

It does not violate the Establishment Clause for a public university to grant access to its facilities on a religion-neutral basis to a wide spectrum of student groups, including groups that use meeting rooms for sectarian activities, accompanied by some devotional exercises. This is so even where the upkeep, maintenance, and repair of the facilities [843] attributed to those uses is paid from a student activities fund to which students are required to contribute. . . .

[844] Were the dissent's view to become law, it would require the University, in order to avoid a constitutional violation, to scrutinize the content of student speech, lest the expression in question—speech otherwise protected by the Constitution—contain too great a religious content. The dissent, in fact, anticipates such censorship as "crucial" in distinguishing between "works characterized by the evangelism of *Wide Awake* and writing that merely happens to express views that a given religion might approve." *Post*, at 896. That eventuality raises the specter of governmental censorship, to ensure that all student writings and publications meet some baseline standard of secular orthodoxy. To impose that [845] standard on student speech at a university is to imperil the very sources of free speech and expression. As we recognized in *Widmar*, official censorship would be far more inconsistent with the Establishment Clause's dictates than would governmental provision of secular printing services on a religion-blind basis.

> "[T]he dissent fails to establish that the distinction [between 'religious' speech and speech 'about' religion] has intelligible content. There is no indication when 'singing hymns, reading scripture, and teaching biblical principles' cease to be 'singing, teaching, and reading'—all apparently forms of 'speech,' despite their religious subject matter—and become unprotected 'worship.' . . .
>
> [E]ven if the distinction drew an arguably principled line, it is highly doubtful that it would lie within the judicial competence to administer. Merely to draw the distinction would require the university—and ultimately the courts—to inquire into the significance of words and practices to different religious faiths, and in varying circumstances by the same faith. Such inquiries would tend inevitably to entangle the State with religion in a manner forbidden by our cases. *E.g.*, *Walz v. Tax Comm'n of City of New York*, 397 U.S. 664 (1970)." 454 U.S. at 269–270, n. 6.

* * *

To obey the Establishment Clause, it was not necessary for the University to deny eligibility to student publications because of their viewpoint. The neutrality commanded of the State by the separate Clauses of the First Amendment was compromised by the University's course of action. The viewpoint discrimination inherent in the University's regulation required public officials to scan and interpret student publications to discern their underlying philosophic assumptions respecting religious theory and belief. That course of action was a denial of the right of free speech and would risk [846] fostering a pervasive bias or hostility to religion, which could undermine the very neutrality the Establishment Clause requires. There is no Establishment Clause violation in the University's honoring its duties under the Free Speech Clause.

JUSTICE O'CONNOR, concurring.

. . . [847] This case lies at the intersection of the principle of government neutrality and the prohibition on state funding of religious activities. It is clear that the University has established a generally applicable program to encourage the free exchange of ideas by its students, an expressive marketplace that includes some 15 student publications with predictably divergent viewpoints. It is equally clear that petitioners' viewpoint is religious and that publication of *Wide Awake* is a religious activity, under both the University's regulation and a fair reading of our precedents. Not to finance *Wide Awake*, according to petitioners, violates the principle of neutrality by sending a message of hostility toward religion. To finance *Wide Awake*, argues the University, violates the prohibition on direct state funding of religious activities.

When two bedrock principles so conflict, understandably neither can provide the definitive answer. Reliance on categorical platitudes is unavailing. Resolution instead depends on the hard task of judging—sifting through the details and determining whether the challenged program offends the Establishment Clause. Such judgment requires courts to draw lines, sometimes quite fine, based on the particular facts of each case. As Justice Holmes observed in a different [848] context: "Neither are we troubled by the question where to draw the line. That is the question in pretty much everything worth arguing in the law. Day and night, youth and age are only types." *Irwin v. Gavit*, 268 U.S. 161, 168 (1925). . . .

[849] So it is in this case. The nature of the dispute does not admit of categorical answers, nor should any be inferred from the Court's decision today, see *ante*, at 838–839. Instead, certain considerations specific to the program at issue lead me to conclude that by providing the same assistance to *Wide Awake* that it does to other publications, the University would not be endorsing the magazine's religious perspective.

First, the student organizations, at the University's insistence, remain strictly independent of the University. The University's agreement with the Contracted Independent Organizations (CIO)—i.e., student groups—provides:

> "The University is a Virginia public corporation and the CIO is not part of that corporation, but rather exists and operates independently of the University. . . .
> The parties understand and agree that this Agreement is the only source of any control the University may have over the CIO or its activities. . . ."

. . . [850] Second, financial assistance is distributed in a manner that ensures its use only for permissible purposes. A student organization seeking assistance must submit disbursement requests; if approved, the funds are paid directly to the third-party vendor and do not pass through the organization's coffers. This safeguard accompanying the University's financial assistance, when provided to a publication with a religious viewpoint such as *Wide Awake*, ensures that the funds are used only to further the University's purpose in maintaining a free and robust marketplace of ideas, from whatever perspective. This feature also makes this case analogous to a school providing equal access to a generally available printing press (or other physical facilities), *ante*, at 843, and unlike a block grant to religious organizations.

Third, assistance is provided to the religious publication in a context that makes improbable any perception of government endorsement of the religious message. *Wide Awake* does not exist in a vacuum. It competes with 15 other magazines and newspapers for advertising and readership. The widely divergent viewpoints of these many purveyors of opinion, all supported on an equal basis by the University, significantly diminishes the danger that the message of any one publication is perceived as endorsed by the University. Besides the general news publications, for example, the University has provided support to *The Yellow Journal*, a humor magazine that has targeted Christianity as a subject of satire, and *Al-Salam*, a publication to "promote a better understanding of Islam to the University Community." Given this wide array of nonreligious, anti-religious and competing religious viewpoints in the forum supported by the University, any perception that the University endorses one particular viewpoint would be illogical. This is not the harder case where religious speech threatens [851] to dominate the forum. . . .

[852] The Court's decision today therefore neither trumpets the supremacy of the neutrality principle nor signals the demise of the funding prohibition in Establishment Clause jurisprudence. As I observed last Term, "experience proves that the Establishment Clause, like the Free Speech Clause, cannot easily be reduced to a single test." *Kiryas Joel*, 512 U.S. at 720 (opinion concurring in part and concurring in judgment). When bedrock principles collide, they test the limits of categorical obstinacy and expose the flaws and dangers of a Grand Unified Theory that may turn out to be neither grand nor unified. The Court today does only what courts must do in many Establishment Clause cases—focus on specific features of a particular government action to ensure that it does not violate the Constitution. By withholding from *Wide Awake* assistance that the University provides generally to all other student publications, the University has discriminated on the basis of the magazine's religious viewpoint in violation of the Free Speech Clause. And particular features of the University's program—such as the explicit disclaimer, the disbursement of funds directly to third-party vendors, the vigorous nature of the forum at issue, and the possibility for objecting students to opt out—convince me that providing such assistance in this case would not carry the danger of impermissible use of public funds to endorse *Wide Awake*'s religious message.

Subject to these comments, I join the opinion of the Court.

JUSTICE THOMAS, concurring.

I agree with the Court's opinion and join it in full, but I write separately to express my disagreement with the historical analysis put forward by the dissent. Although the dissent starts down the right path in consulting the original meaning of the Establishment Clause, its misleading application of history yields a principle that is inconsistent with our Nation's long tradition of allowing religious adherents [853] to participate on equal terms in neutral government programs.

Even assuming that the Virginia debate on the so-called "Assessment Controversy" was indicative of the principles embodied in the Establishment Clause, this incident hardly compels the dissent's conclusion that government must actively discriminate against religion. The dissent's historical discussion glosses over the fundamental characteristic of the Virginia assessment bill that sparked the controversy: The assessment was to be imposed for the support of clergy in the performance of their function of teaching religion. Thus, the "Bill Establishing a Provision for Teachers of the Christian Religion" provided for the collection of a specific tax, the proceeds of which were to be appropriated "by the Vestries, Elders, or Directors of each religious society . . . to a provision for a Minister or Teacher of the Gospel of their denomination, or the providing places of divine worship, and to none other use whatsoever." . . .

[854] James Madison's "Memorial and Remonstrance against Religious Assessments" (hereinafter Madison's "Remonstrance") must be understood in this context. Contrary to the dissent's suggestion, Madison's objection to the assessment bill did not rest on the premise that religious entities may never participate on equal terms in neutral government programs. Nor did Madison embrace the argument that forms the linchpin of the dissent: that monetary subsidies are constitutionally different from other neutral benefits programs. Instead, Madison's comments are more consistent with the neutrality principle that the dissent inexplicably discards. According to Madison, the Virginia assessment was flawed because it "violated that equality which ought to be the basis of every law." Madison's *Remonstrance* ¶ 4. The assessment violated the "equality" principle not because [855] it allowed religious groups to participate in a generally available government program, but because the bill singled out religious entities for special benefits. See *ibid.* (arguing that the assessment violated the equality principle "by subjecting some to peculiar burdens" and "by granting to others peculiar exemptions"). . . .

[856] Under any understanding of the Assessment Controversy, the history cited by the dissent cannot support the conclusion that the Establishment Clause "categorically condemn[s] state programs directly aiding religious activity" when that aid is part of a neutral program available to a wide array of beneficiaries. *Post*, at 875. Even if Madison believed that the principle of nonestablishment of religion precluded government financial support for religion per se (in the sense of government benefits specifically targeting religion), there is no indication that at the time of the framing [857] he took the dissent's extreme view that the government must discriminate against religious adherents by excluding them from more generally available financial subsidies.[2] . . .

[858] Stripped of its flawed historical premise, the dissent's argument is reduced to the claim that our Establishment Clause jurisprudence permits neutrality in the context of access to government facilities but requires discrimination in access to government funds. The dissent purports to locate the prohibition against "direct public funding" at the "heart" of the Establishment Clause, see *post*, at 878, but this conclusion fails to confront historical examples of funding that date back to the time of the founding. To take but one famous example, both Houses of the First Congress elected chaplains, and that Congress enacted legislation providing for an annual salary of $500 to be paid out of the Treasury. Madison himself was a member of the committee that recommended the chaplain system in the House. This same system of "direct public funding" of congres-

---

2. To the contrary, Madison's Remonstrance decried the fact that the assessment bill would require civil society to take "cognizance" of religion. Madison's Remonstrance ¶ 1. Respondents' exclusion of religious activities from SAF funding creates this very problem. It requires University officials to classify publications as "religious activities," and to discriminate against the publications that fall into that category. Such a policy also contravenes the principles expressed in Madison's Remonstrance by encouraging religious adherents to cleanse their speech of religious overtones, thus "degrading from the equal rank of Citizens all those whose opinions in Religion do not bend to those of the Legislative authority." Madison's Remonstrance ¶ 9.

sional chaplains has "continued without interruption ever since that early session of Congress." *Marsh v. Chambers*, 463 U.S. 783, 788 (1983).

[859] The historical evidence of government support for religious entities through property tax exemptions is also overwhelming. As the dissent concedes, property tax exemptions for religious bodies "have been in place for over 200 years without disruption to the interests represented by the Establishment Clause." *Post*, at 881, n. 7. In my view, the dissent's acceptance of this tradition puts to rest the notion that the Establishment Clause bars monetary aid to religious groups even when the aid is equally available to other groups. A tax exemption in many cases is economically and functionally indistinguishable from a direct monetary subsidy. In one instance, the government relieves religious [860] entities (along with others) of a generally applicable tax; in the other, it relieves religious entities (along with others) of some or all of the burden of that tax by returning it in the form of a cash subsidy. Whether the benefit is provided at the front or back end of the taxation process, the financial aid to religious groups is undeniable. The analysis under the Establishment Clause must also be the same: "Few concepts are more deeply embedded in the fabric of our national [861] life, beginning with pre-Revolutionary colonial times, than for the government to exercise at the very least this kind of benevolent neutrality toward churches and religious exercise. . . ." *Walz*, at 676–677. . . .

Though our Establishment Clause jurisprudence is in hopeless disarray, this case provides an opportunity to reaffirm one basic principle that has enjoyed an uncharacteristic degree of consensus: The Clause does not compel the exclusion of religious groups from government benefits programs that are generally available to a broad class of participants. Under the dissent's view, however, the University of Virginia may provide neutral access to the University's own printing press, but it may not provide the same service when the press is owned by a third party. Not surprisingly, [862] the dissent offers no logical justification for this conclusion, and none is evident in the text or original meaning of the First Amendment.

If the Establishment Clause is offended when religious adherents benefit from neutral programs such as the University of Virginia's Student Activities Fund, it must also be offended when they receive the same benefits in the form of in-kind subsidies. The constitutional demands of the Establishment Clause may be judged against either a baseline of "neutrality" or a baseline of "no aid to religion," but the appropriate baseline surely cannot depend on the fortuitous circumstances surrounding the form of aid. The contrary rule would lead to absurd results that would jettison centuries of practice respecting the right of religious adherents to participate on neutral terms in a wide variety of government-funded programs.

Our Nation's tradition of allowing religious adherents to participate in evenhanded government programs is hardly limited to the class of "essential public benefits" identified by the dissent. See *post*, at 879, n. 5. A broader tradition can be traced at least as far back as the First Congress, which ratified the Northwest Ordinance of 1787. Article III of that famous enactment of the Confederation Congress had provided: "Religion, morality, and knowledge . . . being necessary to good government and the happiness of mankind, schools and the means of education shall forever be encouraged." Congress subsequently set aside federal lands in the Northwest Territory and other territories for the use of schools. Many of the schools that enjoyed the benefits of these land grants undoubtedly were church-affiliated sectarian institutions as there was no requirement that the schools be "public." [863] Nevertheless, early Congresses found no problem with the provision of such neutral benefits.

Numerous other government benefits traditionally have been available to religious adherents on neutral terms. Several examples may be found in the work of early Congresses, including copyright protection for "the author and authors of any map, chart, book or books," and a privilege allowing "every printer of newspapers [to] send one paper to each and every other printer of newspapers within the United States, free of postage." Neither of these laws made any exclusion for the numerous authors or printers who manifested a belief in or about a deity.

Thus, history provides an answer for the constitutional question posed by this case, but it is not the one given by the dissent. The dissent identifies no evidence that the Framers intended to disable religious entities from participating on neutral terms in evenhanded government programs. The evidence that does exist points in the opposite direction and provides ample support for today's decision.

JUSTICE SOUTER, with whom JUSTICE STEVENS, JUSTICE GINSBURG, and JUSTICE BREYER join, dissenting.

The Court today, for the first time, approves direct funding of core religious activities by an arm of the State. It does so, however, only after erroneous treatment of some familiar principles of law implementing the First Amendment's Establishment and Speech Clauses, and by viewing the very funds in question as beyond the reach of the Establishment Clause's funding restrictions as such. Because there is no [864] warrant for distinguishing among public funding sources for purposes of applying the First Amendment's prohibition of religious establishment, I would hold that the University's refusal to support petitioners' religious activities is compelled by the Establishment Clause. . . .

I . . .

[865] A

The Court's difficulties will be all the more clear after a closer look at *Wide Awake* than the majority opinion affords. The character of the magazine is candidly disclosed on the opening page of the first issue, where the editor-in-chief announces *Wide Awake*'s mission in a letter to the readership signed, "Love in Christ": it is "to challenge Christians to live, in word and deed, according to the faith they proclaim and to encourage students to consider what a personal relationship with Jesus Christ means." The masthead of every issue bears St. Paul's exhortation, that "the hour has come for you to awake from your slumber, because our salvation is nearer now than when we first believed. Romans 13:11." . . .

[866] Even featured essays on facially secular topics become platforms from which to call readers to fulfill the tenets of Christianity in their lives. Although a piece on racism has some general discussion on the subject, it proceeds beyond even the analysis and interpretation of biblical texts to conclude [867] with the counsel to take action because that is the Christian thing to do:

> "God calls us to take the risks of voluntarily stepping out of our comfort zones and to take joy in the whole richness of our inheritance in the body of Christ. We must take the love we receive from God and share it with all peoples of the world.
>
> Racism is a disease of the heart, soul, and mind, and only when it is extirpated from the individual consciousness and replaced with the love and peace of God will true per-

sonal and communal healing begin." Liu, Rosenberger, Mourad, and Prince, *"Eracing" Mistakes*, Nov./Dec. 1990, p. 14. . . .

This writing is no merely descriptive examination of religious doctrine or even of ideal Christian practice in confronting life's social and personal problems. Nor is it merely the expression of editorial opinion that incidentally coincides with Christian ethics and reflects a Christian view of human obligation. It is straightforward exhortation to enter into a relationship with God as revealed in Jesus Christ, and to satisfy a series of moral obligations derived from the teachings of Jesus Christ. These are not the words of "student news, information, opinion, entertainment, or academic communication . . ." (in the language of the University's funding [868] criterion), but the words of "challenge [to] Christians to live, in word and deed, according to the faith they proclaim and . . . to consider what a personal relationship with Jesus Christ means" (in the language of *Wide Awake*'s founder). The subject is not the discourse of the scholar's study or the seminar room, but of the evangelist's mission station and the pulpit. It is nothing other than the preaching of the word, which (along with the sacraments) is what most branches of Christianity offer those called to the religious life.

Using public funds for the direct subsidization of preaching the word is categorically forbidden under the Establishment Clause, and if the Clause was meant to accomplish nothing else, it was meant to bar this use of public money. Evidence on the subject antedates even the Bill of Rights itself, as may be seen in the writings of Madison, whose authority on questions about the meaning of the Establishment Clause is well settled. Four years before the First Congress proposed the First Amendment, Madison gave his opinion on the legitimacy of using public funds for religious purposes, in the "Memorial and Remonstrance against Religious Assessments," which played the central role in ensuring the defeat of the Virginia tax assessment bill in 1786 and framed the debate upon which the Religion Clauses stand:

> "Who does not see that . . . the same authority which can force a citizen to contribute three pence only of his property for the support of any one establishment, may force him to conform to any other establishment in all cases whatsoever?" James Madison, *Memorial and Remonstrance against Religious Assessments* ¶ 3 (hereinafter Madison's "Remonstrance").

[869] Madison wrote against a background in which nearly every Colony had exacted a tax for church support, *Everson*, at 10, n. 8, the practice having become "so commonplace as to shock the freedom-loving colonials into a feeling of abhorrence," 330 U.S. at 11. Madison's "Remonstrance" captured the colonists' "conviction that individual religious liberty could be achieved best under a government which was stripped of all power to tax, to support, or otherwise to assist any or all religions, or to interfere with the beliefs of any religious individual or group." *Ibid.*[1] Their sentiment, as expressed by

---

1. . . . [870] Nor is it fair to argue that Madison opposed the bill only because it treated religious groups unequally. *Ante*, at 854–855 (THOMAS, J., concurring). In various paragraphs of the Remonstrance, Madison did complain about the bill's peculiar burdens and exemptions, but to identify this factor as the sole point of Madison's opposition to the bill is unfaithful to the Remonstrance's text. Madison strongly inveighed against the proposed aid for religion for a host of reasons (the Remonstrance numbers 15 paragraphs, each containing at least one point in opposition), and crucial here is the fact that many of those reasons would have applied whether or not the state aid was being distributed equally among sects, and whether or not the aid was going to those sects in the context of an evenhanded government program. See, e. g., Madison's Remonstrance ¶ 1 ("In matters of Religion, no man's right is abridged by the institution of Civil Society, and . . . Religion is wholly exempt from its cognizance"); ¶ 6 (arguing that State support of religion "is a contradiction to the Christian

Madison in Virginia, [870] led not only to the defeat of Virginia's tax assessment bill, but also directly to passage of the Virginia Bill for Establishing Religious Freedom, written by Thomas Jefferson. That [871] bill's preamble declared that "to compel a man to furnish contributions of money for the propagation of opinions which he disbelieves, is sinful and tyrannical," and its text provided "that no man shall be compelled to frequent or support any religious worship, place, or ministry whatsoever. . . ." We have "previously recognized that the provisions of the First Amendment, in the drafting and adoption of which Madison and Jefferson played such leading roles, had the same objective and were intended to provide the same protection against governmental intrusion on religious liberty as the Virginia statute." *Ibid.*; see also Laycock, *"Nonpreferential" Aid to Religion: A False Claim about Original Intent*, 27 Wm. & Mary L. Rev. 875, 921, 923 (1986) ("If the debates of the 1780s support any proposition, it is that the Framers opposed government financial support for religion. . . . They did not substitute small taxes for large taxes; three pence was as bad as any larger sum. The principle was what mattered. With respect to money, religion was to be wholly voluntary. Churches either would support [872] themselves or they would not, but the government would neither help nor interfere"); T. Curry, *The First Freedoms* 217 (1986) (At the time of the framing of the Bill of Rights, "the belief that government assistance to religion, especially in the form of taxes, violated religious liberty had a long history"); J. Choper, *Securing Religious Liberty* 16 (1995) ("There is broad consensus that a central threat to the religious freedom of individuals and groups—indeed, in the judgment of many the most serious infringement upon religious liberty—is posed by forcing them to pay taxes in support of a religious establishment or religious activities").[2]

Religion itself; for every page of it disavows a dependence on the powers of this world"); ¶ 7 ("Experience witnesseth that ecclesiastical establishments, instead of maintaining the purity and efficacy of Religion, have had a contrary operation"). Madison's objections were supplemented by numerous other petitions in opposition to the bill that likewise do not suggest that the lack of evenhandedness was its dispositive flaw. For example, the petition that received the largest number of signatories was motivated by the view that religion should only be supported voluntarily. Indeed, Madison's Remonstrance did not argue for a bill distributing aid to all sects and religions on an equal basis, and the [871] outgrowth of the Remonstrance and the defeat of the Virginia assessment was not such a bill; rather, it was the Virginia Bill for Establishing Religious Freedom, which, as discussed in the text, proscribed the use of tax dollars for religious purposes.

In attempting to recast Madison's opposition as having principally been targeted against "governmental preferences for *particular* religious faiths," *ante*, at 856 (emphasis in original), JUSTICE THOMAS wishes to wage a battle that was lost long ago, for "this Court has rejected unequivocally the contention that the Establishment Clause forbids only governmental preference of one religion over another," *School Dist. of Abington Township v. Schempp*, 374 U.S. 203, 216 (1963); see also *Texas Monthly, Inc. v. Bullock*, 489 U.S. 1, 17, (1989) (plurality opinion); *id.*, at 28 (Blackmun, J., concurring in judgment); *Wallace v. Jaffree*, 472 U.S. 38, 52–53 (1985); *Torcaso v. Watkins*, 367 U.S. 488, 495 (1961); *Engel v. Vitale*, 370 U.S. 421, 430 (1962); *Everson*, at 15; see generally *Lee v. Weisman*, 505 U.S. 577, 609–616 (1992) (SOUTER, J., concurring).

2. JUSTICE THOMAS attempts to cast doubt on this accepted version of Establishment Clause history by reference to historical facts that are largely inapposite. *Ante*, at 857–858, 862–863 (concurring opinion). As I have said elsewhere, individual Acts of Congress, especially when they are few and far between, scarcely serve as an authoritative guide to the meaning of the Religion Clauses, for "like other politicians, [members of the early Congresses] could raise constitutional ideals one day and turn their backs on them the next. [For example,] . . . ten years after proposing the First Amendment, Congress passed the Alien and Sedition Acts, measures patently unconstitutional by modern standards. If the early Congress's political actions were determinative, and not merely relevant, evidence of constitutional meaning, we would have to gut our current First Amendment doctrine to make room for political censorship." *Lee v. Weisman*, at 626 (concurring opinion). The legislation cited by JUSTICE THOMAS, including the Northwest Ordinance, is no more dispositive than the Alien and Sedition Acts in interpreting the First Amendment. Even less persuasive, then, are citations to constitutionally untested Acts dating from the mid-19th century, for without some rather innovative argument, they cannot be offered as providing an authoritative gloss on the Framers' intent.

JUSTICE THOMAS's references to Madison's actions as a legislator also provide little support for his cause. JUSTICE THOMAS seeks to draw a significant lesson out of the fact that, in seeking to disestablish the Anglican

[873] The principle against direct funding with public money is patently violated by the contested use of today's student activity fee. Like today's taxes generally, the fee is Madison's three pence. The University exercises the power of the State to compel a student to pay it, see Jefferson's *Preamble*, and the use of any part of it for the direct support of religious activity thus strikes at what we have repeatedly [874] held to be the heart of the prohibition on establishment. *Everson*, at 15–16 ("The 'establishment of religion' clause . . . means at least this. . . . No tax in any amount, large or small, can be levied to support any religious activities or institutions, whatever they may be called, or whatever form they may adopt to teach or practice religion"); see *School Dist. of Grand Rapids v. Ball*, 473 U.S. 373, 385 (1985) ("Although Establishment Clause jurisprudence is characterized by few absolutes, the Clause does absolutely prohibit government-financed or government-sponsored indoctrination into the beliefs of a particular religious faith"); *Committee for Public Ed. v. Nyquist*, 413 U.S. at 780 ("In the absence of an effective means of guaranteeing that the state aid derived from public funds will be used exclusively for secular, neutral, and nonideological purposes, it is clear from our cases that direct aid in whatever form is invalid"); *id.*, at 772 ("Primary among those evils" against which the Establishment Clause guards "have been sponsorship, financial support, and active involvement of the sovereign in religious activity"); see also *Lee v. Weisman*, 505 U.S. 577, 640 (1992) (SCALIA, J., dissenting) ("The coercion that was a hallmark of historical establishments of religion was coercion of religious orthodoxy and of financial support by force of law and threat of penalty") (emphasis deleted).

The Court, accordingly, has never before upheld direct state funding of the sort of proselytizing published in *Wide* [875] *Awake* and, in fact, has categorically condemned state programs directly aiding religious activity.

Even when the Court has upheld aid to an institution performing both secular and sectarian functions, it has always made a searching enquiry to ensure that the institution kept the secular activities separate from its sectarian ones, with any direct aid flowing only to the former and never the latter.

[876] Reasonable minds may differ over whether the Court reached the correct result in each of these cases, but their common principle has never been questioned or repudiated. "Although Establishment Clause jurisprudence is characterized by few absolutes, the Clause does absolutely prohibit government-financed . . . indoctrination into the beliefs of a particular religious faith." *School Dist. v. Ball*, 473 U.S. at 385.

Church in Virginia in 1776, Madison did not inveigh against state funding of religious activities. *Ante*, at 857 (concurring opinion). That was not the task at hand, however. Madison was acting with the specific goal of eliminating the special privileges enjoyed by Virginia Anglicans, and he made no effort to lay out the broader views of church and state that came to bear in his drafting of the First Amendment some 13 years later. That Madison did not speak in more expansive terms than necessary in 1776 was hardly surprising for, as it was, his proposal was defeated by the Virginia Convention as having gone too far. *Ibid.*

Similarly, the invocation of Madison's tenure on the congressional committee that approved funding for legislative chaplains provides no support for more general principles that run counter to settled Establishment Clause jurisprudence. As I have previously pointed out, Madison, upon retirement, "insisted that 'it was not with my approbation, that the deviation from [the immunity of religion from civil jurisdiction] took place in Congs., when they appointed Chaplains, to be paid from the Natl. Treasury.'" *Lee*, 505 U.S. at 625, n. 6, quoting Letter from J. Madison to E. Livingston (July 10, 1822). And when we turned our attention to deciding whether funding of legislative chaplains posed an establishment problem, we did not address the practice as one instance of a larger class of permissible government funding of religious activities. Instead, *Marsh v. Chambers*, 463 U.S. 783, 791 (1983), explicitly relied on the singular, 200-year pedigree of legislative chaplains, noting that "this unique history" justified carving out an exception for the specific practice in question. Given that the decision upholding this practice was expressly limited to its facts, then, it would stand the Establishment Clause on its head to extract from it a broad rule permitting the funding of religious activities.

B

Why does the Court not apply this clear law to these clear facts and conclude, as I do, that the funding scheme here is a clear constitutional violation? The answer must be in part that the Court fails to confront the evidence set out in the preceding section. Throughout its opinion, the Court refers uninformatively to *Wide Awake*'s "Christian viewpoint," *ante*, at 826, or its "religious perspective," *ante*, at 832, and in distinguishing funding of *Wide Awake* from the funding of a church, the Court maintains that "[*Wide Awake*] is not a religious institution, at least in the usual sense," *ante*, at [877] 844; see also *ante*, at 826. The Court does not quote the magazine's adoption of Saint Paul's exhortation to awaken to the nearness of salvation, or any of its articles enjoining readers to accept Jesus Christ, or the religious verses, or the religious textual analyses, or the suggested prayers. And so it is easy for the Court to lose sight of what the University students and the Court of Appeals found so obvious, and to blanch the patently and frankly evangelistic character of the magazine by unrevealing allusions to religious points of view.

Nevertheless, even without the encumbrance of detail from *Wide Awake*'s actual pages, the Court finds something sufficiently religious about the magazine to require examination under the Establishment Clause, and one may therefore ask why the unequivocal prohibition on direct funding does not lead the Court to conclude that funding would be unconstitutional. The answer is that the Court focuses on a subsidiary body of law, which it correctly states but ultimately misapplies. That subsidiary body of law accounts for the Court's substantial attention to the fact that the University's funding scheme is "neutral," in the formal sense that it makes funds available on an evenhanded basis to secular and sectarian applicants alike. *Ante*, at 839–842. While this is indeed true and relevant under our cases, it does not alone satisfy the requirements of the Establishment Clause, as the Court recognizes when it says that evenhandedness is only a "significant factor" in certain Establishment Clause analysis, not a dispositive one. [878] This recognition reflects the Court's appreciation of two general rules: that whenever affirmative government aid ultimately benefits religion, the Establishment Clause requires some justification beyond evenhandedness on the government's part; and that direct public funding of core sectarian activities, even if accomplished pursuant to an evenhanded program, would be entirely inconsistent with the Establishment Clause and would strike at the very heart of the Clause's protection.

In order to understand how the Court thus begins with sound rules but ends with an unsound result, it is necessary to explore those rules in greater detail than the Court does. As the foregoing quotations from the Court's opinion indicate, the relationship between the prohibition on direct aid and the requirement of evenhandedness when affirmative government aid does result in some benefit to religion reflects the relationship between basic rule and marginal criterion. At the heart of the Establishment Clause stands the prohibition against direct public funding, but that prohibition does not answer the questions that occur at the margins of the Clause's application. Is any government activity that provides any incidental benefit to religion likewise unconstitutional? Would it be wrong to put out fires in burning churches, wrong to pay the bus fares of students on the way [879] to parochial schools, wrong to allow a grantee of special education funds to spend them at a religious college? These are the questions that call for drawing lines, and it is in drawing them that evenhandedness becomes important. However the Court may in the past have phrased its line-drawing test, the question whether such benefits are provided on an evenhanded basis has been relevant, for the question addresses one aspect of the issue whether a law is truly neutral with respect to religion (that is, whether the law either "advances [or] inhibits religion." In *Widmar v. Vincent*, 454 U.S. 263 (1981), for example, we noted that "the provision of benefits to [a] broad . . . spectrum of [religious and nonreligious] groups is an important index of secular effect." In the doubtful cases (those not involving direct public funding), where there is initially room for argument about a law's effect, evenhandedness serves to weed out those laws that impermissibly advance religion by channelling aid to it exclusively. Evenhandedness is therefore a prerequisite to further enquiry into the constitutionality of a doubtful law, but evenhandedness goes no further. It does not guarantee success under Establishment Clause scrutiny. . . .

[882] Evenhandedness as one element of a permissibly attenuated benefit is, of course, a far cry from evenhandedness as a sufficient condition of constitutionality for direct financial support of religious proselytization, and our cases have unsurprisingly repudiated any such attempt to cut the Establishment Clause down to a mere prohibition against unequal direct aid. . . .

D

[891] Nothing in the Court's opinion would lead me to end this enquiry into the application of the Establishment Clause any [892] differently from the way I began it. The Court is ordering an instrumentality of the State to support religious evangelism with direct funding. This is a flat violation of the Establishment Clause.

II

Given the dispositive effect of the Establishment Clause's bar to funding the magazine, there should be no need to decide whether in the absence of this bar the University would violate the Free Speech Clause by limiting funding as it has done. But the Court's speech analysis may have independent application, and its flaws should not pass unremarked. . . .

[895] There is no viewpoint discrimination in the University's application of its Guidelines to deny funding to *Wide Awake*. Under those Guidelines, a "religious activity," which is not eligible for funding is "an activity which primarily promotes or manifests a particular belief(s) in or about a deity or an ultimate reality." It is clear that this is the basis on which Wide Awake Productions was denied funding. Letter from Student Council to Ronald W. Rosenberger ("In reviewing the request by Wide Awake Productions, the Appropriations Committee determined your organization's request could not be funded as it is a religious activity"). The discussion of *Wide Awake*'s content, *supra*, at 865–868, shows beyond any question that it "primarily promotes or manifests a particular belief(s) in or about a deity . . . ," in the very specific sense that its manifest function is to call students to repentance, to commitment to Jesus Christ, and to particular moral action because of its Christian character.

If the Guidelines were written or applied so as to limit only such Christian advocacy and no other evangelical efforts that might compete with it, the discrimination would be based on viewpoint. But that is not what the regulation authorizes; it applies to Muslim and Jewish and Buddhist advocacy as well as to Christian. And since it limits funding to activities promoting or manifesting a particular belief not only "in" but "about" a deity or ultimate reality, it applies to agnostics and atheists as well as it does to deists and theists. [896] The Guidelines, and their application to *Wide Awake*, thus do not skew debate by funding one position but not its competitors. As understood by their application to *Wide Awake*, they simply deny funding for hortatory speech that "primarily promotes or manifests" any view on the merits of religion; they deny funding for the entire subject matter of religious apologetics. . . .

III

[899] Since I cannot see the future I cannot tell whether today's decision portends much more than making a shambles out of student activity fees in public colleges. Still, my apprehension is whetted by Chief Justice Burger's warning in *Lemon v. Kurtzman*, 403 U.S. 602, 624 (1971): "in constitutional adjudication some steps, which when taken were thought to approach 'the verge,' have become the platform for yet further steps. A certain momentum develops in constitutional theory and it can be a 'downhill thrust' easily set in motion but difficult to retard or stop."

I respectfully dissent.

Agostini v. Felton*

521 U.S. 203 (1997)

Vote: 5—*Rehnquist, O'Connor, Scalia, Kennedy, Thomas*
     4—*Stevens, Souter, Ginsburg, Breyer*

Opinion announcing the opinion of the Court: O'Connor
Dissenting opinions: Souter, Ginsburg

In Aguilar v. Felton, *473 U.S. 402 (1985), a five-member majority of the Supreme Court found aspects of New York City's expenditures of federal Title I funds unconstitutional. Specifically, the Court held that the city's program that sent public school teachers into parochial schools to provide remedial education to disadvantaged children necessitated an unconstitutional entanglement of church and state. In* Agostini, *the Supreme Court revisited and reversed that decision.*

    Title I of the federal Elementary and Secondary Education Act of 1965 channels federal funds through the states to "local educational agencies" (LEAs) to provide remedial education, guidance, and job counseling. Students eligible to receive Title I funding are those who (1) reside within the attendance boundaries of a public school located in a low-income area, and (2) are failing, or are at risk of failing, the state's student performance standards. Federal law requires that Title I funds be made available to all eligible children, regardless of whether they attend public schools. It also requires that the services provided to private school pupils be "equitable in comparison to services and other benefits for public school children." An LEA providing services to children enrolled in private schools must retain complete control over Title I funds, retain title to all materials used to provide Title I services, and provide those services through public employees or other persons independent of the private school and any religious institution. The Title I services themselves, moreover, must be "secular, neutral, and nonideological" and must "supplement, and in no case supplant, the level of services" already provided by the private school.

    *In its pre-*Aguilar *implementation of Title I funding, the city of New York sent public school teachers into parochial schools during regular school hours to provide remedial education to all disadvantaged children who met Title I's eligibility requirements, regardless of the students' religious beliefs or where the students went*

---

*Together with No. 96-553, *Board of Education of the City of New York v. Felton, *also on certiorari to the same court.

to school. In order to ensure compliance with the city's rules against compromising the program's secular purpose, a publicly employed field supervisor was to attempt to make at least one unannounced visit to each teacher's classroom every month. After the Aguilar decision, the city provided Title I services to parochial school students at public school sites, at leased sites, and in vans parked near the parochial schools. These alternative arrangements led to a dramatic increase in costs and a reduction in eligible student participation.

In 1995, the city and a group of parents commenced litigation asking the courts to review the Aguilar ruling in light of developments in the Supreme Court's Establishment Clause jurisprudence.

O'CONNOR, J., delivered the opinion of the Court, in which REHNQUIST, C. J., and SCALIA, KENNEDY, and THOMAS, JJ., joined.

[208] In *Aguilar v. Felton*, 473 U.S. 402 (1985), this Court held that the Establishment Clause of the First Amendment barred the city of New York from sending public school teachers into parochial schools to provide remedial education to disadvantaged children pursuant to a congressionally mandated program. On remand, the District Court for the Eastern District of New York entered a permanent injunction reflecting our ruling. Twelve years later, petitioners—the parties bound by that injunction—seek relief from its operation. Petitioners maintain that *Aguilar* cannot be [209] squared with our intervening Establishment Clause jurisprudence and ask that we explicitly recognize what our more recent cases already dictate: *Aguilar* is no longer good law. We agree with petitioners that *Aguilar* is not consistent with our subsequent Establishment Clause decisions and further conclude that, on the facts presented here, petitioners are entitled under Federal Rule of Civil Procedure 60 (b)(5) to relief from the operation of the District Court's prospective injunction. . . .

[218] III

A

In order to evaluate whether *Aguilar* has been eroded by our subsequent Establishment Clause cases, it is necessary to understand the rationale upon which *Aguilar*, as well as its companion case, *School Dist. of Grand Rapids v. Ball*, 473 U.S. 373 (1985), rested. . . .

[222] Distilled to essentials, the Court's conclusion that the Shared Time program in *Ball* had the impermissible effect of advancing religion rested on three assumptions: (i) any public employee who works on the premises of a religious school is presumed to inculcate religion in her work; (ii) the presence of public employees on private school premises creates a symbolic union between church and state; and (iii) any and all public aid that directly aids the educational function of religious schools impermissibly finances religious indoctrination, even if the aid reaches such schools as a consequence of private decisionmaking. Additionally, in *Aguilar* there was a fourth assumption: that New York City's Title I program necessitated an excessive government entanglement with religion because public employees who teach on the premises of religious schools must be closely monitored to ensure that they do not inculcate religion.

B

Our more recent cases have undermined the assumptions upon which *Ball* and *Aguilar* relied. To be sure, the general principles we use to evaluate whether government aid violates the Establishment Clause have not changed since *Aguilar* was decided. For example, we continue to ask whether the government acted with the purpose of advancing [223] or inhibiting religion, and the nature of that inquiry has remained largely unchanged. Likewise, we continue to explore whether the aid has the "effect" of advancing or inhibiting religion. What has changed since we decided *Ball* and *Aguilar* is our understanding of the criteria used to assess whether aid to religion has an impermissible effect.

I

As we have repeatedly recognized, government inculcation of religious beliefs has the impermissible effect of advancing religion. Our cases subsequent to *Aguilar* have, however, modified in two significant respects the approach we use to assess indoctrination. First, we have abandoned the presumption erected in *Meek* and *Ball* that the placement of public employees on parochial school grounds inevitably results in the impermissible effect of state-sponsored indoctrination or constitutes a symbolic union between government and religion. In *Zobrest v. Catalina Foothills School Dist.*, 509 U.S. 1 (1993), we examined whether the IDEA, 20 U.S.C. § 1400 *et seq.*, was constitutional as applied to a deaf student who sought to bring his state-employed sign-language interpreter with him to his Roman Catholic high school. We held that this was permissible, expressly disavowing the notion that "the Establishment Clause [laid] down [an] absolute bar to the placing of a public employee in a sectarian school." 509 U.S. at 13. "Such a flat rule, smacking of antiquated notions of 'taint,' would indeed exalt [224] form over substance." *Ibid.* . . .

[225] Second, we have departed from the rule relied on in *Ball* that all government aid that directly aids the educational function of religious schools is invalid. In *Witters v. Washington Dept. of Servs. for Blind*, 474 U.S. 481 (1986), we held that the Establishment Clause did not bar a State from issuing a vocational tuition grant to a blind person who wished to use the grant to attend a Christian college and become a pastor, missionary, or youth director. Even though the grant recipient clearly would use the money to obtain religious education, we observed that the tuition grants were "made available generally without regard to the sectarian-nonsectarian, or public-nonpublic nature of the institution benefited." *Id.*, at 487 (quoting *Committee for Public Ed. & Religious Liberty v. Nyquist*, 413 U.S. 756, 782–783 [226] [1973]). The grants were disbursed directly to students, who then used the money to pay for tuition at the educational institution of their choice. In our view, this transaction was no different from a State's issuing a paycheck to one of its employees, knowing that the employee would donate part or all of the check to a religious institution. In both situations, any money that ultimately went to religious institutions did so "only as a result of the genuinely independent and private choices of" individuals. *Ibid.* . . .

Zobrest and *Witters* make clear that, under current law, the Shared Time program in *Ball* and New York City's Title I program in *Aguilar* will not, as a matter of law, be deemed to have the effect of advancing religion through indoctrination. Indeed, each of the premises upon which we relied in *Ball* to reach a contrary conclusion is no longer valid. First, there is no reason to presume that, simply because she enters a parochial school classroom, a full-time public employee such as a Title I teacher will depart from her assigned duties and instructions and embark on religious indoctrination, any more than there was a reason in *Zobrest* to think an interpreter would inculcate religion by altering her translation of classroom lectures. Certainly, no evidence has ever shown that any New York City Title I instructor teaching on parochial school premises attempted to inculcate religion in students. [227] Thus, both our precedent and our experience require us to reject respondents' remarkable argument that we must presume Title I instructors to be "uncontrollable and sometimes very unprofessional." Tr. of Oral Arg. 39. . . .

[230] 2

Although we examined in *Witters* and *Zobrest* the criteria by which an aid program identifies its beneficiaries, we did so solely to assess whether any use of that aid to indoctrinate religion could be attributed to the State. A number of our Establishment Clause cases have found that the criteria used for identifying beneficiaries are relevant in a second respect, apart from enabling a court to evaluate whether the program [231] subsidizes religion. Specifically, the criteria might themselves have the effect of advancing religion by creating a financial incentive to undertake religious indoctrination. This incentive is not present, however, where the aid is allocated on the basis of neutral, secular criteria that neither favor nor disfavor religion, and is made available to both religious and secular beneficiaries on a nondiscriminatory basis. Under such circumstances, the aid is less likely to have the effect of advancing religion. . . .

[232] Applying this reasoning to New York City's Title I program, it is clear that Title I services are allocated on the basis of criteria that neither favor nor disfavor religion. The services are available to all children who meet the Act's eligibility requirements, no matter what their religious beliefs or where they go to school. The Board's program does not, therefore, give aid recipients any incentive to modify their religious beliefs or practices in order to obtain those services.

3

We turn now to *Aguilar*'s conclusion that New York City's Title I program resulted in an excessive entanglement between church and state. Whether a government aid program results in such an entanglement has consistently been an aspect of our Establishment Clause analysis. . . .

[233] The pre-*Aguilar* Title I program does not result in an "excessive" entanglement that advances or inhibits religion. As discussed previously, the Court's finding of "excessive" entanglement in *Aguilar* rested on three grounds: (i) the program would require "pervasive monitoring by public authorities" to ensure that Title I employees did not inculcate religion; (ii) the program required "administrative cooperation" between the Board and parochial schools; and (iii) the program might increase the dangers of "political divisiveness." 473 U.S. at 413–414. Under our current understanding of the Establishment Clause, the last two considerations are insufficient by themselves to create an "excessive" [234] entanglement. They are present no matter where Title I services are offered, and no court has held that Title I services cannot be offered off-campus. Further, the assumption underlying the first consideration has been undermined. In *Aguilar*, the Court presumed that full-time public employees on parochial school grounds would be tempted to inculcate religion, despite the ethical standards they were required to uphold. Because of this risk *pervasive* monitoring would be

required. But after *Zobrest* we no longer presume that public employees will inculcate religion simply because they happen to be in a sectarian environment. Since we
have abandoned the assumption that properly instructed public employees will fail to
discharge their duties faithfully, we must also discard the assumption that *pervasive*
monitoring of Title I teachers is required. There is no suggestion in the record before
us that unannounced monthly visits of public supervisors are insufficient to prevent
or to detect inculcation of religion by public employees. Moreover, we have not found
excessive entanglement in cases in which States imposed far more onerous burdens on
religious institutions than the monitoring system at issue here.

To summarize, New York City's Title I program does not run afoul of any of three
primary criteria we currently use to evaluate whether government aid has the effect
of advancing religion: it does not result in governmental indoctrination; define its recipients by reference to religion; or create an excessive entanglement. We therefore
hold that a federally funded program providing supplemental, remedial instruction to
disadvantaged children on a neutral basis is not invalid under the Establishment Clause
when such instruction [235] is given on the premises of sectarian schools by government
employees pursuant to a program containing safeguards such as those present here. The
same considerations that justify this holding require us to conclude that this carefully
constrained program also cannot reasonably be viewed as an endorsement of religion.
Accord, *Witters*, 474 U.S. at 488–489 ("The mere circumstance that [an aid recipient] has
chosen to use neutrally available state aid to help pay for [a] religious education [does
not] confer any message of state endorsement of religion"); *Bowen*, at 613–614 (finding
no "symbolic link" when Congress made federal funds neutrally available for adolescent
counseling). Accordingly, we must acknowledge that *Aguilar*, as well as the portion of
Ball addressing Grand Rapids' Shared Time program, are no longer good law. . . .

[240] JUSTICE SOUTER, with whom JUSTICE STEVENS and JUSTICE GINSBURG join, and with whom JUSTICE BREYER joins as to Part II, dissenting.

In this novel proceeding, petitioners seek relief from an injunction the District Court
entered 12 years ago to implement our decision in *Aguilar v. Felton*, 473 U.S. 402 (1985).
For the reasons given by JUSTICE GINSBURG, the Court's holding that petitioners are
entitled to relief under Rule 60 (b) is seriously mistaken. The Court's misapplication of
the rule is tied to its equally erroneous reading of our more recent Establishment Clause
cases, which the Court describes as having rejected the underpinnings of *Aguilar* and
portions of *Aguilar*'s companion case, *School Dist. of Grand Rapids v. Ball*, 473 U.S.
373 (1985). The result is to repudiate the very reasonable line drawn in *Aguilar* and *Ball*,
and to authorize direct state aid to religious institutions on an unparalleled [241] scale,
in violation of the Establishment Clause's central prohibition against religious subsidies
by the government.

I respectfully dissent.

I

. . . [242] As I will indicate as I go along, I believe *Aguilar* was a correct and sensible
decision, and my only reservation about its opinion is that the emphasis on the excessive entanglement produced by monitoring religious instructional content obscured

those facts that independently called for the application of two central tenets of Establishment Clause jurisprudence. The State is forbidden to subsidize religion directly and is just as surely forbidden to act in any way that could reasonably be viewed as religious endorsement.

[243] As is explained elsewhere, the flat ban on subsidization antedates the Bill of Rights and has been an unwavering rule in Establishment Clause cases, qualified only by the conclusion two Terms ago that state exactions from college students are not the sort of public revenues subject to the ban. See *Rosenberger v. Rector and Visitors of Univ. of Va.*, 515 U.S. 819 (1995). The rule expresses the hard lesson learned over and over again in the American past and in the experiences of the countries from which we have come, that religions supported by governments are compromised just as surely as the religious freedom of dissenters is burdened when the government supports religion. "When the government favors a particular religion or sect, the disadvantage to all others is obvious, but even the favored religion may fear being 'tainted . . . with corrosive secularism.' The favored religion may be compromised as political figures reshape the religion's beliefs for their own purposes; it may be reformed as government largesse brings government regulation." *Lee v. Weisman*, 505 U.S. 577, 608 (1992) (Blackmun, J., concurring) (quoting *Ball*, at 385); see also *Memorial and Remonstrance against Religious Assessments* (1785), in *The Complete Madison* 299, 309 (S. Padover ed. 1953) ("Religion flourishes in greater purity, without than with the aid of Government"); M. Howe, *The Garden and the Wilderness* 6 (1965) (noting Roger Williams's view that "worldly corruptions . . . might consume the churches if sturdy fences against the wilderness were not maintained"). The ban against state endorsement of religion addresses the same historical lessons. Governmental approval of religion tends to reinforce the religious message (at least in the short run) and, by the same token, to carry a message of exclusion to those of less favored views. [244] The human tendency, of course, is to forget the hard lessons, and to overlook the history of governmental partnership with religion when a cause is worthy, and bureaucrats have programs. That tendency to forget is the reason for having the Establishment Clause (along with the Constitution's other structural and libertarian guarantees), in the hope of stopping the corrosion before it starts.

These principles were violated by the programs at issue in *Aguilar* and *Ball*, as a consequence of several significant features common to both Title I, as implemented in New York City before *Aguilar*, and the Grand Rapids Shared Time program: each provided classes on the premises of the religious schools, covering a wide range of subjects including some at the core of primary and secondary education, like reading and mathematics; while their services were termed "supplemental," the programs and their instructors necessarily assumed responsibility for teaching subjects that the religious schools would otherwise have been obligated to provide [245]; and, finally, aid under Title I and Shared Time flowed directly to the schools in the form of classes and programs, as distinct from indirect aid that reaches schools only as a result of independent private choice.

What, therefore, was significant in *Aguilar* and *Ball* about the placement of state-paid teachers into the physical and social settings of the religious schools was not only the consequent temptation of some of those teachers to reflect the schools' religious missions in the rhetoric of their instruction, with a resulting need for monitoring and the certainty of entanglement. What was so remarkable was that the schemes in issue assumed a teaching responsibility indistinguishable from the responsibility of the schools themselves. The obligation of primary and secondary schools to teach reading necessarily extends to teaching those who are having a hard time at it, and the same is true of math. Calling some classes remedial does not distinguish their subjects from the schools' basic subjects, [246] however inadequately the schools may have been addressing them.

What was true of the Title I scheme as struck down in *Aguilar* will be just as true when New York reverts to the old practices with the Court's approval after today. There is simply no line that can be drawn between the instruction paid for at taxpayers' expense and the instruction in any subject that is not identified as formally religious. While it would be an obvious sham, say, to channel cash to religious schools to be credited only against the expense of "secular" instruction, the line between "supplemental" and general education is likewise impossible to draw. If a State may constitutionally enter the schools to teach in the manner in question, it must in constitutional principle be free to assume, or assume payment for, the entire cost of instruction provided in any ostensibly secular subject in any religious school. This Court explicitly recognized this in *Ball*, at 394, 396, and although in *Aguilar* the Court concentrated on entanglement it noted the similarity to *Ball*, see *Aguilar*, at 409, and Judge Friendly's opinion for the Second Circuit made it expressly clear that there was no stopping place in principle once the public teacher entered the religious schools to teach their secular subjects. See *Felton v. Secretary, U.S. Dept. of Education*, 739 F.2d 48, 66–67 (CA2 1984), aff'd *sub. nom.* . . .

[247] In sum, if a line is to be drawn short of barring all state aid to religious schools for teaching standard subjects, the *Aguilar-Ball* line was a sensible one capable of principled adherence. It is no less sound, and no less necessary, today. . . .

City of Boerne v. Flores

521 U.S. 507 (1997)

Vote: 6—Rehnquist, Stevens, Scalia, Kennedy, Thomas, Ginsburg
*   3—O'Connor, Souter, Breyer*
Opinion announcing the opinion of the Court: Kennedy
Concurring opinion: Stevens
Opinion concurring in part: Scalia
Dissenting opinions: O'Connor, Souter, Breyer

In his capacity as archbishop of San Antonio, Father Patrick Fernández Flores applied for a building permit to enlarge St. Peter Catholic Church in Boerne, Texas. Built in 1923, the church's structure replicated the mission architectural style of the region's history. At the time, the church sat about 230 worshippers, which left some 40–60 parishioners unaccommodated at some Sunday masses.

City zoning authorities denied the building permit, relying on an ordinance governing historic preservation in a district, which, they argued, included the church. The archbishop brought this suit challenging the permit denial under the Religious Freedom Restoration Act of 1993 (RFRA). Among other things, the Supreme Court considered whether Congress possessed power under § 5 of the Fourteenth Amendment to apply RFRA to the states.

Congress passed the Religious Freedom Restoration Act of 1993 in response to the Supreme Court's decision in Employment Division, Department of Human Resources of Oregon v. Smith *(1990). In the House of Representatives, the bill passed unanimously by voice vote; in the Senate, ninety-seven senators voted in favor of the legislation.*

The relevant text of the Religious Freedom Restoration Act of 1993 is presented here, along with excerpts of the opinions written in the Supreme Court case.

Religious Freedom Restoration Act of 1993, Public Law (P.L.) 103-141

One Hundred Third Congress of the United States of America AT THE FIRST SESSION Begun and held at the City of Washington on Tuesday, the fifth day of January, one thousand nine hundred and ninety-three.

TITLE: To protect the free exercise of religion.

Be it enacted by the Senate and House of Representatives of the United States of America in Congress assembled,

SECTION 1. SHORT TITLE.

This Act may be cited as the "Religious Freedom Restoration Act of 1993."

SEC. 2. CONGRESSIONAL FINDINGS AND DECLARATION OF PURPOSES.

(a) Findings: The Congress finds that—

(1) the framers of the Constitution, recognizing free exercise of religion as an unalienable right, secured its protection in the First Amendment to the Constitution;

(2) laws "neutral" toward religion may burden religious exercise as surely as laws intended to interfere with religious exercise;

(3) governments should not substantially burden religious exercise without compelling justification;

(4) in *Employment Division v. Smith*, 494 U.S. 872 (1990), the Supreme Court virtually eliminated the requirement that the government justify burdens on religious exercise imposed by laws neutral toward religion; and

(5) the compelling interest test as set forth in prior Federal court rulings is a workable test for striking sensible balances between religious liberty and competing prior governmental interests.

(b) Purposes: The purposes of this Act are—

(1) to restore the compelling interest test as set forth in *Sherbert v. Verner*, 374 U.S. 398 (1963), and *Wisconsin v. Yoder*, 406 U.S. 205 (1972), and to guarantee its application in all cases where free exercise of religion is substantially burdened; and

(2) to provide a claim or defense to persons whose religious exercise is substantially burdened by government.

SEC. 3. FREE EXERCISE OF RELIGION PROTECTED.

(a) In General: Government shall not substantially burden a person's exercise of religion even if the burden results from a rule of general applicability, except as provided in subsection (b).

(b) Exception: Government may substantially burden a person's exercise of religion only if it demonstrates that application of the burden to the person—

(1) is in furtherance of a compelling governmental interest; and

(2) is the least restrictive means of furthering that compelling governmental interest.

(c) Judicial Relief: A person whose religious exercise has been burdened in violation of this section may assert that violation as a claim or defense in a judicial proceeding and obtain appropriate relief against a government. Standing to assert a claim or defense under this section shall be governed by the general rules of standing under article III of the Constitution. . . .

SEC. 7. ESTABLISHMENT CLAUSE UNAFFECTED.

Nothing in this Act shall be construed to affect, interpret, or in any way address that portion of the First Amendment prohibiting laws respecting the establishment of religion (referred to in this section as the "Establishment Clause"). Granting government funding, benefits, or exemptions, to the extent permissible under the Establishment Clause, shall not constitute a violation of this Act. As used in this section, the term "granting," used with respect to government funding, benefits, or exemptions, does not include the denial of government funding, benefits, or exemptions.

Speaker of the House of Representatives. Vice President of the United States and President of the Senate.

City of Boerne v. Flores, 521 U.S. 507 (1997)

KENNEDY, J., delivered the opinion of the Court, in which REHNQUIST, C. J., and STEVENS, THOMAS, and GINSBURG, JJ., joined, and in all but Part III-A-1 of which SCALIA, J., joined.

[511] A decision by local zoning authorities to deny a church a building permit was challenged under the Religious Freedom Restoration Act of 1993 (RFRA). The case calls into question the authority of Congress to enact RFRA. We conclude the statute exceeds Congress' power. . . .

[516] III

A

. . . [519] In assessing the breadth of § 5's enforcement power, we begin with its text. Congress has been given the power "to enforce" the "provisions of this article." We agree with respondent, of course, that Congress can enact legislation under § 5 enforcing the constitutional right to the free exercise of religion. The "provisions of this article," to which § 5 refers, include the Due Process Clause of the Fourteenth Amendment. Congress' power to enforce the Free Exercise Clause follows from our holding in *Cantwell v. Connecticut*, 310 U.S. 296, 303 (1940), that the "fundamental concept of liberty embodied in [the Fourteenth Amendment's Due Process Clause] embraces the liberties guaranteed by the First Amendment." Congress' power under § 5, however, extends only to "enforcing" the provisions of the Fourteenth Amendment. The Court has described this power as "remedial," *South Carolina v. Katzenbach*, at 326. The design of the Amendment and the text of § 5 are inconsistent with the suggestion that Congress has the power to decree the substance of the Fourteenth Amendment's restrictions on the States. Legislation which alters the meaning of the Free Exercise Clause cannot be said to be enforcing the Clause. Congress does not enforce a constitutional right by changing what the right is. It has been given the power "to enforce," not the power to determine what constitutes a constitutional violation. Were it not so, what Congress would be enforcing would no longer be, in any meaningful sense, the "provisions of [the Fourteenth Amendment]." . . .

[529] B

. . . [532] Regardless of the state of the legislative record, RFRA cannot be considered remedial, preventive legislation, if those terms are to have any meaning. RFRA is so out of proportion to a supposed remedial or preventive object that it cannot be understood as responsive to, or designed to prevent, unconstitutional behavior. It appears, instead, to attempt a substantive change in constitutional protections. Preventive measures prohibiting certain types of laws may be appropriate when there is reason to believe that many of the laws affected by the congressional enactment have a significant likelihood of being unconstitutional. Remedial legislation under § 5 "should be adapted to the mischief and wrong which the [Fourteenth] Amendment was intended to provide against." *Civil Rights Cases*, 109 U.S. at 13. RFRA is not so confined. Sweeping coverage ensures its intrusion at every level of government, displacing laws and prohibiting official actions of almost every description and regardless of subject matter. RFRA's restrictions apply to every agency and official of the Federal, State, and local Governments. RFRA applies to all federal and state law, statutory or otherwise, whether adopted before or after its enactment. RFRA has no termination date or termination mechanism. Any law is subject to challenge at any time by any individual who alleges a substantial burden on his or her free exercise of religion. The reach and scope of RFRA distinguish it from other measures passed under Congress' enforcement power, even in the area of voting rights. . . .

[534] Simply put, RFRA is not designed to identify and counteract state laws likely to be unconstitutional because of [535] their treatment of religion. In most cases, the state laws to which RFRA applies are not ones which will have been motivated by religious bigotry. If a state law disproportionately burdened a particular class of religious observers, this circumstance might be evidence of an impermissible legislative motive. RFRA's substantial burden test, however, is not even a discriminatory effects or disparate impact test. It is a reality of the modern regulatory state that numerous state laws, such as the zoning regulations at issue here, impose a substantial burden on a large class of individuals. When the exercise of religion has been burdened in an incidental way by a law of general application, it does not follow that the persons affected have been burdened any more than other citizens, let alone burdened because of their religious beliefs. In addition, the Act imposes in every case a least restrictive means requirement—a requirement that was not used in the pre-*Smith* jurisprudence RFRA purported to codify—which also indicates that the legislation is broader than is appropriate if the goal is to prevent and remedy constitutional violations. . . .

[536] JUSTICE STEVENS, concurring.

In my opinion, the Religious Freedom Restoration Act of 1993 (RFRA) is a "law respecting an establishment of religion" that violates the First Amendment to the Constitution.

[537] If the historic landmark on the hill in Boerne happened to be a museum or an art gallery owned by an atheist, it would not be eligible for an exemption from the city ordinances that forbid an enlargement of the structure. Because the landmark is owned by the Catholic Church, it is claimed that RFRA gives its owner a federal statutory entitlement to an exemption from a generally applicable, neutral civil law. Whether the Church would actually prevail under the statute or not, the statute has provided the Church with a legal weapon that no atheist or agnostic can obtain. This governmental preference for religion, as opposed to irreligion, is forbidden by the First Amendment.

JUSTICE SCALIA, with whom JUSTICE STEVENS joins, concurring in part.

I write to respond briefly to the claim of JUSTICE O'CONNOR's dissent (hereinafter "the dissent") that historical materials support a result contrary to the one reached in *Employment Div., Dept. of Human Resources of Ore. v. Smith*. We held in *Smith* that the Constitution's Free Exercise Clause "does not relieve an individual of the obligation to comply with a 'valid and neutral law of general applicability on the ground that the law proscribes (or prescribes) conduct that his religion prescribes (or proscribes).'" 494 U.S. at 879. The material that the dissent claims is at odds with *Smith* either has little to say about the issue or is in fact more consistent with *Smith* than with the dissent's interpretation of the Free Exercise Clause. The dissent's extravagant claim that the historical record shows *Smith* to have been wrong should be compared with the assessment of the most prominent scholarly critic of *Smith*, who, after an extensive review of the historical record, was willing to venture no more than that "constitutionally [538] compelled exemptions [from generally applicable laws regulating conduct] were *within the contemplation* of the framers and ratifiers as a *possible interpretation* of the free exercise clause." McConnell, *The Origins and Historical Understanding of Free Exercise of Religion*, 103 Harv. L. Rev. 1409, 1415 (1990) (emphasis added); see also Hamburger, *A Constitutional Right of Religious Exemption: An Historical Perspective*, 60 Geo. Wash. Law Rev. 915 (1992) (arguing that historical evidence supports *Smith*'s interpretation of free exercise). . . .

[539] Assuming, however, that the affirmative protection of religion accorded by the early "free exercise" enactments sweeps as broadly as the dissent's theory would require, those enactments do not support the dissent's view, since they contain "provisos" that significantly qualify the affirmative protection they grant. According to the dissent, the "provisos" support its view because they would have been "superfluous" if "the Court was correct in *Smith* that generally applicable laws are enforceable regardless of religious conscience." I disagree. In fact, the most plausible reading of the "free exercise" enactments (if their affirmative provisions are read broadly, as the dissent's view requires) is a virtual restatement of *Smith*: Religious exercise shall be permitted so long as it does not violate general laws governing conduct. The "provisos" in the enactments negate a license to act in a manner "unfaithful to the Lord Proprietary" (Maryland Act Concerning Religion of 1649), or "behave" in other than a "peaceable and quiet" manner (Rhode Island Charter of 1663), or "disturb the public peace" (New Hampshire Constitution), or interfere with the "peace [and] safety of the State" (New York, Maryland, and Georgia Constitutions), or "demean" oneself in other than a "peaceable and orderly manner" (Northwest Ordinance of 1787). At the time these provisos were enacted, keeping "peace" and "order" seems to have meant, precisely, obeying the laws. "Every breach of law is against the peace." *Queen v. Lane*, 6 Mod. 128, 87 Eng. Rep. 884, 885 (Q. B. 1704). Even as late as 1828, when Noah Webster published his *American Dictionary of the English Language*, he gave as one of the meanings of "peace": "8. Public [540] tranquility; that quiet, order and security which is guaranteed by the laws; as, to keep the peace; to break the peace." 2 *An American Dictionary of the English Language* 31 (1828). This limitation upon the scope of religious exercise would have been in accord with the background political philosophy of the age (associated most prominently with John Locke), which regarded freedom as the right "to do only what was not lawfully prohibited," West, *The Case against a Right to Religion-Based Exemptions*, 4 Notre Dame J. of Law, Ethics & Public Policy 591, 624 (1990). "Thus, the disturb-the-peace caveats apparently permitted government to deny religious freedom, not merely in the event of violence or force, but, more generally, upon the occurrence of illegal actions." Hamburger, at 918–919. And while, under this interpretation, these early "free exercise" enactments support the Court's judgment in *Smith*, I see no sensible interpretation that could cause them to support what I understand to be the position of JUSTICE O'CONNOR, or any of

Smith's other critics. No one in that camp, to my knowledge, contends that their favored "compelling state interest" test conforms to any possible interpretation of "breach of peace and order"—i.e., that only violence or force, or any other category of action (more limited than "violation of law") which can possibly be conveyed by the phrase "peace and order," justifies state prohibition of religiously motivated conduct.

[541] Apart from the early "free exercise" enactments of Colonies, States, and Territories, the dissent calls attention to those bodies', and the Continental Congress's, legislative accommodation of religious practices prior to ratification of the Bill of Rights. This accommodation—which took place both before and after enactment of the state constitutional protections of religious liberty—suggests (according to the dissent) that "the drafters and ratifiers of the First Amendment . . . assumed courts would apply the Free Exercise Clause similarly." But that legislatures sometimes (though not always) found it "appropriate" to accommodate religious practices does not establish that accommodation was understood to be constitutionally mandated by the Free Exercise Clause. As we explained in *Smith*, "To say that a nondiscriminatory religious-practice exemption is permitted, or even that it is desirable, is not to say that it is constitutionally required." 494 U.S. at 890. "Values that are protected against government interference through enshrinement in the Bill of Rights are not thereby banished from the political process." *Ibid.*

The dissent's final source of claimed historical support consists of statements of certain of the Framers in the context of debates about proposed legislative enactments or debates over general principles (not in connection with the drafting of State or Federal Constitutions). Those statements are subject to the same objection as was the evidence about legislative accommodation: There is no reason to think they were meant to describe what was constitutionally required (and judicially enforceable), as opposed to what was thought to be legislatively or even morally desirable. Thus, for example, the pamphlet written by James Madison opposing Virginia's proposed general assessment for support of religion [542] does not argue that the assessment would violate the "free exercise" provision in the Virginia Declaration of Rights, although that provision had been enacted into law only eight years earlier; rather the pamphlet argues that the assessment wrongly placed civil society ahead of personal religious belief and, thus, should not be approved by the legislators. Likewise, the letter from George Washington to the Quakers by its own terms refers to Washington's "wish and desire" that religion be accommodated, not his belief that existing constitutional provisions required accommodation. These and other examples offered by the dissent reflect the speakers' views of the "proper" relationship between government and religion, but not their views (at least insofar as the content or context of the material suggests) of the constitutionally required relationship. The one exception is the statement by Thomas Jefferson that he considered "the government of the United States as interdicted by the Constitution from intermeddling with religious institutions, their doctrines, discipline, or exercises"; but it is quite clear that Jefferson did not in fact espouse the broad principle of affirmative accommodation advocated by the dissent.

It seems to me that the most telling point made by the dissent is to be found, not in what it says, but in what it fails to say. Had the understanding in the period surrounding the ratification of the Bill of Rights been that the various forms of accommodation discussed by the dissent were constitutionally required (either by State Constitutions or by the Federal Constitution), it would be surprising not to find a single state or federal case refusing to enforce a generally applicable statute because of its failure to make accommodation. Yet the dissent cites none—and to my knowledge, and to the knowledge of the academic defenders of the dissent's position, [543] none exists. The closest one can come in the period prior to 1850 is the decision of a New York City municipal court in 1813, holding that the New York Constitution of 1777 required acknowledgement of a priest-penitent privilege, to protect a Catholic priest from being compelled to testify as to the contents of a confession. *People v. Philips*, Court of General Sessions, City of New York (June 14, 1813). Even this lone case is weak authority, not only because it comes from a minor court, but also because it did not involve a statute, and the same result might possibly have been achieved (without invoking constitutional entitlement) by the court's simply modifying the common-law rules of evidence to recognize such a privilege. On the other side of the ledger, moreover, there are two cases, from the Supreme Court of Pennsylvania, flatly rejecting the dissent's view. In *Simon's Executors v. Gratz*, 2 Pen. & W. 412 (Pa. 1831), the court held that a litigant was not entitled to a continuance of trial on the ground that appearing on his Sabbath would violate his religious principles. And in *Stansbury v. Marks*, 2 U.S. 213 (Pa. 1793), decided just two years after the ratification of the Bill of Rights, the court imposed a fine on a witness who "refused to be sworn, because it was his Sabbath."

I have limited this response to the new items of "historical evidence" brought forward by today's dissent. (The dissent's [544] claim that "before *Smith*, our free exercise cases were generally in keeping" with the dissent's view is adequately answered in *Smith* itself.) The historical evidence marshalled by the dissent cannot fairly be said to demonstrate the correctness of *Smith*; but it is more supportive of that conclusion than destructive of it. And, to return to a point I made earlier, that evidence is not compatible with any theory I am familiar with that has been proposed as an alternative to *Smith*. The dissent's approach has, of course, great popular attraction. Who can possibly be against the abstract proposition that government should not, even in its general, nondiscriminatory laws, place unreasonable burdens upon religious practice? Unfortunately, however, that abstract proposition must ultimately be reduced to concrete cases. The issue presented by *Smith* is, quite simply, whether the people, through their elected representatives, or rather this Court, shall control the outcome of those concrete cases. For example, shall it be the determination of this Court, or rather of the people, whether (as the dissent apparently believes) church construction will be exempt from zoning laws? The historical evidence put forward by the dissent does nothing to undermine the conclusion we reached in *Smith*: It shall be the people.

JUSTICE O'CONNOR, with whom JUSTICE BREYER joins except as to a portion of Part I, dissenting.

I dissent from the Court's disposition of this case. I agree with the Court that the issue before us is whether the Religious Freedom Restoration Act (RFRA) is a proper exercise of Congress' power to enforce § 5 of the Fourteenth Amendment. But as a yardstick for measuring the constitutionality of RFRA, the Court uses its holding in *Employment Div., Dept. of Human Resources of Ore. v. Smith*, the decision that prompted Congress to enact RFRA as a means of more rigorously enforcing the Free Exercise Clause. I remain of the view that *Smith* was [545] wrongly decided, and I would use this case to reexamine the Court's holding there. Therefore, I would direct the parties to brief the question whether *Smith* represents the correct understanding of the Free Exercise Clause and set the case for reargument. If the Court were to correct the misinterpretation of the Free Exercise Clause set forth in *Smith*, it would simultaneously put our First Amendment jurisprudence back on course and allay the legitimate concerns of a majority in Congress who believed that *Smith* improperly restricted religious liberty. We would then be in a position to review RFRA in light of a proper interpretation of the Free Exercise Clause.

I

. . . [546] The Court's analysis of whether RFRA is a constitutional exercise of Congress' § 5 power, set forth in Part III-B of its opinion, is premised on the assumption that *Smith* correctly interprets the Free Exercise Clause. This is an assumption that I do not accept. I continue to believe that *Smith* adopted an improper standard for deciding free exercise claims. In *Smith*, five Members of this Court—without briefing or argument on the issue—interpreted the Free Exercise Clause to permit the government to prohibit, without justification, conduct mandated by an individual's religious beliefs, so long as the prohibition is generally applicable. Contrary to the Court's holding in that case, however, the Free Exercise Clause is not simply an antidiscrimination principle that protects only against those laws that single out religious practice for unfavorable treatment. Rather, the Clause is best understood as an affirmative guarantee of the right to participate in religious practices and conduct without impermissible governmental interference, even when such conduct conflicts with a neutral, generally applicable law. Before *Smith*, our free exercise cases were generally in keeping with this idea: where a law substantially burdened religiously motivated conduct—regardless whether it was specifically targeted at religion or applied generally—we required government to justify that law with a compelling state interest and to use means narrowly tailored to achieve that interest. . . .

[548] Accordingly, I believe that we should reexamine our holding in *Smith*, and do so in this very case. In its place, I would return to a rule that requires government to justify any substantial burden on religiously motivated conduct by a compelling state interest and to impose that burden only by means narrowly tailored to achieve that interest.

II

I shall not restate what has been said in other opinions, which have demonstrated that *Smith* is gravely at odds with our earlier free exercise precedents. Rather, I examine here the early American tradition of religious free exercise to gain insight into the original understanding of the Free Exercise Clause—an inquiry the Court in *Smith* did not undertake. We have previously recognized the importance of interpreting the Religion Clauses in light of their history.

[549] The historical evidence casts doubt on the Court's current interpretation of the Free Exercise Clause. The record instead reveals that its drafters and ratifiers more likely viewed the Free Exercise Clause as a guarantee that government may not unnecessarily hinder believers from freely practicing their religion, a position consistent with our pre-*Smith* jurisprudence.

A

. . . [550] Neither the First Congress nor the ratifying state legislatures debated the question of religious freedom in much detail, nor did they directly consider the scope of the First Amendment's free exercise protection. It would be disingenuous to say that the Framers neglected to define precisely the scope of the Free Exercise Clause because the words "free exercise" had a precise meaning. As is the case for a number of the terms used in the Bill of Rights, it is not exactly clear what the Framers thought the phrase signified. But a variety of sources supplement the legislative history and shed light on the original understanding of the Free Exercise Clause. These materials suggest that—contrary to *Smith*—the Framers did not intend simply to prevent the Government from adopting laws that discriminated against religion. Although the Framers may not have asked precisely the questions about religious liberty that we do today, the historical record indicates that they believed that the Constitution affirmatively protects religious free exercise and that it limits the government's ability to intrude on religious practice.

B

The principle of religious "free exercise" and the notion that religious liberty deserved legal protection were by no [551] means new concepts in 1791, when the Bill of Rights was ratified. To the contrary, these principles were first articulated in this country in the colonies of Maryland, Rhode Island, Pennsylvania, Delaware, and Carolina, in the mid-1600s. These colonies, though established as sanctuaries for particular groups of religious dissenters, extended freedom of religion to groups—although often limited to Christian groups—beyond their own. Thus, they encountered early on the conflicts that may arise in a society made up of a plurality of faiths. . . .

[552] C

The principles expounded in these early charters re-emerged over a century later in state constitutions that were adopted in the flurry of constitution-drafting that followed the American Revolution. By 1789, every State but Connecticut had incorporated some version of a free exercise [553] clause into its constitution. These state provisions, which were typically longer and more detailed than the federal Free Exercise Clause, are perhaps the best evidence of the original understanding of the Constitution's protection of religious liberty. After all, it is reasonable to think that the States that ratified the First Amendment assumed that the meaning of the federal free exercise provision corresponded to that of their existing state clauses. The precise language of these state precursors to the Free Exercise Clause varied, but most guaranteed free exercise of religion or liberty of conscience, limited by particular, defined state interests. For example, the New York Constitution of 1777 provided:

> "The free exercise and enjoyment of religious profession and worship, without discrimination or preference, shall forever hereafter be allowed, within this State, to all mankind: Provided, That the liberty of conscience, hereby granted, *shall not be so construed as to excuse acts of licentiousness, or justify practices inconsistent with the peace or safety of this State.*" N. Y. Const., Art. XXXVIII (1777) (emphasis added).

Similarly, the New Hampshire Constitution of 1784 declared:

> "Every individual has a natural and unalienable right to worship GOD according to the dictates of his own conscience, and reason; and no subject shall be hurt, molested, or restrained in his person, liberty or estate for worshipping GOD, in the manner and season most agreeable to the dictates of his own conscience, . . . *provided he doth not disturb the public peace, or disturb others, in their religious worship.*" N. H. Const., Art. I, § 5 (1784) (emphasis added).

The Maryland Declaration of Rights of 1776 read:

"No person ought by any law to be molested in his person or estate on account of his religious persuasion [554] or profession, or for his religious practice; unless, under colour of religion, *any man shall disturb the good order, peace or safety of the State, or shall infringe the laws of morality, or injure others*, in their natural, civil, or religious rights." Md. Const., Declaration of Rights, Art. XXXIII (emphasis added).

The religious liberty clause of the Georgia Constitution of 1777 stated:

"All persons whatever shall have the free exercise of their religion; provided *it be not repugnant to the peace and safety of the State*." Ga. Const., Art. LVI (1777 (emphasis added).

In addition to these state provisions, the Northwest Ordinance of 1787—which was enacted contemporaneously with the drafting of the Constitution and re-enacted by the First Congress—established a bill of rights for a territory that included what is now Ohio, Indiana, Michigan, Wisconsin, and part of Minnesota. Article I of the Ordinance declared:

"No person, *demeaning himself in a peaceable and orderly manner*, shall ever be molested on account of his mode of worship or religious sentiments, in the said territory." Northwest Territory Ordinance of 1787, Art. I, 1 Stat. 52 (emphasis added).

The language used in these state constitutional provisions and the Northwest Ordinance strongly suggests that, around the time of the drafting of the Bill of Rights, it was generally accepted that the right to "free exercise" required, where possible, accommodation of religious practice. If not—and if the Court was correct in *Smith* that generally applicable laws are enforceable regardless of religious conscience—there would have been no need for these documents to specify, as the New York Constitution did, that rights of conscience should not be "construed as to excuse acts of licentiousness, or justify practices inconsistent with the peace or safety of [the] State." Such a proviso would have been superfluous. [555] Instead, these documents make sense only if the right to free exercise was viewed as generally superior to ordinary legislation, to be overridden only when necessary to secure important government purposes.

The Virginia Legislature may have debated the issue most fully. In May 1776, the Virginia Constitutional Convention wrote a constitution containing a Declaration of Rights with a clause on religious liberty. The initial drafter of the clause, George Mason, proposed the following:

"That religion, or the duty which we owe to our CREATOR, and the manner of discharging it, can be (directed) only by reason and conviction, not by force or violence; and therefore, *that all men should enjoy the fullest toleration in the exercise of religion*, according to the dictates of conscience, unpunished and unrestrained by the magistrate, *unless, under colour of religion, any man disturb the peace, the happiness, or safety of society*. And that it is the mutual duty of all to practice Christian forbearance, love, and charity towards each other." (Emphasis added.)

Mason's proposal did not go far enough for a 26-year-old James Madison, who had recently completed his studies at the Presbyterian College of Princeton. He objected first to Mason's use of the term "toleration," contending that the word implied that the right to practice one's religion was a governmental favor, rather than an inalienable liberty.

Second, Madison thought Mason's proposal countenanced too much state interference in religious matters, since the "exercise of religion" would have yielded whenever it was deemed inimical to "the peace, happiness, or safety of society." Madison suggested the provision read instead:

> "That religion, or the duty we owe our Creator, and the manner of discharging it, being under the direction [556] of reason and conviction only, not of violence or compulsion, *all men are equally entitled to the full and free exercise of it, according to the dictates of conscience;* and therefore that no man or class of men ought on account of religion to be invested with peculiar emoluments or privileges, nor subjected to any penalties or disabilities, *unless under color of religion the preservation of equal liberty, and the existence of the State be manifestly endangered.*" (Emphasis added.)

Thus, Madison wished to shift Mason's language of "toleration" to the language of rights. Additionally, under Madison's proposal, the State could interfere in a believer's religious exercise only if the State would otherwise "be manifestly endangered." In the end, neither Mason's nor Madison's language regarding the extent to which state interests could limit religious exercise made it into the Virginia Constitution's religious liberty clause. Like the federal Free Exercise Clause, the Virginia religious liberty clause was simply silent on the subject, providing only that "all men are equally entitled to the free exercise of religion, according to the dictates of conscience." Virginia Declaration of Rights, Art. XVI (1776). For our purposes, however, it is telling that both Mason's and Madison's formulations envisioned that, when there was a conflict, a person's interest in freely practicing his religion was to be balanced against state interests. Although Madison endorsed a more limited state interest exception than did Mason, the debate would have been irrelevant if either had thought the right to free exercise did not [557] include a right to be exempt from certain generally applicable laws. Presumably, the Virginia Legislature intended the scope of its free exercise provision to strike some middle ground between Mason's narrower and Madison's broader notions of the right to religious freedom.

D

The practice of the colonies and early States bears out the conclusion that, at the time the Bill of Rights was ratified, it was accepted that government should, when possible, accommodate religious practice. Unsurprisingly, of course, even in the American colonies inhabited by people of religious persuasions, religious conscience and civil law rarely conflicted. Most 17th and 18th century Americans belonged to denominations of Protestant Christianity whose religious practices were generally harmonious with colonial law. Moreover, governments then were far smaller and less intrusive than they are today, which made conflict between civil law and religion unusual.

Nevertheless, tension between religious conscience and generally applicable laws, though rare, was not unknown in pre-Constitutional America. Most commonly, such conflicts arose from oath requirements, military conscription, and religious assessments. The ways in which these conflicts were resolved suggest that Americans in the colonies and early States thought that, if an individual's religious scruples prevented him from complying with a generally applicable law, the government should, if possible, excuse the person from the law's coverage. For example, Quakers and certain other Protestant sects refused on Biblical grounds to subscribe to oaths or "swear" allegiance to civil authority. [558] Without accommodation, their beliefs would have prevented them from participating in civic activities involving oaths, including testifying in court. Colonial governments created alternatives to the oath requirement for these individuals. In early decisions, for example, the Carolina proprietors applied the religious liberty provision of the Carolina Charter of 1665 to permit Quakers to enter pledges in a book. Similarly, in 1691, New York enacted a law allowing Quakers to testify by affirmation, and in 1734, it permitted Quakers to qualify to vote by affirmation. *Id.*, at 64. By 1789, virtually all of the States had enacted oath exemptions.

Early conflicts between religious beliefs and generally applicable laws also occurred because of military conscription requirements. Quakers and Mennonites, as well as a few smaller denominations, refused on religious grounds to carry arms. Members of these denominations asserted that liberty of conscience should exempt them from military conscription. Obviously, excusing such objectors from military service had a high public cost, given the importance of the military to the defense of society. Nevertheless, Rhode Island, North Carolina, and Maryland exempted Quakers from military service in the late 1600s. New York, Massachusetts, Virginia, and New Hampshire followed suit in the mid-1700s. The Continental Congress likewise granted exemption from conscription:

> "As there are some people, who, from religious principles, cannot bear arms in any case, this Congress intend no violence to their consciences, but earnestly recommend it to them, to contribute liberally in this time of universal calamity, to the relief of their distressed brethren in the several colonies, and to do all other services to their oppressed Country, which they can consistently [559] with their religious principles." Resolution of July 18, 1775.

Again, this practice of excusing religious pacifists from military service demonstrates that, long before the First Amendment was ratified, legislative accommodations were a common response to conflicts between religious practice and civil obligation. Notably, the Continental Congress exempted objectors from conscription to avoid "violence to their consciences," explicitly recognizing that civil laws must sometimes give way to freedom of conscience.

States and colonies with established churches encountered a further religious accommodation problem. Typically, these governments required citizens to pay tithes to support either the government-established church or the church to which the tithepayer belonged. But Baptists and Quakers, as well as others, opposed all government-compelled tithes on religious grounds. Massachusetts, Connecticut, New Hampshire, and Virginia responded by exempting such objectors from religious assessments. There are additional examples of early conflicts between civil laws and religious practice that were similarly settled through accommodation of religious exercise. Both North Carolina and Maryland excused Quakers from the requirement of removing their hats in court; Rhode Island exempted Jews from the requirements of the state marriage laws; and Georgia allowed groups of European immigrants to organize whole towns according to their own faith.

To be sure, legislatures, not courts, granted these early accommodations. But these were the days before there was a Constitution to protect civil liberties—judicial review did not yet exist. These legislatures apparently believed that the appropriate response to conflicts between civil law and religious scruples was, where possible, accommodation of religious [560] conduct. It is reasonable to presume that the drafters and ratifiers of the First Amendment—many of whom served in state legislatures—assumed courts would apply the Free Exercise Clause similarly, so that religious liberty was safeguarded.

E

The writings of the early leaders who helped to shape our Nation provide a final source of insight into the original understanding of the Free Exercise Clause. The thoughts of James Madison—one of the principal architects of the Bill of Rights—as revealed by the controversy surrounding Virginia's General Assessment Bill of 1784, are particularly illuminating. Virginia's debate over religious issues did not end with its adoption of a constitutional free exercise provision. Although Virginia had disestablished the Church of England in 1776, it left open the question whether religion might be supported on a nonpreferential basis by a so-called "general assessment." In the years between 1776 and 1784, the issue how to support religion in Virginia—either by general assessment or voluntarily—was widely debated.

By 1784, supporters of a general assessment, led by Patrick Henry, had gained a slight majority in the Virginia Assembly. They introduced "A Bill Establishing a Provision for the Teachers of the Christian Religion," which proposed that citizens be taxed in order to support the Christian denomination of their choice, with those taxes not designated for any specific denomination to go to a public fund to aid seminaries. Madison viewed religious assessment as a dangerous infringement of religious liberty and led the opposition to the bill. He took the case against religious assessment to the people of Virginia in his now-famous "Memorial [561] and Remonstrance against Religious Assessments." This pamphlet led thousands of Virginians to oppose the bill and to submit petitions expressing their views to the legislature. The bill eventually died in committee, and Virginia instead enacted a Bill for Establishing Religious Freedom, which Thomas Jefferson had drafted in 1779.

The "Memorial and Remonstrance" begins with the recognition that "the Religion . . . of every man must be left to the conviction and conscience of every man; and it is the right of every man to exercise it as these may dictate." By its very nature, Madison wrote, the right to free exercise is "unalienable," both because a person's opinion "cannot follow the dictates of others," and because it entails "a duty toward the Creator." Madison continued:

> "This duty [owed the Creator] is precedent both in order of time and degree of obligation, to the claims of Civil Society. . . . Every man who becomes a member of any Civil Society, [must] do it with a saving of his allegiance to the Universal Sovereign. We maintain therefore that in matters of Religion, no man's right is abridged by the institution of Civil Society, and that Religion is wholly exempt from its cognizance."

To Madison, then, duties to God were superior to duties to civil authorities—the ultimate loyalty was owed to God above all. Madison did not say that duties to the Creator are precedent only to those laws specifically directed at religion, nor did he strive simply to prevent deliberate acts of persecution or discrimination. The idea that civil obligations are subordinate to religious duty is consonant with the notion that government must accommodate, where possible, those religious practices that conflict with civil law.

[562] Other early leaders expressed similar views regarding religious liberty. Thomas Jefferson, the drafter of Virginia's Bill for Establishing Religious Freedom, wrote in that document that civil government could interfere in religious exercise only "when principles break out into overt acts against peace and good order." In 1808, he indicated that he considered "the government of the United States as interdicted by the Constitution from intermeddling with religious institutions, their doctrines, discipline, or exercises." 11 *The Writings of Thomas Jefferson* 428–429 (A. Lipscomb ed. 1904). Moreover, Jeffer-

son believed that "every religious society has a right to determine for itself the time of these exercises, and the objects proper for them, according to their own particular tenets; and this right can never be safer than in their own hands, where the Constitution has deposited it." *Ibid.*

George Washington expressly stated that he believed that government should do its utmost to accommodate religious scruples, writing in a letter to a group of Quakers:

> "In my opinion the conscientious scruples of all men should be treated with great delicacy and tenderness; and it is my wish and desire, that the laws may always be as extensively accommodated to them, as a due regard to the protection and essential interests of the nation may justify and permit." Letter from George Washington to the Religious Society Called Quakers (Oct. 1789).

Oliver Ellsworth, a Framer of the First Amendment and later Chief Justice of the United States, expressed the similar view that government could interfere in religious matters only when necessary "to prohibit and punish gross immoralities [563] and impieties; because the open practice of these is of evil example and detriment." Oliver Ellsworth, *Landholder*, No. 7 (Dec. 17, 1787). Isaac Backus, a Baptist minister who was a delegate to the Massachusetts ratifying convention of 1788, declared that "every person has an unalienable right to act in all religious affairs according to the full persuasion of his own mind, where others are not injured thereby." Backus, *A Declaration of Rights, of the Inhabitants of the State of Massachusetts-Bay.*

These are but a few examples of various perspectives regarding the proper relationship between church and government that existed during the time the First Amendment was drafted and ratified. Obviously, since these thinkers approached the issue of religious freedom somewhat differently it is not possible to distill their thoughts into one tidy formula. Nevertheless, a few general principles may be discerned. Foremost, these early leaders accorded religious exercise a special constitutional status. The right to free exercise was a substantive guarantee of individual liberty, no less important than the right to free speech or the right to just compensation for the taking of property. As Madison put it in the concluding argument of his "Memorial and Remonstrance":

> "'The equal right of every citizen to the free exercise of his Religion according to the dictates of [his] conscience' is held by the same tenure with all our other rights. . . . It is equally the gift of nature; . . . it cannot be less dear to us; . . . it is enumerated with equal solemnity, [564] or rather studied emphasis."

Second, all agreed that government interference in religious practice was not to be lightly countenanced. Finally, all shared the conviction that "true religion and good morals are the only solid foundation of public liberty and happiness." Curry, *The First Freedoms*, at 219 (quoting Continental Congress). To give meaning to these ideas—particularly in a society characterized by religious pluralism and pervasive regulation—there will be times when the Constitution requires government to accommodate the needs of those citizens whose religious practices conflict with generally applicable law.

III

The Religion Clauses of the Constitution represent a profound commitment to religious liberty. Our Nation's Founders conceived of a Republic receptive to voluntary religious expression, not of a secular society in which religious expression is tolerated only when it does not conflict with a generally applicable law. As the historical sources discussed above show, the Free Exercise Clause is properly understood as an affirmative guarantee of the right to participate in religious activities without impermissible governmental interference, even where a believer's conduct is in tension with a law of general application. Certainly, it is in no way anomalous to accord heightened protection to a right identified in the text of the First Amendment. For example, it has long been the Court's position that freedom of speech—a right enumerated only a few words after the right to free exercise—has special constitutional status. Given the centrality of freedom of speech and religion to the American concept of personal liberty, it is altogether reasonable to conclude [565] that both should be treated with the highest degree of respect.

Although it may provide a bright line, the rule the Court declared in *Smith* does not faithfully serve the purpose of the Constitution. Accordingly, I believe that it is essential for the Court to reconsider its holding in *Smith*—and to do so in this very case. I would therefore direct the parties to brief this issue and set the case for reargument.

I respectfully dissent from the Court's disposition of this case.

54

Santa Fe Independent School District v. Doe

530 U.S. 290 (2000)

Vote: 6—*Stevens, O'Connor, Kennedy, Souter, Ginsburg, Breyer*
       3—*Rehnquist, Scalia, Thomas*

Opinion announcing the opinion of the Court: Stevens
Dissenting opinion: Rehnquist

This case resulted from a challenge to a Texas school district's policy authorizing student-led prayer prior to high school football games.

Prior to 1995, a student elected as Santa Fe High School's student council chaplain delivered a prayer over the public address system before each home varsity football game. In April 1995, Mormon and Catholic students or alumni and their mothers challenged the practice in federal court. The district court entered an interim order providing, among other matters, that students could present a nondenominational prayer.

In August 1995, in response to that order, the school district adopted a policy titled "Prayer at Football Games." The policy authorized two student votes. An initial vote determined whether "invocations" were to be delivered at home football games. If such invocations were affirmatively supported, a second vote was to be held to elect a student spokesperson to deliver them. Pursuant to the August policy, Santa Fe High School's student body voted to allow invocations and elected a spokesperson.

In October 1995, the school district adopted a revised "Pre-Game Ceremonies at Football Games" policy, which was essentially the same as the August policy, except that the title omitted the word "prayer." The October policy (1) authorized the student spokesperson to deliver an "invocation and/or message" during pregame ceremonies; (2) mandated that the spokesperson's "statement or invocation" be consistent with the policy's stated goals and purposes, which were to (a) solemnize the event, (b) promote good sportsmanship and student safety, and (c) establish the appropriate environment for the competition; (3) did not require, as an initial matter, that the content of the invocations be nonsectarian and nonproselytizing; (4) provided that such a limitation would be automatically added—by means of a fallback provision—only if the policy were to be enjoined by a court; and (5) incorporated the two-step student election system set forth in the August policy. The school did not conduct new elections to replace the results of the August votes. The district court subsequently ordered the school district to implement the fallback provision that required the invocations to be nonsectarian and nonproselytizing.

STEVENS, J., delivered the opinion of the Court, in which O'CONNOR, KENNEDY, SOUTER, GINSBURG, and BREYER, JJ., joined.

. . . [301] The first Clause in the First Amendment to the Federal Constitution provides that "Congress shall make no law respecting an establishment of religion, or prohibiting the free exercise thereof." The Fourteenth Amendment imposes those substantive limitations on the legislative power of the States and their political subdivisions. In *Lee v. Weisman* we held that a prayer delivered by a rabbi at a middle school graduation ceremony violated that Clause. Although this case involves student prayer at a different [302] type of school function, our analysis is properly guided by the principles that we endorsed in *Lee.*

As we held in that case:

> "The principle that government may accommodate the free exercise of religion does not supersede the fundamental limitations imposed by the Establishment Clause. It is beyond dispute that, at a minimum, the Constitution guarantees that government may not coerce anyone to support or participate in religion or its exercise, or otherwise act in a way which 'establishes a [state] religion or religious faith, or tends to do so.'" *Id.* at 587.

In this case the District first argues that this principle is inapplicable to its October policy because the messages are private student speech, not public speech. It reminds us that "there is a crucial difference between *government* speech endorsing religion, which the Establishment Clause forbids, and *private* speech endorsing religion, which the Free Speech and Free Exercise Clauses protect." *Board of Ed. of Westside Community Schools (Dist. 66) v. Mergens,* 496 U.S. 226, 250 (1990) (opinion of O'CONNOR, J.). We certainly agree with that distinction, but we are not persuaded that the pregame invocations should be regarded as "private speech."

These invocations are authorized by a government policy and take place on government property at government-sponsored school-related events. Of course, not every message delivered under such circumstances is the government's own. We have held, for example, that an individual's contribution to a government-created forum was not government speech. Although the District relies heavily on *Rosenberger* and similar cases involving such [303] forums, it is clear that the pregame ceremony is not the type of forum discussed in those cases. The Santa Fe school officials simply do not "evince either 'by policy or by practice,' any intent to open the [pregame ceremony] to 'indiscriminate use,' . . . by the student body generally." *Hazelwood School Dist. v. Kuhlmeier,* 484 U.S. 260, 270 (1988). Rather, the school allows only one student, the same student for the entire season, to give the invocation. The statement or invocation, moreover, is subject to particular regulations that confine the content and topic of the student's message. . . .

[304] Granting only one student access to the stage at a time does not, of course, necessarily preclude a finding that a school has created a limited public forum. Here, however, Santa Fe's student election system ensures that only those messages deemed "appropriate" under the District's policy may be delivered. That is, the majoritarian process implemented by the District guarantees, by definition, that minority candidates will never prevail and that their views will be effectively silenced. . . .

[305] Moreover, the District has failed to divorce itself from the religious content in the invocations. It has not succeeded in doing so, either by claiming that its policy is "one of neutrality rather than endorsement" or by characterizing the individual student as the "circuit-breaker" in the process. Contrary to the District's repeated assertions

that it has adopted a "hands-off" approach to the pregame invocation, the realities of the situation plainly reveal that its policy involves both perceived and actual endorsement of religion. In this case, as we found in *Lee*, the "degree of school involvement" makes it clear that the pregame prayers bear "the imprint of the State and thus put school-age children who objected in an untenable position." 505 U.S. at 590.

The District has attempted to disentangle itself from the religious messages by developing the two-step student [306] election process. The text of the October policy, however, exposes the extent of the school's entanglement. The elections take place at all only because the school "board has chosen to permit students to deliver a brief invocation and/or message." The elections thus "shall" be conducted "by the high school student council" and "upon advice and direction of the high school principal." The decision whether to deliver a message is first made by majority vote of the entire student body, followed by a choice of the speaker in a separate, similar majority election. Even though the particular words used by the speaker are not determined by those votes, the policy mandates that the "statement or invocation" be "consistent with the goals and purposes of this policy," which are "to solemnize the event, to promote good sportsmanship and student safety, and to establish the appropriate environment for the competition."

In addition to involving the school in the selection of the speaker, the policy, by its terms, invites and encourages religious messages. The policy itself states that the purpose of the message is "to solemnize the event." A religious message is the most obvious method of solemnizing an event. Moreover, the requirements that the message "promote good citizenship" and "establish the appropriate environment for competition" further narrow the types of message deemed appropriate, suggesting that a solemn, yet nonreligious, message, such as commentary on United States foreign policy, would be prohibited. Indeed, the only type of message that is expressly endorsed in the text is an "invocation"—a term that primarily describes an appeal for divine [307] assistance. In fact, as used in the past at Santa Fe High School, an "invocation" has always entailed a focused religious message. Thus, the expressed purposes of the policy encourage the selection of a religious message, and that is precisely how the students understand the policy. The results of the elections described in the parties' stipulation make it clear that the students understood that the central question before them was whether prayer should be a part of the pregame ceremony. We recognize the important role that public worship plays in many communities, as well as the sincere desire to include public prayer as a part of various occasions so as to mark those occasions' significance. But such religious activity in public schools, as elsewhere, must comport with the First Amendment.

The actual or perceived endorsement of the message, moreover, is established by factors beyond just the text of the policy. Once the student speaker is selected and the message composed, the invocation is then delivered to a large audience assembled as part of a regularly scheduled, school-sponsored function conducted on school property. The message is broadcast over the school's public address system, which remains subject to the control of school officials. It is fair to assume that the pregame ceremony is [308] clothed in the traditional indicia of school sporting events, which generally include not just the team, but also cheerleaders and band members dressed in uniforms sporting the school name and mascot. The school's name is likely written in large print across the field and on banners and flags. The crowd will certainly include many who display the school colors and insignia on their school T-shirts, jackets, or hats and who may also be waving signs displaying the school name. It is in a setting such as this that "the board has chosen to permit" the elected student to rise and give the "statement or invocation."

In this context the members of the listening audience must perceive the pregame message as a public expression of the views of the majority of the student body delivered with the approval of the school administration. In cases involving state participation in a religious activity, one of the relevant questions is "whether an objective observer, acquainted with the text, legislative history, and implementation of the statute, would perceive it as a state endorsement of prayer in public schools." *Wallace*, 472 U.S. at 73, 76 (O'CONNOR, J., concurring in judgment). Regardless of the listener's support for, or objection to, the message, an objective Santa Fe High School student will unquestionably perceive the inevitable pregame prayer as stamped with her school's seal of approval. . . .

[309] Most striking to us is the evolution of the current policy from the long-sanctioned office of "Student Chaplain" to the candidly titled "Prayer at Football Games" regulation. This history indicates that the District intended to preserve the practice of prayer before football games. The conclusion that the District viewed the October policy simply as a continuation of the previous policies is dramatically illustrated by the fact that the school did not conduct a new election, pursuant to the current policy, to replace the results of the previous election, which occurred under the former policy. Given these observations, and in light of the school's history of regular delivery of a student-led prayer at athletic events, it is reasonable to infer that the specific purpose of the policy was to preserve a popular "state-sponsored religious practice." *Lee*, 505 U.S. at 596.

School sponsorship of a religious message is impermissible because it sends the ancillary message to members of the audience who are nonadherents "that they are outsiders, not full members of the political community, and an accompanying [310] message to adherants that they are insiders, favored members of the political community." *Lynch v. Donnelly*, 465 U.S. at 688 (1984) (O'CONNOR, J., concurring). The delivery of such a message—over the school's public address system, by a speaker representing the student body, under the supervision of school faculty, and pursuant to a school policy that explicitly and implicitly encourages public prayer—is not properly characterized as "private" speech. . . .

[313] The Religion Clauses of the First Amendment prevent the government from making any law respecting the establishment of religion or prohibiting the free exercise thereof. By no means do these commands impose a prohibition on all religious activity in our public schools. Indeed, the common purpose of the Religion Clauses "is to secure religious liberty." *Engel v. Vitale*, 370 U.S. 421, 430 (1962). Thus, nothing in the Constitution as interpreted by this Court prohibits any public school student from voluntarily praying at any time before, during, or after the schoolday. But the religious liberty protected by the Constitution is abridged when the State affirmatively sponsors the particular religious practice of prayer. . . .

[318] CHIEF JUSTICE REHNQUIST, with whom JUSTICE SCALIA and JUSTICE THOMAS join, dissenting.

The Court distorts existing precedent to conclude that the school district's student-message program is invalid on its face under the Establishment Clause. But even more disturbing than its holding is the tone of the Court's opinion; it bristles with hostility to all things religious in public life. Neither the holding nor the tone of the opinion is faithful to the meaning of the Establishment Clause, when it is recalled that George Washington himself, at the request of the very Congress which passed the Bill of Rights, proclaimed a day of "public thanksgiving and prayer, to be observed by acknowledging with grateful hearts the many and signal favors of Almighty God."

We do not learn until late in the Court's opinion that respondents in this case challenged the district's student-message program at football games before it had been put into practice. As the Court explained in *United States v. Salerno*, 481 U.S. 739, 745 (1987), the fact that a policy might "operate unconstitutionally under some conceivable set of circumstances is insufficient to render it wholly invalid." While there is an exception to this principle in the First Amendment overbreadth context because of our concern that people may refrain from speech out of fear of prosecution, there is no similar justification for Establishment Clause cases. No speech will be "chilled" by the existence of a government policy that might unconstitutionally endorse religion over nonreligion. Therefore, the question is not whether the district's policy may be applied in violation of the Establishment Clause, but whether it inevitably will be. . . .

[323] The Court bases its conclusion that the true purpose of the policy is to endorse student prayer on its view of the school district's history of Establishment Clause violations and the context in which the policy was written, that is, as "the latest step in developing litigation brought as a challenge to institutional practices that unquestionably violated the Establishment Clause." But the context—attempted compliance with a District Court order—actually demonstrates that the school district was acting diligently to come within the governing constitutional law. The District Court ordered the school district to formulate a policy consistent with Fifth Circuit precedent, which permitted a school district to have a prayer-only policy. But the school district went further than required by the District Court order and eventually settled on a policy that gave the student speaker a choice to deliver either an [324] invocation or a message. In so doing, the school district exhibited a willingness to comply with, and exceed, Establishment Clause restrictions. Thus, the policy cannot be viewed as having a sectarian purpose.

The Court also relies on our decision in *Lee v. Weisman* (1992) to support its conclusion. In *Lee*, we concluded that the content of the speech at issue, a graduation prayer given by a rabbi, was "directed and controlled" by a school official. *Id.* at 588. In other words, at issue in *Lee* was government speech. Here, by contrast, the potential speech at issue, if the policy had been allowed to proceed, would be a message or invocation selected or created by a student. That is, if there were speech at issue here, it would be private speech. The "crucial difference between *government* speech endorsing religion, which the Establishment Clause forbids, and *private* speech endorsing religion, which the Free Speech and Free Exercise Clauses protect," applies with particular force to the question of endorsement. *Board of Ed. of Westside Community Schools (Dist. 66) v. Mergens*, 496 U.S. 226, 250 (1990) (emphasis in original).

Had the policy been put into practice, the students may have chosen a speaker according to wholly secular criteria—like good public speaking skills or social popularity—and the student speaker may have chosen, on her own accord, to deliver a religious message. Such an application of the policy [325] would likely pass constitutional muster. . . .

55

Mitchell v. Helms

530 U.S. 793 (2000)

Vote: 6—Rehnquist, O'Connor, Scalia, Kennedy, Thomas, Breyer
*   3—Stevens, Souter, Ginsburg*

Opinion announcing the judgment of the Court: Thomas
Opinion concurring in the judgment: O'Connor
Dissenting opinion: Souter

Under Chapter 2 of the Education Consolidation and Improvement Act of 1981 (20 USCS 7301–7373), the federal government distributed funds to state and local governmental agencies, which in turn loaned educational materials and equipment, such as library books and computer software and hardware, to elementary and secondary schools. Chapter 2 provided that (1) Chapter 2 assistance had to be offered to both public and private schools; (2) Chapter 2 funds could only supplement—and could not supplant—funds from nonfederal sources; (3) the "services, materials, and equipment" provided to private schools had to be "secular, neutral, and nonideological"; and (4) private schools could not acquire control of Chapter 2 funds or title to Chapter 2 materials, equipment, or property. Participating private schools received Chapter 2 aid based on the number of students enrolled in each school. Private schools received materials and equipment by submitting to local educational agencies an application detailing the items the school sought and how it planned to use them. If the local educational agencies approved the application, it purchased the items from the school's allocation of funds and then loaned them to that school.

In 1985, taxpayers brought a federal suit alleging that federal educational aid as applied in Jefferson Parish, a local governmental unit in Louisiana, violated the Establishment Clause of the U.S. Constitution's First Amendment.

Private schools in Jefferson Parish used their allocations primarily for nonrecurring expenses, usually materials and equipment. During the 1986–1987 fiscal year, local education agencies spent 44 percent of the money budgeted for private schools in Jefferson Parish on library and media materials and 48 percent on instructional equipment. The materials and equipment provided included library books, computers, computer software, slide and movie projectors, overhead projectors, television sets, tape recorders, videocassette recorders, projection screens, laboratory equipment, maps, globes, filmstrips, slides, and cassette recordings.

In an average year in the mid-1980s, about 30 percent of Chapter 2 funds spent in Jefferson Parish were allocated for private schools. During the 1986–1987 fiscal year, forty-six private schools participated in Chapter 2. Of these forty-six, thirty-four were Roman Catholic, seven were otherwise religiously affiliated, and five were not religiously affiliated.

JUSTICE THOMAS announced the judgment of the Court and delivered an opinion, in which THE CHIEF JUSTICE, JUSTICE SCALIA, and JUSTICE KENNEDY join.

[801] As part of a longstanding school aid program known as Chapter 2, the Federal Government distributes funds to state and local governmental agencies, which in turn lend educational materials and equipment to public and private schools, with the enrollment of each participating school determining the amount of aid that it receives. The question is whether Chapter 2, as applied in Jefferson Parish, Louisiana, is a law respecting an establishment of religion, because many of the private schools receiving Chapter 2 aid in that parish are religiously affiliated. We hold that Chapter 2 is not such a law. . . .

[807] The Establishment Clause of the First Amendment dictates that "Congress shall make no law respecting an establishment of religion." In the over 50 years since *Everson*, we have consistently struggled to apply these simple words in the context of governmental aid to religious schools. As we admitted in *Tilton v. Richardson*, "candor compels the acknowledgment that we can only dimly perceive the boundaries of permissible government activity in this sensitive area." 403 U.S. at 678 (plurality opinion).

In *Agostini*, however, we brought some clarity to our case law, by overruling two anomalous precedents (one in whole, the other in part) and by consolidating some of our previously disparate considerations under a revised test. Whereas in *Lemon* we had considered whether a statute (1) has a secular purpose, (2) has a primary effect of advancing or inhibiting religion, or (3) creates an excessive entanglement between government and religion, in *Agostini* we modified *Lemon* for purposes of evaluating aid to schools and examined only the first and second factors. We acknowledged [808] that our cases discussing excessive entanglement had applied many of the same considerations as had our cases discussing primary effect, and we therefore recast *Lemon*'s entanglement inquiry as simply one criterion relevant to determining a statute's effect. We also acknowledged that our cases had pared somewhat the factors that could justify a finding of excessive entanglement. We then set out revised criteria for determining the effect of a statute:

> "To summarize, New York City's Title I program does not run afoul of any of three primary criteria we currently use to evaluate whether government aid has the effect of advancing religion: It does not result in governmental indoctrination; define its recipients by reference to religion; or create an excessive entanglement." 521 U.S. at 234.

In this case, our inquiry under *Agostini*'s purpose and effect test is a narrow one. Because respondents do not challenge the District Court's holding that Chapter 2 has a secular purpose, and because the Fifth Circuit also did not question that holding, we will consider only Chapter 2's effect. Further, in determining that effect, we will consider only the first two *Agostini* criteria, since neither respondents nor the Fifth Circuit has questioned the District Court's holding that Chapter 2 does not create an excessive entanglement. Considering Chapter 2 in light of our more recent case law, we conclude that it neither results in religious indoctrination by the government nor defines its recipients by reference to religion. We therefore hold that Chapter 2 is not a "law respecting an establishment of religion." In so holding, we acknowledge what both the Ninth and Fifth Circuits saw was inescapable—*Meek* and *Wolman* are anomalies in our case law. We therefore conclude that they are no longer good law.

[809] As we indicated in *Agostini*, and have indicated elsewhere, the question whether governmental aid to religious schools results in governmental indoctrination is ultimately a question whether any religious indoctrination that occurs in those schools could reasonably be attributed to governmental action. We have also indicated that the answer to the question of indoctrination will resolve the question whether a program of educational aid "subsidizes" religion, as our religion cases use that term.

In distinguishing between indoctrination that is attributable to the State and indoctrination that is not, we have consistently turned to the principle of neutrality, upholding aid that is offered to a broad range of groups or persons without regard to their religion. If the religious, irreligious, and areligious are all alike eligible for governmental aid, no one would conclude that any indoctrination that any particular recipient conducts has been done at the behest of the government. For attribution of indoctrination is a relative question. If the government is offering assistance to recipients who provide, so to speak, a broad range of indoctrination, the government itself is not thought responsible for any particular [810] indoctrination. To put the point differently, if the government, seeking to further some legitimate secular purpose, offers aid on the same terms, without regard to religion, to all who adequately further that purpose, then it is fair to say that any aid going to a religious recipient only has the effect of furthering that secular purpose. The government, in crafting such an aid program, has had to conclude that a given level of aid is necessary to further that purpose among secular recipients and has provided no more than that same level to religious recipients.

As a way of assuring neutrality, we have repeatedly considered whether any governmental aid that goes to a religious institution does so "only as a result of the genuinely independent and private choices of individuals." *Agostini*, at 226. We have viewed as significant whether the "private choices of individual parents," as opposed to the "unmediated" will of government, *Ball*, 473 U.S. at 395, n. 13, determine what schools ultimately benefit from the governmental aid, and how much. For if numerous private choices, rather than the single choice of a government, determine the distribution of aid pursuant to neutral eligibility criteria, then a government cannot, or at least cannot easily, grant special favors that might lead to a religious establishment. Private choice also helps guarantee neutrality by mitigating the preference for pre-existing recipients that is arguably inherent in any governmental aid program and that could lead to a program inadvertently favoring one religion or favoring religious private schools in general over nonreligious ones. . . .

[813] *Agostini*'s second primary criterion for determining the effect of governmental aid is closely related to the first. The second criterion requires a court to consider whether an aid program "defines its recipients by reference to religion." 521 U.S. at 234. As we briefly explained in *Agostini*, this second criterion looks to the same set of facts as does our focus, under the first criterion, on neutrality, but the second criterion uses those facts to answer a somewhat different question—whether the criteria for allocating the aid "create a financial incentive to undertake religious indoctrination." *Id.* at 231. In *Agostini* we set out the following rule for answering this question:

> "This incentive is not present, however, where the aid is allocated on the basis of neutral, secular criteria that neither favor nor disfavor religion, and is made available to both reli-

gious and secular beneficiaries on a nondiscriminatory basis. Under such circumstances, the aid is less likely to have the effect of advancing religion." *Ibid.*

[814] The cases on which *Agostini* relied for this rule, and *Agostini* itself, make clear the close relationship between this rule, incentives, and private choice. For to say that a program does not create an incentive to choose religious schools is to say that the private choice is truly "independent," *Witters*, 474 U.S. at 487. When such an incentive does exist, there is a greater risk that one could attribute to the government any indoctrination by the religious schools.

We hasten to add, what should be obvious from the rule itself, that simply because an aid program offers private schools, and thus religious schools, a benefit that they did not previously receive does not mean that the program, by reducing the cost of securing a religious education, creates, under *Agostini*'s second criterion, an "incentive" for parents to choose such an education for their children. For any aid will have some such effect. . . .

Respondents inexplicably make no effort to address Chapter 2 under the *Agostini* test. Instead, dismissing *Agostini* as factually distinguishable, they offer two rules that they contend should govern our determination of whether Chapter 2 has the effect of advancing religion. They argue first, and chiefly, that "direct, nonincidental" aid to the primary educational mission of religious schools is always impermissible. Second, they argue that provision to religious schools of aid that is divertible to religious use is similarly impermissible. [815] Respondents' arguments are inconsistent with our more recent case law, in particular *Agostini* and *Zobrest*, and we therefore reject them. . . .

[820] Respondents also contend that the Establishment Clause requires that aid to religious schools not be impermissibly religious in nature or be divertible to religious use. We agree with the first part of this argument but not the second. Respondents' "no divertibility" rule is inconsistent with our more recent case law and is unworkable. So long as the governmental aid is not itself "unsuitable for use in the public schools because of religious content," *Allen*, 392 U.S. at 245, and eligibility for aid is determined in a constitutionally permissible manner, any use of that aid to indoctrinate cannot be attributed to the government and is thus not of constitutional concern. And, of course, the use to which the aid is put does not affect the criteria governing the aid's allocation and thus does not create any impermissible incentive under *Agostini*'s second criterion. . . .

[822] The issue is not divertibility of aid but rather whether the aid itself has an impermissible content. Where the aid would be suitable for use in a public school, it is also suitable for use in any private school. Similarly, the prohibition against the government providing impermissible content resolves the Establishment Clause concerns that exist if aid is actually diverted to religious uses. In *Agostini*, we explained *Zobrest* by making just this distinction between the content of aid and the use of that aid: "Because the only *government* aid in *Zobrest* was the interpreter, who was *herself not inculcating* any religious messages, no *government* indoctrination took place." 521 U.S. at 224 (second emphasis added). *Agostini* also acknowledged that what the dissenters in *Zobrest* had charged was essentially true: *Zobrest* did effect a "shift . . . in our Establishment Clause law." 521 U.S. at 225. The interpreter herself, assuming that she [823] fulfilled her assigned duties, had "no inherent religious significance," *Allen*, 392 U.S. at 244, and so it did not matter (given the neutrality and private choice involved in the program) that she "would be a mouthpiece for religious instruction," *Agostini, supra*, at 226. And just as a government interpreter does not herself inculcate a religious message—even when she is conveying one—so also a government computer or overhead projector does not itself inculcate a religious message, even when it is conveying one. . . .

[824] A concern for divertibility, as opposed to improper content, is misplaced not only because it fails to explain why the sort of aid that we have allowed is permissible, but also because it is boundless—enveloping all aid, no matter how trivial—and thus has only the most attenuated (if any) link to any realistic concern for preventing an "establishment of religion." Presumably, for example, government-provided lecterns, chalk, crayons, pens, paper, and paintbrushes would have to be excluded from religious schools under respondents' proposed rule. But we fail to see how indoctrination by means of (i.e., diversion of) such aid could be attributed to the government. In fact, the risk of improper attribution is less when the aid lacks content, for there is no risk (as there is with books) of the government inadvertently providing improper content. Finally, any aid, with or without content, is "divertible" in the sense that it allows schools to "divert" resources. Yet we have "not accepted the recurrent argument that all aid is forbidden because aid to one aspect of an institution frees it to spend its other resources on religious ends." *Regan*, 444 U.S. at 658.

[825] It is perhaps conceivable that courts could take upon themselves the task of distinguishing among the myriad kinds of possible aid based on the ease of diverting each kind. But it escapes us how a court might coherently draw any such line. It not only is far more workable, but also is actually related to real concerns about preventing advancement of religion by government, simply to require, as did *Zobrest*, *Agostini*, and *Allen*, that a program of aid to schools not provide improper content and that it determine eligibility and allocate the aid on a permissible basis. . . .

[829] Applying the two relevant *Agostini* criteria, we see no basis for concluding that Jefferson Parish's Chapter 2 program "has the effect of advancing religion." *Agostini*, *supra*, at 234. Chapter 2 does not result in governmental indoctrination, because it determines eligibility for aid neutrally, allocates that aid based on the private choices of the parents of schoolchildren, and does not provide aid that has an impermissible content. Nor does Chapter 2 define its recipients by reference to religion.

Taking the second criterion first, it is clear that Chapter 2 aid "is allocated on the basis of neutral, secular criteria that neither favor nor disfavor religion, and is made available to both religious and secular beneficiaries on a nondiscriminatory basis." *Agostini*, *supra*, at 231. Aid is allocated based on enrollment. . . .

[830] Chapter 2 also satisfies the first *Agostini* criterion. The program makes a broad array of schools eligible for aid without regard to their religious affiliations or lack thereof. We therefore have no difficulty concluding that Chapter 2 is neutral with regard to religion. . . .

[831] Finally, Chapter 2 satisfies the first *Agostini* criterion because it does not provide to religious schools aid that has an impermissible content. The statute explicitly bars anything of the sort, providing that all Chapter 2 aid for the benefit of children in private schools shall be "secular, neutral, and nonideological," § 7372 (a)(1), and the record indicates that the Louisiana SEA and the Jefferson Parish LEA have faithfully enforced this requirement insofar as relevant to this case. The chief aid at issue is computers, computer software, and library books. The computers presumably have no pre-existing content, or at least none that would be impermissible for use in public schools. Respondents do not contend [832] otherwise. Respondents also offer no evidence that religious schools have received software from the government that has an impermissible content. . . .

[867] JUSTICE SOUTER, with whom JUSTICE STEVENS and JUSTICE GINSBURG join, dissenting.

The First Amendment's Establishment Clause prohibits Congress (and, by incorporation, the States) from making any law respecting an establishment of religion. It has been [868] held to prohibit not only the institution of an official church, but any government act favoring religion, a particular religion, or for that matter irreligion. Thus it bars the use of public funds for religious aid.

The establishment prohibition of government religious funding serves more than one end. It is meant to guarantee the right of individual conscience against compulsion, to protect the integrity of religion against the corrosion of secular support, and to preserve the unity of political society against the implied exclusion of the less favored and the antagonism of controversy over public support for religious causes.

These objectives are always in some jeopardy since the substantive principle of no aid to religion is not the only limitation on government action toward religion. Because the First Amendment also bars any prohibition of individual free exercise of religion, and because religious organizations cannot be isolated from the basic government functions that create the civil environment, it is as much necessary as it is difficult to draw lines between forbidden aid and lawful benefit. For more than 50 years, this Court has been attempting to draw these lines. Owing to the variety of factual circumstances in which the lines must be drawn, not all of the points creating the boundary have enjoyed self-evidence.

So far as the line drawn has addressed government aid to education, a few fundamental generalizations are nonetheless possible. There may be no aid supporting a sectarian school's religious exercise or the discharge of its religious mission, while aid of a secular character with no discernible benefit to such a sectarian objective is allowable. Because the religious and secular spheres largely overlap in the life of many such schools, the Court has tried to identify some facts likely to reveal the relative religious or secular intent or effect of the government benefits in particular circumstances. We have asked whether the government is acting neutrally in distributing its money, and about the form of the aid itself, its path from government to religious institution, [869] its divertibility to religious nurture, its potential for reducing traditional expenditures of religious institutions, and its relative importance to the recipient, among other things.

In all the years of its effort, the Court has isolated no single test of constitutional sufficiency, and the question in every case addresses the substantive principle of no aid: what reasons are there to characterize this benefit as aid to the sectarian school in discharging its religious mission? Particular factual circumstances control, and the answer is a matter of judgment.

In what follows I will flesh out this summary, for this case comes at a time when our judgment requires perspective on how the Establishment Clause has come to be understood and applied. It is not just that a majority today mistakes the significance of facts that have led to conclusions of unconstitutionality in earlier cases, though I believe the Court commits error in failing to recognize the divertibility of funds to the service of religious objectives. What is more important is the view revealed in the plurality opinion, which espouses a new conception of neutrality as a practically sufficient test of constitutionality that would, if adopted by the Court, eliminate enquiry into a law's effects. The plurality position breaks fundamentally with Establishment Clause principle, and with the methodology painstakingly worked out in support of it. I mean to revisit that principle and describe the methodology at some length, lest there be any question about the rupture that the plurality view would cause. From that new view of the law, and from a majority's mistaken application of the old, I respectfully dissent. . . .

[870] At least three concerns have been expressed since the founding and run throughout our First Amendment jurisprudence. First, compelling an individual to support religion violates the fundamental principle of freedom of conscience. Madison's and Jefferson's now familiar words establish clearly that liberty of personal conviction requires freedom from coercion to support religion, and this means that the government can compel no aid to fund it. Madison put it simply: "The same authority which can force a citizen to [871] contribute three pence only of his property for the support of any one establishment, may force him to conform to any other establishment." *Memorial and Remonstrance* ¶ 3. Any tax to establish religion is antithetical to the command "that the minds of men always be wholly free."

Second, government aid corrupts religion. Madison argued that establishment of religion weakened the beliefs of adherents so favored, strengthened their opponents, and generated "pride and indolence in the Clergy; ignorance and servility in the laity; [and] in both, superstition, bigotry and persecution." *Memorial and Remonstrance* ¶ 7. "Experience witnesseth that ecclesiastical establishments, instead of maintaining the purity and efficacy of religion, have had a contrary operation." *Ibid.* In a variant of Madison's concern, we have repeatedly noted that a government's favor to a particular religion or sect threatens to taint it with "corrosive secularism." *Lee v. Weisman*, 505 U.S. 577, 608 (1992).

> [872] "Government and religion have discrete interests which are mutually best served when each avoids too close a proximity to the other. It is not only the nonbeliever who fears the injection of sectarian doctrines and controversies into the civil polity, but in as high degree it is the devout believer who fears the secularization of a creed which becomes too deeply involved with and dependent upon the government." *School Dist. of Abington Township v. Schempp*, 374 U.S. 203, 259 (1963) (Brennan, J., concurring).

Third, government establishment of religion is inextricably linked with conflict. In our own history, the turmoil thus produced has led to a rejection of the idea that government should subsidize religious education, a position that illustrates the Court's understanding that any implicit endorsement of religion is unconstitutional.

[873] These concerns are reflected in the Court's classic summation delivered in *Everson v. Board of Education*, its first opinion directly addressing standards governing aid to religious schools:

> "The 'establishment of religion' clause of the First Amendment means at least this: Neither a state nor the Federal Government can set up a church. Neither can pass laws which aid one religion, aid all religions, or prefer one religion over another. Neither can force nor influence a person to go to or to remain away from church against his will or force him to profess a belief or disbelief in any religion. No person can be punished for entertaining or professing religious beliefs or disbeliefs, for church attendance or non-attendance. No tax in any amount, large or small, can be levied to support any religious activities or institutions, whatever they may be called, or whatever form they may adopt to teach or practice religion. Neither a state nor the Federal Government can, openly or secretly, participate in the affairs of any religious organizations or groups and vice versa. In the words of Jefferson, the clause against establishment of religion by law was intended to erect 'a wall of separation between Church and State.'" 330 U.S. at 15–16.

The most directly pertinent doctrinal statements here are these: no government "can pass laws which aid one religion [874] [or] all religions. . . . No tax in any amount . . . can be levied to support any religious activities or institutions . . . whatever form they may adopt to teach . . . religion." 330 U.S. at 16. Thus, the principle of "no aid," with which no one in *Everson* disagreed.

Immediately, however, there was the difficulty over what might amount to "aid" or "support." The problem for the *Everson* Court was not merely the imprecision of the words, but the "other language of the [First Amendment that] commands that [government] cannot hamper its citizens in the free exercise of their own religion," *ibid.*, with the consequence that government must "be a neutral in its relations with groups of religious believers and non-believers," *id.* at 18. Since withholding some public benefits from religious groups could be said to "hamper" religious exercise indirectly, and extending other benefits said to aid it, an argument-proof formulation of the no-aid principle was impossible, and the Court wisely chose not to attempt any such thing. Instead it gave definitive examples of public benefits provided pervasively throughout society that would be of some value to organized religion but not in a way or to a degree that could sensibly be described as giving it aid or violating the neutrality requirement: there was no Establishment Clause concern with "such general government services as ordinary police and fire protection, connections for sewage disposal, public highways and sidewalks." *Id.* at 17–18. These "benefits of public welfare legislation," *id.* at 16, extended in modern times to virtually every member of the population and valuable to every person and association, were the paradigms of advantages that religious organizations [875] could enjoy consistently with the prohibition against aid, and that governments could extend without deserting their required position of neutrality. . . .

Everson is usefully understood in the light of a successor case two decades later, *Board of Ed. of Central School Dist. No. 1 v. Allen* (1968), in which the challenged government practice was lending textbooks to pupils of schools both public and private, including religious ones (as to which there was no evidence that they had previously supplied books to their classes and some evidence that they had not). By the time of *Allen*, the problem of classifying the state benefit, as between aid to religion and general public service consistent with government neutrality, [876] had led to the formulation of a "test" that required secular, primary intent and effect as necessary conditions of any permissible scheme. *Id.* at 243. Again the Court split, upholding the state law in issue, but with *Everson*'s majority author, Justice Black, now in dissent. What is remarkable about *Allen* today, however, is not so much its division as its methodology, for the consistency in the way the Justices went about deciding the case transcended their different conclusions. Neither side rested on any facile application of the "test" or any simplistic reliance on the generality or evenhandedness of the state law. Disagreement concentrated on the true intent inferable [*sic*] behind the law, the feasibility of distinguishing in fact between religious and secular teaching in church schools, and the reality or sham of lending books to pupils instead of supplying books to schools. The majority, to be sure, cited the provision for books to all schoolchildren, regardless of religion, just as the *Everson* majority had spoken of the transportation reimbursement as going to all, in each case for the sake of analogy to the provision of police and fire services. But the stress was on the practical significance of the actual benefits received by the schools. As *Everson* had rested on the understanding that no money and no support went to the school, *Allen* emphasized that the savings to parents were devoid of any measurable effect in teaching religion. Justice Harlan, concurring, summed up the approach with his observations that the required government "neutrality is . . . a coat of many colors," and quoted Justice

Goldberg's conclusion, that there was "'no simple and clear measure' . . . by which this or any [religious school aid] case may readily be decided," *id.* at 249.

[877] After *Everson* and *Allen*, the state of the law applying the Establishment Clause to public expenditures producing some benefit to religious schools was this:

1. Government aid to religion is forbidden, and tax revenue may not be used to support a religious school or religious teaching.
2. Government provision of such paradigms of universally general welfare benefits as police and fire protection does not count as aid to religion.
3. Whether a law's benefit is sufficiently close to universally general welfare paradigms to be classified with them, as distinct from religious aid, is a function of the purpose and effect of the challenged law in all its particularity. The judgment is not reducible to the application of any formula. Evenhandedness of distribution as between religious and secular beneficiaries is a relevant factor, but not a sufficiency test of constitutionality. There is no rule of religious equal protection to the effect that any expenditure for the benefit of religious school students is necessarily constitutional so long as public school pupils are favored on ostensibly identical terms.
4. Government must maintain neutrality as to religion, "neutrality" being a conclusory label for the required position of government as neither aiding religion nor impeding religious exercise by believers. "Neutrality" was not the name of any test to identify permissible action, and in particular, was not synonymous with evenhandedness in conferring benefit on the secular as well as the religious.

Today, the substantive principle of no aid to religious mission remains the governing understanding of the Establishment Clause as applied to public benefits inuring to religious schools. The governing opinions on the subject in the 35 years since *Allen* have never challenged this principle. The [878] cases have, however, recognized that in actual Establishment Clause litigation over school aid legislation, there is no pure aid to religion and no purely secular welfare benefit; the effects of the laws fall somewhere in between, with the judicial task being to make a realistic allocation between the two possibilities. The Court's decisions demonstrate its repeated attempts to isolate considerations relevant in classifying particular benefits as between those that do not discernibly support or threaten support of a school's religious mission, and those that cross or threaten to cross the line into support for religion.

The most deceptively familiar of those considerations is "neutrality," the presence or absence of which, in some sense, we have addressed from the moment of *Everson* itself. I say "some sense," for we have used the term in at least three ways in our cases, and an understanding of the term's evolution will help to explain the concept as it is understood today, as well as the limits of its significance in Establishment Clause analysis. "Neutrality" has been employed as a term to describe the requisite state of government equipoise between the forbidden encouragement and discouragement of religion; to characterize a benefit or aid as secular; and to indicate evenhandedness in distributing it.

As already mentioned, the Court first referred to neutrality in *Everson*, simply stating that government is required "to be a neutral" among religions and between religion and nonreligion. 330 U.S. at 18. Although "neutral" may have carried a hint of inaction when we indicated that the First Amendment "does not require the state to be [the] adversary" of religious believers, *ibid.*, or to cut off general government services from religious organizations, *Everson* provided no explicit definition of the term or further indication of what the government was required to do or not do to be [879] a "neutral" toward religion. In practical terms, "neutral" in *Everson* was simply a term for government in its required median position between aiding and handicapping religion. The second major case on aid to religious schools, *Allen*, used "neutrality" to describe an adequate state of balance between government as ally and as adversary to religion. The term was not further defined, and a few subsequent school cases used "neutrality" simply to designate the required relationship to religion, without explaining how to attain it.

The Court began to employ "neutrality" in a sense different from equipoise, however, as it explicated the distinction between "religious" and "secular" benefits to religious schools, the latter being in some circumstances permissible. Even though both *Everson* and *Allen* had anticipated some such distinction, neither case had used the term "neutral" in this way. In *Everson*, Justice Black indicated that providing [880] police, fire, and similar government services to religious institutions was permissible, in part because they were "so separate and so indisputably marked off from the religious function." 330 U.S. at 18. *Allen* similarly focused on the fact that the textbooks lent out were "secular" and approved by secular authorities and assumed that the secular textbooks and the secular elements of education they supported were not so intertwined with religious instruction as "in fact [to be] instrumental in the teaching of religion," 392 U.S. at 248. Such was the Court's premise in *Lemon* for shifting the use of the word "neutral" from labeling the required position of the government to describing a benefit that was nonreligious. We spoke of "our decisions from *Everson* to *Allen* [as] permitting the States to provide church-related schools with secular, neutral, or nonideological services, facilities, or materials," 403 U.S. at 616, and thereafter, we regularly used "neutral" in this second sense of "secular" or "nonreligious."

[881] The shift from equipoise to secular was not, however, our last redefinition, for the Court again transformed the sense of "neutrality" in the 1980s. Reexamining and reinterpreting *Everson* and *Allen*, we began to use the word "neutral" to mean "evenhanded," in the sense of allocating aid on some common basis to religious and secular recipients. Again, neither *Everson* nor *Allen* explicitly used "neutral" in this manner, but just as the label for equipoise had lent itself to referring to the secular characteristic of what a government might provide, it was readily adaptable to referring to the generality of government services, as in *Everson*'s paradigms, to which permissible benefits were compared. . . .

[882] In sum, "neutrality" originally entered this field of jurisprudence as a conclusory term, a label for the required relationship [883] between the government and religion as a state of equipoise between government as ally and government as adversary. Reexamining *Everson*'s paradigm cases to derive a prescriptive guideline, we first determined that "neutral" aid was secular, nonideological, or unrelated to religious education. Our subsequent reexamination of *Everson* and *Allen*, beginning in *Nyquist* and culminating in *Mueller* and most recently in *Agostini*, recast neutrality as a concept of "evenhandedness."

There is, of course, good reason for considering the generality of aid and the evenhandedness of its distribution in making close calls between benefits that in purpose or effect support a school's religious mission and those that do not. This is just what *Everson* did. Even when the disputed practice falls short of *Everson*'s paradigms, the breadth of evenhanded distribution is one pointer toward the law's purpose, since on the face of it aid distributed generally and without a religious criterion is less likely to be meant to aid religion than a benefit going only to religious institutions or people. And, depending on the breadth of distribution, looking to evenhandedness is a way of asking whether a benefit can reasonably be seen to aid religion in fact; we do not regard the postal system as aiding religion, even though parochial schools get mail. Given the legitimacy of considering evenhandedness, then, there is no reason to avoid the term "neutrality" to refer to it. But one crucial point must be borne in mind.

In the days when "neutral" was used in *Everson*'s sense of equipoise, neutrality was tantamount to constitutionality; the term was conclusory, but when it applied it meant that the government's position was constitutional under the Establishment Clause. This is not so at all, however, under the most recent use of "neutrality" to refer to generality or evenhandedness of distribution. This kind of neutrality is relevant in judging whether a benefit scheme so characterized should be seen as aiding a sectarian school's religious [884] mission, but this neutrality is not alone sufficient to qualify the aid as constitutional. It is to be considered only along with other characteristics of aid, its administration, its recipients, or its potential that have been emphasized over the years as indicators of just how religious the intent and effect of a given aid scheme really is. Thus, the basic principle of establishment scrutiny of aid remains the principle as stated in *Everson*, that there may be no public aid to religion or support for the religious mission of any institution. . . .

[885] Hence, if we looked no further than evenhandedness, and failed to ask what activities the aid might support, or in fact did support, religious schools could be blessed with government funding as massive as expenditures made for the benefit of their public school counterparts, and religious missions would thrive on public money. This is why the consideration of less than universal neutrality has never been recognized as dispositive and has always been teamed with attention to other facts bearing on the substantive prohibition of support for a school's religious objective.

At least three main lines of enquiry addressed particularly to school aid have emerged to complement evenhandedness neutrality. First, we have noted that two types of aid recipients heighten Establishment Clause concern: pervasively religious schools and primary and secondary religious schools. Second, we have identified two important characteristics of the method of distributing aid: directness or indirectness of distribution and distribution by genuinely independent choice. Third, we have found relevance in at least five characteristics of the aid itself: its religious content; its cash form; its divertibility or actually diversion to religious support; its supplantation of traditional items of religious school expense; and its substantiality.

Two types of school aid recipients have raised special concern. First, we have recognized the fact that the overriding religious mission of certain schools, those sometimes called [886] "pervasively sectarian," is not confined to a discrete element of the curriculum. Based on record evidence and long experience, we have concluded that religious teaching in such schools is at the core of the instructors' individual and personal obligations, and that individual religious teachers will teach religiously. [887] As religious teaching cannot be separated from secular education in such schools or by such teachers, we have concluded that direct government subsidies to such schools are prohibited because they will inevitably and impermissibly support religious indoctrination.

Second, we have expressed special concern about aid to primary and secondary religious schools. On the one hand, we have understood how the youth of the students in such schools makes them highly susceptible to religious indoctrination. On the other, we have recognized that the religious element in the education offered in most sectarian primary and secondary schools is far more intertwined with the secular than in university teaching, where the natural and academic skepticism of most older students may separate the two. Thus, government benefits accruing to these pervasively religious primary and secondary schools raise special dangers of diversion into support for the religious indoctrination of children and the involvement of government in religious training and practice.

[888] We have also evaluated the portent of support to an organization's religious mission that may be inherent in the method by which aid is granted, finding pertinence in at least two characteristics of distribution. First, we have asked whether aid is direct or indirect, observing distinctions between government schemes with individual beneficiaries and those whose beneficiaries in the first instance might be religious schools. Direct aid obviously raises greater risks, although recent cases have discounted this risk factor, looking to other features of the distribution mechanism. . . .

[889] Second, we have distinguished between indirect aid that reaches religious schools only incidentally as a result of numerous individual choices and aid that is in reality directed to religious schools by the government or in practical terms selected by religious schools themselves. In these cases, we have declared the constitutionality of programs providing aid directly to parents or students as tax deductions or scholarship money, where such aid may pay for education at some sectarian institutions, but only as the result of "genuinely independent and private choices of aid recipients," [*Witters,*] 474 U.S. at 487. . . .

In addition to the character of the school to which the benefit accrues, and its path from government to school, a number of features of the aid itself have figured in the classifications [890] we have made. First, we have barred aid with actual religious content, which would obviously run afoul of the ban on the government's participation in religion. In cases where we have permitted aid, we have regularly characterized it as "neutral" in the sense of being without religious content.

Second, we have long held government aid invalid when circumstances would allow its diversion to religious education. The risk of diversion is obviously high when aid in the form of government funds makes its way into the coffers of religious organizations, and so from the start we have understood the Constitution to bar outright money grants of aid to religion. . . .

[893] Divertibility is not, of course, a characteristic of cash alone, and when examining provisions for ostensibly secular supplies we have considered their susceptibility to the service of religious ends.[13] In upholding a scheme to provide students with secular textbooks, we emphasized that "each book loaned must be approved by the public school authorities; only secular books may receive approval." *Allen,* 392 U.S. at 244–245. By the same token, we could not sustain provisions for instructional materials adaptable to teaching a variety of subjects. While the textbooks had a known and fixed secular content not readily divertible [894] to religious teaching purposes, the adaptable materials did not. So, too, we explained the permissibility of busing on public routes to schools but not busing for field trips designed by religious authorities specifically because the latter trips were components of teaching in a pervasively religious school. We likewise were able to uphold underwriting the expenses of standard state testing in religious schools while being forced to strike down aid for testing designed by the school officials, because the latter tests could be used to reinforce religious teaching. . . .

[896] Third, our cases have recognized the distinction, adopted by statute in the Chapter 2 legislation, between aid that merely supplements and aid that supplants expenditures for offerings at religious schools, the latter being barred. Although we have never adopted the position that any benefit that flows to a religious school is impermissible because it frees up resources for the school to engage in religious indoctrination,

---

13. I reject the plurality's argument that divertibility is a boundless principle. Our long experience of evaluating this consideration demonstrates its practical limits. Moreover, the Establishment Clause charges us with making such enquiries, regardless of their difficulty. Finally, the First Amendment's rule permitting only aid with fixed secular content seems no more difficult to apply than the plurality's rule prohibiting only aid with fixed religious content.

from our first decision holding it permissible to provide textbooks for religious schools we have repeatedly explained the unconstitutionality of aid that supplants an item of the school's traditional expense. . . .

[898] Finally, we have recognized what is obvious (however imprecise), in holding "substantial" amounts of aid to be unconstitutional whether or not a plaintiff can show that it supplants a specific item of expense a religious school would have borne. . . .

[899] This stretch of doctrinal history leaves one point clear beyond peradventure: together with James Madison we have consistently understood the Establishment Clause to impose a substantive prohibition against public aid to religion and, hence, to the religious mission of sectarian schools. Evenhandedness neutrality is one, nondispositive pointer toward an intent and (to a lesser degree) probable effect on the permissible side of the line between forbidden aid and general public welfare benefit. Other pointers are facts about the religious mission and education level of benefited schools and their pupils, the pathway by which a benefit travels from public treasury to educational effect, the form and content of the aid, its adaptability to religious ends, and its effects on school budgets. The object of all enquiries into such matters is the same whatever the particular circumstances: is the benefit intended to aid in providing the religious element of the education and is it likely to do so?

The substance of the law has thus not changed since *Everson*. Emphasis on one sort of fact or another has varied depending on the perceived utility of the enquiry, but all that has been added is repeated explanation of relevant considerations, confirming that our predecessors were right in their prophecies that no simple test would emerge to allow easy application of the establishment principle.

The plurality, however, would reject that lesson. The majority misapplies it.

[900] The nub of the plurality's new position is this:

> "If the government, seeking to further some legitimate secular purpose, offers aid on the same terms, without regard to religion, to all who adequately further that purpose, then it is fair to say that any aid going to a religious recipient only has the effect of furthering that secular purpose. The government, in crafting such an aid program, has had to conclude that a given level of aid is necessary to further that purpose among secular recipients and has provided no more than that same level to religious recipients."

As a break with consistent doctrine the plurality's new criterion is unequaled in the history of Establishment Clause interpretation. Simple on its face, it appears to take evenhandedness neutrality and in practical terms promote it to a single and sufficient test for the establishment constitutionality of school aid. Even on its own terms, its errors are manifold, and attention to at least three of its mistaken assumptions will show the degree to which the plurality's proposal would replace the principle of no aid with a formula for generous religious support.

First, the plurality treats an external observer's attribution of religious support to the government as the sole impermissible effect of a government aid scheme. While perceived state endorsement of religion is undoubtedly a relevant concern under the Establishment Clause [901] it is certainly not the only one. *Everson* made this clear from the start: secret aid to religion by the government is also barred. State aid not attributed to the government would still violate a taxpayer's liberty of conscience, threaten to corrupt religion, and generate disputes over aid. In any event, since the same-terms feature of the scheme would, on the plurality's view, rule out the attribution or perception of endorsement, adopting the plurality's rule of facial evenhandedness would convert neutrality into a dispositive criterion of establishment constitutionality and eliminate the effects enquiry directed by *Allen, Lemon*, and other cases. Under the plurality's rule of neutrality, if a program met the first part of the *Lemon* enquiry, by declining to define a program's recipients by religion, it would automatically satisfy the second, in supposedly having no impermissible effect of aiding religion.[19]

Second, the plurality apparently assumes as a fact that equal amounts of aid to religious and nonreligious schools will have exclusively secular and equal effects, on both external perception and on incentives to attend different schools. But there is no reason to believe that this will be the case; the effects of same-terms aid may not be confined to the secular sphere at all. This is the reason that we have long recognized that unrestricted aid to religious schools will support religious teaching in addition [902] to secular education, a fact that would be true no matter what the supposedly secular purpose of the law might be.

Third, the plurality assumes that per capita distribution rules safeguard the same principles as independent, private choices. But that is clearly not so. We approved university scholarships in *Witters* because we found them close to giving a government employee a paycheck and allowing him to spend it as he chose, but a per capita aid program is a far cry from awarding scholarships to individuals, one of whom makes an independent private choice. Not the least of the significant differences between per capita aid and aid individually determined and directed is the right and genuine opportunity of the recipient to choose not to give the aid. To hold otherwise would be to license the government to donate funds to churches based on the number of their members, on the patent fiction of independent private choice.

The plurality's mistaken assumptions explain and underscore its sharp break with the Framers' understanding of establishment and this Court's consistent interpretative course. Under the plurality's regime, little would be left of the right of conscience against compelled support for religion; the more massive the aid the more potent would be the influence of the government on the teaching mission; the more generous the support, the more divisive would be the resentments of those resisting religious support, and those religions without school systems ready to claim their fair share.

The plurality's conception of evenhandedness does not, however, control the case, whose disposition turns on the misapplication of accepted categories of school aid analysis. The facts most obviously relevant to the Chapter 2 scheme [903] in Jefferson Parish are those showing divertibility and actual diversion in the circumstance of pervasively sectarian religious schools. The type of aid, the structure of the program, and the lack of effective safeguards clearly demonstrate the divertibility of the aid. While little is known about its use, owing to the anemic enforcement system in the parish, even the thin record before us reveals that actual diversion occurred.

The aid that the government provided was highly susceptible to unconstitutional use. Much of the equipment provided under Chapter 2 was not of the type provided for individual students, but included "slide projectors, movie projectors, overhead projectors, television sets, tape recorders, projection screens, maps, globes, filmstrips, cassettes, computers," and computer software and peripherals. The videocassette players, overhead projectors, and other instructional aids were of the sort that we have found can easily be used by religious teachers for religious purposes. The same was true of the computers, which were as readily employable for religious teaching as the other equipment,

---

19. Adopting the plurality's rule would permit practically any government aid to religion so long as it could be supplied on terms ostensibly comparable to the terms under which aid was provided to nonreligious recipients. As a principle of constitutional sufficiency, the manipulability of this rule is breathtaking. A legislature would merely need to state a secular objective in order to legalize massive aid to all religions, one religion, or even one sect, to which its largess could be directed through the easy exercise of crafting facially neutral terms under which to offer aid favoring that religious group. Short of formally replacing the Establishment Clause, a more dependable key to the public fisc or a cleaner break with prior law would be difficult to imagine.

and presumably as immune to any countervailing safeguard. Although library books, like textbooks, have fixed content, religious teachers can assign secular library books for religious critique, and books for libraries may be religious, as any divinity school library would demonstrate. The sheer number and variety of books that could be and were ordered gave ample opportunity for such diversion.

The divertibility thus inherent in the forms of Chapter 2 aid was enhanced by the structure of the program in Jefferson Parish. Requests for specific items under Chapter 2 came not from secular officials [904] but from officials of the religious schools (and even parents of religious school pupils). The sectarian schools decided what they wanted and often ordered the supplies to be forwarded directly to themselves. It was easy to select whatever instructional materials and library books the schools wanted, just as it was easy to employ computers for the support of the religious content of the curriculum infused with religious instruction.

The concern with divertibility thus predicated is underscored by the fact that the religious schools in question here covered the primary and secondary grades, the grades in which the sectarian nature of instruction is characteristically the most pervasive, and in which pupils are the least critical of the schools' religious objectives. No one, indeed, disputes the trial judge's findings, based on a detailed record, that the Roman Catholic schools, which made up the majority of the private schools participating, were pervasively sectarian, that [905] their common objective and mission was to engage in religious education, and that their teachers taught religiously, making them precisely the kind of primary and [906] secondary religious schools that raise the most serious Establishment Clause concerns. The threat to Establishment Clause values was accordingly at its highest in the circumstances of this case. Such precautionary features as there were in the Jefferson Parish scheme were grossly inadequate to counter the threat. To be sure, the disbursement of the aid was subject to statutory admonitions against diversion and was supposedly subject to a variety of safeguards. But the provisions for onsite monitoring visits, labeling of government property, and government oversight cannot be accepted as sufficient in the face of record evidence that the safeguard provisions proved to be empty phrases in Jefferson Parish.

The plurality has already noted at length the ineffectiveness of the government's monitoring program. Monitors visited a nonpublic school only sporadically, discussed the program with a single contact person, observed nothing more than attempts at recordkeeping, and failed to inform the teachers of the restrictions involved. Although Chapter 2 required labeling of government property, it occurred haphazardly at best, and the government's sole monitoring system for computer use amounted to nothing more [907] than questioning school officials and examining the location of computers at the schools. No records of software and computer use were kept, and no such recordkeeping was even planned. State and local officials in Jefferson Parish admitted that nothing prevented the Chapter 2 computers from being used for religious instruction, and although they knew of methods of monitoring computer usage, such as locking the computer functions, they implemented no particular policies, instituted no systems, and employed no technologies to minimize the likelihood of diversion to religious uses. The watchdogs did require the religious schools to give not so much as an assurance that they would use Chapter 2 computers solely for secular purposes. Government officials themselves admitted that there was no way to tell whether instructional materials had been diverted, and, as the plurality notes, the only screening mechanism in the library book scheme was a review of titles by a single government official. The government did not even have a policy on the consequences of noncompliance. . . .

[908] Providing such governmental aid without effective safeguards against future diversion itself offends the Establishment Clause, and even without evidence of actual diversion, our cases have repeatedly held that a "substantial risk" of it suffices to invalidate a government aid program on establishment grounds. [909] A substantial risk of diversion in this case was more than clear, as the plurality has conceded. The First Amendment was violated.

But the record here goes beyond risk, to instances of actual diversion. What one would expect from such paltry efforts at monitoring and enforcement naturally resulted, and the record strongly suggests that other, undocumented diversions probably occurred as well. First, the record shows actual diversion in the library book program. Although only limited evidence exists, it contrasts starkly with the records of the numerous textbook programs that we have repeatedly upheld, where there was no evidence of any actual diversion. Here, discovery revealed that under Chapter 2, nonpublic schools requested and the government purchased at least 191 religious books with taxpayer funds by December 1985. Books such as *A Child's Book of Prayers* and *The Illustrated Life of Jesus* [910] were discovered among others that had been ordered under the program. . . .

[911] The plurality would break with the law. The majority misapplies it. That misapplication is, however, the only consolation in the case, which reaches an erroneous result but does not stage a doctrinal coup. But there is no mistaking the abandonment of doctrine that would occur if the plurality were to become a majority. It is beyond question that the plurality's notion of evenhandedness neutrality as a practical guarantee of the validity of aid to sectarian schools would be the end of the principle of no aid to the schools' religious mission. And if that were not so obvious it would become so after reflecting on the plurality's thoughts about diversion [912] and about giving attention to the pervasiveness of a school's sectarian teaching.

The plurality is candid in pointing out the extent of actual diversion of Chapter 2 aid to religious use in the case before us and equally candid in saying it does not matter. To the plurality there is nothing wrong with aiding a school's religious mission; the only question is whether religious teaching obtains its tax support under a formally evenhanded criterion of distribution. The principle of no aid to religious teaching has no independent significance.

And if this were not enough to prove that no aid in religious school aid is dead under the plurality's First Amendment, the point is nailed down in the plurality's attack on the legitimacy of considering a school's pervasively sectarian character when judging whether aid to the school is likely to aid its religious mission. The relevance of this consideration is simply a matter of common sense: where religious indoctrination pervades school activities of children and adolescents, it takes great care to be able to aid the school without supporting the doctrinal effort. This is obvious. The plurality nonetheless condemns any enquiry into the pervasiveness of doctrinal content as a remnant of anti-Catholic bigotry (as if evangelical Protestant schools and Orthodox Jewish yeshivas were never pervasively sectarian), and it equates a refusal to aid religious schools with hostility to religion (as if aid to religious teaching were not [913] opposed in this very case by at least one religious respondent and numerous religious *amici curiae* in a tradition claiming descent from Roger Williams). My concern with these arguments goes not so much to their details as it does to the fact that the plurality's choice to employ imputations of bigotry and irreligion as terms in the Court's debate makes one point clear: that in rejecting the principle of no aid to a school's religious mission the plurality is attacking the most fundamental assumption underlying the Establishment Clause, that government can in fact operate with neutrality in its relation to religion. I believe that it can, and so respectfully dissent.

56

Good News Club v. Milford Central School

533 U.S. 98 (2001)

Vote: 6—Rehnquist, O'Connor, Scalia, Kennedy, Thomas, Breyer
  3—Stevens, Souter, Ginsberg

Opinion announcing the opinion of the Court: Thomas
Concurring opinions: Scalia, Breyer (in part)
Dissenting opinions: Stevens, Souter

New York state law authorized local school boards to adopt regulations governing use of their school facilities, including regulations pertaining to use of school facilities by the public. In 1992, Milford Central School enacted a community-use policy that included seven purposes for after-school use of its building. Two of those purposes were relevant to the case at hand: district residents could use the school for "instruction in any branch of education, learning or the arts," and the school was available for "social, civic and recreational meetings and entertainment events, and other uses pertaining to the welfare of the community, provided that such uses shall be nonexclusive and shall be opened to the general public."

In September 1996, Stephen and Darleen Fournier, residents within Milford's district, submitted a request to hold weekly Good News Club after-school meetings in the school cafeteria. The Good News Club is a private Christian organization for children ages six to twelve. The Fourniers' proposed meeting activities included singing songs, hearing a Bible lesson, and memorizing scripture. The interim superintendent of the district denied the Fourniers' request on the grounds that the proposed use was "the equivalent of religious worship" and that Milford community-use policy prohibited use "by any individual or organization for religious purposes."

In an effort to have the decision reversed, the Fourniers' Good News Club had legal counsel contact Milford officials. In a response to a letter submitted by the club's attorney, Milford's attorney requested information to clarify the nature of the club's activities. The club sent a set of materials used or distributed at the meetings and the following description of its meeting:

> *The Club opens its session with Ms. Fournier taking attendance. As she calls a child's name, if the child recites a Bible verse the child receives a treat. After attendance, the Club sings songs. Next Club members engage in games that involve, inter alia, learning Bible verses. Ms. Fournier then relates a Bible story and explains how it applies to Club*

members' lives. The Club closes with prayer. Finally, Ms. Fournier distributes treats and the Bible verses for memorization.

The interim superintendent and Milford's attorney reviewed the materials and concluded that "the kinds of activities proposed to be engaged in by the Good News Club were not a discussion of secular subjects such as child rearing, development of character and development of morals from a religious perspective, but were in fact the equivalent of religious instruction itself."

In February 1997, the Milford Board of Education adopted a resolution rejecting the club's request to use Milford's facilities "for the purpose of conducting religious instruction and Bible study." In March 1997, the Good News Club, Ms. Fournier, and her daughter Andrea Fournier (collectively, the Club) filed a legal action that led to the Supreme Court decision below.

THOMAS, J., delivered the opinion of the Court, in which REHNQUIST, C. J., and O'CONNOR, SCALIA, and KENNEDY, JJ., joined, and in which BREYER, JJ., joined in part.

[102] This case presents two questions. The first question is whether Milford Central School violated the free speech rights of the Good News Club when it excluded the Club from meeting after hours at the school. The second question is whether any such violation is justified by Milford's concern that permitting the Club's activities would violate the Establishment Clause. We conclude that Milford's restriction violates the Club's free speech rights and that no Establishment Clause concern justifies that violation. . . .

[106] II

The standards that we apply to determine whether a State has unconstitutionally excluded a private speaker from use of a public forum depend on the nature of the forum. If the forum is a traditional or open public forum, the State's restrictions on speech are subject to stricter scrutiny than are restrictions in a limited public forum. We have previously declined to decide whether a school district's opening of its facilities pursuant to N. Y. Educ. Law § 414 creates a limited or a traditional public forum. Because the parties have agreed that Milford created a limited public forum when it opened its facilities in 1992, we need not resolve the issue here. Instead, we simply will assume that Milford operates a limited public forum.

When the State establishes a limited public forum, the State is not required to and does not allow persons to engage in every type of speech. The State may be justified "in reserving [its forum] for certain groups or for the discussion of certain topics." *Rosenberger v. Rector and Visitors of Univ. of Va.*, 515 U.S. 819, 829 (1995). The State's power to restrict speech, however, is not without limits. The restriction must not discriminate against speech on the basis of viewpoint, [107] and the restriction must be "reasonable in light of the purpose served by the forum," *Cornelius v. NAACP Legal Defense & Ed. Fund, Inc.*, 473 U.S. 788, 806 (1985).

III

Applying this test, we first address whether the exclusion constituted viewpoint discrimination. We are guided in our analysis by two of our prior opinions, *Lamb's Chapel* and *Rosenberger*. In *Lamb's Chapel*, we held that a school district violated the Free Speech Clause of the First Amendment when it excluded a private group from presenting films at the school based solely on the films' discussions of family values from a religious perspective. Likewise, in *Rosenberger*, we held that a university's refusal to fund a student publication because the publication addressed issues from a religious perspective violated the Free Speech Clause. Concluding that Milford's exclusion of the Good News Club based on its religious nature is indistinguishable from the exclusions in these cases, we hold that the exclusion constitutes viewpoint discrimination. Because the restriction is viewpoint discriminatory, we need not decide whether it is unreasonable in light of the purposes served by the forum. . . .

[108] Milford has opened its limited public forum to activities that serve a variety of purposes, including events "pertaining to the welfare of the community." Milford interprets its policy to permit discussions of subjects such as child rearing, and of "the development of character and morals from a religious perspective." For example, this policy would allow someone to use Aesop's Fables to teach children moral values. Additionally, a group could sponsor a debate on whether there should be a constitutional amendment to permit prayer in public schools and the Boy Scouts could meet "to influence a boy's character, development and spiritual growth." In short, any group that "promotes the moral and character development of children" is eligible to use the school building.

Just as there is no question that teaching morals and character development to children is a permissible purpose under Milford's policy, it is clear that the Club teaches morals and character development to children. For example, no one disputes that the Club instructs children to overcome feelings of jealousy, to treat others well regardless of how they treat the children, and to be obedient, even if it does so in a nonsecular way. Nonetheless, because Milford found the Club's activities to be religious in nature—"the equivalent of religious instruction itself," 202 F.3d at 507—it excluded the Club from use of its facilities.

[109] Applying *Lamb's Chapel*, we find it quite clear that Milford engaged in viewpoint discrimination when it excluded the Club from the afterschool forum. . . .

Like the church in *Lamb's Chapel*, the Club seeks to address a subject otherwise permitted under the rule, the teaching of morals and character, from a religious standpoint. Certainly, one could have characterized the film presentations in *Lamb's Chapel* as a religious use, as the Court of Appeals did. And one easily could conclude that the films' purpose to instruct that "society's slide toward humanism . . . can only be counterbalanced by a loving home where Christian values are instilled from an early age," [959 F.2d 381,] at 384, was "quintessentially religious," 202 F.3d at 510. The only apparent difference [110] between the activity of Lamb's Chapel and the activities of the Good News Club is that the Club chooses to teach moral lessons from a Christian perspective through live storytelling and prayer, whereas Lamb's Chapel taught lessons through films. This distinction is inconsequential. Both modes of speech use a religious viewpoint. Thus, the exclusion of the Good News Club's activities, like the exclusion of Lamb's Chapel's films, constitutes unconstitutional viewpoint discrimination.

Our opinion in *Rosenberger* also is dispositive. In *Rosenberger*, a student organization at the University of Virginia was denied funding for printing expenses because its publication, *Wide Awake*, offered a Christian viewpoint. Just as the Club emphasizes the role of Christianity in students' morals and character, *Wide Awake* "challenged Christians to live, in word and deed, according to the faith they proclaim and . . . encouraged students to consider what a personal relationship with Jesus Christ means." 515 U.S. at 826. Because the university "selected for disfavored treatment those student journalistic efforts with religious editorial viewpoints," we held that the denial of funding was unconstitutional. *Id.* at 831. Although in *Rosenberger* there was no prohibition on religion as a subject matter, our holding did not rely on this factor. Instead, we concluded simply that the university's denial of funding to print *Wide Awake* was viewpoint discrimination, just as the school district's refusal to allow Lamb's Chapel to show its films was viewpoint discrimination. *Ibid.* Given the obvious religious content of *Wide Awake*, we cannot say that the Club's activities are any more "religious" or deserve any less First Amendment protection than did the publication of *Wide Awake* in *Rosenberger*. . . .

[111] [W]e reaffirm our holdings in *Lamb's Chapel* and *Rosenberger* [112] that speech discussing otherwise permissible subjects cannot be excluded from a limited public forum on the ground that the subject is discussed from a religious viewpoint. Thus, we conclude that Milford's exclusion of the Club from use of the school, pursuant to its community use policy, constitutes impermissible viewpoint discrimination. . . .

IV

Milford argues that, even if its restriction constitutes viewpoint discrimination, its interest in not violating the Establishment Clause outweighs the Club's interest in gaining equal access to the school's facilities. In other words, according to Milford, its restriction was required to avoid violating the Establishment Clause. We disagree.

We have said that a state interest in avoiding an Establishment Clause violation "may be characterized as compelling," and therefore may justify content-based discrimination. [113] *Widmar v. Vincent*, 454 U.S. 263, 271 (1981). However, it is not clear whether a State's interest in avoiding an Establishment Clause violation would justify viewpoint discrimination. We need not, however, confront the issue in this case, because we conclude that the school has no valid Establishment Clause interest. . . .

[114] First, we have held that "a significant factor in upholding governmental programs in the face of Establishment Clause attack is their *neutrality* towards religion." *Rosenberger*, 515 U.S. at 839 (emphasis added). Milford's implication that granting access to the Club would do damage to the neutrality principle defies logic. For the "guarantee of neutrality is respected, not offended, when the government, following neutral criteria and evenhanded policies, extends benefits to recipients whose ideologies and viewpoints, including religious ones, are broad and diverse." *Rosenberger*, at 839. The Good News Club seeks nothing more than to be treated neutrally and given access to speak about the same topics as are other groups. Because allowing the Club to speak on school grounds would ensure neutrality, not threaten it, Milford faces an uphill battle in arguing that the Establishment Clause compels it to exclude the Good News Club.

[115] Second, to the extent we consider whether the community would feel coercive pressure to engage in the Club's activities, the relevant community would be the parents, not the elementary school children. It is the parents who choose whether their children will attend the Good News Club meetings. Because the children cannot attend without their parents' permission, they cannot be coerced into engaging in the Good News Club's religious activities. Milford does not suggest that the parents of elementary school children would be confused about whether the school was endorsing religion. Nor do we believe that such an argument could be reasonably advanced.

Third, whatever significance we may have assigned in the Establishment Clause context to the suggestion that elementary school children are more impressionable than adults, we have never extended our Establishment Clause jurisprudence to foreclose private religious conduct during nonschool hours merely because it takes place on school premises where elementary school children may be present. . . .

[117] Fourth, even if we were to consider the possible misperceptions by schoolchildren in deciding whether Milford's permitting the Club's activities would violate the Establishment Clause, the facts of this case simply do not support Milford's conclusion. There is no evidence that young children are permitted to loiter outside classrooms after the schoolday has ended. Surely even young children are aware of events for which their parents must sign permission [118] forms. The meetings were held in a combined high school resource room and middle school special education room, not in an elementary school classroom. The instructors are not schoolteachers. And the children in the group are not all the same age as in the normal classroom setting; their ages range from 6 to 12. In sum, these circumstances simply do not support the theory that small children would perceive endorsement here.

Finally, even if we were to inquire into the minds of schoolchildren in this case, we cannot say the danger that children would misperceive the endorsement of religion is any greater than the danger that they would perceive a hostility toward the religious viewpoint if the Club were excluded from the public forum. This concern is particularly acute given the reality that Milford's building is not used only for elementary school children. Students, from kindergarten through the 12th grade, all attend school in the same building. There may be as many, if not more, upperclassmen than elementary school children who occupy the school after hours. For that matter, members of the public writ large are permitted in the school after hours pursuant to the community use policy. Any bystander could conceivably be aware of the school's use policy and its exclusion of the Good News Club, and could suffer as much from viewpoint discrimination as elementary school children could suffer from perceived endorsement.

[119] We cannot operate, as Milford would have us do, under the assumption that any risk that small children would perceive endorsement should counsel in favor of excluding the Club's religious activity. We decline to employ Establishment Clause jurisprudence using a modified heckler's veto, in which a group's religious activity can be proscribed on the basis of what the youngest members of the audience might misperceive. There are countervailing constitutional concerns related to rights of other individuals in the community. In this case, those countervailing concerns are the free speech rights of the Club and its members. And, we have already found that those rights have been violated, not merely perceived to have been violated, by the school's actions toward the Club.

We are not convinced that there is any significance in this case to the possibility that elementary school children may witness the Good News Club's activities on school premises, and therefore we can find no reason to depart from our holdings in *Lamb's Chapel* and *Widmar*. Accordingly, we conclude that permitting the Club to meet on the school's premises would not have violated the Establishment Clause.

[120] V

When Milford denied the Good News Club access to the school's limited public forum on the ground that the Club was religious in nature, it discriminated against the Club because of its religious viewpoint in violation of the Free Speech Clause of the First Amendment. Because Milford has not raised a valid Establishment Clause claim, we do not address the question whether such a claim could excuse Milford's viewpoint discrimination.

JUSTICE SCALIA, concurring.

I join the Court's opinion but write separately to explain further my views on two issues.

I

First, I join Part IV of the Court's opinion, regarding the Establishment Clause issue, with the understanding that its consideration of coercive pressure and perceptions of endorsement, "to the extent" that the law makes such factors relevant, [121] is consistent with the belief (which I hold) that in this case that extent is zero. As to coercive pressure: Physical coercion is not at issue here; and so-called "peer pressure," if it can even be considered coercion, is, when it arises from private activities, one of the attendant consequences of a freedom of association that is constitutionally protected. What is at play here is not coercion, but the compulsion of ideas—and the private right to exert and receive that compulsion (or to have one's children receive it) is protected by the Free Speech and Free Exercise Clauses, not banned by the Establishment Clause. A priest has as much liberty to proselytize as a patriot.

As to endorsement, I have previously written that "religious expression cannot violate the Establishment Clause where it (1) is purely private and (2) occurs in a traditional or designated public forum, publicly announced and open to all on equal terms." *Capitol Square Review and Advisory Bd. v. Pinette*, 515 U.S. 753, 770 (1995). The same is true of private speech that occurs in a limited public forum, publicly announced, whose boundaries are not drawn to favor religious groups but instead permit a cross-section of uses. In that context, which is this case, "erroneous conclusions [about endorsement] do not count." *Id.* at 765.

[122] II

Second, since we have rejected the only reason that respondent gave for excluding the Club's speech from a forum that clearly included it (the forum was opened to any "use pertaining to the welfare of the community"), I do not suppose it matters whether the exclusion is characterized as viewpoint or subject-matter discrimination. Lacking any legitimate reason for excluding the Club's speech from its forum—"because it's religious" will not do—respondent would seem to fail First Amendment scrutiny regardless of how its action is characterized. Even subject-matter limits must at least be "reasonable in light of the purpose served by the forum," *Cornelius v. NAACP Legal Defense & Ed. Fund, Inc.*, 473 U.S. 788, 806 (1985). But I agree, in any event, that respondent did discriminate on the basis of viewpoint.

As I understand it, the point of disagreement between the Court and the dissenters (and the Court of Appeals) [123] with regard to petitioner's Free Speech Clause claim is not whether the Good News Club must be permitted to present religious viewpoints on morals and character in respondent's forum, which has been opened to secular discussions of that subject. The answer to that is established by our decision in *Lamb's Chapel*. The point of disagreement is not even whether some of the Club's religious speech fell within the protection of *Lamb's Chapel*. It certainly did.

The disagreement, rather, regards the portions of the Club's meetings that are not "purely" "discussions" of morality and character from a religious viewpoint. The Club, for example, urges children "who already believe in the Lord Jesus as their Savior" to "stop and ask God for the strength and the 'want' . . . to obey Him," and it invites children who "don't know Jesus as Savior" to "trust the Lord Jesus to be [their] Savior from sin." The dissenters and the Second Circuit say that the presence of such additional speech, because it is purely religious, transforms the Club's meetings into something different in kind from other, nonreligious activities that teach moral and character development. Therefore, the argument goes, excluding the Club is not viewpoint discrimination. I disagree.

Respondent has opened its facilities to any "use pertaining to the welfare of the community, provided that such use shall be nonexclusive and shall be opened to the general [124] public." Shaping the moral and character development of children certainly "pertains to the welfare of the community." Thus, respondent has agreed that groups engaged in the endeavor of developing character may use its forum. The Boy Scouts, for example, may seek "to influence a boy's character, development and spiritual growth," and a group may use Aesop's Fables to teach moral values. When the Club attempted to teach Biblical-based moral values, however, it was excluded because its activities "did not involve merely a religious perspective on the secular subject of morality" and because "it [was] clear from the conduct of the meetings that the Good News Club goes far beyond merely stating its viewpoint." 202 F.3d at 510.

From no other group does respondent require the sterility of speech that it demands of petitioners. The Boy Scouts could undoubtedly buttress their exhortations to keep "morally straight" and live "clean" lives, by giving reasons why that is a good idea—because parents want and expect it, because it will make the scouts "better" and "more successful" people, because it will emulate such admired past Scouts as former President Gerald Ford. The Club, however, may only discuss morals and character, and cannot give its reasons why they should be fostered—because God wants and expects it, because it will make the Club members "saintly" people, and because it emulates Jesus Christ. The Club may not, in other words, independently discuss the religious premise on which its views are based—that God exists and His assistance is necessary to morality. It may not defend the premise, and it absolutely must not seek to persuade the children that the premise is true. The children must, so to say, take it on faith. This is blatant viewpoint discrimination. [125] Just as calls to character based on patriotism will go unanswered if the listeners do not believe their country is good and just, calls to moral behavior based on God's will are useless if the listeners do not believe that God exists. Effectiveness in presenting a viewpoint rests on the persuasiveness with which the speaker defends his premise—and in respondent's facilities every premise but a religious one may be defended. . . .

The right to present a viewpoint based on a religion premise carried with it the right to defend the premise.

The dissenters emphasize that the religious speech used by the Club as the foundation for its views on morals and character is not just any type of religious speech—although they cannot agree exactly what type of religious speech it is. In JUSTICE STEVENS' view, it is speech "aimed principally at proselytizing or inculcating belief in a particular religious faith." This does not, to begin with, distinguish *Rosenberger*, which [126] also involved proselytizing speech, as the above quotations show. But in addition, it does not distinguish the Club's activities from those of the other groups using respondent's forum—which have not, as JUSTICE STEVENS suggests, been restricted to round-table "discussions" of moral issues. Those groups may seek to inculcate children with their beliefs, and they may furthermore "recruit others to join their respective groups."

The Club must therefore have liberty to do the same, even if, as JUSTICE STEVENS fears without support in the record, its actions may prove (shudder!) divisive.

JUSTICE SOUTER, while agreeing that the Club's religious speech "may be characterized as proselytizing," thinks that it is even more clearly excludable from respondent's forum because it is essentially "an evangelical service of worship." But we have previously rejected the attempt to distinguish worship from other religious speech, saying that "the distinction has [no] intelligible content," and further, no "relevance" to the constitutional issue. Those holdings [127] are surely proved correct today by the dissenters' inability to agree, even between themselves, into which subcategory of religious speech the Club's activities fell. If the distinction did have content, it would be beyond the courts' competence to administer. And if courts (and other government officials) were competent, applying the distinction would require state monitoring of private, religious speech with a degree of pervasiveness that we have previously found unacceptable. I will not endorse an approach that suffers such a wondrous diversity of flaws.

* * *

With these words of explanation, I join the opinion of the Court.

. . . [130] JUSTICE STEVENS, dissenting.

The Milford Central School has invited the public to use its facilities for educational and recreational purposes, but not for "religious purposes." Speech for "religious purposes" may reasonably be understood to encompass three different categories. First, there is religious speech that is simply speech about a particular topic from a religious point of view. The film in *Lamb's Chapel v. Center Moriches Union Free School Dist.* (1993) illustrates this category. See *id.* at 388 (observing that the film series at issue in that case "would discuss Dr. [James] Dobson's views on the undermining influences of the media that could only be counterbalanced by returning to traditional, Christian family values instilled at an early stage"). Second, there is religious speech that amounts to worship, or its equivalent. Our decision in *Widmar v. Vincent* (1981), concerned such speech. See *id.* at 264–265 (describing the speech in question as involving "religious worship"). Third, there is an intermediate category that is aimed principally at proselytizing or inculcating belief in a particular religious faith.

A public entity may not generally exclude even religious worship from an open public forum. Similarly, a public entity that creates a limited public forum for the discussion of certain specified topics may not exclude a speaker simply because she approaches those topics from a religious point of view. Thus, in *Lamb's Chapel* we held that a public school that permitted its facilities to be used for the discussion of family issues and child rearing could not deny access to speakers presenting a religious point of view on those issues.

But, while a public entity may not censor speech about an authorized topic based on the point of view expressed [131] by the speaker, it has broad discretion to "preserve the property under its control for the use to which it is lawfully dedicated." *Greer v. Spock*, 424 U.S. 828, 836 (1976). Accordingly, "control over access to a nonpublic forum can be based on subject matter and speaker identity so long as the distinctions drawn are reasonable in light of the purpose served by the forum and are viewpoint neutral." *Cornelius v. NAACP Legal Defense & Ed. Fund, Inc.*, 473 U.S. 788, 806. The novel question that this case presents concerns the constitutionality of a public school's attempt to limit the scope of a public forum it has created. More specifically, the question is whether a school can, consistently with the First Amendment, create a limited public forum that admits the first type of religious speech without allowing the other two.

Distinguishing speech from a religious viewpoint, on the one hand, from religious proselytizing, on the other, is comparable to distinguishing meetings to discuss political issues from meetings whose principal purpose is to recruit new members to join a political organization. If a school decides to authorize after school discussions of current events in its classrooms, it may not exclude people from expressing their views simply because it dislikes their particular political opinions. But must it therefore allow organized political groups—for example, the Democratic Party, the Libertarian Party, or the Ku Klux Klan—to hold meetings, the principal purpose of which is not to discuss the current-events topic from their own unique point of view but rather to recruit others to join their respective groups? I think not. Such recruiting meetings may introduce divisiveness and [132] tend to separate young children into cliques that undermine the school's educational mission.

School officials may reasonably believe that evangelical meetings designed to convert children to a particular religious faith pose the same risk. And, just as a school may allow meetings to discuss current events from a political perspective without also allowing organized political recruitment, so too can a school allow discussion of topics such as moral development from a religious (or nonreligious) perspective without thereby opening its forum to religious proselytizing or worship. Moreover, any doubt on a question such as this should be resolved in a way that minimizes "intrusion by the Federal Government into the operation of our public schools," *Mergens*, 496 U.S. at 290 (STEVENS, J., dissenting).

The particular limitation of the forum at issue in this case is one that prohibits the use of the school's facilities for "religious purposes." It is clear that, by "religious purposes," the school district did not intend to exclude all speech from a religious point of view. [133] Instead, it sought only to exclude religious speech whose principal goal is to "promote the gospel." In other words, the school sought to allow the first type of religious speech while excluding the second and third types. As long as this is done in an evenhanded manner, I see no constitutional violation in such an effort. The line between the various categories of religious speech may be difficult to draw, but I think that the distinctions are valid, and that a school, particularly an elementary school, must be permitted to draw them.

This case is undoubtedly close. Nonetheless, regardless of whether the Good News Club's activities amount to "worship," it does seem clear, based on the facts in the record, that the school district correctly classified those activities as falling within the third category of religious speech and therefore beyond the scope of the school's limited public forum. In short, I am persuaded that the school district [134] could (and did) permissibly exclude from its limited public forum proselytizing religious speech that does not rise to the level of actual worship. I would therefore affirm the judgment of the Court of Appeals. . . .

Zelman v. Simmons-Harris

536 U.S. 639 (2002)

Vote: 5—Rehnquist, O'Connor, Scalia, Kennedy, Thomas
4—Stevens, Souter, Ginsburg, Breyer

Opinion announcing the opinion of the Court: Rehnquist
Concurring opinions: O'Connor, Thomas
Dissenting opinions: Stevens, Souter, Breyer

In 1995, a federal district court declared a "crisis of magnitude" and placed the entire Cleveland City School District under state control. Only one in ten district ninth graders could pass a basic proficiency examination, and more than two-thirds of district high school students either dropped or failed out before graduation. Of those students who managed to reach their senior year, one in every four still failed to graduate. At the time of litigation, more than seventy-five thousand children were enrolled in the Cleveland City School District, the majority of whom were from low-income and minority families.

As part of a broader undertaking to enhance the educational options of Cleveland's schoolchildren, the state of Ohio enacted the Pilot Project Scholarship Program. The program provided two forms of aid to parents in a covered district: (1) tuition aid in the form of scholarship vouchers for students to attend a participating public or private school of their parent's choosing, and (2) tutorial assistance grants for Cleveland students who chose to remain enrolled in public school. The program was open to religious and nonreligious schools in the Cleveland district, as well as to public schools in adjacent school districts. Participating private schools had to agree not to discriminate on the basis of race, religion, or ethnic background or to "advocate or foster unlawful behavior or teach hatred of any person or group on the basis of race, ethnicity, national origin, or religion." All participating schools, whether public or private, were required to accept students in accordance with rules and procedures established by the state superintendent.

Tuition aid was distributed to parents according to financial need. Families with incomes below 200 percent of the poverty line were given priority and were eligible to receive 90 percent of private school tuition up to $2,250. For these lowest-income families, participating private schools could not charge a parental copayment greater than $250. For all other families, the program paid 75 percent of tuition costs, up to $1,875, with *no copayment cap. These families received tuition aid only if the number of available scholarships (determined annually by the Ohio superintendent for public instruction) exceeded the number of low-income children who chose to participate. Where tuition aid was spent depended solely on where parents who received tuition aid chose to enroll their child. If parents chose a private school, checks were made payable to the parents, who then endorsed the checks over to the chosen school.*

The tutorial aid portion of the program provided tutorial assistance through grants to any student in a covered district who chose to remain in public school. Parents arranged for registered tutors to provide assistance to their children and then submitted bills for those services to the state for payment. Students from low-income families received 90 percent of the amount charged for such assistance up to $360. All other students received 75 percent of that amount. The number of tutorial assistance grants offered to students in a covered district had to equal the number of tuition aid scholarships provided to students enrolled at participating private or adjacent public schools.

Adjacent public schools were eligible to receive a $2,250 tuition grant for each program student accepted, in addition to the full amount of per-pupil state funding attributable to each additional student.

The program began operation within the Cleveland City School District during the 1996–1997 school year. In the 1999–2000 school year, fifty-six private schools participated in the program, forty-six (82 percent) of which had a religious affiliation. None of the public schools in districts adjacent to Cleveland elected to participate. At the time of litigation, more than thirty-seven hundred students participated in the scholarship program, most of whom (96 percent) enrolled in religiously affiliated schools. Of these students, 60 percent were from families at or below the poverty line. In the 1998–1999 school year, approximately fourteen hundred Cleveland public school students received tutorial aid.

REHNQUIST, C. J., delivered the opinion of the Court, in which O'CONNOR, SCALIA, KENNEDY, and THOMAS, JJ., joined.

[643] The State of Ohio has established a pilot program designed to provide educational choices to families with children who [644] reside in the Cleveland City School District. The question presented is whether this program offends the Establishment Clause of the United States Constitution. We hold that it does not. . . .

[648] The Establishment Clause of the First Amendment, applied to the States through the Fourteenth Amendment, prevents a State from enacting laws that have the "purpose" [649] or "effect" of advancing or inhibiting religion. *Agostini v. Felton*, 521 U.S. 203, 222–223 (1997). There is no dispute that the program challenged here was enacted for the valid secular purpose of providing educational assistance to poor children in a demonstrably failing public school system. Thus, the question presented is whether the Ohio program nonetheless has the forbidden "effect" of advancing or inhibiting religion.

To answer that question, our decisions have drawn a consistent distinction between government programs that provide aid directly to religious schools and programs of true private choice, in which government aid reaches religious schools only as a result of the genuine and independent choices of private individuals. While our jurisprudence with respect to the constitutionality of direct aid programs has "changed significantly" over the past two decades, *Agostini*, at 236, our jurisprudence with respect to true private choice programs has remained consistent and unbroken. Three times we have confronted Establishment Clause challenges to neutral government programs that provide aid directly to a broad class of individuals, who, in turn, direct the aid to religious schools or institutions of their own choosing. Three times we have rejected such challenges.

In *Mueller*, we rejected an Establishment Clause challenge to a Minnesota program authorizing tax deductions for various educational expenses, including private school tuition [650] costs, even though the great majority of the program's beneficiaries (96%) were parents of children in religious schools. We began by focusing on the class of beneficiaries, finding that because the class included "*all* parents," including parents with "children [who] attend nonsectarian private schools or sectarian private schools," 463 U.S. at 397 (emphasis in original), the program was "not readily subject to challenge under the Establishment Clause," *id.*, at 399. Then, viewing the program as a whole, we emphasized the principle of private choice, noting that public funds were made available to religious schools "only as a result of numerous, private choices of individual parents of school-age children." 463 U.S. at 399–400. This, we said, ensured that "'no imprimatur of state approval' can be deemed to have been conferred on any particular religion, or on religion generally." *Id.*, at 399. We thus found it irrelevant to the constitutional inquiry that the vast majority of beneficiaries were parents of children in religious schools, saying:

> "We would be loath to adopt a rule grounding the constitutionality of a facially neutral law on annual reports reciting the extent to which various classes of private citizens claimed benefits under the law." 463 U.S. at 401.

That the program was one of true private choice, with no evidence that the State deliberately skewed incentives toward religious schools, was sufficient for the program to survive scrutiny under the Establishment Clause.

In *Witters*, we used identical reasoning to reject an Establishment Clause challenge to a vocational scholarship program that provided tuition aid to a student studying at a religious institution to become a pastor. . . .

[651] Finally, in *Zobrest*, we applied *Mueller* and *Witters* to reject an Establishment Clause challenge to a federal program that permitted sign-language interpreters to assist deaf children enrolled in religious schools. . . .

[652] *Mueller*, *Witters*, and *Zobrest* thus make clear that where a government aid program is neutral with respect to religion, and provides assistance directly to a broad class of citizens who, in turn, direct government aid to religious schools wholly as a result of their own genuine and independent private choice, the program is not readily subject to challenge under the Establishment Clause. A program that shares these features permits government aid to reach religious institutions only by way of the deliberate choices of numerous individual recipients. The incidental advancement of a religious mission, or the perceived endorsement of a religious message, is reasonably attributable to the individual recipient, not to the government, whose role ends with the disbursement of benefits. As a plurality of this Court recently observed:

> "If numerous private choices, rather than the single choice of a government, determine the distribution of aid, pursuant to neutral eligibility criteria, then a government cannot, or at least cannot easily, grant special [653] favors that might lead to a religious establishment." *Mitchell*, 530 U.S. at 810.

It is precisely for these reasons that we have never found a program of true private choice to offend the Establishment Clause.

We believe that the program challenged here is a program of true private choice, consistent with *Mueller*, *Witters*, and *Zobrest*, and thus constitutional. As was true in those cases, the Ohio program is neutral in all respects toward religion. It is part of a general and multifaceted undertaking by the State of Ohio to provide educational opportunities to the children of a failed school district. It confers educational assistance directly to a broad class of individuals defined without reference to religion, i.e., any parent of a school-age child who resides in the Cleveland City School District. The program permits the participation of *all* schools within the district, religious or nonreligious. Adjacent public schools also may participate and have a financial incentive to do so. Program benefits are available to participating families on neutral terms, with no reference to religion. The only preference stated anywhere in the program is a preference for low-income families, who receive greater assistance and are given priority for admission at participating schools. . . .

[656] JUSTICE SOUTER speculates that because more private religious schools currently participate in the program, the program itself must somehow discourage the participation of private nonreligious schools. But Cleveland's preponderance of religiously affiliated [657] private schools certainly did not arise as a result of the program; it is a phenomenon common to many American cities. Indeed, by all accounts the program has captured a remarkable cross-section of private schools, religious and nonreligious. It is true that 82% of Cleveland's participating private schools are religious schools, but it is also true that 81% of private schools in Ohio are religious schools. To attribute constitutional significance to this figure, moreover, would lead to the absurd result that a neutral school-choice program might be permissible in some parts of Ohio, such as Columbus, where a lower percentage of private schools are religious schools but not in inner-city Cleveland, where Ohio has deemed such programs most sorely needed, but where the preponderance of religious schools happens to be greater. Likewise, an identical private choice program might be constitutional in some States, such as Maine or Utah, where less [658] than 45% of private schools are religious schools, but not in other States, such as Nebraska or Kansas, where over 90% of private schools are religious schools.

Respondents and JUSTICE SOUTER claim that even if we do not focus on the number of participating schools that are religious schools, we should attach constitutional significance to the fact that 96% of scholarship recipients have enrolled in religious schools. They claim that this alone proves parents lack genuine choice, even if no parent has ever said so. We need not consider this argument in detail, since it was flatly rejected in *Mueller*, where we found it irrelevant that 96% of parents taking deductions for tuition expenses paid tuition at religious schools. Indeed, we have recently found it irrelevant even to the constitutionality of a direct aid program that a vast majority of program benefits went to religious schools. The constitutionality of a neutral educational aid program simply does not turn on whether and why, in a particular area, at a particular time, most private schools are run by religious organizations, or most recipients choose to use the aid at a religious school. As we said in *Mueller*, "such an approach would scarcely provide the certainty that this field stands in need of, nor can we perceive principled standards by which such statistical evidence might be evaluated." 463 U.S. at 401. . . .

[662] In sum, the Ohio program is entirely neutral with respect to religion. It provides benefits directly to a wide spectrum of individuals, defined only by financial need and residence in a particular school district. It permits such individuals to exercise genuine choice among options public and private, secular and religious. The program is therefore a program of true private choice. In keeping with an unbroken line of [663] decisions rejecting challenges to similar programs, we hold that the program does not offend the Establishment Clause.

. . . [676] JUSTICE THOMAS, concurring.

Frederick Douglass once said that "education . . . means emancipation. It means light and liberty. It means the uplifting of the soul of man into the glorious light of truth, the light by which men can only be made free."[1] Today many of our inner-city public schools deny emancipation to urban minority students. Despite this Court's observation nearly 50 years ago in *Brown v. Board of Education* that "it is doubtful that any child may reasonably be expected to succeed in life if he is denied the opportunity of an education," 347 U.S. 483, 493 (1954), urban children have been forced into a system that continually fails them. These cases present an [677] example of such failures. Besieged by escalating financial problems and declining academic achievement, the Cleveland City School District was in the midst of an academic emergency when Ohio enacted its scholarship program.

The dissents and respondents wish to invoke the Establishment Clause of the First Amendment, as incorporated through the Fourteenth, to constrain a State's neutral efforts to provide greater educational opportunity for underprivileged minority students. Today's decision properly upholds the program as constitutional, and I join it in full.

I

This Court has often considered whether efforts to provide children with the best educational resources conflict with constitutional limitations. Attempts to provide aid to religious schools or to allow some degree of religious involvement in public schools have generated significant controversy and litigation as States try to navigate the line between the secular and the religious in education. We have recently decided several cases challenging federal aid programs that include religious schools. To determine whether a federal program survives scrutiny under the Establishment Clause, we have considered whether it has a secular purpose and whether it has the primary effect of advancing or inhibiting religion. I agree with the Court that Ohio's program easily passes muster under our stringent test, but, as a matter of first principles, I question whether this test should be applied to the States.

[678] The Establishment Clause of the First Amendment states that "Congress shall make no law respecting an establishment of religion." On its face, this provision places no limit on the States with regard to religion. The Establishment Clause originally protected States, and by extension their citizens, from the imposition of an established religion by the Federal Government. Whether and how this Clause should constrain state action under the Fourteenth Amendment is a more difficult question.

The Fourteenth Amendment fundamentally restructured the relationship between individuals and the States and ensured that States would not deprive citizens of liberty without due process of law. It guarantees citizenship to all individuals born or naturalized in the United States and provides that "no State shall make or enforce any law which shall abridge the privileges or immunities of citizens of the United States; nor shall any State deprive any person of life, liberty, or property, without due process of law; nor deny to any person within its jurisdiction the equal protection of the laws." As Justice Harlan noted, the Fourteenth Amendment "added greatly to the dignity and glory of American citizenship, and to the security of personal liberty." *Plessy v. Ferguson*, 163 U.S. 537, 555

---

1. The Blessings of Liberty and Education: An Address Delivered in Manassas, Virginia, on 3 September 1894, in 5 *The Frederick Douglass Papers* 623 (J. Blassingame & J. McKivigan eds. 1992) (hereinafter *Douglass Papers*).

(1896) (dissenting opinion). When rights are incorporated against the States through the Fourteenth Amendment they should advance, not constrain, individual liberty.

Consequently, in the context of the Establishment Clause, it may well be that state action should be evaluated on different terms than similar action by the Federal Government. "States, while bound to observe strict neutrality, should be freer to experiment with involvement [in religion]—on a neutral [679] basis—than the Federal Government." *Walz v. Tax Comm'n of City of New York*, 397 U.S. 664, 699 (1970) (Harlan, J., concurring). Thus, while the Federal Government may "make no law respecting an establishment of religion," the States may pass laws that include or touch on religious matters so long as these laws do not impede free exercise rights or any other individual religious liberty interest. By considering the particular religious liberty right alleged to be invaded by a State, federal courts can strike a proper balance between the demands of the Fourteenth Amendment on the one hand and the federalism prerogatives of States on the other.

Whatever the textual and historical merits of incorporating the Establishment Clause, I can accept that the Fourteenth Amendment protects religious liberty rights.[4] But I [680] cannot accept its use to oppose neutral programs of school choice through the incorporation of the Establishment Clause. There would be a tragic irony in converting the Fourteenth Amendment's guarantee of individual liberty into a prohibition on the exercise of educational choice.

II

The wisdom of allowing States greater latitude in dealing with matters of religion and education can be easily appreciated in this context. Respondents advocate using the Fourteenth Amendment to handcuff the State's ability to experiment with education. But without education one can hardly exercise the civic, political, and personal freedoms conferred by the Fourteenth Amendment. Faced with a severe educational crisis, the State of Ohio enacted wide-ranging educational reform that allows voluntary participation of private and religious schools in educating poor urban children otherwise condemned to failing public schools. The program does not force any individual to submit to religious indoctrination or education. It simply gives parents a greater choice as to where and in what manner to educate their children. This is a choice that those with greater means have routinely exercised.

[681] Cleveland parents now have a variety of educational choices. There are traditional public schools, magnet schools, and privately run community schools, in addition to the scholarship program. Currently, 46 of the 56 private schools participating in the scholarship program are church affiliated (35 are Catholic), and 96 percent of students in the program attend religious schools. Thus, were the Court to disallow the inclusion of religious schools, Cleveland children could use their scholarships at only 10 private schools. . . .

---

4. In particular, these rights inhere in the Free Exercise Clause, which unlike the Establishment Clause protects individual liberties of religious worship. "That the central value embodied in the First Amendment—and, more particularly, in the guarantee of 'liberty' contained in the Fourteenth—is the safeguarding of an individual's right to free exercise of his religion has been consistently recognized." *Schempp*, at 312 (Stewart, J., dissenting). See also Amar, *The Bill of Rights as a Constitution*, 100 Yale L. J. 1131, 1159 (1991) ("The free exercise clause was paradigmatically about citizen rights, not state rights; it thus invites incorporation. Indeed, this clause was specially concerned with the plight of minority religions, and thus meshes especially well with the minority-rights thrust of the Fourteenth Amendment"); Lietzau, *Rediscovering the Establishment Clause: Federalism and the Rollback of Incorporation*, 39 DePaul L. Rev. 1191, 1206–1207 (1990).

* * *

[683] Ten States have enacted some form of publicly funded private school choice as one means of raising the quality of education provided to underprivileged urban children. These programs address the root of the problem with failing urban public schools that disproportionately affect minority students. Society's other solution to these educational failures is often to provide racial preferences in higher education. Such preferences, however, run afoul of the Fourteenth Amendment's prohibition against distinctions based on race. By contrast, school choice programs that involve religious schools [684] appear unconstitutional only to those who would twist the Fourteenth Amendment against itself by expansively incorporating the Establishment Clause. Converting the Fourteenth Amendment from a guarantee of opportunity to an obstacle against education reform distorts our constitutional values and disserves those in the greatest need.

As Frederick Douglass poignantly noted, "no greater benefit can be bestowed upon a long benighted people, than giving to them, as we are here earnestly this day endeavoring to do, the means of an education."[10]

JUSTICE STEVENS, dissenting.

Is a law that authorizes the use of public funds to pay for the indoctrination of thousands of grammar school children in particular religious faiths a "law respecting an establishment of religion" within the meaning of the First Amendment? In answering that question, I think we should ignore three factual matters that are discussed at length by my colleagues.

First, the severe educational crisis that confronted the Cleveland City School District when Ohio enacted its voucher program is not a matter that should affect our appraisal of its constitutionality. In the 1999–2000 school year, that program provided relief to less than five percent of the students enrolled in the district's schools. The solution to the disastrous conditions that prevented over 90 percent of the student body from meeting basic proficiency standards obviously required massive improvements unrelated to the voucher program. Of course, the emergency may have [685] given some families a powerful motivation to leave the public school system and accept religious indoctrination that they would otherwise have avoided, but that is not a valid reason for upholding the program.

Second, the wide range of choices that have been made available to students *within the public school system* has no bearing on the question whether the State may pay the tuition for students who wish to reject public education entirely and attend private schools that will provide them with a sectarian education. The fact that the vast majority of the voucher recipients who have entirely rejected public education receive religious indoctrination at state expense does, however, support the claim that the law is one "respecting an establishment of religion." The State may choose to divide up its public schools into a dozen different options and label them magnet schools, community schools, or whatever else it decides to call them, but the State is still required to provide a public education and it is the State's decision to fund private school education over and above its traditional obligation that is at issue in these cases.

Third, the voluntary character of the private choice to prefer a parochial education over an education in the public school system seems to me quite irrelevant to the question

---

10. *Douglass Papers* 623.

whether the government's choice to pay for religious indoctrination is constitutionally permissible. Today, however, the Court seems to have decided that the mere fact that a family that cannot afford a private education wants its children educated in a parochial school is a sufficient justification for this use of public funds.

For the reasons stated by JUSTICE SOUTER and JUSTICE BREYER, I am convinced that the Court's decision is profoundly misguided. Admittedly, in reaching that conclusion [686] I have been influenced by my understanding of the impact of religious strife on the decisions of our forbears to migrate to this continent, and on the decisions of neighbors in the Balkans, Northern Ireland, and the Middle East to mistrust one another. Whenever we remove a brick from the wall that was designed to separate religion and government, we increase the risk of religious strife and weaken the foundation of our democracy.

I respectfully dissent.

JUSTICE SOUTER, with whom JUSTICE STEVENS, JUSTICE GINSBURG, and JUSTICE BREYER join, dissenting.

The Court's majority holds that the Establishment Clause is no bar to Ohio's payment of tuition at private religious elementary and middle schools under a scheme that systematically provides tax money to support the schools' religious missions. The occasion for the legislation thus upheld is the condition of public education in the city of Cleveland. The record indicates that the schools are failing to serve their objective, and the vouchers in issue here are said to be needed to provide adequate alternatives to them. If there were an excuse for giving short shrift to the Establishment Clause, it would probably apply here. But there is no excuse. Constitutional limitations are placed on government to preserve constitutional values in hard cases, like these. "Constitutional lines have to be drawn, and on one side of every one of them is an otherwise sympathetic case that provokes impatience with the Constitution and with the line. But constitutional lines are the price of constitutional government." *Agostini v. Felton*, 521 U.S. 203, 254 (1997) (SOUTER, J., dissenting). I therefore respectfully dissent.

The applicability of the Establishment Clause to public funding of benefits to religious schools was settled in *Everson v. Board of Ed. of Ewing*, 330 U.S. 1 (1947), which inaugurated [687] the modern era of establishment doctrine. The Court stated the principle in words from which there was no dissent:

> "No tax in any amount, large or small, can be levied to support any religious activities or institutions, whatever they may be called, or whatever form they may adopt to teach or practice religion." *Id.*, at 16.

The Court has never in so many words repudiated this statement, let alone, in so many words, overruled *Everson*.

Today, however, the majority holds that the Establishment Clause is not offended by Ohio's Pilot Project Scholarship Program, under which students may be eligible to receive as much as $2,250 in the form of tuition vouchers transferable to religious schools. In the city of Cleveland the overwhelming proportion of large appropriations for voucher money must be spent on religious schools if it is to be spent at all, and will be spent in amounts that cover almost all of tuition. The money will thus pay for eligible students' instruction not only in secular subjects but in religion as well, in schools that can fairly be characterized as founded to teach religious doctrine and to imbue teaching in all subjects with a religious dimension. Public tax money will pay at a systemic level for teaching the covenant with Israel and Mosaic law in Jewish schools, the primacy of the Apostle Peter and the Papacy in Catholic schools, the truth of reformed Christianity in Protestant schools, and the revelation to the Prophet in Muslim schools, to speak only of major religious groupings in the Republic.

[688] How can a Court consistently leave *Everson* on the books and approve the Ohio vouchers? The answer is that it cannot. It is only by ignoring *Everson* that the majority can claim to rest on traditional law in its invocation of neutral aid provisions and private choice to sanction the Ohio law. It is, moreover, only by ignoring the meaning of neutrality and private choice themselves that the majority can even pretend to rest today's decision on those criteria. . . .

II

. . . [703] It is not, of course, that I think even a genuine choice criterion is up to the task of the Establishment Clause when substantial state funds go to religious teaching; the discussion in Part III shows that it is not. The point is simply that if the majority wishes to claim that choice is a criterion, it must define choice in a way that can function as a criterion with a practical capacity to screen something out.

If, contrary to the majority, we ask the right question about genuine choice to use the vouchers, the answer shows that something is influencing choices in a way that aims the money in a religious direction: of 56 private schools in the district participating in the voucher program (only 53 of which accepted voucher students in 1999–2000), 46 of them are religious; 96.6% of all voucher recipients go to religious schools, only 3.4% to nonreligious ones. Unfortunately for the majority position, there is no explanation for this that suggests the religious direction results simply from free choices by parents. One answer to these statistics, for example, which would be consistent with the genuine choice claimed to be operating, might be that 96.6% of families choosing to avail themselves of vouchers choose to educate their children in schools of their own religion. This would not, in my view, render the scheme constitutional, but it would speak to the majority's choice criterion. [704] Evidence shows, however, that almost two out of three families using vouchers to send their children to religious schools did not embrace the religion of those schools.[11] The families made it clear they had not chosen the schools because they wished their children to be proselytized in a religion not their own, or in any religion, but because of educational opportunity.[12]

Even so, the fact that some 2,270 students chose to apply their vouchers to schools of other religions might be consistent with true choice if the students "chose" their religious schools over a wide array of private nonreligious options, or if it could be shown generally that Ohio's program had no effect on educational choices and thus no impermissible effect of advancing religious education. But both possibilities are contrary to fact. First, even if all existing nonreligious private schools in Cleveland were willing to accept large numbers of voucher students, only a few more than the 129 currently enrolled in such schools would be able to attend, as the total enrollment at all nonreligious

---

11. For example, 40% of families who sent their children to private schools for the first time under the voucher program were Baptist, but only one school, enrolling 44 voucher students, is Baptist.

12. When parents were surveyed as to their motives for enrolling their children in the voucher program, 96.4% cited a better education than available in the public schools, and 95% said their children's safety. When asked specifically in one study to identify the most important factor in selecting among participating private schools, 60% of parents mentioned academic quality, teacher quality, or the substance of what is taught (presumably secular); only 15% mentioned the religious affiliation of the school as even a consideration.

private schools in Cleveland for kindergarten through eighth grade is only 510 children and there is no indication that these schools have many open seats. Second, the [705] $2,500 cap that the program places on tuition for participating low-income pupils has the effect of curtailing the participation of nonreligious schools: "nonreligious schools with higher tuition (about $4,000) stated that they could afford to accommodate just a few voucher students." By comparison, the average tuition at participating Catholic schools in Cleveland in 1999–2000 was $1,592, almost $1,000 below the cap.

[706] Of course, the obvious fix would be to increase the value of vouchers so that existing nonreligious private and non-Catholic religious schools would be able to enroll more voucher students, and to provide incentives for educators to create new such schools given that few presently exist. Private choice, if as robust as that available to the seminarian in *Witters*, would then be "true private choice" under the majority's criterion. But it is simply unrealistic to presume that parents of elementary and middle schoolchildren in Cleveland will have a range of secular and religious choices even arguably comparable to the statewide program for vocational and higher education in *Witters*. And to get to that hypothetical point would require that such massive financial support be made available to religion as to disserve every objective of the Establishment Clause even more than the present scheme does.[16]

[707] There is, in any case, no way to interpret the 96.6% of current voucher money going to religious schools as reflecting a free and genuine choice by the families that apply for vouchers. The 96.6% reflects, instead, the fact that too few nonreligious school desks are available and few but religious schools can afford to accept more than a handful of voucher students. And contrary to the majority's assertion, public schools in adjacent districts hardly have a financial incentive to participate in the Ohio voucher program, and none has. For the overwhelming number of children in the voucher scheme, the only alternative to the public schools is religious. And it is entirely irrelevant that the State did not deliberately design the network of private schools for the sake of channeling money into religious institutions. The criterion is one of genuinely free choice on the part of the private individuals who choose, and a Hobson's choice is not a choice, whatever the reason for being Hobsonian.

III

I do not dissent merely because the majority has misapplied its own law, for even if I assumed *arguendo* that the [708] majority's formal criteria were satisfied on the facts, today's conclusion would be profoundly at odds with the Constitution. Proof of this is clear on two levels. The first is circumstantial, in the now discarded symptom of violation, the substantial dimension of the aid. The second is direct, in the defiance of every objective supposed to be served by the bar against establishment.

A

The scale of the aid to religious schools approved today is unprecedented, both in the number of dollars and in the proportion of systemic school expenditure supported. . . .

---

16. The majority notes that I argue both that the Ohio program is unconstitutional because the voucher amount is too low to create real private choice and that any greater expenditure would be unconstitutional as well. The majority is dead right about this, and there is no inconsistency here: any voucher program that satisfied the majority's requirement of "true private choice" would be even more egregiously unconstitutional than the current scheme due to the substantial amount of aid to religious teaching that would be required.

[710] The Cleveland voucher program has cost Ohio taxpayers $33 million since its implementation in 1996 ($28 million in voucher payments, $5 million in administrative costs), and its cost was expected to exceed $8 million in the 2001–2002 school year. These tax-raised funds are on top of the textbooks, reading and math tutors, laboratory equipment, and the like that Ohio provides to private schools, worth roughly $600 per child.

The gross amounts of public money contributed are symptomatic of the scope of what the taxpayers' money buys for a broad class of religious-school students. In paying for practically the full amount of tuition for thousands of qualifying students, the scholarships purchase everything that tuition purchases, be it instruction in math or indoctrination in faith. The consequences [711] of "substantial" aid hypothesized in *Meek* are realized here: the majority makes no pretense that substantial amounts of tax money are not systematically underwriting religious practice and indoctrination.

B

It is virtually superfluous to point out that every objective underlying the prohibition of religious establishment is betrayed by this scheme, but something has to be said about the enormity of the violation. I anticipated these objectives earlier in discussing *Everson*, which cataloged them, the first being respect for freedom of conscience. Jefferson described it as the idea that no one "shall be compelled to . . . support any religious worship, place, or ministry whatsoever," *A Bill for Establishing Religious Freedom*, even a "teacher of his own religious persuasion," *ibid.*, and Madison thought it violated by any "authority which can force a citizen to contribute three pence . . . of his property for the support of any . . . establishment." *Memorial and Remonstrance* ¶ 3. "Any tax to establish religion is antithetical to the command that the minds of men always be wholly free," *Mitchell*, 530 U.S. at 871 (SOUTER, J., dissenting). Madison's objection to three pence has simply been lost in the majority's formalism.

As for the second objective, to save religion from its own corruption, Madison wrote of the "experience . . . that ecclesiastical [712] establishments, instead of maintaining the purity and efficacy of Religion, have had a contrary operation." *Memorial and Remonstrance* ¶ 7. In Madison's time, the manifestations were "pride and indolence in the Clergy; ignorance and servility in the laity[,] in both, superstition, bigotry and persecution," *ibid.*; in the 21st century, the risk is one of "corrosive secularism" to religious schools, *Ball*, 473 U.S. at 385, and the specific threat is to the primacy of the schools' mission to educate the children of the faithful according to the unaltered precepts of their faith. Even "the favored religion may be compromised as political figures reshape the religion's beliefs for their own purposes; it may be reformed as government largesse brings government regulation." *Lee v. Weisman*, 505 U.S. 577, 608 (1992) (Blackmun, J., concurring).

The risk is already being realized. In Ohio, for example, a condition of receiving government money under the program is that participating religious schools may not "discriminate on the basis of . . . religion," Ohio Rev. Code Ann. § 3313.976 (A)(4) (West Supp. 2002), which means the school may not give admission preferences to children who are members of the patron faith; children of a parish are generally consigned to the same admission lotteries as non-believers. This indeed was the exact object of a 1999 amendment repealing the portion of a predecessor statute that had allowed an admission preference for "children . . . whose parents are affiliated with any organization that provides financial support to the school, at the discretion of the school." § 3313.977 (A)(1)(d) (West 1999). Nor is the State's religious antidiscrimination restriction limited to student admission policies:

by its terms, a participating religious school may well be forbidden to choose a member of its own clergy to serve as teacher or principal over a layperson of a different religion claiming [713] equal qualification for the job. Indeed, a separate condition that "the school . . . not . . . teach hatred of any person or group on the basis of . . . religion," § 3313.976 (A)(6) (West Supp. 2002), could be understood (or subsequently broadened) to prohibit religions from teaching traditionally legitimate articles of faith as to the error, sinfulness, or ignorance of others, if they want government money for their schools.

[714] For perspective on this foot-in-the-door of religious regulation, it is well to remember that the money has barely begun to flow. . . .

[715] When government aid goes up, so does reliance on it; the only thing likely to go down is independence. If Justice Douglas in *Allen* was concerned with state agencies, influenced by powerful religious groups, choosing the textbooks that parochial schools would use, 392 U.S. at 265 (dissenting opinion), how much more is there reason to wonder when dependence will become great enough to give the State of Ohio an effective veto over basic decisions on the content of curriculums? A day will come when religious schools will learn what political leverage can do, just as Ohio's politicians are now getting a lesson in the leverage exercised by religion.

Increased voucher spending is not, however, the sole portent of growing regulation of religious practice in the school, for state mandates to moderate religious teaching may well be the most obvious response to the third concern behind the ban on establishment, its inextricable link with social conflict. As appropriations for religious subsidy rise, competition for the money will tap sectarian religion's capacity for discord. "Public money devoted to payment of religious costs, educational or other, brings the quest for more. It brings too the struggle of sect against sect for the larger share or for any. Here one by numbers alone will benefit most, there another." *Id.*, at 53. (Rutledge, J., dissenting).

JUSTICE BREYER has addressed this issue in his own dissenting opinion, which I join, and here it is enough to say that the intensity of the expectable friction can be gauged by realizing that the scramble for money will energize not only contending sectarians, but taxpayers who take their liberty of conscience seriously. Religious teaching at taxpayer [716] expense simply cannot be cordoned from taxpayer politics, and every major religion currently espouses social positions that provoke intense opposition. Not all taxpaying Protestant citizens, for example, will be content to underwrite the teaching of the Roman Catholic Church condemning the death penalty. Nor will all of America's Muslims acquiesce in paying for the endorsement of the religious Zionism taught in many religious Jewish schools, which combines "a nationalistic sentiment" in support of Israel with a "deeply religious" element. Nor will every secular taxpayer be content to support Muslim views on differential treatment of the sexes, or, for that matter, to fund the espousal of a wife's obligation of obedience to her husband, presumably taught in any schools adopting the articles of faith of the Southern Baptist Convention. Views like these, and innumerable others, have been safe in the sectarian pulpits and classrooms of this Nation not only because the Free Exercise Clause protects them directly, but because the ban on supporting religious establishment has protected free exercise, by keeping it relatively private. With the arrival of vouchers in religious schools, that privacy will go, and along with it will go confidence that religious disagreement will stay moderate.

* * *

If the divisiveness permitted by today's majority is to be avoided in the short term, it will be avoided only by action [717] of the political branches at the state and national levels. Legislatures not driven to desperation by the problems of public education may be able to see the threat in vouchers negotiable in sectarian schools. Perhaps even cities with problems like Cleveland's will perceive the danger, now that they know a federal court will not save them from it.

My own course as a judge on the Court cannot, however, simply be to hope that the political branches will save us from the consequences of the majority's decision. *Everson*'s statement is still the touchstone of sound law, even though the reality is that in the matter of educational aid the Establishment Clause has largely been read away. True, the majority has not approved vouchers for religious schools alone, or aid earmarked for religious instruction. But no scheme so clumsy will ever get before us, and in the cases that we may see, like these, the Establishment Clause is largely silenced. I do not have the option to leave it silent, and I hope that a future Court will reconsider today's dramatic departure from basic Establishment Clause principle.

JUSTICE BREYER, with whom JUSTICE STEVENS and JUSTICE SOUTER join, dissenting.

I join JUSTICE SOUTER's opinion, and I agree substantially with JUSTICE STEVENS. I write separately, however, to emphasize the risk that publicly financed voucher programs pose in terms of religiously based social conflict. I do so because I believe that the Establishment Clause concern for protecting the Nation's social fabric from religious conflict poses an overriding obstacle to the implementation of this well-intentioned school voucher program. And by explaining the nature of the concern, I hope to demonstrate why, in my view, "parental choice" cannot significantly alleviate the constitutional problem.

I

The First Amendment begins with a prohibition, that "Congress shall make no law respecting an establishment of [718] religion," and a guarantee, that the government shall not prohibit "the free exercise thereof." These Clauses embody an understanding, reached in the 17th century after decades of religious war, that liberty and social stability demand a religious tolerance that respects the religious views of all citizens, permits those citizens to "worship God in their own way," and allows all families to "teach their children and to form their characters" as they wish. C. Radcliffe, *The Law & Its Compass* 71 (1960). The Clauses reflect the Framers' vision of an American Nation free of the religious strife that had long plagued the nations of Europe. Whatever the Framers might have thought about particular 18th century school funding practices, they undeniably intended an interpretation of the Religion Clauses that would implement this basic First Amendment objective.

In part for this reason, the Court's 20th century Establishment Clause cases—both those limiting the practice of religion in public schools and those limiting the public funding of private religious education—focused directly upon social conflict, potentially created when government becomes involved in religious education. In *Engel v. Vitale*, 370 U.S. 421 (1962), the Court held that the Establishment Clause forbids prayer in public elementary and secondary schools. It did so in part because it recognized the "anguish, hardship and bitter strife that could come when zealous religious groups struggle with one another to obtain the Government's stamp of approval. . . ." *Id.*, at 429. And it added:

"The history of governmentally established religion, both in England and in this country, showed that whenever [719] government had allied itself with one particular form of religion, the inevitable result had been that it had incurred the hatred, disrespect and even contempt of those who held contrary beliefs." *Id.*, at 431.

In *Lemon v. Kurtzman*, 403 U.S. 602, 29 L. Ed. 2d 745, 91 S. Ct. 2105 (1971), the Court held that the Establishment Clause forbids state funding, through salary supplements, of religious school teachers. It did so in part because of the "threat" that this funding would create religious "divisiveness" that would harm "the normal political process." *Id.*, at 622. The Court explained:

"Political debate and division . . . are normal and healthy manifestations of our democratic system of government, but political division along religious lines was one of the principal evils against which [the First Amendment's religious clauses were] . . . intended to protect." *Ibid.*

And in *Committee for Public Ed. & Religious Liberty v. Nyquist*, 413 U.S. 756, 794 (1973), the Court struck down a state statute that, much like voucher programs, provided aid for parents whose children attended religious schools, explaining that the "assistance of the sort here involved carries grave potential for . . . continuing political strife over aid to religion." . . .

[721] These historical circumstances suggest that the Court, applying the Establishment Clause through the Fourteenth Amendment to 20th century American society, faced an interpretive dilemma that was in part practical. The Court appreciated the religious diversity of contemporary American society. It realized that the status quo favored some religions at the expense of others. And it understood the Establishment Clause to prohibit (among other things) any such favoritism. Yet *how* did the Clause achieve that objective? Did it simply require the government to give each religion an equal chance to introduce religion into the primary schools—a kind of "equal opportunity" approach to the interpretation of the Establishment Clause? Or, did that Clause avoid government favoritism of some religions by insisting upon "separation"—that the government achieve [722] equal treatment by removing itself from the business of providing religious education for children? This interpretive choice arose in respect both to religious activities in public schools and government aid to private education.

In both areas the Court concluded that the Establishment Clause required "separation," in part because an "equal opportunity" approach was not workable. With respect to religious activities in the public schools, how could the Clause require public primary and secondary school teachers, when reading prayers or the Bible, *only* to treat all religions alike? In many places there were too many religions, too diverse a set of religious practices, too many whose spiritual beliefs denied the virtue of formal religious training. This diversity made it difficult, if not impossible, to devise meaningful forms of "equal treatment" by providing an "equal opportunity" for all to introduce their own religious practices into the public schools.

With respect to government aid to private education, did not history show that efforts to obtain equivalent funding for the private education of children whose parents did not hold popular religious beliefs only exacerbated religious strife? As Justice Rutledge recognized:

"Public money devoted to payment of religious costs, educational or other, brings the quest for more. It brings too the struggle of sect against sect for the larger share or for any. Here one [religious sect] by numbers [of adherents] alone will benefit most, there another. This is precisely the history of societies which have had an established religion and dissident groups." *Everson v. Board of Ed. of Ewing*, 330 U.S. 1, 53–54 (1947) (dissenting opinion).

The upshot is the development of constitutional doctrine that reads the Establishment Clause as avoiding religious strife, *not* by providing every religion with an *equal opportunity* (say, to secure state funding or to pray in the public [723] schools), but by drawing fairly clear lines of *separation* between church and state—at least where the heartland of religious belief, such as primary religious education, is at issue.

II

The principle underlying these cases—avoiding religiously based social conflict—remains of great concern. As religiously diverse as America had become when the Court decided its major 20th century Establishment Clause cases, we are exponentially more diverse today. America boasts more than 55 different religious groups and subgroups with a significant number of members. Major religions include, among others, Protestants, Catholics, Jews, Muslims, Buddhists, Hindus, and Sikhs. And several of these major religions contain different subsidiary sects with different religious beliefs. Newer Christian immigrant groups are "expressing their Christianity in languages, customs, and independent churches that are barely recognizable, and often controversial, for European-ancestry Catholics and Protestants." H. Ebaugh & J. Chafetz, *Religion and the New Immigrants: Continuities and Adaptations in Immigrant Congregations* 4 (Abridged Student ed. 2002).

Under these modern-day circumstances, how is the "equal opportunity" principle to work—without risking the "struggle of sect against sect" against which Justice Rutledge warned? School voucher programs finance the religious education of the young. And, if widely adopted, they may well provide billions of dollars that will do so. Why will different religions not become concerned about, and seek to influence, the criteria used to channel this money to religious schools? Why will they not want to examine the implementation of the programs that provide this money—to determine, for example, [724] whether implementation has biased a program toward or against particular sects, or whether recipient religious schools are adequately fulfilling a program's criteria? If so, just how is the State to resolve the resulting controversies without provoking legitimate fears of the kinds of religious favoritism that, in so religiously diverse a Nation, threaten social dissension?

Consider the voucher program here at issue. That program insists that the religious school accept students of all religions. Does that criterion treat fairly groups whose religion forbids them to do so? The program also insists that no participating school "advocate or foster unlawful behavior or teach hatred of any person or group on the basis of race, ethnicity, national origin, or religion." Ohio Rev. Code Ann. § 3313.976 (A)(6) (West Supp. 2002). And it requires the State to "revoke the registration of any school if, after a hearing, the superintendent determines that the school is in violation" of the program's rules. § 3313.976 (B). As one *amicus* argues, "it is difficult to imagine a more divisive activity" than the appointment of state officials as referees to determine whether a particular religious doctrine "teaches hatred or advocates lawlessness."

How are state officials to adjudicate claims that one religion or another is advocating, for example, civil disobedience in response to unjust laws, the use of illegal drugs in a religious ceremony, or resort to force to call attention to what it views as an immoral social practice? What kind of public hearing will there be in response to claims that one religion or another is continuing to teach a view of history that casts members of other religions in the worst possible light? How will the public react to government funding for schools that take controversial religious positions on topics that are of current popular interest—say, the conflict in the Middle East or the war on terrorism? Yet any major funding program [725] for primary religious education will require criteria. And the selection of those criteria, as well as their application, inevitably pose problems that are divisive. Efforts to respond to these problems not only will seriously entangle church and state but also will promote division among religious groups, as one group or another fears (often legitimately) that it will receive unfair treatment at the hands of the government.

I recognize that other nations, for example Great Britain and France, have in the past reconciled religious school funding and religious freedom without creating serious strife. Yet British and French societies are religiously more homogeneous—and it bears noting that recent waves of immigration have begun to create problems of social division there as well.

In a society as religiously diverse as ours, the Court has recognized that we must rely on the Religion Clauses of the First Amendment to protect against religious strife, particularly when what is at issue is an area as central to religious belief as the shaping, through primary education, of the next generation's minds and spirits.

[726] III

I concede that the Establishment Clause currently permits States to channel various forms of assistance to religious schools, for example, transportation costs for students, computers, and secular texts. States now certify the nonsectarian educational content of religious school education. Yet the consequence has not been great turmoil.

School voucher programs differ, however, in both *kind* and *degree* from aid programs upheld in the past. They differ in kind because they direct financing to a core function of the church: the teaching of religious truths to young children. For that reason the constitutional demand for "separation" is of particular constitutional concern.

Private schools that participate in Ohio's program, for example, recognize the importance of primary religious education, for they pronounce that their goals are to "communicate the gospel," "provide opportunities to . . . experience a faith community," "provide . . . for growth in prayer," and "provide [727] instruction in religious truths and values." History suggests, not that such private school teaching of religion is undesirable, but that *government funding* of this kind of religious endeavor is far more contentious than providing funding for secular textbooks, computers, vocational training, or even funding for adults who wish to obtain a college education at a religious university. Contrary to JUSTICE O'CONNOR's opinion, history also shows that government involvement in religious primary education is far more divisive than state property tax exemptions for religious institutions or tax deductions for charitable contributions, both of which come far closer to exemplifying the neutrality that distinguishes, for example, fire protection on the one hand from direct monetary assistance on the other. Federal aid to religiously based hospitals is even further removed from education, which lies at the heartland of religious belief.

Vouchers also differ in *degree*. The aid programs recently upheld by the Court involved limited amounts of aid to religion. But the majority's analysis here appears to permit a considerable shift of taxpayer dollars from public secular schools to private religious schools. That fact, combined with the use to which these dollars will be put, exacerbates the conflict problem. State aid that takes the form of peripheral secular items, with prohibitions against diversion of funds to religious teaching, holds significantly less potential for social division. In this respect as well, the secular aid upheld in *Mitchell* differs dramatically from the present case. Although it was conceivable that minor amounts of money could have, contrary to the statute, found their way to the religious activities of the recipients, that case is at worst the camel's nose, while the litigation before us is the camel itself.

[728] IV

I do not believe that the "parental choice" aspect of the voucher program sufficiently offsets the concerns I have mentioned. Parental choice cannot help the taxpayer who does not want to finance the religious education of children. It will not always help the parent who may see little real choice between inadequate nonsectarian public education and adequate education at a school whose religious teachings are contrary to his own. It will not satisfy religious minorities unable to participate because they are too few in number to support the creation of their own private schools. It will not satisfy groups whose religious beliefs preclude them from participating in a government-sponsored program, and who may well feel ignored as government funds primarily support the education of children in the doctrines of the dominant religions. And it does little to ameliorate the entanglement problems or the related problems of social division that Part II describes. Consequently, the fact that the parent may choose which school can cash the government's voucher check does not alleviate the Establishment Clause concerns associated with voucher programs.

V

The Court, in effect, turns the clock back. It adopts, under the name of "neutrality," an interpretation of the Establishment Clause that this Court rejected more than half a century ago. In its view, the parental choice that offers each religious group a kind of equal opportunity to secure government funding overcomes the Establishment Clause concern for social concord. An earlier Court found that "equal opportunity" principle insufficient; it read the Clause as insisting upon greater separation of church and state, at least in respect to primary education. In a society composed of many different religious creeds, I fear that this present departure from the Court's earlier understanding risks creating a form of religiously [729] based conflict potentially harmful to the Nation's social fabric. Because I believe the Establishment Clause was written in part to avoid this kind of conflict, and for reasons set forth by JUSTICE SOUTER and JUSTICE STEVENS, I respectfully dissent.

58

Locke v. Davey

540 U.S. 712 (2004)

Vote: 7—Rehnquist, Stevens, O'Connor, Kennedy, Souter, Ginsburg, Breyer
   2—Scalia, Thomas

Opinion announcing the opinion of the Court: Rehnquist
Dissenting opinions: Scalia, Thomas

In 1999, the state of Washington established its Promise Scholarship Program to assist academically gifted students with college education expenses. Scholarship eligibility was based on academic, income, and enrollment requirements. Eligible students, first, had to graduate from a Washington public or private high school and either graduate in the top 15 percent of their graduating class or attain on the first attempt a cumulative score of at least twelve hundred on the Scholastic Assessment Test I (or, in lieu of the SAT, a score of twenty-seven or better on the American College Test). Second, the student's family income had to be less than 135 percent of the state's median. Finally, the student had to enroll "at least half time in an eligible postsecondary institution in the state of Washington" and could not pursue a degree in "theology" at that institution while receiving the scholarship. Private postsecondary institutions, including those religiously affiliated, qualified as "eligible postsecondary institution[s]" if they were accredited by a nationally recognized accrediting body. The scholarship was worth $1,125 for academic year 1999–2000 and $1,542 for 2000–2001.

The "theology" degree exclusion was instituted to comply with Washington's state constitution, which contained the following provisions:

> Art. I, § 11: "No public money or property shall be appropriated for or applied to any religious worship, exercise or instruction, or the support of any religious establishment."

> Art. IX, § 4: "All schools maintained or supported wholly or in part by the public funds shall be forever free from sectarian control or influence."

A degree in "theology" was not defined in the statute; as implemented, it was understood to encompass majors that were "devotional in nature or designed to induce religious faith."

Joshua Davey was awarded a Promise Scholarship and chose to attend Northwest College, a private Christian college affiliated with the Assemblies of God denomination. According to trial records, Davey had "planned for many years to attend a Bible *college and to prepare [himself] through that college training for a lifetime of ministry, specifically as a church pastor." When he enrolled in Northwest College, Davey declared a double major in pastoral ministries and business management/administration.*

At the beginning of the 1999–2000 academic year, Davey learned from school administrators that he could not use his scholarship to pursue a devotional theology degree and that to receive the funds appropriated for his use he would have to certify in writing that he would not pursue such a degree at Northwest College. Davey refused to sign the form and did not receive any scholarship funds. Davey, in turn, filed litigation that resulted in the Supreme Court opinions below.

Rehnquist, C. J., delivered the opinion of the Court, in which Stevens, O'Connor, Kennedy, Souter, Ginsburg, and Breyer, JJ., joined.

[715] The State of Washington established the Promise Scholarship Program to assist academically gifted students with postsecondary education expenses. In accordance with the State Constitution, students may not use the scholarship at an institution where they are pursuing a degree in devotional theology. We hold that such an exclusion from an otherwise inclusive aid program does not violate the Free Exercise Clause of the First Amendment. . . .

[718] The Religion Clauses of the First Amendment provide: "Congress shall make no law respecting an establishment of religion, or prohibiting the free exercise thereof." These two Clauses, the Establishment Clause and the Free Exercise Clause, are frequently in tension. Yet we have long said that "there is room for play in the joints" between them. *Walz v. Tax Comm'n of City of New York*, 397 U.S. 664, 669 (1970). In [719] other words, there are some state actions permitted by the Establishment Clause but not required by the Free Exercise Clause.

This case involves that "play in the joints" described above. Under our Establishment Clause precedent, the link between government funds and religious training is broken by the independent and private choice of recipients. As such, there is no doubt that the State could, consistent with the Federal Constitution, permit Promise Scholars to pursue a degree in devotional theology and the State does not contend otherwise. The question before us, however, is whether Washington, pursuant to its own constitution, which has been authoritatively interpreted as prohibiting even indirectly funding religious instruction that will prepare students for the ministry, can deny them such funding without violating the Free Exercise Clause.

[720] Davey urges us to answer that question in the negative. He contends that under the rule we enunciated in *Church of Lukumi Babalu Aye, Inc. v. Hialeah* the program is presumptively unconstitutional because it is not facially neutral with respect to religion. We reject his claim of presumptive unconstitutionality, however; to do otherwise would extend the *Lukumi* line of cases well beyond not only their facts but their reasoning. In *Lukumi*, the city of Hialeah made it a crime to engage in certain kinds of animal slaughter. We found that the law sought to suppress ritualistic animal sacrifices of the Santeria religion. In the present case, the State's disfavor of religion (if it can be called that) is of a far milder kind. It imposes neither criminal nor civil sanctions on any type of religious service or rite. It does not deny to ministers the right to participate in the political affairs of the community. And it does not require students to choose between their religious beliefs and [721] receiving a government benefit. The State has merely chosen not to fund a distinct category of instruction.

Justice Scalia argues, however, that generally available benefits are part of the "baseline against which burdens on religion are measured." Because the Promise Scholarship Program funds training for all secular professions, Justice Scalia contends the State must also fund training for religious professions. But training for religious professions and training for secular professions are not fungible. Training someone to lead a congregation is an essentially religious endeavor. Indeed, majoring in devotional theology is akin to a religious calling as well as an academic pursuit. And the subject of religion is one in which both the United States and state constitutions embody distinct views—in favor of free exercise, but opposed to establishment—that find no counterpart with respect to other callings or professions. That a State would deal differently with religious education for the ministry than with education for other callings is a product of these views, not evidence of hostility toward religion.

[722] Even though the differently worded Washington Constitution draws a more stringent line than that drawn by the United States Constitution, the interest it seeks to further is scarcely novel. In fact, we can think of few areas in which a State's antiestablishment interests come more into play. Since the founding of our country, there have been popular uprisings against procuring taxpayer funds to support church leaders, which was one of the hallmarks of an "established" religion.

[723] Most States that sought to avoid an establishment of religion around the time of the founding placed in their constitutions formal prohibitions against using tax funds to support the ministry. *E.g.*, Ga. Const., Art. IV, § 5 (1789) ("All persons shall have the free exercise of religion, without being obliged to contribute to the support of any religious profession but their own"); Pa. Const., Art. II (1776) ("[N]o man ought or of right can be compelled to attend any religious worship, or erect or support any place of worship, or maintain any ministry, contrary to, or against, his own free will and consent"). . . . The plain text of these constitutional provisions prohibited any tax dollars from supporting the clergy. We have found nothing to indicate, as Justice Scalia contends, that these provisions would not have applied so long as the State equally supported other professions or if the amount at stake was *de minimis*. That early state constitutions saw no problem in explicitly excluding only the ministry from receiving state dollars reinforces our conclusion that religious instruction is of a different ilk. . . .

[725] In short, we find neither in the history or text of Article I, § 11 of the Washington Constitution, nor in the operation of the Promise Scholarship Program, anything that suggests animus towards religion. Given the historic and substantial state interest at issue, we therefore cannot conclude that the denial of funding for vocational religious instruction alone is inherently constitutionally suspect.

Without a presumption of unconstitutionality, Davey's claim must fail. The State's interest in not funding the pursuit of devotional degrees is substantial and the exclusion of such funding places a relatively minor burden on Promise Scholars. If any room exists between the two Religion Clauses, it must be here. We need not venture further into this difficult area in order to uphold the Promise Scholarship Program as currently operated by the State of Washington.

[726] Justice Scalia, with whom Justice Thomas joins, dissenting.

In *Church of Lukumi Babalu Aye, Inc. v. Hialeah* (1993), the majority opinion held that "[a] law burdening religious practice that is not neutral . . . must undergo the most rigorous of scrutiny," *id.* at 546, and that "the minimum requirement of neutrality is that a law not discriminate on its face," *id.* at 533. The concurrence of two Justices stated that "[w]hen a law discriminates against religion as such, . . . it automatically will fail strict scrutiny." *Id.* at 579 (Blackmun, J., joined by O'Connor, J., concurring in judgment). And the concurrence of a third Justice endorsed the "noncontroversial principle" that "formal neutrality" is a "necessary conditio[n] for free-exercise constitutionality." *Id.* at 563 (Souter, J., concurring in part and concurring in judgment). These opinions are irreconcilable with today's decision, which sustains a public benefits program that facially discriminates against religion.

I

We articulated the principle that governs this case more than 50 years ago in *Everson v. Board of Ed. of Ewing* (1947):

> "New Jersey cannot hamper its citizens in the free exercise of their own religion. Consequently, it cannot exclude individual Catholics, Lutherans, Mohammedans, Baptists, Jews, Methodists, Non-believers, Presbyterians, or the members of any other faith, because of their faith, or lack of it, from receiving the benefits of public welfare legislation." *Id.*, at 16 (emphasis deleted).

When the State makes a public benefit generally available, that benefit becomes part of the baseline against which burdens on religion are measured; and when the State withholds [727] that benefit from some individuals solely on the basis of religion, it violates the Free Exercise Clause no less than if it had imposed a special tax.

That is precisely what the State of Washington has done here. It has created a generally available public benefit, whose receipt is conditioned only on academic performance, income, and attendance at an accredited school. It has then carved out a solitary course of study for exclusion: theology. No field of study but religion is singled out for disfavor in this fashion. Davey is not asking for a special benefit to which others are not entitled. He seeks only equal treatment—the right to direct his scholarship to his chosen course of study, a right every other Promise Scholar enjoys.

The Court's reference to historical "popular uprisings against procuring taxpayer funds to support church leaders" is therefore quite misplaced. That history involved not the inclusion of religious ministers in public benefits programs like the one at issue here, but laws that singled them out for financial aid. For example, the Virginia bill at which Madison's "Remonstrance" was directed provided: "[F]or the support of Christian teachers . . . [a] sum payable for tax on the property within this Commonwealth, is hereby assessed. . . ." Laws supporting the clergy in other States operated in a similar fashion. One can concede the Framers' hostility to funding the clergy specifically, but that says nothing about whether the clergy had to be excluded from benefits the State made available to all. No one would seriously contend, for example, that the Framers [728] would have barred ministers from using public roads on their way to church.[1]

---

1. Equally misplaced is the Court's reliance on founding-era state constitutional provisions that prohibited the use of tax funds to support the ministry. There is no doubt what these provisions were directed against: measures of the sort discussed earlier in text, singling out the clergy for public support. The Court offers no historical support for the proposition that they were meant to exclude clergymen from general benefits available to all citizens. In choosing to interpret them in that fashion, the Court needlessly gives them a meaning that not only is contrary to our Religion Clause jurisprudence, but has no logical stopping point short of the absurd. No State with such a constitutional provision has, so far as I know, ever prohibited the hiring of public employees who use their salary to conduct ministries, or excluded ministers from generally available disability or unemployment benefits. Since the Court cannot identify any instance in which these provisions were applied in such a discriminatory fashion, its appeal to their "plain text" adds nothing whatever to the "plain text" of Washington's own Constitution.

The Court does not dispute that the Free Exercise Clause places some constraints on public benefits programs, but finds none here, based on a principle of "play in the joints." I use the term "principle" loosely, for that is not so much a legal principle as a refusal to apply any principle when faced with competing constitutional directives. There is nothing anomalous about constitutional commands that abut. A municipality hiring public contractors may not discriminate against blacks or in favor of them; it cannot discriminate a little bit each way and then plead "play in the joints" when haled into court. If the Religion Clauses demand neutrality, we must enforce them, in hard cases as well as easy ones. . . .

[729] What is the nature of the State's asserted interest here? It cannot be protecting the pocketbooks of its citizens; given the tiny fraction of Promise Scholars who would pursue theology degrees, the amount of any citizen's tax bill at stake is *de minimis*. It cannot be preventing mistaken appearance of endorsement; where a State merely declines to penalize students for selecting a religious major, "[n]o reasonable observer is likely to draw . . . an inference that the State itself is endorsing a religious practice or belief." [*Witters v. Washington Deptartment of Services for the Blind*], at 493 (O'Connor, J., concurring in part and concurring in judgment). Nor can Washington's exclusion be defended as a means of assuring that the State will neither favor nor disfavor Davey in his religious calling. Davey will throughout his life contribute to the public fisc through sales taxes on [730] personal purchases, property taxes on his home, and so on; and nothing in the Court's opinion turns on whether Davey winds up a net winner or loser in the State's tax-and-spend scheme.

No, the interest to which the Court defers is not fear of a conceivable Establishment Clause violation, budget constraints, avoidance of endorsement, or substantive neutrality—none of these. It is a pure philosophical preference: the State's opinion that it would violate taxpayers' freedom of conscience not to discriminate against candidates for the ministry. This sort of protection of "freedom of conscience" has no logical limit and can justify the singling out of religion for exclusion from public programs in virtually any context. The Court never says whether it deems this interest compelling (the opinion is devoid of any mention of standard of review) but, self-evidently, it is not.

[731] II

. . . [733] In *McDaniel v. Paty*, we considered a Tennessee statute that disqualified clergy from participation in the state constitutional convention. That statute, like the one here, was based upon a state constitutional provision—a clause in the 1796 Tennessee Constitution that disqualified clergy from sitting in the legislature. The State defended the statute as an attempt to be faithful to its constitutional separation of church and state, and we accepted that claimed benevolent purpose as bona fide. Nonetheless, because it did not justify facial discrimination against religion, we invalidated the restriction.

It may be that Washington's original purpose in excluding the clergy from public benefits was benign, and the same might be true of its purpose in maintaining the exclusion today. But those singled out for disfavor can be forgiven for suspecting more invidious forces at work. Let there be no doubt: This case is about discrimination against a religious minority. Most citizens of this country identify themselves as professing some religious belief, but the State's policy poses no obstacle to practitioners of only a tepid, civic version of faith. Those the statutory exclusion actually affects—those whose belief in their religion is so strong that they dedicate their study and their lives to its ministry—are a far narrower set. One need not delve too far into modern popular culture to perceive a trendy disdain for deep religious conviction. In an era when the Court is so quick to come to the aid of other disfavored groups, see, *e.g.*, *Romer v. Evans*, 517 U.S. 620, 635 (1996), its indifference in this case, which involves a form of discrimination to which the Constitution actually speaks, is exceptional.

[734] * * *

Today's holding is limited to training the clergy, but its logic is readily extendible, and there are plenty of directions to go. What next? Will we deny priests and nuns their prescription-drug benefits on the ground that taxpayers' freedom of conscience forbids medicating the clergy at public expense? This may seem fanciful, but recall that France has proposed banning religious attire from schools, invoking interests in secularism no less benign than those the Court embraces today. When the public's freedom of conscience is invoked to justify denial of equal treatment, benevolent motives shade into indifference and ultimately into repression. Having accepted the justification in this case, the Court is less well equipped to fend it off in the future. I respectfully dissent.

59

Elk Grove Unified
School District v. Newdow

542 U.S. I (2004)

Vote: 8—Rehnquist, Stevens, O'Connor, Kennedy, Souter, Thomas, Ginsburg, Breyer
   0

Opinion announcing the opinion of the Court: Stevens
Opinions concurring in the judgment: Rehnquist, O'Connor, Thomas
Not participating in the case: Scalia

This case resulted from an Establishment Clause challenge to teacher-led recitations of the Pledge of Allegiance by a professed atheist with a daughter in a California public school.

   California law required public elementary schools to "conduc[t] . . . appropriate patriotic exercises" at the beginning of the school day and noted that the "giving of the Pledge of Allegiance to the Flag of the United States of America shall satisfy the requirements of this section." Elk Grove Unified School District complied with this requirement by instructing that "each elementary school class recite the Pledge of Allegiance to the Flag once each day." Students who objected on religious or other grounds were allowed to abstain from the recitation.

   The history of the Pledge of Allegiance dates to nationwide interest in commemorating the four hundredth anniversary of Christopher Columbus's discovery of America. A widely circulated national magazine for youth proposed in 1892 that pupils recite the following affirmation: "I pledge allegiance to my flag and the republic for which it stands: one nation indivisible, with liberty and justice for all."

   In the 1920s, the National Flag Conferences replaced the phrase "my flag" with "the flag of the United States of America." In 1942, in the midst of World War II, Congress adopted, and the president signed, a joint resolution codifying a detailed set of "rules and customs pertaining to the display and use of the flag of the United States of America." Section 7 of this codification provided the following text for the pledge: "I pledge allegiance to the flag of the United States of America and to the Republic for which it stands, one Nation indivisible, with liberty and justice for all."

   In 1954, Congress amended the text to add the words "under God" (Act of June 14, 1954, ch. 297, 68 Stat. 249). The House report that accompanied the legislation observed that "from the time of our earliest history our peoples and our institutions have reflected the traditional concept that our Nation was founded on a fundamental belief in God" (H. R. Rep. No. 1693, 83d Cong., 2d Sess., 2 [1954]). The resulting text was the pledge as it is currently recited: "I pledge allegiance to the flag of the United States of America, and to the Republic for which it stands, one nation under God, indivisible, with liberty and justice for all."

Stevens, J., delivered the opinion of the Court, in which Kennedy, Souter, Ginsburg, and Breyer, JJ., joined.

[4] Each day elementary school teachers in the Elk Grove Unified School District (School District) lead their classes in [5] a group recitation of the Pledge of Allegiance. Respondent, Michael A. Newdow, is an atheist whose daughter participates in that daily exercise. Because the Pledge contains the words "under God," he views the School District's policy as a religious indoctrination of his child that violates the First Amendment. A divided panel of the Court of Appeals for the Ninth Circuit agreed with Newdow. In light of the obvious importance of that decision, we granted *certiorari* to review the First Amendment issue and, preliminarily, the question whether Newdow has standing to invoke the jurisdiction of the federal courts. We conclude that Newdow lacks standing and therefore reverse the Court of Appeals' decision. . . .

[7] In March 2000, Newdow filed suit in the United States District Court for the Eastern District of California against the United States Congress, the President of the United States, the State of California, and the School District and its superintendent. At the time of filing, Newdow's daughter was enrolled in kindergarten in the School District and participated in the daily recitation of the Pledge. Styled as a mandamus action, the complaint explains that Newdow is an atheist who was ordained more than 20 years ago in a ministry that "espouses the religious philosophy that the true and eternal bonds of righteousness and virtue stem from reason rather than mythology." The complaint seeks a declaration that the 1954 Act's addition of the words "under God" violated the Establishment and Free Exercise Clauses of the United States Constitution as well as an injunction against the School District's policy requiring daily recitation of the Pledge. It alleges that Newdow has standing to sue on his own behalf and on behalf of his daughter as "next friend." . . .

[9] After the Court of Appeals' initial opinion was announced, Sandra Banning, the mother of Newdow's daughter, filed a motion for leave to intervene, or alternatively to dismiss the complaint. She declared that although she and Newdow shared "physical custody" of their daughter, a state-court order granted her "exclusive legal custody" of the child, "including the sole right to represent [the daughter's] legal interests and make all decision[s] about her education" and welfare. Banning further stated that her daughter is a Christian who believes in God and has no objection either to reciting or hearing others recite the Pledge of Allegiance, or to its reference to God. Banning expressed the belief that her daughter would be harmed if the litigation were permitted to proceed, because others might incorrectly perceive the child as sharing her father's atheist views. Banning [10] accordingly concluded, as her daughter's sole legal custodian, that it was not in the child's interest to be a party to Newdow's lawsuit. . . .

[13] As explained briefly above, the extent of the standing problem raised by the domestic relations issues in this case was not apparent until August 5, 2002, when Banning filed [14] her motion for leave to intervene or dismiss the complaint following the Court of Appeals' initial decision. At that time, the child's custody was governed by a February 6, 2002, order of the California Superior Court. That order provided that Banning had

"sole legal custody as to the rights and responsibilities to make decisions relating to the health, education and welfare of" her daughter. The order stated that the two parents should "consult with one another on substantial decisions relating to" the child's "psychological and educational needs," but it authorized Banning to "exercise legal control" if the parents could not reach "mutual agreement."

That family court order was the controlling document at the time of the Court of Appeals' standing decision. After the Court of Appeals ruled, however, the Superior Court held another conference regarding the child's custody. At a hearing on September 11, 2003, the Superior Court announced that the parents have "joint legal custody," but that Banning "makes the final decisions if the two . . . disagree." . . .

[15] Newdow contends that despite Banning's final authority, he retains "an unrestricted right to inculcate in his daughter—free from governmental interference—the atheistic beliefs he finds persuasive." The difficulty with that argument is that Newdow's rights, as in many cases touching upon family relations, cannot be viewed in isolation. This case concerns not merely Newdow's interest in inculcating his child with his views on religion, but also the rights of the child's mother as a parent generally and under the Superior Court orders specifically. And most important, it implicates the interests of a young child who finds herself at the center of a highly public debate over her custody, the propriety of a widespread national ritual, and the meaning of our Constitution.

The interests of the affected persons in this case are in many respects antagonistic. Of course, legal disharmony in family relations is not uncommon, and in many instances that disharmony poses no bar to federal-court adjudication of proper federal questions. What makes this case different is that Newdow's standing derives entirely from his relationship with his daughter, but he lacks the right to litigate as her next friend. In marked contrast to our case law on *jus tertii*, the interests of this parent and this child are not parallel and, indeed, are potentially in conflict. . . .

[17] In our view, it is improper for the federal courts to entertain a claim by a plaintiff whose standing to sue is founded on family law rights that are in dispute when prosecution of the lawsuit may have an adverse effect on the person who is the source of the plaintiff's claimed standing. When hard questions of domestic relations are sure to affect the outcome, the prudent course is for the federal court to stay its hand rather than reach out to resolve a weighty question of federal constitutional law. There is a vast difference between Newdow's right to communicate with his child—which both California law and the First Amendment recognize—and his claimed right to shield his daughter from influences to which she is exposed in school despite the terms of the custody order. We conclude that, having been deprived under California law of the right to sue as next friend, Newdow [18] lacks prudential standing to bring this suit in federal court.

Chief Justice Rehnquist, with whom Justice O'Connor joins, and with whom Justice Thomas joins as to Part I, concurring in the judgment.

The Court today erects a novel prudential standing principle in order to avoid reaching the merits of the constitutional claim. I dissent from that ruling. On the merits, I conclude that the Elk Grove Unified School District (School District) policy that requires teachers to lead willing students in reciting the Pledge of Allegiance, which includes the words "under God," does not violate the Establishment Clause of the First Amendment. . . .

[25] II

. . . As part of an overall effort to "codify and emphasize existing rules and customs pertaining to the display and use of the flag of the United States of America," Congress amended the Pledge to include the phrase "under God" in 1954. The amendment's sponsor, Representative Rabaut, said its purpose was to contrast this country's belief in God with the Soviet Union's embrace of atheism. We do not know what [26] other Members of Congress thought about the purpose of the amendment. Following the decision of the Court of Appeals in this case, Congress passed legislation that made extensive findings about the historic role of religion in the political development of the Nation and reaffirmed the text of the Pledge. To the millions of people who regularly recite the Pledge, and who have no access to, or concern with, such legislation or legislative history, "under God" might mean several different things: that God has guided the destiny of the United States, for example, or that the United States exists under God's authority. How much consideration anyone gives to the phrase probably varies, since the Pledge itself is a patriotic observance focused primarily on the flag and the Nation, and only secondarily on the description of the Nation.

The phrase "under God" in the Pledge seems, as a historical matter, to sum up the attitude of the Nation's leaders, and to manifest itself in many of our public observances. Examples of patriotic invocations of God and official acknowledgments of religion's role in our Nation's history abound.

At George Washington's first inauguration on April 30, 1789, he

"stepped toward the iron rail, where he was to receive the oath of office. The diminutive secretary of the Senate, Samuel Otis, squeezed between the President and Chancellor Livingston and raised up the crimson cushion with a Bible on it. Washington put his right hand on the Bible, opened to Psalm 121:1: 'I raise my eyes toward the hills. Whence shall my help come.' The Chancellor proceeded with the oath: 'Do you solemnly swear that you will faithfully execute the office of President of the United States and will to the best of your ability preserve, protect and defend the Constitution of the United States?' The President responded, 'I solemnly swear,' and repeated the oath, adding, 'So help me God.' [27] He then bent forward and kissed the Bible before him." M. Riccards, *A Republic, If You Can Keep It: The Foundation of the American Presidency, 1700–1800*, pp. 73–74 (1987). . . .

Later Presidents, at critical times in the Nation's history, have likewise invoked the name of God. Abraham Lincoln, concluding his masterful Gettysburg Address in 1863, used the very phrase "under God":

"It is rather for us to be here dedicated to the great task remaining before us—that from these honored dead we take increased devotion to that cause for which they [28] gave the last full measure of devotion—that we here highly resolve that these dead shall not have died in vain—that this nation, under God, shall have a new birth of freedom—and that government of the people, by the people, for the people, shall not perish from the earth."

Lincoln's equally well-known second inaugural address, delivered on March 4, 1865, makes repeated references to God, concluding with these famous words:

"With malice toward none, with charity for all, with firmness in the right as God gives us to see the right, let us strive on to finish the work we are in, to bind up the nation's wounds, to care for him who shall have borne the battle and for his widow and his orphan, to do all which may achieve and cherish a just and lasting peace among ourselves and with all nations." . . .

[29] President Franklin Delano Roosevelt, taking the office of the Presidency in the depths of the Great Depression, concluded his first inaugural address with these words: "In this dedication of a nation we humbly ask the blessing of God. May He protect each and every one of us! May He guide me in the days to come!" . . .

The motto "In God We Trust" first appeared on the country's coins during the Civil War. Secretary of the Treasury Salmon P. Chase, acting under the authority of an Act of Congress passed in 1864, prescribed that the motto should appear on the two cent coin. The motto was placed on more and more denominations, and since 1938 all United States coins bear the motto. Paper currency followed suit at a slower pace; Federal Reserve notes were so inscribed during the decade of the 1960s. Meanwhile, in 1956, Congress declared that the motto of the United States would be "In God We Trust."

Our Court Marshal's opening proclamation concludes with the words "God save the United States and this honorable Court." The language goes back at least as far as 1827.

[30] All of these events strongly suggest that our national culture allows public recognition of our Nation's religious history and character. In the words of the House Report that accompanied the insertion of the phrase "under God" in the Pledge: "From the time of our earliest history our peoples and our institutions have reflected the traditional concept that our Nation was founded on a fundamental belief in God." H. R. Rep. No. 1693, 83d Cong., 2d Sess., 2 (1954). . . .

Notwithstanding the voluntary nature of the School District policy, the Court of Appeals, by a divided vote, held that the policy violates the Establishment Clause of the First Amendment because it "impermissibly coerces a religious [31] act." To reach this result, the court relied primarily on our decision in *Lee v. Weisman*, 505 U.S. 577 (1992). That case arose out of a graduation ceremony for a public high school in Providence, Rhode Island. The ceremony began with an invocation and ended with a benediction, both given by a local rabbi. The Court held that even though attendance at the ceremony was voluntary, students who objected to the prayers would nonetheless feel coerced to attend and to stand during each prayer. But the Court throughout its opinion referred to the prayer as "an explicit religious exercise," *id.*, at 598, and "a formal religious exercise," *id.*, at 589.

As the Court notes in its opinion, "the Pledge of Allegiance evolved as a common public acknowledgment of the ideals that our flag symbolizes. Its recitation is a patriotic exercise designed to foster national unity and pride in those principles."

I do not believe that the phrase "under God" in the Pledge converts its recital into a "religious exercise" of the sort described in *Lee*. Instead, it is a declaration of belief in allegiance and loyalty to the United States flag and the Republic that it represents. The phrase "under God" is in no sense a prayer, nor an endorsement of any religion, but a simple recognition of the fact noted in H. R. Rep. No. 1693, at 2: "From the time of our earliest history our peoples and our institutions have reflected the traditional concept that our Nation was founded on a fundamental belief in God." Reciting the Pledge, or listening to others recite it, is a patriotic exercise, not a religious one; participants promise fidelity to our flag and our Nation, not to any particular God, faith, or church.

[32] There is no doubt that respondent is sincere in his atheism and rejection of a belief in God. But the mere fact that he disagrees with this part of the Pledge does not give him a veto power over the decision of the public schools that willing participants should pledge allegiance to the flag in the manner prescribed by Congress. There may be

others who disagree, not with the phrase "under God," but with the phrase "with liberty and justice for all." But surely that would not give such objectors the right to veto the holding of such a ceremony by those willing to participate. Only if it can be said that the phrase "under God" somehow tends to the establishment of a religion in violation of the First Amendment can respondent's claim succeed, where one based on objections to "with liberty and justice for all" fails. Our cases have broadly interpreted this phrase, but none have gone anywhere near as far as the decision of the Court of Appeals in this case. The recital, in a patriotic ceremony pledging allegiance to the flag and to the Nation, of the descriptive phrase "under God" cannot possibly lead to the establishment of a religion, or anything like it. . . .

[33] Justice O'Connor, concurring in the judgment.

I join the concurrence of the Chief Justice in full. Like him, I would follow our policy of deferring to the Federal Courts of Appeals in matters that involve the interpretation of state law and thereby conclude that respondent Newdow does have standing to bring his constitutional claim before a federal court. Like the Chief Justice, I believe that we must examine those questions, and, like him, I believe that petitioner school district's policy of having its teachers lead students in voluntary recitations of the Pledge of Allegiance does not offend the Establishment Clause. But while the history presented by the Chief Justice illuminates the constitutional problems this case presents, I write separately to explain the principles that guide my own analysis of the constitutionality of that policy. . . .

As I have said before, the Establishment Clause "cannot easily be reduced to a single test. There are different categories of Establishment Clause cases, which may call for different approaches." *Board of Ed. of Kiryas Joel Village School Dist. v. Grumet*, 512 U.S. 687, 720 (1994) (concurring opinion). When a court confronts a challenge to [34] government-sponsored speech or displays, I continue to believe that the endorsement test "captures the essential command of the Establishment Clause, namely, that government must not make a person's religious beliefs relevant to his or her standing in the political community by conveying a message 'that religion or a particular religious belief is favored or preferred.'" *County of Allegheny v. American Civil Liberties Union, Greater Pittsburgh Chapter*, 492 U.S. 573, 627 (1989) (opinion concurring in part and concurring in judgment). In that context, I repeatedly have applied the endorsement test, and I would do so again here. . . .

[36] For centuries, we have marked important occasions or pronouncements with references to God and invocations of divine assistance. Such references can serve to solemnize an occasion instead of to invoke divine provenance. The reasonable observer discussed above, fully aware of our national history and the origins of such practices, would not perceive these acknowledgments as signifying a government endorsement of any specific religion, or even of religion over nonreligion.

There are no *de minimis* violations of the Constitution—no constitutional harms so slight that the courts are obliged [37] to ignore them. Given the values that the Establishment Clause was meant to serve, however, I believe that government can, in a discrete category of cases, acknowledge or refer to the divine without offending the Constitution. This category of "ceremonial deism" most clearly encompasses such things as the national motto ("In God We Trust"), religious references in traditional patriotic songs such as The Star-Spangled Banner, and the words with which the Marshal of this Court opens each of its sessions ("God save the United States and this honorable Court"). These references are not minor trespasses upon the Establishment Clause to which I turn a blind eye. Instead, their history, character, and context prevent them from being constitutional violations at all.

This case requires us to determine whether the appearance of the phrase "under God" in the Pledge of Allegiance constitutes an instance of such ceremonial deism. Although it is a close question, I conclude that it does, based on my evaluation of the following four factors.

History and Ubiquity

The constitutional value of ceremonial deism turns on a shared understanding of its legitimate nonreligious purposes. That sort of understanding can exist only when a given practice has been in place for a significant portion of the Nation's history, and when it is observed by enough persons that it can fairly be called ubiquitous. By contrast, novel or uncommon references to religion can more easily be perceived as government endorsements because the reasonable observer cannot be presumed to be fully familiar with their origins. As a result, in examining whether a given practice constitutes an instance of ceremonial deism, its "history and ubiquity" will be of great importance. . . .

[38] Fifty years have passed since the words "under God" were added, a span of time that is not inconsiderable given the relative youth of our Nation. In that time, the Pledge has become, alongside the singing of The Star-Spangled Banner, our most routine ceremonial act of patriotism; countless schoolchildren recite it daily, and their religious heterogeneity reflects that of the Nation as a whole. As a result, the Pledge and the context in which it is employed are familiar and nearly inseparable in the public mind. No reasonable observer could have been surprised to learn the words of the Pledge, or that petitioner school district has a policy of leading its students in daily recitation of the Pledge. . . .

[39] Absence of Worship or Prayer

"[O]ne of the greatest dangers to the freedom of the individual to worship in his own way [lies] in the Government's placing its official stamp of approval upon one particular kind of prayer or one particular form of religious services." [40] *Engel v. Vitale*, 370 U.S. 421, 429 (1962). Because of this principle, only in the most extraordinary circumstances could actual worship or prayer be defended as ceremonial deism. We have upheld only one such prayer against Establishment Clause challenge, and it was supported by an extremely long and unambiguous history. See *Marsh v. Chambers* (1983) (upholding Nebraska Legislature's 128-year-old practice of opening its sessions with a prayer offered by a chaplain). Any statement that has as its purpose placing the speaker or listener in a penitent state of mind, or that is intended to create a spiritual communion or invoke divine aid, strays from the legitimate secular purposes of solemnizing an event and recognizing a shared religious history.

Of course, any statement can be imbued by a speaker or listener with the qualities of prayer. But, as I have explained, the relevant viewpoint is that of a reasonable observer, fully cognizant of the history, ubiquity, and context of the practice in question. Such an observer could not conclude that reciting the Pledge, including the phrase "under God," constitutes an instance of worship. I know of no religion that incorporates the Pledge into its canon, nor one that would count the Pledge as a meaningful expression of religious faith. Even if taken literally, the phrase is merely descriptive; it purports only to identify the United States as a Nation subject to divine authority. That cannot be seen as a serious invocation of God or as an expression of individual submission to divine authority. . . .

[42] Absence of Reference to Particular Religion

. . . [N]o religious acknowledgment could claim to be an instance of ceremonial deism if it explicitly favored one particular religious belief system over another.

The Pledge complies with this requirement. It does not refer to a nation "under Jesus" or "under Vishnu," but instead acknowledges religion in a general way: a simple reference to a generic "God." Of course, some religions—Buddhism, for instance—are not based upon a belief in a separate Supreme Being. See Brief for Buddhist Temples, et al. as Amici Curiae 15–16. But one would be hard pressed to imagine a brief solemnizing reference to religion that would adequately encompass every religious belief expressed by any citizen of this Nation. The phrase "under God," conceived and added at a time when our national religious diversity was neither as robust nor as well recognized as it is now, represents a tolerable attempt to acknowledge religion and to invoke its solemnizing power without favoring any individual religious sect or belief system.

Minimal Religious Content

A final factor that makes the Pledge an instance of ceremonial deism, in my view, is its highly circumscribed reference to God. In most of the cases in which we have struck down government speech or displays under the Establishment Clause, the offending religious content has been much more [43] pervasive. Of course, a ceremony cannot avoid Establishment Clause scrutiny simply by avoiding an explicit mention of God. But the brevity of a reference to religion or to God in a ceremonial exercise can be important for several reasons. First, it tends to confirm that the reference is being used to acknowledge religion or to solemnize an event rather than to endorse religion in any way. Second, it makes it easier for those participants who wish to "opt out" of language they find offensive to do so without having to reject the ceremony entirely. And third, it tends to limit the ability of government to express a preference for one religious sect over another.

The reference to "God" in the Pledge of Allegiance qualifies as a minimal reference to religion; Newdow's challenge focuses on only two of the Pledge's 31 words. Moreover, the presence of those words is not absolutely essential to the Pledge, as demonstrated by the fact that it existed without them for over 50 years. As a result, students who wish to avoid saying the words "under God" still can consider themselves meaningful participants in the exercise if they join in reciting the remainder of the Pledge. . . .

[45] Justice Thomas, concurring in the judgment.

We granted *certiorari* in this case to decide whether the Elk Grove Unified School District's Pledge policy violates the Constitution. The answer to that question is: "no." But in a testament to the condition of our Establishment Clause jurisprudence, the Court of Appeals reached the opposite conclusion based on a persuasive reading of our precedent, especially *Lee v. Weisman*. In my view, *Lee* adopted an expansive definition of "coercion" that cannot be defended however one decides the "difficult question" of "[w]hether and how th[e Establishment] Clause should constrain state action under the Fourteenth Amendment." *Zelman v. Simmons-Harris*, 536 U.S. 639, 678 (2002) (Thomas, J., concurring). The difficulties with our Establishment Clause cases, however, run far deeper than *Lee*.

Because I agree with the Chief Justice that respondent Newdow has standing, I would take this opportunity to begin the process of rethinking the Establishment Clause. I would acknowledge that the Establishment Clause is a federalism provision, which, for this reason, resists incorporation. [46] Moreover, as I will explain, the Pledge policy is not implicated by any sensible incorporation of the Establishment Clause, which would probably cover little more than the Free Exercise Clause.

I

In *Lee*, the Court held that invocations and benedictions could not, consistent with the Establishment Clause, be given at public secondary school graduations. The Court emphasized "heightened concerns with protecting freedom of conscience from subtle coercive pressure in the elementary and secondary public schools." 505 U.S., at 592. It brushed aside both the fact that the students were not required to attend the graduation and the fact that they were not compelled, in any meaningful sense, to participate in the religious component of the graduation ceremony, see *id.*, at 593. The Court surmised that the prayer violated the Establishment Clause because a high school student could—in light of the "peer pressure" to attend graduation and "to stand as a group or, at least, maintain respectful silence during the invocation and benediction," *ibid.*—have "a reasonable perception that she is being forced by the State to pray in a manner her conscience will not allow," *ibid.*

Adherence to *Lee* would require us to strike down the Pledge policy, which, in most respects, poses more serious difficulties than the prayer at issue in *Lee*. A prayer at graduation is a one-time event, the graduating students are almost (if not already) adults, and their parents are usually present. By contrast, very young students, removed from the protection of their parents, are exposed to the Pledge each and every day. . . .

[48] The Chief Justice would distinguish *Lee* by asserting "that the phrase 'under God' in the Pledge [does not] conver[t] its recital into a 'religious exercise' of the sort described in *Lee*." In *Barnette*, the Court addressed a state law that compelled students to salute and pledge allegiance to the flag. The Court described this as "compulsion of students to declare a belief." 319 U.S., at 631. The Pledge "require[d] affirmation of a belief and an attitude of mind." *Id.*, at 633. In its current form, reciting the Pledge entails pledging allegiance to "the Flag of the United States of America, and to the Republic for which it stands, one Nation under God." Under *Barnette*, pledging allegiance is "to declare a belief" that now includes that this is "one Nation under God." It is difficult to see how this does not entail an affirmation that God exists. Whether or not we classify affirming the existence of God as a "formal religious exercise" akin to prayer, it must present the same or similar constitutional problems.

To be sure, such an affirmation is not a prayer, and I admit that this might be a significant distinction. But the Court has squarely held that the government cannot require a person to "declare his belief in God." *Torcaso v. Watkins*, 367 U.S. 488, 489 (1961). And the Court has said, in my view questionably, that the Establishment Clause "prohibits government from appearing to take a position on questions of religious belief." *County of Allegheny v. American Civil Liberties Union, Greater Pittsburgh Chapter*, 492 U.S. 573, 594.

[49] I conclude that, as a matter of our precedent, the Pledge policy is unconstitutional. I believe, however, that *Lee* was wrongly decided. *Lee* depended on a notion of "coercion" that, as I discuss below, has no basis in law or reason. The kind of coercion implicated by the Religion Clauses is that accomplished "by force of law and threat of penalty." 505 U.S., at 640 (Scalia, J., dissenting). Peer pressure, unpleasant as it may be, is not coercion. But rejection of *Lee*-style "coercion" does not suffice to settle this case. Although children are not coerced to pledge their allegiance, they are legally coerced to attend school. Because what is at issue is a state action, the question becomes whether the Pledge policy implicates a religious liberty right protected by the Fourteenth Amendment.

II

I accept that the Free Exercise Clause, which clearly protects an individual right, applies against the States through the Fourteenth Amendment. But the Establishment Clause is another matter. The text and history of the Establishment Clause strongly suggest that it is a federalism provision intended to prevent Congress from interfering with state establishments. Thus, unlike the Free Exercise Clause, which does protect an individual right, it makes little sense to incorporate the Establishment Clause. In any case, I do not believe that the Pledge policy infringes any religious liberty right that would arise from incorporation of the Clause. Because the Pledge policy also does not infringe any free-exercise rights, I conclude that it is constitutional.

A

The Establishment Clause provides that "Congress shall make no law respecting an establishment of religion." [50] As a textual matter, this Clause probably prohibits Congress from establishing a national religion. Perhaps more importantly, the Clause made clear that Congress could not interfere with state establishments, notwithstanding any argument that could be made based on Congress' power under the Necessary and Proper Clause.

Nothing in the text of the Clause suggests that it reaches any further. The Establishment Clause does not purport to protect individual rights. By contrast, the Free Exercise Clause plainly protects individuals against congressional interference with the right to exercise their religion, and the remaining Clauses within the First Amendment expressly disable Congress from "abridging [particular] *freedom[s]*." (Emphasis added.) This textual analysis is consistent with the prevailing view that the Constitution left religion to the States. History also supports this understanding: At the founding, at least six States had established religions. Nor has this federalism point escaped the notice of Members of this Court.

Quite simply, the Establishment Clause is best understood as a federalism provision—it protects state establishments from federal interference but does not protect any individual right. These two features independently make incorporation of the Clause difficult to understand. The best argument in favor of incorporation would be that, by disabling Congress from establishing a national religion, the Clause protected an individual right, enforceable against the Federal [51] Government, to be free from coercive federal establishments. Incorporation of this individual right, the argument goes, makes sense. I have alluded to this possibility before. See *Zelman*, at 679.

But even assuming that the Establishment Clause precludes the Federal Government from establishing a national religion, it does not follow that the Clause created or protects any individual right. For the reasons discussed above, it is more likely that States and only States were the direct beneficiaries. Moreover, incorporation of this putative individual right leads to a peculiar outcome: It would prohibit precisely what the Establishment Clause was intended to protect—state establishments of religion. Nevertheless, the potential right against federal establishments is the only candidate for incorporation.

I would welcome the opportunity to consider more fully the difficult questions whether and how the Establishment Clause applies against the States. One observation suffices for now: As strange as it sounds, an incorporated Establishment Clause prohibits exactly what the Establishment Clause protected—state practices that pertain to "an establishment of religion." At the very least, the burden of persuasion rests with anyone who claims that the term took on a different meaning upon incorporation. We must therefore determine whether the Pledge policy pertains to an "establishment of religion."

[52] B

The traditional "establishments of religion" to which the Establishment Clause is addressed necessarily involve actual legal coercion:

> "The coercion that was a hallmark of historical establishments of religion was coercion of religious orthodoxy and of financial support by force of law and threat of penalty. Typically, attendance at the state church was required; only clergy of the official church could lawfully perform sacraments; and dissenters, if tolerated, faced an array of civil disabilities. L. Levy, *The Establishment Clause* 4 (1986). Thus, for example, in the Colony of Virginia, where the Church of England had been established, ministers were required by law to conform to the doctrine and rites of the Church of England; and all persons were required to attend church and observe the Sabbath, were tithed for the public support of Anglican ministers, and were taxed for the costs of building and repairing churches. *Id.*, at 3–4." *Lee*, 505 U.S., at 640–641 (Scalia, J., dissenting).

Even if "establishment" had a broader definition, one that included support for religion generally through taxation, the element of legal coercion (by the State) would still be present.

It is also conceivable that a government could "establish" a religion by imbuing it with governmental authority or by "delegat[ing] its civic authority to a group chosen according to a religious criterion," *Board of Ed. of Kiryas Joel Village School Dist. v. Grumet*, 512 U.S. 687, 698 (1994). A religious organization that carries some measure of the authority of the State begins to look like a traditional "religious establishment," at least when that authority can be used coercively.

[53] It is difficult to see how government practices that have nothing to do with creating or maintaining the sort of coercive state establishment described above implicate the possible liberty interest of being free from coercive state establishments. In addressing the constitutionality of voluntary school prayer, Justice Stewart made essentially this point, emphasizing that "we deal here not with the establishment of a state church, . . . but with whether school children who want to begin their day by joining in prayer must be prohibited from doing so." *Engel*, 370 U.S., at 445 (dissenting opinion).

To be sure, I find much to commend the view that the Establishment Clause "bar[s] governmental preferences for particular religious faiths." *Rosenberger v. Rector and Visitors of Univ. of Va.*, 515 U.S. 819, 856 (1995) (Thomas, J., concurring). But the position I suggest today is consistent with this. Legal compulsion is an inherent component of "preferences" in this context. James Madison's "Memorial and Remonstrance against Religious Assessments," [54] which extolled the no-preference argument, concerned coercive taxation to support an established religion, much as its title implies. And, although "more extreme notions of the separation of church and state [might] be attribut[able] to Madison, many of them clearly stem from 'arguments reflecting the concepts of natural law, natural rights, and the social contract between government and a civil society,' [R. Cord, *Separation of Church and State: Historical Fact and Current Fiction* 22 (1982)], rather than the principle of nonestablishment in the Constitution." *Rosenberger*, at 856 (Thomas, J., concurring).

C

Through the Pledge policy, the State has not created or maintained any religious establishment, and neither has it granted government authority to an existing religion. The Pledge policy does not expose anyone to the legal coercion associated with an established religion. Further, no other free-exercise rights are at issue. It follows that religious liberty rights are not in question and that the Pledge policy fully comports with the Constitution.

60

Van Orden v. Perry

545 U.S. 677 (2005)

Vote: 5—Rehnquist, Scalia, Kennedy, Thomas, Breyer
4—Stevens, O'Connor, Souter, Ginsburg

Opinion announcing the opinion of the Court: Rehnquist
Concurring opinions: Scalia, Thomas
Opinion concurring in the judgment: Breyer
Dissenting opinions: Stevens, O'Connor, Stevens

Decided on the same day as McCreary County v. American Civil Liberties Union
of Kentucky, *this case involved an Establishment Clause challenge to a 6-foot-high,
3.5-foot-wide monument located on the grounds of the Texas State Capitol. The monument's primary content was the text of the Ten Commandments. The space above
the text included an eagle grasping the American flag, an eye inside a pyramid, and
two small tablets with ancient script. Below the text were two Stars of David and the
superimposed Greek letters chi and rho, which represent Christ. The bottom of the
monument included the inscription, "Presented to the people and youth of Texas by the
Fraternal Order of Eagles of Texas 1961."*

*The granite monument was donated to the state in 1961 by the Fraternal Order
of Eagles, a private civic organization. The organization's stated goal in donating the
monument was to highlight the Ten Commandments' role in shaping civic morality, as
part of the organization's efforts to combat juvenile delinquency. Records indicate that
after accepting the monument, the state selected a site for it based on the recommendation of the state organization that maintains the capitol grounds. The Eagles paid the
cost of erecting the monument.*

*At the time of litigation, the twenty-two acres surrounding the Texas State Capitol
contained seventeen monuments (including the one at issue) and twenty-one historical
markers commemorating the "people, ideals, and events that compose Texan identity"
(Tex. H. Con. Res. 38, 77th Leg., Reg. Sess. [2001]). Among such displays were monuments to "Heroes of the Alamo" and veterans of various wars.*

REHNQUIST, C. J., announced the judgment of the Court and delivered an opinion, in which SCALIA, KENNEDY, and THOMAS, JJ., joined.

[681] The question here is whether the Establishment Clause of the First Amendment allows the display of a monument inscribed with the Ten Commandments on the Texas State Capitol grounds. We hold that it does. . . .

[683] Our cases, Januslike, point in two directions in applying the Establishment Clause. One face looks toward the strong role played by religion and religious traditions throughout our Nation's history. . . .

The other face looks toward the principle that governmental intervention in religious matters can itself endanger religious freedom.

This case, like all Establishment Clause challenges, presents us with the difficulty of respecting both faces. Our institutions presuppose a Supreme Being, yet these institutions must not press religious observances upon their citizens. One face looks to the past in acknowledgment of our Nation's heritage, while the other looks to the present in demanding a separation between church and state. Reconciling these two faces requires that we neither abdicate our [684] responsibility to maintain a division between church and state nor evince a hostility to religion by disabling the government from in some ways recognizing our religious heritage:

> "When the state encourages religious instruction or cooperates with religious authorities by adjusting the schedule of public events to sectarian needs, it follows the best of our traditions. For it then respects the religious nature of our people and accommodates the public service to their spiritual needs. To hold that it may not would be to find in the Constitution a requirement that the government show a callous indifference to religious groups. . . . [W]e find no constitutional requirement which makes it necessary for government to be hostile to religion and to throw its weight against efforts to widen the effective scope of religious influence." *Zorach v. Clauson*, 343 U.S. 306, 313–314 (1952).[3]

[685] These two faces are evident in representative cases both upholding and invalidating laws under the Establishment Clause. Over the last 25 years, we have sometimes pointed [686] to *Lemon v. Kurtzman* as providing the governing test in Establishment Clause challenges. Yet, just two years after *Lemon* was decided, we noted that the factors identified in *Lemon* serve as "no more than helpful signposts." *Hunt v. McNair*, 413 U.S. 734, 741 (1973). Many of our recent cases simply have not applied the *Lemon* test. See, *e.g.*, *Zelman v. Simmons-Harris*, *Good News Club v. Milford Central School*. Others have applied it only after concluding that the challenged practice was invalid under a different Establishment Clause test.

Whatever may be the fate of the *Lemon* test in the larger scheme of Establishment Clause jurisprudence, we think it not useful in dealing with the sort of passive monument that Texas has erected on its Capitol grounds. Instead, our analysis is driven both by the nature of the monument and by our Nation's history. . . .

[688] In this case we are faced with a display of the Ten Commandments on government property outside the Texas State Capitol. Such acknowledgments of the role played by the Ten Commandments in our Nation's heritage are common throughout America.

---

3. Despite Justice Stevens' recitation of occasional language to the contrary, we have not, and do not, adhere to the principle that the Establishment Clause bars any and all governmental preference for religion over irreligion. Even the dissenters do not claim that the First Amendment's Religion Clauses forbid all governmental acknowledgments, preferences, or accommodations of religion.

We need only look within our own Courtroom. Since 1935, Moses has stood, holding two tablets that reveal portions of the Ten Commandments written in Hebrew, among other lawgivers in the south frieze. Representations of the Ten Commandments adorn the metal gates lining the north and south sides of the Courtroom as well as the doors leading into the Courtroom. Moses also sits on the exterior east facade of the building holding the Ten Commandments tablets. . . .

[689] Our opinions, like our building, have recognized the role the Decalogue plays in America's heritage. [690] The Executive and Legislative Branches have also acknowledged the historical role of the Ten Commandments. These displays and recognitions of the Ten Commandments bespeak the rich American tradition of religious acknowledgments.

Of course, the Ten Commandments are religious—they were so viewed at their inception and so remain. The monument, therefore, has religious significance. According to Judeo-Christian belief, the Ten Commandments were given to Moses by God on Mt. Sinai. But Moses was a lawgiver as well as a religious leader. And the Ten Commandments have an undeniable historical meaning, as the foregoing examples demonstrate. Simply having religious content or promoting a message consistent with a religious doctrine does not run afoul of the Establishment Clause.

There are, of course, limits to the display of religious messages or symbols. For example, we held unconstitutional a Kentucky statute requiring the posting of the Ten Commandments in every public schoolroom. *Stone v. Graham* (1980). In the classroom context, we found that the Kentucky statute had an improper and plainly religious purpose. As evidenced by *Stone*'s almost exclusive reliance upon two of our school [691] prayer cases, *id.*, at 41–42 (citing *School Dist. of Abington Township v. Schempp* and *Engel v. Vitale*), it stands as an example of the fact that we have "been particularly vigilant in monitoring compliance with the Establishment Clause in elementary and secondary schools," *Edwards v. Aguillard*, 482 U.S. 578, 583–584 (1987). Indeed, *Edwards v. Aguillard* recognized that *Stone*—along with *Schempp* and *Engel*—was a consequence of the "particular concerns that arise in the context of public elementary and secondary schools." 482 U.S., at 584–585. Neither *Stone* itself nor subsequent opinions have indicated that *Stone*'s holding would extend to a legislative chamber or to capitol grounds.

The placement of the Ten Commandments monument on the Texas State Capitol grounds is a far more passive use of those texts than was the case in *Stone*, where the text confronted elementary school students every day. Indeed, Van Orden, the petitioner here, apparently walked by the monument for a number of years before bringing this lawsuit. The monument is therefore also quite different from the prayers involved in *Schempp* and *Lee v. Weisman*. Texas has treated its Capitol grounds monuments as representing the several strands in the State's political and legal history. The inclusion of the Ten Commandments monument in this [692] group has a dual significance, partaking of both religion and government. We cannot say that Texas' display of this monument violates the Establishment Clause of the First Amendment.

Justice Scalia, concurring.

I join the opinion of the Chief Justice because I think it accurately reflects our current Establishment Clause jurisprudence—or at least the Establishment Clause jurisprudence we currently apply some of the time. I would prefer to reach the same result by adopting an Establishment Clause jurisprudence that is in accord with our Nation's past and present practices, and that can be consistently applied—the central relevant feature of which is that there is nothing unconstitutional in a State's favoring religion generally, honoring God through public prayer and acknowledgment, or, in a nonproselytizing manner, venerating the Ten Commandments.

Justice Thomas, concurring.

The Court holds that the Ten Commandments monument found on the Texas State Capitol grounds does not violate the Establishment Clause. Rather than trying to suggest meaninglessness where there is meaning, the Chief Justice rightly recognizes that the monument has "religious significance." He properly recognizes the role of religion in this Nation's history and the permissibility of government displays acknowledging that history. For those reasons, I join the Chief Justice's opinion in full.

This case would be easy if the Court were willing to abandon the inconsistent guideposts it has adopted for addressing [693] Establishment Clause challenges, and return to the original meaning of the Clause. I have previously suggested that the Clause's text and history "resis[t] incorporation" against the States. See *Elk Grove Unified School Dist. v. Newdow*, 542 U.S. 1, 45–46 (2004) (opinion concurring in judgment); see also *Zelman v. Simmons-Harris*, 536 U.S. 639, 677–680, and n. 3 (2002) (concurring opinion). If the Establishment Clause does not restrain the States, then it has no application here, where only state action is at issue.

Even if the Clause is incorporated, or if the Free Exercise Clause limits the power of States to establish religions, our task would be far simpler if we returned to the original meaning of the word "establishment" than it is under the various approaches this Court now uses. The Framers understood an establishment "necessarily [to] involve actual legal coercion." *Newdow, supra*, at 52 (Thomas, J., concurring in judgment). "In other words, establishment at the founding involved, for example, mandatory observance or mandatory payment of taxes supporting ministers." *Cutter*, at 729 (Thomas, J., concurring). And "government practices that have nothing to do with creating or maintaining . . . coercive state establishments" simply do not "implicate the possible liberty interest of being [694] free from coercive state establishments." *Newdow*, at 53 (Thomas, J., concurring in judgment).

There is no question that, based on the original meaning of the Establishment Clause, the Ten Commandments display at issue here is constitutional. In no sense does Texas compel petitioner Van Orden to do anything. The only injury to him is that he takes offense at seeing the monument as he passes it on his way to the Texas Supreme Court Library. He need not stop to read it or even to look at it, let alone to express support for it or adopt the Commandments as guides for his life. The mere presence of the monument along his path involves no coercion and thus does not violate the Establishment Clause.

Returning to the original meaning would do more than simplify our task. It also would avoid the pitfalls present in the Court's current approach to such challenges. This Court's precedent elevates the trivial to the proverbial "federal case," by making benign signs and postings subject to challenge. Yet even as it does so, the Court's precedent attempts to avoid declaring all religious symbols and words of longstanding tradition unconstitutional, by counterfactually declaring them of little religious significance. Even when the Court's cases recognize that such symbols have religious meaning, they adopt an unhappy compromise that fails fully to account for either the adherent's or the non-adherent's beliefs, and provides no principled way to choose between them. Even worse, the incoherence of the Court's decisions in this area renders the Establishment Clause impenetrable and incapable of consistent application. All told, this Court's jurisprudence leaves courts, governments, and believers and nonbelievers alike confused—an observation that is hardly new. . . .

[697] Much, if not all, of this would be avoided if the Court would return to the views of the Framers and adopt coercion as the touchstone for our Establishment Clause inquiry. Every acknowledgment of religion would not give rise to an Establishment Clause claim. Courts would not act as theological commissions, judging the meaning of religious matters. Most important, our precedent would be capable of consistent and coherent application. While the Court correctly [698] rejects the challenge to the Ten Commandments monument on the Texas Capitol grounds, a more fundamental rethinking of our Establishment Clause jurisprudence remains in order.

Justice Breyer, concurring in the judgment.

In *School Dist. of Abington Township v. Schempp* (1963), Justice Goldberg, joined by Justice Harlan, wrote, in respect to the First Amendment's Religion Clauses, that there is "no simple and clear measure which by precise application can readily and invariably demark the permissible from the impermissible." *Id.*, at 306 (concurring opinion). One must refer instead to the basic purposes of those Clauses. They seek to "assure the fullest possible scope of religious liberty and tolerance for all." *Id.*, at 305. They seek to avoid that divisiveness based upon religion that promotes social conflict, sapping the strength of government and religion alike. *Zelman v. Simmons-Harris*, 536 U.S. 639, 717–729 (2002) (Breyer, J., dissenting). They seek to maintain that "separation of church and state" that has long been critical to the "peaceful dominion that religion exercises in [this] country," where the "spirit of religion" and the "spirit of freedom" are productively "united," "reign[ing] together" but in separate spheres "on the same soil." A. de Tocqueville, *Democracy in America*. They seek to further the basic principles set forth today by Justice O'Connor in her concurring opinion in *McCreary County v. Am. Civil Liberties Union*.

The Court has made clear, as Justices Goldberg and Harlan noted, that the realization of these goals means that government must "neither engage in nor compel religious practices," that it must "effect no favoritism among sects or between religion and non-religion," and that it must "work deterrence of no religious belief." *Schempp*, at 305. [699] The government must avoid excessive interference with, or promotion of, religion. But the Establishment Clause does not compel the government to purge from the public sphere all that in any way partakes of the religious. Such absolutism is not only inconsistent with our national traditions, but would also tend to promote the kind of social conflict the Establishment Clause seeks to avoid.

Thus, as Justices Goldberg and Harlan pointed out, the Court has found no single mechanical formula that can accurately draw the constitutional line in every case. Where the Establishment Clause is at issue, tests designed to measure "neutrality" alone are insufficient, both because it is sometimes difficult to determine when a legal rule is "neutral," and because

> "untutored devotion to the concept of neutrality can lead to invocation or approval of results which partake not simply of that noninterference and noninvolvement with the religious which the Constitution commands, but of a brooding and pervasive devotion to the secular and a passive, or even active, hostility to the religious." *Ibid.*

Neither can this Court's other tests readily explain the Establishment Clause's tolerance, for example, of the prayers that open legislative meetings, see *Marsh*; certain references to, and invocations of, the Deity in the public words of public officials; the public references to God on coins, decrees, and buildings; or the attention paid to the religious objectives of certain holidays, including Thanksgiving.

[700] If the relation between government and religion is one of separation, but not of mutual hostility and suspicion, one will inevitably find difficult borderline cases. And in such cases, I see no test-related substitute for the exercise of legal judgment. That judgment is not a personal judgment. Rather, as in all constitutional cases, it must reflect and remain faithful to the underlying purposes of the Clauses, and it must take account of context and consequences measured in light of those purposes. While the Court's prior tests provide useful guideposts—and might well lead to the same result the Court reaches today—no exact formula can dictate a resolution to such fact-intensive cases.

The case before us is a borderline case. It concerns a large granite monument bearing the text of the Ten Commandments located on the grounds of the Texas State Capitol. On the one hand, the Commandments' text undeniably has a religious message, invoking, indeed emphasizing, the [701] Deity. On the other hand, focusing on the text of the Commandments alone cannot conclusively resolve this case. Rather, to determine the message that the text here conveys, we must examine how the text is used. And that inquiry requires us to consider the context of the display.

In certain contexts, a display of the tablets of the Ten Commandments can convey not simply a religious message but also a secular moral message (about proper standards of social conduct). And in certain contexts, a display of the tablets can also convey a historical message (about a historic relation between those standards and the law)—a fact that helps to explain the display of those tablets in dozens of courthouses throughout the Nation, including the Supreme Court of the United States.

Here the tablets have been used as part of a display that communicates not simply a religious message, but a secular message as well. The circumstances surrounding the display's placement on the capitol grounds and its physical setting suggest that the State itself intended the latter, nonreligious aspects of the tablets' message to predominate. And the monument's 40-year history on the Texas state grounds indicates that that has been its effect.

The group that donated the monument, the Fraternal Order of Eagles, a private civic (and primarily secular) organization, while interested in the religious aspect of the Ten Commandments, sought to highlight the Commandments' role in shaping civic morality as part of that organization's efforts to combat juvenile delinquency. The Eagles' consultation with a committee composed of members of several faiths in order to find a nonsectarian text underscores the group's ethics-based motives. The tablets, as displayed on the monument, prominently acknowledge that the Eagles donated the display, a factor which, though not sufficient, thereby further distances [702] the State itself from the religious aspect of the Commandments' message.

The physical setting of the monument, moreover, suggests little or nothing of the sacred. The monument sits in a large park containing 17 monuments and 21 historical markers, all designed to illustrate the "ideals" of those who settled in Texas and of those who have lived there since that time. The setting does not readily lend itself to meditation or any other religious activity. But it does provide a context of history and moral ideals. It (together with the display's inscription about its origin) communicates to visitors that the State sought to reflect moral principles, illustrating a relation between ethics and law that the State's citizens, historically speaking, have endorsed. That is to say, the context suggests that the State intended the display's moral message—an illustrative message reflecting the historical "ideals" of Texans—to predominate.

If these factors provide a strong, but not conclusive, indication that the Commandments' text on this monument conveys a predominantly secular message, a further factor is determinative here. As far as I can tell, 40 years passed in which the presence of this monument, legally speaking, went unchallenged (until the single legal objection raised by petitioner). And I am not aware of any evidence suggesting that this was due to a climate of intimidation. Hence, those 40 years suggest more strongly than can any set of formulaic tests that few individuals, whatever their system of beliefs, are likely to have understood the monument as amounting, in any significantly detrimental way, to a government effort to favor a particular religious sect, primarily to promote religion over nonreligion, to "engage in" any "religious practic[e]," to "compel" any "religious practic[e]," or to "work deterrence" of any "religious belief." *Schempp*, 374 U.S., at 305. Those 40 years suggest that [703] the public visiting the capitol grounds has considered the religious aspect of the tablets' message as part of what is a broader moral and historical message reflective of a cultural heritage.

This case, moreover, is distinguishable from instances where the Court has found Ten Commandments displays impermissible. The display is not on the grounds of a public school, where, given the impressionability of the young, government must exercise particular care in separating church and state. This case also differs from *McCreary County*, where the short (and stormy) history of the courthouse Commandments' displays demonstrates the substantially religious objectives of those who mounted them, and the effect of this readily apparent objective upon those who view them. That history there indicates a governmental effort substantially to promote religion, not simply an effort primarily to reflect, historically, the secular impact of a religiously inspired document. And, in today's world, in a Nation of so many different religious and comparable nonreligious fundamental beliefs, a more contemporary state effort to focus attention upon a religious text is certainly likely to prove divisive in a way that this longstanding, pre-existing monument has not.

For these reasons, I believe that the Texas display—serving a mixed but primarily nonreligious purpose, not primarily "advanc[ing]" or "inhibit[ing] religion," and not creating an "excessive government entanglement with religion"—might satisfy this Court's more formal Establishment Clause tests. But, as I have said, in reaching the conclusion that the Texas display falls on the permissible side of the constitutional line, I rely less upon a literal application of any particular [704] test than upon consideration of the basic purposes of the First Amendment's Religion Clauses themselves. This display has stood apparently uncontested for nearly two generations. That experience helps us understand that as a practical matter of degree this display is unlikely to prove divisive. And this matter of degree is, I believe, critical in a borderline case such as this one.

At the same time, to reach a contrary conclusion here, based primarily on the religious nature of the tablets' text would, I fear, lead the law to exhibit a hostility toward religion that has no place in our Establishment Clause traditions. Such a holding might well encourage disputes concerning the removal of longstanding depictions of the Ten Commandments from public buildings across the Nation. And it could thereby create the very kind of religiously based divisiveness that the Establishment Clause seeks to avoid.

Justices Goldberg and Harlan concluded in *Schempp* that

"[t]he First Amendment does not prohibit practices which by any realistic measure create none of the dangers which it is designed to prevent and which do not so directly or substantially involve the state in religious exercises or in the favoring of religion as to have meaningful and practical impact." 374 U.S., at 308 (concurring opinion).

That kind of practice is what we have here. I recognize the danger of the slippery slope. Still, where the Establishment Clause is at issue, we must "distinguish between real threat and mere shadow." *Ibid.* Here, we have only the shadow.

In light of these considerations, I cannot agree with today's plurality's analysis. Nor can I agree with Justice Scalia's dissent in *McCreary County*. I do agree with Justice O'Connor's statement of principles in *McCreary County*, though I disagree with [705] her evaluation of the evidence as it bears on the application of those principles to this case.

I concur in the judgment of the Court.

. . . [707] Justice Stevens, with whom Justice Ginsburg joins, dissenting.

The sole function of the monument on the grounds of Texas' State Capitol is to display the full text of one version of the Ten Commandments. The monument is not a work of art and does not refer to any event in the history of the State. . . .

Viewed on its face, Texas' display has no purported connection to God's role in the formation of Texas or the founding of our Nation; nor does it provide the reasonable observer with any basis to guess that it was erected to honor any individual or organization. The message transmitted by Texas' chosen display is quite plain: This State endorses the divine code of the "Judeo-Christian" God.

[708] For those of us who learned to recite the King James version of the text long before we understood the meaning of some of its words, God's Commandments may seem like wise counsel. The question before this Court, however, is whether it is counsel that the State of Texas may proclaim without violating the Establishment Clause of the Constitution. If any fragment of Jefferson's metaphorical "wall of separation between church and State" is to be preserved—if there remains any meaning to the "wholesome 'neutrality' of which this Court's [Establishment Clause] cases speak," *School Dist. of Abington Township v. Schempp*, 374 U.S. 203, 222 (1963)—a negative answer to that question is mandatory.

I

In my judgment, at the very least, the Establishment Clause has created a strong presumption against the display of religious symbols on public property. The adornment of our public spaces with displays of religious symbols and messages undoubtedly provides comfort, even inspiration, to many individuals who subscribe to particular faiths. Unfortunately, the practice also runs the risk of "offend[ing] nonmembers of the faith being advertised as well as adherents who consider the particular advertisement disrespectful." *Allegheny County*, 492 U.S., at 651 (Stevens, J., concurring in part and dissenting in part).

[709] Government's obligation to avoid divisiveness and exclusion in the religious sphere is compelled by the Establishment and Free Exercise Clauses, which together erect a wall of separation between church and state. This metaphorical wall protects principles long recognized and often recited in this Court's cases. The first and most fundamental of these principles, one that a majority of this Court today affirms, is that the Establishment Clause demands religious neutrality—government may not exercise a preference for one religious faith over another. This essential command, however, is

not merely a prohibition [710] against the government's differentiation among religious sects. We have repeatedly reaffirmed that neither a State nor the Federal Government "can constitutionally pass laws or impose requirements which aid all religions as against non-believers, and neither can aid those religions based on a belief in the existence of God as against those religions founded on different beliefs." *Torcaso v. Watkins*, 367 U.S. 488, 495 (1961). This principle is based on the straightforward notion that governmental promotion of orthodoxy is not saved by the aggregation of several orthodoxies under the State's banner. . . .

[712] The monolith displayed on Texas Capitol grounds cannot be discounted as a passive acknowledgment of religion, nor can the State's refusal to remove it upon objection be explained as a simple desire to preserve a historic relic. This Nation's resolute commitment to neutrality with respect to religion is flatly inconsistent with the plurality's wholehearted validation of an official state endorsement of the message that there is one, and only one, God.

II

When the Ten Commandments monument was donated to the State of Texas in 1961, it was not for the purpose of commemorating a noteworthy event in Texas history, signifying [713] the Commandments' influence on the development of secular law, or even denoting the religious beliefs of Texans at that time. To the contrary, the donation was only one of over a hundred largely identical monoliths, and of over a thousand paper replicas, distributed to state and local governments throughout the Nation over the course of several decades. This ambitious project was the work of the Fraternal Order of Eagles, a well-respected benevolent organization whose good works have earned the praise of several Presidents. . . .

[714] The [monument's] donors were motivated by a desire to "inspire the youth" and curb juvenile delinquency by providing children with a "code of conduct or standards by which to govern their actions." It is the Eagles' belief that disseminating the message conveyed by the Ten Commandments will help to persuade young men and women to observe civilized standards of behavior, and will lead to more productive lives. Significantly, although the Eagles' organization is nonsectarian, eligibility for membership is premised on a belief in the existence of a "Supreme Being." . . .

[715] The desire to combat juvenile delinquency by providing guidance to youths is both admirable and unquestionably secular. But achieving that goal through biblical teachings injects a religious purpose into an otherwise secular endeavor. By spreading the word of God and converting heathens to Christianity, missionaries expect to enlighten their converts, enhance their satisfaction with life, and improve their behavior. Similarly, by disseminating the "law of God"—directing fidelity to God and proscribing murder, theft, and adultery—the Eagles hope that this divine guidance will help wayward youths conform their behavior and improve their lives. In my judgment, the significant secular byproducts that are intended consequences of religious instruction—indeed, of the establishment of most religions—are not the type of "secular" purposes that justify government promulgation of sacred religious messages.

Though the State of Texas may genuinely wish to combat juvenile delinquency, and may rightly want to honor the Eagles for their efforts, it cannot effectuate these admirable purposes through an explicitly religious medium. . . .

[717] The profoundly sacred message embodied by the text inscribed on the Texas monument is emphasized by the especially large letters that identify its author: "I AM

the LORD thy God." It commands present worship of Him and no other deity. It directs us to be guided by His teaching in the current and future conduct of all of our affairs. It instructs us to follow a code of divine law, some of which has informed and been integrated into our secular legal code ("Thou shalt not kill"), but much of which has not ("Thou shalt not make to thyself any graven images. . . . Thou shalt not covet").

Moreover, despite the Eagles' best efforts to choose a benign nondenominational text, the Ten Commandments display projects not just a religious, but an inherently sectarian, message. There are many distinctive versions of the Decalogue, ascribed to by different religions and even different denominations within a particular faith; to a pious and learned observer, these differences may be of enormous religious [718] significance. In choosing to display this version of the Commandments, Texas tells the observer that the State supports this side of the doctrinal religious debate. The reasonable observer, after all, has no way of knowing that this text was the product of a compromise, or that there is a rationale of any kind for the text's selection.

The Establishment Clause, if nothing else, prohibits government from "specifying details upon which men and women who believe in a benevolent, omnipotent Creator and Ruler of the world are known to differ." *Lee v. Weisman*, 505 U.S. 577, 641 (1992) (Scalia, J., dissenting). Given that the chosen text inscribed on the Ten Commandments monument invariably places the State at the center of a serious [719] sectarian dispute, the display is unquestionably unconstitutional under our case law. See *Larson v. Valente*, 456 U.S. 228, 244 (1982) ("The clearest command of the Establishment Clause is that one religious denomination cannot be officially preferred over another").

Even if, however, the message of the monument, despite the inscribed text, fairly could be said to represent the belief system of all Judeo-Christians, it would still run afoul of the Establishment Clause by prescribing a compelled code of conduct from one God, namely, a Judeo-Christian God, that is rejected by prominent polytheistic sects, such as Hinduism, as well as nontheistic religions, such as Buddhism. And, at the very least, the text of the Ten Commandments impermissibly commands a preference for religion over irreligion. [720] Any of those bases, in my judgment, would be sufficient to conclude that the message should not be proclaimed by the State of Texas on a permanent monument at the seat of its government.

I do not doubt that some Texans, including those elected to the Texas Legislature, may believe that the statues displayed on the Texas Capitol grounds, including the Ten Commandments monument, reflect the "ideals . . . that compose Texan identity." But Texas, like our entire country, is now a much more diversified community than it was when it became a part of the United States or even when the monument was erected. Today there are many Texans who do not believe in the God whose Commandments are displayed at their seat of government. Many of them worship a different god or no god at all. Some may believe that the account of the creation in the Book of Genesis is less reliable than the views of men like Darwin and Einstein. The monument is no more an expression of the views of every true Texan than was the "Live Free or Die" motto that the State of New Hampshire placed on its license plates in 1969 an accurate expression of the views of every citizen of New Hampshire.

Recognizing the diversity of religious and secular beliefs held by Texans and by all Americans, it seems beyond peradventure that allowing the seat of government to serve as a stage for the propagation of an unmistakably Judeo-Christian message of piety would have the tendency to make nonmonotheists and nonbelievers "feel like [outsiders] in matters of faith, and [strangers] in the political community." *Pinette*, 515 U.S., at 799 (Stevens, J., dissenting). "[D]isplays of this kind inevitably have a greater tendency to emphasize sincere and deeply felt differences among individuals than to achieve an ecumenical goal." *Allegheny County*, 492 U.S., at 651 [721] (Stevens, J., concurring in part and dissenting in part).

Even more than the display of a religious symbol on government property, displaying this sectarian text at the state capitol should invoke a powerful presumption of invalidity. As Justice Souter's opinion persuasively demonstrates, the physical setting in which the Texas monument is displayed—far from rebutting that presumption—actually enhances the religious content of its message. The monument's permanent fixture at the seat of Texas government is of immense significance. The fact that a monument

> "is installed on public property implies official recognition and reinforcement of its message. That implication is especially strong when the sign stands in front of the seat of the government itself. The 'reasonable observer' of any symbol placed unattended in front of any capitol in the world will normally assume that the sovereign—which is not only the owner of that parcel of real estate but also the lawgiver for the surrounding territory—has sponsored and facilitated its message." *Pinette*, 515 U.S., at 801–802 (Stevens, J., dissenting).

Critical examination of the Decalogue's prominent display at the seat of Texas government, rather than generic citation [722] to the role of religion in American life, unmistakably reveals on which side of the "slippery slope" this display must fall. God, as the author of its message, the Eagles, as the donor of the monument, and the State of Texas, as its proud owner, speak with one voice for a common purpose—to encourage Texans to abide by the divine code of a "Judeo-Christian" God. If this message is permissible, then the shining principle of neutrality to which we have long adhered is nothing more than mere shadow.

III

The plurality relies heavily on the fact that our Republic was founded, and has been governed since its nascence, by leaders who spoke then (and speak still) in plainly religious rhetoric. The Chief Justice cites, for instance, George Washington's 1789 Thanksgiving Proclamation in support of the proposition that the Establishment Clause does not proscribe official recognition of God's role in our Nation's heritage. Further, the plurality emphatically endorses the seemingly timeless recognition that our "institutions presuppose a Supreme Being." Many of the submissions made to this Court by the parties and *amici*, in accord with the plurality's opinion, have relied on the ubiquity of references to God throughout our history.

The speeches and rhetoric characteristic of the founding era, however, do not answer the question before us. I have already explained why Texas' display of the full text of the Ten Commandments, given the content of the actual display [723] and the context in which it is situated, sets this case apart from the countless examples of benign government recognitions of religion. But there is another crucial difference. Our leaders, when delivering public addresses, often express their blessings simultaneously in the service of God and their constituents. Thus, when public officials deliver public speeches, we recognize that their words are not exclusively a transmission from the government because those oratories have embedded within them the inherently personal views of the speaker as an individual member of the polity. The permanent placement of a textual religious display on state property is different in kind; it amalgamates otherwise discordant individual views into a collective statement of government approval. Moreover, the message never ceases to transmit itself to objecting viewers whose only choices are to accept the message or to ignore the offense by averting their gaze. In this sense, although Thanksgiving Day proclamations and inaugural speeches undoubtedly seem official, in most circumstances they will not constitute the sort of governmental endorsement of religion at which the separation of church and state is aimed.

[724] The plurality's reliance on early religious statements and proclamations made by the Founders is also problematic because those views were not espoused at the Constitutional Convention in 1787 nor enshrined in the Constitution's text. Thus, the presentation of these religious statements as a unified historical narrative is bound to paint a misleading picture. It does so here. In according deference to the statements of George Washington and John Adams, the Chief Justice and Justice Scalia fail to account for the acts and publicly espoused views of other influential leaders of that time. Notably absent from their historical snapshot is the fact that Thomas Jefferson refused to issue the Thanksgiving proclamations that Washington had so readily embraced based on the argument that to do so would violate the Establishment Clause. The Chief Justice and Justice Scalia disregard the substantial debates that took place regarding the constitutionality of the early proclamations and acts they cite [725] and paper over the fact that Madison more than once repudiated the views attributed to him by many, stating unequivocally that with respect to government's involvement with religion, the "tendency to a usurpation on one side, or the other, or to a corrupting coalition or alliance between them, will be best guarded against by an entire abstinence of the Government from interference, in any way whatever, beyond the necessity of preserving public order, & protecting each sect against trespasses on its legal rights by others."

These seemingly nonconforming sentiments should come as no surprise. Not insignificant numbers of colonists came to this country with memories of religious persecution by [726] monarchs on the other side of the Atlantic. Others experienced religious intolerance at the hands of colonial Puritans, who regrettably failed to practice the tolerance that some of their contemporaries preached. The Chief Justice and Justice Scalia ignore the separationist impulses—in accord with the principle of "neutrality"—that these individuals brought to the debates surrounding the adoption of the Establishment Clause.[27]

Ardent separationists aside, there is another critical nuance lost in the plurality's portrayal of history. Simply put, many of the Founders who are often cited as authoritative expositors of the Constitution's original meaning understood the Establishment Clause to stand for a narrower proposition than the plurality, for whatever reason, is willing to accept. Namely, many of the Framers understood the word "religion" in the Establishment Clause to encompass only the various sects of Christianity.

The evidence is compelling. Prior to the Philadelphia Convention, the States had begun to protect "religious freedom" in their various constitutions. Many of those provisions, however, restricted "equal protection" and "free exercise" [727] to Christians, and invocations of the divine were commonly understood to refer to Christ. That historical background likely informed the Framers' understanding of the First Amendment. Accordingly, one influential thinker wrote of the First Amendment that "[t]he meaning

---

27. The contrary evidence cited by The Chief Justice and Justice Scalia only underscores the obvious fact that leaders who have drafted and voted for a text are eminently capable of violating their own rules. The first Congress was—just as the present Congress is—capable of passing unconstitutional legislation. Thus, it is no answer to say that the Founders' separationist impulses were "plainly rejected" simply because the first Congress enacted laws that acknowledged God. To adopt such an interpretive approach would misguidedly give authoritative weight to the fact that the Congress that proposed the Fourteenth Amendment also enacted laws that tolerated segregation, and the fact that 10 years after proposing the First Amendment, Congress enacted the Alien and Sedition Act, which indisputably violated our present understanding of the First Amendment.

of the term 'establishment' in this amendment unquestionably is, the preference and establishment given by law to one sect of Christians over every other." Jasper Adams, *The Relation of Christianity to Civil Government in the United States* (Feb. 13, 1833). That definition tracked the understanding of the text Justice Story adopted in his famous Commentaries, in which he wrote that the "real object" of the Clause was

> "not to countenance, much less to advance Mahometanism, or Judaism, or infidelity, by prostrating Christianity; but to exclude all rivalry among Christian sects, and to prevent any national ecclesiastical establishment, which should give to an hierarchy the exclusive patronage of the national government. It thus sought to cut off the means of religious persecution (the vice and pest of former ages) and the power of subverting the rights of conscience in matters of religion, which had been trampled upon almost from the days of the Apostles to the present age." J. Story, *Commentaries on the Constitution of the United States* § 991.

[728] Along these lines, for nearly a century after the Founding, many accepted the idea that America was not just a religious nation, but "a Christian nation." *Church of Holy Trinity v. United States*, 143 U.S. 457, 471 (1892).

The original understanding of the type of "religion" that qualified for constitutional protection under the Establishment Clause likely did not include those followers of Judaism and Islam who are among the preferred "monotheistic" religions Justice Scalia has embraced in his *McCreary County* opinion. [729] The inclusion of Jews and Muslims inside the category of constitutionally favored religions surely would have shocked Chief Justice Marshall and Justice Story. Indeed, Justice Scalia is unable to point to any persuasive historical evidence or entrenched traditions in support of his decision to give specially preferred constitutional status to all monotheistic religions. Perhaps this is because the history of the Establishment Clause's original meaning just as strongly supports a preference for Christianity as it does a preference for monotheism. Generic references to "God" hardly constitute evidence that those who spoke the word meant to be inclusive of all monotheistic believers; nor do such references demonstrate that those who heard the word spoken understood it broadly to include all monotheistic faiths. Justice Scalia's inclusion of Judaism and Islam is a laudable act of religious tolerance, but it is one that is unmoored from the Constitution's history and text, and moreover one that is patently arbitrary in its inclusion of some, but exclusion of other (e.g., Buddhism), widely practiced non-Christian religions. Given the original understanding of the men who championed our "Christian nation"—men who had no cause to view anti-Semitism or contempt for atheists as problems worthy of civic concern—one must ask whether Justice Scalia "has not had the courage (or the foolhardiness) to apply [his originalism] principle consistently."

Indeed, to constrict narrowly the reach of the Establishment Clause to the views of the Founders would lead to more than this unpalatable result; it would also leave us with an unincorporated constitutional provision—in other words, one that limits only the federal establishment of "a national religion." [730] Under this view, not only could a State constitutionally adorn all of its public spaces with crucifixes or passages from the New Testament, it would also have full authority to prescribe the teachings of Martin Luther or Joseph Smith as the official state religion. Only the Federal Government would be prohibited from taking sides (and only then as between Christian sects).

A reading of the First Amendment dependent on either of the purported original meanings expressed above would eviscerate the heart of the Establishment Clause. It would replace Jefferson's "wall of separation" with a perverse wall of exclusion—Christians inside, non-Christians out. It would permit States to construct walls of their own choosing—Baptists inside, Mormons out; Jewish Orthodox inside, Jewish Reform out. A Clause so understood might be faithful to the expectations of some of our Founders, but it is plainly not worthy of a society whose enviable hallmark over the course of two centuries has been the continuing expansion of religious pluralism and tolerance.

Unless one is willing to renounce over 65 years of Establishment Clause jurisprudence and cross back over the incorporation bridge, appeals to the religiosity of the Framers ring hollow. But even if there were a coherent way to embrace [731] incorporation with one hand while steadfastly abiding by the Founders' purported religious views on the other, the problem of the selective use of history remains. As the widely divergent views espoused by the leaders of our founding era plainly reveal, the historical record of the preincorporation Establishment Clause is too indeterminate to serve as an interpretive North Star.

It is our duty, therefore, to interpret the First Amendment's command that "Congress shall make no law respecting an establishment of religion" not by merely asking what those words meant to observers at the time of the founding, but instead by deriving from the Clause's text and history the broad principles that remain valid today. . . .

[733] The principle that guides my analysis is neutrality.[35] The basis for that principle is firmly rooted in our Nation's [734] history and our Constitution's text. I recognize that the requirement that government must remain neutral between religion and irreligion would have seemed foreign to some of the Framers; so too would a requirement of neutrality between Jews and Christians. Fortunately, we are not bound by the Framers' expectations—we are bound by the legal principles they enshrined in our Constitution. Story's vision that States should not discriminate between Christian sects has as its foundation the principle that government must remain neutral between valid systems of belief. As religious pluralism has expanded, so has our acceptance of what constitutes valid belief systems. The evil of discriminating today against atheists, "polytheists[,] and believers in unconcerned deities," *McCreary County* at 893 (Scalia, J., dissenting), is in my view a direct descendent of the evil of discriminating among Christian sects. The Establishment Clause [735] thus forbids it and, in turn, prohibits Texas from displaying the Ten Commandments monument the plurality so casually affirms.

IV

The Eagles may donate as many monuments as they choose to be displayed in front of Protestant churches, benevolent organizations' meeting places, or on the front lawns

---

35. Justice Thomas contends that the Establishment Clause cannot include such a neutrality principle because the Clause reaches only the governmental coercion of individual belief or disbelief. In my view, although actual religious coercion is undoubtedly forbidden by the Establishment Clause, that cannot be the full extent of the provision's reach. Jefferson's "wall" metaphor and his refusal to issue Thanksgiving proclamations would have been nonsensical if the Clause reached only direct coercion. Further, under the "coercion" view, the Establishment Clause would amount to little more than a replica of our compelled speech doctrine, see, e.g., *West Virginia Bd. of Ed. v. Barnette*, 319 U.S. 624, 639 (1943), with a religious flavor. A Clause so interpreted would not prohibit explicit state endorsements of religious orthodoxies of particular sects, actions that lie at the heart of what the Clause was meant to regulate. The government could, for example, take out television advertisements lauding Catholicism as the only pure religion. Under the reasoning endorsed by Justice Thomas, those programs would not be coercive because the viewer could simply turn off the television or ignore the ad. Further, the notion that the application of a "coercion" principle would somehow lead to a more consistent jurisprudence is dubious. Enshrining coercion as the Establishment Clause touchstone fails to eliminate the difficult judgment calls regarding "the form that coercion must take." *McCreary County*, at 909 (Scalia, J., dissenting). Coercion may seem obvious to some, while appearing nonexistent to others. It may be a legal requirement or an effect that is indirectly inferred from a variety of factors. In short, "reasonable people could, and no doubt would, argue about whether coercion existed in a particular situation." Feldman, 77 N. Y. U. L. Rev., at 415.

of private citizens. The expurgated text of the King James version of the Ten Commandments that they have crafted is unlikely to be accepted by Catholic parishes, Jewish synagogues, or even some Protestant denominations, but the message they seek to convey is surely more compatible with church property than with property that is located on the government side of the metaphorical wall.

The judgment of the Court in this case stands for the proposition that the Constitution permits governmental displays of sacred religious texts. This makes a mockery of the constitutional ideal that government must remain neutral between religion and irreligion. If a State may endorse a particular deity's command to "have no other gods before me," it is difficult to conceive of any textual display that would run afoul of the Establishment Clause.

The disconnect between this Court's approval of Texas' monument and the constitutional prohibition against preferring religion to irreligion cannot be reduced to the exercise of plotting two adjacent locations on a slippery slope. Rather, it is the difference between the shelter of a fortress and exposure to "the winds that would blow" if the wall were allowed to crumble. That wall, however imperfect, remains worth preserving.

I respectfully dissent.

. . . [737] Justice Souter, with whom Justice Stevens and Justice Ginsburg join, dissenting.

Although the First Amendment's Religion Clauses have not been read to mandate absolute governmental neutrality toward religion, the Establishment Clause requires neutrality as a general rule and thus expresses Madison's condemnation of "employ[ing] Religion as an engine of Civil policy," *Memorial and Remonstrance against Religious Assessments*. A governmental display of an obviously religious text cannot be squared with neutrality, except in a setting that plausibly indicates that the statement is not placed in view with a predominant purpose on the part of government either to adopt the religious message or to urge its acceptance by others.

Until today, only one of our cases addressed the constitutionality of posting the Ten Commandments, *Stone v. Graham*, 449 U.S. 39, 41–42 (1980) (*per curiam*). A Kentucky statute required posting the Commandments on the walls of public school classrooms, and the Court described the State's purpose (relevant under the tripartite test laid out in *Lemon v. Kurtzman*) as being at odds with the obligation of religious neutrality.

> "The pre-eminent purpose for posting the Ten Commandments on schoolroom walls is plainly religious in nature. The Ten Commandments are undeniably a sacred text in the Jewish and Christian faiths, and no legislative recitation of a supposed secular purpose can blind us to that fact. The Commandments do not confine [738] themselves to arguably secular matters, such as honoring one's parents, killing or murder, adultery, stealing, false witness, and covetousness. Rather, the first part of the Commandments concerns the religious duties of believers: worshipping the Lord God alone, avoiding idolatry, not using the Lord's name in vain, and observing the Sabbath Day." 449 U.S., at 41–42.

What these observations underscore are the simple realities that the Ten Commandments constitute a religious statement, that their message is inherently religious, and that the purpose of singling them out in a display is clearly the same.

Thus, a pedestrian happening upon the monument at issue here needs no training in religious doctrine to realize that the statement of the Commandments, quoting God himself, proclaims that the will of the divine being is the source of obligation to obey the rules, including the facially secular ones. In this case, moreover, the text is presented to give particular prominence to the Commandments' first sectarian [739] reference, "I am the Lord thy God." That proclamation is centered on the stone and written in slightly larger letters than the subsequent recitation. To ensure that the religious nature of the monument is clear to even the most casual passerby, the word "Lord" appears in all capital letters (as does the word "am"), so that the most eye-catching segment of the quotation is the declaration "I AM the LORD thy God." What follows, of course, are the rules against other gods, graven images, vain swearing, and Sabbath breaking. And the full text of the fifth Commandment puts forward filial respect as a condition of long life in the land "which the Lord thy God giveth thee." These "words . . . make [the] . . . religious meaning unmistakably clear." *County of Allegheny v. American Civil Liberties Union, Greater Pittsburgh Chapter*, 492 U.S. 573, 598 (1989).

To drive the religious point home, and identify the message as religious to any viewer who failed to read the text, the engraved quotation is framed by religious symbols: two tablets with what appears to be ancient script on them, two Stars of David, and the superimposed Greek letters Chi and Rho as the familiar monogram of Christ. Nothing on the monument, in fact, detracts from its religious nature.[2]

[740] The monument's presentation of the Commandments with religious text emphasized and enhanced stands in contrast to any number of perfectly constitutional depictions of them, the frieze of our own Courtroom providing a good example, where the figure of Moses stands among history's great lawgivers. While Moses holds the tablets of the Commandments showing some Hebrew text, no one looking at the lines of figures in marble relief is likely to see a religious purpose behind the assemblage or take away a religious message from it. Only one other depiction represents a religious leader, and the historical personages are mixed with symbols of moral and intellectual abstractions like Equity and Authority. Since Moses enjoys no especial prominence on the frieze, viewers can readily take him to be there as a lawgiver in the company of other lawgivers; and the viewers may just as naturally see the tablets of the Commandments (showing the later ones, forbidding things like killing and theft, but without the divine preface) as background from which the concept of law [741] emerged, ultimately having a secular influence in the history of the Nation. Government may, of course, constitutionally call attention to this influence, and may post displays or erect monuments recounting this aspect of our history no less than any other, so long as there is a context and that context is historical. Hence, a display of the Commandments accompanied by an exposition of how they have influenced modern law would most likely be constitutionally unobjectionable. [742] And the Decalogue could, as *Stone* suggested, be integrated constitutionally into a course of study in public schools.

Texas seeks to take advantage of the recognition that visual symbol and written text can manifest a secular purpose in secular company, when it argues that its monument (like Moses in the frieze) is not alone and ought to be viewed as only 1 among 17 placed on the 22 acres surrounding the State Capitol. Texas, indeed, says that the Capitol grounds are like a museum for a collection of exhibits, the kind of setting that several Members of the Court have said can render the exhibition of religious artifacts permis-

---

2. That the monument also surrounds the text of the Commandments with various American symbols (notably the U. S. flag and a bald eagle) only underscores the impermissibility of Texas's actions: by juxtaposing these patriotic symbols with the Commandments and other religious signs, the monument sends the message that being American means being religious (and not just being religious but also subscribing to the Commandments, i.e., practicing a monotheistic religion).

sible, even though in other circumstances their display would be seen as meant to convey a religious message forbidden to the State. So, for example, the Government of the United States does not violate the Establishment Clause by hanging Giotto's Madonna on the wall of the National Gallery.

But 17 monuments with no common appearance, history, or esthetic role scattered over 22 acres is not a museum, and anyone strolling around the lawn would surely take each memorial on its own terms without any dawning sense that some purpose held the miscellany together more coherently [743] than fortuity and the edge of the grass. One monument expresses admiration for pioneer women. One pays respect to the fighters of World War II. And one quotes the God of Abraham whose command is the sanction for moral law. The themes are individual grit, patriotic courage, and God as the source of Jewish and Christian morality; there is no common denominator. In like circumstances, we rejected an argument similar to the State's, noting in *County of Allegheny* that "[t]he presence of Santas or other Christmas decorations elsewhere in the . . . [c]ourthouse, and of the nearby gallery forum, fail to negate the [creche's] endorsement effect. . . . The record demonstrates . . . that the creche, with its floral frame, was its own display distinct from any other decorations or exhibitions in the building." 492 U.S., at 598–599.

If the State's museum argument does nothing to blunt the religious message and manifestly religious purpose behind it, neither does the plurality's reliance on generalities culled from cases factually different from this one. [744] In fact, it is not until the end of its opinion that the plurality turns to the relevant precedent of *Stone*, a case actually dealing with a display of the Decalogue.

When the plurality finally does confront *Stone*, it tries to avoid the case's obvious applicability by limiting its holding to the classroom setting. The plurality claims to find authority for limiting *Stone*'s reach this way in the opinion's citations of two schoolprayer cases, *School Dist. of Abington Township v. Schempp* (1963) and *Engel v. Vitale* (1962). But *Stone* relied on those cases for widely applicable notions, not for any concept specific to schools. The opinion quoted *Schempp*'s statements that "it is no defense to urge that the religious practices here may be relatively minor encroachments on the First Amendment," *Schempp*, at 225; and that "the place of the Bible as an instrument of religion cannot be gainsaid," *Schempp*, at 224. And *Engel* was cited to support the proposition that the State was responsible for displaying the Commandments, even though their framed, printed texts were bought with private subscriptions. Thus, the schoolroom was beside the point of the citations, and that is presumably why the *Stone* Court failed to discuss the educational setting, as other opinions had done when school was significant. *Stone* did not, for example, speak of children's impressionability or their captivity as an audience in a school class. In fact, *Stone*'s reasoning reached the classroom only in noting the lack of support for the claim that the State had brought the Commandments into schools in order to "integrat[e] [them] into the school curriculum." 449 U.S., at 42. [745] Accordingly, our numerous prior discussions of *Stone* have never treated its holding as restricted to the classroom.

Nor can the plurality deflect *Stone* by calling the Texas monument "a far more passive use of [the Decalogue] than was the case in *Stone*, where the text confronted elementary school students every day." Placing a monument on the ground is not more "passive" than hanging a sheet of paper on a wall when both contain the same text to be read by anyone who looks at it. The problem in *Stone* was simply that the State was putting the Commandments there to be seen, just as the monument's inscription is there for those who walk by it.

To be sure, Kentucky's compulsory-education law meant that the school-children were forced to see the display every day, whereas many see the monument by choice, and those who customarily walk the Capitol grounds can presumably avoid it if they choose. But in my judgment (and under our often inexact Establishment Clause jurisprudence, such matters often boil down to judgment), this distinction should make no difference. The monument in this case sits on the grounds of the Texas State Capitol. There is something significant in the common term "statehouse" to refer to a state capitol building: it is the civic home of every one of the State's citizens. If neutrality in religion means something, any citizen should be able to visit that civic home without having to confront religious expressions clearly meant to convey an official religious position that may be at odds with his own [746] religion, or with rejection of religion.

Finally, though this too is a point on which judgment will vary, I do not see a persuasive argument for constitutionality in the plurality's observation that Van Orden's lawsuit comes "[f]orty years after the monument's erection . . . ," an observation that echoes the State's contention that one fact cutting in its favor is that "the monument had stood in Austin . . . for some forty years without generating any controversy or litigation." It is not that I think the passage of time is necessarily irrelevant in Establishment Clause analysis. We have approved framing-era practices because they must originally have been understood as constitutionally permissible, *e.g.*, *Marsh v. Chambers*, and we have recognized that Sunday laws have grown recognizably secular over time, *McGowan v. Maryland*. There is also an analogous argument, not yet evaluated, that ritualistic religious expression can become so numbing over time that its initial Establishment Clause violation becomes at some point too diminished for notice. But I do not understand any of these to be the State's argument, which rather seems to be that 40 years without a challenge shows that as a factual matter the religious expression is too tepid to provoke a serious reaction and constitute a violation. Perhaps, but the writer of Exodus chapter 20 was not lukewarm, and other explanations may do better in accounting [747] for the late resort to the courts. Suing a State over religion puts nothing in a plaintiff's pocket and can take a great deal out, and even with volunteer litigators to supply time and energy, the risk of social ostracism can be powerfully deterrent. I doubt that a slow walk to the courthouse, even one that took 40 years, is much evidentiary help in applying the Establishment Clause.

I would reverse the judgment of the Court of Appeals.

61

McCreary County v. American Civil Liberties Union of Kentucky

545 U.S. 844 (2005)

Vote: 5—Stevens, O'Connor, Souter, Ginsburg, Breyer
4—Rehnquist, Scalia, Kennedy, Thomas

Opinion announcing the opinion of the Court: Souter
Concurring opinion: O'Connor
Dissenting opinions: Scalia

This case, one of two Supreme Court decisions pertaining to the Ten Commandments handed down on the last day of the Supreme Court's 2004 term, involved evolving Ten Commandment displays posted in Kentucky county courthouses.

In the summer of 1999, McCreary County and Pulaski County, Kentucky, erected in their respective courthouses large, gold-framed copies of an abridged text of the King James version of the Ten Commandments. In McCreary County, the county legislative body ordered the display "[to] be posted in 'a very high traffic area' of the courthouse." In Pulaski County, amid reported controversy over its propriety, the display was hung in a ceremony presided over by the county judge-executive, who called them "good rules to live by."

In November 1999, the American Civil Liberties Union of Kentucky sued the counties in federal district court and sought a preliminary injunction against maintaining the displays. Within a month, and before the district court had responded to the request for injunction, the legislative body of each county passed nearly identical resolutions authorizing a second, expanded display. Those resolutions asserted that the Ten Commandments are "the precedent legal code upon which the civil and criminal codes of . . . Kentucky are founded" and stated several grounds for taking that position, including that "the Ten Commandments are codified in Kentucky's civil and criminal laws," that the Kentucky House of Representatives had in 1993 "voted unanimously . . . to adjourn . . . 'in remembrance and honor of Jesus Christ, the Prince of Ethics,'" and that the "Founding Father[s] [had an] explicit understanding of the duty of elected officials to publicly acknowledge God as the source of America's strength and direction."

As directed by the resolutions, the counties expanded the displays. In addition to the first display's large framed copy of the edited King James version of the Ten Commandments, the second set of displays included the following eight other documents in smaller frames, each either having a religious theme or excerpted to highlight a religious element: the "endowed by their Creator" passage from the Declaration of Independence; the Preamble to the Constitution of Kentucky; the national motto, "In God We Trust"; a page from the Congressional Record of February 2, 1983, proclaiming the Year of the Bible; a proclamation by President Abraham Lincoln designating April 30, 1863, a National Day of Prayer and Humiliation; an excerpt from President Lincoln's "Reply to Loyal Colored People of Baltimore upon Presentation of a Bible," reading that "the Bible is the best gift God has ever given to man"; a proclamation by President Reagan marking 1983 the Year of the Bible; and the Mayflower Compact.

On May 5, 2000, the district court entered a preliminary injunction ordering that the "display . . . be removed from [each] County Courthouse IMMEDIATELY" and that no county official "erect or cause to be erected similar displays."

Subsequently, the counties both installed a third display titled "The Foundations of American Law and Government Display." These displays consisted of nine equally sized framed documents: the Ten Commandments (explicitly identified as the "King James Version"), the Magna Carta, the Declaration of Independence, the Bill of Rights, the lyrics of the "Star-Spangled Banner," the Mayflower Compact, the national motto, the Preamble to the Kentucky Constitution, and a picture of Lady Justice. Each document included a statement about its historical and legal significance. The statement accompanying the Ten Commandments read as follows:

> The Ten Commandments have profoundly influenced the formation of Western legal thought and the formation of our country. That influence is clearly seen in the Declaration of Independence, which declared that "We hold these truths to be self-evident, that all men are created equal, that they are endowed by their Creator with certain unalienable Rights, that among these are Life, Liberty, and the pursuit of Happiness." The Ten Commandments provide the moral background of the Declaration of Independence and the foundation of our legal tradition.

The federal district court, when issuing a modified injunction to include the third set of displays, concluded the following: (1) the counties' objective of proclaiming the Commandments' foundational value had a religious, rather than secular, purpose; and (2) the assertion that the counties' broader educational goals were secular failed upon an examination of the history of the litigation at hand and in light of the counties' decisions to (a) post the Commandments by themselves in the first instance, and (b) later accentuate the religious objective by surrounding the Commandments with specific references to Christianity. The United States Court of Appeals for the Sixth Circuit, in affirming the district court's decision, expressed the view that (1) the counties' purpose was religious, not educational, given the nature of the Commandments as an active symbol of religion; and (2) the history of the litigation itself was evidence of the counties' religious objective.

Souter, J., delivered the opinion of the Court, in which Stevens, O'Connor, Ginsburg, and Breyer, JJ., joined.

. . . [859] II

Twenty-five years ago in a case prompted by posting the Ten Commandments in Kentucky's public schools, this Court recognized that the Commandments "are undeniably a sacred text in the Jewish and Christian faiths" and held that their display in public classrooms violated the First Amendment's bar against establishment of religion. *Stone*, 449 U.S., at 41. *Stone* found a predominantly religious purpose in the government's posting of the Commandments, given their prominence as "an instrument of religion," *id.*, at 41. The Counties ask for a different approach here by arguing that official purpose is unknowable and the search for it inherently vain. In the alternative, the Counties would avoid the District Court's conclusion by having us limit the scope of the purpose enquiry so severely that any trivial rationalization would suffice, under a standard oblivious to the history of religious government action like the progression of exhibits in this case.

Ever since *Lemon v. Kurtzman* summarized the three familiar considerations for evaluating Establishment Clause claims, looking to whether government action has "a secular legislative purpose" has been a common, albeit seldom dispositive, element. Though we have found government action motivated by an illegitimate purpose only four times since *Lemon*, and "the secular purpose requirement alone may rarely be determinative . . . , it nevertheless serves an important function."[10] *Wallace v.* [860] *Jaffree*, 472 U.S. 38, 75 (1985) (O'Connor, J., concurring in judgment).

The touchstone for our analysis is the principle that the "First Amendment mandates governmental neutrality between religion and religion, and between religion and nonreligion." *Epperson v. Arkansas*, 393 U.S. 97, 104 (1968). When the government acts with the ostensible and predominant purpose of advancing religion, it violates that central Establishment Clause value of official religious neutrality, there being no neutrality when the government's ostensible object is to take sides. Manifesting a purpose to favor one faith over another, or adherence to religion generally, clashes with the "understanding, reached . . . after decades of religious war, that liberty and social stability demand a religious tolerance that respects the religious views of all citizens. . . ." *Zelman v. Simmons-Harris*, 536 U.S. 639, 718 (2002) (Breyer, J., dissenting). By showing a purpose to favor religion, the government "sends the . . . message to . . . nonadherents 'that they are outsiders, not full members of the political community, and an accompanying message to adherents that they are insiders, favored members. . . .'" *Santa Fe Independent School Dist. v. Doe*, 530 U.S. 290, 309–310 (2000). . . .

[866] 2

[The Counties] argue that purpose in a case like this one should be inferred, if at all, only from the latest news about the last in a series of governmental actions, however close they may all be in time and subject. But the world is not made brand new every morning, and the Counties are simply asking us to ignore perfectly probative evidence; they want an absentminded objective observer, not one presumed to be familiar with the history of the government's actions and competent to learn what history has to show. The Counties' position just bucks common sense: reasonable observers have reasonable memories, and our precedents sensibly forbid an observer "to turn a blind eye to the context in which [the] policy arose."[14] *Santa Fe*, at 315. . . .

---

10. At least since *Everson v. Board of Ed. of Ewing*, it has been clear that Establishment Clause doctrine lacks the comfort of categorical absolutes. In special instances we have found good reason to hold governmental action legitimate even where its manifest purpose was presumably religious. See, e.g., *Marsh v. Chambers* (1983) (upholding legislative prayer despite its religious nature). No such reasons present themselves here.

14. One consequence of taking account of the purpose underlying past actions is that the same government action may be constitutional if taken in the first instance and unconstitutional if it has a sectarian heritage. This presents no incongruity, however, because purpose matters. Just as Holmes's dog could tell the difference between being kicked and being stumbled over, it will matter to objective observers whether posting the Commandments follows on the heels of displays motivated by sectarianism, or whether it lacks a history

[867] We take *Stone* as the initial legal benchmark, our only case dealing with the constitutionality of displaying the Commandments. *Stone* recognized that the Commandments are an "instrument of religion" and that, at least on the facts before it, the display of their text could presumptively be understood as meant to advance religion: although state law specifically required their posting in public school classrooms, their isolated exhibition did not leave room even for an argument that secular education explained their being there. But *Stone* did not purport to decide the constitutionality of every possible way the Commandments might be set out by the government, and under the Establishment Clause detail is key. [868] Hence, we look to the record of evidence showing the progression leading up to the third display of the Commandments.

The display rejected in *Stone* had two obvious similarities to the first one in the sequence here: both set out a text of the Commandments as distinct from any traditionally symbolic representation, and each stood alone, not part of an arguably secular display. *Stone* stressed the significance of integrating the Commandments into a secular scheme to forestall the broadcast of an otherwise clearly religious message, and for good reason, the Commandments being a central point of reference in the religious and moral history of Jews and Christians. They proclaim the existence of a monotheistic god (no other gods). They regulate details of religious obligation (no graven images, no sabbath breaking, no vain oath swearing). And they unmistakably rest even the universally accepted prohibitions (as against murder, theft, and the like) on the sanction of the divinity proclaimed at the beginning of the text. Displaying that text is thus different from a symbolic depiction, like tablets with 10 roman numerals, which could be seen as alluding to a general notion of law, not a sectarian conception of faith. Where the text is set out, the insistence of the religious message is hard to avoid in the absence of a context plausibly suggesting a message going beyond an excuse to promote the religious point of view. The display in *Stone* had no context that might have indicated an object beyond the religious character of the text, and the Counties' solo exhibit here did nothing more to counter the sectarian implication than the [869] postings at issue in *Stone*. Actually, the posting by the Counties lacked even the *Stone* display's implausible disclaimer that the Commandments were set out to show their effect on the civil law. What is more, at the ceremony for posting the framed Commandments in Pulaski County, the county executive was accompanied by his pastor, who testified to the certainty of the existence of God. The reasonable observer could only think that the Counties meant to emphasize and celebrate the Commandments' religious message.

This is not to deny that the Commandments have had influence on civil or secular law; a major text of a majority religion is bound to be felt. The point is simply that the original text viewed in its entirety is an unmistakably religious statement dealing with religious obligations and with morality subject to religious sanction. When the government initiates an effort to place this statement alone in public view, a religious object is unmistakable. . . .

---

demonstrating that purpose. The dissent, apparently not giving the reasonable observer as much credit as Holmes's dog, contends that in practice it will be "absur[d]" to rely upon differences in purpose in assessing government action. As an initial matter, it will be the rare case in which one of two identical displays violates the purpose prong. In general, like displays tend to show like objectives and will be treated accordingly. But where one display has a history manifesting sectarian purpose that the other lacks, it is appropriate that they be treated differently, for the one display will be properly understood as demonstrating a preference for one group of religious believers as against another. While posting the Commandments may not have the effect of causing greater adherence to them, an ostensible indication of a purpose to promote a particular faith certainly will have the effect of causing viewers to understand the government is taking sides.

[870] After the Counties changed lawyers, they mounted a third display, without a new resolution or repeal of the old one. The result was the "Foundations of American Law and Government" [871] exhibit, which placed the Commandments in the company of other documents the Counties thought especially significant in the historical foundation of American government. In trying to persuade the District Court to lift the preliminary injunction, the Counties cited several new purposes for the third version, including a desire "to educate the citizens of the county regarding some of the documents that played a significant role in the foundation of our system of law and government."[18] 145 F. Supp. 2d, at 848. The Counties' claims did not, however, persuade the court, intimately familiar with the details of this litigation, or the Court of Appeals, neither of which found a legitimizing secular purpose in this third version of the display. "When both courts [that have already passed on the case] are unable to discern an arguably valid secular purpose, this Court normally should hesitate to find one." *Edwards*, 482 U.S., at 594. The conclusions of the two courts preceding us in this case are well warranted.

These new statements of purpose were presented only as a litigating position, there being no further authorizing action by the Counties' governing boards. And although repeal of the earlier county authorizations would not have erased them from the record of evidence bearing on current purpose, the extraordinary resolutions for the second display passed just months earlier were not repealed or otherwise [872] repudiated. Indeed, the sectarian spirit of the common resolution found enhanced expression in the third display, which quoted more of the purely religious language of the Commandments than the first two displays had done. No reasonable observer could swallow the claim that the Counties had cast off the objective so unmistakable in the earlier displays. . . .

[875] The First Amendment has not one but two clauses tied to "religion," the second forbidding any prohibition on "the free exercise thereof," and sometimes the two clauses compete: spending government money on the clergy looks like establishing religion, but if the government cannot pay for military chaplains a good many soldiers and sailors would be kept from the opportunity to exercise their chosen religions. At other times, limits on governmental action that might make sense as a way to avoid establishment could arguably limit freedom of speech when the speaking is done under government auspices. The dissent, then, is wrong to read cases like *Walz v. Tax Comm'n of City of New York* (1970) as a rejection of neutrality on its own terms, for tradeoffs are inevitable, and an elegant interpretative rule to draw the line in all the multifarious situations is not to be had.

Given the variety of interpretative problems, the principle of neutrality has provided a good sense of direction: the government may not favor one religion over another, or religion over irreligion, religious choice being the prerogative of individuals [876] under the Free Exercise Clause. The principle has been helpful simply because it responds to one of the major concerns that prompted adoption of the Religion Clauses. The Framers and the citizens of their time intended not only to protect the integrity of individual conscience in religious matters but to guard against the civic divisiveness that follows when the government weighs in on one side of religious debate; nothing does a better job of roiling society, a point that needed no explanation to the descendants of English Puritans and Cavaliers (or Massachusetts Puritans and Baptists). A sense of the past thus points

---

18. The Counties' other purposes were: "to erect a display containing the Ten Commandments that is constitutional; . . . to demonstrate that the Ten Commandments were part of the foundation of American Law and Government; . . . [to include the Ten Commandments] as part of the display for their significance in providing 'the moral background of the Declaration of Independence and the foundation of our legal tradition.'" 145 F. Supp. 2d, at 848.

to governmental neutrality as an objective of the Establishment Clause and a sensible standard applying it. To be sure, given its generality as a principle, an appeal to neutrality alone cannot possibly lay every issue to rest, or tell us what issues on the margins are substantial enough for constitutional significance, a point that has been clear from the founding era to modern times. But invoking neutrality is a prudent way of keeping sight of something the Framers of the First Amendment thought important.

The dissent, however, puts forward a limitation on the application of the neutrality principle, with citations to historical evidence said to show that the Framers understood the [877] ban on establishment of religion as sufficiently narrow to allow the government to espouse submission to the divine will. The dissent identifies God as the God of monotheism, all of whose three principal strains (Jewish, Christian, and Muslim) acknowledge the religious importance of the Ten Commandments. On the dissent's view, it apparently follows that even rigorous espousal of a common element of this common monotheism is consistent with the establishment ban.

But the dissent's argument for the original understanding is flawed from the outset by its failure to consider the full range of evidence showing what the Framers believed. The dissent is certainly correct in putting forward evidence that some of the Framers thought some endorsement of religion was compatible with the establishment ban; the dissent quotes the first President as stating that "[n]ational morality [cannot] prevail in exclusion of religious principle," for example, and it cites his first Thanksgiving proclamation giving thanks to God. Surely if expressions like these from Washington and his contemporaries were all we had to go on, there would be a good case that the neutrality principle has the effect of broadening the ban on establishment beyond the Framers' understanding of it (although there would, of course, still be the question of whether the historical case could overcome some 60 years of precedent taking neutrality as its guiding principle).

[878] But the fact is that we do have more to go on, for there is also evidence supporting the proposition that the Framers intended the Establishment Clause to require governmental neutrality in matters of religion, including neutrality in statements acknowledging religion. The very language of the Establishment Clause represented a significant departure from early drafts that merely prohibited a single national religion, and the final language instead "extended [the] prohibition to state support for 'religion' in general." See *Lee v. Weisman*, 505 U.S. 577, 614–615 (1992) (Souter, J., concurring).

The historical record, moreover, is complicated beyond the dissent's account by the writings and practices of figures no less influential than Thomas Jefferson and James Madison. Jefferson, for example, refused to issue Thanksgiving Proclamations because he believed that they violated the Constitution. And Madison, whom the dissent claims as supporting its thesis, criticized Virginia's general assessment tax not just because it required people to donate "three pence" to religion, but because "it is itself a signal of persecution. It degrades from the equal rank of Citizens all those whose opinions in Religion do not bend to those of the Legislative authority."

[879] The fair inference is that there was no common understanding about the limits of the establishment prohibition, and the dissent's conclusion that its narrower view was the original understanding stretches the evidence beyond tensile capacity. What the evidence does show is a group of statesmen, like others before and after them, who proposed a guarantee with contours not wholly worked out, leaving the Establishment Clause with edges still to be determined. And none the worse for that. Indeterminate edges are the kind to have in a constitution meant to endure, and to meet "exigencies which, if foreseen at all, must have been seen dimly, and which can be best provided for as they occur." *McCulloch v. Maryland*, 17 U.S. 316 (1819). . . .

[881] Historical evidence thus supports no solid argument for changing course (what-ever force the argument might have when directed at the existing precedent), whereas public discourse at the present time certainly raises no doubt about the value of the interpretative approach invoked for 60 years now. We are centuries away from the St. Bartholomew's Day massacre and the treatment of heretics in early Massachusetts, but the divisiveness of religion in current public life is inescapable. This is no time to deny the prudence of understanding the Establishment Clause to require the government to stay neutral on religious belief, which is reserved for the conscience of the individual. . . .

[885] Justice Scalia, with whom the Chief Justice and Justice Thomas join, and with whom Justice Kennedy joins as to Parts II and III, dissenting.

I would uphold McCreary County and Pulaski County, Kentucky's (hereinafter Counties) displays of the Ten Commandments. I shall discuss, first, why the Court's oft repeated assertion that the government cannot favor religious practice is false; second, why today's opinion extends the scope of that falsehood even beyond prior cases; and third, why even on the basis of the Court's false assumptions the judgment here is wrong.

I

A

On September 11, 2001, I was attending in Rome, Italy, an international conference of judges and lawyers, principally from Europe and the United States. That night and the next morning virtually all of the participants watched, in their hotel rooms, the address to the Nation by the President of the United States concerning the murderous attacks upon the Twin Towers and the Pentagon, in which thousands of Americans had been killed. The address ended, as Presidential addresses often do, with the prayer "God bless America." The next afternoon I was approached by one of the judges from a European country, who, after extending his profound condolences for my country's loss, sadly observed: "How I wish that the Head of State of my country, at a similar time of national tragedy and distress, could conclude his address 'God bless ____.' It is of course absolutely forbidden."

[886] That is one model of the relationship between church and state—a model spread across Europe by the armies of Napoleon, and reflected in the Constitution of France, which begins, "France is [a] . . . secular . . . Republic." France Const., Art. 1. Religion is to be strictly excluded from the public forum. This is not, and never was, the model adopted by America. George Washington added to the form of Presidential oath prescribed by Art. II, § 1, cl. 7, of the Constitution, the concluding words "so help me God." The Supreme Court under John Marshall opened its sessions with the prayer "God save the United States and this Honorable Court." The First Congress instituted the practice of beginning its legislative sessions with a prayer. The same week that Congress submitted the Establishment Clause as part of the Bill of Rights for ratification by the States, it enacted legislation providing for paid chaplains in the House and Senate. The day after the First Amendment was proposed, the same Congress that had proposed it requested the President to proclaim "a day of public thanksgiving and prayer, to be observed, by acknowledging, with grateful hearts, the many signal favours of Almighty God." President Washington offered the first Thanksgiving Proclamation shortly there-

after, devoting November 26, 1789, on behalf of the American people "to the service of that great and glorious Being who is the beneficent author of all the good that was, that is, or that will be," thus beginning a tradition of offering gratitude to [887] God that continues today. The same Congress also reenacted the Northwest Territory Ordinance of 1787, Article III of which provided: "Religion, morality, and knowledge, being necessary to good government and the happiness of mankind, schools and the means of education shall forever be encouraged." And of course the First Amendment itself accords religion (and no other manner of belief) special constitutional protection.

These actions of our First President and Congress and the Marshall Court were not idiosyncratic; they reflected the beliefs of the period. Those who wrote the Constitution believed that morality was essential to the well-being of society and that encouragement of religion was the best way to foster morality. . . .

[888] Nor have the views of our people on this matter significantly changed. Presidents continue to conclude the Presidential oath with the words "so help me God." Our legislatures, state and national, continue to open their sessions with prayer led by official chaplains. The sessions of this Court continue to open with the prayer "God save the United States and this Honorable Court." Invocation of the Almighty by our public figures, at all levels of government, [889] remains commonplace. Our coinage bears the motto, "IN GOD WE TRUST." And our Pledge of Allegiance contains the acknowledgment that we are a Nation "under God." As one of our Supreme Court opinions rightly observed, "We are a religious people whose institutions presuppose a Supreme Being." *Zorach v. Clauson*, 343 U.S. 306, 313 (1952), repeated with approval in *Lynch v. Donnelly* (1984); *Marsh*, 463 U.S., at 792; *Abington Township*, at 213.

With all of this reality (and much more) staring it in the face, how can the Court possibly assert that "the First Amendment mandates governmental neutrality between . . . religion and nonreligion," and that "[m]anifesting a purpose to favor . . . adherence to religion generally" is unconstitutional? Who says so? Surely not the words of the Constitution. Surely not the history and traditions that reflect our society's constant understanding of those words. Surely not even the current sense of our society, recently reflected in an Act of Congress adopted unanimously by the Senate and with only five nays in the House of Representatives, criticizing a Court of Appeals opinion that had held "under God" in the Pledge of Allegiance unconstitutional. Nothing stands behind the Court's assertion that governmental affirmation of the society's belief in God is unconstitutional except the Court's own say-so, citing as support only the unsubstantiated say-so of earlier Courts going back no further than the mid-20th century. [890] And it is, moreover, a thoroughly discredited say-so. It is discredited, to begin with, because a majority of the Justices on the current Court (including at least one Member of today's majority) have, in separate opinions, repudiated the brain-spun "*Lemon* test" that embodies the supposed principle of neutrality between religion and irreligion. And it is discredited because the Court has not had the courage (or the foolhardiness) to apply the neutrality principle consistently.

What distinguishes the rule of law from the dictatorship of a shifting Supreme Court majority is the absolutely indispensable [891] requirement that judicial opinions be grounded in consistently applied principle. That is what prevents judges from ruling now this way, now that—thumbs up or thumbs down—as their personal preferences dictate. Today's opinion forthrightly (or actually, somewhat less than forthrightly) admits that it does not rest upon consistently applied principle. In a revealing footnote, n. 10, the Court acknowledges that the "Establishment Clause doctrine" it purports to be applying "lacks the comfort of categorical absolutes." What the Court means by this lovely euphemism is that sometimes the Court chooses to decide cases on the principle that government cannot favor religion, and sometimes it does not. The footnote goes on to say that "[i]n special instances we have found good reason" to dispense with the principle, but "[n]o such reasons present themselves here." *Ibid.* It does not identify all of those "special instances," much less identify the "good reason" for their existence.

I have cataloged elsewhere the variety of circumstances in which this Court—even after its embrace of *Lemon*'s stated prohibition of such behavior—has approved government action "undertaken with the specific intention of improving the position of religion," *Edwards v. Aguillard*, 482 U.S. 578, 616 (1987) (Scalia, J., dissenting). Suffice it to say here that when the government relieves churches from the obligation to pay property taxes, when it allows students to absent themselves from public school to take religious classes, and when it exempts religious organizations from generally applicable prohibitions of religious discrimination, it surely means to bestow a benefit on religious practice—but we have approved it. [892] Indeed, we have even approved (post-*Lemon*) government-led prayer to God. In *Marsh v. Chambers*, the Court upheld the Nebraska State Legislature's practice of paying a chaplain to lead it in prayer at the opening of legislative sessions. The Court explained that "[t]o invoke Divine guidance on a public body entrusted with making the laws is not . . . an 'establishment' of religion or a step toward establishment; it is simply a tolerable acknowledgment of beliefs widely held among the people of this country." 463 U.S., at 792. (Why, one wonders, is not respect for the Ten Commandments a tolerable acknowledgment of beliefs widely held among the people of this country?)

The only "good reason" for ignoring the neutrality principle set forth in any of these cases was the antiquity of the practice at issue. That would be a good reason for finding the neutrality principle a mistaken interpretation of the Constitution, but it is hardly a good reason for letting an unconstitutional practice continue. We did not hide behind that reason in *Reynolds v. Sims* (1964), which found unconstitutional bicameral state legislatures of a sort that had existed since the beginning of the Republic. And almost monthly, it seems, the Court has not shrunk from invalidating aspects of criminal procedure and penology of similar vintage. What, then, could be the genuine "good reason" for occasionally ignoring the neutrality principle? I suggest it is the instinct for self-preservation, and the recognition that the Court, which "has no influence over either the sword or the purse," *The Federalist No. 78*, cannot go [893] too far down the road of an enforced neutrality that contradicts both historical fact and current practice without losing all that sustains it: the willingness of the people to accept its interpretation of the Constitution as definitive, in preference to the contrary interpretation of the democratically elected branches.

Besides appealing to the demonstrably false principle that the government cannot favor religion over irreligion, today's opinion suggests that the posting of the Ten Commandments violates the principle that the government cannot favor one religion over another. That is indeed a valid principle where public aid or assistance to religion is concerned or where the free exercise of religion is at issue, but it necessarily applies in a more limited sense to public acknowledgment of the Creator. If religion in the public forum had to be entirely nondenominational, there could be no religion in the public forum at all. One cannot say the word "God," or "the Almighty," one cannot offer public supplication or thanksgiving, without contradicting the beliefs of some people that there are many gods, or that God or the gods pay no attention to human affairs. With respect to public acknowledgment of religious belief, it is entirely clear from our Nation's historical practices that the Establishment Clause permits this disregard of polytheists and believers in unconcerned deities, just as it permits the disregard of devout atheists. The Thanksgiving Proclamation issued by George Washington at the instance of the First Congress was scrupulously nondenominational—but it was monotheistic. In *Marsh v.* [894] *Chambers,* we said that the fact the particular prayers offered in the Nebraska Legislature were "in the Judeo-Christian tradition," at 793, posed no additional problem, because "there is no indication that the prayer opportunity has been exploited to proselytize or advance any one, or to disparage any other, faith or belief," at 794–795.

Historical practices thus demonstrate that there is a distance between the acknowledgment of a single Creator and the establishment of a religion. The former is, as *Marsh v. Chambers* put it, "a tolerable acknowledgment of beliefs widely held among the people of this country," at 792. The three most popular religions in the United States, Christianity, Judaism, and Islam—which combined account for 97.7% of all believers—are monotheistic. All of them, moreover (Islam included), believe that the Ten Commandments were given by God to Moses, and are divine prescriptions for a virtuous life. Publicly honoring the Ten Commandments is thus indistinguishable, insofar as discriminating against other religions is concerned, from publicly honoring God. Both practices are recognized across such a broad and diverse range of the population—from Christians to Muslims—that they cannot be reasonably understood as a government endorsement of a particular religious viewpoint.[4]

[895] B

A few remarks are necessary in response to the criticism of this dissent by the Court, as well as Justice Stevens' criticism in the related case of *Van Orden v. Perry.* Justice Stevens' writing is largely devoted to an attack upon a straw man. "[R]eliance on early religious proclamations and statements made by the Founders is . . . problematic," he says, "because those views were not espoused at the Constitutional Convention in 1787 nor enshrined in the Constitution's text." But I have not relied upon (as he and the Court in this case do) mere "proclamations and statements" of the Founders. I have relied primarily upon official acts and official proclamations of the United States or of the component branches of its Government, including the First Congress's beginning of the tradition of legislative prayer to God, its appointment of congressional chaplains, its legislative proposal of a Thanksgiving Proclamation, and its reenactment of the Northwest Territory Ordinance; our first President's issuance of a Thanksgiving Proclamation; and invocation of God at the opening of sessions of the Supreme Court. The only mere "proclamations and statements" of the Founders I have relied upon were statements of Founders who occupied federal office, and spoke in at least a quasi-official capacity—Washington's prayer at the opening of his Presidency and his Farewell Address, President John Adams' letter to the Massachusetts Militia, and Jefferson's and Madison's inaugural addresses. The Court and Justice Stevens, by contrast, appeal to no official or even quasi-official action in support of their view of the Establishment Clause—only James Madison's "Memorial and Remonstrance against Religious Assessments," written before the Federal Constitution had even been proposed, [896] two letters written by Madison long after he was President, and the quasi-official inaction of Thomas Jefferson in refusing to

---

4. This is not to say that a display of the Ten Commandments could never constitute an impermissible endorsement of a particular religious view. The Establishment Clause would prohibit, for example, governmental endorsement of a particular version of the Decalogue as authoritative. Here the display of the Ten Commandments alongside eight secular documents, and the plaque's explanation for their inclusion, make clear that they were not posted to take sides in a theological dispute.

issue a Thanksgiving Proclamation. The Madison "Memorial and Remonstrance," dealing as it does with enforced contribution to religion rather than public acknowledgment of God, is irrelevant; one of the letters is utterly ambiguous as to the point at issue here, and should not be read to contradict Madison's statements in his first inaugural address, quoted earlier; even the other letter does not disapprove public acknowledgment of God, unless one posits (what Madison's own actions as President would contradict) that reference to God contradicts "the equality of all religious sects." And as to Jefferson: The notoriously self-contradicting Jefferson did not choose to have his nonauthorship of a Thanksgiving Proclamation inscribed on his tombstone. What he did have inscribed was his authorship of the Virginia Statute for Religious Freedom, a governmental act which begins "Whereas, Almighty God hath created the mind free. . . ."

It is no answer for Justice Stevens to say that the understanding that these official and quasi-official actions reflect was not "enshrined in the Constitution's text." The Establishment Clause, upon which Justice Stevens would rely, was enshrined in the Constitution's text, and these official actions show what it meant. There were doubtless some who thought it should have a broader meaning, but those views were plainly rejected. Justice Stevens says that reliance on these actions is "bound to paint a misleading picture," but it is hard to see why. What is more probative of the meaning of the Establishment Clause than the actions of [897] the very Congress that proposed it, and of the first President charged with observing it? . . .

[898] Justice Stevens says that if one is serious about following the original understanding of the Establishment Clause, he must repudiate its incorporation into the Fourteenth Amendment, and hold that it does not apply against the States. This is more smoke. This is more smoke. Justice Stevens did not feel that way last Term, when he joined an opinion insisting upon the original meaning of the Confrontation Clause, but nonetheless applying it against the State of Washington. See *Crawford v. Washington* (2004). The notion that incorporation empties the incorporated provisions of their original meaning has no support in either reason or precedent.

[899] Justice Stevens argues that original meaning should not be the touchstone anyway, but that we should rather "expoun[d] the meaning of constitutional provisions with one eye toward our Nation's history and the other fixed on its democratic aspirations." This is not the place to debate the merits of the "living Constitution," though I must observe that Justice Stevens' quotation from *McCulloch v. Maryland* refutes rather than supports that approach. Even assuming, however, that the meaning of the Constitution ought to change according to "democratic aspirations," why are those aspirations to be found in Justices' notions of what the Establishment Clause ought to mean, rather than in the democratically adopted dispositions of our current society? As I have observed above, numerous provisions of our laws and numerous continuing practices of our people demonstrate that the government's invocation of God (and hence the government's invocation of the Ten Commandments) is unobjectionable—including a statute enacted by Congress almost unanimously less than three years ago, stating that "under God" in the Pledge of Allegiance is constitutional. To ignore all this is not to give effect to "democratic aspirations" but to frustrate them.

Finally, I must respond to Justice Stevens' assertion that I would "marginaliz[e] the belief systems of more than 7 million Americans" who adhere to religions that are not monotheistic. Surely that is a gross exaggeration. The beliefs of those citizens are entirely protected by the Free Exercise Clause, and by those aspects of the Establishment Clause that do not relate to government acknowledgment of the Creator. Invocation of God despite their beliefs is permitted not because nonmonotheistic religions cease to be religions recognized by the Religion Clauses of the First Amendment, [900] but because governmental invocation of God is not an establishment. Justice Stevens fails to recognize that in the context of public acknowledgments of God there are legitimate competing interests: On the one hand, the interest of that minority in not feeling "excluded"; but on the other, the interest of the overwhelming majority of religious believers in being able to give God thanks and supplication as a people, and with respect to our national endeavors. Our national tradition has resolved that conflict in favor of the majority. It is not for this Court to change a disposition that accounts, many Americans think, for the phenomenon remarked upon in a quotation attributed to various authors, including Bismarck, but which I prefer to associate with Charles de Gaulle: "God watches over little children, drunkards, and the United States of America."

II

As bad as the *Lemon* test is, it is worse for the fact that, since its inception, its seemingly simple mandates have been manipulated to fit whatever result the Court aimed to achieve. Today's opinion is no different. In two respects it modifies *Lemon* to ratchet up the Court's hostility to religion. First, the Court justifies inquiry into legislative purpose, not as an end itself, but as a means to ascertain the appearance of the government action to an "objective observer." Because in the Court's view the true danger to be guarded against is that the objective observer would feel like an "outside[r]" or "not [a] full membe[r] of the political community," its inquiry focuses not on [901] the actual purpose of government action, but the "purpose apparent from government action." Under this approach, even if a government could show that its actual purpose was not to advance religion, it would presumably violate the Constitution as long as the Court's objective observer would think otherwise.

I have remarked before that it is an odd jurisprudence that bases the unconstitutionality of a government practice that does not actually advance religion on the hopes of the government that it would do so. But that oddity pales in comparison to the one invited by today's analysis: the legitimacy of a government action with a wholly secular effect would turn on the misperception of an imaginary observer that the government officials behind the action had the intent to advance religion.

Second, the Court replaces *Lemon*'s requirement that the government have "*a* secular . . . purpose," 403 U.S., at 612 (emphasis added), with the heightened requirement that the secular purpose "predominate" over any purpose to advance religion. The Court treats this extension as a natural outgrowth of the longstanding requirement that the government's secular purpose not be a sham, but simple logic shows the two to be unrelated. If the government's proffered secular purpose is not genuine, then the government has no secular purpose at all. The new demand that secular purpose predominate contradicts *Lemon*'s more limited requirement, and finds no support in our cases. In all but one of the five cases in which this Court has invalidated a government practice on the basis of its purpose to [902] benefit religion, it has first declared that the statute was motivated entirely by the desire to advance religion. See *Santa Fe Independent School Dist. v. Doe*, 530 U.S. 290, 308–309 (2000) (dismissing the school district's proffered secular purposes as shams); *Wallace*, 472 U.S., at 56 (finding "*no* secular purpose" [emphasis in original]); *Stone v. Graham*, 449 U.S. 39, 41 (1980) (*per curiam*) (finding that "Kentucky's statute requiring the posting of the Ten Commandments in public school rooms has *no secular legislative purpose*" [emphasis added]); *Epperson v. Arkansas*, 393 U.S. 97, 107–109 (1968). In *Edwards*, the Court did say that the state action was invalid because its "primary" or "preeminent" purpose was to advance a particular religious belief, 482 U.S., at 590, 593, 594, but that statement was unnecessary to the result, since the Court rejected the State's only proffered secular purpose as a sham.

I have urged that *Lemon*'s purpose prong be abandoned, because (as I have discussed in Part I) even an exclusive purpose to foster or assist religious practice is not necessarily invalidating. But today's extension makes things even worse. By shifting the focus of *Lemon*'s purpose prong from the search for a genuine, secular motivation to the hunt for a predominantly religious purpose, the Court converts what has in the past been a fairly limited inquiry into a rigorous review of the full record. Those responsible for the [903] adoption of the Religion Clauses would surely regard it as a bitter irony that the religious values they designed those Clauses to protect have now become so distasteful to this Court that if they constitute anything more than a subordinate motive for government action they will invalidate it.

III

Even accepting the Court's *Lemon*-based premises, the displays at issue here were constitutional.

A

To any person who happened to walk down the hallway of the McCreary or Pulaski County Courthouse during the roughly nine months when the Foundations Displays were exhibited, the displays must have seemed unremarkable—if indeed they were noticed at all. The walls of both courthouses were already lined with historical documents and other assorted portraits; each Foundations Display was exhibited in the same format as these other displays and nothing in the record suggests that either County took steps to give it greater prominence.

Entitled "The Foundations of American Law and Government Display," each display consisted of nine equally sized documents. . . .

[904] B

On its face, the Foundations Displays manifested the purely secular purpose that the Counties asserted before the District Court: "to display documents that played a significant role in the foundation of our system of law and government." That the displays included the Ten Commandments did not transform their apparent secular purpose into one of impermissible advocacy for Judeo-Christian beliefs. Even an isolated display of the Decalogue conveys, at worst, "an equivocal message, perhaps of respect for Judaism, for religion in general, or for law." *Allegheny County*, 492 U.S., at 652 (Stevens, J., [905] concurring in part and dissenting in part). But when the Ten Commandments appear alongside other documents of secular significance in a display devoted to the foundations of American law and government, the context communicates that the Ten Commandments are included, not to teach their binding nature as a religious text, but to show their unique contribution to the development of the legal system. This is doubly true when the display is introduced by a document that informs passersby that it "contains documents that played a significant role in the foundation of our system of law and government." . . .

[907] Perhaps in recognition of the centrality of the Ten Commandments as a widely recognized symbol of religion in public life, the Court is at pains to dispel the impression

that its decision will require governments across the country to sandblast the Ten Commandments from the public square. The constitutional problem, the Court says, is with the Counties' purpose in erecting the Foundations Displays, not the displays themselves. The Court adds in a footnote: "One consequence of taking account of the purpose underlying past actions is that the same government action may be constitutional if taken in the first instance and unconstitutional if it has a sectarian heritage," *Ante*, at n. 14.

This inconsistency may be explicable in theory, but I suspect that the "objective observer" with whom the Court is so concerned will recognize its absurdity in practice. By virtue of details familiar only to the parties to litigation and their lawyers, McCreary and Pulaski Counties, Kentucky, and Rutherford County, Tennessee, have been ordered to remove the same display that appears in courthouses from Mercer County, Kentucky, to Elkhart County, Indiana. [908] Displays erected in silence (and under the direction of good legal advice) are permissible, while those hung after discussion and debate are deemed unconstitutional. Reduction of the Establishment Clause to such minutiae trivializes the Clause's protection against religious establishment; indeed, it may inflame religious passions by making the passing comments of every government official the subject of endless litigation.

C

In any event, the Court's conclusion that the Counties exhibited the Foundations Displays with the purpose of promoting religion is doubtful. In the Court's view, the impermissible motive was apparent from the initial displays of the Ten Commandments all by themselves: When that occurs, the Court says, "a religious object is unmistakable." Surely that cannot be. If, as discussed above, the Commandments have a proper place in our civic history, even placing them by themselves can be civically motivated—especially when they are placed, not in a school (as they were in the *Stone* case upon which the Court places such reliance), but in a courthouse. And the fact that at the posting of the exhibit a clergyman was present is unremarkable; and even more unremarkable the fact that the clergyman "testified to the certainty of the existence of God."

The Court has in the past prohibited government actions that "proselytize or advance any one, or . . . disparage any other, faith or belief," *Marsh*, 463 U.S., at 794–795, or that apply some level of coercion (though I and others have disagreed [909] about the form that coercion must take). The passive display of the Ten Commandments, even standing alone, does not begin to do either. . . .

Nor is it the case that a solo display of the Ten Commandments advances any one faith. They are assuredly a religious symbol, but they are not so closely associated with a single religious belief that their display can reasonably be understood as preferring one religious sect over another. The Ten Commandments are recognized by Judaism, Christianity, and Islam alike as divinely given.

[910] The Court also points to the Counties' second displays, which featured a number of statements in historical documents reflecting a religious influence, and the resolutions that accompanied their erection, as evidence of an impermissible religious purpose. In the Court's view, "[t]he [second] display's unstinting focus . . . on religious passages, show[s] that the Counties were posting the Commandments precisely because of their sectarian content." No, all it necessarily shows is that the exhibit was meant to focus upon the historic role of religious belief in our national life—which is entirely permissible. And the same can be said of the resolution. To forbid any government focus upon this aspect of our history is to display what Justice Goldberg called "untutored devotion

to the concept of neutrality," *Abington Township*, 374 U.S., at 306 (concurring opinion), that would commit the Court (and the Nation) to a revisionist agenda of secularization.

[911] Turning at last to the displays actually at issue in this case, the Court faults the Counties for not repealing the resolution expressing what the Court believes to be an impermissible intent. Under these circumstances, the Court says, "[n]o reasonable observer could swallow the claim that the Counties had cast off the objective so unmistakable in the earlier displays." Even were I to accept all that the Court has said before, I would not agree with that assessment. To begin with, of course, it is unlikely that a reasonable observer would even have been aware of the resolutions, so there would be nothing to "cast off." The Court implies that the Counties may have been able to remedy the "taint" from the old resolutions by enacting a new one. But that action would have been wholly unnecessary in light of the explanation that the Counties included with the displays themselves: A plaque next to the documents informed all who passed by that each display "contains documents that played a significant role in the foundation of our system of law and government." Additionally, there was no reason for the Counties to repeal or repudiate the resolutions adopted with the hanging of the second displays, since they related only to the second displays. After complying with the District Court's order to remove the second displays "immediately," and erecting new displays that in content and by express assertion reflected a different purpose from that identified in the resolutions, the Counties had no reason to believe that their previous resolutions would be deemed to be the basis for their actions. After the Counties [912] discovered that the sentiments expressed in the resolutions could be attributed to their most recent displays (in oral argument before this Court), they repudiated them immediately.

In sum: The first displays did not necessarily evidence an intent to further religious practice; nor did the second displays, or the resolutions authorizing them; and there is in any event no basis for attributing whatever intent motivated the first and second displays to the third. Given the presumption of regularity that always accompanies our review of official action, the Court has identified no evidence of a purpose to advance religion in a way that is inconsistent with our cases. The Court may well be correct in identifying the third displays as the fruit of a desire to display the Ten Commandments but neither our cases nor our history support its assertion that such a desire renders the fruit poisonous. . . .

62

*Christian Legal Society v. Martinez**

130 S. Ct. 2971 (2010)

Vote: 5—Stevens, Kennedy, Ginsburg, Breyer, Sotomayor
4—Roberts, Scalia, Thomas, Alito

Opinion announcing the opinion of the Court: Ginsburg
Concurring opinions: Stevens, Kennedy
Dissenting opinion: Alito

In 2004, a small group of students sought to register a chapter of the Christian Legal Society (CLS) at Hastings College of the Law. A national organization of Christian lawyers and law students, the CLS requires all members to sign a statement of faith affirming belief in fundamental Christian doctrines, including the belief that the Bible is "the inspired Word of God." In early 2004, the national organization adopted a resolution stating that "in view of the clear dictates of Scripture, unrepentant participation in or advocacy of a sexually immoral lifestyle is inconsistent with an affirmation of the Statement of Faith, and consequently may be regarded by CLS as disqualifying such an individual from CLS membership." The resolution made it clear that, in CLS's view, "a sexually immoral lifestyle" includes "acts of sexual conduct outside of God's design for marriage between one man and one woman."

Founded in 1878, Hastings was the first law school in the University of California public school system. Like many institutions of higher education, the school encourages students to form extracurricular associations that "contribute to the Hastings community and experience." Through its Registered Student Organization (RSO) program, Hastings extends official recognition to student groups. Several benefits attend school-approved status. RSOs are eligible to seek financial assistance from the law school (which subsidizes their events using funds from a mandatory student-activity fee imposed on all students), to apply for permission to use the school's facilities for meetings and office space, to use the law school's name and logo, to use official law school channels to communicate with students, and to recruit new members at the annual student organizations fair. In exchange for these benefits, RSOs must abide by certain conditions: only a noncommercial organization whose membership is limited to Hast-

---

*At the time of publication, the volume and page numbers for the decision in *Christian Legal Society v. Martinez* in the *United States Reports* were unavailable. The citation and page numbers used in this case refer to the *Supreme Court Reporter*.

ings students may become an RSO, a prospective RSO must submit its bylaws to Hastings for approval, and all RSOs must undertake to comply with Hastings's "Policies and Regulations Applying to College Activities, Organizations and Students."

The law school's policy on nondiscrimination, which binds RSOs, states that Hastings shall not discriminate unlawfully on the basis of race, color, religion, national origin, ancestry, disability, age, sex, or sexual orientation. This nondiscrimination policy covers admission, access, and treatment in Hastings-sponsored programs and activities.

During litigation, the school contended the nondiscrimination policy mandates that all school-approved groups allow any student to participate, become a member, and seek leadership positions in the organization, regardless of status or beliefs.

In September 2004, a group of Hastings students applied for RSO status as a group affiliated with the Christian Legal Society. School officials informed them that the group's proposed bylaws did not comply with the school's nondiscrimination policy because they barred students based on religion and sexual orientation. CLS formally requested an exemption from the nondiscrimination policy, which Hastings declined to grant. When the students refused to alter the group's bylaws, which reflected the national organization's standards for CLS membership, Hastings denied the request for RSO status.

In October 2004, CLS filed suit against various Hastings officers and administrators, alleging that Hastings's refusal to grant the organization RSO status violated CLS's First and Fourteenth Amendment rights to free speech, expressive association, and free exercise of religion.

Justice GINSBURG delivered the opinion of the Court.

[2978] In a series of decisions, this Court has emphasized that the First Amendment generally precludes public universities from denying student organizations access to school-sponsored forums because of the groups' viewpoints. This case concerns a novel question regarding student activities at public universities: May a public law school condition its official recognition of a student group—and the attendant use of school funds and facilities—on the organization's agreement to open eligibility for membership and leadership to all students?

In the view of petitioner Christian Legal Society (CLS), an accept-all-comers policy impairs its First Amendment rights to free speech, expressive association, and free exercise of religion by prompting it, on pain of relinquishing the advantages of recognition, to accept members who do not share the organization's core beliefs about religion and sexual orientation. From the perspective of respondent Hastings College of the Law (Hastings or the Law School), CLS seeks special dispensation from an across-the-board open-access requirement designed to further the reasonable educational purposes underpinning the school's student-organization program.

In accord with the District Court and the Court of Appeals, we reject CLS's First Amendment challenge. Compliance with Hastings' all-comers policy, we conclude, is a reasonable, viewpoint-neutral condition on access to the student-organization forum. In requiring CLS—in common with all other student organizations—to choose between welcoming all students and forgoing the benefits of official recognition, we hold, Hastings did not transgress constitutional limitations. CLS, it bears emphasis, seeks not parity with other organizations, but a preferential exemption from Hastings' policy. The First Amendment shields CLS against state prohibition of the organization's expressive activity, however exclusionary that activity may be. But CLS enjoys no constitutional right to state subvention of its selectivity. . . .

[2984] III . . .

[2988] C

We first consider whether Hastings' policy is reasonable taking into account the RSO [Registered Student Organization] forum's function and "all the surrounding circumstances." *Cornelius*, 473 U.S., at 809. . . .

[2989] 2

With appropriate regard for school administrators' judgment, we review the justifications Hastings offers in defense of its all-comers requirement. First, the open-access policy "ensures that the leadership, educational, and social opportunities afforded by [RSOs] are available to all students." Brief for Hastings 32. Just as "Hastings does not allow its professors to host classes open only to those students with a certain status or belief," so the Law School may decide, reasonably in our view, "that the . . . educational experience is best promoted when all participants in the forum must provide equal access to all students." Brief for Hastings 32. RSOs, we count it significant, are eligible for financial assistance drawn from mandatory student-activity fees; the all-comers policy ensures that no Hastings student is forced to fund a group that would reject her as a member.

[2990] Second, the all-comers requirement helps Hastings police the written terms of its Nondiscrimination Policy without inquiring into an RSO's motivation for membership restrictions. To bring the RSO program within CLS's view of the Constitution's limits, CLS proposes that Hastings permit exclusion because of *belief* but forbid discrimination due to *status*. But that proposal would impose on Hastings a daunting labor. How should the Law School go about determining whether a student organization cloaked prohibited status exclusion in belief-based garb? If a hypothetical Male-Superiority Club barred a female student from running for its presidency, for example, how could the Law School tell whether the group rejected her bid because of her sex or because, by seeking to lead the club, she manifested a lack of belief in its fundamental philosophy?

This case itself is instructive in this regard. CLS contends that it does not exclude individuals because of sexual orientation, but rather "on the basis of a conjunction of conduct and the belief that the conduct is not wrong." Brief for Petitioner 35–36 (emphasis deleted). Our decisions have declined to distinguish between status and conduct in this context. See *Lawrence v. Texas*, 539 U.S. 558, 575 ("When homosexual *conduct* is made criminal by the law of the State, that declaration in and of itself is an invitation to subject homosexual *persons* to discrimination" [emphasis added]).

Third, the Law School reasonably adheres to the view that an all-comers policy, to the extent it brings together individuals with diverse backgrounds and beliefs, "encourages tolerance, cooperation, and learning among students." App. 349. And if the policy sometimes produces discord, Hastings can rationally rank among RSO-program goals development of conflict-resolution skills, toleration, and readiness to find common ground.

Fourth, Hastings' policy, which incorporates—in fact, subsumes—state-law proscriptions on discrimination, conveys the Law School's decision "to decline to subsidize with public monies and benefits conduct of which the people of California disapprove." Brief for Hastings 35. State law, of course, may not *command* [2991] that public universities take action impermissible under the First Amendment. But so long as a public university does not contravene constitutional limits, its choice to advance state-law goals through the school's educational endeavors stands on firm footing.

In sum, the several justifications Hastings asserts in support of its all-comers requirement are surely reasonable in light of the RSO forum's purposes. . . .

[2993] D

We next consider whether Hastings' all-comers policy is viewpoint neutral.

I

Although this aspect of limited-public-forum analysis has been the constitutional sticking point in our prior decisions, as earlier recounted, we need not dwell on it here. It is, after all, hard to imagine a more viewpoint-neutral policy than one requiring *all* student groups to accept *all* comers. In contrast to *Healy*, *Widmar*, and *Rosenberger*, in which universities singled out organizations for disfavored treatment because of their points of view, Hastings' all-comers requirement draws no distinction between groups based on their message or perspective. An all-comers condition on access to RSO status, in short, is textbook viewpoint neutral.

[2994] 2

Conceding that Hastings' all-comers policy is "nominally neutral," CLS attacks the regulation by pointing to its effect: The policy is vulnerable to constitutional assault, CLS contends, because "it systematically and predictably burdens most heavily those groups whose viewpoints are out of favor with the campus mainstream." Brief for Petitioner 51. This argument stumbles from its first step because "[a] regulation that serves purposes unrelated to the content of expression is deemed neutral, even if it has an incidental effect on some speakers or messages but not others." *Ward v. Rock Against Racism*, 491 U.S. 781, 791 (1989).

Even if a regulation has a differential impact on groups wishing to enforce exclusionary membership policies, "[w]here the [State] does not target conduct on the basis of its expressive content, acts are not shielded from regulation merely because they express a discriminatory idea or philosophy." *R. A. V. v. St. Paul*, 505 U.S. 377, 390 (1992). . . .

CLS's conduct—not its Christian perspective—is, from Hastings' vantage point, what stands between the group and RSO status. "In the end," as Hastings observes, "CLS is simply confusing its *own* viewpoint-based objections to . . . nondiscrimination laws (which it is entitled to have and [to] voice) with viewpoint *discrimination*." Brief for Hastings 31.

[2995] Finding Hastings' open-access condition on RSO status reasonable and viewpoint neutral, we reject CLS' free-speech and expressive-association claims.[27] . . .

---

27. CLS briefly argues that Hastings' all-comers condition violates the Free Exercise Clause. Our decision in *Smith*, 494 U.S. 872, forecloses that argument. In *Smith*, the Court held that the Free Exercise Clause does not inhibit enforcement of otherwise valid regulations of general application that incidentally burden religious conduct. In seeking an exemption from Hastings' across-the-board all-comers policy, CLS, we repeat, seeks preferential, not equal, treatment; it therefore cannot moor its request for accommodation to the Free Exercise Clause.

* * *

For the foregoing reasons, we affirm the Court of Appeals' ruling that the all-comers policy is constitutional and remand the case for further proceedings consistent with this opinion.

[3000] Justice ALITO, with whom the CHIEF JUSTICE, Justice SCALIA, and Justice THOMAS join, dissenting.

The proudest boast of our free speech jurisprudence is that we protect the freedom to express "the thought that we hate." *United States v. Schwimmer*, 279 U.S. 644, 654–655 (1929) (Holmes, J., dissenting). Today's decision rests on a very different principle: no freedom for expression that offends prevailing standards of political correctness in our country's institutions of higher learning.

The Hastings College of the Law, a state institution, permits student organizations to register with the law school and severely burdens speech by unregistered groups. Hastings currently has more than 60 registered groups and, in all its history, has denied registration to exactly one: the Christian Legal Society (CLS). CLS claims that Hastings refused to register the group because the law school administration disapproves of the group's viewpoint and thus violated the group's free speech rights.

Rejecting this argument, the Court finds that it has been Hastings' policy for 20 years that all registered organizations must admit *any* student who wishes to join. Deferring broadly to the law school's judgment about the permissible limits of student debate, the Court concludes that this "accept-all-comers" policy is both viewpoint-neutral and consistent [3001] with Hastings' proclaimed policy of fostering a diversity of viewpoints among registered student groups.

The Court's treatment of this case is deeply disappointing. The Court does not address the constitutionality of the very different policy that Hastings invoked when it denied CLS's application for registration. Nor does the Court address the constitutionality of the policy that Hastings now purports to follow. And the Court ignores strong evidence that the accept-all-comers policy is not viewpoint neutral because it was announced as a pretext to justify viewpoint discrimination. Brushing aside inconvenient precedent, the Court arms public educational institutions with a handy weapon for suppressing the speech of unpopular groups—groups to which, as Hastings candidly puts it, these institutions "do not wish to . . . lend their name[s]." Brief for Respondent Hastings College of Law 11. . . .

[3013] VI

I come now to the version of Hastings' policy that the Court has chosen to address. This is not the policy that Hastings invoked when CLS was denied registration. Nor is it the policy that Hastings now proclaims—and presumably implements. It is a policy that, as far as the record establishes, was in force only from the time when it was first disclosed by the former dean in July 2005 until Hastings filed its brief in this Court in March 2010. Why we should train our attention on this particular policy and not the other two is a puzzle. But in any event, it is clear that the accept-all-comers policy is not reasonable in light of the purpose of the RSO forum, and it is impossible to say on the present record that it is viewpoint neutral.

A

Once a state university opens a limited forum, it "must respect the lawful boundaries it has itself set." *Rosenberger*, 515 U.S., at 829. Hastings' regulations on the registration of student groups impose only two substantive limitations: A group seeking registration must have student members and must be non-commercial. Access to the forum is not limited to groups devoted to particular purposes. The regulations provide that a group applying for registration must submit an official document including "a statement of *its purpose*" (emphasis added), but the regulations make no attempt to define the limits of acceptable purposes. The regulations do not require a group seeking registration to show that it has a certain number of members or that its program is of interest to any particular number of Hastings students. Nor do the regulations require that a group serve a need not met by existing groups.

The regulations also make it clear that the registration program is not meant to stifle unpopular speech. They proclaim that "[i]t is the responsibility of the Dean to ensure an ongoing opportunity for the expression of a variety of viewpoints." They also emphatically disclaim any endorsement of or responsibility for views that student groups may express.

Taken as a whole, the regulations plainly contemplate the creation of a forum within which Hastings students are free to form and obtain registration of essentially the same broad range of private groups that nonstudents may form off campus. That is precisely what the parties in this case stipulated: The RSO forum "seeks to promote a diversity of viewpoints *among* registered student organizations, including viewpoints on religion and human sexuality" (emphasis added).

The way in which the RSO forum actually developed corroborates this design. As noted, Hastings had more than 60 RSOs in 2004–2005, each with its own independently devised purpose. Some addressed serious social issues; others—for example, the wine appreciation and ultimate Frisbee clubs—were simply recreational. Some organizations focused on a subject but did [3014] not claim to promote a particular viewpoint on that subject (for example, the Association of Communications, Sports & Entertainment Law); others were defined, not by subject, but by viewpoint. The forum did not have a single Party Politics Club; rather, it featured both the Hastings Democratic Caucus and the Hastings Republicans. There was no Reproductive Issues Club; the forum included separate pro-choice and pro-life organizations. Students did not see fit to create a Monotheistic Religions Club, but they have formed the Hastings Jewish Law Students Association and the Hastings Association of Muslim Law Students. In short, the RSO forum, true to its design, has allowed Hastings students to replicate on campus a broad array of private, independent, noncommercial organizations that is very similar to those that nonstudents have formed in the outside world.

The accept-all-comers policy is antithetical to the design of the RSO forum for the same reason that a state-imposed accept-all-comers policy would violate the First Amendment rights of private groups if applied off campus. As explained above, a group's First Amendment right of expressive association is burdened by the "forced inclusion" of members whose presence would "affec[t] in a significant way the group's ability to advocate public or private viewpoints." *Dale*, 530 U.S., at 648. The Court has therefore held that the government may not compel a group that engages in "expressive association" to admit such a member unless the government has a compelling interest, "unrelated to the suppression of ideas, that cannot be achieved through means significantly less restrictive of associational freedoms." *Ibid.* (quoting *Roberts*, 468 U.S., at 623).

There can be no dispute that this standard would not permit a generally applicable law mandating that private religious groups admit members who do not share the groups' beliefs. Religious groups like CLS obviously engage in expressive association, and no legitimate state interest could override the powerful effect that an accept-all-comers law would have on the ability of religious groups to express their views. The State of California surely could not demand that all Christian groups admit members who believe that Jesus was merely human. Jewish groups could not be required to admit anti-Semites and Holocaust deniers. Muslim groups could not be forced to admit persons who are viewed as slandering Islam.

While there can be no question that the State of California could not impose such restrictions on all religious groups in the State, the Court now holds that Hastings, a state institution, may impose these very same requirements on students who wish to participate in a forum that is designed to foster the expression of diverse viewpoints. The Court lists four justifications offered by Hastings in defense of the accept-all-comers policy and, deferring to the school's judgment, the Court finds all those justifications satisfactory. If we carry out our responsibility to exercise our own independent judgment, however, we must conclude that the justifications offered by Hastings and accepted by the Court are insufficient.

The Court first says that the accept-all-comers policy is reasonable because it helps Hastings to ensure that "leadership, educational, and social opportunities" are afforded to all students. The RSO forum, however, is designed to achieve these laudable ends in a very different way—by permitting groups of students, no matter how small, to form the groups they want. In this way, the forum multiplies the opportunity [3015] for students to serve in leadership positions; it allows students to decide which educational opportunities they wish to pursue through participation in extracurricular activities; and it permits them to create the "social opportunities" they desire by forming whatever groups they wish to create.

Second, the Court approves the accept-all-comers policy because it is easier to enforce than the Nondiscrimination Policy that it replaced. It would be "a daunting labor," the Court warns, for Hastings to try to determine whether a group excluded a member based on belief as opposed to status.

This is a strange argument, since the Nondiscrimination Policy prohibits discrimination on substantially the same grounds as the antidiscrimination provisions of many States, including California, and except for the inclusion of the prohibition of discrimination based on sexual orientation, the Nondiscrimination Policy also largely tracks federal antidiscrimination laws. Moreover, Hastings now willingly accepts greater burdens under its latest policy, which apparently requires the school to distinguish between certain "conduct requirements" that are allowed and others that are not. Nor is Hastings daunted by the labor of determining whether a club admissions exam legitimately tests knowledge or is a pretext for screening out students with disfavored beliefs. Asked at oral argument whether CLS could require applicants to pass a test on the Bible, Hastings' attorney responded: "If it were truly an objective knowledge test, it would be okay." The long history of disputes about the meaning of Bible passages belies any suggestion that it would be an easy task to determine whether the grading of such a test was "objective."

Third, the Court argues that the accept-all-comers policy, by bringing together students with diverse views, encourages tolerance, cooperation, learning, and the development of conflict-resolution skills. These are obviously commendable goals, but they are not undermined by permitting a religious group to restrict membership to persons who share the group's faith. Many religious groups impose such restrictions. Such practices are not manifestations of "contempt" for members of other faiths. Nor do they thwart the objectives that Hastings endorses. Our country as a whole, no less than the Hastings College of Law, values tolerance, cooperation, learning, and the amicable [3016] resolution of conflicts. But we seek to achieve those goals through "[a] confident pluralism that conduces to civil peace and advances democratic consensus-building," not by abridging First Amendment rights. Brief for Gays and Lesbians for Individual Liberty as *Amicus Curiae* 35.

Fourth, the Court observes that Hastings' policy "incorporates—in fact, subsumes—state-law proscriptions on discrimination." Because the First Amendment obviously takes precedence over any state law, this would not justify the Hastings policy even if it were true—but it is not. The only Hastings policy considered by the Court—the accept-all-comers policy—goes far beyond any California antidiscrimination law. Neither Hastings nor the Court claims that California law demands that state entities must accept all comers. Hastings itself certainly does not follow this policy in hiring or student admissions. . . .

In sum, Hastings' accept-all-comers policy is not reasonable in light of the stipulated purpose of the RSO forum: to promote a diversity of viewpoints *"among"*—not within—"registered student organizations."

B

The Court is also wrong in holding that the accept-all-comers policy is viewpoint neutral. The Court proclaims that it would be "hard to imagine a more viewpoint-neutral policy," but I would not be so quick to jump to this conclusion. Even if it is assumed that the policy is viewpoint neutral on its face, [3017] there is strong evidence in the record that the policy was announced as a pretext.

The adoption of a facially neutral policy for the purpose of suppressing the expression of a particular viewpoint is viewpoint discrimination. A simple example illustrates this obvious point. Suppose that a hated student group at a state university has never been able to attract more than 10 members. Suppose that the university administration, for the purpose of preventing that group from using the school grounds for meetings, adopts a new rule under which the use of its facilities is restricted to groups with more than 25 members. Although this rule would be neutral on its face, its adoption for a discriminatory reason would be illegal.

Here, CLS has made a strong showing that Hastings' sudden adoption and selective application of its accept-all-comers policy was a pretext for the law school's unlawful denial of CLS's registration application under the Nondiscrimination Policy.

Shifting policies. When Hastings denied CLS's application in the fall of 2004, the only policy mentioned was the Nondiscrimination Policy. In July 2005, the former dean suggested in a deposition that the law school actually followed the very different accept-all-comers policy. In March of this year, Hastings' brief in this Court rolled out still a third policy. As is recognized in the employment discrimination context, where issues of pretext regularly arise, "[s]ubstantial changes over time in [an] employer's proffered reason for its employment decision support a finding of pretext." *Kobrin v. University of Minnesota*, 34 F.3d 698, 703 (CA8 1994).

Timing. The timing of Hastings' revelation of its new policies closely tracks the law school's litigation posture. When Hastings denied CLS registration, it cited only the Nondiscrimination Policy. Later, after CLS alleged that the Nondiscrimination [3018] Policy discriminated against religious groups, Hastings unveiled its accept-all-comers policy. Then, after we granted *certiorari* and CLS's opening brief challenged the constitutionality—and the plausibility—of the accept-all-comers policy, Hastings disclosed a new policy. As is true in the employment context, "[w]hen the justification for an adverse . . . action changes during litigation, that inconsistency raises an issue whether the proffered reason truly motivated the defendant's decision." *Cicero*, at 592.

Lack of documentation. When an employer has a written policy and then relies on a rule for which there is no written documentation, that deviation may support an inference of pretext.

Here, Hastings claims that it has had an accept-all-comers policy since 1990, but it has not produced a single written document memorializing that policy. Nor has it cited a single occasion prior to the dean's deposition when this putative policy was orally disclosed to either student groups interested in applying for registration or to the Office of Student Services, which was charged with reviewing the bylaws of applicant groups to ensure that they were in compliance with the law school's policies.

Nonenforcement. Since it appears that no one was told about the accept-all-comers policy before July 2005, it is not surprising that the policy was not enforced. The record is replete with evidence that Hastings made no effort to enforce the all-comers policy until after it was proclaimed by the former dean. If the record here is not sufficient to permit a finding of pretext, then the law of pretext is dead. . . .

[3019] C

One final aspect of the Court's decision warrants comment. In response to the argument that the accept-all-comers-policy would permit a small and unpopular group to be taken over by students who wish to silence its message, the Court states that the policy would permit a registered group to impose membership requirements "designed to ensure that students join because of their commitment to a group's vitality, not its demise." With this concession, the Court tacitly recognizes that Hastings does not really have an accept-all-comers policy—it has an accept-some-dissident-comers policy—and the line between members who merely seek to change a group's message (who apparently must be admitted) and those who seek a group's "demise" (who may be kept out) is hopelessly vague. . . .

In the end, the Court refuses to acknowledge the consequences of its holding. A true accept-all-comers policy permits small unpopular groups to be taken over by students who wish to change the views that the group expresses. Rules requiring that members attend meetings, pay dues, and behave politely would not eliminate this threat.

The possibility of such takeovers, however, is by no means the most important effect of the Court's holding. There are religious groups that cannot in good conscience agree in their bylaws that they will admit persons who do not share their faith, and for these groups, the consequence of an accept-all-comers policy is marginalization. [3020] This is where the Court's decision leads.

* * *

I do not think it is an exaggeration to say that today's decision is a serious setback for freedom of expression in this country. Our First Amendment reflects a "profound national commitment to the principle that debate on public issues should be uninhibited, robust, and wide-open." *New York Times Co. v. Sullivan*, 376 U.S. 254, 270 (1964). Even if the United States is the only Nation that shares this commitment to the same extent, I would not change our law to conform to the international norm. I fear that the Court's decision marks a turn in that direction. Even those who find CLS's views objectionable should be concerned about the way the group has been treated—by Hastings, the Court of Appeals, and now this Court. I can only hope that this decision will turn out to be an aberration.

63

Arizona Christian School
Tuition Organization v. Winn*

131 S. Ct. 1436 (2011)

Vote: 5—*Roberts, Scalia, Kennedy, Thomas, Alito*
     4—*Ginsburg, Breyer, Sotomayor, Kagan*

Opinion announcing opinion of the Court: Kennedy
Concurring opinion: Scalia
Dissenting opinion: Kagan

At the time of this case, state law allowed Arizona taxpayers a dollar-for-dollar tax credit of up to $500 per person and $1,000 per married couple for contributions to student tuition organizations (STOs), charitable organizations that provided scholarships to students attending private schools, including religious schools. A charitable organization could be deemed an STO under Arizona law upon meeting three conditions: (1) the organization was exempt from federal taxation as a not-for-profit entity under § 501 (c)(3) of the Internal Revenue Code; (2) it did not limit its scholarships to students attending only one school; and (3) it allocated at least 90 percent of its annual revenue for educational scholarships or tuition grants to children attending qualified schools. A qualified school was defined in part as a private school in Arizona that did not discriminate on the basis of race, color, handicap, familial status, or national origin.

A group of Arizona taxpayers challenged the STO tax credit as a violation of Establishment Clause principles under the First and Fourteenth Amendments. The Court considered whether, as a threshold matter, the group had legal standing to bring the lawsuit in the first place. The case unfolded in the shadow of two previous Supreme Court decisions. Flast v. Cohen, *392 U.S. 83 (1968), an overview of which is provided in the following excerpt, held that under certain circumstances taxpayers have standing to challenge government expenditures that raise Establishment Clause concerns.* Hein v. Freedom from Religion Foundation, Inc., *551 U.S. 587 (2007), however, held that taxpayers lack standing to bring Establishment Clause challenges against discretionary expenditures by the executive branch.*

---

*At the time of publication, the volume and page numbers for *Winn* in the *United States Reports* were unavailable. The citation and page numbers used in this case refer to the *Supreme Court Reporter*.

KENNEDY, J., delivered the opinion of the Court, in which ROBERTS, C. J., and SCALIA, THOMAS, and ALITO, JJ., joined.

. . . [1440] To obtain a determination on the merits in federal court, parties seeking relief must show that they have standing under Article III of the Constitution. Standing in Establishment Clause cases may be shown in various ways. Some plaintiffs may demonstrate standing based on the direct harm of what is claimed to be an establishment of religion, such as a mandatory prayer in a public school classroom. Other plaintiffs may demonstrate standing on the ground that they have incurred a cost or been denied a benefit on account of their religion. Those costs and benefits can result from alleged discrimination in the tax code, such as when the availability of a tax exemption is conditioned on religious affiliation.

For their part, respondents contend that they have standing to challenge Arizona's STO tax credit for one and only one reason: because they are Arizona taxpayers. But the mere fact that a plaintiff is a taxpayer is not generally deemed sufficient to establish standing in federal court. To overcome that rule, respondents must rely on an exception created in *Flast v. Cohen*, 392 U.S. 83 (1968). For the reasons discussed below, respondents cannot take advantage of *Flast*'s narrow exception to the general rule against taxpayer standing. As a consequence, respondents lacked standing to commence this action, and their suit must be dismissed for want of jurisdiction. . . .

II

[1441] The concept and operation of the separation of powers in our National Government have their principal foundation in the first three Articles of the Constitution. Under Article III, the Federal Judiciary is vested with the "Power" to resolve not questions and issues but "Cases" or "Controversies." This language restricts the federal judicial power "to the traditional role of the Anglo-American courts." *Summers v. Earth Island Institute*, 555 U.S. 488 (2009). In the English legal tradition, the need to redress an injury resulting from a specific dispute taught the efficacy of judicial resolution and gave legitimacy to judicial decrees. . . .

[1442] Continued adherence to the case-or-controversy requirement of Article III maintains the public's confidence in an unelected but restrained Federal Judiciary. If the judicial power were "extended to every *question* under the constitution," Chief Justice Marshall once explained, federal courts might take possession of "almost every subject proper for legislative discussion and decision." 4 *Papers of John Marshall* 95 (C. Cullen ed. 1984) (quoted in *DaimlerChrysler Corp. v. Cuno*, 547 U.S. 332, 341 [2006]). The legislative and executive departments of the Federal Government, no less than the judicial department, have a duty to defend the Constitution. See U.S. Const., Art. VI, cl. 3. That shared obligation is incompatible with the suggestion that federal courts might wield an "unconditioned authority to determine the constitutionality of legislative or executive acts." *Valley Forge Christian College v. Americans United for Separation of Church and State, Inc.*, 454 U.S. 464, 471 (1982). For the federal courts to decide questions of law arising outside of cases and controversies would be inimical to the Constitution's democratic character. And the resulting conflict between the judicial and the political branches would not, "in the long run, be beneficial to either." *United States v. Richardson*, 418 U.S. 166 (1974) (Powell, J., concurring). Instructed by Chief Justice Marshall's admonition, this Court takes care to observe the "role assigned to the judiciary" within the Constitution's "tripartite allocation of power." *Valley Forge*, at 474.

III

To state a case or controversy under Article III, a plaintiff must establish standing. The minimum constitutional requirements for standing were explained in *Lujan v. Defenders of Wildlife*, 504 U.S. 555 (1992).

> "First, the plaintiff must have suffered an 'injury in fact'—an invasion of a legally protected interest which is (a) concrete and particularized, and (b) 'actual or imminent, not "conjectural" or "hypothetical."' Second, there must be a causal connection between the injury and the conduct complained of—the injury has to be 'fairly . . . trace[able] to the challenged action of the defendant, and not . . . th[e] result [of] the independent action of some third party not before the court.' Third, it must be 'likely,' as opposed to merely 'speculative,' that the injury will be 'redressed by a favorable decision.'" *Id.*, at 560–561.

In requiring a particular injury, the Court meant "that the injury must affect the plaintiff in a personal and individual way." *Id.*, at 560. The question now before the Court is whether respondents, the plaintiffs in the trial court, satisfy the requisite elements of standing.

A

Respondents suggest that their status as Arizona taxpayers provides them with standing to challenge the STO tax credit. Absent special circumstances, however, standing cannot be based on a plaintiff's mere status as a taxpayer. This Court has rejected the general proposition that an individual who has paid taxes has a "continuing, legally cognizable interest in ensuring that those funds are not *used* by the Government in a way that violates the [1443] Constitution." *Hein v. Freedom from Religion Foundation, Inc.*, 551 U.S. 587, 599 (2007) (plurality opinion). This precept has been referred to as the rule against taxpayer standing. . . .

[1445] B

The primary contention of respondents, of course, is that, despite the general rule that taxpayers lack standing to object to expenditures alleged to be unconstitutional, their suit falls within the exception established by *Flast v. Cohen*. It must be noted at the outset that, as this Court has explained, *Flast*'s holding provides a "narrow exception" to "the general rule against taxpayer standing." *Bowen v. Kendrick*, 487 U.S. 589, 618 (1988).

At issue in *Flast* was the standing of federal taxpayers to object, on First Amendment grounds, to a congressional statute that allowed expenditures of federal funds from the General Treasury to support, among other programs, "instruction in reading, arithmetic, and other subjects in religious schools, and to purchase textbooks and other instructional materials for use in such schools." 392 U.S., at 85–86. *Flast* held that taxpayers have standing when two conditions are met.

The first condition is that there must be a "logical link" between the plaintiff's taxpayer status "and the type of legislative enactment attacked." *Id.*, at 102. . . .

The second condition for standing under *Flast* is that there must be "a nexus" between the plaintiff's taxpayer status and "the precise nature of the constitutional infringement alleged." 392 U.S., at 102. . . .

After stating the two conditions for taxpayer standing, *Flast* considered them together, explaining that individuals suffer a particular injury for standing purposes when, in violation of the Establishment Clause and by means of "the taxing and [1446] spending power," their property is transferred through the Government's Treasury to a sectarian entity. 392 U.S., at 105–106. As *Flast* put it: "The taxpayer's allegation in such cases would be that his tax money is being extracted and spent in violation of specific constitutional protections against such abuses of legislative power." *Id.*, at 106. *Flast* thus "understood the 'injury' alleged in Establishment Clause challenges to federal spending to be the very 'extract[ion] and spen[ding]' of 'tax money' in aid of religion alleged by a plaintiff." *DaimlerChrysler*, 547 U.S., at 348 (quoting *Flast*, 392 U.S., at 106). "Such an injury," *Flast* continued, is unlike "generalized grievances about the conduct of government" and so is "appropriate for judicial redress." *Id.*, at 106.

Flast found support for its finding of personal injury in "the history of the Establishment Clause," particularly James Madison's "Memorial and Remonstrance against Religious Assessments." . . .

In the "Memorial and Remonstrance," Madison objected to the proposed assessment on the ground that it would coerce a form of religious devotion in violation of conscience. In Madison's view, government should not "force a citizen to contribute three pence only of his property for the support of any one establishment." *Flast*, at 103 (quoting 2 *Writings of James Madison* 183, 186 [G. Hunt ed. 1901]). This Madisonian prohibition does not depend on the amount of property conscripted for sectarian ends. Any such taking, even one amounting to "three pence only," violates conscience. 392 U.S., at 103. . . .

[1447] Respondents contend that these principles demonstrate their standing to challenge the STO tax credit. In their view the tax credit is, for *Flast* purposes, best understood as a governmental expenditure. That is incorrect.

It is easy to see that tax credits and governmental expenditures can have similar economic consequences, at least for beneficiaries whose tax liability is sufficiently large to take full advantage of the credit. Yet tax credits and governmental expenditures do not both implicate individual taxpayers in sectarian activities. A dissenter whose tax dollars are "extracted and spent" knows that he has in some small measure been made to contribute to an establishment in violation of conscience. *Flast*, at 106. In that instance the taxpayer's direct and particular connection with the establishment does not depend on economic speculation or political conjecture. The connection would exist even if the conscientious dissenter's tax liability were unaffected or reduced. When the government declines to impose a tax, by contrast, there is no such connection between dissenting taxpayer and alleged establishment. Any financial injury remains speculative. And awarding some citizens a tax credit allows other citizens to retain control over their own funds in accordance with their own consciences.

The distinction between governmental expenditures and tax credits refutes respondents' assertion of standing. When Arizona taxpayers choose to contribute to STOs, they spend their own money, not money the State has collected from respondents or from other taxpayers. . . .

Furthermore, respondents cannot satisfy the requirements of causation and redressability. When the government collects and spends taxpayer money, governmental choices are responsible for the transfer of wealth. In that case a resulting subsidy of religious activity is, for purposes of *Flast*, traceable to the government's expenditures. And an injunction [1448] against those expenditures would address the objections of conscience raised by taxpayer-plaintiffs. Here, by contrast, contributions result from the decisions of private taxpayers regarding their own funds. Private citizens create private STOs; STOs choose beneficiary schools; and taxpayers then contribute to STOs. While the State, at the outset, affords the opportunity to create and contribute to an

STO, the tax credit system is implemented by private action and with no state intervention. Objecting taxpayers know that their fellow citizens, not the State, decide to contribute and in fact make the contribution. These considerations prevent any injury the objectors may suffer from being fairly traceable to the government. And while an injunction against application of the tax credit most likely would reduce contributions to STOs, that remedy would not affect noncontributing taxpayers or their tax payments. As a result, any injury suffered by respondents would not be remedied by an injunction limiting the tax credit's operation. . . .

[1449] Justice SCALIA, with whom Justice THOMAS joins, concurring.

Taxpayers ordinarily do not have standing to challenge federal or state expenditures that allegedly violate the Constitution. In *Flast v. Cohen*, 392 U.S. 83 (1968), we created a narrow exception for taxpayers raising Establishment Clause challenges to government expenditures. Today's majority and dissent struggle with whether respondents' challenge to the Arizona [1450] tuition tax credit falls within that narrow exception. Under a principled reading of Article III, their struggles are unnecessary. *Flast* is an anomaly in our jurisprudence, irreconcilable with the Article III restrictions on federal judicial power that our opinions have established. I would repudiate that misguided decision and enforce the Constitution.

I nevertheless join the Court's opinion because it finds respondents lack standing by applying *Flast* rather than distinguishing it away on unprincipled grounds.

Justice KAGAN, with whom Justice GINSBURG, Justice BREYER, and Justice SOTOMAYOR join, dissenting.

Since its inception, the Arizona private-school-tuition tax credit has cost the State, by its own estimate, nearly $350 million in diverted tax revenue. The Arizona taxpayers who instituted this suit (collectively, Plaintiffs) allege that the use of these funds to subsidize school tuition organizations (STOs) breaches the Establishment Clause's promise of religious neutrality. Many of these STOs, the Plaintiffs claim, discriminate on the basis of a child's religion when awarding scholarships.

For almost half a century, litigants like the Plaintiffs have obtained judicial review of claims that the government has used its taxing and spending power in violation of the Establishment Clause. Beginning in *Flast v. Cohen*, 392 U.S. 83 (1968), and continuing in case after case for over four decades, this Court and others have exercised jurisdiction to decide taxpayer-initiated challenges not materially different from this one. Not every suit has succeeded on the merits, or should have. But every taxpayer-plaintiff has had her day in court to contest the government's financing of religious activity.

Today, the Court breaks from this precedent by refusing to hear taxpayers' claims that the government has unconstitutionally subsidized religion through its tax system. These litigants lack standing, the majority holds, because the funding of religion they challenge comes from a tax credit, rather than an appropriation. A tax credit, the Court asserts, does not injure objecting taxpayers, because it "does not extract and spend [their] funds in service of an establishment."

This novel distinction in standing law between appropriations and tax expenditures has as little basis in principle as it has in our precedent. Cash grants and targeted tax breaks are means of accomplishing the same government objective—to provide financial support to select individuals or organizations. Taxpayers who oppose state aid of religion have equal reason to protest whether that aid flows from the one form of subsidy or the other. Either way, the government has financed the religious activity. And so either way, taxpayers should be able to challenge the subsidy.

Still worse, the Court's arbitrary distinction threatens to eliminate *all* occasions for a taxpayer to contest the government's monetary support of religion. Precisely because appropriations and tax breaks can achieve identical objectives, the government can easily substitute one for the other. Today's opinion thus enables the government to end-run *Flast's* guarantee of access to the Judiciary. From now on, the government need follow just one simple rule—subsidize through the tax system—to preclude taxpayer challenges to state funding of religion.

[1451] And that result—the effective demise of taxpayer standing—will diminish the Establishment Clause's force and meaning. Sometimes, no one other than taxpayers has suffered the injury necessary to challenge government sponsorship of religion. Today's holding therefore will prevent federal courts from determining whether some subsidies to sectarian organizations comport with our Constitution's guarantee of religious neutrality. Because I believe these challenges warrant consideration on the merits, I respectfully dissent from the Court's decision. . . .

[1462] III

Today's decision devastates taxpayer standing in Establishment Clause cases. The government, after all, often uses tax expenditures to subsidize favored persons and activities. Still more, the government almost *always* has this option. Appropriations and tax subsidies are readily interchangeable; what is a cash grant today can be a tax break tomorrow. The Court's opinion thus offers a roadmap—more truly, just a one-step instruction—to any government that wishes to insulate its financing of religious activity from legal challenge. Structure the funding as a tax expenditure, and *Flast* will not stand in the way. No taxpayer will have standing to object. However blatantly the government may violate the Establishment Clause, taxpayers cannot gain access to the federal courts.

And by ravaging *Flast* in this way, today's decision damages one of this Nation's defining constitutional commitments. "Congress shall make no law respecting an establishment of religion"—ten simple words that have stood for over 200 years as a foundation stone of American religious liberty. Ten words that this Court has long understood, as James Madison did, to limit (though by no means eliminate) the government's power to finance religious activity. The Court's ruling today will not shield all state subsidies for religion from review; as the Court notes, some persons alleging Establishment Clause violations have suffered individualized injuries, and therefore have standing, independent of their taxpayer status. But *Flast* arose because "the taxing and spending power [may] be used to favor one religion over another or to support religion in general," 392 U.S., at 103, without causing particularized harm to discrete persons. It arose because state sponsorship of religion sometimes harms individuals only (but this "only" is no small matter) in their capacity as contributing members of our national [1463] community. In those cases, the *Flast* Court thought, our Constitution's guarantee of religious neutrality still should be enforced.

Because that judgment was right then, and remains right today, I respectfully dissent.

64

Hosanna-Tabor Evangelical Lutheran Church and School v. Equal Employment Opportunity Commission*

132 S. Ct. 694 (2012)

Vote: 9—Roberts, Scalia, Kennedy, Thomas, Ginsburg, Breyer, Alito, Sotomayor, Kagan
0

Opinion announcing the opinion of the Court: Roberts
Concurring opinions: Thomas, Alito

This case resulted from an unlawful-termination action filed by the Equal Employment Opportunity Commission (EEOC) against Hosanna-Tabor Evangelical Lutheran Church and School.

A member of the Lutheran Church–Missouri Synod, Hosanna-Tabor classified its schoolteachers into two categories: "called" and "lay." "Called" teachers, who received the formal title "minister of religion, commissioned," were regarded as having been called by God to their vocation. To be eligible to be considered "called," a teacher had to complete certain academic requirements, including a course of theological study. "Lay," or "contract," teachers, by contrast, were not required to be trained by the synod or even to be Lutheran. Although lay and called teachers at Hosanna-Tabor generally performed the same duties, lay teachers were hired only when called teachers were unavailable.

Cheryl Perich was first employed by Hosanna-Tabor as a lay teacher. Soon after hiring her in 1999, Hosanna-Tabor asked Perich to become a called teacher, which she did. After completing the required training, Perich received a "diploma of vocation" designating her as a commissioned minister. She taught kindergarten during her first four years at Hosanna-Tabor and fourth grade during the 2003–2004 school year. Her subjects included math, language arts, social studies, science, gym, art, and music. She also taught a religion class four days a week, led the students in prayer and devotional exercises each day, and attended a weekly school-wide chapel service, a service that Perich herself led about twice a year.

In June 2004, Perich developed narcolepsy with symptoms including sudden and deep sleeps from which she could not be roused. She began the 2004–2005 school year on disability leave. On January 27, 2005, Perich notified the school principal, Stacey

---

*At the time of publication, the volume and page numbers for *Hosanna-Tabor* in the *United States Reports* were unavailable. The citation and page numbers used in this case refer to the *Supreme Court Reporter*.

Hoeft, that she would be able to report to work the following month. Hoeft responded that the school had already contracted with a lay teacher to fill Perich's position for the remainder of the school year. Hoeft also expressed concern that Perich was not yet ready to return to the classroom. The Hosanna-Tabor congregation voted to offer Perich a "peaceful release" from her call, whereby the congregation would pay a portion of her health insurance premiums in exchange for her resignation as a "called" teacher. Perich refused to resign and, instead, produced a note from her doctor stating that she would be able to return to work on February 22, 2005.

On the morning of February 22, Perich presented herself at the school. Hoeft asked her to leave, but Perich would not do so until she obtained written documentation that she had reported to work. Later that afternoon, Hoeft called Perich at home and told her that she would likely be fired. Perich responded that she had spoken with an attorney and intended to assert her legal rights. In a subsequent letter to Perich, the chairman of the school board advised her that the congregation would consider whether to rescind her call at its next meeting. As grounds for possible termination, the letter cited Perich's "insubordination and disruptive behavior," as well as the damage she had done to her "working relationship" with the school by "threatening to take legal action." The congregation voted to rescind Perich's call, and Hosanna-Tabor sent her a letter of termination.

In response, Perich filed a charge with the Equal Employment Opportunity Commission, claiming that her employment had been terminated in violation of the Americans with Disabilities Act (ADA). The EEOC subsequently brought suit against Hosanna-Tabor, claiming that it fired Perich in retaliation for threating to bring an ADA lawsuit.

Chief Justice ROBERTS delivered the opinion of the Court.

[699] Certain employment discrimination laws authorize employees who have been wrongfully terminated to sue their employers for reinstatement and damages. The question presented is whether the Establishment and Free Exercise Clauses of the First Amendment bar such an action when the employer is a religious group and the employee is one of the group's ministers. . . .

[702] II

The First Amendment provides, in part, that "Congress shall make no law respecting an establishment of religion, or prohibiting the free exercise thereof." We have said that these two Clauses "often exert conflicting pressures," *Cutter v. Wilkinson*, 544 U.S. 709, 719 (2005), and that there can be "internal tension . . . between the Establishment Clause and the Free Exercise Clause," *Tilton v. Richardson*, 403 U.S. 672, 677 (1971) (plurality opinion). Not so here. Both Religion Clauses bar the government from interfering with the decision of a religious group to fire one of its ministers. . . .

[703] Familiar with life under the established Church of England, the founding generation sought to foreclose the possibility of a national church. By forbidding the "establishment of religion" and guaranteeing the "free exercise thereof," the Religion Clauses ensured that the new Federal Government—unlike the English Crown—would have no role in filling ecclesiastical offices. The Establishment Clause prevents the Government from appointing ministers, and the Free Exercise Clause prevents it from interfering with the freedom of religious groups to select their own.

This understanding of the Religion Clauses was reflected in two events involving James Madison, "the leading architect of the religion clauses of the First Amendment." *Arizona Christian School Tuition Organization v. Winn*, 131 S. Ct. 1436, 1446 (2011) (quoting *Flast v. Cohen*, 392 U.S. 83, 103 [1968]). The first occurred in 1806, when John Carroll, the first Catholic bishop in the United States, solicited the Executive's opinion on who should be appointed to direct the affairs of the Catholic Church in the territory newly acquired by the Louisiana Purchase. After consulting with President Jefferson, then–Secretary of State Madison responded that the selection of church "functionaries" was an "entirely ecclesiastical" matter left to the Church's own judgment. Letter from James Madison to Bishop Carroll (Nov. 20, 1806). The "scrupulous policy of the Constitution in guarding against a political interference with religious affairs," Madison explained, prevented the Government from rendering an opinion on the "selection of ecclesiastical individuals."

The second episode occurred in 1811, when Madison was President. Congress had passed a bill incorporating the Protestant Episcopal Church in the town of Alexandria in what was then the District of Columbia. Madison vetoed the bill, on the ground that it "exceeds the rightful authority to which Governments are limited, by the essential distinction between civil [704] and religious functions, and violates, in particular, the article of the Constitution of the United States, which declares, that 'Congress shall make no law respecting a religious establishment.'" 22 Annals of Cong. 982–983 (1811). Madison explained:

> "The bill enacts into, and establishes by law, sundry rules and proceedings relative purely to the organization and polity of the church incorporated, and comprehending even the election and removal of the Minister of the same; so that no change could be made therein by the particular society, or by the general church of which it is a member, and whose authority it recognises." *Id.*, at 983 (emphasis added). . . .

[705] Until today, we have not had occasion to consider whether this freedom of a religious organization to select its ministers is implicated by a suit alleging discrimination in employment. The Courts of Appeals, in contrast, have had extensive experience with this issue. Since the passage of Title VII of the Civil Rights Act of 1964, 42 U.S.C. § 2000e *et seq.*, and other employment discrimination laws, the Courts of Appeals have uniformly recognized the existence of a "ministerial exception," grounded in the First Amendment, that precludes application of such legislation to claims concerning the employment relationship between a religious institution and its ministers.

[706] We agree that there is such a ministerial exception. The members of a religious group put their faith in the hands of their ministers. Requiring a church to accept or retain an unwanted minister, or punishing a church for failing to do so, intrudes upon more than a mere employment decision. Such action interferes with the internal governance of the church, depriving the church of control over the selection of those who will personify its beliefs. By imposing an unwanted minister, the state infringes the Free Exercise Clause, which protects a religious group's right to shape its own faith and mission through its appointments. According the state the power to determine which individuals will minister to the faithful also violates the Establishment Clause, which prohibits government involvement in such ecclesiastical decisions. . . .

[707] III

Having concluded that there is a ministerial exception grounded in the Religion Clauses of the First Amendment, we consider whether the exception applies in this case. We hold that it does.

Every Court of Appeals to have considered the question has concluded that the ministerial exception is not limited to the head of a religious congregation, and we agree. We are reluctant, however, to adopt a rigid formula for deciding when an employee qualifies as a minister. It is enough for us to conclude, in this our first case involving the ministerial exception, that the exception covers Perich, given all the circumstances of her employment.

To begin with, Hosanna-Tabor held Perich out as a minister, with a role distinct from that of most of its members. When Hosanna-Tabor extended her a call, it issued her a "diploma of vocation" according her the title "Minister of Religion, Commissioned." She was tasked with performing that office "according to the Word of God and the confessional standards of the Evangelical Lutheran Church as drawn from the Sacred Scriptures." The congregation prayed that God "bless [her] ministrations to the glory of His holy name, [and] the building of His church." In a supplement to the diploma, the congregation undertook to periodically review Perich's "skills of ministry" and "ministerial responsibilities," and to provide for her "continuing education as a professional person in the ministry of the Gospel."

Perich's title as a minister reflected a significant degree of religious training followed by a formal process of commissioning. To be eligible to become a commissioned minister, Perich had to complete eight college-level courses in subjects including biblical interpretation, church doctrine, and the ministry of the Lutheran teacher. She also had to obtain the endorsement of her local Synod district by submitting a petition that contained her academic transcripts, letters of recommendation, personal statement, and written answers to various ministry-related questions. Finally, she had to pass an oral examination by a faculty committee at a Lutheran college. It took Perich six years to fulfill these requirements. And when she eventually did, she was commissioned as a minister only upon election by the congregation, which recognized God's call to her to teach. At that point, her call could be rescinded only upon a supermajority vote of the congregation—a protection designed to allow her to "preach the Word of God boldly."

Perich held herself out as a minister of the Church by accepting the formal call to religious service, according to its terms. [708] She did so in other ways as well. For example, she claimed a special housing allowance on her taxes that was available only to employees earning their compensation "in the exercise of the ministry." In a form she submitted to the Synod following her termination, Perich again indicated that she regarded herself as a minister at Hosanna-Tabor, stating: "I feel that God is leading me to serve in the teaching ministry. . . . I am anxious to be in the teaching ministry again soon."

Perich's job duties reflected a role in conveying the Church's message and carrying out its mission. Hosanna-Tabor expressly charged her with "lead[ing] others toward Christian maturity" and "teach[ing] faithfully the Word of God, the Sacred Scriptures, in its truth and purity and as set forth in all the symbolical books of the Evangelical Lutheran Church." In fulfilling these responsibilities, Perich taught her students religion four days a week, and led them in prayer three times a day. Once a week, she took her students to a school-wide chapel service, and—about twice a year—she took her turn leading it, choosing the liturgy, selecting the hymns, and delivering a short message based on verses from the Bible. During her last year of teaching, Perich also led her fourth graders in a brief devotional exercise each morning. As a source of religious instruction, Perich performed an important role in transmitting the Lutheran faith to the next generation.

In light of these considerations—the formal title given Perich by the Church, the substance reflected in that title, her own use of that title, and the important religious functions she performed for the Church—we conclude that Perich was a minister covered by the ministerial exception. . . .

[709] Because Perich was a minister within the meaning of the exception, the First Amendment requires dismissal of this employment discrimination suit against her religious employer. . . .

[710] * * *

The interest of society in the enforcement of employment discrimination statutes is undoubtedly important. But so too is the interest of religious groups in choosing who will preach their beliefs, teach their faith, and carry out their mission. When a minister who has been fired sues her church alleging that her termination was discriminatory, the First Amendment has struck the balance for us. The church must be free to choose those who will guide it on its way.

Justice THOMAS, concurring.

I join the Court's opinion. I write separately to note that, in my view, the Religion Clauses require civil courts to apply the ministerial exception and to defer to a religious organization's good-faith understanding of who qualifies as its minister. As the Court explains, the Religion Clauses guarantee religious organizations autonomy in matters of internal governance, including the selection of those who will minister the faith. A religious organization's right to choose its ministers would be hollow, however, if secular courts could second-guess the organization's sincere determination that a given employee is a "minister" under the organization's theological tenets. Our country's religious landscape includes organizations with different leadership structures and doctrines that influence their conceptions of ministerial status. The question whether an employee is a minister is itself religious in nature, and the answer will vary widely. [711] Judicial attempts to fashion a civil definition of "minister" through a bright-line test or multi-factor analysis risk disadvantaging those religious groups whose beliefs, practices, and membership are outside of the "mainstream" or unpalatable to some. Moreover, uncertainty about whether its ministerial designation will be rejected, and a corresponding fear of liability, may cause a religious group to conform its beliefs and practices regarding "ministers" to the prevailing secular understanding. These are certainly dangers that the First Amendment was designed to guard against.

The Court thoroughly sets forth the facts that lead to its conclusion that Cheryl Perich was one of Hosanna-Tabor's ministers, and I agree that these facts amply demonstrate Perich's ministerial role. But the evidence demonstrates that Hosanna-Tabor sincerely considered Perich a minister. That would be sufficient for me to conclude that Perich's suit is properly barred by the ministerial exception.

Justice ALITO, with whom Justice KAGAN joins, concurring.

I join the Court's opinion, but I write separately to clarify my understanding of the significance of formal ordination and designation as a "minister" in determining whether an "employee" of a religious group falls within the so-called "ministerial" exception. The term "minister" is commonly used by many Protestant denominations to refer to members of their clergy, but the term is rarely if ever used in this way by Catholics, Jews, Muslims, Hindus, or Buddhists. In addition, the concept of ordination as understood by most Christian churches and by Judaism has no clear counterpart in some Christian denominations and some other religions. Because virtually every religion in the world is represented in the population of the United States, it would be a mistake if the term "minister" or the concept of ordination were viewed as central to the important issue of religious autonomy that is presented in cases like this one. Instead, courts should focus on the function performed by persons who work for religious bodies.

The First Amendment protects the freedom of religious groups to engage in certain key religious activities, including the conducting of worship services and other [712] religious ceremonies and rituals, as well as the critical process of communicating the faith. Accordingly, religious groups must be free to choose the personnel who are essential to the performance of these functions.

The "ministerial" exception should be tailored to this purpose. It should apply to any "employee" who leads a religious organization, conducts worship services or important religious ceremonies or rituals, or serves as a messenger or teacher of its faith. If a religious group believes that the ability of such an employee to perform these key functions has been compromised, then the constitutional guarantee of religious freedom protects the group's right to remove the employee from his or her position. . . .

[714] The ministerial exception applies to respondent because, as the Court notes, she played a substantial role in "conveying the Church's message and carrying out its mission." *Ante*, at 708. She taught religion to her students four days a week and took them to chapel on the fifth day. She led them in daily devotional exercises, and led them in prayer three times a day. She [715] also alternated with the other teachers in planning and leading worship services at the school chapel, choosing liturgies, hymns, and readings, and composing and delivering a message based on Scripture.

It makes no difference that respondent also taught secular subjects. While a purely secular teacher would not qualify for the "ministerial" exception, the constitutional protection of religious teachers is not somehow diminished when they take on secular functions in addition to their religious ones. What matters is that respondent played an important role as an instrument of her church's religious message and as a leader of its worship activities. Because of these important religious functions, Hosanna-Tabor had the right to decide for itself whether respondent was religiously qualified to remain in her office.

A Bill for Establishing Religious Freedom in Virginia (1777, 1786)

Thomas Jefferson

According to Merrill D. Peterson, Jefferson initially drafted his bill for religious freedom sometime in 1777.[1] In 1779, the Virginia House of Delegates debated but did not adopt the bill. It was amended and then adopted by the Virginia General Assembly on January 16, 1786. The italicized words were deleted during the October 1785 session of the Virginia General Assembly.

Well aware that the opinions and belief of men depend not on their own will, but follow involuntarily the evidence proposed to their minds; that Almighty God hath created the mind free, *and manifested his supreme will that free it shall remain by making it altogether insusceptible of restraint*; that all attempts to influence it by temporal punishments, or burthens, or by civil incapacitations, tend only to beget habits of hypocrisy and meanness, and are a departure from the plan of the holy author of our religion, who being lord both of body and mind, yet chose not to propagate it by coercions on either, as was in his Almighty power to do, *but to extend it by its influence on reason alone*; that the impious presumption of legislators and rulers, civil as well as ecclesiastical, who, being themselves but fallible and uninspired men, have assumed dominion over the faith of others, setting up their own opinions and modes of thinking as the only true and infallible, and as such endeavoring to impose them on others, hath established and maintained false religions over the greatest part of the world and through all time: That to compel a man to furnish contributions of money for the propagation of opinions which he disbelieves *and abhors*, is sinful and tyrannical; that even the forcing him to support this or that teacher of his own religious persuasion, is depriving him of the comfortable liberty of giving his contributions to the particular pastor whose morals he would make his pattern, and whose powers he feels most persuasive to righteousness; and is withdrawing from the ministry those temporary [temporal] rewards, which proceeding from an approbation of their personal conduct, are an additional incitement to earnest and unremitting labours for the instruction of mankind; that our civil rights have no dependance [sic] on our religious opinions, any more than [on] our opinions in physics or geometry; that therefore the proscribing any citizen as unworthy the public confidence by laying upon him an incapacity of being called to offices of trust and emolument, unless he profess or renounce this or that religious opinion, is depriving him injuriously of those privileges

---

1. Merrill D. Peterson, ed., *The Portable Thomas Jefferson* (New York: Viking Penguin, 1975), 251.

and advantages to which, in common with his fellow citizens, he has a natural right; that it tends also[2] to corrupt the principles of that *very* religion it is meant to encourage, by bribing, with a monopoly of worldly honours and emoluments, those who will externally profess and conform to it; that though indeed these are criminal who do not withstand such temptation, yet neither are those innocent who lay the bait in their way; *that the opinions of men are not the object of civil government, nor under its jurisdiction;* that to suffer the civil magistrate to intrude his powers into the field of opinion and to restrain the profession or propagation of principles on supposition of their ill tendency is a dangerous falacy, [*sic*] which at once destroys all religious liberty, because he being of course judge of that tendency will make his opinions the rule of judgment, and approve or condemn the sentiments of others only as they shall square with or differ from his own; that it is time enough for the rightful purposes of civil government for its officers to interfere when principles break out into overt acts against peace and good order; and finally, that truth is great and will prevail if left to herself; that she is the proper and sufficient antagonist to error, and has nothing to fear from the conflict unless by human interposition disarmed of her natural weapons, free argument and debate; errors ceasing to be dangerous when it is permitted freely to contradict them.

We the General Assembly of Virginia do enact[3] that no man shall be compelled to frequent or support any religious worship, place, or ministry whatsoever, nor shall be enforced, restrained, molested, or burthened in his body or goods, nor shall otherwise suffer, on account of his religious opinions or belief; but that all men shall be free to profess, and by argument to maintain, their opinions in matters of religion, and that the same shall in no wise diminish, enlarge, or affect their civil capacities.

And though we well know that this Assembly, elected by the people for the ordinary purposes of legislation only, have no power to restrain the acts of succeeding Assemblies, constituted with powers equal to our own, and that therefore to declare this act [to be] irrevocable would be of no effect in law; yet we are free to declare, and do declare, that the rights hereby asserted are of the natural rights of mankind, and that if any act shall be hereafter passed to repeal the present or to narrow its operation, such act will be an infringement of natural right.

Source: Daniel L. Dreisbach, *Thomas Jefferson and the Wall of Separation between Church and State* (New York: New York University Press, 2002), 133–135.

---

2. The act replaced "also" with "only." See Dreisbach, *Thomas Jefferson and the Wall of Separation*, 243, n. 3.

3. The act started the paragraph with "Be it enacted by the General Assembly . . ." Ibid., 243, n. 4.

B

Memorial and Remonstrance against Religious Assessments (1785)

James Madison

James Madison drafted the "Memorial and Remonstrance" in the spring of 1785 in the midst of a statewide debate over Patrick Henry's proposed legislation "Establishing a Provision for Teachers of the Christian Religion." Henry's bill was a property tax designed to fund religious Christian ministers in the state of Virginia. Under the bill's provisions, each property owner was to specify the Christian denomination to which he wished his tax directed. If a taxpayer failed or refused to specify a Christian society, his tax would go to the public treasury "to be disposed of under the direction of the General Assembly, for the encouragement of seminaries of learning . . . and to no other use or purpose whatsoever." Similarly, the taxes received by the various denominations were to be "appropriated to a provision for a Minister or Teacher of the Gospel, or the providing of places of divine worship, and to none other use whatsoever." An exception to this rule was made for Quakers and Mennonites, who were allowed to place their distribution in their general funds because they lacked the requisite clergy.

Madison published his remonstrance anonymously. It helped defeat Henry's proposal in 1785. The following year, in 1786, the Virginia legislature, guided by Madison, adopted Thomas Jefferson's statute for religious freedom.

To the Honorable the General Assembly of the Commonwealth of Virginia. A Memorial and Remonstrance.

We the subscribers, citizens of the said Commonwealth, having taken into serious consideration, a Bill printed by order of the last Session of General Assembly, entitled "A Bill establishing a provision for Teachers of the Christian Religion," and conceiving that the same if finally armed with the sanctions of a law, will be a dangerous abuse of power, are bound as faithful members of a free State to remonstrate against it, and to declare the reasons by which we are determined. We remonstrate against the said Bill,

1. Because we hold it for a fundamental and undeniable truth, "that religion or the duty which we owe to our Creator and the manner of discharging it, can be directed only by reason and conviction, not by force or violence." The Religion then of every man must be left to the conviction and conscience of every man; and it is the right of every man to exercise it as these may dictate. This right is in its nature an unalienable right. It is unalienable; because the opinions of men, depending only on the evidence contemplated by their own minds cannot follow the dictates

of other men: It is unalienable also, because what is here a right towards men, is a duty towards the Creator. It is the duty of every man to render to the Creator such homage and such only as he believes to be acceptable to him. This duty is precedent, both in order of time and in degree of obligation, to the claims of Civil Society. Before any man can be considered as a member of Civil Society, he must be considered as a subject of the Governor of the Universe: And if a member of Civil Society, do it with a saving of his allegiance to the Universal Sovereign. We maintain therefore that in matters of Religion, no man's right is abridged by the institution of Civil Society and that Religion is wholly exempt from its cognizance. True it is, that no other rule exists, by which any question which may divide a Society, can be ultimately determined, but the will of the majority; but it is also true that the majority may trespass on the rights of the minority.

2. Because if religion be exempt from the authority of the Society at large, still less can it be subject to that of the Legislative Body. The latter are but the creatures and vicegerents of the former. Their jurisdiction is both derivative and limited: it is limited with regard to the co-ordinate departments, more necessarily is it limited with regard to the constituents. The preservation of a free Government requires not merely, that the metes and bounds which separate each department of power be invariably maintained; but more especially that neither of them be suffered to overleap the great Barrier which defends the rights of the people. The Rulers who are guilty of such an encroachment, exceed the commission from which they derive their authority, and are Tyrants. The People who submit to it are governed by laws made neither by themselves nor by an authority derived from them, and are slaves.

3. Because it is proper to take alarm at the first experiment on our liberties. We hold this prudent jealousy to be the first duty of Citizens, and one of [the] noblest characteristics of the late Revolution. The free men of America did not wait till usurped power had strengthened itself by exercise, and entangled the question in precedents. They saw all the consequences in the principle, and they avoided the consequences by denying the principle. We revere this lesson too much, soon to forget it. Who does not see that the same authority which can establish Christianity, in exclusion of all other Religions, may establish with the same ease any particular sect of Christians, in exclusion of all other Sects? That the same authority which can force a citizen to contribute three pence only of his property for the support of any one establishment, may force him to conform to any other establishment in all cases whatsoever?

4. Because the Bill violates the equality which ought to be the basis of every law, and which is more indispensible, in proportion as the validity or expediency of any law is more liable to be impeached. If "all men are by nature equally free and independent," all men are to be considered as entering into Society on equal conditions; as relinquishing no more, and therefore retaining no less, one than another, of their natural rights. Above all are they to be considered as retaining an "*equal* title to the free exercise of Religion according to the dictates of conscience." Whilst we assert for ourselves a freedom to embrace, to profess and to observe the Religion which we believe to be of divine origin, we cannot deny an equal freedom to those whose minds have not yet yielded to the evidence which has convinced us. If this freedom be abused, it is an offence against God, not against man: To God, therefore, not to man, must an account of it be rendered. As the Bill violates equality by subjecting some to peculiar burdens, so it violates

the same principle, by granting to others peculiar exemptions. Are the Quakers and Menonists the only sects who think a compulsive support of their religions unnecessary and unwarrantable? Can their piety alone be entrusted with the care of public worship? Ought their Religions to be endowed above all others with extraordinary privileges, by which proselytes may be enticed from all others? We think too favorably of the justice and good sense of these denominations to believe that they either covet pre-eminencies over their fellow citizens or that they will be seduced by them from the common opposition to the measure.

5. Because the bill implies either that the Civil Magistrate is a competent Judge of Religious Truth; or that he may employ Religion as an engine of Civil policy. The first is an arrogant pretension falsified by the contradictory opinions of Rulers in all ages, and throughout the world: The second an unhallowed perversion of the means of salvation.

6. Because the establishment proposed by the Bill is not requisite for the support of the Christian Religion. To say that it is, is a contradiction to the Christian Religion itself; for every page of it disavows a dependence on the powers of this world: it is a contradiction to fact; for it is known that this Religion both existed and flourished, not only without the support of human laws, but in spite of every opposition from them, and not only during the period of miraculous aid, but long after it had been left to its own evidence and the ordinary care of Providence: Nay, it is a contradiction in terms; for a Religion not invented by human policy, must have pre-existed and been supported, before it was established by human policy. It is moreover to weaken in those who profess this Religion a pious confidence in its innate excellence and the patronage of its Author; and to foster in those who still reject it, a suspicion that its friends are too conscious of its fallacies to trust it to its own merits.

7. Because experience witnesseth that ecclesiastical establishments, instead of maintaining the purity and efficacy of Religion, have had a contrary operation. During almost fifteen centuries has the legal establishment of Christianity been on trial. What have been its fruits? More or less in all places, pride and indolence in the Clergy; ignorance and servility in the laity, in both, superstition, bigotry and persecution. Enquire of the Teachers of Christianity for the ages in which it appeared in its greatest lustre; those of every sect, point to the ages prior to its incorporation with Civil policy. Propose a restoration of this primitive State in which its Teachers depended on the voluntary rewards of their flocks, many of them predict its downfall. On which side ought their testimony to have greatest weight, when for or when against their interest?

8. Because the establishment in question is not necessary for the support of Civil Government. If it be urged as necessary for the support of Civil Government only as it is a means of supporting Religion, and it be not necessary for the latter purpose, it cannot be necessary for the former. If Religion be not within the cognizance of Civil Government how can its legal establishment be necessary to civil Government? What influence in fact have ecclesiastical establishments had on Civil Society? In some instances they have been seen to erect a spiritual tyranny on the ruins of the Civil authority; in many instances they have been seen upholding the thrones of political tyranny: in no instance have they been seen the guardians of the liberties of the people. Rulers who wished to subvert the public liberty, may have found an established Clergy convenient auxiliaries. A just Government instituted to secure & perpetuate it needs them not. Such a Government will be best supported by pro-

tecting every Citizen in the enjoyment of his Religion with the same equal hand which protects his person and his property; by neither invading the equal rights of any Sect, nor suffering any Sect to invade those of another.

9. Because the proposed establishment is a departure from the generous policy, which, offering an Asylum to the persecuted and oppressed of every Nation and Religion, promised a lustre to our country, and an accession to the number of its citizens. What a melancholy mark is the Bill of sudden degeneracy? Instead of holding forth an Asylum to the persecuted, it is itself a signal of persecution. It degrades from the equal rank of Citizens all those whose opinions in Religion do not bend to those of the Legislative authority. Distant as it may be in its present form from the Inquisition, it differs from it only in degree. The one is the first step, the other the last in the career of intolerance. The magnanimous sufferer under this cruel scourge in foreign Regions, must view the Bill as a Beacon on our Coast, warning him to seek some other haven, where liberty and philanthropy in their due extent, may offer a more certain repose from his Troubles.

10. Because it will have a like tendency to banish our Citizens. The allurements presented by other situations are every day thinning their number. To superadd a fresh motive to emigration by revoking the liberty which they now enjoy, would be the same species of folly which has dishonoured and depopulated flourishing kingdoms.

11. Because it will destroy that moderation and harmony which the forbearance of our laws to intermeddle with Religion, has produced among its several sects. Torrents of blood have been split in the old world, by vain attempts of the secular arm, to extinguish Religious discord, by proscribing all difference in Religious opinion. Time has at length revealed the true remedy. Every relaxation of narrow and rigorous policy, wherever it has been tried, has been found to assuage the disease. The American Theatre has exhibited proofs, that equal and compleat liberty, if it does not wholly eradicate it, sufficiently destroys its malignant influence on the health and prosperity of the State. If with the salutary effects of this system under our own eyes, we begin to contract the bounds of Religious freedom, we know no name that will too severely reproach our folly. At least let warning be taken at the first fruits of the threatened innovation. The very appearance of the Bill has transformed "that Christian forbearance, love and charity," which of late mutually prevailed, into animosities and jealousies, which may not soon be appeased. What mischiefs may not be dreaded should this enemy to the public quiet be armed with the force of a law?

12. Because the policy of the Bill is adverse to the diffusion of the light of Christianity. The first wish of those who enjoy this precious gift, ought to be that it may be imparted to the whole race of mankind. Compare the number of those who have as yet received it with the number still remaining under the dominion of false Religions; and how small is the former! Does the policy of the Bill tend to lessen the disproportion? No; it at once discourages those who are strangers to the light of [revelation] from coming into the Region of it; and countenances by example the nations who continue in darkness, in shutting out those who might convey it to them. Instead of levelling as far as possible, every obstacle to the victorious progress of Truth, the Bill with an ignoble and unchristian timidity would circumscribe it with a wall of defence against the encroachments of error.

13. Because attempts to enforce by legal sanctions, acts obnoxious to so great a proportion of Citizens, tend to enervate the laws in general, and to slacken the

bands of Society. If it be difficult to execute any law which is not generally deemed necessary or salutary, what must be the case, where it is deemed invalid and dangerous? And what may be the effect of so striking an example of impotency in the Government, on its general authority?

14. Because a measure of such singular magnitude and delicacy ought not to be imposed, without the clearest evidence that it is called for by a majority of citizens: and no satisfactory method is yet proposed by which the voice of the majority in this case may be determined, or its influence secured. "The people of the respective countries are indeed requested to signify their opinion respecting the adoption of the Bill to the next Session of Assembly." But the representation must be made equal, before the voice either of the Representatives of the Counties, will be that of the people. Our hope is that neither of the former will, after due consideration, espouse the dangerous principle of the Bill. Should the event disappoint us, it will still leave us in full confidence, that a fair appeal to the latter will reverse the sentence against our liberties.

15. Because finally, "the equal right of every citizen to the free exercise of his Religion according to the dictates of conscience" is held by the same tenure with all our other rights. If we recur to its origin, it is equally the gift of nature; if we weigh its importance, it cannot be less dear to us; if we consult the Declaration of those rights which pertain to the good people of Virginia, "as the basis and foundation of Government," it is enumerated with equal solemnity, or rather studied emphasis. Either then, we must say, that the will of the Legislature is the only measure of their authority; and that in the plentitude of this authority, they may sweep away all our fundamental rights; or, that they are bound to leave this particular right untouched and sacred: Either we must say, that they may control the freedom of the press, may abolish the trial by jury, may swallow up the Executive and Judiciary Powers of the State; nay that they may despoil us of our very right of suffrage, and erect themselves into an independent and hereditary assembly: or we must say, that they have no authority to enact into the law the Bill under consideration. We the Subscribers say, that the General Assembly of this Commonwealth have no such authority: And that no effort may be omitted on our part against so dangerous an usurpation, we oppose to it, this remonstrance; earnestly praying, as we are in duty bound, that the Supreme Lawgiver of the Universe, by illuminating those to whom it is addressed, may on the one hand, turn their councils from every act which would affront his holy prerogative, or violate the trust committed to them: and on the other, guide them into every measure which may be worthy of his [blessing, may re]dound to their own praise, and may establish more firmly the liberties, the prosperity and the Happiness of the Commonwealth.

The Massachusetts Constitution of 1780 and *Barnes v. Falmouth* (1810)

The declaration of rights in the Massachusetts Constitution of 1780 recognized the right of all individuals to worship according to conscience (Art. II) and the right of the people to authorize their legislatures to collect taxes to support "public Protestant teachers of piety, religion, and morality" (Art. III).

Pursuant to Article III, Massachusetts provided for a system of local taxation to support religious clergy. The arrangement was the subject of several lawsuits, including one by Thomas Barnes, a Universalist minister. The ministerial taxes paid by Barnes's followers were directed not to Barnes but to the local Congregational minister. Barnes filed suit in an attempt to receive these tax dollars. The Supreme Judicial Court of Massachusetts decided against Barnes, ruling that Article III ministerial taxes could be directed only to ministers of incorporated religious societies, a criterion Barnes failed to meet.

In the opinion of the court, Chief Justice Theophilus Parsons set forth a justification of Article III that defended the wisdom, propriety, and reasonableness of Massachusetts's arrangement of taxpayer support of religion. Reproduced here are the first three articles of the declaration of rights of the Massachusetts Constitution of 1780 and excerpts of Chief Justice Parsons's defense of Article III's provision for taxpayer-funded ministers.

Massachusetts Constitution of 1780

A Declaration of the Rights of the Inhabitants of the Commonwealth of Massachusetts

Article I. All men are born free and equal, and have certain natural, essential, and unalienable rights; among which may be reckoned the right of enjoying and defending their lives and liberties; that of acquiring, possessing, and protecting property; in fine, that of seeking and obtaining their safety and happiness.

Art. II. It is the right as well as the duty of all men in society, publicly and at stated seasons, to worship the Supreme Being, the great Creator and Preserver of the universe. And no subject shall be hurt, molested, or restrained, in his person, liberty, or estate, for worshipping God in the manner and season most agreeable to the dictates of his own conscience, or for his religious profession or sentiments, provided he doth not disturb the public peace or obstruct others in their religious worship.

Art. III. As the happiness of a people and the good order and preservation of civil government essentially depend upon piety, religion, and morality, and as these cannot be generally diffused through a community but by the institution of the public worship of God and of the public instructions in piety, religion, and morality: Therefore, To promote their happiness and to secure the good order and preservation of their government, the people of this commonwealth have a right to invest their legislature with power to authorize and require, and the legislature shall, from time to time, authorize and require, the several towns, parishes, precincts, and other bodies-politic or religious societies to make suitable provision, at their own expense, for the institution of the public worship of God and for the support and maintenance of public Protestant teachers of piety, religion, and morality in all cases where such provision shall not be made voluntarily.

And the people of this commonwealth have also a right to, and do, invest their legislature with authority to enjoin upon all the subjects an attendance upon the instructions of the public teachers aforesaid, at stated times and seasons, if there be any on whose instructions they can conscientiously and conveniently attend.

Provided, notwithstanding, That the several towns, parishes, precincts, and other bodies-politic, or religious societies, shall at all times have the exclusive right of electing their public teachers and of contracting with them for their support and maintenance.

And all moneys paid by the subject to the support of public worship and of public teachers aforesaid shall, if he require it, be uniformly applied to the support of the public teacher or teachers of his own religious sect or denomination, provided there be any on whose instructions he attends; otherwise it may be paid toward the support of the teacher or teachers of the parish or precinct in which the said moneys are raised.

And every denomination of Christians, demeaning themselves peaceably and as good subjects of the commonwealth, shall be equally under the protection of the law; and no subordination of any sect or denomination to another shall ever be established by law.

Thomas Barnes v. The Inhabitants of the First Parish in Falmouth, 6 Mass. 401 (1810)

Supreme Judicial Court of Massachusetts

PARSONS, C. J.

. . . [404] The object of a free civil government is the promotion and security of the happiness of the citizens. These effects cannot be produced, but by the knowledge and practice [405] of our moral duties, which comprehend all the social and civil obligations of man to man, and of the citizen to the state. If the civil magistrate in any state could procure by his regulations a uniform practice of these duties, the government of that state would be perfect.

To obtain that perfection, it is not enough for the magistrate to define the rights of the several citizens, as they are related to life, liberty, property, and reputation, and to punish those by whom they may be invaded. Wise laws, made to this end, and faithfully executed, may leave the people strangers to many of the enjoyments of civil and social life, without which their happiness will be extremely imperfect. Human laws cannot oblige to the performance of the duties of imperfect obligation; as the duties of charity and hospitality, benevolence and good neighborhood; as the duties resulting from the relation of husband and wife, parent and child; of man to man, as children of a common parent; and of real patriotism, by influencing every citizen to love his country, and to obey all its laws. These are moral duties, flowing from the disposition of the heart, and not subject to the control of human legislation.

Neither can the laws prevent, by temporal punishment, secret offences, committed without witness, to gratify malice, revenge, or any other passion, by assailing the most important and most estimable rights of others. For human tribunals cannot proceed against any crimes, unless ascertained by evidence; and they are destitute of all power to prevent the commission of offences, unless by the feeble examples exhibited in the punishment of those who may be detected.

Civil government, therefore, availing itself only of its own powers, is extremely defective; and unless it could derive assistance from some superior power, whose laws extend to the temper and disposition of the human heart, and before whom no offence is secret, wretched indeed would be the [406] state of man under a civil constitution of any form.

This most manifest truth has been felt by legislators in all ages; and as man is born, not only a social, but a religious being, so, in the pagan world, false and absurd systems of religion were adopted and patronized by the magistrate, to remedy the defects necessarily existing in a government merely civil.

On these principles, tested by the experience of mankind, and by the reflections of reason, the people of *Massachusetts*, in the frame of their government, adopted and patronized a religion, which, by its benign and energetic influences, might cooperate with human institutions, to promote and secure the happiness of the citizens, so far as might be consistent with the imperfections of man.

In selecting a religion, the people were not exposed to the hazard of choosing a false and defective religious system. Christianity had long been promulgated, its pretensions and excellences well known, and its divine authority admitted. This religion was found to rest on the basis of immortal truth; to contain a system of morals adapted to man, in all possible ranks and conditions, situations and circumstances, by conforming to which he would be meliorated and improved in all the relations of human life; and to furnish the most efficacious sanctions, by bringing to light a future state of retribution. And this religion, as understood by Protestants, tending, by its effects, to make every man submitting to its influence, a better husband, parent, child, neighbor, citizen, and magistrate, was by the people established as a fundamental and essential part of their constitution.

The manner in which this establishment was made, is liberal, and consistent with the rights of conscience on religious subjects. As religious opinions, and the time and manner of expressing the homage due to the Governor of the universe, are points depending on the sincerity and belief of each individual, and do not concern the public [407] interest, care is taken, in the second article of the declaration of rights, to guard these points from the interference of the civil magistrate; and no man can be hurt, molested, or restrained, in his person, liberty, or estate, for worshipping God in the manner and season most agreeable to the dictates of his own conscience, or for his religious profession or sentiment, provided he does not disturb the public peace, or obstruct others in their religious worship; in which case he is punished, not for his religious opinions or worship, but because he interrupts others in the enjoyment of the rights he claims for himself, or because he has broken the public peace.

Having secured liberty of conscience, on the subject of religious opinion and worship, for every man, whether Protestant or Catholic, Jew, Mahometan, or Pagan, the constitution then provides for the public teaching of the precepts and maxims of the religion, of Protestant Christians to all the people. And for this purpose it is made the right and the duty of all corporate religious societies, to elect and support a public Protestant teacher of piety, religion, and morality; and the election and support of the teacher depend exclusively on the will of a majority of each society incorporated for those purposes. As public instruction requires persons who may be taught, every citizen may be enjoined to attend on some one of these teachers, at times and seasons to be stated by law, if there be any on whose instructions he can conscientiously attend.

In the election and support of a teacher, every member of the corporation is bound by the will of the majority; but as the great object of this provision was to secure the election and support of public Protestant teachers by corporate societies, and as some members of any corporation might be of a sect or denomination of Protestant Christians different from the majority of the members, and might choose to unite with other Protestant Christians of their own sect or denomination, in maintaining a public teacher, who by law was entitled to support, and on whose [408] instructions they usually attended, indulgence was granted, that persons thus situated might have the money they contributed to the support of public worship, and of the public teachers aforesaid, appropriated to the support of the teacher on whose instructions they should attend.

Several objections have at times been made to this establishment, which may be reduced to three: that when a man disapproves of any religion, or of any supported doctrines of any religion, to compel him by law to contribute money for public instruction in such religion or doctrine, is an infraction of his liberty of conscience; that to compel a man to pay for public religious instructions, on which he does not attend, and from which he can therefore derive no benefit, is unreasonable and intolerant; and that it is antichristian for any state to avail itself of the precepts and maxims of Christianity, to support civil government, because the Founder of it has declared that his kingdom is not of this world.

These objections go to the authority of the people to make this constitution, which is not proper nor competent for us to bring into question. And although we are not able, and have no inclination, to assume the character of theologians, yet it may not be improper to make a few short observations, to defend our constitution from the charges of persecution, intolerance, and impiety.

When it is remembered that no man is compellable to attend on any religious instruction, which he conscientiously disapproves, and that he is absolutely protected in the most perfect freedom of conscience in his religious opinions and worship, the first objection seems to mistake a man's conscience for his money, and to deny the state a right of levying and of appropriating the money of the citizens, at the will of the legislature, in which they all are represented. But as every citizen derives the security of his property, and the fruits of his industry, from the power of the state, so, as the price of this protection, he is bound to contribute, in common with his fellow-citizens, [409] for the public use, so much of his property, and for such public uses, as the state shall direct. And if any individual can lawfully withhold his contribution, because he dislikes the appropriation, the authority of the state to levy taxes would be annihilated; and without money it would soon cease to have any authority. But all moneys raised and appropriated for public uses, by any corporation, pursuant to powers derived from the state, are raised and appropriated substantially by the authority of the state. And the people, in their constitution, instead of devolving the support of public teachers on the corporations, by whom they should be elected, might have directed their support to be defrayed out of the public treasury, to be reimbursed by the levying and collection of state taxes. And against this mode of support, the objection of an individual, disapproving of the object of the public taxes, would have the same weight it can have against the mode of public support through the medium of corporate taxation. In either case, it can have no weight to maintain a charge of persecution for conscience' sake. The great error lies in not distinguishing between liberty of conscience in religious opinions and worship, and the right of appropriating money by the state. The former is an unalienable right; the latter is surrendered to the state, as the price of protection.

The second objection is, that it is intolerant to compel a man to pay for religious instruction, from which, as he does not hear it, he can derive no benefit. This objection is founded wholly in mistake. The object of public religious instruction is to teach, and to enforce by suitable arguments, the practice of a system of correct morals among the people, and to form and cultivate reasonable and just habits and manners; by which every man's person and property are protected from outrage, and his personal and social enjoyments promoted and multiplied. From these effects every man derives the most important benefits; and whether he be, or be not, an auditor of any public [410] teacher, he receives more solid and permanent advantages from this public instruction, than the administration of justice in courts of law can give him. The like objection may be made by any man to the support of public schools, if he have no family who attend; and any man, who has no lawsuit, may object to the support of judges and jurors on the same ground; when, if there were no courts of law, he would unfortunately find that causes for lawsuits would sufficiently abound.

The last objection is founded upon the supposed antichristian conduct of the state, in availing itself of the precepts and maxims of Christianity, for the purposes of a more excellent civil government. It is admitted that the Founder of this religion did not intend to erect a temporal dominion, agreeably to the prejudices of his countrymen; but to reign in the hearts of men, by subduing their irregular appetites and propensities, and by moulding their passions to the noblest purposes. And it is one great excellence of his religion, that, not pretending to worldly pomp and power, it is calculated and accommodated to meliorate the conduct and condition of man, under any form of civil government.

The objection goes further, and complains that Christianity is not left, for its promulgation and support, to the means designed by its Author, who requires not the assistance of man to effect his purposes and intentions. Our constitution certainly provides for the punishment of many breaches of the laws of Christianity, not for the purpose of propping up the Christian religion, but because those breaches are offences against the laws of the state; and it is a civil, as well as a religious duty of the magistrate, not to bear the sword in vain. But there are many precepts of Christianity, of which the violation cannot be punished by human laws; and as obedience to them is beneficial to civil society, the state has wisely taken care that they should be taught, and also enforced by explaining their moral and religious sanctions, as they cannot be enforced by temporal [411] punishments. And from the genius and temper of this religion, and from the benevolent character of its Author, we must conclude that it is his intention that man should be benefited by it in his civil and political relations, as well as in his individual capacity. And it remains for the objector to prove, that the patronage of Christianity by the civil magistrate, induced by the tendency of its precepts to form good citizens, is not one of the means by which the knowledge of its doctrines was intended to be disseminated and preserved among the human race.

The last branch of the objection rests on the very correct position that the faith and precepts of the Christian religion are so interwoven, that they must be taught together; whence it is inferred that the state, by enjoining instruction in its precepts, interferes with its doctrines, and assumes a power not intrusted to any human authority.

If the state claimed the absurd power of directing or controlling the faith of its citizens, there might be some ground for the objection. But no such power is claimed.

The authority derived from the constitution extends no further than to submit to the understandings of the people the evidence of truths deemed of public utility, leaving the weight of the evidence, and the tendency of those truths, to the conscience of every man.

Indeed, this objection must come from a willing objector; for it extends, in its consequences, to prohibit the state from providing for public instruction in many branches of useful knowledge which naturally tend to defeat the arguments of infidelity, to illustrate the doctrines of the Christian religion, and to confirm the faith of its professors.

As Christianity has the promise not only of this, but of a future life, it cannot be denied that public instruction in piety, religion, and morality, by Protestant teachers, may have a beneficial effect beyond the present state of existence. And the people are to be applauded, as well for their benevolence as for their wisdom, that, in selecting a religion whose precepts and sanctions might supply the [412] defects in civil government, necessarily limited in its power, and supported only by temporal penalties, they adopted a religion founded in truth; which in its tendency will protect our property here, and may secure to us an inheritance in another and a better country.

These objections to our constitution cannot be made by the plaintiff, who, having sought his remedy by an action at law, must support it as resting on our religious establishment, or his claim can have no legal foundation. . . .

[415] Again, it is asked, What relief can a few conscientious men have, who are of a religious sect, different from that of the parish in which they live, and have no teacher of any corporate society in their neighborhood, of their own sect or denomination, on whose instructions they can conscientiously attend?

The rights of conscience, in matters of religious opinion and worship, are protected by the second article; and by the third article, they are not obliged to attend on the instructions of any teacher, whom they cannot conscientiously hear. The inconvenience, therefore, is merely pecuniary, and of no great magnitude. In this case, they ought, as good citizens, to submit to those laws, from which they derive protection for their persons and property, and which must regulate the disposition of all assessments made [416] by their authority. When their numbers are large, and they are able and willing to submit to the obligation of electing and supporting a public teacher, the liberality of the legislature will grant them relief, by vesting them with corporate powers; when, in consequence of those powers, other corporations will not be disabled from discharging the duties already imposed on them by law. And it seems a mistake to suppose that the legislature cannot grant any further relief in particular cases, which in its discretion it may consider as deserving relief. Quakers are not provided for by the third article, because they have no teacher, and they resist the payment of any ministerial taxes. But they were exempted from ministerial assessments by the provisions of a provincial statute now expired; and those provisions are reënacted by the statute of 1799, c. 87.

But the object of the constitution was to settle general principles and to secure general rights, and not to legislate in all cases. If particular cases should arise, which might claim relief, consistently with the constitution, those cases were left to the discretion of the legislature, to whom the interests of the citizens are intrusted.

The last paragraph of the third article has also been pressed upon us. It provides that "every denomination of Christians, demeaning themselves peaceably, and as good subjects of the commonwealth, shall be equally under the protection of law; and no subordination of one sect or denomination to another shall ever be established by law."

In our opinion, this paragraph has no relation to the subject before us. Its object was to prevent any hierarchy, or ecclesiastical jurisdiction of one sect of Christians over any other sect; and the sect of Roman Catholics are as fully entitled to the benefit of this clause, as any society of Protestant Christians. It was also intended to prevent any religious test, as a qualification for office. Therefore those Catholics, who renounce all obedience and subjection to the pope, as a foreign prince or prelate, may, notwithstanding [417] their religious tenets, hold any civil office, although the constitution has not provided for the support of any public teacher of the Popish religion.

If this paragraph can be considered as relating to the provision for public teachers, a Catholic teacher of a Catholic congregation might maintain an action to recover the parish taxes of his hearers, as well as a public Protestant teacher of any incorporated religious society.

The only inferiority, created by the third article, is founded on a social principle, essential to the existence of any society—the submission of the minority to the majority. This submission is required, without any regard to sects or denominations of Christians. In the present case, if the plaintiff was of the same sect as the inhabitants of the first parish in *Falmouth*, and they were of the denomination to which he belongs, the law would be precisely the same.

This construction, which we find ourselves obliged to give to the constitution on this subject, is agreeable to the construction adopted by the legislature, as expressed in the statute of 1799, c. 87, before cited. Thus all citizens, except Quakers, are obliged to contribute to the support of public teachers; and when any member of any society, but of a different sect, shall request to have his taxes paid to the teacher of his own sect, but of another society, his request cannot prevail, but on his producing a certificate signed by his public teacher, and by a committee of the society, purporting in substance such facts as entitle him to the obtaining of his request; and the assessors of the society in which he dwells may afterwards omit him in their assessments.

This construction is not denied; but it is argued that the legislature cannot, by any construction, control the constitution. This is true; but where any part of the constitution is of doubtful construction, the opinion of the legislature deserves to be heard, and is entitled to due consideration. And in the present case, their construction [418] appears to us to be correct. Certainly no conclusion can be drawn from it, that the statute intended to exempt any citizen, except Quakers, from contributing to the support of some public Protestant teacher.

It is our opinion that the verdict do stand, and that judgment be rendered upon it.

D

Records of the First Congress Pertaining to the Drafting of the Religion Clauses of the First Amendment (1789)

The records below from the House of Representatives are reproduced from the Annals of the Congress of the United States, *volume 1, published by Gales & Seaton in Washington, DC, in 1834.* The* Annals *were compiled using the best records available, primarily newspaper accounts. Speeches are paraphrased and cannot be considered verbatim accounts of the House debate.*

The records below from the Senate are reproduced from the Journal of the Senate of the United States of America, *published by Gales & Seaton in Washington, DC, in 1820.** Unfortunately, the* Journal of the Senate *lacks detailed information about, or even a paraphrased transcription of, the debates that took place on the Senate floor. It notes only the matters considered and the votes taken by the Senate.*

The House of Representatives

MONDAY, June 8

[448] MR. MADISON.—. . .

[450] The amendments which have occurred to me, proper to be recommended by Congress to the State Legislatures, are these:

[451] First, That there be prefixed to the Constitution a declaration, that all power is originally vested in, and consequently derived from, the people.

That Government is instituted and ought to be exercised for the benefit of the people; which consists in the enjoyment of life and liberty, with the right of acquiring and using property, and generally of pursuing and obtaining happiness and safety.

That the people have an indubitable, unalienable, and indefeasible right to reform or change their Government, whenever it be found adverse or inadequate to the purposes of its institution. . . .

Fourthly. That in article 1st, section 9, between clauses 3 and 4, be inserted these clauses, to wit: The civil rights of none shall be abridged on account of religious belief or

---

*Available online at "Annals of Congress," Library of Congress, http://memory.loc.gov/ammem/amlaw/lwac.html.

**Available online at "Annals of Congress," Library of Congress, http://memory.loc.gov/ammem/amlaw/lwsj.html.

worship, nor shall any national religion be established, nor shall the full and equal rights of conscience be in any manner, or on any pretext, infringed.

The people shall not be deprived or abridged of their right to speak, to write, or to publish their sentiments; and the freedom of the press, as one of the great bulwarks of liberty, shall be inviolable.

The people shall not be restrained from peaceably assembling and consulting for their common good; nor from applying to the Legislature by petitions, or remonstrances, for redress of their grievances.

The right of the people to keep and bear arms shall not be infringed; a well armed and well regulated militia being the best security of a free country: but no person religiously scrupulous of bearing arms shall be compelled to render military service in person. . . .

[452] Fifthly. That in article 1st, section 10, between clauses 1 and 2, be inserted this clause, to wit:

> No State shall violate the equal rights of conscience, or the freedom of the press, or the trial by jury in criminal cases. . . .

Saturday, August 15

AMENDMENTS TO THE CONSTITUTION

[757] The House again went into a Committee of the whole, on the proposed amendments to the constitution, Mr. BOUDINOT in the chair.

The fourth proposition under consideration being as follows:

Article 1. Sect. 9. Between paragraph two and three insert "no religion shall be established by law, nor shall the equal rights of conscience be infringed."

Mr. SYLVESTER had some doubts of the propriety of the mode of expression used in this paragraph. He apprehended that it was liable to a construction different from what had been made by the committee. He feared it might be thought to have a tendency to abolish religion altogether.

Mr. VINING suggested the propriety of transposing the two members of the sentence.

Mr. GERRY said it would read better if it was, that no religious doctrine shall be established by law.

Mr. SHERMAN thought the amendment altogether unnecessary, inasmuch as Congress had no authority whatever delegated to them by the constitution to make religious establishments; he would, therefore, move to have it struck out.

Mr. CARROLL.—As the rights of conscience are, in their nature, of peculiar delicacy, and will little bear the gentlest touch of the governmental hand; and as many sects have concurred [758] in opinion that they are not well secured under the present constitution, he said he was much in favor of adopting the words. He thought it would tend more toward conciliating the minds of the people to the Government than almost any other amendment he had heard proposed. He would not contend with gentlemen about the phraseology, his object was to secure the substance in such a manner as to satisfy the wishes of the honest part of the community.

Mr. MADISON said, he apprehended the meaning of the words to be, that Congress should not establish a religion, and enforce the legal observation of it by law, nor compel men to worship God in any manner contrary to their conscience. Whether the words were necessary or not he did not mean to say, but they had been required by some of the State Conventions, who seemed to entertain an opinion that under the clause of the constitution, which gave power to Congress to make all laws necessary and proper to carry into execution the constitution, and the laws made under it, enabled them to make laws of such a nature as might infringe the rights of conscience, and establish a national religion; to prevent these effects he presumed the amendment was intended, and he thought it as well expressed as the nature of the language would admit.

Mr. HUNTINGTON said that he feared, with the gentleman first up on this subject, that the words might be taken in such a latitude as to be extremely hurtful to the cause of religion. He understood the amendment to mean what had been expressed by the gentleman from Virginia; but others might find it convenient to put another construction upon it. The ministers of their congregations to the Eastward were maintained by the contributions of those who belonged to their society; the expense of building meeting-houses was contributed in the same manner. These things were regulated by by-laws. If an action was brought before a Federal Court on any of these cases, the person who had neglected to perform his engagements could not be compelled to do it; for a support of ministers, or building of places of worship might be construed into a religious establishment.

By the charter of Rhode Island, no religion could be established by law; he could give a history of the effects of such a regulation; indeed the people were now enjoying the blessed fruits of it. He hoped, therefore, the amendment would be made in such a way as to secure the rights of conscience, and a free exercise of the rights of religion, but not to patronize those who professed no religion at all.

Mr. MADISON thought, if the word national was inserted before religion, it would satisfy the minds of honorable gentlemen. He believed that the people feared one sect might obtain a pre-eminence, or two combine together, and establish a religion to which they would compel others to conform. He thought if the word national was introduced, it would point the [759] amendment directly to the object it was intended to prevent.

Mr. LIVERMORE was not satisfied with that amendment; but he did not wish them to dwell long on the subject. He thought it would be better if it was altered, and made to read in this manner, that Congress shall make no laws touching religion, or infringing the rights of conscience.

Mr. GERRY did not like the term national, proposed by the gentleman from Virginia, and he hoped it would not be adopted by the House. It brought to his mind some observations that had taken place in the conventions at the time they were considering the present constitution. It had been insisted upon by those who were called antifederalists, that this form of Government consolidated the Union; the honorable gentleman's motion shows that he considers it in the same light. Those who were called antifederalists at that time complained that they had injustice done them by the title, because they were in favor of a Federal Government, and the others were in favor of a national one; the federalists were for ratifying the constitution as it stood, and the others not until amendments were made. Their names then ought not to have been distinguished by federalists and antifederalists, but rats and antirats.

Mr. MADISON withdrew his motion, but observed that the words "no national religion shall be established by law," did not imply that the Government was a national one; the question was then taken on Mr. Livermore's motion, and passed in the affirmative, thirty-one for, and twenty against it. . . .

MONDAY, August 17

AMENDMENTS TO THE CONSTITUTION

[778] The House went into a committee, Mr. BOUDINOT in the chair, on the proposed amendments to the constitution. The third clause of the fourth proposition in the report

was taken into consideration, being as follows: "A well regulated militia, composed of the body of the people, being the best security of a free state, the right of the people to keep and bear arms shall not be infringed; but no person, religiously scrupulous, shall be compelled to bear arms."

Mr. GERRY.—This declaration of rights, I take it, is intended to secure the people against the mal-administration of the Government; if we could suppose that, in all cases, the rights of the people would be attended to, the occasion for guards of this kind would be removed. Now I am apprehensive, sir, that this clause would give an opportunity to the people in power to destroy the constitution itself. They can declare who are those religiously scrupulous, and prevent them from bearing arms.

What, sir, is the use of a militia? It is to prevent the establishment of a standing army, the bane of liberty. Now it must be evident, that under this provision, together with their other powers, Congress could take such measures with respect to a militia, as make a standing army necessary. Whenever Governments mean to invade the rights and liberties of the people, they always attempt to destroy the militia, in order to raise an army upon their ruins. This was actually done by Great Britain at the commencement of the late revolution. They used every means in their power to prevent the establishment of an effective militia to the eastward. The Assembly of Massachusetts, seeing the rapid progress that administration were making, to divest them of their inherent privileges, endeavored to counteract them by the organization of the militia, but they were always defeated by the influence of the Crown.

Mr. SENEY wished to know what question there was before the committee, in order to ascertain the point upon which the gentleman was speaking.

Mr. GERRY replied that he meant to make a motion, as he disapproved of the words as they [779] stood. He then proceeded. No attempts that they made were successful, until they engaged in the struggle which emancipated them at once from their thraldom. Now, if we give a discretionary power to exclude those from militia duty who have religious scruples, we may as well make no provision on this head. For this reason he wished the words to be altered so as to be confined to persons belonging to a religious sect, scrupulous of bearing arms.

Mr. JACKSON did not expect that all the people of the United States would turn Quakers or Moravians; consequently, one part would have to defend the other, in case of invasion. Now this, in his opinion, was unjust, unless the constitution secured an equivalent: for this reason he moved to amend the clause, by inserting at the end of it, "upon paying an equivalent to be established by law."

Mr. SMITH, of South Carolina, inquired what were the words used by the conventions respecting this amendment. If the gentleman would conform to what was proposed by Virginia and Carolina, he would second him. He thought they were to be excused provided they found a substitute.

Mr. JACKSON was willing to accommodate. He thought the expression was, "No one, religiously scrupulous of bearing arms, shall be compelled to render military service in person, upon paying an equivalent."

Mr. SHERMAN conceived it difficult to modify the clause and make it better. It is well known that those who are religiously scrupulous of bearing arms, are equally scrupulous of getting substitutes or paying an equivalent. Many of them would rather die than do either one or the other; but he did not see an absolute necessity for a clause of this kind. We do not live under an arbitrary Government, said he, and the States, respectively, will have the government of the militia, unless when called into actual service; besides, it would not do to alter it so as to exclude the whole of any sect, because there are men amongst the Quakers who will turn out, notwithstanding the religious principles of the society, and defend the cause of their country. Certainly it will be improper to prevent the exercise of such favorable dispositions, at least whilst it is the practice of nations to determine their contests by the slaughter of their citizens and subjects.

Mr. Vining hoped the clause would be suffered to remain as it stood, because he saw no use in it if it was amended so as to compel a man to find a substitute, which, with respect to the Government, was the same as if the person himself turned out to fight.

Mr. Stone inquired what the words "religiously scrupulous" had reference to: was it of bearing arms? If it was, it ought so to be expressed.

Mr. Benson moved to have the words "but no person religiously scrupulous shall be compelled to bear arms," struck out. He would always leave it to the benevolence of the Legis- [780] lature, for, modify it as you please, it will be impossible to express it in such a manner as to clear it from ambiguity. No man can claim this indulgence of right. It may be a religious persuasion, but it is no natural right, and therefore ought to be left to the discretion of the Government. If this stands part of the constitution, it will be a question before the Judiciary, on every regulation you make with respect to the organization of the militia, whether it comports with this declaration or not? It is extremely injudicious to intermix matters of doubt with fundamentals.

I have no reason to believe but the Legislature will always possess humanity enough to indulge this class of citizens in a matter they are so desirous of; but they ought to be left to their discretion.

The motion for striking out the whole clause being seconded, was put, and decided in the negative—22 members voting for it, and 24 against it. . . .

[783] The committee then proceeded to the fifth proposition:

Article I, section 10, between the first and second paragraph insert "no State shall infringe the equal rights of conscience, nor the freedom of speech, or of the press, nor of the right of trial by jury in criminal cases."

Mr. Tucker.—This is offered, I presume, as an amendment to the constitution of the United States, but it goes only to the alteration of the constitutions of particular States. It will be much better, I apprehend, to leave the State Governments to themselves, and not to interfere with them more than we already do; [784] and that is thought by many to be rather too much. I therefore move, sir, to strike out these words.

Mr. Madison conceived this to be the most valuable amendment on the whole list. If there was any reason to restrain the Government of the United States from infringing upon these essential rights, it was equally necessary that they should be secured against the State Governments. He thought that if they provided against the one, it was as necessary to provide against the other, and was satisfied that it would be equally grateful to the people.

Mr. Livermore had no great objection to the sentiment, but he thought it not well expressed. He wished to make it an affirmative proposition; "the equal rights of conscience, the freedom of speech, or of the press, and the right of trial by jury in criminal cases, shall not be infringed by any State."

This transposition being agreed to, and Mr. Tucker's motion being rejected, the clause was adopted. . . .

Thursday, August 20

[795] AMENDMENTS TO THE CONSTITUITON

The House resumed the consideration of the report of the Committee of the whole on the subject of amendment to the constitution.

Mr. Ames's proposition was taken up. Five or six other members introduced propositions on the same point, and the whole were, by mutual [796] consent, laid on the table. After which, the House proceeded to the third amendment, and agreed to the same.

On motion of Mr. Ames, the fourth amendment was altered so as to read "Congress shall make no law establishing religion, or to prevent the free exercise thereof, or to infringe the rights of conscience." This being adopted.

The first proposition was agreed to.

Mr. Scott objected to the clause in the sixth amendment, "No person religiously scrupulous shall be compelled to bear arms." He observed that if this becomes part of the constitution, such persons can neither be called upon for their services, nor can an equivalent be demanded; it is also attended with still further difficulties, for a militia can never be depended upon. This would lead to the violation of another article in the constitution, which secures to the people the right of keeping arms, and in this case recourse must be had to a standing army. I conceive it, said he, to be a legislative right altogether. There are many sects I know, who are religiously scrupulous in this respect; I do not mean to deprive them of any indulgence the law affords; my design is to guard against those who are of no religion. It has been urged that religion is on the decline; if so, the argument is more strong in my favor, for when the time comes that religion shall be discarded, the generality of persons will have recourse to these pretexts to get excused from bearing arms.

Mr. Boudinot thought the provision in the clause, or something similar to it, was necessary. Can any dependence, said he, be placed in men who are conscientious in this respect? or what justice can there be in compelling them to bear arms, when, according to their religious principles, they would rather die than use them? He adverted to several instances of oppression on this point, that occurred during the war. In forming a militia, an effectual defence ought to be calculated, and no characters of this religious description ought to be compelled to take up arms. I hope that in establishing this Government, we may show the world that proper care is taken that the Government may not interfere with the religious sentiments of any person. Now, by striking out the clause, people may be led to believe that there is an intention in the General Government to compel all its citizens to bear arms.

Some further desultory conversation arose, and it was agreed to insert the words "in person" to the end of the clause; after which, it was adopted, as was the fourth, fifth, sixth, seventh, and eighth clauses of the fourth proposition; then the fifth, sixth, and seventh propositions were agreed to, and the House adjourned.

The Senate

Thursday, September 3, 1789

[70] . . . The Senate resumed the consideration of the Resolve of the House of Representatives on the Amendments to the Constitution of the United States. . . .

On motion to amend article third, and to strike out these words: "religion, or prohibiting the free Exercise thereof," and insert, "one religious sect or society in preference to others";

It passed in the negative.

On motion for reconsideration:

It passed in the Affirmative.

On motion that article the third be striken out:

It passed in the negative.

On motion to adopt the following, in lieu of the third Article: "Congress shall not make any law infringing the rights of conscience, or establishing any religious sect or society":

It passed in the negative.

On motion to amend the third article, to read thus: "Congress shall make no law establishing any particular denomination of religion in preference to another, or prohibiting the free exercise thereof, nor shall the rights of conscience be infringed";

It passed in the Negative.

On the question upon the third Article as it came from the House of Representatives:

It passed in the Negative.

On motion to adopt the third Article proposed in the Resolve of the House of Representatives, amended by striking out these words, "nor shall the rights of conscience be infringed";

It passed in the affirmative. . . .

WEDNESDAY, September 9, 1789

[76] . . . Proceeded in the consideration of the Resolve of the House of Representatives of [77] the 24th of August, on "Articles to be proposed to the legislatures of the several states as amendments to the Constitution of the United States"; and,

On motion to amend article the third, to read as follows: "Congress shall make no law establishing articles of faith or a mode of worship, or prohibiting the free exercise of religion, or abridging the freedom of speech, or the press, or the right of the people peaceably to assemble, and petition to the Government for the redress of grievances":

It passed in the Affirmative. . . .

On motion, on article the fifth, to strike out the word "fifth," after "article the," and insert "fourth," and to amend the article to read as follows: "A well regulated militia being the security of a free state, the right of the people to keep and bear arms, shall not be infringed."

It passed in the affirmative. . . .

On motion to strike out the tenth and the eleventh articles:

It passed in the affirmative.

Letter to the Annual Meeting of Quakers (1789)

George Washington

September 1789

Government being, among other purposes, instituted to protect the persons and consciences of men from oppression, it certainly is the duty of rulers, not only to abstain from it themselves, but, according to their stations, to prevent it in others.

The liberty enjoyed by the people of these states of worshipping Almighty God agreeably to their consciences, is not only among the choicest of their *blessings*, but also of their *rights*. While men perform their social duties faithfully, they do all that society or the state can with propriety demand or expect; and remain responsible only to their Maker for their religion, or modes of faith, which they may prefer or profess.

Your principles and conduct are well known to me; and it is doing the people called Quakers no more than justice to say, that (except their declining to share with others the burden of the common defense) there is no denomination among us, who are more exemplary and useful citizens.

I assure you very explicitly, that in my opinion the conscientious scruples of all men should be treated with great delicacy and tenderness; and it is my wish and desire, that the laws may always be as extensively accommodated to them, as a due regard to the protection and essential interests of the nation may justify and permit.

Letter to the Hebrew Congregation at Newport (1790)

George Washington

1790

Gentlemen:

While I received with much satisfaction your address replete with expressions of esteem, I rejoice in the opportunity of assuring you that I shall always retain grateful remembrance of the cordial welcome I experienced on my visit to Newport from all classes of citizens.

The reflection on the days of difficulty and danger which are past is rendered the more sweet from a consciousness that they are succeeded by days of uncommon prosperity and security.

If we have wisdom to make the best use of the advantages with which we are now favored, we cannot fail, under the just administration of a good government, to become a great and happy people.

The citizens of the United States of America have a right to applaud themselves for having given to mankind examples of an enlarged and liberal policy—a policy worthy of imitation. All possess alike liberty of conscience and immunities of citizenship.

It is now no more that toleration is spoken of as if it were the indulgence of one class of people that another enjoyed the exercise of their inherent natural rights, for, happily, the Government of the United States, which gives to bigotry no factions, to persecution no assistance, requires only that they who live under its protection should demean themselves as good citizens in giving it on all occasions their effectual support.

It would be inconsistent with the frankness of my character not to avow that I am pleased with your favorable opinion of my administration and fervent wishes for my felicity.

May the children of the stock of Abraham who dwell in this land continue to merit and enjoy the good will of the other inhabitants—while every one shall sit in safety under his own vine and fig tree and there shall be none to make him afraid.

May the father of all mercies scatter light, and not darkness, upon our paths, and make us all in our several vocations useful here, and in His own due time and way everlastingly happy.

G. Washington

G

Letter to the Danbury Baptist Association (1802)

Thomas Jefferson

Jan. 1, 1802.

To messrs. Nehemiah Dodge, Ephraim Robbins, & Stephen S. Nelson, a committee of the Danbury Baptist association in the state of Connecticut.

Gentlemen,

The affectionate sentiments of esteem and approbation which you are so good as to express towards me, on behalf of the Danbury Baptist association, give me the highest satisfaction. My duties dictate a faithful & zealous pursuit of the interests of my constituents, & in proportion as they are persuaded of my fidelity to those duties, the discharge of them becomes more and more pleasing.

Believing with you that religion is a matter which lies solely between Man & his God, that he owes account to none other for his faith or his worship, that the legitimate powers of government reach actions only, & not opinions, I contemplate with sovereign reverence that act of the whole American people which declared that their legislature should "make no law respecting an establishment of religion, or prohibiting the free exercise thereof," thus building a wall of separation between Church & State. Adhering to this expression of the supreme will of the nation in behalf of the rights of conscience, I shall see with sincere satisfaction the progress of those sentiments which tend to restore to man all his natural rights, convinced he has no natural right in opposition to his social duties.

I reciprocate your kind prayers for the protection & blessing of the common father and creator of man, and tender you for yourselves & your religious association, assurances of my high respect & esteem.

Th: Jefferson

Index